Talk Radio
Wants You

Talk Radio Wants You

An Intimate Guide to 700 Shows and How to Get Invited

FRANCINE SILVERMAN

McFarland & Company, Inc., Publishers
Jefferson, North Carolina, and London

LIBRARY OF CONGRESS CATALOGUING-IN-PUBLICATION DATA

Silverman, Francine.
Talk radio wants you : an intimate guide to 700 shows and how to get invited / Francine Silverman.
      p.   cm.
Includes bibliographical references and index.

ISBN 978-0-7864-4033-7
softcover : 50# alkaline paper ∞

1. Radio talk shows — United States — Handbooks, manuals, etc.
2. Radio talk shows — United States — Directories.   I. Title.
PN1991.8.T35S55   2009   791.45'6 — dc22   2008053063

British Library cataloguing data are available

©2009 Francine Silverman. All rights reserved

No part of this book may be reproduced or transmitted in any form or by any means, electronic or mechanical, including photocopying or recording, or by any information storage and retrieval system, without permission in writing from the publisher.

Cover photograph ©2009 Shutterstock

Manufactured in the United States of America

McFarland & Company, Inc., Publishers
Box 611, Jefferson, North Carolina 28640
www.mcfarlandpub.com

To Ronnie and Amy for their everlasting love and support. My newsletter subscriber, Eileen Bodoh, bears mention for her continuous interest in providing me with new shows to contact.

I would also like to thank the responsive hosts who offered their help with this book or invited me to be a guest on their shows, or both, and the producers and radio execs who kindly forwarded my questionnaire to their hosts, especially Jeff Weber, executive vice-president of Business TalkRadio Network and Lifestyle TalkRadio Network; Celeste Selwyn, former program director of Radio Sandy Springs; Pat Lynch, editor-in-chief, WomensRadio; Wade Andrews, station manager at Hold 'Em Radio; Georgiann Kiricoples, formerly in management at The Mix Radio Network, LLC, which airs TheMix Talk.com and TheMixRock.com; Jason Greenly, chair of the programming committee at WEFT 90.1 FM, Champaign, Illinois; Frank J. Hogan, general manager at Rowen Radio, WGLS-FM; Paul Baroli, program director at WBCB 1490 AM; and Donald Newsom, president and chairman of BBS Network.

TABLE OF CONTENTS

Preface 1

Addiction and Recovery
The Blazing Grace Show 3
Last Call 3
The Prescription Addiction Radio Show 4
Steppin' Out 4

African American
The Bev Smith Show 5
Conscious Rasta Report 5
Empowered Black Perspectives 6

Animals
The All Pets Radio Show 6
Animal Hour 7
Animal Radio 7
Animal Rescue: Where to Go, What to Do, How to Help! 7
Animal Talk Naturally 8
Animals Aloud 9
Dog Cast Radio 10
Dr. Carol on Pets 11
Dr. Shawn — The Natural Vet 11
Friesian Ink Radio 11
Horse Talk 12
The KAHI Corral 12
Nature's Translator 13
Talk with Your Animals 13
Talkin' Pets 14
Wendy's Animal Talk 14

Antiques and Collectibles
APS Stamp Talk 14
Burchard Galleries Antiques and Collectibles Radio Show 15
Card Corner 15
Collectors Coach Show 16
Comic Zone 16
Inkstuds 17
Whatcha Got? 17

Art and Design
Art and Technology 17
The Art Full Life 18
Change Your Home — Change Your Life 18
Design Talk 19
The Emy Louie Show 19
The Home Show 19
Living Large 20
Organization Nation 20
Scrappers Talk Radio 20
Smart City 21
Your House Chicago 21

Authors
Adirondack Book House 22
AuthorB-Known 22
Author's Voice 23
Beyond Words 23
The Book Babes Program 24
Book Bites for Kids 24
The Book Guys 25
The Book Squad 25
Book Talk 26
Calling All Authors 27
Cherry Picking 27
The Compulsive Reader 28
Dr. Maxine 29
Katz Pajamas 29
On the Bookshelf 29
Poetry & Prose & Anything Goes with Dr. Ni 30
The Reader's Round Table 30

Reading with Robin — 31
Sound Authors — 32
Today's Author — 32
Vin Smith's Midday Book Break — 32
Writers FM — 33
Writers in the Sky — 34
Writers on Writing — 34
The Writing Show — 35

Beauty, Style and Fashion
A Fashionable Life — 35
Let's Talk Makeup — 36
Make Me Over Eb Show — 36

Business, Finance and Marketing
The American Dream — 36
Business at Night — 37
Business in Motion — 37
Business Matters — 38
Business Success Coaching — 38
The Career Engineers Radio Broadcast — 38
CEO Lounge — 39
The China Business Show — 39
Cover Your Assets — 40
The Cranky Middle Manager Show — 40
Demystifying Non-Profits — 41
eBay Radio — 41
The Gabe Wisdom Show — 42
Goldseek Radio — 42
The Growth Strategist — 43
Home Base Business 101 — 44
Indie Business Radio Show — 44
The Innovation Zone — 45
Insight on Coaching — 45
Integrity in Business — 46
Job You Deserve Radio — 46
The John Adam Show — 47
Legends of Success — 47
Let's Talk Marketing Show — 48
Life Business and Money, with Steven Kay — 48
Making a Living with Maggie — 49
Mind Your BIZness — 49
Money Matters Financial Network Radio — 50
The Money Thing — 50
Networking with the Blindguy from Gorilla Central — 51
Online Marketing — 51
Powerfull Living — 52
PowerSellingMom's Radio Show: Let's Talk eBay — 52
PricewaterhouseCoopers Start Up Show — 52
The Ryan C. Greene Show — 53
The Small Business Big Ideas Show — 53
Small Business Power Hour — 54
SmallBizAmerica Radio — 54
Sound Investing — 55
Stu Taylor — 55
Taking Care of Business — 56
The Tom O'Brien Show — 57
Traders Nation — 57
Unlock Your Sales Potential — 58
Where Wall Street Meets Main Street — 58
Women in Business Radio — 59
Work at Home Family Talk Radio — 59
Work Matters with Nan Russell — 59
Work with Marty Nemko — 60

Cars
America on the Road — 60
Bobby Likis Car Clinic — 61

Crime and Child Abuse
Breaking the Conspiracy of Silence — 61
Crime and Punishment — 62
Las Vegas and the Mob — 62

Disabilities
Disability Beat — 63
Making Life Easier — 63
The Rose Moore Show — 63
The Yvonne Pierre Show — 64

Entertainment
Barry Reisman Show — 65
Celebrity Stars — 65
Dr. Blogstein's Radio Happy Hour — 65
DRC-FM Morning Show — 66
Entertainment and the Arts — 66
Everyday People's Entertainment Guide — 67
A Fistful of Quarters — 67
Gary B. Duglin Talks with the Stars — 67
Holder Tonight — 68
The Indie Music Showcase — 68
Jay Grayce Variety Show — 69
The Jiggy Jaguar Show — 69
The Jim Cates Show — 70
The Jordan Rich Show — 70
Judy Carmichael's Jazz Inspired — 71
The Kathleen Show — 72
The Mark and Brian Program — 72
Movie Addict Headquarters — 73

The Movie Show	73
Mr. Media	74
The Music Connection	74
Now Showing with Bill Wilson	74
Out and About with Richard G.	74
Poppoff	75
Pride Radio	76
The Radio Host Show	76
Radio Rickshaw	76
Red Bar Radio	77
Rick's Picks	77
Sassy Sistah Radio Show	78
Show Business 101	78
Six Degrees	78
Talk to Me ... Conversations with Creative, Unconventional People	79
The TV of Tomorrow Show LIVE	79
Ultrasonic Film	80

Environment
Healing the Earth Radio	80
Healthy Planet, Healthy Me!	81
Science in Action	81
Tomorrow Matters	81

Food and Wine
America's Dining and Travel Guide	82
Beyond the Measuring Cup	82
Culinary Confessions	83
The Curious Cook on Tastebuds Food Show	84
Deconstructing Dinner	84
Dr. Tea! Show	85
Ed Hitzel's Radio Show	85
Food Chain Radio	85
The Good Food Hour	86
The Good Life	86
GrapeRadio	87
Grapevine Radio	87
Judy a la Carte	88
Life Bites News	88
Mouthful	88
Raw Inspirations Radio	89
Seattle Kitchen	89
Table Talk	90
The Urban Herbalist	90
Vegan Radio	91
Wine and Dine Radio	91

Gardening
Arbor Talk	92
Bob Tanem in the Garden	92
Florida Gardening	93
Garden Girls	93
Garden Mama	94
The Gardener	94
The Gestalt Gardener	94
The Mike Nowak Show	95

Gay and Lesbian
Queer FM	96
This Way Out	96

Health and Fitness
Autism: Help, Hope and Healing	97
The Balancing Point	97
Beyond Health	98
Caregiving 101	98
Coping with Caregiving	99
Create Abundance Now!	99
Deborah "Doc" Watson	99
Dr. Fred Bell's Health, Science and Energy Show	100
The Dr. Meg Jordan Show	101
Fitness and Nutrition Radio	101
Fitness Business Radio	102
Full Power Living	102
Heal Yourself Talk Radio	103
The Healing Sounds Show	104
The Health and Beauty Revolution Show	104
Health in 30	105
Health Matters	106
Health Matters with Dr G.	106
Healthy Lifestyles	106
Healthy Talk Radio	107
Healthy Woman	107
Herb Talk Live	108
In Short Order	108
Insights	109
Living on Purpose	109
"The New You" Radio Show	110
No Bones About It	110
Nutrition and Health	111
The Patient's Voice	111
The Peter K Show	112
The Positive Mind	112
Problems and Solutions	113
Psychiatry Today with Dr. Scot	113
The Real World of Autism with Chantal	114
Spencer Power Hour	114

x   Table of Contents

Turn on Your Inner Light 115
Vibrant Living 115
Wake Up America 116
The Wellness Roadshow: Searching for Whole Being 116
What's Ailing America? 117
Your Doctor Said What? 118
Your Health Matters 118

History
Civil War Talk Radio 119
The Oopa Loopa Café 119

Labor
The Heartland Labor Forum 120
The Labor Show 120

Law and Law Enforcement
The Dailey and Stearn Law Show 121
The Expert Witness 121
The Power of Attorney 122
The Watering Hole 122

Men and Women
Cosmolicious with Diana 122
The Divorced Fathers Network Radio 123

Military
Army Wife Talk Radio 123
The Captain's America 124
Career Call 124

Nautical
Nautical Talk Radio 125

New Age
Ageless Lifestyles: Cutting Edge Thinking on Being Youthful at Every Age 125
All Things That Matter 126
Another Reality Show 126
Ask the Psychic 127
Between Two Worlds Radio 127
Beyond Reality 128
Blog Talk Radio's Holistic Integrative Energy Medicine 128
Breaking Through 129
Bridging Heaven and Earth 129
Brightlights Pathfinder 130
Calling All Angels 130
The Candia Sanders Hour 130
Connect 131

Connecting the Light 132
Conscious Healing 132
Conversations from Beyond 133
Conversations of the Quantum Age 133
Creative Health and Spirit 134
Dimensions of Light 134
Divine Awakening 135
Divine Manifesting 136
The Dr. Anne Marie Evers Show 136
Dynamic Transformations Where Intuition and Inspiration Collide 137
Earth Angel 137
Earth Harmony Divinations 138
Embracing Mother Earth 138
Going Global for Spirit 139
GoofyGoddess Radio 139
Happy Hour Radio 140
The Heart and Home Healing Show 140
Intuitive Living 140
Just Energy Radio 141
Knowing Spirit Radio 141
Lanto's Lantern 142
Life Beyond Reason 143
Lights On! 143
Live Your Purpose Radio 144
Manifest Change Now 144
Manifesting Miracles in Your Life 144
Marketing as a Spiritual Practice 145
Mastering Ourselves 145
The Messengerfiles 146
Metaphysical World and Beyond 146
The Michael Gogger Show 147
My Spiritual Healer 148
Myth or Logic Radio 148
News for the Soul 149
Now That's What I'm Talking About! 149
Peaceful Planet Show 150
Quantum Health 151
The Robert Scott Bell Show 151
SAGE: Spirit, Angels and Guides Entertainment 151
Soul Connections 152
Soul Journeys Live 153
Spirit Connections 153
Spirit Is Speaking 154
Spiritual Hollywood 154
Terry Nazon Talks Astrology 154
A Time to Heal 155
The Truth About Life 155
Truth from the Source 156

Turning of the Wheel	156
Visible by Numbers	156
Walking with Spirit	157
Wellness, Wholeness and Wisdom	157
When Pigs Fly	158
Windows to Wellness	158
Wings of Love	159
You Are What You Love	160

Outdoor Life

Big Outdoors	160
Outdoor Talk Network	161
The Outdoors Experience	161

Paranormal

As You Wish Talk Radio	161
Celtic Seers	162
Dark Matters Radio	162
Darkness on the Edge of Town	163
Ghostly Talk	163
A Glimpse Through the Veil	164
Haunted Voices Radio	164
Journeys with Rebecca	165
Kevin Smith Show	165
Matthew and Friends	166
P.O.R.T.A.L. Paranormal Talk Radio	167
The Sasquatch Experience	167
UFO Radio	168
The Unexplained World	169
The Vike Report	169
The "X" Zone Radio Show (and TV Show)	169

Parents and Children

Chit Chat with Kat	170
Creating a Family: Talk About Infertility and Adoption	170
Friend of the Family	171
Growing Up with Dr. Jerry Brodlie	171
Just One More Book!	172
The Kevin and Trudie Show	172
Mom Talk Radio	173
Parents Rule!	173
Work at Home Moms Talk Radio	174

Politics

Action Point	174
AM South Florida	175
The Andrew Carter Show	175
Battle Line with Alan Nathan	175
Behind the News	176
Beneath the Surface	176
The Big Sauce Radio Show	177
Bill Dwight Show	177
The Bill Handel Show	178
The Bob Frantz Show	178
The Brad Show	179
The Breakfast Show	179
BullDog and the Rude Awakening Show	180
Canadian Voices	180
Capitol Talk	181
CBS Weekend Roundup	181
Charlotte's Morning News Weekend	182
The Chuck Morse Show	182
CHUM Radio Ottawa	182
A Community Affair	182
Connecting the Dots	183
The Dark Side	183
The Dave Elswick Show	184
Deace in the Afternoon	184
The Dom Giordano Show	184
Evening Edition	184
Face the Tribune	184
First News with Bob Steel	185
Fix Your Conflicts!	185
The Flipside Show	186
Focus580 (and) The Afternoon Magazine	186
Free Forum	186
Free Range Thought	187
Freedom Works!/The Paul Molloy Show	187
Howard Monroe and the Morning Show	188
It Takes a Village	188
The Jeff Farias Show	188
The Jeff Katz Show	189
Jefferson City's Morning News with Jay Kersting	189
Jim Bohannon Show	190
KnightTime Radio Show	190
Laurie and Olga Show	190
The Lee Rodgers Show	190
The Leslie Marshall Show	191
Liberalpro	192
Liberty Watch	192
Lighting the Fires of Liberty	192
The Lionel Show	193
Madely in the Morning	193
Mancow	194

The Mark Reardon Show	194
The Media Lizzy Show	194
Media Matters	195
The Meria Show	195
The Midwatch	196
The Morning Show	196
My Point Radio	196
Mytalkshow	197
New Dimensions	197
New World Order Disorder	197
Nightside Project	198
NightSide with Dan Rea	198
The Norm Jones Show	199
One Hour of Hope	199
The Pamela Furr Show	199
The Party Line	200
ProAmerica Radio	200
Quinn and Rose	200
Radio Free Volusia	201
The Right Perspective	201
The Roth Show	202
The Scooter McGee Show	202
The Sean Leslie Show	203
Shakedown Street	203
Situation Awareness	203
Sound Off Connecticut	204
Soundingboard	204
Speak Up	204
The Steve Gill Show	205
The Steve Yuhas Show	205
StraitTalks	206
Talk It Over	206
The Things That Matter Most	207
The Todd Feinburg Show	207
The Tom Becka Show	207
Trevor Carey Show	208
Trey Ware Morning Show	208
The Uncooperative Radio Show	208
Vannah and Collins	209
Visibility 9–11	209
Y Talk Radio	210
You Are the Guest	210
Your Call	211

Real Estate
The Future of Real Estate	211
J.T. Foxx Show	212
The Real Estate Guys	212
Real Estate, Real Advice	212
Real Talk "With the Experts"	213
The Townstone Financial Show	213
Your Home — Your Money Mortgage and Real Estate Radio	213

Regional
Aboriginal Connections	214
Caribbean Crossroads	214
Eight Forty-Eight	214
Eye on Toledo	215
The FOG	215
The Graduates	216
Inside New Orleans	216
The Jim Brown Show	217
The Kaare Johnson Show	217
Lunch Pail Logic	217
Mac's World	218
Madison in the Morning	218
Remember When	218
Sante Fe Radio Café	219
Welcome to My World	219

Relationships
Ask Dr. Jackie	220
Bride's Night Out	220
A Fresh Start with Sallie Felton	221
Infinitelove Talk Radio	221
Love by Intuition Show	222
Love Mechanics	223
Passion	223
Quality of Life	224
Relationships for Life	224
Sex with Emily	224
Sex with Sassy Radio Show	225
Single Talk	226
Your Dream Wedding	226

Religion and Atheism
The Allen Hunt Show	227
Answers in Atheism	227
Awake, Alive and Jewish	228
Bob Enyart Live	228
The Christian Women's View	228
The Christian Worldview	229
God Unplugged	229
The Infidel Guy Show	230
Interfaith Voices	230
Jewish Digest	231
The Jewish Experience	231
The JPEG Show	232
Need a Word	232
The Steve Duignan Show	232

Table of Contents xiii

This Gospel of the Kingdom (and) I
   Saw the Light Ministries 232
WJEW Talk Hour 233

Science
Biota Live 233
The Groks Science Show 234
Infinite Consciousness 234
Planetary Radio 234
This Week in Science 235
X-Squared Radio 235

Science Fiction
SyFy Radio 236

Self Help
Alivewiredu Talk Radio Show 237
At Home with Cheryll Gillespie 237
The BottomLine 237
The Brad Neufeld Show 238
Bright Spot! 238
Celebrating Your Potential 239
Conscious Discussions 239
Conversations Live with Vicki St. Clair 240
The Creativity Salon 241
The Daring Dreamers Showcase 241
The Donna Seebo Show 242
The Dr. Pat Show 242
The Father John Walsh Show 243
The Florida Show 244
Goddess Radio 244
Good News Broadcast 244
The Harry Wolf Show 244
In the Know 245
The Inez Bracy Show: Living Smart
   and Well 245
The Iris Fanning Show 245
Journey to Self 246
Let's Talk It Through 246
Lisa's Walk the Talk Show 247
Live the Day 247
Live! With Lisa Radio 248
Living and Loving Life 248
The Louie Jones Show 249
Never Settle for Less 249
On the Verve 249
Point of Life 250
Positive Changes 250
Positively Incorrect! 251
Power Talk 252
The Power Within You 252

Radio Good Spirited 253
Reaching Peak Show 253
Results Radio Show 254
Seeing Beyond 254
Shelia Smoot on Your Side 254
Shrink Rap Radio 255
Something You Should Know 256
Starstyle: Be the Star You Are! 256
Take Charge of Your Life 257
U Smile Radio 257

Seniors
Aging Outside the Box 258
Senior Legal Strategies 258
The Third Age 259

Sports
The Adventure Show 259
BBD Talk Radio 260
Big Nation Radio 260
The Big Wild 261
Broad Minded Poker 261
Dick Santino's Fantasy Sports Show 262
The Drive on Fox 262
The EquiSport Report 262
The Extreme Scene 263
Fightin' Words 263
The Golf Connection 264
Hockey Hour/Canadian Sport 264
Kidz 'n' Sports 264
Minor League Baseball Radio 265
NY Baseball Digest 265
The Performance Nutrition Show 265
Pit Pass Radio 266
Pratt and Taylor 266
The Professor and Mary Ann Talk
   NASCAR 266
Ringside Live 266
Rod and Reel Radio 267
Signs of Speed/Thursday Night
   Thunder 267
Sports Heaven with Mark and Evan 268
The Sports Opinions Show 268
Sports Talk Live 268
The Strength-Power Hour 269
Takedown Radio 269
Tee It Up 269
Teebox Golf Show 269
The Tournament Trail 270
Twisted Metal 270
The UltraFlight Radio Show 270

WSB 120	271	**Women**	
Yankee Fan Club Radio	271	Amazing Women	281
		And the Women Gather Radio Show	282
Technology		Bob and Sheri	282
Ask the Technology Therapist	271	Chat with Women	283
Breakfast Bytes	272	Coach K! Talk Radio Show for Women	283
Computer America	272	Cocoa Mode	284
Computer and Technology Radio	273	Conversations with Coach Yvonne	284
Computer Corner	273	Eve's Third Wave	285
Computer Outlook	273	eWomenNetwork Radio Show	285
Digital Nation Radio	274	How She Really Does It	286
Into Tomorrow	274	Just Between Us	286
Let's Talk Computers	274	The Ladies Room with Lolis	287
My Computer Show	275	The Life Lounge	287
Podcaster Training from Two Beams	275	Loving Life Radio Show	287
TechForum LIVE!	276	Metrochick Radio	288
		The Mother Daughter Club	288
Travel and Living Abroad		Roaring Women Radio	289
The Chris Robinson Travel Show	276	Speak Up!	289
The Expat Show	277	Strong Woman Hiding	290
Get a Life with Françoise	277	Timeless Women Speak	290
Talking Travel	278	Whatever Live!	291
Tilley Talks Travel	278	Wise Women Talk	291
Travel Queen Show	279	A Woman's Spirit	291
The Travel Show	279	Women Power Talk Radio	292
Travel Talk: Escapes!	280	The Women's Community Talk Radio	293
Travel'n On Radio Show	280		
Whirl with Merle	281		

Appendices:

1. *The 100 Top Radio Talk Shows*   295

2. *33 Interview Tips (by Scott Lorenz)*   301

3. *Top 10 Telephone Tips (by Joe Sabah)*   302

4. *Getting Invited Back*
(by Judith Sherven and Jim Sniechowski)   303

Further Reading   305

Index   307

Preface

As an online publicist for more than 100 authors, I know how difficult it can be to get the attention of talk radio hosts. Even when I do receive a reply to an email, it sometimes takes a while before the match between host and guest is made.

Add to this the problem what I call "rookie radio." This does not refer to the quality of the programs or the station, but the poor quality of radio websites. This is especially true of terrestrial radio — those on the air with call letters. More often than not, the site contains biographies of its hosts but neither the theme of their shows nor the guest criteria — or even *if* they welcome guests.

On the other hand, it's a lot easier to get a guest spot on radio than to get newspaper coverage.

As a radio advocate, I encourage people to use radio as their voice for promoting books, businesses and services. After all, it's free and easy.

Talk Radio Wants You is divided into 40 categories so you can hone in on the subjects that match your specialties. Bear in mind that hosts are people just like you and me, except they have an audience to please. As Michael Harrison, publisher of *Talkers Magazine*, writes in the foreword of Ellen Ratner's book *Ready, Set, Talk!*, "If you have a story to tell, information to pass along, and someone interesting to talk about it, the odds are good that there are a whole bunch of talk shows out there waiting to hear from you."

Each entry in this book contains all the information you'll need before contacting a host: The name of the show and host, email, telephone number (unless withheld upon request), website, the show's theme and guest criteria, the host's description of the worst guest, contact's name and best method of contact, what to do if there's no response and who gets invited back.

The questionnaires emailed to hosts asked these questions:

What do you look for in a guest?

What is your idea of a guest from hell?

What do you want to know about potential guests, i.e., past interview experiences, credentials, sound of their voice?

What determines if guests are invited back?

How should someone approach you? By calling with a pitch? Emailing a bio? Sending you a press kit?

What happens if a guest emails you and you don't respond within a reasonable time? Should the person email or call you?

These more detailed answers from stations or the hosts were incorporated into the basic information.

Entries continue with comments from listeners and guests and biographical information about the hosts, all provided by the radio stations. This way, you will get to learn about the hosts in their own words. Information is correct as of December 2008.

Appendix 1 contains the major shows selected by *Talkers Magazine*, the bible of the radio industry. Questionnaires were emailed to all of the shows that welcome guests, but only a few responded, probably because they have more guest requests than they need. In those cases, only basic information is provided. Additional appendices offer tips.

I hope you will find many shows to contact and report your experience to me at franalive@optonline.net. I'd also like to know what radio shows I have omitted.

Good luck on the air.

The Categories

Addiction and Recovery

"Addictions are the number one health problem in our country today and we are all affected in some way." — From the **Last Call** website

The Blazing Grace Show with Jayson Graves of Healing for the Soul and Taff Wennik of Legend Counseling on iTunes and on 103 FM, Glenstantia, Pretoria, South Africa (the station runs 9-week cycles).
Theme: Sexual addiction and recovery.
Guest Profile: Authors, therapists, ministry leaders. We want expertise, faith, inspirational story and something related to our theme. Also, credentials, faith background and current ministry status/info.
Guest from Hell: Argumentative, hostile and boring. Somebody who drones on without effectively making their point concisely.
Contact: mike@blazinggrace.org, help@healingforthesoul.org; 719-590-7685; www.blazinggrace.org/radio.htm; either host or cohost. Best method: E-mail. Press kits are helpful but not totally necessary. No response? That doesn't happen unless we're not interested and don't have enough time to get back with them but it's rare if it takes place at all.
Invited Back? Are they compelling? Do they want to partner with us in our common interests and goals? Were they prompt and respectful?
Listener Comment: "I'm a college student and I've been listening to the *Blazing Grace* podcast ever since I saw a link posted on my e-mail accountability group several months ago. I just wanted to write you all and tell you how thankful I am for your ministry. I've struggled with porn since I was in middle school. God has done some amazing things in my life recently, and your ministry has played a huge part in it. I tend to listen to your podcast whenever I'm feeling tempted or even just bored. Sometimes (like right now) I'm just cleaning my room. No matter when or why I listen to your show, I am always tremendously blessed....

"I wanted to especially thank you for a couple of specific episodes. First, thank you for the episodes interviewing former porn stars. These interviews, which I first listened to prior to my relationship with my future wife, marked a HUGE turning point in my recovery. Hearing the stories of women like Shelley Lubben breathed the humanity back into these women who have been reduced to objects in my mind through pictures and movies. Thank you so much.

"Second, thank you for your interviews with wives of men with sexual addiction. Hearing their stories has been a huge blessing for me in this time of engagement. God is using the pain they've experienced to help my fiancée and I tackle issues even before we're married." — Anonymous

Bio of Jayson Graves: Both founder and host of his radio show, Jayson is a Christian psychotherapist specializing in Sexual Addictions Recovery and Unwanted Same-Gender Attractions. He enjoys helping his clients from both a clinical and personal frame as a person in recovery himself. Founder and director of international counseling ministry "Healing for the Soul Counseling and Coaching, LLC" (http://www.healingforthesoul.org), Jayson offers telephone therapy and his first original idea: Teleconference Recovery Groups for men and for wives in recovery worldwide. He also serves as a national program director for New Life Ministry's Every Man's Battle intensive workshops http://www.everymansbattle.com.

Jayson and his wife, Susan, are the parents of Selah.
Bio of Taff Wennik: Taff is the owner and president of Legend Professional Counseling, Inc. He has a unique ability to help people find the language of their truest heart. His desire is to see individuals, couples, and families become healthy, strong, and thriving ... full of purpose and hope. Originally from West Texas, Taff and his family moved to Colorado Springs in the summer of 2002. He and his wife have been together since 1989. They have two beautiful children and love living in the Rocky Mountains.

Full bio at http://www.oneplace.com/ministries/Blazing_Grace_Radio/host_bio.asp?show_id=551

Last Call with Dan Murphy on Fox News 1450 KZNU, St George, UT, and Internet Stream.
Theme: Education and prevention of addictions/Substance and abuse issues.
Guest Profile: All knowledgeable persons re: above

subjects. Able guests should possess knowledge and understanding of addictions and related issues. Otherwise it should be someone who suffers or has suffered as a result of addictions, directly or indirectly.

Guest from Hell: A guest who basically has nothing to offer, and/or answers with yes/no responses.

Contact: lastcall2005@msn.com, dan@mylastcall.com; 435-467-8096; http://www.mylastcall.com; Dan Murphy. Best method: E-mail and/or phone. Call us with your pitch, provide brief bio, send a press kit and tell us what motivates you to be on the program. No response? I try to respond to viable requests within 48 hours. If I should fail, I encourage them to resubmit their request.

Invited Back? If the guest offered tangible content and how listeners responded. E-mail and personal input from various sources also helps make determination.

Guest Comments: "We're all addicts of one sort or another, and Dan offers a fabulous forum to address the ones you know best."— Sheldon Norberg, author of *Confessions of a Dope Dealer* (Ronin Publishing 2005). http://www.sheldonnorberg.com

"I've done over 250 TV and radio interviews discussing my Self-Coaching series of books. The number one best host on my list is Dan Murphy—without a close second. Imagine sitting in your living room with your best friend. You're having a chat about the issues and ideas that interest you most. Your friend is both gracious and enthusiastic to hear everything you have to say, and best of all, your friend is aggressively helping you sell your books (Dan never forgets to mention your books, what you're working on and your web site). Dan Murphy is talented, entertaining, and never overbearing. I've run into many rude, obnoxious, incompetent hosts — if you ask me, doing an interview with Dan Murphy will spoil you rotten."— Dr. Joe Luciani, author of *Self-Coaching: The Powerful Program to Beat Anxiety and Depression* (Wiley 2004), http://www.self-coaching.net

Bio of Dan Murphy: Dan started in broadcast (radio) in 1969 in the LA area. In the late 1980s he produced and hosted approximately 10 Public Access Cable TV programs with a primary emphasis on addictions. He moved to southern Utah in 1997 and created *Last Call* in 1998.

Full bio at http://www.mylastcall.com/?pg=about

The Prescription Addiction Radio Show with "Larry G" (Larry Golbom) on WGUL 860 AM, http://www.860wgul.com, covering the entire Tampa-St. Petersburg-Clearwater area, Florida, and airing Sundays, 9–10 PM.

Theme: Prescription drug misuse (only show with this concept in country). The show focuses on the hypocrisy of the prescription drug message in our society. Almost every person knows someone who is affected by the overuse or misuse of a prescription drug(s).

Guest Profile: Anybody affected by prescription drug misuse? I'd like to know the title of the book or focus ... I can do the homework quickly.

Guest from Hell: Show welcomes diverging ideas. My goal is to have the guest be comfortable. If I disagree, my strength is diplomacy.

Contact: Larry@PrescriptionAddictionRadio.com; 727-463-0067; http://www.prescriptionaddictionradio.com; Larry Golbom. Best method: My radio program is still small and growing. I am limited in my time. E-mail with a brief description would be adequate. No response? If I miss an opportunity, please let me know again.

Invited Back? "Friends of the Show"

Guest Comment: "Larry G. from *The Prescription Addiction Radio Show* is a kind and compassionate man who understands exactly what my passion for unnecessary drugging of America is all about. He is well educated in his field and tells it like it is. Being on his show is so comfortable because he lets me talk about my issues with benzodiazepines, welcomes guest callers as if he is welcoming you into his living room and has drug facts that many unsuspecting people are not aware of to help in their own decisions about taking addictive medications."— Geraldine Burns, http://www.allaboutanxiety.net, http://www.benzobookreview.com

Bio of Larry Golbom: Larry is a pharmacist and MBA whose family is affected by prescription drug misuse.

Steppin' Out with Scott Clark airs weekends on Powerful Radio, http://www.powerfulradio.com and carried on 17 affiliate stations.

Theme: 12 step meeting on the radio.

Guest Profile: Experts in addiction, i.e., sex, drugs, alcohol, food, nicotine and gambling; however, any topic of transforming one's life. Speakers with something new to say and compelling content. Like to know guests' past interview experiences, credentials, and sound of their voice.

Guest from Hell: Someone who is boring, low energy, no enthusiasm.

Contact: denise@powerfulradio.com; 845-359-3299; http://www.12stepmeeting.com; Denise McIntee. Best method: E-mail only, please. No response? E-mail again.

Invited Back? Great speakers.

Listener Comments: "It was late on a Saturday night. I had just had a fight with my girlfriend and was about to get into the car and go lookin' for booze ... flippin' around on the radio dial, I heard the meeting and forgot about buying my bottle."— Hal H., Brooklyn, New York

"I was at my wit's end, always trying to get my boyfriend to stop using drugs. He's stubborn, though. When we heard your show last weekend, he got inspired and went to a meeting. Thank you."— Penny J., New York, New York

Bio of Denise McIntee: While taking psychology courses in college, Denise attended 12 Step meetings and found them more fascinating than many of the stories currently on the air. That is how *Steppin' Out* was born. In 2000, she formed Powerful Radio Productions, Inc., the broadcast company, with one goal: to produce powerful radio programs.

Denise served for 17 years as operations manager at WABC-AM radio in New York. In 1997, she joined Geller Media International, where she finds, trains and develops on-air personalities for Geller's radio and TV clients around the word.

She lives in Rockland County, New York, with her twin daughters Danielle and Dominique and her husband Mike, who works for CBS TV's "Late Show with David Letterman."

Full bio at http://www.powerfulradio.com

African American

"There is a terrible crisis within the African (Black) communities all around the world with regards to independent media. All too often, the media we get our information from is not seriously taking on the critical issues that affect our lives."— From the **Conscious Rasta Report** website

The Bev Smith Show on American Urban Radio Networks is syndicated nationally. Rated #41 in the 2008 Talkers Heavy Hundred.

Theme: News and information of the day, primarily as it affects the African American audience

Guest Profile: VIPs, authors, academic and experienced experts, community-level persons and activists. Engaging and informative people who can connect to our listeners on a "real" and even emotional level for the more serious issues; we turn to people with direct and/or expert knowledge and opinion, especially as they pertain to the national African American community and perspective. Credentials and experience (expert or layman) are vital.

Guest from Hell: A) A guest that doesn't show up; B) A guest whose delivery is dry, whose answers are more generic than specific, and whose answers prove them less than knowledgeable.

Contact: bevsmith@thebevsmithshow.com; http://www.aurn.com (corporate), http://www.myspace.com/bevsmithonline (bev smith myspace page); LIVE 7–10 PM caller line 1-888-331-1210; Show offices 412-560-4109; Laurence Gaines, executive producer. Best method: E-mail: bevsmith OR lgaines @thebevsmithshow.com. Best pitches are short and concise e-mails, with additional info as attachments. Long phone message "pitches" are a turn-off. No response? You should follow up with either a short e-mail or call. But don't keep doing it.

Invited Back? If they gave a dynamic, engaging and in some cases, entertaining, segment.

Bio of Bev Smith: Bev began her television and radio career in 1971 when she was named Pittsburgh's first African American consumer affairs investigative reporter for WPXI Television, an NBC affiliate. Among her nearly 300 awards for contributions in radio and TV, she received the 1980 and 1989 Pennsylvania Social Security Outstanding Journalist Award for consumer investigation reporting, never before or after presented to any journalist. Bev wrote a weekly consumer advice column, called "Bev Sez" for *The Pittsburgh Courier,* the nation's oldest African American newspaper. She also hosted a television talk show, "Vibrations," for KDKA TV.

In 1975, she was named news and public affairs director for the Sheridan Broadcasting Company (now the American Urban Radio Networks). She's hosted many radio and TV shows and was a guest host on the *Larry King Show* and *Kathy Hughes Show* on WOL Radio in Washington.

Conscious Rasta Report (now ***Culturally Conscious Communications***) with Keidi Obi Awadu on LIBRadio.com, airing weekdays, 6–8 AM (PT) 9–11 AM (ET)

Theme: Culturally conscious communications.

Guest Profile: Experts in all areas, authors, NGO leaders, community based activists. We prefer people of African descent, progressives and experts in their fields. We need to know that the guest has earned their credibility or has convincing communication skills.

Guest from Hell: Guest from hell has no verifiable facts, is argumentative or says "uuuhh" repeatedly.

Contact: info@libradio.net; 323-902-2919, 800-842-1409, London 0208.002.9096; http://www.LIBRadio.com; Keidi Obi Awadu. Best method: E-mail or phone. Press kit, web sites, copy of latest published book, CD or DVD all receive maximum attention. No response? Guests should be persistent as we get quite busy.

Invited Back? Our audience will respond quite enthusiastically to a guest who connects with them.

Bio of Keidi Obi Awadu: Keidi is founder and CEO of Black Star Media, a multi-media company specializing in web design, streaming media, audio and video production, and graphic design services. He is also founder of LIBRadio.com, an Internet radio station along with the complementary LIBtv.com web television.

During 1990–2006, Keidi authored 18 books and traveled throughout the U.S. and Canada lecturing from his *Conscious Rasta Report*. He has appeared on major television shows and talk radio throughout the U.S. and Canada.

Earlier in his career, he was a record producer and recording artist, producing more than 25 record albums for various artists. Skilled on a number of musical instruments and production tools, he was widely received in Jamaica, France and Spain. As a musician, he's traveled to 45 U.S. states.

Keidi has been a member of the D.C.–based think tank Information Project for Africa (Africa2000.com) for over a decade. On the west coast, he has been affiliated with the Afrikan Culture and Research Center Long Beach for over a dozen years. He is founder of the 7th Millennium Academy of Consciousness, a youth advocacy organization.

Empowered Black Perspectives with Rachel S. Ramone on Blog Talk Radio

Theme: Topic relating to issues pertaining to developments in Black communities.

Guest Profile: Diverse panel of guests who have an empowered perspective on various topics regardless of race, gender or religious beliefs. Commitment to empowering communities and advocating social awareness. Credentials and past interview experiences are essential. A prominent guest was Janks Morton, producer and filmmaker of the highly acclaimed film *What Black Men Think*.

We have a rate card for guests that request specific advertising support. This is because we advertise and promote all broadcasts via our book club as well as over 150 different Internet network affiliate groups. Our book club meets each month in Atlanta and currently has close to 550 members (both Black and White and all income levels) that meet at the local Barnes and Noble. We submit the names of the books we wish to have read and they make the purchases at the bookstore and later meet there to discuss them.

Invited guests are given the opportunity to be on a show without paying for advertising. They must, however, provide giveaways for listeners as well as a link to our website from theirs up to a year. These guests are usually doing something in the community, have a book or endeavor that we believe our listeners would be interested in knowing more about. For example, we host shows with everyone from filmmakers and authors to bloggers and health professionals. As stated before, they must be willing to give as they wish to receive. We believe that promoting businesses without requesting any form of remuneration weakens the integrity of our shows. Therefore we are able to be more selective as to who we invite as well as who we are promoting on our broadcasts.

Guest from Hell: Obnoxious behavior.

Contact: Empoweredblack@aol.com; 1-888-425-8298; Empoweredblackperspectives.com; Best method: E-mailing a bio and a press kit. No response? Resend e-mail with SECOND REQUEST in the subject field.

Invited Back? Rapport with host and listener requests

Bio of Rachel Ramone: Rachel is the executive director of the Empowered Black Women's Network Alliance. The format and weekly broadcasts for her radio show were established in 2005 under the auspice of the Alliance in order to create social awareness. Broadcasts are structured to inform and disseminate information pertaining to issues affecting Black communities throughout the global diaspora.

Rachel has hosted hundreds of broadcasts which are promoted via her listening audience, network affiliates and social events that are held each year in conjunction with EBWN's empowerment conventions. She is also the president of the Atlanta Book Club (the largest and most diverse book club in Atlanta), and publicity director for the National Black Writers and Artists Association.

She has been a featured columnist for magazines and e-zines and is developing a print magazine to complement her radio broadcasts.

Animals

Have a tail waggin' day! — Kim Bloomer's signature line

The All Pets Radio Show with Bill Clanton, Steven Clanton and Mike Sheck airs on WRRW, Virginia Beach, Va. and has been featured on WHFR in Detroit, Mich.

The All Pets Radio Show also produces these shows: *All Pets Spotlight*: a talk program about anything pet related; *The Pet Lover's Oldies Show*: a music program for pet lovers that do interviews; *All Pets News Break*: a short form program that usually features edited versions of *All Pets Spotlight*.

Theme: Pets.

Guest Profile: All types of guests; typically our guests range from authors to doctors to even CEOs of pet companies. The ideal guest would be someone who really wants to talk about their product. We want the WHO — WHAT — WHY.

Guest from Hell: One that doesn't know their product or book very well. I would expect the person to be willing to talk. Sometimes we get guests that we have to kinda pull teeth with to get them to speak.

Contact: info@allpetsradio.com; http://www.allpetsradio.com; Bill Clanton, program director. Best method: Bio via e-mail. No response? A second e-mail is fine. Often the amount of requests for interviews is overwhelming, so it may take as much as 2–3 days for me to get back to someone.

Invited Back? Depends on the quality of the content of the interview.

Bio of Bill Clanton: Bill is program director and co-founder of his show. Having worked in broadcast radio for the past 15 years and always living around pets of all kinds, he felt that bringing these two loves together would be a perfect match.

Bill lives with his wife Natercia, 6-year-old son William, Ringo (German short hair mix), Donut (pit bull terrier), and two beautiful cats (Sassy and Shadow). His mission in the pet world is to help pet owners and non–pet owners around the world understand the concept of unconditional love. Whether you are happy, sad, mad or glad, your dog will always be there for you with a smile and a wagging tail.

Animal Hour with Susie Aga on Tuesday at 2 PM (ET), aired on 1620 AM, Sandy Springs, Ga. and live and archived at http://www.radiosandysprings.com

Theme: Animal interest, behavior and dog training solutions, aggression management, etc.

Guest Profile: Experts, Dept. of Natural Resources experts from Georgia. We want them outgoing, friendly and knowledgeable — plus of course talkative. Usually how they answer my pre-interview questions is most important.

Guest from Hell: Someone that answers with yes and no and does not elaborate or someone that does not know their material.

Contact: Atlantadogtrainer@yahoo.com; 770-754-9178; http://www.atlantadogtrainer.com; Susie Aga. Best method: E-mail. No response? They should call me. I answer all e-mails within a 24 hour period so if I did not reply I did not get it.

Invited Back? If the guest is fun and informative.

Bio of Susie Aga: Susie is a certified canine behavior and training specialist who received her certification from Triple Crown Academy, a world leader in pet education. She has 20 years' experience with dogs and is recommended by more than 45 veterinarians in the metro Atlanta area.

As "Pet Expert" for Pet Doctor Online — http://www.petdoctoronline.com, she is interviewed by veterinarians about behavioral problems, such as separation anxiety, cage aggression and other hard to define issues facing many owners and their dogs.

A popular guest speaker in the psychology department at Georgia State University, Susie lectures on canine behavior and the similarities of conditioning behaviors in humans and animals.

She has six rescue dogs of her own and donates much of her time and services to rescue organizations. You can truly say her life has gone to the dogs and that is just the way SHE WANTS IT.

Full bio at http://www.dogcastradio.com/episode/152_episode_52__freestyle_and_aggression.htm

Animal Radio with Hal Abrams and Judy Francis, airing on 94 stations from KOST 103.5 in Los Angeles to WXBA, NY.

Theme: Animals — celebrities and their pets, caller questions.

Guest Profile: Celebs, authors, animal experts. One popular guest is Marty Becker, a veterinarian who also appears on ABC's "Good Morning America." (Becker credits *Animal Radio*'s website with carrying the first wide-ranging database on news about the pet-food recall before the Food and Drug Administration got up to speed). Recognition, expertise, charisma, uniqueness are important qualities. We want as much information as possible.

Guest from Hell: When host does more talking than guest ... hate trying to "jump-start" guests. I'll fire the producer first.

Contact: Hal@AnimalRadio.com; 435-644-5992; http://www.AnimalRadio.com. Best method: E-mail. Call with a pitch to follow up on a media kit. No response? Call me and engage me.

Invited Back? If they are fun on the air and get the phones ringing.

Bio of Hal Abrams: Hal is a major-market radio veteran turned operations manager of Animal Radio Network and a long-time animal advocate, spending weeks inside doghouses (literally) to raise money for SPCAs throughout the U.S.

In 1999, Hal gave up a 17-year morning-radio routine to create the largest and most listened to animal radio programming. Hal lives with his wife and four cats near the Best Friends Animal Sanctuary in Kanab, Utah — home to 1800 animals at any one time.

Animal Rescue: Where to Go, What to Do, How to Help! with Barbara Niven and Phyllis Botti on Big Media USA, http://www.bigmediausa.com/show.asp?sid=524 and also on iTunes and podcast. Barbara's other show is *Show Business 101* on page 78.

Theme: Animal rescue.

Guest Profile: Animal rescue organizations and animal advocates, people who are passionate about helping to rescue, help and save animals of all kinds. Someone who is passionate about what they do, and who wants to share that passion with the audience. A pay it forward situation. Someone who loves to talk and have fun is fantastic, but you don't know that until they're actually sitting in front of you at the microphone. You just cross your fingers.

Their bio and what they do tell me a lot. Their personality and passion can come through even in an e-mail. It's helpful to know if they've been interviewed before so that they have a sense about how it all works. I also ask guests to send me 20 questions they want me to ask them, so that I make sure we get their message out in the time allotted. It's easy to get caught up in chit-chat unless I'm very organized, and time goes by very quickly.

Guest from Hell: Someone who answers with short yes or no answers. It's scary when you realize that's what you're up against in the first few moments of the interview, and then you know you are going to have to scramble to fill the black hole of dead air space. It's not fun then, it's work. You can't play and make magic.

Contact: barbara@barbaraniven.com; Withheld upon request; http://www.barbaraniven.com; Barbara Niven. Best method: E-mailing me with a bio and/or press kit. No response? If I don't get back in a reasonable amount of time, please e-mail me again. Sometimes I lose it in the amount of e-mail I get, and I'm sorry. I'm also an actress and do film projects out of town for weeks at a time. I've got a pretty good system to keep me organized, but it's not perfect. I do like people to follow up with a second e-mail. They are not bugging me — and I will get back to them ASAP.

Invited Back? If we're having so much fun that I know we have enough to talk about for FIVE shows. I need people with personality — because I find the more fun we have during the interview, the more fun the audience has. That energy is magic. I love having guests return with new information and updates.

Guest Comment: "My experience on *Animal Rescue* was very worthwhile and enjoyable. Barbara and Phyllis were very gracious hostesses, and they did an excellent job in structuring the interview to ensure we captured important details concerning the topic under discussion. As a result of their show, we have received a number of visitors to our website, some of which have made contributions to our campaign" [banning puppy mills and dog auctions in Ohio].— Mary O'Connor-Shaver, Columbus Top Dogs (Shure Pets), http://www.columbustopdogs.com, http://www.BanOhioDogAuctions.com

Bio of Barbara Niven: One of Hollywood's busiest actresses, shooting 18 films and several TV guest star roles in the past three years, Barbara is on the national board of directors for the Screen Actors Guild.

Her motto is: "Live your dreams! Don't settle for less than wonderful in your life. And don't give up five minutes before the miracle."

If you're not living the life you've always dreamed of, it's not too late to start a rewrite, she believes. She has created a program called "ACT as If!" that uses acting techniques to help people design what they want and to start living it right now. It's the secret to getting the techniques from "The Secret" out of our thoughts and into our physical realities. You must redesign your "character" and your lifestyle from the inside out, just like an actor does, so that your belief system starts to kick in. Then the more you believe, the more you experience, and the more you experience, the more you believe. You actually begin to transform into that character and that lifestyle. It's powerful and it's fun and anyone can learn to do it.

Barbara was almost 30 when she began her acting career, after becoming a wife and mother. One day she received notice about her ten year high school reunion and asked herself, "Have you achieved what you thought you would in your life so far?" It hit her like a ton of bricks that she was living everybody else's idea of who she should be.

So she set aside the "what ifs" and refused to take "no" for an answer. She talked her way into a news internship at Portland's NBC affiliate, selling her first story to network. Then she discovered her real passion, acting, and has been making a living at it, against all odds, for more than 20 years now.

Her love of animals began early on. A native of Portland, Oregon, Barbara had a horse in her backyard and went hunting and fishing with the guys.

She's proud her daughter is going after her own dreams now, which are very different from hers. "That is the best gift I could have given her, watching me fight for my dreams, so that she now has the courage to make her own dreams and destiny come true."

Animal Talk Naturally with Kim Bloomer and Jeannie Thomason on Tuesday and Wednesday at 2:30 PM (ET) on BlogTalk Radio at http://www.blogtalkradio.com/animaltalknaturally or use this url if it is easier to remember http://www.Holistic-Pet-Audio.com. The podcast version can be listened to at http://www.AnimalTalkNaturally.com or on the Blog Talk Radio show site following the live version of the show. The duo also hosts *The Dog View*, together with friend and like-minded dog lover, Jan Cooper. This is not a regular weekly show but a special show reserved just for special needs or stories to help dogs or how dogs help humans. http://www.TheDogView.com

Theme: Empowering pet owners with UNlearning to care for their animals naturally.

Guest Profile: We look for guests who have knowledge of and experience with working with animals in a natural health capacity — holistic veterinarians, natural health practitioners, behavior experts based on the nature of animals, etc., and those focused on the human-animal bond. Authors we look for have books on natural animal care and health, animal nature or the human-animal bond.

Our ideal guest is one who is willing to work outside the box, meaning traditional radio and take the experience of online radio (podcasting) as a new and vital way to gain an additional audience for their book and/or passion/mission. We want to know their passions, their experiences, their credentials and most DEFINITELY the sound of their voice and how they field questions in a natural conversational setting. We have a variety of repeat guests back by popular demand and they ALL have a natural knack and passion for educating pet owners, sharing vital information that leaves our audience knowing that they've received valuable information they can take home and apply to the care of their animals.

Guest from Hell: Mostly those who won't commit to a deadline. We don't chase guests. Also overly self-promotional guests. We will promote our guests so they don't have to do so repeatedly during the show. If they don't comply with our time frame, then we move on to those who will. We rarely have any trouble with guests. A few pet peeves? Those who answer in monosyllables, who don't provide us information to research them, such as articles, websites and blogs, or authors who have a book they want us to promote on the show but don't realize we must read the book first to review it before we can interview them. Courtesy to hosts is to send in the book for review without being prompted to do so. Guests who continue to promote their product or service DURING the show will not be asked back on the show. We promote our guests well, so anyone doing that is all about themselves and not sharing their knowledge with our audience to better help the animals. If a guest wants to offer something special to our listeners that is definitely welcome.

Contact: info@animaltalknaturally.com; 505-554-1476; http://www.AnimalTalkNaturally.com; http://www.aspenbloompetcare.com

Blogs: Bark 'N' Blog, A Dog's View (http://www.bark-n-blog.com and http://www.adogsview.com

Contact (for media or press): Dr. Kim Bloomer. Best method: E-mail is preferred and we prefer potential guests include their website and blogs links for us to research them. If they are an author we need for them to send us each a copy of their book for review. We make our decision based upon if they are in line with the theme of our show and their educational focus. We honestly don't like pitches but we do need bios and press kits if we determine they will be a guest on our show. If they have done their homework and researched our show (listened) they will know that Dr. Jeannie and I prefer them to contact us via e-mail with how they can be of help to our listeners. We're not interested in their agenda or how great they are but how what they share can empower and enrich our audience that is applicable to helping their animals. We don't like being pitched. A bio is great but tell us why you're sending a bio first because otherwise it may end up in File 13. We also like guests to be referred by others. Others who can vouch for their work. Most of our guests come to us through referral.

To schedule an appearance contact: Dr. Jeannie Thomason at thewholedog@gmail.com. No response? If we don't get back to them, then we most likely do not feel they are a good fit for our show.

Invited Back? Those who have a genuine care and concern for the animals, in teaching and educating their owners on how to properly care for them, who aren't afraid to buck the status quo with professional aplomb (not vulgarity), who don't have an agenda but a heartfelt concern and love for natural animal care, animal nature, the human-animal bond and the animals receiving the care. Some of our guests are asked back repeatedly such as Ron Hevener, Dr. Hugh Bassham, Dr. Stephen Blake, Dr. Myrna Milani, Maggie Wright, and Tallgrass Institute among just a few because of their genuine concern and care for and of animals.

Guest Comments: "Thanks guys for what you do and who you are. The talk is easy, the walk more challenging and who you are not what you say."—Dr. Stephen Blake, author of *The Pet Whisperer* (The Pet Whisperer Publishing Co., 2003)

"I can't thank you enough for allowing me to speak on your show. I must say that of all the TV shows, radio shows, and magazines we've been written up in, your show focused more on the meat of the subject instead of just the frills than all the other shows put together... I wish that all the other media that we have been exposed to could have at least covered even 10 percent of what your show did."—Irena Schulz, owner of the famous dancing Cockatoo, Snowball Bird Lovers Only Rescue

Bios of Dr. Kim Bloomer and Dr. Jeannie Thomason: Kim is a veterinary naturopath and proficient blogger and writer on natural pet health. She is co-author of *Whole Health for Happy Dogs* (Quarry Books 2006) and has worked in traditional veterinary medicine for many years and continues to do extensive research into natural health care for dogs and cats.

Dr. Kim is currently enrolled in the Clayton College of Natural Health. She finished her bachelor of science degree in human holistic nutrition in January 2008 and has begun her studies for her human doctor of naturopathy degree. She earned her doctor of veterinary naturopathy degree from the Kingdom College of Natural Health.

Jeannie is a veterinary naturopath and former licensed veterinarian technician. She worked in the veterinary field for many years and continues to study animal nutrition and holistic animal husbandry. Dr. Jeannie has been breeding and showing dogs for more than 20 years and practices what she preaches in maintaining her beloved dogs' health. Her love for animals and passion for natural health led her to create her website, The Whole Dog (http://www.thewholedog.org).

She also has a blog where she shares her passion for natural dog health and the issues surrounding the industry at Whole Dog News (http://www.wholedognews.com). Dr. Jeannie earned her doctor of veterinary naturopathy degree from the Kingdom College of Natural Health. She is also the founder of the Natural Rearing Breeders Association (http://www.nrbreedersassociation.org).

Animals Aloud with Deirdre Kennedy, podcast.

Theme: The complex bond between humans and animals, from bees to bears, from cats to dogs.

Guest Profile: Authors, animal experts, filmmakers, entertainers, biologists, and anyone with a compelling story about animals. People who are good story-tellers, articulate, concise, preferably a pleasant way of speaking. I usually do a pre-interview so that I can determine if they will be interesting on air. They don't necessarily have to have past interview experience. I want to know if they have credentials to talk about their subject.

But sometimes that can just be someone who's got a very good story about an encounter with an animal and can recall it in a very funny way. When I'm dealing with scientific experts, I look for people who have good anecdotes and who can speak in a lay person's language about scientific issues. Her celebrity guests have included Isabella Rossellini, actress and Wildlife Conservation Network advocate, and Normand La Tourelle, founder of Cirque du Soleil.

Guest from Hell: Someone who punctuates their sentences with "um, you know uh" or who repeats words before delivering a sentence.

Contact: dk@animalsaloud.net; 415-474-4449; http://www.animalsaloud.net. Best method: The best way is to e-mail a press release with a bio and some background information. It's great if you have photos we can post on the website. No response? Yes, it's good to e-mail and check back but if I don't respond after the second e-mail, it probably means I'm not going to line up an interview.

Invited Back? I don't often have guests back on the show. I have a regular veterinarian on who can talk about various different types of animal diseases.

Guest Comment: "*Animals Aloud* is a radio show with a mission — to take a compelling look at the plight of animals and their role in society. This show has the potential to awaken millions of listeners to critical issues that impact animals and all of us" — Wayne Pacelle, president and CEO, The Humane Society of the United States, wpacelle@hsus.org

Bio of Deirdre Kennedy: Deirdre has spent 20 years as a broadcast journalist. She has written and produced radio stories for *All Things Considered, Morning Edition, Marketplace, Living on Earth, On the Media, Performance Today, The Infinite Mind, Latino USA, This American Life*, and the *BBC World Service's Outlook*.

For nine years, she was a reporter and news anchor for KQED FM and KALW FM in San Francisco.

In her early career, she was a desk editor and writer for NBC's London bureau and ITN's World News and Channel 4 News in London, England. She later worked in the San Francisco Bay Area as a news writer for KRON TV and KTVU Channel 2 Oakland. She is host and executive producer of her radio show, which aired on XM Satellite Radio for a year and is now available as a podcast.

DogCast Radio with Julie Hill on http://www.DogCastRadio.com and through iTunes. Worldwide audience — 80 percent U.S. The show airs twice monthly on the second and fourth Saturday.

Theme: Dogs. Breed profiles, dog-related interviews and news from around the world, training advice, kids' section, website reviews, fiction, etc., all dog related.

Guest Profile: People with expertise and experience of dogs. For example we talk to breeders and people who show their dogs for our breed profiles. We talk to trainers about training. We have interviewed dog owners with interesting stories or stories that have hit the headlines.

We want someone with something interesting to say about dogs. This can vary from someone who has spent years amassing expert knowledge about their specialist subject, to a first time dog owner. Experts who have built up a name for themselves are good, as they have authority. We have interviewed some people who just happen to have unusual dogs — for example Jude Stringfellow about her three legged dog Faith. We have also talked to people who offer unique dog related vacation experiences. If we feel a person has something to say that will interest, educate and/or entertain our listeners they're a good guest. We always try to inspire responsible dog ownership. It is always great when the guest has a clear idea of what they want to say, and is articulate and confident. Having said that, I always start off an interview just with a quick chat to settle the interviewee if I feel that will help.

I need to know at least an outline of what the person has to offer. Do they have a book, if so what is it about and what inspired it? What makes their dog special? I need the basic idea that is going to make them interesting to an audience, then we can explore further as we chat. It doesn't matter to us whether someone has never been interviewed before, or they are a seasoned professional. Sound of voice isn't too important — it is the content of what they say, but of course very strong accents might be a problem as we have an international audience.

Guest from Hell: A cat person. Seriously, someone monosyllabic would be a problem. I always try to do enough research that I have some questions to prompt a guest with. Since the interviews are not broadcast live, we can edit and so at worst if it's a bad interview for whatever reason we just wouldn't use it.

Contact: Julie@DogCastRadio.com; 315-849-2022 (UK number 0121 288 0922); http://www.DogCastRadio.com. Best method: In the first place an e-mail is good, with the outline of why they/their dog would be of interest to our audience. A website link or other reference is useful, as well as photos. As well as longer interviews, we also like to hear from people with dog related problems, that we can find expert help with. No response? Remind us again with an e-mail, or leave a phone message.

Invited Back? How much they have to say of interest basically. Mim Edwards is an excellent trainer from Adelaide, Australia, and we have talked to her several times because her advice is sound, and she puts in down-to-earth terms with a lot of humor. Dr. Stanley Coren has been on a couple of times, and is always fascinating and amusing.

Guest Comment: "My experience was wonderful as a guest on the *DogCast radio* show. The show is Internet-only and pre-taped several weeks in advance, however. The hosts were professional and they allowed me to discuss my book (which I was promoting) in great detail" — Jason Rich, author of *Pampering Your Pooch: Discover What Your Dog Wants, Needs and Loves* (Howell Book House 2006).

Bio of Julie Hill: Julie is a dog enthusiast who falls into conversation with people easily and decided to turn a fault into a job. She lives in the UK with her three dogs and assorted humans. She began her program in 2005. "Basically, if you like dogs we're the show for you," she says "If you don't like dogs, maybe we can convert you."

Dr. Carol on Pets with Dr. Carol Osborne. She is also host of *Anti-Pet Aging* on blogtalkradio.

Theme: Pets.

Guest Profile: Pet professionals both traditional and alternative. Want interesting commentary, credentials, good on air.

Contact: drcarol@drcarol.com; 866-372-2765; http://www.carolonpets.com; Dr. Carol Osborne — 440-287-6787. Best method: E-mail preferred but phone is fine — 440-287-6787. A press kit is appreciated. No response? E-mail or call.

Invited Back? Response to former segment.

Bio of Dr. Carol Osborne: Dr. Osborne earned her B.S. degree from John Carroll University and graduated summa cum laude. She received her D.V.M. degree with honors from the Ohio State University College of Veterinary Medicine and is the nation's first veterinarian to be a board certified diplomat in anti-aging medicine. Dr. Osborne has pioneered the exploration of new therapies for the treatment and prevention of age related degenerative disease, as well as promotion of optimum health and performance for pets. Currently, she devotes much of her time to the research and development of advanced biosciences for the benefit of animal health and welfare.

Licensed from coast to coast, Dr. Osborne has been in private clinical practice in Chagrin Falls, Ohio, for over 20 years.

She is the founder and president of the American Pet Institute, a non-profit organization dedicated to the promotion of animal health and welfare and president of PAAWS, Pet Anti-Aging Wellness System.

She is the author of international best sellers, *Dr. Carol's Naturally Healthy Dogs* and *Dr. Carol's Naturally Healthy Cats*, both published in 2006 by Marshall Editions.

Dr. Shawn — The Natural Vet with Shawn Messonnier, DVM, aired on Martha Stewart Radio Sirius Channel 112, on Tuesday, 8–9 PM (ET) and repeated Saturday, 8–9:30 PM (ET).

Theme: Natural pet care.

Guest Profile: Anything related to people or pet health, especially with a natural approach. Guests should have an interesting topic and be a good talker. We like to know their past interview experiences, credentials and sound of their voice.

Guest from Hell: A boring guest, someone who answers yes or no w/o expounding on the answer, or someone who is so well prepared that he does a lecture and I can't get a question into what should be a discussion and not a one-sided pitch.

Contact: shawnvet@sbcglobal.net; 972-867-8800; http://www.petcarenaturally.com. Best method: E-mail any info and mail any products, books, etc. No response? Follow-up e-mail ... I'm very busy and need frequent reminders...

Invited Back? If they sound interesting and exciting.

Bio of Shawn Messonnier, D.V. M.: Dr. Messonnier is a holistic pet columnist for Animal Wellness, Body + Soul, and Veterinary Forum. His weekly newspaper column, The Holistic Pet, is read by millions of pet owners across North America each week. Dr. Messonnier owns Paws and Claws Animal Hospital in Plano, Texas.

He is author of *The Natural Vet's Guide to Preventing and Treating Cancer in Dogs* (New World Library 2006), *8 Weeks to a Healthy Pet* (Rodale Books 2003); *The Natural Health Bible for Dogs and Cats* (Three Rivers Press 2001), *The Allergy Solution for Dogs* (Prima Lifestyles 2000); and *The Arthritis Solution for Dogs and Cats* (Prima Lifestyles 2000).

Dr. Messonnier is a graduate of Texas A&A College of Veterinary Medicine.

Friesian Ink Radio with Melissa Alvarez (monthly) on Blog Talk Radio, http://blogtalkradio.com/FriesianInkRadio. Melissa is also host of two other shows on Blog Talk Radio: *The Reader's Round Table* on page 30 and *Celtic Seers* on page 162.

Theme: To interview those involved with horses, whether they're trainers, riders or just horse lovers. Special emphasis on Friesians and dressage.

Guest Profile: Equestrians, trainers, riders, vets, anyone involved with horses who has a message that will teach our listeners. Someone who is knowledgeable about a topic that deals with horses or someone who has information that would be of interest *to horse owners*. Do they have knowledge that will be beneficial to those in the horse world?

Guest from Hell: Someone with a bad attitude who hasn't prepared for the show or someone who doesn't show up without giving prior notice.

Contact: melissa@friesianink.com; 561-776-0758; http://FriesianInk.com, http://FriesianInkCommunity.com, http://blogtalkradio.com/FriesianInkRadio, http://TopHatFriesians, http://EquineBarnSupply.com; Melissa Alvarez. Best method: By sending me an e-mail with a short bio and letting me know what they can offer my listeners. Do they have a following, will they bring new listeners to the show? No response? They should contact me through the Friesian Ink Community if they've e-mailed and I haven't answered. They can call as well but I'm at the barn quite a bit and it may take a while for me to get back to them.

Invited Back? If I have time on the schedule, if they are engaging, and if they've helped to promote their segment to bring more listeners. Boring guests without a sense of humor probably won't get invited back.

Bio of Melissa Alvarez: Melissa and her husband Jorge are the owners of FriesianInk.com, a new online advertising site for horses and horse related products.

They wanted to create a community for horse enthusiasts so they also started the Friesian Ink Community and Friesian Ink Radio to go along with the launch of Friesian Ink. Melissa and Jorge are breeders of Friesian horses with their website at http://www.TopHatFriesians.com and also run an online retail store at http://www.EquineBarnSupply.com.

For a bio of Melissa's publishing career, see *The Reader's Round Table* on page 30.

Horse Talk with June Evers, Chip Watson and Peter Cashman aired on WTBQ, Orange County, NY, on Saturday, 7:30–8:30 AM (ET).

Theme: Basically horses all the time.

Guest Profile: Must be equine related. We do prefer in-studio local Orange County, NY, guests but do love to hear from well-known horse people, people offering something totally new and different to the horse world. Not too interested in authors unless the book is something totally new rather than the run of the mill horse trainer, etc. Please not a non-horse person selling something to horse people. It will come out on air in about 5 minutes that the interviewee is not horsey. Definitely provide credentials, small bio, horse experience bio and what you want to talk about.

Guest from Hell: We have not really had any bad guests but I guess guests who call on cell phones. We usually just get rid of them quickly. Oh and one that did not really tell us the correct credentials. But we pulled it through once we figured it out. Nonetheless, she will not be invited back.

Contact: jevers@warwick.net or info@horseholowpress.com; 845-651-1110; http://www.wtbq.com; June Evers. Best method: Please do NOT call or mail; use e-mail only. No response? We are not interested then.

Invited Back? We usually invite humorous people back.

Bio of June Evers: June is a horse person of more than 38 years. She is a graduate of the Rhode Island School of Design and author of the following horse books, all published by Horse Hollow Press: *The Original Book of Horse Treats* (1994), *The Ultimate Guide to Pampering Your Horse* (1996), *Horse Lover's Birthday Book* (2006), *Anyone Can Draw Horses* (2003), *The Squeamish Person's Guide to Pulling Your Horse's Mane* (2007) and *The Horse of My Dreams* (2007).

Bio of Chip Watson: Chip is Mid-Hudson regional director for the New York State Horse Council and member of most horse clubs in the area. His goal is to preserve and protect the horse industry by providing to the public awareness and appreciation of the impact of the equine industry on the community.

The KAHI Corral with B.K. England and Margot Farrelly on AM 950 KAHI, Auburn, CA, with live stream on the Internet.

Theme: Horses, sometimes dogs and other farm and domestic animals, but 90 percent+ about horses.

Guest Profile: Authors and equine artists, trainers. Passion about the subject + personality are prime. Credentials are important; they must be knowledgeable about horses. Sometimes enthusiastic amateurs make the best guests.

Guest from Hell: A guest who may start to answer a question, then just have nothing more to say, and you just can't drag the desired info out of them. No monotones, please.

Contact: bkequiart@jps.net; 916-663-1211; http://www.bkenglandart.net; B.K (Betty) England. Best method: E-mailing or a press kit would be best. No response? I hope I'd have the courtesy to respond in a timely manner, but I might be away, overwhelmed, etc., so another e-mail would be appreciated.

Invited Back? If we had a good time, and they obviously did, too, we'd love to chat again!

Guest Comment: "As the illustrator of *The Way of the Horse—Equine Archetypes for Self Discovery*, I was interviewed on *KAHI Corral* radio with B.K. England and Margot Farrelly. Our conversation was delightful. It was like having a chat with two old friends and our conversation naturally evolved without ever seeming contrived, yet somehow they managed to fit in interesting questions that kept the flow going, while explaining in detail my product which isn't an easy thing to explain. We didn't want the time to end and I'm sure the listeners felt that way too."—Kim McElroy, http://www.spiritofhorse.com

Bios of B.K. England and Margot Farrelly: Born in Wenatchee, Washington, B.K. grew up on a ranch, where an eclectic herd of horses pranced through her childhood. She and her father shared a love of all horses, and her grandfathers were both horsemen. One had farmed with draft teams and took B.K. to harness races; the other especially loved gaited horses.

B.K. is an artist who has had many one-artist shows. She has been poster artist for such varied California events as the Auburn Wild West Stampede, the Draft Horse Classic, and the Cowpoke Poetry Gathering. Her portrait titled "The Spanish Ambassador" was accepted by the American Academy of Equine Arts, and hung in the Kentucky Derby Museum. She has also designed a logo and been yearbook artist for the American Endurance Ride Conference. Each year, B.K. designs an equine art t-shirt for the Loomis Basin Horsemen's Association Benefit Horse Show, held each October in northern California.

Horses are definitely B.K.'s favorite subject. Her equine portraits can be found in private collections from coast to coast, and in England, and she has been featured columnist for *Equine Images* magazine. Her "cowboy" and equine poetry has been published in *Western Horseman* and *American Cowboy Poet*.

Margot is a long time breeder of quarter horses, photographer, equine event planner, AQHA officer, etc., and has been with the show for a few years. She recently returned to *KAHI*, after being co-host of the original *Horsetalk* show in the 1990s.

Nature's Translator with Tracy Ann aired Thursdays on Contact Talk Radio.

Theme: Any topic which is or can be related to animals, nature and spirituality.

Guest Profile: Guests range from natural healing and natural products to spirituality, metaphysics, authors, musicians, animal related businesses including non profits. Someone with unique perspectives and experiences, has integrity and is genuinely sincere. Want their biography and credentials.

Guest from Hell: One that takes over the show — talking over the host, not open to dialogue.

Contact: tracyann@naturestranslator.com; 360-895-8800; http://contacttalkradio.com and http://www.naturestranslator.com; Tracy Ann. Best method: E-mail a bio, website link (if possible) with a presentation of topic. No response? Do not e-mail or call.

Invited Back? The content of what they have to offer the listeners and their behavior on the show.

Guest Comment: "Thank you for last night's interview/dialogue. I realized afterwards how many aspects I managed to articulate for the first time, i.e., like the colors of the CD covers, etc. Yes, you are a conduit for translation. A real gift. No wonder words are important to you and their power as well. So I thank you for that all. I hope it was well received. It takes time, I believe for people to respond as the last time. Have a great day and again thank you for the opportunity to connect with you again and your listeners." — Janet Marlow, *Music for Pets and People*, http://www.musicforpetsandpeople.com

"I, too, enjoyed being on your program, and I'm so grateful to you for featuring this important topic for your listeners. I've received some very nice feedback about the program... In any event, I thank you once again for the opportunity you've given me to shine some more light on the important topic of pet loss." — Marty Tousley, author and originator of on-line courses on grief, http://www.griefhealing.com

Bio of Tracy Ann: Tracy Ann, nature's translator, is an animal communicator and Zimbaté practitioner. She began to pursue a career in animal communication in the late 1990's as a result of her own animal's behavioral issues. Tracy Ann had originally been skeptical of a person's ability to "talk" with animals, but after asking an animal communicator to speak with her own animals and witnessing results, her skepticism became a curiosity which then became her career.

After a year of practicing animal communication, another of her dogs became terminally ill. As a result her journey as an animal communicator was now to include the healing arts with the focus on Zimbaté. Tracy Ann has studied Bach flower remedies, essential oils, Pranic energy, the use of stones for their healing qualities, and the most amazing healing technique of all, Zimbaté.

Talk with Your Animals with Joy Turner airs Wednesdays, 12–1 PM (PT) on KKNW 1150 AM in western Washington, http://www.1150kknw.com, or re-broadcast on the Animal Radio Network http://www.animalradio.com

Theme: Animal communication and alternative ways of relating to the animal companions you share life with.

Guest Profile: Sometimes the guests are authors — if the book is extremely educational and would warrant more information from the author — or if it contains information not generally in consideration. Specialties are literally anything relating to animals and their companions. I look for someone who knows their topic, is passionate about animals and their topic, can talk to the level that works best for the radio (no jargonese, etc.), and can be asked a question and expound on it.

Guest from Hell: Someone who uses jargon people don't understand, who talks without pauses, who wants to be interviewed only to promote themselves without revealing any information about their topic. I like to talk over the phone with the potential guest to get the feel of them and see if we would be a good match.

Contact: joy@talkwithyouranimals.com; http://www.TalkWithYourAnimals.com, http://www.UniversalLight.net, http://www.JoyTurner.com; 425-867-1779. Best method: I prefer not to be upchucked on initially. Just a simple e-mail providing some basic information about what they do and a way to contact them both by e-mail and phone. No response? It depends on what they consider reasonable time. We usually book out a few months in advance so it would not be unusual for them to hear from us even after a month or two. Sometimes we have so many guests to choose from we take the ones first we think will have the most interest to our listeners and others may be called even a year later. So, if they don't hear from us, e-mail us again and then wait. We will either get back to them to schedule or we are not interested in their topic.

Invited Back? Listener interest and, of course, the way we work together.

Bio of Joy Turner: Throughout her life, Joy has been the bridge between thousands of animals and their humans. She is a spiritual teacher and leading animal communicator with clients around the world.

"About 12 years ago, I began offering my services professionally," she says. "Over the years I have honed my abilities with the help of all the animals I have communed with. I can speak with all levels of Beings — personality, mental, emotional and Soul — speak with both animals and humans who have crossed over, and Spiritual Guides as well as teach others to speak with their animals."

Joy also hosted the television show, "Talk with Your Animals," writes columns in three magazines: *Holistic Horse*, *IGTimes* and *Modern Dog*, and is the author of the book series, *The Spiritual Principles of Con-*

sciousness and Manifestation (Authorhouse 2001). (Book I—*Living Happily in 3D*—is available for order in your local book stores.)

Talkin' Pets with Jon Patch, syndicated on 100 stations nationwide. Jon also covers remote broadcasts from national zoos, animal preserves, dog events like Westminster Kennel Club, the Genesis Awards in LA.

Theme: Medical and behavioral advice, discussions and comments about pets, wildlife and the environment.

Guest Profile: Authors, celebrities, organizations and foundations. Pleasant, well versed and entertaining. Would like to know as much as possible along with sample questions if applicable.

Guest from Hell: Yes or no answers to questions

Contact: jonpatch@talkinpets.com; 813-888-5043; http://www.talkinpets.com and http://www.myspace.com/talkinpets; Jon Patch. Best method: E-mail or send a press kit. No response? Do not call or e-mail.

Invited Back? Content.

Bio of Jon Patch: Jon graduated from Penn State University in 1983 with a degree in communications and broadcasting. He began hosting his show in 1989, first distributed through Sun Radio Network and later through USA Radio Networks and finally Business TalkRadio Network.

"I have been a believer that the animals on this planet are the true aspects of beauty and am proud to be a defender in helping their medical, behavior and overall existence here on earth," he says.

Wendy's Animal Talk with Wendy Nan Rees airing on Tuesdays, 1–2 PM, PT on http://www.healthylife.net

Theme: Animal talk.

Guest Profile: Must be in the pet world, such as authors who write books about animals or have a radio show. They know their topic very well. Nice to know a lot and they are fun to have on; easy going. Past interview experiences, credentials and sounds of their voice are all important.

Guest from Hell: Someone who is not ready.

Contact: wenan@aol.com; 310-344-6532; http://www.wendynanrees.com; Wendy Nan Rees or producer Ruthie Bently at 507-835-0021, thedogs8myemail@yahoo.com. Best method: Phone and press kit. No response? Please call me.

Invited Back? It depends on how they do on the show and feedback from listeners. Also, we do themes and if a former guest fits in with that theme they may be invited back.

Guest Comments: "It is always such a great pleasure being on *Wendy's Animal Talk Radio Show*. Wendy is wonderful and has great love for the animals. Her show is such a treat for animal lovers everywhere"—Joy Turner, host of *Talk with Your Animals*, see page 13.

Guest Comment from Wendy's former program, *The Wild Life Radio*: "I thought that working with Wendy was extremely rewarding. She is a well-informed host that focuses on key issues and gives pet owners helpful opinions. It was a pleasure to work with her."—Jessica Waldman, VMD, CCRTJ, Waldman@CalAnimalRehab.com

Bio of Wendy Rees: Wendy has been involved in the pet industry for over 25 years, starting when she founded Lip Smackers, Inc., a company dedicated to providing healthy, all natural treats to consumers who are concerned about the well-being of their pets. The Lip Smackers bakery still operates today out of the Pet Care Company located in Hermosa Beach, CA.

While creating her healthy products, Wendy created so many different recipes she was inspired to write her first book. *No Barking at the Table: Canine Recipes Most Begged For* (Lip Smackers 1991). Written to give dog owners some fresh and creative recipes on how to feed their best friends, the book was so well-received she co-authored two books published by Howell Book House—*No Barking at the Table 2* (1996) and *No Catnapping in the Kitchen* (1996).

Moving in a different direction, Wendy co-authored *The Name Game* (Howell Books 1996), a collection of over 100 celebrity essays along with over 1,000 suggestions of names. This fun book offers pet owners an entertaining and unique take on how and why people name their pets. A percentage of the proceeds from *The Name Game* went directly to PAWS, a non-profit organization dedicated to helping people with HIV/AIDS to care for their pets. Her latest collaboration is *The Natural Pet Food Cookbook* (Howell Book House 2007).

Wendy's success as an author and dog-treat creator led to numerous television appearances. She was the "Pet Lifestyle Advisor" on Animal Planet's *Pets burgh, USA* and has also appeared on The Home Shopping Network. Wendy also wrote a monthly column called "In the Kitchen with Wendy" for *Your Pet Magazine*.

Not one to rest on her laurels, Wendy returned to her entrepreneurial side, helping to create Cedar Green, a line of all natural odor eliminators created with pet owners in mind. The signature product is Freshen Vac; a heat activated natural odor eliminator that can be used in vacuum cleaners, dog beds, any air vent in your home and cars.

Antiques and Collectibles

APS Stamp Talk with Nancy Clark on WS Radio, http://www.wsradio.com/apsstamptalk (San Diego, CA).

Theme: Postage stamps, shows, collectors and dealers.

Guest Profile: Collectors, dealers, educators, authors, exhibitors and judges of philatelic materials. Interesting story to tell, interaction with collecting community, and/or postage issuing entities. Voice timbre and credentials in the world of stamp collecting are vital.

Guest from Hell: One who either answers with fewer than two words or one who has their own agenda and attempts to force it on the listeners.

Contact: nancy@stamps.org; 814-933-3803 (society telephone number); http://www.stamps.org; Nancy Clark. Best method: E-mailing a bio and pitch. No response? E-mail.

Invited Back? Their bon homme and their knowledge.

Bio of Nancy B. Clark: Nancy's extensive service to the American Philatelic Society goes back to 1982, which includes her chairmanship of the APS Youth Activities Committee (1982–86), and National and International philatelic juror, from 1982 until the present. During this time she developed materials for CD-ROMs produced by the APS Education Department and from 2002-3 she taught a course for teachers with APS director of education, Kim Kowalczyk, called Stamps in the Classroom.

From 2000–4, Nancy was director of the American Association of Philatelic Exhibitors and has founded stamp clubs and shows, and hosted conferences and exhibits.

Among her legion of honors is the Ernest Kehr Award, American Philatelic Society, 2006.

Burchard Galleries Antiques and Collectibles Radio Show with Jeffrey Burchard on WGUL 860 AM, Tampa Bay, FL, aired Sunday, 10–11 AM (ET) and on http://boss.streamos.com/wmedia-live/swn/9344/20_swn-20_wgul_0905_050913.asx

Theme: Discussing current market trends and values of antiques and fine art. Callers can learn the value of their treasures and gain information to help them in their collecting decision making.

Guest Profile: Guests include callers that wish information as to value and age of antiques. Someone who is handling an estate who needs advice and has an item(s) that may have exceptional value and we are able to make the discovery on the air. Someone who calls the show with an item of unknown value, consigns that item to one of our auctions and it sells for huge amounts of money, kind of like the Road show. As for experts in the field, which we occasionally have on the show, past interview experiences, credentials and sound of their voice are important. Other than that it is no holds barred, the more real it is the better.

Guest from Hell: Someone who is a doubting Thomas and has had a bad auction experience somewhere else or their item is so sentimentally valuable no one could possibly make them happy.

Contact: mail@burchardgalleries.com; 727-821-1167; http://www.burchardgalleries.com; Jeffrey Burchard. Best method: E-mail. No response? E-mail again.

Invited Back? Popular demand or response to a record-breaking sale of their items.

Bio of Jeffrey A. Burchard: Jeffrey is owner of Burchard Galleries/Auctioneers in St. Petersburg, Florida, since 1981.

Burchard is a full service estate liquidation entity to banks, attorneys and major estates, not only in the Tampa Bay area, but throughout the United States as well as in the International Fine Arts Auction Arena.

Jeffrey is graduate of Indiana University, where he completed CAI Advanced Auctioneer Training.

Jon Waldman and Russ Cohen host three shows: *XM Hockey Hour, Card Corner* and *Canadian Sport— The Magazine.*

Card Corner with Jon Waldman and Russ Cohen at http://www.sportsology.net

Theme: Collectibles.

Guest Profile: Authors and other personalities associated with the sport and non-sport memorabilia industries, such as cards, figurines, books and game-used paraphernalia. For me, a guest needs to be able to talk more than I do. They need to take my 10 to 20-word question and turn it into a 100-word answer. There's enough time that people hear my voice on a show. I like to know as little as possible about my first-time guests. If I know about them beforehand, chances are a lot of their hardcore fans do as well.

Guest from Hell: Someone who takes sports too seriously. You have to realize that sports is ultimately about leisure and entertainment.

Contact: Bookings are done through Russ — rcohen@sportsology.net or Jon at jwaldman@mts.net; Withheld upon request; http://www.sportsology.net; Jon Waldman. Best method: Best way is to either shoot me an e-mail with a press release and a direct contact or send a press kit in the mail. Out-of-the-blue is best done today electronically, hands down. No response? If that happens, send a second e-mail with a high priority marker. That will catch my eye, even if it's in a junk mail bin.

Invited Back? While there are guests I can talk to over and over because I've built a kinship with them, I always like to have someone on who has news or a deep perspective that can be applied to an ever-changing topic, such as new rules in hockey or innovations in the hobby.

Guest Comments: "Russ Cohen has run a great series of websites and a radio show related to all major sports. My experience with Russ and Doug Cataldo involved my activity and advocacy in trying to free Ted Williams from his frozen fate in AZ. Russ and his colleagues were and are sympathetic to my attempts to help Ted's daughter grant her father his desire to be cremated and dispersed over the FLA Keys. I appeared on Russ's show on occasion to discuss the hope that Ted's wishes would be respected. They also discussed my books on Ted Williams... Russ and colleagues are pros at asking great questions. They are knowledgeable in their sports-related fields, pick great topics and know both former and current players' records and current issues. They are fun to interact with and offer intelligent debates about sports in general. It has been my pleasure to interact with Russ for over five years." — Jack Polidoro, author of two novels involving Ted Williams, *Brain Freeze* (Xlibris Corporation 2005) and *Project Samuel* (Longtail Publishing 2001).

"Working so closely with the Sportsology group over the years has helped Upper Deck Sports Cards and Upper Deck Authenticated to really tap into a passionate group of collectors. Their *Card Corner* show has developed a loyal following of these collectors so we value the opportunity we have to appear on the show and use it as a way to share upcoming products and promotions with them." — Chris Carlin, hobby marketing manager

Bio of Jon Waldman: Jon has been a co-host on the Sportsology Radio Network for three years, and XM Radio for one year, doing both taped and live shows. He has been a regular contributor to *The Hockey News*, *Hockey Business News*, *The Hot Dog Hockey Post*, *The Winnipeg Free Press*, *The Winnipeg Sun*, *Winnipeg Men's Magazine*, *SLAM! Sports* and others since graduating from Ryerson University in 2002. Jon is also an editor with Matrix Group, Inc., a trade publication company, and has done contract work for Sport Media Group and Topps among others. Jon lives in Winnipeg with his wife, Elana.

Bio of Russ Cohen: Russ has co-authored a hockey book called *100 Ranger Greats*, as well as working solo on an upcoming baseball book called *The Resurrection of Baseball*. He has numerous articles published on NHL.com and other team websites as well as Slam and FoxSports.com. His articles have appeared in *Canadian Sports: The Magazine*, *Goalie News*, *New England Hockey Journal*, *The Hockey News* and he has a monthly column in *Center Ice Magazine* that is distributed to every amateur hockey rink in Pennsylvania.

His AM radio experience is extensive and he has been asked to be a guest or host on several radio shows, including two hockey shows on XM Satellite radio.

Collectors Coach Show with Jack DeAngelis at 5 PM (ET) on Business Talk Radio and WWDJ 970am, New York.

For a complete list of stations, visit http://www.collectorscoachshow.com/radioshowlist.htm

Theme: Money, memories, life.

Guest Profile: Expert financial, collectibles, life coach, business coach and manager of sales executives, books written on history, decision making. Good content and emotion towards his statements. A quick bio and direction the guest wants to go helps. Let him talk about his story.

Guest from Hell: The crazier the better — that's real radio. I haven't had that bad of experience yet — I normally will get what I want from them, but a shy speaker needs help.

Contact: imakemoneyjack@aol.com; 949-439-7527; http://www.businesstalkradio.net; archives — http://www.businesstalkradio.net/weekend_host/Archives/cc.shtml; Jack DeAngelis. Best method: E-mail or phone with a presentation, but you need cash to really make things happen, ideas we all have, the money ... show me the money, then the idea and we can talk about the future; ideas are great but sweat and money are the two great players. No response? Call me, something is wrong.

Invited Back? If they help acquire advertisers and my listeners respond well to the interview.

Bio of Jack DeAngelis: Jack started his career on Wall Street as a margin clerk, quickly working his way up the ladder. A history buff, he later pursued his passion for collectibles. Jack has 25 years experience in buying and selling coins, antiques, art, and collectibles. He sees the need to inform people about the world's most private investment sector — tangible assets. Called the "Collector's Coach," Jack answers questions like "what is it worth?" or "where do I sell?"

Comic Zone with Vincent Zurzolo on World Talk Radio, http://www.worldtalkradio.com, http://www.metropoliscomics.com/comiczone.php

Theme: Comic books, pop culture and entertainment.

Guest Profile: Authors welcome, along with artists, directors, actors, inkers, collectors, dealers and convention promoters. I like to interview creators who are relevant, have broad appeal in comics or pop culture. When interviewing other comic dealers I want the ones with the great stories about the big collection they brought to the market. I want to know what makes them tick, what's important to them, why they love what they are doing. Better yet, if they love what they are doing. Past guests include Stan Lee, chairman emeritus of Marvel Comics; Frank Miller, a writer and artist who has done work for all major publishers in the comic industry; and Bryan Singer, a producer and/or director of such films as *Superman Returns* and *The Usual Suspects*.

Guest from Hell: A guest who gives short answers or completely skirts the answer to the question. I had a guest on who didn't even pay attention to my questions and just kept speaking about nonsense ... it was funny yet agonizing; http://www.metropoliscomics.com

Contact: vincentz@metropolisent.com; 212-260-4147; Vincent Zurzolo. Best method: E-mail a bio, call with a pitch, send a press kit. No response? E-mail or call.

Invited Back? How much I enjoyed the interview, if I feel there is more to say and how fans react to the guest.

Bio of Vincent Zurzolo: Vincent is one of the nation's leading comic book aficionados. He joined Metropolis as a partner and co-owner in 1999. He has been interviewed on NYC radio shows, international TV programs and by many national and trade newspapers. In 1996, he created and promoted Big Apple Conventions, the largest and most successful comic book and multi-media convention on the East Coast.

Inkstuds with Robin McConnell on CiTR, Vancouver, Canada.
Theme: Interviews with comics creators.
Guest Profile: Cartoonists. An artist who is really into the work that they do, and has a good understanding of other related works. Only interested in their body of comic work.
As Canada's only English language radio show devoted to comix, *Inkstuds* strives to interview the best and brightest in alternative comix.
Guest from Hell: Anyone who answers with one word.
Contact: inkstuds@inkstuds.com; 604-822-2487; http://www.inkstuds.com; Robin McConnell. Best method: E-mail. No response? They should e-mail me again.
Invited Back? If I have time, and if they have something else to say that is interesting.
Bio of Robin McConnell: Robin has been reading comix since a young age with a tattered 12-cent Batman he found at a fleamarket. He was propelled further into the four colored world when he came across a copy of *A Velvet Glove Cast in Iron* at his local library.

Whatcha Got? with Harry L. Rinker on Sunday from 8:00–10:00 AM (ET) and 50+ affiliates nationwide. Steams live on the Internet at http://www.goldenbroadcasters.com.
Theme: Antiques and collectibles.
Guest Profile: Individuals involved in the antiques and collectibles field, including but not limited to, auctioneers, authors, collectors, dealers, show promoters, etc. Entertaining and fun, enthusiastic, shares knowledge yet keeps it simple and basic to appeal to widest audience, willingness to provide insider tips, short concise answers that answer questions asked, allow host to promote book and website.
Guest from Hell: Answers in phrases and not sentences, goes off on tangents, and attempts to promote his book or himself in every answer, argumentative, flat monotone voice, know-it-all attitude.
Contact: harrylrinker@aol.com; 484-695-5628; http://www.harryrinker.com; Harry L. Rinker. Best method: Initial approach should be via e-mail. Short bio, copy of book or other material to be discussed a minimum of two weeks before interview. Note: No author booked prior to receipt of review copy of book. Prefer to do actual booking by telephone. The more people in the middle, the more difficult to get a booking. No response? Yes. I maintain an active personal appearance schedule. Several days can pass when I do not have access to a computer. When in doubt, phone.
Invited Back? Personality, knowledge, and/or new title.
Guest Comment: "I was very nervous but your comments and questions helped to put me at ease ... thank you for your comments about liking my book and my website, that is very important to me."—Ann Mitchell Pitman, author of *Inside the Jewelry Box: A Collector's Guide to Costume Jewelry: Identification and Values, Volume 2* (Collector Books 2007)
Bio of Harry Rinker: Harry is a principal in Rinker Enterprises, Inc., a firm specializing in providing appraisal, consulting, editorial, educational, media, personal appearance, research, and writing services in the antiques and collectibles field. He has authored, co-authored, and edited close to 60 books about antiques and collectibles. His latest is *Sell, Keep, or Toss?: How to Downsize a Home, Settle an Estate, and Appraise Personal Property* (House of Collectibles/ Random House Information Group, 2007).

Art and Design

"Decorating one's Lifespace whether it be a home or office, is very personal and must reflect the personality and lifestyle of the people occupying the space."—Lydia Costa

Art and Technology with Daniel Durning on http://www.ps1.org; danieldurning.com. WPS Art Radio is the Internet station of P.S. 1 Contemporary Art Center, a MOMA (Museum of Modern Art) affiliate. The MOMA archives are available online at WPS1.org as part of a shared service. The program is recorded at the WPS1 Studios in the clock tower in lower Manhattan; however, Daniel has a portable rig and can set it up anywhere — at events, for example. The show is in the process of a name change to Art International Radio on http://www.artonair.org
Theme: Artist interview program, discussing the use and influence of technology on their artwork.
Guest Profile: Artist, innovators, technologists working with and influencing the use of new media and digital technologies. I look for artists who are currently exhibiting artwork that is created with or exhibited using innovative technologies. My guests for theme based panel discussions also include innovators, educators, and experts in the specific fields discussed on the program such as future technological breakthroughs, directions of animation, and arts education and technology. I work to familiarize myself with potential guests researching their background, current projects and relevant history. I often pre-screen guests with studio and site visits or pre interview discussions. The sound of their voice has not been a problem.
See http://www.danielduring.com/html/Page_Guests.html for guest list.

18 Art and Design

Guest from Hell: A quiet, soft spoken, and shy person who does not respond to any of my questions. Another guest type that I find problematic is one that refuses to participate with other artists in the discussion at hand and dominates the conversation taking the majority of time of the show.

Contact: daniel@danieldurning.com; 646-298-9251; http://www.danieldurning.com; Daniel Durning. Best method: E-mail me with upcoming exhibits or projects specific to my show. Artist groups may suggest panel ideas for discussion on my program. Bios and other support materials are needed upon request. No response? Follow up e-mails are suggested with art and technology in the subject line. No calls please.

Invited Back? My return guests are active members of the field that have new shows or have relevant options and experiences for specific topic discussions.

Bio of Daniel Durning: Daniel is an independent producer and his program has become a scholarly resource for the digital art community. He interviewed more than 40 guests his first season and has delivered interview programming from various venues including Live from the Armory Show, The International Fair for New Art in NYC, and SIGGRAPH International Computer Conference in Los Angeles.

The Art Full Life with Melissa Galt on 1620 AM, Sandy Springs, Ga., and http://www.radiosandysprings.com; now off the air.

Theme: How art and artists inspire daily living

Guest Profile: Artists, gallery owners, collectors. Colorful, comfortable talking about themselves and their work, excited about art, passionate about their pursuits. Brief bio and website are vital, interesting personal anecdotes are always good, sound of voice helpful, it isn't important if they've been interviewed before, formal credentials are interesting but not essential.

Guest from Hell: Too quiet, shy, won't divulge details.

Contact: Melissa@melissagalt.com; 404-788-6528; http://www.melissagalt.com; Melissa Galt. Best method? E-mail or call. Send me a website to review; while radio is auditory, art has a visual component I want to know about. No response? Always e-mail or call me. I am very responsive so if you don't get a reply please try alternate method.

Invited Back? Level of enthusiasm, engagement and ability to speak well.

Guest Comments: "Melissa, I just want you to know how much fun I had today—thank you so much!"—Catherine Kelleghan McGee, Catherine Kelleghan Gallery

"Hi Melissa, Many thanks for having me on your show. The interview was fun, comfortable and went incredibly fast. You are very good at what you're doing and make it easy for the interviewee."—Joel Barr (artist)

Bio of Melissa Galt: Melissa is a national lifestyle designer, speaker, author and coach known for her comprehensive no-nonsense philosophy and approach to working with clients and audiences to design their signature lives. She established her firm in 1994 and her mission is to use interior design and one's interior surroundings as a springboard.

Melissa empowers others to create their own signature life, including focusing on their career, relationships, wellbeing, style, interior environments and legacy. According to Melissa, we can enjoy the life we want most by learning how to 1) establish the architecture of our lives, 2) design the experiences we want to have, 3) build the strategy and support systems for getting there, 4) decorate our lives with the results we seek.

Her latest book is *Celebrate Your Life! The Art of Celebrating Every Day* (Publishing by Design 2006) and she is developing a series of books on life design. Often referred to as "America's Lifestyle Diva," Melissa keynotes and conducts workshops at conferences and corporate events nationwide.

Like her great-grandfather, famous architect Frank Lloyd Wright, Melissa has an insatiable appetite for life and guides others on the path to creating a unique life by design. Raised by a single, working mother, the late Academy Award–winning actress Anne Baxter, Melissa learned that with focus and determination, every problem has a solution. She often solves problems for her clients and keeps them from obsessing over a design project by saying, "remember decorate for living, don't live to decorate."

Change Your Home — Change Your Life with Lydia Costa on WARL 1320AM, aired in Attleboro, MA/Providence, RI.

Theme: Thoughts, suggestions, ideas on home decorating.

Guest Profile: Any person that would bring ideas for home interiors not only to include the physical aspects of decorating but the emotional aspect as well. Companies and or people that are involved in any way with home interiors such as fabric companies, furniture companies, kitchen companies, carpet companies, artistes, color specialists, feng shui, etc. Want to know their past interview experiences, credentials, sounds of their voice, their attitude about life and exactly what they do as a profession.

Guest from Hell: One that would contradict EVERY suggestion or idea I had. They certainly wouldn't have to agree with everything but have a professional way of presenting their point of view.

Contact: Interiors@lydiacosta.com; 508-336-2572; http://www.lydiacosta.com; Lydia. Best method: E-mail a bio and/or press kit. No response? E-mail, as I would normally respond one way or another.

Invited Back? I am not able to answer this yet. (The show is too new.)

Bio of Lydia Costa: Lydia was a nurse before starting her decorating business in 1987.

She is a graduate of the Rhode Island School of Design.

Design Talk with Tracy Self, Jim Johnson, Joe Self (producer) on 88.7 The Choice from TCU, Fort Worth, TX.

Theme: All types of design (i.e. house, office, web page design, lighting, furniture, landscape, etc.).

Guest Profile: Designers and crafts people in all fields. We look for guests who are knowledgeable and articulate in their field of expertise with an animated quality. We like to meet our guests personally and or see work they have done to evaluate their appropriateness for the show.

Guest from Hell: A guest from hell would be a monotone, humorless inarticulate person.

Contact: info@designtalkradio.net; http://www.FIRM817.com; 817-921-2111; Tracy Self; http://www.designtalkradio.net. Best method: Someone can approach us by calling or e-mailing us with a proposal or photos of their work. No response? If we don't respond in a reasonable amount of time they should e-mail us again and give us a call.

Invited Back? Guests might be invited back if we ran out of time or if they are in the middle of a project and we want to follow up.

Guest Comments: "At first I was a little concerned about the hour you wanted us on. I wasn't sure if I had an hour's worth of comments. You two were so professional and engaging that the hour flew by. I really appreciate the work you do to bring design to the public. I think that what you convey to people, that they can be involved in good design and it doesn't have to be cost prohibitive, is something this community needs." — Mike Reznikoff, Reznikoff Custom Furniture Inc.

"Tracy and Joe made us feel at ease and made the entire experience enjoyable and fun. They have great chemistry and I think this translates on the air and to their guests. Their knowledge on the subject of design allows them to ask the right questions to guide the guest through the interview. I found myself feeling nervous about being on the radio but never at a loss for words because of their insightful comments and questions. They seem to really enjoy what they are doing and are obviously very passionate about design. We would love to be guests on their show again in the future." — Lorie and Michael Kinler, Redenta's landscape design

Bio of Tracy Self: Tracy is a designer practicing with Joe. She received a BSN from the University of Texas at Arlington and took interior design coursework at TCU.

The Emy Louie Show on BBS Radio, http:www.bbsradio.com, airing Friday at 1 PM (ET); now off the air.

Theme: Feng shui, sustainable living, green building ranging from mystical to mundane topics: green and sustainable architecture; healthy living and feng shui.

Guest Profile: Feng shui consultants and architects. The most influential person for the topic I can find: heads of schools, authors, specialists and experts that one doesn't normally speak to under normal circumstances, nationally and internationally known experts. Credentials are important.

Guest from Hell: I never really had any probably because I screen them. All of my guests have good reputations so they wouldn't want to jeopardize the situation.

Contact: emylouie@hotmail.com; (office) 919-845-8205: (mobile) 919-880-4545; http://www.bbsradio.com/emylouieshow/emy_louie_show.php; Emy. Best method: Phone or e-mail. No response? Call or e-mail.

Invited Back? If we "complete each other's sentences" and if I feel that much more needs to be said.

Bio of Emy Louie: Emy is a feng shui architect — a feng shui practitioner and a licensed architect.

The Home Show with Natalie Weinstein on WALK 1370 AM, Long Island, NY, Sunday at 10 AM (ET).

Theme: Decorating, lifestyles, interesting Long Island personalities.

Guest Profile: Knowledgeable in areas of applicable subject matter. Someone knowledgeable and passionate about their topic. A sense of humor doesn't hurt. Do they know their subject matter? Don't need to have past experience. I'm an experienced interviewer. Phone calls discouraged some. Someone will call them if we are interested. Other methods are fine.

Guest from Hell: "One Word" Charlie.

Contact: Nataliesclub@aol.com; http://www.NatalieWeinstein.com and http://www.Nataliesclub.com; Office # 631-862-6198; Cell # 516-242-9242. Best method: E-mail. No response? Contact my assistant, Jenny.

Invited Back? Good interaction with host, fun for listeners, more to say.

Bio of Natalie Weinstein, Allied ASID: Natalie is a veteran interior designer whose energy and dynamism have powered both a vast client base and more than 15,000 members in her Home Decorating Club. Her mission is clear — make the world a better place, one person at a time, through the home environment, the place that nurtures and empowers.

Her commitment to her club members is as great as to her clients. She appears at Home and Gardens Shows, moderating and providing seminars. Her often-published design work has appeared in *House, Newsday, The New York Times, Palm Beach Life, Nite Life* and *Distinction* magazines. Her "Long Island Focus" feature in *House Magazine* highlights Long Island's historic sites, as well as her love for L.I. She is a frequent guest expert on Long Island Cable TV.

Her most recent book was inspired by her many

years of teaching and lecturing entitled *The 100 Most Often Asked Interior Design Questions* (Images for Presentation 2006), as well as a children's book on interior design entitled *Katrina's New Room* (Images for Presentation 2004).

Living Large with Karen Mills on News Radio 980 KMBZ, Sunday at 10 AM (CT) and Classical 1660 KXTR, Saturday at 10:30 AM (CT), in Kansas City area (Kansas and Missouri), plus streams live around the world. We're currently working on expansion to other states.

Theme: Interior design and lifestyle.

Guest Profile: Celebrity designers, actors/actresses, network television personalities, shelter magazine editors, design, garden and home improvement authors, design expert. We look for guests who are not only informative, but also enthusiastic, with interesting content and the ability to speak well. First, we want to know a guest's credentials and then their ability to speak well plus share interesting content.

Guest from Hell: Our least preferred guest would be someone who can't hold a conversation or give interesting and informative content in response to questions.

Contact: Karen@karenmills.net; 913-764-5915 or station: 913-744-3600; http://www.karenmills.net, http://www.interiorsbydesigninc.com, http://www.entercomkc.com/livinglarge; Karen Mills. Best method: E-mail a bio and a pitch or angle. Authors/publicists should also offer to mail us a book for review. No response? Send a second e-mail or call.

Invited Back? Guests are usually invited back if they are informative, interesting, friendly and have something new to say the next time.

Guest Comments: "What a pleasant interview! Thank you so much for your time and interest!"— Chris Madden, author of 16 design books, celebrity designer and TV personality

"...it was so much fun to have done two radio interviews with you and I totally appreciate the copies that you have forwarded on to me. *Living Large* was a wonderful experience!"— Monica Pedersen, host of HGTV's "Designed to Sell" show

Bio of Karen Mills: After designing and staging sets for television productions, Karen turned her designer's eye to private homes in the Kansas City area. She specializes in making homes more attractive, using existing furnishings and often uses her skills to stage homes for resale.

Karen's creative approach to design has been widely covered in the media, which led to a co-production deal with Entercom Broadcasting for her design show. Recent media coverage includes the *Kansas City Star*, NBC 41, Fox 4 TV, *Symphony Designers' Showhouse*, KCHandG magazine, Time Warner Cable, *Olathe Daily News*, *Olathe Sun*, *The X* magazine, *Shawnee/Lenexa Sun*, *Flourish* magazine, and the *Kansan*.

Karen was also the first designer in Kansas City to be invited to the exclusive "Kohler Experience" at the Kohler Design Center and Waters Spa. She is a graduate of the University of Kansas where she studied Interior Design and Radio/Television/Film.

Organization Nation with Monica Ricci aired on 1620 AM in Atlanta and the Internet at www.radiosandysprings.com; now off the air.

Theme: Organizing all aspects of life.

Guest Profile: Professionals who have accomplished great results through focus and superior personal productivity and/or time management. I prefer guests who are upbeat, lively and fun. Of course, they have to be knowledgeable in whatever we're discussing but personality is very important. I'd love a basic bio that would tell me their experience in their field, credentials, and if there is audio of their voice that's a bonus.

Guest from Hell: A guest who answers questions with single word or very short answers or who is talking about/pitching their product or service every ten minutes.

Contact: monica@catalystorganizing.com; 770-569-2642; http://www.catalystorganizing.com; Monica Ricci. Best method: Call with a pitch, e-mail a bio and send a press kit. No response? E-mail or call. I am often occupied with many high-priority items so sometimes guests can get put on the back burner unintentionally. I love proactive people who follow up.

Invited Back? If their subject matter is broad enough to warrant a second show, *and* their personality is terrific. Some guests have great personalities but their subject matter is adequately covered in a single show, so there is no real logical reason to have them back. But some guests have several topics to cover.

Guest Comment: "Thank you Monica for the opportunity to be a guest on your show. Our website has already seen increased hits after the show aired."— Pat Bowen, http://www.getreadyfortomorrow.com

Bio of Monica Ricci: Monica founded Catalyst Organizing Solutions in 1998 and is committed to helping individuals change their lives by changing their home and work environments.

She is author of *Organize Your Office in No Time* (Que Publishing 2006), past president of the Georgia Chapter of the National Association of Professional Organizers, and named one of the nation's "Organizing Elite" by *Forbes Magazine*. She has been an expert guest on radio and television, including the nationally syndicated *Clark Howard Radio Show*, WAGA TV's "Good Day Atlanta" and is a regular expert organizer on the popular home and garden television show, "MISSION: Organization."

Scrappers Talk Radio with Vera Raposo on http://www.scrapperstalkradio.com

Theme: Scrapbooking.

Guest Profile: Scrapbook business owners, enthusiasts, manufacturers. I look for someone who will help create an interesting show by sharing their story and relating it to the industry. I've worked with people who have done many interviews and some who haven't done any, but I'd say one of the most important parts is if they can keep their voice lively during the interview. They can send me their credentials or past interviews, but even a simple e-mail to me can get them on the show. I just want to know their story and what they can offer my listeners.

Guest from Hell: Ah yes, the guest from you know where ... I would have to say those with "yes or no" type answers.

Contact: vera@scrapperstalkradio.com; 778-240-6578; http://www.scrapperstalkradio.com; Vera Raposo. Best method: E-mail. No response? They can call or e-mail me anytime.

Invited Back? I look at the response of the show listeners and how the flow of the show went. If I felt that it was a great interview, I invite them back.

Bio of Vera Raposo: Vera has been an entrepreneur since age 22, when she negotiated a lease for her first retail store in 1997. By the summer of 2000, her stores grew to five retail locations in Vancouver, British Columbia. By the age of 29 she re-evaluated her life and sold and closed all store locations.

Since 2003, Vera has developed marketing plans for her own online business and has landed inside books and magazines for her hobby of scrapbooking.

"I've never ever believed in the word 'can't,'" she says. "I have always had big dreams for myself and my family which has caused me to strive for excellence in everything.

"Today, my Scrap Venture (http://www.scrapventure.com) brand includes information products, individual consulting and a premium membership site.... I am living out an entrepreneur's dream, having successfully turned a hobby I love into a profitable business."

Smart City with Carol Coletta aired on public radio stations throughout the U.S.

Theme: What is happening in design, planning, architecture, business, technology, urban issues, as they affect cities.

Guest Profile: Urban leaders and decision makers, authors of related books. I look for someone who has something fresh and new to say about what makes cities successful. I want to see the guest's research, book or experience that shows he/she is learning something new that ought to be shared.

Guest from Hell: Someone who doesn't know his or her subject.

Contact: carol@smartcityradio.com; withheld upon request; http://www.smartcityradio.com; Scotty Iseri, producer, at siseri@ceosforcities.org, or Carol at carol@smartcityradio.com. Best method: Easiest way to reach me is via e-mail. A short pitch with relevant bio and info attached is great. If the guest is promoting a book, send the book. If guest has new research, send the link. No response? I am happy to have someone e-mail me a second time. When I am on the road for weeks at a time, it's easy to overlook important opportunities.

Invited Back? When there is something new to be said about what has been learned.

Bio of Carol Coletta: Carol is president and CEO of CEOs for Cities. Before moving to Chicago to head CEOs for Cities, she served as president of Coletta and Company in Memphis. In addition, she served as executive director of the Mayors' Institute on City Design, a partnership of the National Endowment for the Arts, U.S. Conference of Mayors and American Architectural Foundation.

Carol hosted The Vine, a three-day gathering of internationally recognized speakers for the Pacific Coast Builders Conference; she created and hosted the Memphis Manifesto Summit with Richard Florida, the first gathering of the creative class to write their call to action for cities; she conceived and wrote the *Talent Magnet Report*, the first city blueprint aimed at attracting and retaining the creative class; and she co-authored *Cultural Development in Creative Communities for Americans for the Arts*.

Your House Chicago with Rich and Dawn on AM 560 WIND, Chicago, Illinois, airing Sunday 12–1 PM (CT).

Theme: Home improvement, repair, maintenance for callers/homeowners.

Guest Profile: Anyone affiliated with home repair and improvement (i.e., window dealers, electricians, plumbers, mortgage specialists, decorator, designers, concrete/brick pavers, appliances, etc.) Must be knowledgeable and expert of their product or service — no previous radio experience is necessary. Potential for sponsorship of show to communicate with their potential customers. Specifics of their product/service, credentials and a sincere interest in sponsoring the show to grow and advertise their products/services is appreciated.

Guest from Hell: Someone who doesn't know their product or service.

Contact: richanddawn@yourhousechicago.com or dtuskey@ihmremodeling.com; 630-926-5739 — Dawn's Cell or 847-956-8255 (TALK) call-in number during show; http://www.yourhousechicago.com; Dawn M. Tuskey, Sales/Marketing or Rich Cowgill, Certified Remodeler/Topic Content. Best method: E-mail or phone. No response? Absolutely call and send e-mail again. Must be able to prove they sent e-mail in the first place by providing original e-mail.

Invited Back? Their product/service and knowledge of that product/service. Ability to interact with hosts.

Bio of Dawn M. Tuskey: Growing up on the South Side of Chicago, Dawn preferred being in the garage and workshop with her steelworker grandfather to avoid doing the dishes. Always in his shadow, she was the "gopher" for his tools and materials. When the family moved to Westmont, she and her grandfather repaired and maintained the family's suburban home and cars. Well into her adult years, Dawn worked professional positions that required extensive client contact, management, and service.

In 1989, she and her husband bought their first home, the beginning of many home purchases that they would make in order to work hand-in-hand to completely gut and remodel while living in each home during all the projects. As a result of their first purchase and rehab, they opened IHM Remodeling Repair Contractors in 2000.

Dawn is CEO/President and co-owner of IHM Remodeling which holds a prestigious service record with the Better Business Bureau of Chicago. She has been awarded several nominations for customer service, and a nomination to *Remodeling Magazine*'s Top 50 remodelers in the nation. Recently, IHM was nominated for The Better Business Bureau's Torch Award for 2007 and The Business Ledger's best business practices award. She is an active member of NARI, NAHB, NKBA, BBB, and a founding member of the Downers Grove Chamber's Woman to Woman Leads Group which strives to build clients and business for other women business owners in the area.

Bio of Rich Cowgill: As one of three sons of a construction project manager growing up in the southwest suburbs of Chicago, Rich was destined to become an expert in the industry. Working with his dad on subdivisions throughout the southland and in the family home and garage, he spent an even greater amount of time perfecting his "hands on" techniques of the various crafts of the construction trades. As a freelance computer programmer during high school, Rich started his first professional company called Computer Talk. After college, he went to work rehabbing various buildings into sought-after commercial office space. He purchased his first home by the age of 21 and then followed up with building his first home a year later.

In 1990, Rich opened Cowgill Builders Inc. and in 1998, he opened Vision Design and Build, Inc.

Rich and his wife still live in the south suburbs.

Authors

"Many people love to go on radio and television. In fact, I think some people write books just to get on the air." —Dan Poynter, from *Self-Publishing Manual*

Adirondack Book House with Peter "Pete" Klein on Blog Talk Radio http://www.blogtalkradio.com/The-Dancing-Valkyrie, Saturdays, 6:30 PM (ET).

Theme: Author interviews and general book talk. I have an open policy. Anyone can schedule a show to promote their book/books. Anyone can call in.

Guest Profile: Authors. I want to know the name of the book so I can check it out online. If they want to provide a bio or why they wrote the book, that would be helpful.

Guest from Hell: I can listen to anyone to death as long as they don't use words that are meant to hurt others or words I would censor myself from using on air.

Contact: kleinpete@hotmail.com; 518-648-0104; http://www.lulu.com/ravenwolfpublish; Pete Klein. Best method: E-mail a bio and/or the name of book and a short "what's it about?" No response? To me a reasonable response time is within a few days. If I were not to respond within a couple of days, e-mail again just in case I accidentally deleted their e-mail.

Invited Back? As long as they enjoyed talking with me and I with them, they could return for a second show after a few months. Always, anyone can call in.

Guest Comment: "Pete Klein's style is interesting because he has a conversation with you rather than a typical interview where he just asks questions about your work. For instance, in *Night Crimes*, Lara, the heroine, is being pursued by a man she never sees but who is on the subway train with her. Instead of Pete asking about the novel, he begins to talk about riding the subway and how spooky it can be." — Judith Columbo, author of two novels — *The Fablesinger*, a fantasy set among the myth and magic of the Caribbean, published by The Crossing Press in 1989 and republished as an Authors Guild Backinprint.Com Edition in June 2001, and *Night Crimes* (PublishAmerica 2001), a mystery/suspense tale, http://odin.prohosting.com/night01

Bio of Pete Klein: Pete has been living in the Adirondacks of northern New York for the past 21 years and a reporter for the *Hamilton County News* for the past six years. He has been married for 40 years, has three children and two granddaughters.

Born in Detroit, Mich., he served in the U.S. Navy as a hospital corpsman, studied acting at the American Academy of Dramatic Arts, NY, attended night school (English and Philosophy at NYU) and has held numerous jobs when first living in NYC (wood and metal fabricator, stock clerk for NY Stock Exchange, and automotive whse. parts manager). He has also been employed as an assistant to a blacksmith, part-time disc jockey in high school, bank teller and manager of a summer resort.

Pete is author of *Adirondack Hikes in Hamilton County* and the vampire novels *The Dancing Valkyrie* (Lulu.com 2006), *The Vampire Valkyrie* (Lulu.com 2008).

AuthorB-Known with Lillian Cauldwell on Passionate Internet Voices Talk Radio (PIVTR) on InternetVoicesRadio.com

Theme: Promoting and marketing published mid-list and unknown authors to the media and the world

Guest Profile: Non-fiction and fiction, poets, dramatists, essayists, musicians, playwrights writing quality information, entertainment, and benefits so that people can turn around and use their content in their spiritual, personal, and business lives. Guests must have the ability to express themselves and speak about their topic that relates to the current political, social and economical state of the world. Do they know how to hold a conversation, answer questions without reacting emotionally?

Guest from Hell: Someone who can't string two or three words together, let alone a full sentence. Someone who says, "you know," "like uh," and "and, and, and hmmmmm."

Contact: LCauldwell@internetvoicesradio.com; 734-332-5902; http://internetvoicesradio.com; Lillian Cauldwell. Best method: Call with a pitch, e-mail a bio and send a press kit. No response? Person should try calling. E-mail sometimes doesn't always work.

Invited Back? Passion. Expertise. Sharing their knowledge and mistakes.

Guest Comments: "Your questions were interesting and entertaining. I hope you enjoyed the interview as much as I did." — Bob Avey, author of *Twisted Perception* (Deadly Niche Press 2006), http://www.bobavey.com

"I thoroughly enjoyed the interview." — Carla J. Curtis, author of *A Single Woman's Parenting Journey: Survival Tactics* (2001) and *Grip the Rope: Prayers for Single Mothers* (2003), both published by TRC Communications, http://www.carlajcurtis.com

Bio of Lillian Cauldwell: Lillian owns the Internet talk radio station, Passionate Internet Voices Talk Radio. She is author of *Teenagers! A Bewildered Parent's Guide* (Silvercat Publishing 1996), which Atrium ranked number 10 in its top newly published books, and the book went into a second printing. Her second book, *Sacred Honor* (2003), is an historical science fiction published by a Print-on-Demand publisher.

Between 1996 and 2003, Lillian wrote short stories, published by Simegen.com for its Do A Good Deed Charitable Section. She is working on three plays, "Betty, Death by Starvation," "A Camp David Christmas," and "Faithless Angels," "The Anna Mae Mysteries — King Solomon's Ark," and "Camazotz," a vampire story set in South America.

Author's Voice with Joe Carroccio on Achieve Radio, http://www.achieveradio.com

Theme: Interview authors.

Guest Profile: Any type of author, published or self-published. Background, book info and any other fun item.

Guest from Hell: One who answers with one word.

Contact: joe@azgoodlife.com; 480 816-5908; http://www.AzGoodlife.com and http://www.achieveradio.com/goodlife/; Joe Carroccio. Best method: E-mail. No response? I always respond in 48 to 72 hours.

Invited Back? Anytime they have a new book.

Guest Comments: "I found Joe to be charismatic, interesting and fun to chat with live ... he kept the pace of the show pleasant and we covered quite a bit of material in a very short time. Afterwards he invited my girlfriend and I to a concert he was hosting and lead singing in, we accepted and found his concert delightful as well. As I told him during the break at his concert, I'm of fan for life..." — Brando Quin, a musician and author of *The Master Painter* (Lulu 2006)

"Joe was a delightful interviewer.... His show provided me with a wonderful opportunity to discuss my latest book" [*Six Spiritual Steps to Mend a Broken Heart: Learn to Love Again* (Cyan Communications 2007)]. — Fiona Taylor, Mystic, Olympian and metaphysical counselor, http://www.barakaya.com

Bio of Joe Carroccio: Joe is founder and president of the Good Life News, Inc. and has more than 30 years of marketing, sales, media, management and operational experience in technology and communications. As a management consultant for more than 16 years, Joe worked with various industries from Washington, D.C., to Boston, Mass. For 6 years he was a director for the Social Services Agency, HRA, City of New York. Joe has performed as a vocalist, musician, and promoter/manager of many musical productions.

Beyond Words with Frances Halpern airs Saturday at 2 PM (PT) on KCLU, an NPR affiliate, which broadcasts to 88.3 in Ventura County, CA, and 102.3 in Santa Barbara County, CA, and on the web at http://www.kclu.org. Calls and e-mail responses are welcome during and after the broadcast at 805/493-9200.

Theme: Literary toilers and readers.

Guest Profile: Mainly authors; however, everyone connected to the word — bestselling authors of fiction and non-fiction and others who interpret the word, i.e., creators of crossword puzzles, producers, directors, actors, literary agents, screen writers, publishers, book sellers. We encourage writers of how-to publishing guides to contact us. We are not interested in inspiration, spirituality, 12 steps to improving life titles. Please no psychic stuff. First they must be entertaining. Ideal guests are articulate, with clear and pleasant voices who are prepared for any questions the host tosses their way. (Hosts should of course be thoroughly prepared and knowledgeable.) Do they have an entertaining or compelling tale? Celebrity authors with career credentials are particularly welcome.

Guest from Hell: Guests from hell are yep and nope types. Or who are over-prepped and rigid. The worst of course is the no-show guest. This can happen for any one of a dozen reasons. So, we hosts must be prepared to fill in the time with intelligent conversation, and if the show is live, encourage listeners to participate — big time.

Contact: fjsaga@cox.net; withheld upon request;

http://www.kclu.org; Frances Halpern. Best method: E-mail a proposal or send a press kit. Don't send a book unless requested. No response? Send a second e-mail. I generally respond immediately.

Invited Back? Seldom happens; however, a new book or that compelling story which listeners will welcome hearing again.

Guest Comments: "You are a gracious interviewer. You read my book and understood its message. And you inspired interesting conversation."— Karen Taleen-Lawton, author of *Canyon Voices* (Mission Creek Studios 2006)

"Always enjoy being on *Beyond Words*. Let's do it again."— Ray Bradbury, whose latest book is *Farewell Summer* (Harper 2007)

Bio of Frances Halpern: Frances is an award-winning journalist, lecturer and author of *Writer's Guide to Publishing in the West* (Pinnacle Books 1982). She wrote the "Words and Images" column for the Ventura Calendar section of the *Los Angeles Times* for six years.

Among her many freelance credits are chapters in writer's guides including her essay "The Obsession" in *Chicken Soup for the Writer's Soul*. She also moderates panels for the annual Los Angeles Times Festival of Books.

The Book Babes Program with Margo Hammond and Ellen Heltzel on WMNF-FM, aired the 3rd Wednesday of every month, 11:30–12 PM (ET) on Florida's West Coast (Tampa Bay, Sarasota).

Theme: Books.

Guest Profile: Current authors or book-related persons. The hosts want to talk to writers whose books are a jumping-off place for all sorts of topics — current events, women's lives, the media, contemporary culture, medicine, history — and who can express ideas and relate them to their books. Most important: What they've done to make themselves authoritative on the topics their books address. We wouldn't interview self-published authors — unless we're doing a show on self-publishing. Recent guests have included Dave Eggers, author of *What Is the What* (Vintage 2007), Susan Shapiro, author of *Only as Good as Your Word: Writing Lessons from My Favorite Literary Gurus* (Seal Press 2007) and Dee Dee Myers, author of *Why Women Should Rule the World* (Harper 2008).

Guest from Hell: People who think they have something to say but don't.

Contact: thebookbabes@yahoo.com; withheld upon request; http://www.thebookbabes.com; Margo Hammond or Ellen Heltzel. Best method: E-mail information about the author and his or her book and when the author is available to be interviewed. No response? We are usually contacted by publicist, not directly by authors. Publicists understand if they haven't heard back, we're probably not interested. Sometimes they might send a follow-up e-mail, in case the first was waylaid. We try to answer as promptly as possible.

Invited Back? What they have to say the first time around. It's not their point of view, but how convincingly they can express it.

Bio of "The Book Babes": Prizewinning journalists and book critics Margo Hammond and Ellen Heltzel are "The Book Babes." Margo lives in St. Petersburg, Florida; Ellen in Portland, Ore. In addition to their radio show they blog at www.thebookbabes.com. Their book of recommendations is *Between the Covers: The Book Babes' Guide to Women's Reading Pleasures* (Da Capo Press Nov 2008).

They began as a team in 2002, writing a weekly column for Poynter Online, the website of the Poynter Institute for Media Studies. They have also written columns about books for *The Book Standard* and http://www.goodhousekeeping.com

Book Bites for Kids with Suzanne Lieurance on http://www.blogtalkradio.com/bookbitesforkids

Theme: Interviews with successful children's authors and/or illustrators with tips for aspiring children's authors/illustrators.

Guest Profile: Published children's authors and/or illustrators, editors, publishers, or anyone else involved with children's publishing. Someone who is articulate enough to talk about their work and the writing process in general. Generally, I like to read their books, so I ask that review copies be sent to our P.O. box several weeks ahead of the author's appearance on the show (Suzanne Lieurance, founder, director, and coaching coordinator, The National Writing for Children Center P.O. Box 8422 Kansas City, Missouri 64114). I also like to visit the guest's website to find out as much about him or her as I possibly can before the show.

Guest from Hell: I can't imagine a children's writer being a guest from hell. I have such fun speaking with each of my guests. But I suppose a guest from hell would be someone who doesn't show up for the live show, or doesn't say anything, so I have to fill the dead air time.

Contact: suzanne@workingwriterscoach.com; 816-361-4103; http://www.writingforchildrencenter.com; Suzanne Lieurance. Best method: E-mail. Children's authors and/or illustrators who wish to be guests on *Book Bites for Kids* can submit a letter of interest (via e-mail) and then have their publicist send their current book(s) to our P.O. box for review. It's also good to send a short bio, their website URL, and any photos or book cover illustrations (as .jpg files) that we can use to promote their appearance on the show. No response? Give us a week to respond. We always respond within a week. After a week, feel free to send a follow-up e-mail.

Invited Back? Guests are invited back when they have a new book or other item to promote and they were an interesting guest the first time they were on the show.

Guest Comment: "Suzanne has such an easy style

of questioning her guests that it makes the time fly by. In fact, a number of people e-mailed me to say they sat down to listen and, before they knew it, the half hour was over. Even though the advanced notice for my interview was short, she had taken the time to read up on my work and was well prepared for the interview." — Max Elliot Anderson, author of eight books for readers 8 and up, especially boys, all published by Baker Trittin Press. His latest is *Reckless Runaway* (2006), http://maxbooks.9k.com

Bio of Suzanne Lieurance: Suzanne is a full time freelance writer, children's author, and writing coach. She has published over a dozen books for children, and several books for adults. She is an instructor with the Institute of Children's Literature, a former regional advisor for the Society of Children's Writers and Illustrators (SCBWI), and founder and director of the National Writing for Children Center at http://www.writingforchildrencenter.com

The Book Guys with Mike Cuthbert and Allan Stypeck syndicated nationally on public radio stations and on http://www.bookguys.com

Theme: Everything about the book.

Guest Profile: Authors, collectors, historians, librarians, preservationists, agents, printers, bibliophiles of all sorts. Articulate and knowledgeable about books or their subject matter. Somebody with a good sense of humor who can speak in a relaxed manner. Helps if they have been on the air before, but not a requirement. We want to know their bona fides are legit. "Professional Pitchmen" with a tight presentation don't work well in our informal environment.

Guest from Hell: Someone who is NOT up on their subject, dull and wordy.

Contact: mjcuth@comcast.net; 301-770-0477 ext.16; http://www.bookguys.com; Warren Wigutow, Producer, at warren@secondstorybooks.com. Best method: E-mail basic information to warren@secondstorybooks.com or e-mail link from our website (mjcuth@comcast.net) with details on subject and some bio on guest. No response? Safest to e-mail again. We're pretty good at responding if the e-mail is addressed to us rather than a mailing in general.

Invited Back? Knowledgeability and glibness but willingness and ability to go deep into subjects. Sense of humor and breadth of interest in the world in general.

Guest Comment: "I have been a guest twice on *The Book Guys*, the first time in 2002 for my book, *Saving Monticello* (University of Virginia Press 2003), and then in 2007 for *Desperate Engagement* (Thomas Dunne Books). Both times were great experiences. Mike and Alan asked good questions and lots of them. They gave me plenty of time to answer and there was a good deal of interaction among the three of us. They made me feel very welcomed and the hour flew by each time. Any type of broadcast media generates sales, and *Book Guys* was no exception." — Marc Leepson, http://www.marcleepson.com, http://www.flagbiography.com, http://www.savingmonticello.com

Bio of Allan Stypeck: President of Second Story Books, Allan has been providing appraisal services for more than 20 years. He has taught seminars and classes on the subject for such groups as the Smithsonian Institution, University of Florida and George Washington University. In addition, Allan does appraisals for the White House, U.S. Senate, Supreme Court and other major branches of government as well as the Library of Congress and the Smithsonian Institution. He has also conducted appraisals for colleges, universities and museums around the country. Allan provides appraisals on books, manuscripts, records, stamps, all printed material, antiquities, Oriental art, fine art, photography and *objets d'art*. He has been seen on the PBS show *Antiques Roadshow* and C-SPAN's *About Books*.

Allan lives in a farmhouse in Poolesville, MD, with his wife and two daughters.

Bio of Mike Cuthbert: Mike is a trained musician who, after teaching music at high schools in Wisconsin and Illinois and a college in Wisconsin, got back into radio. He had started radio in high school and took his first full-time job at WCWC radio in Ripon, Wisconsin, followed by program director at WGMS in Washington, WRC Talk Radio in D.C., WCKY in Cincinnati, WAMU in Washington and WRKO in Boston. He left full-time radio in the late 90s to serve as host of "Prime Time Radio" for AARP and to co-host *The Book Guys* while setting up Second Story Books' web presence and cataloging of inventory.

Mike lives in the Kentlands section of Gaithersburg, MD, and is working on several unpublished novels.

The Book Squad with Karyn Langhorne and Wendy Coakley-Thompson on WMET 1160 AM, Washington, D.C., on Fridays, noon to 1:00 PM (ET), and at http://www.wmet1160.com

Theme: *The Book Squad*'s tag line is "We track down the hottest authors ... and bring them in for questioning."

Guest Profile: There is no guest profile for the show. The only proviso is that guests must be authors. We profile authors of all genres. A guest whose work falls within the theme of the show for that particular day. While we're open to less well-known authors, we do try to entice best selling authors with a following that they can bring with them to the show. We just want to know if they have a great book on a topic that interests us and we think would interest our listeners. Among prominent guests were Walter Mosley, Robin Givens and David Baldacci.

Guest from Hell: We haven't had any guests from Hell yet. However, any guests who don't maximize the opportunity and leave us with a mound of dead air is a challenge.

Contact: info@thebooksquad.com; karynfolan@comcast.net; me@wendycoakley-thompson.com; karyn@thebooksquad.com; wendy@thebooksquad.com; Studio: 866-369-1160; Karyn: 240-543-6109; Wendy: 703-568-3492; http://www.thebooksquad.com; http://thebooksquad.blogspot.com; http://www.wendycoakley-thompson.com; http://wendycoakley-thompson.blogspot.com; Karyn Langhorne or Wendy Coakley-Thompson. Best method: E-mail. For information on being a guest, visit the website and click "Contact Us." No response? It generally means that their work does not fit within our theme at that given time. However, that is subject to change.

Invited Back? We don't usually invite guests back. We would entertain the thought if they have a new project to discuss.

Guest Comments: "I have done a zillion radio guest spots in recent years, and I must say that *The Book Squad* rates right up there with the best of them. The interview process was easy and stress-free. Talking with Karyn and Wendy was just like chatting with a couple of my best buddies in the living room. They were well prepared and totally focused on the core messages of my book. The next time they call, I'm there in a flash." — Jeff Brendenberg, whose latest book is *How to Cheat at Cleaning* (Taunton 2007), http://www.jeffbredenberg.com

"I really enjoyed [the interview]. Karyn Langhorne and Wendy Coakley-Thompson were hilarious, and they put me at ease and asked questions about my book and about myself.

"Sometimes they did deviate, but nothing that made me feel uncomfortable or that wasn't in some way relevant to the overall topic. Humor is a big part of their interview process, and it worked very well. Also, because we were all African American, I probably felt more comfortable automatically just because of that. Also, I am younger and a new author, but I didn't feel intimidated while talking to them. Nervous, yes, but not intimidated, and the nervousness eased as the conversation continued. I wouldn't hesitate to go on their show again. It's a very relaxing and engaging format." — Savannah J. Frierson, author of *Being Plumville* (iUniverse 2007), http://sjfbooks.com

Bio of Karyn Langhorne: Karyn is a graduate of Harvard Law School and a former law professor who no longer practices law. When she's not interviewing other authors, she writes. Her publications include four novels, *A Personal Matter* (Harper Torch 2004), *Street Level* (Harper Torch 2005), *Diary of an Ugly Duckling* (Harper Torch 2006) and *Unfinished Business* (Avon 2007), articles on writing for *Writers Digest* and AbsoluteWrite.com, a weekly "American Idol" column (during show season) as well as several books of nonfiction, a dozen screenplays and an off–Broadway play. She lives in the Washington, D.C., suburbs with her husband and two daughters.

Bio of Wendy Coakley-Thompson: Wendy is the author of the novels *Back to Life* (Kensington 2005), a 2004 *Romantic Times* Award nominee, and *What You Won't Do for Love* (Dafina 2006), (recently optioned for a cable television movie). She has also written articles and fiction for music and fashion/lifestyle magazines in New Jersey, her adopted home state, and in Nassau, Bahamas, where she was raised. She graduated from Syracuse University with a Ph.D. in Education. Her work as a commentator for *Metro Connection* on WAMU, a Washington, D.C., National Public Radio affiliate, earned a 2003 Associated Press/Chesapeake Award in the editorial category.

Book Talk with Gail Cohn aired on 1620 am, Sandy Springs, GA.

Theme: Books and authors.

Guest Profile: Authors of all genres. The ideal guest is one who speaks to the theme of the show/books and is comfortable elaborating on a variety of questions asked by the host and is passionate about his/her work. I want to know about his/her credentials and the message he/she would like to impart.

Guest from Hell: The guest from hell is one that is very talkative before they get in front of a microphone, and the day of the show (since we are live) seems to freeze and gives short and one-word answers to most of your questions.

Contact: gcohn11406@aol.com or gail@gailcohn.com; 404-252-5441; http://www.gailcohn.com or http://www.radiosandysprings.com; Gail Cohn. Best method: I prefer to be approached by e-mail or telephone and then receive a press kit. No response? He/She should continue to contact me via telephone and e-mail.

Invited Back? The ease in which he/she is able to respond to questions. Enthusiasm is also a great voice ingredient.

Guest Comment: "Being on air with Gail Cohn was a pleasure from start to finish. She is a consummate professional and made me feel totally at ease. Our hour together flew by, and I had a delightful time. Another benefit of her show is that the web link stays up indefinitely so others can listen well after the broadcast, and you can purchase a CD of the program for promotional." — Man Martin, cartoonist and creator of the syndicated comic strip "Sibling Revelry" and author of *Days of the Endless Corvette* (Carroll and Graf 2007), http://www.manmartin.net

"My experience with Gail Cohn was a very pleasant one. It was done via phone, thus a bit more impersonal on my part, since I could not see the interviewer. Gail is a very fine interviewer, she read my book and the questions were right on the money. I have also listened to some of her other interviews and they seem to be as thorough and professional as with my own." — Eric Lamet, author of *A Gift from the Enemy: Childhood Memories of Wartime Italy* (Syracuse University Press 2007), http://www.ericlamet.com

Bio of Gail Cohn: Gail is a consultant with more than 20 years' experience in both corporate and non-profit environments, who guides clients through processes that are proven to increase productivity and facilitate excellence. She has presented her customized workshops in more than 400 forums covering 40+ topics and served for eight years on the Georgia Human Relations Commission. Uniquely qualified to master complete information specific to industry and client needs, she delivers materials in a timeline convenient to the organization — be it a law firm, government association, educational institution, bank, non-profit entity or Fortune 500 company. Ultimately, Gail helps her clients to help themselves. She is an expert in guiding the process of acquisition and application of invaluable skills. She will design, create and implement an effective program tailored to meet your needs.

Calling All Authors with Valerie Connelly aired Tuesday at 4 PM (CT) on Global Talk Radio.

Theme: Highlighting authors and their books; authors choose the interview topic. Highlighting experts in publishing and marketing; interviews address topics such as publishing trends, marketing success, outside the box promotional techniques, and writing. And in the weekly Publisher's Corner segment, Valerie comments about insider perspectives on hot topics such as technology, legal issues, marketing techniques, copyright piracy, international publishing trends and writing to inform listeners.

There is no fee to appear. You will receive at least 16 minutes of interview time, a prepared e-mail letter for you to use to send to your friends and colleagues announcing your appearance time and date. Each show is archived for on-demand streaming so your show is available to listeners 24/7 for a year or more. Valerie does offer optional display ads and 60-second commercials for a fee.

Guest Profile: Authors in all genres, experts in publishing, writing, marketing books. The ideal guest is cheerful, knows what they want to say, actually responds to the questions, whether planned or impromptu, and is spontaneous when talking about their work. We supply a form requiring 10 talking points which we use to guide the conversation. This helps us talk about everything the guest wants to get across to the audience.

Guest from Hell: The guest from hell reads a prepared text, ignores the host's efforts to engage in a true conversation, answers with one word replies, and has a monotone voice that could put the dead to sleep.

Contact: publisher@nightengalepress.biz or info@callingallauthors.org; 847-810-8498; http://www.callingallauthors.org, http://www.globaltalkradio.com/shows/callingallauthors, http://www.valerieconnelly.com; Valerie Connelly. Best method: Just e-mail a bio and a short synopsis with a website I can look at as well. We'll respond in 24 hours. No response? We respond within 24 hours. A second e-mail is appropriate if we goof.

Invited Back? The scope of the topic, their ability to have a great conversation, the depth of their interest in communicating and if there is more to say than possible in the first interview. Perhaps, too, if they have a new book coming out, we'd be happy to have them on the show again to assist in the launch of the book.

Guest Comments: "Thank you for a wonderful interview. I had a great time and you are an excellent host." — Kathleen Gage, author of *The Law of Achievement* (Maxwell Publishing 2006)

"Just wanted to thank you for the opportunity to be on your show, it was a lot of fun! And I stayed and listened to your other guests, I felt I was in such good company. I learned a few things about the authenticity of writing and the use of your second guest's contacts with vets to make sure her stories about horses are accurate. I was also surprised that your final guest had such an interesting invention and a wonderful story about her own life! (Please forgive me I didn't catch their names!) Thanks again and I look forward to being on your show again in the fall!" — Bea Joyner, author of *Don't Need No Soaps, My Life Is Soap Enough!* (Busy as a Bea Productions 1999)

Bio of Valerie Connelly: Life experience, travel, a love of French literature, and a consuming habit of reading American and English literature all came together to ignite the spark of Valerie's writing career. Her years as an advertising copywriter, graphic designer and print shop owner served her well as she founded Nightengale Press in July of 2003.

Nightengale Press serves more than 50 authors, with 65 books among them, and several more coming through the process into print every month. The company has evolved into Nightengale Media LLC offering its authors a first class website, bookstore, marketing opportunites and more.

Valerie's mystery-thrillers *Sacred Night* (2003) and *Sidetracks* (2004), her most recent title *Calling All Authors — How to Publish with Your Eyes Wide Open* (2007) and her children's book *Arthur, The Christmas Elf* (2006) are all available at http://www.nightengalepress.com and all online bookstores. http://www.arthurthechristmaself.com

Cherry Picking with Rowena Cherry on Passionate Internet Voices Talk Radio.

Theme: Authors with special interests or authors whose book have environmentally topical themes. Throughout the year, the show puts on two-hour Sunday night specials including skits, reviews, excerpts, and "deep" thoughts about alien and shapeshifter romances involving heroes from under the sea — selkies, kelpies, hunks with gills, during Sea Otter Awareness week, and Manatee Awareness month with Mermen heroes, sea gods, Atlantans, Neptune types, ... and more.

Guest Profile: Romance authors of all shades, from science fiction romance, through paranormal romance, fantasy romance, to exotic oriental historical romance. A great guest is entertaining. Though not necessarily experienced, she is enthusiastic, knowledgeable and willing to open up about her work, what influences her choice of hero and heroine, where she finds inspiration, and she is ready to answer any surprise questions with good humor and respect for the audience. If a guest is nervous about a regional accent, or loss of voice, I also invite a volunteer to read excerpts on her behalf. I prefer to have three or four guests who know (and preferably like) each other, so we can all pinch hit and encourage each other. I invite authors whose books I have read or who are from author loops I'm on, and reviewers whom I've known in cyberspace. I don't mind about past interview experience, credentials, or sound of their voice. We all want to do ourselves credit, be likeable, and strike a chord with booklovers. Guests have included such multiple published authors as Linnea Sinclair, author of *Shades of Dark* (Bantam 2008), Susan Kearney, author of *Solar Heat* (Tor Paranormal Romance 2008) and Jade Lee, *Dragonborn* (Love Spell 2008).

Guest from Hell: I've never had a guest from hell, but I imagine it would be someone who sounded surly and who managed to answer open ended questions with Yes/No or Um. Also hellish would be a guest who hung up, or one on a cellphone who felt free to use the toilet while on air. I came close to that, once.

Contact: rowena@rowenacherry.com; 248-642-0438; http://www.rowenacherry.com; Rowena Cherry. Best method: E-mail if they have a book, an idea and a celebration on the calendar (horse week, gopher month, lion heat week, shark summer ... that sort of event would be worth a show), and suggestions for other authors/reviewers who have similar themes in their books, or who have recently reviewed similar themes (with phone follow up if no response within 12 hours... AOL is not always reliable). No response? If I'm not expecting an e-mail, the spam might pick it up. A guest should choose a sensible subject line. Cherry Picking will work for a while, until the spammers cotton on. A week would be my idea of "a reasonable time." A potential guest should try a second e-mail, possibly "poke" me on Facebook, or message me on MySpace. Phoning me should be a last resort. This applies to guests. Journalists, TV producers and publishers can always call me.

Invited Back? When their subject matter is topical, whether they have the time and inclination, if they are easy to talk with, if they are supportive of other guests. I would not invite back an author who was an "air hog" or one who used her time to criticize other people.

Guest Comment: "Thanks so much, Rowena. What a sweetie you are!"— Jacquie Rogers http://www.JacquieRogers.com, 2006 PEARL Award Winner, 2006 RIO Award Nominee, Faery Special Romances (May 2007)

Bio of Rowena Cherry: Award winning author Rowena is a self-described lifelong lurker and fact magpie. Her youth was spent on the tiny British island of Guernsey: a mystical, idyllic setting with its prehistoric earth-goddess, historic Martello towers, underground gun emplacements, and legends of faery men emerging from a cleft in the Hommet Headland to mate with human women.

A school chess champion and winner of the Duke of Edinburgh's Gold Award, Rowena went to ancient Cambridge University for her four-year combined honors degree in English and Education, after which she taught at exclusive boarding schools, first in Dorset, then in London. Eventually Rowena met and married her auto designer husband, who whirled her off to Germany to live the glamorous life of an alien abroad.

Reassigned to America, she rode in pace cars at the Indy 500 and Brickyard and has flown in corporate jets to exotic locations. Her life so far has been fantastic inspiration for romance novel scenes and alien-world building.

The Compulsive Reader with Magdalena Ball on Blog Talk Radio, http://www.blogtalkradio.com/compulsivereader

Theme: Books! Author interviews, readings, chat.

Guest Profile: Authors of literary fiction and poetry (mainly). I mainly look for an author with high quality work. As we would also be discussing issues of a general literary nature, a vibrant, chatty, interesting personality is also very highly sought.

I like to read their books first. Their literary profile (what they've written, where they've been, who they're networking with) is also useful. The sound of their voice isn't too important, but if I've heard them speak or spoken to them before and know they've got plenty to say, that is very helpful.

Guest from Hell: Someone who is not interested in talking at all. It isn't common, but I've interviewed authors like that and getting them to respond to questions in more than a monosyllable yes or no can often be a challenge — you find yourself answering their questions for them, which isn't good.

Contact: maggieball@compulsivereader.com; Skype: maggieball; http://www.compulsivereader.com; Magdalena Ball. Best method: E-mailing a pitch would be the perfect first start. If I'm interested I can take it further and obtain books and press kits. No response? A second e-mail is the best way to go (never phone, as I'm not in an easy time zone for Americans, and have been woken a few times at 2 AM. I'm usually a lucid speaker but not at that hour. Skype is fine though, as I will only answer if I'm online and that means I'm awake). I'm very responsive and quick, so if I haven't responded within a few days, the e-mail may well have gone astray.

Invited Back? How interesting they are to speak with! And of course new releases they want to promote.

Bio of Magdalena Ball: Magdalena runs *The Compulsive Reader* http://www.compulsivereader.com/html. Her stories, poetry, reviews and articles have appeared in many printed anthologies and journals, and have won several awards.

She is the author of *The Art of Assessment* (Mountain Mist Productions 2003) (nonfiction), *Quark Soup* (Picaro Press 2006) (poetry), awarded a 2006 "NOBLE" PRIZE!—for books that "exhibit exceptional writing skills and explore the human condition," and a novel, *Sleep Before Evening* (BeWrite Books 2007), which can be found at http://tinyurl.com/3crnk5

Dr. Maxine with Dr. Maxine Thompson on Artist first.com on Monday, 6 P.M. (PT)

Theme: Literary and publishing (including self-publishing).

Guest Profile: Authors of all genres who are informative, personable, and articulate. They should provide credentials and their past interviews in press release.

Guest from Hell: One who answers in one sentence.

Contact: maxtho@aol.com; http://www.maxinethompson.com/artistfirst.html; 323-242-9917; http://www.maxinethompson.com; Dr. Maxine Thompson. Best method: E-mail a pitch, a bio, and a press kit. No response? Call.

Invited Back? The feedback of the audience helps.

Guest Comment: "If you want a relaxing environment for your radio show interview, the Maxine Thompson Show is the show for you. Dr. Thompson interviews her guests with a soothing style, making the guests feel at ease and peace in mind, body and spirit."— Shirley Cheng, a blind and physically disabled poet and author who authored five books before age 23. Her latest, with highly acclaimed experts like Dr. Wayne Dyer, Tony Robbins, and Brian Tracy, is *Wake Up ... Live the Life You Love: Finding Your Life's Passion*, second edition (2007), http://www.shirleycheng.com

Bio of Maxine Thompson: Called a "Renaissance Woman" by her peers, Maxine is largely self-taught in the areas of e-book publishing, book doctoring, ghostwriting, story editing, literary coaching, column writing, information marketing, and Internet radio show hosting. She is the author of nine titles, an up and coming literary agent and owner of Black Butterfly Press. Maxine supports artists through her non-profit Maxine Thompson's Literary and Education Services and is opening doors once closed to black writers.

Maxine is author of the anthology, *Secret Lovers* (Urban Mass Paper 2006), which made the Black Expressions' Book Club Bestseller's List. Her novella *Second Chances* is one of the stories published in the anthology. She has an anthology, *All in the Family*, (novella: *Summer of Salvation*) being sold through Walmart and on-line book stores. She also has another anthology, *Never Knew Love Like This Before* (novella: *Katrina Blues*), which was picked up by Black Expressions' Book Club.

Katz Pajamas with Michael Katz on KCBX, aired along California's Central Coast (Santa Barbara and San Luis Obispo County, and on http://www.storytellermichael.com

Theme: Storytelling for all ages.

Guest Profile: Quality and experience in the art of storytelling. I want to have examples of their material from the past as well as the present, and what they are currently working on.

Guest from Hell: Short answers and an attitude.

Contact: mkatzstory@yahoo.com; 805-284-5906, 510-649-0631; http://www.storytellermichael.com; Michael Katz. Best method: E-mail and send me recordings of their work. No Response? They can e-mail me again.

Invited Back? That we run out of time and more topics are left to be touched on.

Bio of Michael Katz: Michael has been on the radio since 1984 with his storytelling program. He has been performing all over the world and was a featured teller at the openings of both the Getty Museum and the Disney Concert Hall in L.A. Michael's CD "Far Away and Close to Home" won a prestigious Parents' Choice Silver Honor Award.

On the Bookshelf with Dave (Doc) Kirby on WTBF-FM, aired in southeast Alabama, on Sundays at 9:30 AM and WTBF-AM, Sun at 7:30. Doc also hosts **Book Bits**, a daily 2–3 minute review/report.

Theme: Reading is important.

Guest Profile: Authors (traditionally or self-published), generally of religious, historical or health books. Articulate, relaxed, friendly, personable and knowledgeable of the subject of their book. I like for the interview to be a dialog, a discussion, so I always read the entire book and make notes prior to interview. Tell me a little about the book they wrote, and why they were qualified to write it. I hate to admit it, but if they have been on TV plugging it I take notice, but it is certainly no requirement.

Guest from Hell: Answers with short sentences or "yeah" all the time. I host the show and do my homework but I don't want to do all the talking (or even MOST of the talking).

Contact: wtbfdoc@yahoo.com; 334-566-0300 or cell 334-372-1441; http://www.wtbf.com; Dave Kirby. Best method: Either phone or e-mail is fine. E-mail is probably easier to find me and, I must admit, I will keep an e-mail that intrigues me and consider calling about it. But I like the personal touch, too. No response? What is reasonable? Also, is there a timeframe within which you as the publicist is working? Also remember that I will schedule the show when I feel it does the most good for my listeners, not merely when it suits any PR campaign, but I don't ignore your needs either.

Invited Back? If the next book is good, too. If I connected with them during the first interview. If the publicist contacts me again.

Guest Comment: "Doc Kirby ... what memories those two words bring back. One of the first radio talk hosts who ever interviewed me back when *Christmas in My Heart* was in its infancy (2008 will see the release of our 17th collection). What impressed me then — and still does now — was how well he did his homework before we went on the air. Unbelievable as it may seem, there are interviewers who go on the air without even having seen your book — much less actually read it. Such "interviewers" (if one can call them by such a name) usually have some cookie-cutter questions to ask so it won't be clear to the audience that they haven't even scanned the book in question.

"Then we have the other end of the spectrum: Interviewers who are a joy to talk to: so full of the book they don't even need you. So excited you wonder if they're airborne. That's the kind of interviewer Doc Kirby is. The reason why out of the several thousand radio interviews I've given, his name stands out against the years. And perish the thought I'd ever come out with a book without hearing his warm, excited voice on the line, eager to get another interview going." — Joe Wheeler, Ph.D., author/editor, http://www.JoeWheelerBooks.com

Bio of Dave (Doc) Kirby: Doc has been in radio since 1973, and a bi-vocational United Methodist minister since 1990. He holds degrees in music, musical theater, and ministry. He has been a high school teacher, TV cameraman/producer, newspaper columnist, and university journalism professor.

Doc has been reviewing books since 1988, and his weekly 30-minute interview show has been on the air at WTBF-AM/FM (where he is the Operations and Program Manager) since 1991. BOOK BITS, his daily 3 minute book review show, began airing in 1992.

Poetry & Prose & Anything Goes with Dr. Ni with Dr. Niama L. Williams on Blog Talk Radio, http://www.blogtalkradio.com/drni on Saturdays, 3–4 PM (ET).

Theme: Interview guest authors about their new books. The best in contemporary poetry and prose.

Guest Profile: New or continually publishing authors. Guests who write this type of work: The best in contemporary literature, period. It's got to be very, very good. I want depth, complexity, multiple layers and levels of meaning, metaphor and simile that leap off the page and haunt the readers' minds. I think part of my DNA comes from T. S. Eliot whose poetry I adore. I want my readers and my listeners to have to, to WANT to think when they hear the work on my show. All I am interested in is the quality of their work.

Guest from Hell: Have not had this experience.

Contact: niamapers@gmail.com; 484-231-1768; http://www.blowingupbarriers.com; Dr. Niama L. Williams. Best method: E-mail me your interest in being on the show and a 5-pg minimum (10-pg maximum) writing sample of poetry, prose or memoir. No scripty fonts, no bold fonts and no italic fonts. Fiction, prose, poetry or memoir only. 12 point font size. No response? E-mail me once more; I am a very polite e-mail correspondent and if I have not gotten back to someone within a reasonable amount of time I will usually apologize and try to get right to their submission.

Invited Back? The continued quality of their work.

Guest Comment: "Dr. Ni was a gracious, informed, and inviting interviewer. She had taken the time to familiarize herself with my work and made sharing ideas and information so easy that I had absolutely no stress. She was so inspiring that I found myself wanting to share more of myself and find out more about her. My time with Dr. Ni was all too short, and I would happily join her again, on the phone or in person." — Gary Earl Ross, fiction writer, playwright and essayist, http://www.angelfire.com/journal/garyearlross

Bio of Niama Leslie Williams: A June 2006 Leeway Foundation Art and Social Change Grant recipient and a 2006 participant in a Sable Literary Magazine/Arvon Foundation residential course in Shropshire, UK, Niama has a doctorate in African American literature from Temple University, a bachelor's in comparative literature from Occidental College, and a master's in professional writing from the University of Southern California. She was born and raised in Los Angeles, California, and resides in Philadelphia, Pennsylvania.

Niama is author of three books published by Lulu.com in 2007: *The Journey, Steven* and *Famous Faces*. In addition, she's had essays and short stories published in numerous publications. Her short story "The Embrace" was selected for the 2006–2007 Writing Aloud series at the InterAct Theatre Company in Philadelphia, PA.

Niama explains the purpose of her writing: "I frequently do not err on the side of caution in my writing, but I believe in the purpose of it: to speak to the things others do not want to speak of, with the hopes of reaching that one woman, or her lover, or her friend, who refuses to deal with her pain, who hides from it, who doesn't think she'll survive it. That's the audience I hope to reach."

The Reader's Round Table with Melissa Alvarez (monthly) on Blog Talk Radio, http://blogtalkradio.com/MelissaAlvarez. Melissa also hosts two other shows on Blog Talk Radio: *Friesian Ink Radio* (see page 11) and *Celtic Seers* (see page 162).

Theme: To bring readers and authors together and to bring psychic readers to our listeners.

Guest Profile: Authors who write in any genre and anyone involved in new age or paranormal type topics. I want to know what they've written or what they do that is involved in the paranormal etc. What can they offer my listeners?

Guest from Hell: Someone with a bad attitude who hasn't prepared for the show or someone who doesn't show up without giving prior notice.

Contact: contact@melissa.com; 561-776-0758; http://melissa.com, http://apsychichaven.com, http://blogtalkradio.com/MelissaAlvarez; Melissa Alvarez. Best method: By sending me an e-mail with a short bio and letting me know what they can offer my listeners. Are they willing to promote their segment? No response? They should e-mail me again.

Invited Back? If I have time on the schedule, if they are engaging, and if they've helped to promote their segment to bring more listeners. Boring guests without a sense of humor probably won't get invited back.

Bio of Melissa Alvarez: Melissa is an award winning author, graphic artist and website designer who obtained a Bachelor of Arts from Virginia Tech. She has always been an entrepreneur and owned several successful businesses with her husband. She became involved in the publishing industry in 2000 by forming New Age Dimensions to self-publish her first book, *The Phoenix's Guide to Self-Renewal,* released in 2001. It quickly landed in Amazon.com's Top 1000 where it stayed until it went out of print. At the time, Melissa was manufacturing the 416-page book in her home and couldn't keep up with the demand. "The learning process that went with the publication of this book was phenomenal," she says. "I jumped into the industry in an unconventional way but it was fun and worthwhile."

From 2004 to 2006, Melissa operated New Age Dimensions as a small press, with 40 authors and over 70 titles released. Melissa designed the book covers, created the print book layouts and e-book files, designed and maintained websites for the company as well as some of the authors. She had the final decision on contracted books. The company won awards for website design and the books published received numerous five star reviews and won many awards including EPPIE'S, the Oscars of e-publishing.

Because of the industry contacts made when Melissa worked as The Guide to Romance Fiction at About.com, she decided to release her first paranormal romantic suspense novel, *Night Visions,* under the pen name Ariana Dupré. She wanted the book to stand on its own, to receive good or bad reviews because of the writing, not because she knew a lot of people in the romance industry or because she owned the publishing company. Melissa didn't want her jobs, past or present, to affect the reviews in any way (good or bad). So she kept Ariana's real identity a secret until enough reviews came in that she knew the book had indeed earned success on its own. *Night Visions* became a multiple award winning title that is currently published by Cerridwen Press.

Reading with Robin with Robin Kall on 920 AM, WHJJ, Providence, RI, also streaming live at www.920whjj.com, aired Saturday, 7–8 AM (ET).

Theme: Books, author interviews (with traditionally published authors only).

Guest Profile: Adult fiction for the most part — also YA books discussed — whatever is interesting to me — women's issues, family life, etc. Lively chat — interesting — that sort of thing. I don't really need to know about potential guests — I read up on their sites and of course have read the books. That's enough. Some of her memorable author guests include Jodi Picoult, Sue Monk Kidd, Jennifer Weiner, David Baldacci, and such children's authors as Aliki, Lois Lowry, Meg Cabot, Mary Jane Begin, Margie Palatini and Lois Lowry.

Guest from Hell: I really haven't had any. I guess someone who is boring — oh, also guests who interrupt or come on with an agenda as opposed to answering the questions and following the conversation.

Contact: robin@readingwithrobin.com; 401-952-0660; http://www.readingwithrobin.com; Robin. Best method: Phone or e-mail — press kit/book is good. No response? If I don't e-mail in a reasonable amount of time the guest can assume I didn't get the e-mail or some tragic event has occurred. I am really good about responding.

Invited Back? If they have another book that's come out and if we had fun the first time. My favorite authors are always invited back w/the next book if we can fit it in.

Guest Comments: "I was delighted to be on Reading with Robin. Robin is a generous, energetic and informed host. She had read my book before the show and asked me thoughtful questions that lead to a terrific discussion. She's a warm and intimate interviewer and, with her enthusiasm, helped sell my book to her listeners. I can't wait to visit her show again!"— Leslie Schnur, author of *Late Night Talking* (Atria 2007) and *The Dog Walker* (Washington Square Press 2005), http://www.leslieschnur.com

Bio of Robin Kall: Robin grew up during the 60s and 70s on Long Island in a close family of five. She developed a love of reading from her mom, and among her favorite books as a youngster were Judy Blume's *Are You There, God, It's Me, Margaret* and *Gone with the Wind.*

She graduated from the State University of New York at Binghamton with a degree in Sociology. Robin, and her husband Burt, their two teenage children and their dog make their home in East Greenwich, R.I. While her family has a lot of diverse interests, everyone enjoys reading (except the dog, who won't sit still long enough), and all are enthusiastic supporters of her book-related endeavors.

Robin has always been active in the community and has been attracted most to those activities that involve reading. As a volunteer at Women and Infants Hospital of RI, she was an auxilian who worked on their first Storybook Ball in the 80s, and its Festival of Authors. She organized Moses Brown School book fairs that brought in leading children's authors, and continues to lead the reading circle that she initiated at Temple Beth El in Providence, and a mother/daughter book club. She serves on the Board of Directors of Reading Across Rhode Island and the Rhode Island Center for the Book, and is the guest at book club meetings throughout the state.

Sound Authors with Dr. Kent Gustavson on World Talk Radio Network, http://www.worldtalkradio.com

Theme: Authors and their interests.

Guest Profile: Authors of all types; Interesting book/subject matter. Credentials, past interview experiences and relevant life experiences are important.

Guest from Hell: Obnoxious and plugging their product every minute.

Contact: amber@offsitebusinesssolutions.com; 813-657-5995; http://www.soundauthors.com, http://www.kentgustavson.com; Amber Bean. Best method: E-mail Amber with all the info. No response? E-mail again.

Invited Back? If their first appearance was a success.

Guest Comment: "Thank you for the opportunity to present my unique perspective to your listeners. They do not get it from the general media ... I correctly suspected [that Dr. Gustavson] spoke Arabic from the way he pronounced my name (exactly as it is pronounced in Arabic). It is a rare and a pleasant surprise."— Saul Silas Fathi, author of *Full Circle: Escape from Baghdad and the Return* (Xlibris 2006), http://www.saulsilasfathi.com

Bio of Kent Gustavson: Kent is a man with as many hats as a Dr. Seuss cat... author, publisher, professional musician, classical composer, professor at two New York universities, speaker, owner of the independent publisher Blooming Twig Books LLC, and author of the *Book Publishing Bible* (Blooming Twig Books 2007).

Kent also has more than a dozen acclaimed commercial recordings, and conducts workshops around the world in both music and publishing.

His musical and literary background have driven him towards a life and career committed to altruism and charity. His radio show is an extension of his wish to bring a bit of light into the often hopelessly dark and complex world of publishing, and help authors get their stories heard.

Today's Author with David K. Ewen, M.Ed., aired live on Sunday afternoons on http://www.ewenprime.com — archived recorded shows are also available

Theme: Talk show with writers — How did they do it and why?

Guest Profile: A guest is a writer or author. Someone who has a strong passion for what they do. I want to know what inside them made them want to write the book. I'd also like to know their publishing experience.

Guest from Hell: All of a sudden they get stage fright and it was unexpected.

Contact: TodaysAuthor@yahoo.com; 877-414-5096; http://www.ewenprime.com; David K. Ewen. Best method: The best way is to go directly to http://www.ewenprime.com to get booking information. The initial method of contact is by e-mail. No response? The booking information tells the potential guest that if they don't hear a response within two weeks, give us a call or e-mail us again.

Invited Back? If a lot of listeners call in, then it's a sure bet the guest will be back.

Guest Comment: "David goes the extra mile and downloads a video of your audio interview onto Google with photos you provide him as well as media from your website. While the images morph into each other, viewers can listen to the interview which makes for a more interesting experience. David also downloads the audio interview to various blog sites. Within 20 minutes of doing the interview on *Today's Author*, I got 84 hits on my website from all over the world."— Laurel Dewey, author of *Protector* (Safe Goods 2006), http://www.laureldewey.com

Bio of David K. Ewen: David started in publishing in 1994 in Natick, Massachusetts. In 1998, he launched the New England Publishers Association that became affiliated with PMA and SPAN. He volunteered and donated his time to run the association for two years. He had special guests like Mary Westheimer of Bookzone, Tom and Marilyn Ross of SPAN and Jim Cox of Midwest Book Review.

David conducted a year-long speaking tour in all six New England states to promote self-publishing and the independent press industry. He produced and hosted a live show on WORC 1310 AM and WGFP 940 AM called *Author of the Week*, which aired Thursdays for an hour before going to ABC News. In 2004, his speaking turned to a regular workshop seminar called "Publish Your Book — Guaranteed" held at 10 universities and colleges in four states.

Vin Smith's Midday Book Break (now ***The Midnight Bookworm***) on America First Radio, flagship stations KCAA, Loma Linda/San Bernardino/Riverside, Cal, and KTAE, Cameron, Texas (the show is part of the Night Shift Program starring Uncle Buck on KCAA America First Radio, http://www.kcaaradio.com). Vin also hosts *Beyond the Paranormal*, Saturday, 8–10 PM (PT), which is aired on the same stations and Internet as his other show.

Theme: MB brings the finest authors on the planet right into your home.

Guest Profile: Usually authors talking about their books; on occasion, experts on a subject (who have not written a book), at which point we suggest a reading list on the subject to the listeners. We handle both fiction and non-fiction. We only interview authors who can write well. That's one of the major reasons for the need for review copies. Sometimes self-published writers cannot, in fact, write well, and we do not include them on our book shows. However, the same can be said of mainstream royalty published authors; some cannot write up to our standards. We look only for quality. The first quality is the ability to be verbally liquid — that is, able to keep pace with the pacing of the show; think on one's feet; the second quality is to be extremely familiar with the subject; questions may well overwhelm those who write books without really knowing the subject. And finally, we look for personality. Those who come across flat will not be invited back. We want to know past interview experiences, credentials, and sound of their voice and more. We usually do a pre-interview, at which time the author is literally auditioning. If I like what I hear, then I know the author is going to help me make good radio, and in the process add to his/her fan base. If I don't like what I hear, then radio is probably not the way for the author to go. I would suggest in those cases to try and get newspaper coverage and dip into the pocket for advertising dollars for one medium or another.

We don't reveal information about guests, as that immediately puts them on contact lists which they do not appreciate. However, if an author wishes to get a handle on the style, they may send $5.00 to cover costs, and an air check will be sent to the author for any of 82 archived programs of the old *Midnight Bookworm* program. Or, wait a few weeks, and every brand new *Vin Smith's Midday Book Break* will be available in perpetuity on the website for America First Radio. Listening to a previous show is the best way to understand what the experience will be like.

Guest from Hell: Any guest who fails any of the above criteria. The idea is to create good radio. Selling books for the author is merely a byproduct of that process.

Contact: midnightbookworm@sbcglobal.net (primary) midnightbookworm@earthlink.net (secondary); 530-842-7672; http://www.midnightbookworm.com; Vin Smith. Best method: The first thing to do is e-mail MBB — due to the volume of inquiries. Then, if it looks good to us from an editorial standpoint, we will invite the author or author's representative to send three review copies, plus 15 to 20 questions. The process goes on from there, including the day when a pre-interview is scheduled. Then, finally, the show booking. Any author who fails to make a show booking will be red flagged and will never again appear on MBB. No response? Send another e-mail. Things go poof sometimes in the cyber world.

Invited Back? This question is answered clearly in the above paragraphs. You collaborate to make good radio, and you get invited back — regularly. Show expertise in any subject that makes great radio, and you get invited back.

Bio of Vin "Doc" Smith: Vin is multimedia artist, freelance novelist, poet, pianist, singer, songwriter, composer, orator, and ventriloquist.

Born in Whittier, California, he grew up among orange and avocado groves in Pico, California. He has degrees and certifications from Cuesta College, Columbia School of Broadcasting, New York Institute of Photography, Cronemiller School of Music, and American School of Piano Tuning.

In the mid-sixties, Vin began his radio career at the small 250 watt station in Frederick, Oklahoma, KTAT. "When I first saw that wonderful town, I almost cried," Vin said a few years ago. "America's heartland at last. I quickly fell in love with the people of Oklahoma, and the wheat and cotton fields that spread as far as the eye could see."

Later, Vin would move to Oklahoma City to star on KOCY as the first midnight radio personality in the station's history. His show was sponsored by Spectro Theaters and the Goodyear Tire and Rubber Company. "One of my duties was to go to the movies every single night of the year. Of all the films that came through town on a sneak preview, the one that sticks in my memory the best is John Wayne in *True Grit*. Nobody realized at the time that *True Grit* would be Wayne's masterpiece." While at KTAT, Vin invented the Countrypolitan Radio Format. It was one of the most successful radio formats ever developed, incorporating music that would one day fuel the crossover movement.

In 1986, Vin won the first of three straight writing awards from the National Writers Club in Aurora, Colorado. Those three books, *Arena of the Mind, Goodbye Stress*, and *The Adventures of Timothy Turtle* were published by 1st Books Library.

Full bio at http://midnightbookworm.com

Writers FM with Karl Moore on http://www.writersfm.com

Theme: Writers, writing, inspiration.

Guest Profile: Authors, screenwriters, poets. Someone who is lively, chatting, and with real information to share. Humble, genuine, honest. I want to know exactly what kooky and interesting things they can share with our listeners. If you've written a book on psychic development and can give me a reading over the air, brilliant! Cool, crazy concepts always welcome. Some great guests have been: Lucinda Hawksley; Edwina Currie; Joe Vitale.

Guest from Hell: An individual who does nothing but talk, talk, talk — without coming up for air. This isn't a platform. Radio should be broadcasting a two-way chat.

Contact: karl@karlmoore.com; 07092 17 18 19; http://www.writersfm.com/; Karl Moore. Best method: An e-mail is probably best, stating your "best features." No response? Do not call or e-mail.

Invited Back? We don't invite many guests back! If they're super interesting and there's a lot of demand, we do a follow-on show.

Guest Comments: "Not only was it fun talking to Karl on the air, but he's the first host who ever sent me an e-mail thanking me for the interview before I had a chance to write him!! As both a radio host and guest, I consider thank-you notes after the show from the guest paramount, but from the host it's extraordinary"—Francine Silverman, host of *The Radio Host Show* (see p. 76) and author of *Radio Wants You: An Intimate Portrait of 700 Shows That Welcome Guests*, http://www.talkradioadvocate.com

"Karl is a great interviewer. He's well-researched and always asks intelligent questions!"—Edwina Currie, best-selling author and former UK health minister

Bio of Karl Moore: Karl is a self-growth writer and officially one of the world's top 100 developers.

Living in Durham, United Kingdom, Karl is the managing director of White Cliff Computing Ltd and controls the entire WCCL Network, currently consisting of over 100 online properties.

Karl is a three-time MVP award winner and the author of two best-selling books—*Karl Moore's Visual Basic .NET* (APress 2002 USA, UK) and *The Ultimate Code Book* (APress 2005 USA, UK).

Writers in the Sky with Yvonne Perry (or associate) on http://www.yvonneperry.net, iTunes and http://yvonneperry.blogspot.com

Theme: Information about the craft and business of writing, publishing and marketing. Features news about books on the market, the publishing industry and book publicity. The purpose is to connect the writing and publishing community with one another and other readers.

Guest Profile: Authors of any genre welcome. Specialties include spirituality, natural healing, how-to or self-help books, fiction and non-fiction literature, children's books, and anything about writing, publishing and marketing books or magazines. The person has a great book or information about writing, publishing and marketing to share. Should be able to answer questions that will help listeners become a better writer or know more about the publishing industry. Non-authors are welcome if they are writers, publishers, literary agents, or book publicists with tips to share about their craft or business. I would like to have their biography. If we are interviewing about a book, I'd like to have information about the book (jpg book cover, author photo, review copy of book if available). Guest fees are charged. Go to www.yvonneperry.net/Writing_Packages.htm#Publicity_Packages_

Guest from Hell: 1. One who monopolizes the conversation or 2. One who answers with a one-word sentence and doesn't seem interested in their own product.

Contact: write_on_yvonne@comcast.net; http://www.yvonneperry.net; 615-884-1224; Yvonne Perry

Theme: The craft and business of writing and news about books, publishing and marketing. Best method: E-mail a short query with a short author bio and book synopsis in the body of the e-mail text. If I am interested in having the person as a guest, I will ask for more material. No response? I always answer e-mail. If a person e-mails and doesn't hear from me within 48 hours, they should try again by e-mail or call me.

Invited Back? The information shared is vital to the writing and publishing community. The author has another book coming to market. The author has a contest they would like to announce.

Listener Comment: "Yvonne, Thank you so much for your podcasts. After having heard the first 12–15 of them, I realized what an outstanding resource you have provided. Thank you so much for the diversity and expertise you have made available. Each and every one of the podcasts contains useful and productive information as well as a load of inspiration from folks who have succeeded by walking their talk. It's way, way more than just a 'how-to' series. I also appreciate that you offer it for free and why you choose to do that. You reap what you sow. Thanks for sowing into the writer's community. It makes for a better world."—MaAnna Stephenson, author-to-be

Bio of Yvonne Perry: Yvonne is the owner of Write On! Creative Writing Services based in Nashville, TN. With her wide variety of freelance writing experience that includes impressive résumés, personal and professional bios, high-quality press releases, articles, books, and business documents, Yvonne and her team are ready to work with you on your next writing project. As a networker, Yvonne loves to share her knowledge and connect writers with one another. One way she does this is through her business, blog, monthly newsletter and weekly podcast about the craft and business of writing.

Yvonne is the author of *More Than Meets the Eye: True Stories About Death, Dying and Afterlife* (BookSurge Publishing 2005), and *Right to Recover: Winning the Political and Religious Wars Over Stem Cell Research in America* (Nightengale Press 2007).

She is a graduate of American Institute of Holistic Theology, where she earned a Bachelor of Science in Metaphysics. She welcomes writers, authors, publishers, literary agents, and publicists to submit literary material and announcements for her monthly newsletter and daily blog post.

Writers on Writing with Barbara DeMarco-Barrett and guest host Marrie Stone on KUCI-FM, http://www.kuci.org, aired in Southern California and podcast at http://writersonwriting.blogspot.com

Theme: Writers and writing.

Guest Profile: Novelists, literary agents, some narrative nonfiction authors. The author must be a novelist of either literary fiction or narrative nonfiction, a literary agent or a poet. I want to know what they've published. I don't book self-published or print-on-demand authors — ever.

Guest from Hell: Someone who is self-published and has a book full of typos.

Contact: penonfire@earthlink.net; withheld upon request; http://www.penonfire.com — Click on radio tower on left side of the screen; Barbara DeMarco-Barrett. Best method: E-mail. Sending a book with a press release is best. It all begins with the book. No response? Do not call or e-mail.

Invited Back? If I like their book and like them.

Guest Comments: "Thanks for having me on your show. An hour seemed like a long time to talk about myself, but you made it fun, especially after I got warmed up." — Billy Collins, U.S. Poet Laureate in 2001

"I really enjoyed talking to you. Thanks for making it such a relaxed and welcoming atmosphere. I had fun, and appreciate all your support and good questions — a lot!" — Aimee Bender, *Willful Creatures* (Doubleday 2005)

Bio of Barbara DeMarco-Barrett: Barbara splits her time between writing, teaching, editing *The ASJA Monthly* and producing and hosting her radio show. Her writing covers writing and writers, travel, parenting, and consumer topics. Her book, *Pen on Fire: A Busy Woman's Guide to Igniting the Writer Within* (Harcourt, 2004) was a *Los Angeles Times* best-seller and won a 2005 ASJA Outstanding Book Award, Service/Self-help. She also has essays in *The ASJA Guide to Freelance Writing* (St. Martin's, 2001) and *Conversations with Clarence Major* (University of Mississippi, 2002). In March of 2008, her essay, "Knitting: My Urban Escape," was published in *Knitting Through It* (Voyageur Press), edited by Lela Nargi.

Barbara's articles and essays have appeared in *The Los Angeles Times, Westways, The Writer, Writer's Digest, Poets and Writers, Sunset, Morning Calm* (Korean Air's inflight), *San Jose Mercury News* and *The Toronto Sun*, among others. For two years she was the "Women's Business" columnist for *OC Metro*, an Orange County business lifestyle magazine. She currently blogs about writers and writing at http://penonfire.blogspot.com

Barbara is also editor of *The ASJA Monthly*, the American Society of Journalists and Authors official publication (http://www.asja.org). She is Southern California chapter president of ASJA and has sat on the board of directors. In 2007 she was co-chair of the ASJA Annual Writers Conference in NYC.

She has taught creative writing at UC-Irvine Extension since 2000, and also teaches in its new online classroom. She teaches online for Gotham Writers Workshop, based in New York City. She also holds writing workshops in corporations for business people who want to jumpstart their creative writing.

The Writing Show with Paula B. on http://www.writingshow.com/Feeds/feed.mrss.xml and through podcast aggregators like iTunes, Zune, etc.

Theme: Information and inspiration for writers.

Guest Profile: Authors, screenwriters, poets, playwrights, publishers, literary agents, etc. An articulate writer or person associated with writing (publisher, agent, filmmaker, attorney, editor, etc.) who can talk knowledgeably about the craft and business of writing. Ability to talk knowledgeably about the craft and business of writing. That may mean credentials, but samples of their work are a better indication.

Guest from Hell: A person who tells me how to do my job.

Contact: paula@writingshow.com; 818-253-5431; http://www.writingshow.com; Paula Berinstein. Best method: Send a query by e-mail that tells me what you can offer my listeners. What can you talk about knowledgeably that we haven't already covered? Do not tell me you want to be on the show because you need to promote your book. No response? E-mail me. Messages can go astray, as we all know.

Invited Back? Since I don't have many openings, I only invite a guest back if their additional content or knowledge (past their first appearance) knocks my socks off. Sometimes a guest is so compelling that I invite them to do commentaries or other special features.

Guest Comment: "I thoroughly enjoyed my experience on *The Writing Show*. Paula Berinstein gets it. She cares about the process, much more than the hype. Paula, you're a true friend to writers." — Scott Fivelson, author of *Tuxes* (Beachside Press 2007)

Bio of Paula Berinstein: Producer and host of her radio show, Paula is the author of seven geeky nonfiction books, including *Making Space Happen* (Medford Press 2002) and *Business Statistics on the Web* (Information Today 2003). She has been "Publishing Trends" columnist for *Searcher* magazine, ran her own research business serving the entertainment and other industries for 15 years, and has been a programmer, systems analyst, and librarian. Paula considers herself first and foremost a journalist. Her heroes are Jim Lehrer and Margaret Warner of the "PBS NewsHour," whom she admires for their low-key manners and thoughtful questions.

Beauty, Style and Fashion

Who Says You Aren't Fabulous? — From the MMOElist.com page of *Make Me Over Eb Show*

A Fashionable Life with Jayne and Jen on 1490 WGCH/BusinessTalkRadio Network.

Theme: Fashion, beauty, interior design, lifestyle.

Guest Profile: Leaders in fashion industry (Candy Pratts Price, Editor Style.Com), beauty (Liz Michael, Freelance make up artist Bumble and Bumble NYC), fashion stylists (Phillip Bloch, Robert Verdi), publishing (DJ Carey, editor of Connecticut Cottages and Gardens), psychologists (Dr. Norma Ross, psychologist VH1), authors (Danielle Ganek, *LuLu Meets God and Doubts Him*). We look for individuals who are the best and the brightest in their fields. Dynamic leaders who can share their expertise and experience in a way that lends to the dynamic of our show and who can inform our listeners in an enlightening way. We are interested in individuals who have experience, valuable insight and information that fits into the content/context of *A Fashionable Life*.

Guest from Hell: We have never had a "guest from hell" as we are very selective of who we choose to have on as our guests.

Contact: Radio@fashionableliferadio.com; http://www.fashionableliferadio.com; Jayne Chase 203-550-9484; Jennifer Goodkind 203-249-8022. Best method: People who are interested in becoming a guest on *A Fashionable Life* should e-mail bio, send a press kit or provide a web site that we feel is of interest to our listening audience. No response? E-mail.

Invited Back? A guest who is "invited back" is someone who is engaging, informative and who has information worth sharing more than once.

Bios of Jayne Chase and Jennifer Goodkind: Jayne started her career at *Glamour* and *Vanity Fair* magazines and ultimately became the international editor at *Harper's Bazaar*. Then, she became the Public relations director at J. Crew. Presently, she is the fashion editor at The Cottages and Gardens Publications, which include Connecticut, Hamptons and Palm Beach.

Jennifer began her successful career as an accessories editor at *Vogue*. Her style and taste quickly caught the eye of many celebrities. She soon became a stylist to the stars as well as clients around the country who wanted to take advantage of her in-depth knowledge and cutting edge fashion sense. In 2000, Jen started JL ROCKS fine jewelry in Greenwich and Westport, Connecticut.

Let's Talk Makeup with Sherry Backman on Blog Talk Radio http//www.blogtalkradio.com.

Theme: Beauty, style fashion, self improvement.

Guest Profile: Makeup artists, image consultants, business owners, beauty bloggers. Someone knowledgeable about their subject matter. Someone easy to converse with. Why they want to be on my show? What do they know about the subject matter? Do they have a blog or website?

Guest from Hell: One who does not speak well. One who goes on and on about nothing.

Contact: sherrybackman@optonline.net; 631-667-6078; http://www.looselipsny.com; Sherry Backman. Best method: E-mail. No response? Keep e-mailing — I will get back to them.

Invited Back? Responses from my audience. If I had fun talking to them.

Guest Comment: "My experience on Sherry Backman's show was great! I've had her on my podcasts and talk radio show. She is great to talk to. We had so much fun, the time flew by." — Ebony Looney, host of *Make Me Over Eb Show* (see below)

Bio of Sherry Backman: Sherry is CEO of Loose Lips New York, http://www.looselipsny.com, a beauty/skincare webstore. She's a podcast host at http://www.blogtalkradio.com/looselipsny

Make Me Over Eb Show with Ebony Looney on BlogTalk Radio, www.blogtalk.radio.com/makemeover

Theme: Beauty and health topics, makeovers.

Guest Profile: We like them all. We have massage therapists, hairstylists, candlemakers, etc. What they have that the public may want. Why they're in business. If they don't mind taking off-the-cuff questions from callers.

Guest from Hell: No talker. If I have to pull things from them to say.

Contact: Eb@MakeMeOverEb.com; 803-467-1905; http://www.MakeMeOverEb.com; Ebony Looney. Best method: E-mail a bio, send a press kit. Just ask. I'm easygoing. No response? E-mail or call. Sometimes, messages can slip through. It doesn't hurt to be persistent.

Invited Back? Good talker, and have an interesting product or service that can better someone.

Bio of Ebony Looney: "I have to admit that I'm in a constant 'makeover' state of mind," says Ebony. "I'm always trying to improve in how I dress, in how I approach work, life and even cooking. I keep coming to the same conclusion — I have it in me to be fabulous. Who says I can't?"

Ebony's experience as an independent beauty consultant with Mary Kay Cosmetics made her realize that women wanted more from a beauty consultant than makeup. So she started a blog and then the radio show.

"I'm just on a quest to bring out the best in everyone who wants to be fabulous," she says.

Full bio at http://www.MakeMeOverEb.com/about.html

Business, Finance and Marketing

"It's about time we celebrate stories of successful business leaders, not the failures." — John Adam, host of The John Adam Show

The American Dream with Stanley El on Rowan Radio 89.7 WGLS FM, Rowan University, Glassboro, New Jersey.

Theme: Patriotic show highlights the dreams and ideals of guests.

Guest Profile: Business and community leaders, grassroots champions, crusaders, pioneers, inventors, trendsetters, authors, idealists. The guests that appear on *The American Dream* represent the true spirit of America — the pursuit of health, happiness and prosperity for all. These folks are patriotic, enthusiastic, highly motivated and passionate about their dreams to succeed. The big qualifier for getting on *The American Dream* is a guest with a passion to do good however big or small.

Guest from Hell: I have no idea of a guest from hell, but if you mean a difficult guest or one that doesn't fit, it would a guest that insists on promoting a product or business.

Contact: stanleyel@gmail.com; 856-845-1575; http://www.nsabo.wordpress.com, http://americandreamradio.wordpress.com; Stanley El. Best method: Phone or e-mail. I prefer talking to a potential guest over the phone. It is the most effective way to learn the motive and passion of an individual. No response? I always respond promptly.

Invited Back? Repeat guests are those who have a passion to serve humanity. They come in various forms — inventors, leaders, entrepreneurs, idealists, mothers, fathers, teenagers.

Guest Comment: "I did an interview with Stanley El on January 10 of this year [2007]. Had a great time in the process. The topic was 'What Is Your American Dream?' Prior to the interview Stanley gave me a general script of the types of questions he was likely to ask and, true to my nature, I ended up with a written 17 page script (with rather extensive answers to each question) of my own. During the broadcast, my 17 page response was a first for *The American Dream*. The show went great, and as I was on a bit of a roll telling my story and reading sample haiku from the book, he was gracious enough to allow my 15 segment to grow well over 20. I really had a ball and he obviously did, as well. Stanley El is a great guy and one of the most personable people I have ever had the good fortune to meet. We still have regular contact and discussions; and I value our friendship greatly. If we were all more like Stanley El, the world would be a much better place." — Rich Hay, author of *Out of My Mind and Back to My Senses: The Object of Life Is to Find Out Who I Am Before Time Runs Out* (Tate Publishing 2006).

His blogs are http://rfhay333.gather.com, http://rfhay333.eons.com and http://myspace.com/rfhay333

Bio of Stanley J. El: A self-proclaimed "Crusader for High Growth and Ideals in American Business," innovator, strategist, facilitator and speaker, Stanley is founder of The National Society of American Business Owners, established in 1996. He is the nation's authority on American Business Ownership Development and staff enrichment. An entrepreneur since age 17, Stanley has led his own marketing firm for nearly 20 years. His work in economic development earned him a national award for Gloucester County. Stanley's creativity began in grade school. His professional career began in the entertainment industry as a promoter, producer, director, dancer, artist and mime. Today, he is an accomplished graphic artist, writer, web designer, musician, poet and multi-media specialist.

Stanley is an adjunct professor at Cumberland County College and teaches at the Rutgers Small Business Development Center and Gloucester County College.

Business at Night with Greg Hebert on CFRA, Ottawa, Ontario, aired weeknights at 7 PM (ET).

Theme: Business and Investing.

Guest Profile: Presidents, CEOs, economists, market analysts, etc. I talk to Canadian and American business leaders. I try to talk to anyone with a newsworthy story that would be of interest to investors. In fact, I'm working on expanding the boundaries of the show to include more content from the U.S. Knowledge first, story telling ability second. Credentials are most important, experience and sound is less important if there's good story to be told.

Guest from Hell: The one-word answer type.

Contact: greg.hebert@chumottawa.com; 613-789-2486 ext 4776; http://www.cfra.com. Best method: E-mailing a pitch is usually sufficient. No response? I appreciate one follow-up e-mail or call, but don't hound me.

Invited Back? If they've managed to impress me with all of the above qualities.

Bio of Greg Hebert: Greg joined the CHUM radio family in 2000 in Montreal and is entering his 10th year in radio. Prior to his radio pursuits, Greg worked in the back office of DPM Financial Planning Group in Montreal. Greg's interest in business and investing runs second only to his passion for radio.

He attended Carleton University in Broadcast Journalism and the Montreal Radio and Television School leading up to his radio career. Greg has worked as the executive producer of the Montreal Expos radio broadcast. He has also worked as a reporter, sports anchor, talk show host and editorialist. His resume includes stations like Montreal's CHOM, CKGM and CJAD. He currently works as senior business editor at CHUM Limited's Ottawa radio stations, which include News Talk Radio 580 CFRA, Majic 100 (CJMJ), 93.9 BOB FM (CKKL) and Sports Radio The Team 1200 (CFGO).

Business in Motion with George Torok on Station 93.3 CFMU, aired Friday at noon (ET), from Hamilton, Ontario, Canada.

Theme: Lessons and inspiration from business for business 30 minute interview. A person dealing with a changing business environment with an interesting story or lesson.

Guest Profile: Business leaders, corporate executives, entrepreneurs, innovators, business authors, experts. Must be able to speak clearly. Prefer in studio interviews. I want them to be able to leave a one or two sentence description of their story on my voice mail.

Guest from Hell: One who is difficult to hear or understand. One who speaks in vague terms and refuses to answer specific questions.

Contact: info@torok.com; 905-335-1997; http://www.BusinessinMotion.ca; http://www.Torok.com; George Torok. Best method: E-mail with link to their site. Then followup with phone message. No response? Followup in a couple weeks by e-mail or phone. Some e-mail gets trapped by spam blockers.

Invited Back? If they were great the first time and there is more to the story.

Bio of George Torok: George was the creator of his show, launched in the fall of 1995.

He is a specialist in communication and thinking skills, and works with organizations and individuals to help them grow.

Full bio at http://www.businessinmotion.ca/host.html

Business Matters with James Max on LBC 97.3 FM, aired in London and the south east of England and nationwide on DAB and through SKY and Virgin Media and on the web, http://www.lbc.co.uk

Theme: Business and fine things.

Guest Profile: Business people, advisers, companies, experts, entrepreneurs, purveyors of fine things from magazine writers to travel writers, authors and celebs. Want to know their past interview experiences, credentials, sound of their voice. All of it — normally have a chat before going on air.

Guest from Hell: I don't have any. Perhaps someone who doesn't talk or is dull.

Contact: james.max@lbc.co.uk; withheld upon request; http://www.lbc.co.uk and personal is http://www.jamesmax.net; Myself or my producer Rajiv Patni. Best method: E-mail. No response? E-mail or call if they must.

Invited Back? If they were good, interesting or relevant.

Bio of James Max: James is a qualified chartered surveyor with 15 years experience in the world of commercial real estate, finance and private equity. He was a semi-finalist on BBC's "The Apprentice" and has adapted his career to radio and TV. He presents his own shows on LBC 97.3 and is also a presenter on TalkSPORT (a national UK talk radio station). He regularly reviews the newspapers on "Sky News" and co-presents Property Pensions and Profit from Property on "Overseas Property TV."

James's level of expertise comes across in his broadcasting where he covers a wide range of topics with authority, empathy and with a sprinkling of wit and humor. He is building up quite a following in the UK and is in demand not only from broadcasters but also corporates for their events, podcasts and events.

Business Success Coaching with John McKee on Womens Radio http://www.WomensRadio.com

Theme: Career success while maintaining a life of balance.

Guest Profile: Senior executives, business owners, recognized experts in the areas such as money management. Real world success and experience providing tips and strategies which can be used by listeners. Experience, credentials, comfort doing interviews.

Guest from Hell: Only wants to do a "commercial" for themselves or their businesses and not provide valuable tips free of charge.

Contact: john@businesssuccesscoach.net; 720-226-9072; http://www.WomensRadio.com; http://www.BusinessSuccessCoach.net; John McKee or Virginia Smith. Best method: E-mail is best so that we can determine if the "fit" is right and then which show would be best for the guest. No response? We always respond quickly.

Invited Back? How many downloads the show gets, if they were entertaining, listener feedback.

Bio of John McKee: John has 30+ years of leadership experience. He was one of the founding senior executives of Directv, leader of national billion dollar corporations in the U.S. and Canada and is a specialist in leadership, executive and career coaching.

The Career Engineers Radio Broadcast with Francina R. Harrison, MSW "The Career Engineer" on TCE Network, http://thecareerengineers/radiotalkshow.html. Francina also does the live *Career Talk Radio* show on Blog Talk Radio on which she interviews authors of career, business or lifestyle intelligence, http://www.blogtalkradio.com/TCE/2008/05/31/How-to-GET-Hustled-in-Your-Business. She also produces an Internet TV Show called "TCE & Friends Presents ... The Career, Life & Business Show" (CLB TV), http://www.thecareerengineers.com

Theme: Don't get anxious — get prepared in your career, business and life.

Guest Profile: (Lifestyle format) — Authors who write on empowering your career, life or business. A "REAL" person who has been there, done that ... now what appeal. Took a healthy risk, made things happen and can help our viewers make Monday morning better. We have a guest form that must be completed, unless I hand select them based on their area of performance and what I see.

Guest from Hell: A person who has one word responses and has no substance, just fluff.

Contact: francina@thecareerengineers.com; 757-420-1109; http://www.thecareerengineers.com; info@careerengineers.com; Francina R. Harrison. Best method: No pitch. Guest form is available on my radio page. I will view a bio, website and would like to hear how they sound. E-mailing is better — then a phone conversation will follow. No response? E-mail or call, plus we are developing other media products as well, so that accounts for our time as well.

Invited Back? How they inspire me.

Guest Comments: "Francina Harrison was actually the first person to invite me on a radio show to discuss my book, *Embracing the Real World: The Black Woman's Guide to Life After College*. I have since been on more than 15 radio shows and can easily say that I enjoyed being on hers the most. She is witty, down-to-earth and has a true 'radio voice/personality.' She is also very professional and friendly. However, what I liked most about Francina was that she really was interested in getting to know me and more about my book. We have since become friends and I still listen to her show." — Chaz Kyser, author of *Embracing the Real World: The Black Woman's Guide to Life After College* (Seshet Press 2006), http://www.embracingtherealworld.com

Bio of Francina Harrison: "The Career Engineer," Francina is a nationally recognized career/workforce expert, media personality, speaker, author and human potential/business building consultant.

She is author of *A Mind to Work: The Life and Career Planning Guide for People Who ~~Want~~ Need to Work* (iUniverse 2004) and contributing author in the 2007 nationally released book *Embracing the Real World: A Black Woman's Guide to Life After College* http://www.embracingtherealworld.com by author/ Langston University journalism instructor, Ms. Chaz Kyser.

Host, creator and executive producer of "Push Up Your Career" on Internet TV, she has appeared on such national media as *The Tavis Smiley* syndicated radio show.

Francina graduated summa cum laude with a Bachelor in Social Work and received her Masters in Social Work (MSW) from Norfolk State University in 1997. She and her husband, a retired Navy senior chief petty officer, have two children and live in Virginia Beach, VA.

CEO Lounge with Michelle Bauer and Brent Britton on WGUL 860 AM, aired by Salem Communications.

Theme: Talk with Tampa CEOs and executives about build to grow, uncommon knowledge and luxe life.

Guest Profile: Authors, CEOs in every business from technology to fitness to education to entertainment. We look for someone with a story to tell. *CEO Lounge* lets you sneak a peek into the businesses of women and men who are driven and successful. We'd like to know if they have experience in subjects of interest to us.

Guest from Hell: Every guest is delightful in her or his own way, of course. A guest from hell is someone who is boring.

Contact: michelle@common-language.com or bcbritton@ssd.com; 727-510-2524 or 813-508-5042; http://www.tampabayceo.com/ceolounge.html; Michelle Bauer and Brent Britton. Best method: E-mail us. We try to package segments according to content. For example, we finished a recent segment all about fitness with guest speaker Dawna Stone, winner of Martha Stewart *Apprentice* and publisher of *Her Sports* magazine, Geoffrey Dyer, CEO of Lifestyle Family Fitness, and David Schlaifer, Center for Community Health Leadership project. No response? We are very busy, so the person can try e-mailing again. Please avoid calling.

Invited Back? We would like to keep expanding our guest list until we speak with every last CEO on the planet. No repeats needed.

Bios of Michelle Bauer and Brent Britton: Michelle is CEO and president of Common Language, a boutique strategic communications firm located in St. Petersburg, Florida. She is responsible for overall direction of the practice, which provides strategic consulting, communications planning, media relations, relationship brokering, and conference development services.

Brent is an attorney in the Tampa office of Squire Sander and Dempsey, LLP, where he provides a broad spectrum of legal services to entrepreneurs, emerging technology companies, and innovative enterprises. He was a founding partner of the San Francisco law firm, Britton Silberman and Cervantez, before coming to Florida. Britton is president of the MIT Club of Tampa Bay and a board member of the Tampa Bay Technology Forum, where he also chairs the Emerging Companies Committee.

The China Business Show with Christine Lu on http://www.wsradio.com

Theme: Doing business in China.

Guest Profile: Entrepreneurs and experts on China business. First and foremost, we try to find a guest who is an expert in their field and articulate in the way they present themselves on-air. We prefer guests who have an interesting background and can speak from a point of view that the listening audience can relate to. We always like to start with their entrepreneurial background story since the experience of our guests is something that fellow listeners who are entrepreneurs can identify with. We will usually give them a ring prior to confirming their guest spot on our show to get a better idea of what type of guest they might be, i.e., do they sound nervous? Do they speak fast and will we need to think up more questions than planned? Are they confident enough of the subject to speak on it with minimal questions asked, etc. etc.

Guest from Hell: The guest that answers questions with just a simple "yes" or "no" and does not elaborate or add any value to the conversation.

Contact: christine@TheChinaBusinessShow.com; Withheld upon request; http://www.TheChinaBusinessShow.com; Christine, executive producer and host. Best method: E-mailing a bio and providing us with 10 questions they would like us to ask them on-air. This usually gives us a good idea of how we can integrate their background into our show programming and guest line-up. No response? Due to the high number of spam, the person should try and re-send just in case it was not received the first time. We make every effort to reply; therefore, e-mail is best.

Invited Back? Whether or not the flow of their first interview went well. If we feel they added value and the topic of the discussion is something that warrants an update or a repeat visit.

Bio of Christine Lu: Christine began her own learning curve in doing business in China 11 years ago as a very driven Boston University undergrad student who flew herself out to Shanghai determined to land the best summer internship she could talk her way into. She convinced The American Chamber of Commerce in Shanghai that they needed the services of an unpaid Chinese-American intern and the rest is history.

Offering a strong blend of creativity and cross cultural insight since 1996, Christine's entrepreneurial career in China has included designing two lines of women's ready to wear clothing, co-founding a dot-com startup, training for 6 months at HSN (Home Shopping Network) International's headquarters in the U.S., developing a catalog and Internet business to complement a TV shopping company's multi-channel retail concept and, through it all, remaining an active member in networking circles within The American Chamber of Commerce in Shanghai.

After a successful five years, Christine was promoted to marketing director for TVSN (TV Shopping Network) in China. In 2004, she returned to the U.S. and is based in San Diego where she lives with her husband and son.

Christine remains true to her entrepreneurial retail spirit as the co-owner of an online kitchenware boutique that maintains an excellent Gold Powerseller status on eBay and is a featured merchant in Amazon.com's Seller Central network.

Cover Your Assets with Vince Rowe on KJCE, 1370 AM (CST), Austin, TX, on Saturday at 1 PM (CT) and on BizRadio.com, 1110 AM, Dallas and Houston, from 11 to noon (CT) weekdays and Sat., 4–6 PM (CT).

Theme: Financial consumer education and advocacy.

Guest Profile: Vince's "take no prisoners" style of ferreting out all the bad financial advice and brutal interviews of folks that would sell it sets him apart from the crowd of financial shows. Someone who is not selling a financial product, especially a software trading system. Guests that like to talk about the skills of investing and trading and understand that their way is not the end all be all in the Stock, FOREX, eMini's or commodities markets. All we need is what they have written (i.e., books, papers, economic dissertation) and their belief structures. I don't like to go based on past performance, rather hold them to task on something in a first interview and then have a second interview booked to bring them back. If they don't show up for the second interview rest assured I won't forget the date they were booked and have the results of their prognostication(s). This is why I have so many downloads of the show, and guests that are good at what they do get massive global response from my show.

Guest from Hell: First and foremost, and by far the worst, someone that comes on and pushes their product, book or software and makes it obvious that's what they are doing. Second, someone that has no substance and can't articulate a point, or roll over when I put them to the test of the point they are trying to sell; http://www.vincerowe.com

Contact: vrowe@tradingacademy.com; 214-476-6656; Vince Rowe. Best method: E-mail me a bulleted talking points sheet on how the potential guest can help investors traders learn a set of skills associated to the market. No response? I get so many pitches that aren't associated to the topic that I just don't respond, so try a second time and if you don't hear back and receive a confirmation that I received it, then you can safely discern from that that I'm not interested. Now, if I am interested I forward it to my producers immediately for booking.

Invited Back? They are all invited back, see above.

Bio of Vince Rowe: Vince is president of Online Trading Academy–Texas.

His experience in education began as an instructor and he finished as COO for companies such as New Horizons Computer Learning Centers, Sylvan Learning Centers, and Fujitsu. As a leader in their Human Capital Management divisions and training support functions, he was responsible for groups of 450 employees and facilitated two large scale mergers.

Next, he bought and sold several businesses with his venture capital partners and continues to hold majority ownership positions in small incubator companies. After retiring at 38, Vince was a professional trader in 2003 and 2004. Combining his education and trading experience, he started Online Trading Academy–Texas in 2005.

Originally from California, Vince now resides in Irving, Texas. He has three children: Brandon, Spencer and Sydney 12, 7 and 4 respectively. He is a decorated Desert Storm veteran and an ex–Army Ranger.

The Cranky Middle Manager Show with Wayne Turmel on http://cmm.thepodcastnetwork.com

Theme: An irreverent but informative look at the functions and duties of a manager in today's workplace.

Guest Profile: Experts in the field of management development and the workplace. Authors, trainers and managers who have something to share with their peers are welcome. A guest should have a strong, passionate point of view about management and making people's lives at work better. Mostly I look for something we haven't heard a thousand times, put a way we've never heard it. A sense of humor is essential. I've interviewed plenty of people without hearing them, sometimes to my detriment. I want to see samples of their work (their blog site, book) and, if they've been interviewed on radio or in podcasts before, let me hear snippets so I know what we're in for.

Guest from Hell: The guest from hell is monotone and monosyllabic, possibly suffering from mononucleosis. Their voice should portray their passion for their topic. Additionally, people who rely on statistics or generalities, rather than real world examples, make me crazy. Also, those who worship at the altar of Jack Welch, prepare for a hard time.

Contact: wayne@crankymiddlemanager.com; 630-347-8369; http://www.crankymiddlemanager.com; Wayne Turmel. Best method: E-mail me a pitch, a bio and links to anything on the web I can check out. If they have a book, odds are better if they send it but be warned, I read each book and if it's not good or not right for my audience you'll have wasted postage. No response? I'm usually pretty good, but if I don't respond, follow up. If I don't respond, odds are it didn't excite me so be prepared to overcome objections and tell me why I should be more excited about having you/your client on the show.

Invited Back? Guests are invited back: a) if we had fun b) our listeners post and respond to them and c) they'll take my call.

Bio of Wayne Turmel: Wayne is a writer, speaker, trainer, stand-up comedian and corporate drone whose latest book is *A Philistine's Journal — An Average Guy Tackles the Classics* (New Leaf Books 2003), which Rebecca's Reads called "One of the best non-fiction books of 2003."

He is currently president of http://www.greatwebmeetings.com, a training and consulting company that helps businesses use web-meeting tools more effectively.

Demystifying Non-Profits with Celeste E. Terry, MSSA, on Global Talk Radio, Wednesdays, 5–6 PM, EST, http://www.globaltalkradio.com

Theme: Non-profits, with authors and music featured from time to time.

Guest Profile: Non-profit leaders, authors and musicians. I look for guests that are enthusiastic about their program, book or music CD and are able to have a great conversation with me during the interview. I like having a brief bio, and if there is a book or CD, a copy to review before the interview.

Guest from Hell: My ideal guest from hell is someone who doesn't do the interview even after they were booked, and a guest who is uncomfortable talking.

Contact: celest@sbcglobal.net; 216-566-9263; http://www.ubfogc.org; Celeste Terry. Best method: People can approach me by sending a press kit, or phone call and e-mail. No response? The person can e-mail me again if I am unable to respond quickly. I do not have a staff. I do everything myself.

Invited Back? Rapport, number of listeners and if I felt the guest provided interesting information.

Guest Comments: "I listened to the interview again yesterday, and I too thought it went great. In fact, I've had several friends and one potential client (whom I had notified beforehand) tell me they learned a lot from the show and that the messages I gave about branding are messages their membership and boards desperately need to hear. Thanks for the opportunity." — Larry, Checco Communications, http://www.checcocomm.net

"I have known your show for some time. You are pioneering a very powerful forum for bringing important information to many people. Thank you for having me as a guest." — Jomo W. Mutegi, Ph.D., Executive Director, Sankore Institute

Bio of Celeste Terry, MSSA: Celeste is Assistant Executive Director of the United Black Fund of Greater Cleveland, Inc., responsible for Special Projects.

She created the unique weekly talk show about non-profits in 2005, blending social work, communication and entertainment. According to Celeste, it's the *only* program devoted to information about non-profits.

Her passion is creating synergy to harness the power of the Internet to market non-profits. Tune in to her podcast, "Digital Sista" on http://imazepod@podomatic.com or you can visit her website at http://www.imazemarketing.com and add comments to the Digital Sista blog.

Celeste has over 23 years of marketing communications experience as voice-over talent and writer and producer of a speaker's series and cable programs.

eBay Radio with Jim "Griff" Griffith and cohost Lee Mirabal on WS Radio http://www.wsradio.com/ebayradio on Tuesdays 11:00 AM–2:00 PM (PT).

Theme: All things eBay.

Guest Profile: eBay sellers, owners of third party service companies which create or offer features, services or information pertinent to eBay buyers and sellers. For example, an experienced eBay PowerSeller to share their expertise and experience running a business on eBay or a representative of a company that provides valuable services or features for an eBay seller. If they are speaking about a product or service, I want to know about that product or service beforehand and how it is relevant to eBay sellers or buyers. If they are an eBay seller, I will visit their listings and feedback to obtain a better perspective of their activity on eBay.

Guest from Hell: That's easy. A guest that is incoherent, shy or awkward or extremely uncomfortable in an interview setting and who cannot be coaxed into a constructive conversation about their segment topic. It happens rarely but it does happen.

Contact: griff@ebay.com; 877-474-3302; http://www.wsradio.com/ebayradio; Chris Murch, President, WSRadio.com, Lee Mirabal Vice President, WSRadio.com. Best method: E-mail cmruch@wsradio.com lee@wsradio.com They should send a detailed e-mail proposal that includes their credentials, the subject of their segment, and, if applicable, information about any product, service or feature they are offering to eBay buyers or sellers. All segment requests should be e-mailed to either Chris Murch at WSRadio (cmurch@wsradio.com) or to me, Jim Griffith (griff@ebay.com). No response? They should send a second e-mail. However, we always respond to interview segment requests with either a "yes" or a "no thank you."

Invited Back? Two factors: 1. If they have something more to say or reveal about their experiences, product or service beyond what they have already covered. 2. If they were "radio friendly," that is, they were engaging, lively, and personable (as opposed to incoherent, shy or awkward or extremely uncomfortable in an interview setting...)

Bio of Jim "Griff" Griffith: "Griff," as he is popularly known, has been the foremost education expert on eBay since 1996 when he was invited to join the company as its first customer support representative. For the past 10 years as both eBay ambassador and instructor, Griff has been traveling around the country leading eBay University seminars and attending community gatherings on how to buy and sell on eBay.

In addition to presenting at dozens of eBay University events, he's made more than 100 local and national television and radio appearances.

Griff is author of the *Official eBay Bible* (Gotham, Third Edition, 2007).

The Gabe Wisdom Show aired weekdays 7–8 PM (ET), on Business Talk Radio Network http://www.businesstalkradio.net, and on its affiliates.

Theme: Stock and financial markets.

Guest Profile: Authors, noted authorities on the financial markets who are colorful and articulate. What is their topic?

Guest from Hell: Boring and bumbling.

Contact: gwisdom@cox.net; 858-755-0909; http://www.gabrielwisdom.com; Gabe Wisdom. Best method: E-mail. No response? Assume we are not interested.

Invited Back? Content.

Bio of Gabriel Wisdom: Gabriel is a seasoned investment advisor and well known broadcaster, who has handled thousands of investment accounts, representing over one billion dollars in assets during the last 24 years.

Gabriel is managing director of American Money Management LLC, an SEC registered investment advisory firm serving individuals and retirement plans in 31 states. He is a portfolio manager of two publicly held no-load funds and president of the Fallen Angels Family of Mutual funds, http://www.fallenangelsfunds.com. Over a 15-year period, he served as an officer of three Wall Street investment houses (Shearson Lehman Brothers, Prudential Bache, and Sutro and Co.) and is a director-shareholder of Monterey Financial, a national finance company headquartered in Oceanside, California.

Gabriel's broadcast career began in 1968 as a young pioneer in "Free-Form" FM radio at KPRI, San Diego. He was one of the prominent on-air personalities for KGB-FM San Diego, and KMET-FM Los Angeles, two legendary Album Oriented Rock stations during the 1970s and early '80s. During his 10 years at KGB and KMET, Gabe was part of many highly successful station promotions including over 100 major concerts and rock festivals.

Gabriel is a graduate of the Harvard Business School's Owner/President Management Program (OPM-Class 26), and is a vice president of the Harvard Business School Alumni Club of San Diego, http://www.hbssandiego.org. Additionally, Gabe has an MBA from Cal Pacific University of San Diego.

He has three daughters and is married to Diana. They live in Rancho Santa Fe, California.

Full bio at http://www.gabrielwisdom.com/about/index.htm

Goldseek Radio with Chris Waltzek aired on Global Satellite Radio.

Theme: Economics, finance, investing.

Guest Profile: Leader in field and passion for helping others to learn. Voice is least important. Ability to express what they do best to the audience. Some of his well-known guests have been Steve Forbes, Jim Rogers, presidential candidate Congressman Ron Paul, and John Perkins.

Guest from Hell: Unfriendly and closed to new ideas.

Contact: goldseekradio@hughes.net; Phone Studio: 828-743-1081; http://www.radio.goldseek.com; Chris Waltzek or Sandra, Assistant: 828-743-7910. Best method: E-mail a bio, send a press kit, call with a pitch. No response? E-mail or call.

Invited Back? Audience response and chemistry.

Listener Comments: "I can't imagine the show getting any better. But, you always surprise us. I love the new high speed downloads. What a difference they make. Also, the new addition of listening to the entire show is good. I'm taking a course at our local University and I can use their language labs to listen to the entire program in one sitting.

"And last, the Spanish guitar music is fabulous. Is it from a CD? Can you provide the name and player?

"Please don't take any vacations."—Judi T.

"First I want to thank you for your show. I live in Karlsruhe, Germany, and each Sunday morning as I get up to start my day with my first coffee, I turn on the Internet and listen to both segments of your show.

Please tell Mr. Chapman I especially like his weekly input as well.

"I also read Mr. Starkey's analysis below and found it highly interesting. I don't recall he was ever on your great show. Any chance you could get him?

"Once again, many, many thanks for a truly fantastic show." — Charles

Bio of Chris Waltzek: Chris graduated from KSU with a dual MBA in Business Economics and Information Systems, only six classes away from a Ph.D. in Business Management. After graduating as a Presidential Scholar, he went to work at one of the nation's largest law firms, Jones Day Reavis Pogue, as the firm-wide industry analyst.

He created a weekly stock market newsletter in 2002, published each week on Clearstation and sent via e-mail to subscribers. Chris is author of a soon-to-be published book on trend following investing, as well as several financial articles. He interviews the world's leading market pundits and economists on an online broadcast, The Gold and Silver Review.

The Growth Strategist with Aldonna R. Ambler, CMC, CSP aired on Voice America Business on Tuesdays at 11:00 AM EST; recent shows are available for download on demand; past shows are available in archives.

Theme: A peer-to-peer program featuring interviews with CEOs/Presidents of mid sized companies (typically between $20 and 200 million/yr) who have successfully executed the growth strategy of the week.

Guest Profile: CEO/presidents of a mid-sized company ($20–200 mil/yr). Willing and able to convey why and how his/her business has grown. Candid. Each prospective guest is interviewed prior to being selected and scheduled to appear on the program. Each prospective guest provides a biography and participates in a phone appt with the host to select the strategy (theme), good questions, etc. Many guests are provided coaching re: how to project and protect his/her voice. Research is conducted about each guest re credibility, authenticity, reputation, etc. Guests are people who are included on published lists of the fastest growing privately held companies around the world (e.g., INC 500). Or they are people who have been referred to us. Consultants, lawyers, accountants, trainers, advertising agencies, venture capitalists refer their clients to us. Most of the people who have asked to be a guest on my show have not done research prior to calling us, are not presidents/CEOs of midsized companies, and don't qualify to be a guest.

Guest from Hell: Acts like he/she has never had a problem, always knew what to do, never made a mistake, etc. Interrupts the host when a question is being asked. Ignores or disregards host's cues to redirect comments or move on. Braggadocios, self promoting, uses "I" language, talks down to the audience, condescending, provides simplistic or vague responses.

Contact: Aldonna@AMBLER.com; 609-567-9669; http://www.TheGrowthStrategist.com; http://www.business.voiceamerica.com; Melissa Norcross at Melissa@AMBLER.com. Best method: E-mail. No response? If we don't respond in a timely manner, chances are the e-mail to us got stuck in a spam filter or is lost in cyberspace. It can be resent or a call should be made to check if we have actually received the e-mail.

Invited Back? Only a few people have been invited back. They were folks who shared information about a new product launch or business expansion. The repeat appearance provided an opportunity for the audience to hear how things worked out.

Guest Comments: "I found a wealth of business experience on the subject of growth strategies. I was impressed with Aldonna's interviewing style which gets to the essence of real life business experience. The topics she chooses can be of enormous value to anyone who has a hand in planning growth strategy and process. And the best part is that a reference library in the form of recorded radio programs on the topic is only a mouse click away." — Art Crowley, Sr., GAREN Products

"I am both a listener and a guest on *The Growth Strategist*. Aldonna always makes people so comfortable that it's easy and a pleasure to talk with her, radio or not. Her questions are so thoughtful and bring out the best practices of her guests. I lean toward being more of the intuitive kind of entrepreneur, and Aldonna helped me understand some of my own business processes better as we talked." — Janet Holloway, Women Leading Kentucky

Bio of Aldonna Ambler, CMC, CSP: Known as the Growth Strategist, Aldonna is an award winning entrepreneur, a frequent speaker at national business conferences and corporate annual meetings, a prolific author, and an intermediary who helps midmarket companies obtain growth financing. President of the international firm AMBLER Growth Strategy Consultants, Inc., in Hammonton, New Jersey, her firm's services include opportunity and resource analysis, organizational design, strategic working sessions, and executive coaching.

Ambler's corporate clients have included IKON, CertainTeed, U.S. Honda, U.S. Homes, H&R Block, Horizon BC/BS, Eastman Kodak, Bank One, Robert Wood Johnson, Bluegreen Resorts, Scott Paper, Knoll International, Resorts International, and Caesars. Over 50 corporations (including IBM, Nortel, Verizon, SBC, Wachovia, *Entrepreneurial Edge* magazine, Business-to-Business Yellow Pages, Bell South, and Pacific Bell) have sponsored multi-city tours (spanning as long as 14 years) featuring her speeches/seminars about business strategy and growth management. She has guided the growth of over 150 professional service firms, over 100 technology-driven businesses, and over 100 construction-related product, service, and distribution companies.

Aldonna was named the lead instructor for IBM's Owners and Presidents Program serving IBM's global network of business partners. She is the official coaching partner for the Philadelphia M.S.A. of Gazelles, Inc. Her latest honor was the Pioneer Award from National Association of Women Business Owners (NAWBO) South Jersey Chapter — 2006.

Home Base Business 101 with Baba Sitawi Kiongozi Jahi on Blog Talk Radio, http://www.blogtalkradio.com/homebasebusiness101

Theme: To help people with the development of their home base business; primary focus is network-marketing businesses, secondary focus is any type of legal business one operates from home.

Guest Profile: Persons who operate a home base business, authors of self-help books and newspaper columnists, tax advisors, personal development coaches and health counselors. Someone who is humble and cares about how they say what they say to people. Plus knows what they are talking about because they have done it! I want to be able to hear past shows that they have done, plus have a copy of their credentials.

Guest from Hell: Someone who trashes my show, and my audience and is not humble!

Contact: Sitawi_Jasari@JahiTravelSite.com; 252-212-0281; http://www.JahiTravelSite.com; Baba Jahi. Best method: One should e-mail me their bio and a press kit, and then schedule a time for me to interview them. No response? They should get back to me by e-mail; most of the time I get back to people in 72 hours.

Invited Back? If I get good reviews from my audience and if they share information that is relevant and exciting concerning my theme.

Guest Comment: "Baba Sitawi Kiongozi Jahi's radio show is not simply inspirational and motivational for those with an entrepreneurial spirit, but it is also a practical guide, overflowing with proven tips on how to germinate and grow a bountiful home-based business, that will continually yield the lifestyle and income that you desire." — Beni Dakar, COO of World Wide WealthNet and a Freelance Journalist http://benidakar.com

Bio of Baba Sitawi Kiongozi Jahi, aka Baba Jahi: Baba is a graduate of the University of New Orleans and completed a seven-week training program at the After School Institute (Advancing youth development). He's been a teacher in elementary and middle school and a theology teacher. Since 2001, he is Seba (Moral Teacher) for Hekalu ya Nia (Temple of Purpose).

He is a writer and columnist, whose subjects cover environmental racism, political education, and health issues.

Since 1990, Baba has worked with youth and also helps parents design a curriculum that will work for their child, in collaboration with the National African American Homeschoolers Alliance (http://www.naaha.com).

Since his return from the Vietnam War, he's been an advocate and follower of Kawaida, the philosophy of Dr. Maulana Karenga (http://www.us-organization.org). In 2001 he became a Seba (a moral teacher — equivalent to preacher, rabbi or imam), and founded Hekalu ya Nia (Temple of Purpose).

"In Kawaida, the Seba takes a vow of five commitments which serve as a ground and guide for the good we seek to bring in the world," he explains. "To be a good person in the world; to be a consistent servant of the people; to be a constant soldier in the struggle; to be a continuous student of the teachings; and to be a tireless teacher of the good, the right and the possible."

He and his wife own their own travel business, http://www.JahiTravelSite.com

Indie Business Radio Show with Donna Maria Coles Johnson on Global Talk Radio and http://www.indiebusinessradio.com

Theme: Enjoy your life, build your business and have your way.

Guest Profile: Donna Maria seeks guests who can share their expertise with listeners and answer their questions about how to maximize success in life and business. A good guest knows their subject matter very well. Additionally, they are passionate and enthusiastic about it. They are comfortable and confident in their expertise and have a heartfelt desire to use their talents, gifts and knowledge to help other people.

If you simply want to plug your product or service, this is not the show for you. Authors preferred but not required. Past interview experience a plus, but not necessary. Guest must have a well maintained website and send a promotional photo. Credentials and experience must be in line with what guest promotes as area(s) of expertise. Must speak clearly and call in from a landline.

Guests must be able to send a head shot and have a well maintained website. Examples: Media personality Paula Deen on going from single mom to mega-successful entrepreneur, psychologist and author Dr. Kathy Marshack on entrepreneurial success for married couples, "Baby Einstein" founder Julie Clark on combining motherhood and business, and search engine marketing guru Catherine Seda on improving search engine rankings.

Guest from Hell: I have never had anything other than ideal guests on my show, but I would venture to say that the guest from hell is one who gives one word answers and makes the host work too hard to get information out of them. Also a guest from hell is all glitz and no substance.

Contact: info@indiebusinessradio.com; http://www.indiebusinessradio.com; 704-291-7280; for archives and past guests, visit http://www.indiebusi

nessradio.com. Best method: E-mail bio, show theme suggestion and sample questions and answers. No response? E-mail again.

Invited Back? That they knew their stuff, answered my questions honestly and fully, without blatant self promotion.

Guest Comments: "Thank you for the wonderful interview. I love that you are teaching these skills to your children, it will make a huge difference for them no matter what career they choose." — Romanus Wolter, author of *Kick Start Your Dream Business* (Ten Speed Press 2001)

"Thanks *so much* for the wonderful interview. My clients Bob and Mel Blanchard *raved* about it and really enjoyed being on with you." — Tammy Richards, LeSure, Richards Public Relations

Bio of Donna Maria Coles Johnson: Donna Maria — the Chief Executive Indie — has hosted and produced her radio show since 2005. She is an author, publisher, motivational speaker, attorney, and the founder and president of the Indie Beauty Network, a worldwide trade organization serving the business and professional needs of manufacturers of handmade beauty products including soaps, cosmetics, fragrances, candles and aromatherapy products. Together with her husband, she also produces the Indie Business Conference and a popular blog at http://www.indiebusinessblog.com.

Donna Maria is the author of *Making Aromatherapy Creams and Lotions* (Storey Books, 2000), *The Lifestyle CEO: How to Break All the Rules, Build Your Own Corporate Ladder and Create the Life You Love* (Lifestyle CEO Media, 2006) and other materials that uplift and encourage women and families.

The Innovation Zone with Thomas Koulopoulos on Blog Talk Radio, http://www.blogtalkradio.com/Innovation

Theme: Innovation in Business, Society and Science.

Guest Profile: Authors, notable business experts. Guests should have a clear crisp idea and opinion on the topic of innovation. Articulate and engaging personality.

Guest from Hell: Someone who cannot dialog and either talks endlessly or provides two-word answers.

Contact: tk@theinnovationzone.com; 617-274-8444; http://www.blogtalkradio.com/Innovation; Thomas Koulopoulos. Best method: E-mail either a press kit or a bio and specific topics for discussion. No response? I always respond one way or the other.

Invited back? Listener response.

Bio of Thomas Koulopoulos: President and founder of The Delphi Group, executive director Babson College Center for Business Innovation, past managing director of Perot Systems Innovation Lab, Thomas is among the industry's six most influential consultants, according to *InformationWeek*, author of eight books, lecturer at the Boston College Graduate School of Management, and frequent contributor to national and international print and broadcast media.

He is one of the industry's most prolific thought leaders. His insights provide a beyond-the-edge view of the turbulence created by the collision of technology and business. Tom Peters has called his writing, "a brilliant vision of where we must take our enterprises to survive and thrive." The late management guru and 20th century business icon Peter Drucker said of Tom's writing, "[It] makes you question not only the way you run your business but the way you run yourself."

Insight on Coaching with Tom Floyd on Voice America Business http://www.modavox.com/VoiceAmericaBusiness, airing Mondays at 11 AM (PT), on http://www.modavox.com/VoiceAmericaBusiness, and podcast on Apple iTunes, Google, Yahoo, Odeo, and via FeedBurner.

Theme: Professional coaching. The program explores coaching issues impacting the corporate workforce and offers practical solutions for those challenges. The show covers a wide range of topics — from how coaching facilitates leadership development to the value of coaching in multi-generational workforces to the importance of coaching in change management.

Guest Profile: Through interviews, audience participation, and lively debate on real case studies, the host showcases experts from a variety of areas within the professional coaching field. We look for four types of guests. Authors, executives from Corporate America who can provide a business perspective on the topic at hand, coaches who specialize in the topic for the show, and members of academia who can provide an academic perspective on the topic. We occasionally feature celebrity personalities for given topics as well. Guests must have established credentials, biographies, and experience participating in interviews, shows, or panel-like discussions. Past interview experiences and sound of voice are also important. All guests go through a screening process with the production team at our PR firm, GolinHarris. Résumés are screened as well, and as host I approve all final guests for each show.

Past guests have included business leaders from AllTel Corporation, BlueCross BlueShield of North Carolina, Booz Allen Hamilton, Capital One, CNA, EDS, Intel, McDonald's, Unilever, Verizon, leading book authors, executive coaching experts and prominent academia from universities, including Elon University, George Washington, Harvard, Johns Hopkins, Pepperdine, UCLA, and the University of Florida.

Guests from Hell: Guests who have inflated senses of themselves and are egotistical, and at the other extreme, guests who are very passive, nervous, and afraid to speak.

Contact: tfloyd@ieconsulting.biz; 408-298-6600; http://www.ieconsulting.biz; Tom Floyd. Best method:

E-mail or phone. Contact our production manager, Jessica del Mundo, JdelMundo@GolinHarris.com (213-438-8772) at GolinHarris (http://www.golinharris.com). Ideally, call with a pitch or inquire about topics for the current season. No response? Guests are directed to our production manager. For either Jessica or myself, guests should follow up with a phone call if they do not receive a response to their original e-mail submitted.

Invited Back? Their on-air personalities, engagement, and ability to make the topic "real" using illustrative examples. Being conversational and interacting with the other guests is a big part of it as well. Guests who let their personalities really shine through tend to do best.

Guest Comments: "It was a real pleasure to be a guest on Tom Floyd's *Insight on Coaching* show. The program content was well researched and thought provoking, incorporating different perspectives and opinions from experts in the field. Tom Floyd, the host, was extremely professional to work with and has a great on-air personality. The staff has done an exceptional job on marketing the show as well as staying in touch with the guests and listeners. This show is a great resource on leadership and business coaching."—Maya Hu-Chan, author of *Global Leadership: The Next Generation* (Financial Times/Prentice Hall 2003), and president of Global Leadership Associates http://www.geocities.com/wayneacp/maya_hu_chan.html

"I was thrilled to be asked to participate on the *Insight on Coaching* radio show. The show was the third in a series about corporate coaching success stories. Someone involved in organizational learning and development; I know how important it is to share lessons learned and success stories. Listening to the other panelists reassured me that we frequently face common challenges — and that we have options for addressing them. I am grateful for the opportunity to expand my professional community and am looking forward to continuing conversations with Tom and the other panelists."—Karol Eller, associate, Booz Allen Hamilton

Bio of Tom Floyd: Tom is founder and CEO of Insight Education Consulting (IEC), a management consulting firm specializing in corporate change and transformation, workforce performance and employee development.

Prior to founding IEC, Tom served as a senior consultant at Crawford and Associates International, where he was responsible for business development, client relations and strategic consulting to top-tier clients.

Full bio at http://www.ieconsulting.biz

Integrity in Business with Kimberley A. Colvard, Ph.D. (The Energy Doctor) aired Mondays, noon–1 PM (ET) on Radio Sandy Springs, 1620 AM, or http://www.radiosandysprings.com

Theme: Speak with business owners and entrepreneurs who left Corporate America to start their own business or individuals who are in business following their dreams and passions.

Guest Profile: Anyone who is *passionate* about what they do for a living.

Guest from Hell: Someone that answers questions with a one sentence answer.

Contact: KimColvard@aol.com; http://www.TheEnergyDoctor.biz and http://www.radiosandysprings.com; 404-728-0005; Kimberley Colvard. Best method: Phone or e-mail, e-mailing a bio with a phone number, and a little about their personal life. No response? We can never count on e-mails getting to where they are going. A phone call would be great.

Invited Back? Our radio station sells advertising, so repeat guests are not looked upon as a good thing. Otherwise, if this person has more enthusiasm and more to talk about, I would have them back.

Bio of Kimberley Colvard, Ph.D.: Kimberley has been referred to as "The Energy Doctor." She is an inspirational speaker, intuitive life coach and a business consultant. She is the author of *Life Is a Perception, What's Yours: How Your Thoughts and Beliefs Determine Your Life* (iUniverse 2006).

Kimberley has educated and motivated individuals and businesses for over two decades.

Job You Deserve Radio with Kristen Hallows on Blog Talk Radio, http://www.blogtalkradio.com

Theme: Career and banishing the "Sunday night blues." The main idea of my show is live career coaching. I'm there to help those experiencing the "Sunday night blues." Ideally, listeners will call to be coached on a career-related goal or issue.

Guest Profile: Career coaches, recruiters, HR professionals. I look for unique knowledge or experience, particularly in the area of career management. Honestly, past experience, credentials and voice quality don't matter to me as much as passion and knowledge. I can tell how much someone cares/knows just by talking with him or her prior to the show. It helps if the guest has a Web site, book, etc., but that's not necessary.

Guest from Hell: Good question. Someone who dominates our time together with self-serving messages such as his or her latest program, especially if it isn't particularly related to our discussion. Or, someone who points out that the question I just asked "wasn't on the list." Hello ... listeners are supposed to think it's organic conversation. LOL

Contact: khallows@jobyoudeserve.com; 614-589-8720; http://www.jobyoudeserve.com; Kristen Hallows. Best method: I don't require more than a simple e-mail or phone call. I just want to know who you are and what you want to talk about. I'm very open-minded and flexible ... I'll consider practically anything/anyone as long as it can be tied back to career development! No response? I can honestly say that I always respond to e-mails and phone calls within 24 hours. But if I haven't, I may be in the hospital ... just kidding. If for some reason I don't respond, the person should definitely call or e-mail again.

Invited Back? Some conversations flow better than others, and of course listener feedback counts for a lot! I go by my general feeling ... was there tons of useful, related info for listeners or not?

Guest Comment: "Kristen was a gracious host; she allowed me to fully articulate my points without attempting to spin my words."— Deborah Jones, Guardian Healthcare Providers, Inc., Brentwood, TN

Bio of Kristin Hallows: Kristin has always been passionate about career satisfaction. She was inspired to launch her radio show in 2007 after observing her recent college graduate friends working as temps, secretaries and bartenders. After four (or more) years of study, being under-employed is unacceptable. Life is too short, and you spend too much time at work to not enjoy it.

What started off as a crusade against underemployment has developed into a holistic enterprise dedicated to all people who feel they deserve better — from college students to executives to retirees wishing to start a second or third career.

Kristin has coached people in New Zealand, Germany, Norway, Canada, and the United States. She has helped people achieve in many areas, including career and workplace, business and Web site development, and health and wellness.

She is also a self-taught Webmaster and the author of *The Recruiter Is Your Friend: This Ain't Your Granddaddy's Job Search* (iUniverse 2006).

Kristin is a Certified Professional Coach, having received her coach training from the International Coach Academy (ICA). She received her BS in Business Administration *magna cum laude* with minors in Human Resources and Finance from Franklin University.

The John Adam Show with John Adam (Kowalski) on KFNN 1510 AM, Phoenix, Arizona. The first hour is broadcast Friday, 9–10 AM (MT), and the second hour is broadcast Saturday, 8–9 AM (MT).

Theme: Entertaining and informative talk radio show; each week focuses on a different business topic.

Guest Profile: Topic guest experts and guest entrepreneurs with knowledge of topic and personality. I always pre-interview my guest for topic knowledge, interesting angle on the topic, outgoing personality, and sense of humor.

Guest from Hell: Nervous guests who over-prepare.

Contact: john@thejohnadamshow.com; 602-319-3190; http://www.thejohnadamshow.com; John Adam Kowalski, executive producer; Brian Jewett, technical producer. Best method: Call with a pitch, e-mail a bio, send a press kit ... to get my attention. I need an interesting angle on a topic. No response? Follow up is not necessary ... all guest recommendations are kept on file as possible matches for upcoming shows.

Invited Back? Guests are rarely invited back because I don't like to repeat topics.

Listener Comments: "I listen to your show instead of music when I am working on projects... I have a notepad with 'Light Bulb' ideas jotted down."— Debbie L., Springfield, OR

"The show is fun and informative and I've been making a list of things that can be discussed at our meetings."— Andrea T., Monterey, CA

Bio of John Adam: John served in the U.S. Navy before earning a B.S. degree in Communication from Northwestern University. While working as an institutional asset financial reporting analyst at the Harris Trust and Savings Bank in Chicago, he did course work at the J. L. Kellogg Graduate School of Management at Northwestern University.

He moved to Phoenix in 1985 and joined Kowalski Construction, Inc., where he rose from financial controller to president and CEO. During this time the company increased revenues over 1,500 percent, opened a branch office in Tucson, expanded to five divisions, and had a workforce of approximately 100 employees.

John left Kowalski Construction in 2001 and has since been available nationally as a business consultant, executive coach, meeting facilitator and speaker.

He specializes in helping people see the relationship between personal development and business results.

Legends of Success with John Resnick, syndicated on more than 80 radio stations and the audio channels of 58 cable TV systems in the U.S. Rated among The Talkers 250.

Theme: Interviews with America's outstanding entrepreneurs, CEOs, members of the Forbes 400 and other acclaimed individuals.

Guest Profile: Those who have overcome obstacles and setbacks to make it to the top and have built household names for themselves or their organizations. Also a passion to help make a difference in other peoples lives; giving back. Want to know everything possible that would be useful content for our listeners. Prominent guests have included Steve Forbes, editor-in-chief of *Forbes Magazine*; Jack Welch, retired chairman of General Electric; William Randolph Hearst III, director of The Hearst Corporation; Bernie Marcus, founder of Home Depot; Evelyn Lauder of The Estee Lauder Co.; legendary entertainer Jerry Lewis; Sandy Weill, chairman emeritus of Citigroup; Jon M. Huntsman; founder of Huntsman Corp; Ed McMahon, longtime sidekick of Johnny Carson; Chris Sullivan, founder of Outback Steakhouse; baseball legend Tommy Lasorda; and American news icon Walter Cronkite.

Guest from Hell: Never had one.

48 Business, Finance and Marketing

Contact: John@legendsofsuccess.com; 717-791-9774; http://www.legendsofsuccess.com; John Resnick or Billie Resnick. Best method: Initially, e-mail a bio and send a press kit. All past guests and their representatives may call anytime. No response? Can e-mail again, but it is impossible to respond to every e-mail and postal mailing we receive. Potential guests should visit website to see what we look for in our guests.

Invited Back? Mostly feedback from listeners.

Guest Comment: "This is something I've looked forward to. Thank you very much for having me on. I've enjoyed being with you." — Howard Schultz, chairman of Starbucks

"I enjoyed the interview and thought you did a very good job covering important issues regarding corporate philanthropy and our work at The Carter Center. Thank you for inviting me back to discuss our continuing efforts in waging peace, fighting disease, and building hope." — President Jimmy Carter

Bio of John Resnick: Having grown tired of only hearing the media's reporting of business scandals and greed, knowing these stories did not represent the real picture of business in America, John debuted his radio show in 2002. With no prior radio experience, he showed his own entrepreneurial spirit by going on air. Within months he was interviewing not just regional but national and global business icons. The show is now heard in many cities from coast to coast. As John says, "It's about time we celebrate stories of successful business leaders, not the failures."

Let's Talk Marketing Show, with Catherine Franz, is a syndicated show that doesn't have a set schedule. The show is recorded in Catherine's studio and then sent to 118 stations to be played as a fill-in.

Theme: *LTM* is a marketing educational show with a side of personal and business development. Every show includes instructional pieces plus guest interviews that can help listeners improve their marketing and business skills. February and March focuses on helping individuals improve their writing and publishing skills and techniques that expand their book sales.

Guest Profile: The majority of the shows invite experts who generally, but not always, have a book on the show's theme. The host also shares her expertise on the topic as well as the latest updates on new software and other materials that will help generate revenue.

Contact: Catherine@abundancecenter.com; http://www.letstalkmarketingshow.com

Listener Comment: "I have found your shows to be engaging, informative and entertaining. As a result of what you have provided, just during the short time I have been listing, this has been an educationally profitable and enlightening experience for me on several levels (personal and professional)." — Steve Walling

Bio of Catherine Franz: Catherine is a master coach, commerical writer and Internet architect, syndicated host and producer, radio and television, and author.

She is a graduate of Coach University, 2003.

Life Business and Money, with Steven Kay on CNN 650 Radio News, Houston, TX.

Theme: Business and more.

Guest Profile: Entrepreneurs, business owners and professionals. Someone who has something of value to teach my audience. I want to know mostly about their topic, what are they going to provide to the listener that can help them achieve success.

Guest from Hell: Someone who gives one word answers.

Contact: me@StevenKayLive.com; 713-STEVEN-K (713-783-8365) / Office #713-278-9109; http://www.StevenKayLive.com; Steven Kay. Best method: Call with a pitch, send a press kit and/or e-mail a bio. No response? E-mail or call.

Invited Back? All of the above.

Bio of Steven Kay: When it comes to achieving success and overcoming obstacles, Steven brings an invaluable wealth of knowledge and experience. Starting his working career straight out of high school, Steven became a top level executive of a marketing company by age 19.

After moving to Texas in 1993 and a few more years of continual growth in the corporate environment as a business manager and project development specialist, Steven decided to start his own marketing company. In 1996, he built his small one-man operation to a full service marketing management and consultation firm, assisting organizations with multi-million dollar campaigns. Then in 1998, Steven decided to pursue another of his passions (hockey), and purchased a roller hockey rink in Houston.

Unfortunately, this business did not become profitable despite his efforts and achievements, and had to be closed down even though he had tripled the revenues. This turn of events almost forced Steven into bankruptcy and left him with nothing. Having to start over, Steven never gave up on achieving his goals and dreams.

In 2000, Steven took up employment with a life insurance company, which led him into the financial services arena. Even with the recent setbacks and obstacles to still overcome, Steven entrepreneurial spirit was still very alive. He learned very quickly that insurance was about helping others secure financial success, and is only a part of a well thought out financial plan.

Steven developed a unique retirement planning system called *The Financial Stronghold*, designed to allow people to create true financial stability from the ground up. Specializing in the area of life and health insurance as a part of this overall system, Steven became an independent broker so that he could represent his client's best interest.

Very early in his new career, Steven was invited on several business radio programs (such as "Mid Day Money Talk") as a featured expert in his field. This instilled in him a new desire to host a radio program of his own that helped people achieve financial success, and in mid 2004 he not only started to work on this concept, but completely devoted himself to it. The show first aired live on April 4th, 2005

Making a Living with Maggie airing on Thursday on Martha Stewart Living Radio, Sirius 112, in the U.S., Canada and Mexico. Host Maggie Mistral occasionally has guests and is a contributor to other shows on the channel.

Theme: Career talk — inspiring career success stories and practical career advice helping people "learn something new" when it comes to their careers — whether that be strategizing for a promotion, making a career change or even how to deal with the daily frustrations of the workplace.

Guest Profile: Expertise, passion for the topic, ability to bullet point the topic into articulate sound bytes, credentials and past interview experience are most important. Authors welcome who are experts in a career-related or work-related fields (networking, mentoring, assertiveness, negotiations, etiquette, conflict mgt, etc.) or have a particular perspective on careers that is new and different (i.e. the power of positive thinking, gender in the workplace, multiple careers, corporate responsibility); also guests who have interesting careers for my "day in the life" segment, including celebrities, pro-athletes, business moguls and everyday people who have exciting/new and different careers. Topics range from following your passion, managing your professional image, dealing with stress and conflict in the office, work/life trends and strategies, making work meaningful, rebounding from layoff/pink slip, to practical advice for resumes, interviews and promotions. Prominent guests have included Martha Stewart, Sally Field, Deepak Chopra and Cynthia Rowley.

Guest from Hell: One that doesn't know the topic or have an authentic interest in it. A guest who talks too quickly, goes off on tangents and doesn't take a breath in between sentences.

Contact: coaching@maggiemistal.com; http://www.maggiemistal.com; 917-886-8029; Marcy Yurick at marcy@maggiemistal.com. Best method: E-mailing a pitch and press kits. No response? E-mail follow-up.

Invited Back? If the topic is deep enough to warrant more conversation and if the listeners/callers enjoyed the topic.

Guest Comments: "I would like to take this opportunity to thank you for inviting me to be on your very informative talk show *Making a Living*. I was enthralled with the content and watching you excite the audience and their participation was inspiring." — Judy George, founder and president of DOMAIN home furnishings

"It was great being on your show. You're a gracious hostess." — Stewart F. Lane, three-time TONY award winning Broadway producer

Bio of Maggie Mistal: Maggie is a certified life purpose and career coach. After serving as Director of Learning and Development for Martha Stewart Living Omnimedia for several years, she became Martha Stewart Living Radio's Career Coach on her radio show. As an expert on careers, Maggie has appeared as a guest on the *Candace Bushnell Show* on SIRIUS Stars Channel, *Morning Living* and *Living Today* on Martha Stewart living Radio.

But Maggie's passion is her career consulting practice, working with individuals to identify their ideal careers and allowing them to make their career change. Along with individuals, such top corporations such as CIGNA, Diageo NA, and Martha Stewart Living Omnimedia seek her help in developing their employees and managers.

Maggie lives in Manhattan.

Mind Your BIZness with Danielle Hampson on http://www.wnbnetworkwest.com

Theme: Business topics focusing on entrepreneurs and micro-businesses.

Guest Profile: All experts in individual fields; all fields are covered as long as the topic to be discussed offers information listeners can use/apply to their business. Guests should have an in-depth knowledge of subject matter, energy, a delivery that is concise, clear and easy to understand and a good voice. I make a point of conducting a pre-interview of guests to check their voice, to get an idea of their demeanor. I check their website to find out more about them and what they do or have done. Although guests with past interview experiences often make for an easier interview, the in-depth knowledge tops my "Guest must have" list.

Guest from Hell: A guest who comes on the show totally unprepared, one who tries to make the interview a commercial for him/herself; a guest who speaks with no energy and who does not exhibit any knowledge of his topic, and who speaks too fast.

Contact: Danielle@mindyourbizness.com; 877-955-8800; http://www.MindYourBIZness.com; Danielle Hampson. Best method: I favor making a pitch by calling or e-mailing, with all relevant information for me to do some research on the guest and his/her activities. Guest must have a website in order to be considered. No response? I get many e-mail requests and often fall behind on responses. A follow up after a month would be wise.

Invited Back? The guest's overall demeanor and level of knowledge, combined. A guest with great knowledge but bad demeanor will never make it back, and a guest with a great demeanor but not much to say will not come back either.

Guest Comments: "Danielle Hampson is an excellent interviewer and a terrific networker. She uses her skills to make everyone feel relaxed and to bring out the best in them. She's an asset to the business community!"— Marcia Fine, author/entrepreneur

"I have had the pleasure of being grilled by Danielle Hampson on more than one occasion, and I must say that she is one of the most considerate, passionate and energetic hosts and interviewers I have worked with. Danielle is delightful, courteous and takes great pains to research her subject prior to the interview, I eagerly look forward to working with her on future projects."— Allan Sabo, president ALTI Consulting

Bio of Danielle Hampson: As an international business consultant speaking several languages, Danielle has traveled the world to assist small and large U.S. and foreign corporations establish a foothold on both sides of the Atlantic and Pacific. In 2004, she founded "The Art of Networking," a business-social networking group that provides a forum for entrepreneurs to build relationships.

In 2006, she added a web-based radio/TV network to her business portfolio — WNB Network West, offering "Edu Training" business and non-business programs. In 2007, she saw the launch of her own webTV production company and produces various TV shows broadcast on her network and syndicated on others, and she hosts some of these TV shows as well.

Money Matters Financial Network Radio with Gary Goldberg, syndicated weekdays 10–11 AM.

Theme: Business, investing, economic issues.

Guest Profile: We interview financial experts, business newsmakers, company CEOs, political leaders, sports and entertainment figures — with a business/money angle. We look for someone who can be informative as well as entertaining. We also look outside "the tunnel" of other money shows, preferring unique angles on stories and issues to stand out as a program. We like to know their past interview experience, credentials, ability to change focus if a story breaks before the show and whether they can take on other angles to what they want to present.

Some prominent guests have included GE CEO Jack Welch, former Dow Chemicals CEO Paul Orrefice, former baseball player, commentator and TV personality Joe Garagiola, Sam Stovall of Standard and Poors and boxing trainer Teddy Atlas (he now runs the Dr. Theodore Atlas Foundation). For more recent guests go to http://www.mmfn.net/Recent.asp

Guest from Hell: A boring "stuffed shirt" who speaks too slowly and doesn't stop.

Contact: chrisc@mmfn.net; (800) 433-0323 x274; http://www.financialtalkshow.com; Chris Cordani, executive producer. Best method: E-mail and telephone are the best ways to contact me. Press kits, however, help authors more because their material would be in my hands for review. No response? I'm not sure if that ever happened, but, if it did, I would hope for any follow-up. That shows the potential guest really wants to come on *Money Matters.*

Invited Back? Overall performance is the top factor; ability to communicate knowledge in an entertaining and informative fashion is also important.

Bio of Gary M. Goldberg: For over 30 years, Gary has been giving financial advice, early on as an institutional trader on Wall Street and later as president and founder of the investment and financial planning firm which bears his name since 1972.

He is a nationally recognized expert on mutual funds, the stock market, and investment planning. Articles about him and quotes of his opinions in publications such as *The Wall Street Journal, Forbes, Fortune, Money,* and *USA Today* offer ample testimony to his reputation.

Gary's financial evaluations and recommendations have also appeared in many other newspapers and on television, including his regular appearances on CNBC and "Wall Street Week." He is constantly providing his audience with thoughtful insights into money and investing, complemented by his in-depth industry knowledge and his unique sense of humor.

The Money Thing with Howard Bono and Gary Mantz on KKNW 1150 airing in the Greater Seattle area.

Theme: Helping people understand their money and tips and techniques to eliminate debt and put some money away.

Guest Profile: We are looking for guests that bring relevant financial information to our listeners — from ways to prepare for retirement to money saving tips to what is coming next in our economy. If a guest has a book or a product, we like it if they would offer a copy of their book to any callers who contribute to the show.

We are looking for guests who bring relevant information based on sound financial principles. We are not looking for some kind of get rich quick scheme or people trying to sell a product or service that does not have real value. Past interview experiences, credentials, sounds of their voice all have value. However, do they bring a viewpoint that you don't find in the conventional media? Do they have passion about what they are talking about? Will they follow our lead and give us the opportunity to direct the show so it has continuity?

Guest from Hell: The guest from hell would be someone who is self-absorbed, does not listen to our audience and/or is pushing something that only benefits the guest.

Contact: garymantz@juno.com or howard@themoneything.com; Gary 206-409-3499 or Howard 425-252-1121; http://www.themoneything.com; Gary Mantz. Best method: Either call with a pitch, e-mail a bio or send a press kit. They should contact Gary and then he and I talk about the potential of the guest and when it fits into the schedule the best. No response? Call or e-mail. We always make the effort to get back to potential guests quickly. Sometimes life makes the time frame a little longer than we would like. By the way, please don't call and leave us a pre-recorded message. I hate those things.

Invited Back? If we can have a good time and our audience gets value from that show.

Guest Comment: "Right from the time I was first contacted by Gary Mantz until the time the program ended, I was totally impressed by the professionalism and courtesy extended to me by Gary, Eric and Howard. However, what impressed me most was that Howard actually took the time to call me the day before to go over the game plan for the program. And, during the commercial breaks, he kept me informed of what to expect next. I found Howard to be very easy to work with — he exhibited interest in the subject, the book AND me, interest that I have found to be lacking sometimes from hosts of other programs I have been on. His friendliness and warmth also allowed me to feel comfortable and eliminate any nervousness I might have had." — Bill Billimoria, author of *On Golden Pond ... Or Up the Creek? Making the Right Choices for Your Retirement Security* (Synergy Books 2007). Bill can be reached at bill@goldenpondretirement.com or at (512) 478-2028.

Bio of Howard Bono: Howard has spent 15 years in the mortgage business as the owner of Old West Mortgage. His book, *The Money Thing Made Easy* (Old West Media 2007), distills years of personal study and educating clients on how they can dump their debt and start building wealth.

After learning from his own financial mistakes and studying how wealthy people do it, Howard has become a self-made millionaire.

Howard is quick to underscore that there is no such thing as "easy money." He has never seen a get-rich-quick scheme that actually worked.

Howard's strategies are based on his success and the success of his students and clients.

Networking with the Blindguy from Gorilla Central with Dr Robin on Blog Talk Radio, http://www.blogtalkradio.com/blindguy at 11 AM (CT).

Theme: Changing the face of network marketing.

Guest Profile: Network marketers, authors, MLMs etc. I want to know just what MLM/networking area they are in.

Guest from Hell: One that does not show up.

Contact: Rrushlo@Marketinggorillas.net; 319-679-3838; http://www.gorillatalkradio.com; Dr. Robin Rushlo. Best method: E-mail or phone. No response? E-mail or call.

Invited Back? Chemistry I get and response from my listeners.

Bio of Dr. Robin Rushlo: Known to his friends as Robin, Dr. Robin, the Blindguy and Dr. Blindguy, Robin is an Army veteran, investor, MLM marketing expert, chief content authority at InternetMarketing Gorillas, LLC. While in the Army, he began building his "honorary" doctorate in the network marketing world. He built a huge Amway organization in the tens of thousands and was later a top producer at A. L. Williams.

He and wife Kathy have two grown daughters and two daughters in the house, 15 and 16, and a granddaughter, 9, and a grandson 14 months old who live with them on 2.2 acres in Hills, Iowa.

Online Marketing with RSS Ray on wsRadio.com

Theme: Radio show brings you world class experts for online marketing success. We bring you the strategy, tactics and measurements that impact your bottom line, the kind of "put to work now" stuff that makes a difference.

Guest Profile: Online marketing experts. Someone who is an expert in topics relating to the show such as online marketing. Also someone who is articulate. Bios, areas of expertise, published works.

Guest from Hell: Someone who freezes and doesn't say anything.

Contact: Ray@RSSRay.com; 877-837-8803; http://www.wsradio.com/internet-talk-radio.cfm/shows/Online-Marketing-with-RSS-Ray.html; http://www.RSSRay.com; Brian Offenberger (aka RSS Ray). Best method: E-mail. No response? E-mail.

Invited Back? Content, articulation, ability to capture audience.

Guest Comments: "Wow. I've been on a lot of radio shows, but this is one of the most professional I have ever been on: RSS Ray. I'm on the air now. I've subscribed. Based on my e-mails lots of you listen to this show, which is for marketers looking to keep up with what's going on in the industry." — Robert Scoble, vice president Media Development at PodTech.net, co-author *Naked Conversations: How Blogs Are Changing the Way Businesses Talk with Customers* (Wiley 2006), and popular blogger at Scobleizer.com

"I just wanted to take a few minutes and thank you for the great work you did with getting my website optimized. The information you provided me with was more effective than I ever thought it would be. Since implementing the changes you recommended my site traffic has gone up about 150 percent. Thank you for the top notch service. I will be calling on your services again." — Andrew Riley, owner, Three Monitor Wallpaper.com

Bio of RSS Ray: Since 1983, RSS Ray has generated millions of dollars in profits and sales for his clients and business partners through sound marketing, sales and management strategies and tactics. He specializes in online marketing and electronic media practices, such as search engine marketing, online advertising, web analytics, blogging, podcasting, RSS marketing, social media marketing, webinars, and teleseminars.

RSS Ray has personally consulted or worked for such companies as Siemens, Mobile Mini, Sonitrol, and Latino Coaches Association.

He is certified as an eMarketing specialist by the eMarketing Association, is top level certified in search engine marketing and advertising by Google and Yahoo, is a certified online testing and paid search management expert by MEC Labs and has received advanced training in web analytics.

RSS Ray is the CEO of BizGrowth Search Engine Solutions, an integrated online marketing agency specializing in search engine marketing, online advertising, analytics and social media marketing. He is also co-founder of Branded Online Solutions, a company providing custom designed e-mail stationery for marketing and branding purposes.

RSS Ray believes any company can do well in marketing-online and offline-by applying his time tested duplicatable strategies, tactics and practices.

RSS Ray lives in Scottsdale, Arizona. When not on the air, he is known as Brian Offenberger.

Powerfull Living with Lorraine Cohen on http://www.internetvoicesradio.com

Theme: Compelling conversations for business and personal success.

Guest Profile: Specialties are marketing, e-commerce, business building and personal development and spirituality. Someone who knows how to have a back and forth conversation with the intent to bring rich content and value to the program. Ideal guests are articulate, personable, entertaining, confident, succinct, professional experts in their field of expertise. They have experience speaking to audiences and have a desire to "be in contribution" to listeners — meaning a "how can I be of help" attitude. Interested in their past interview experiences, credentials and sound of their voice. I meet all the guests I don't know prior to booking them on my show.

Guest from Hell: Guests from hell use the format to "pitch" their business. They ramble and try to make the show "all about them." They lack the skill to flow with a conversation.

Contact: lorraine@powerfull-living.biz; 610-415-1733; http://www.powerfull-living.biz; Lorraine Cohen. Best method: E-mail initially with an interest and a pitch with a bio. No response? E-mail a second time. I always respond if I receive the e-mail. Allow up to two weeks for response if I am out of town and away from e-mail.

Invited Back? If they came on the show and were engaging, articulate, experienced guests who shared great information and know how to be conversational and were fun. I invite people back who come on to add value to my listeners by sharing their expertise without ego or pitching.

Bio of Lorraine Cohen: Lorraine is CEO and founder of Powerfull Living, an organization dedicated to enhancing business development, leadership proficiency, and personal enrichment. She brings more than 25 years' experience in personal and business coaching, psychological counseling, and sales to thousands of business owners, entrepreneurs, executives and managers from a wide range of professional service industries.

An expert in breaking through fear and removing barriers to success, she shows people how to get unstuck; to break through the confusion and roadblocks so that they move forward in all areas of their life. A published writer, Lorraine's articles on personal and business development are featured online, on multiple websites, and local newspapers. She has been a guest expert in the Philadelphia area and national radio and local television programs. Her warm and interactive presentation style makes her a sought-after speaker and seminar leader.

PowerSellingMom's Radio Show: Let's Talk eBay with Danna Crawford on Blog Talk Radio, http://www.blogtalkradio.com/dannacrawford

Theme: eBay.

Guest Profile: eBay sellers, buyers and employees. I look for a down to earth, genuine type of person that can bring warmth and excitement to the table. Experience with eBay is all that matters.

Guest from Hell: Someone that would not speak clearly or does not seem interested to talk to me.

Contact: danna@powersellingmom.com; 352-402-0877; http://www.PowerSellingMom.com; http://www.AskDanna.com; http://www.practicalecommerce.com/blogs/ebay-for-ecommerce/; Danna Crawford. Best method: E-mail or phone. No response? E-mail or call.

Invited Back? How well the show goes.

Bio of Danna Crawford: Danna has been a PowerSellingMom on eBay since 1997! As a stay-at-home-mom, she's proof that the bills can get paid by selling on eBay. Now that her children are off to college and have left the nest, she shares her "wisdom" with others about eBay. "I especially help the 'Moms,'" she says, "encouraging them to learn eBay and put the family first!"

She writes ebooks about selling on eBay and a weekly blog for an on-line magazine as the eBay eCommerce style of writing.

As an eBay education specialist, she teaches several different styles of eBay classes, and has students travel from around the USA to attend her private classes.

"The radio show has opened up a new door of opportunity for myself and my eBay business," says Danna.

PricewaterhouseCoopers Start Up Show with Steve Bengston on http://www.wsradio.com

Theme: Startups.

Guest Profile: Anyone involved with startups, e.g., vc, CEO, authors, service providers.

Guest from Hell: Boring self promoter not that relevant to startups.

Contact: steve.bengston@us.pwc.com; 650-281-9843; http://www.wsradio.com; Steve Bengston. Best method: E-mail. No response? E-mail.

Invited Back? If they are controversial, humorous, or informative.

Bio of Steve Bengston: Steve heads the Emerging Company Services (ECS) group at Pricewaterhouse-Coopers. Prior to joining PwC, he spent 20 years in a variety of marketing, business development and general management roles at several high tech companies in the Bay area. Most recently, he was Pres/CEO of ynot.com, a leading international emarketing and greeting card company. Previously, he was vice president Marketing and Business Development at Worldview Systems, an Internet travel pioneer. At Worldview, Steve helped launch and market Travelocity with Sabre Interactive.

Steve has a BA in Economics and MBA from Stanford University.

The Ryan C. Greene Show with Ryan C. Greene on Blog Talk Radio, http://www.blogtalkradio.com/theryancgreeneshow, first Sunday, 8–10 PM (ET).

Theme: Educate, empower and equip today's leaders.

Guest Profile: Guests with an uplifting message to help listeners be more successful in business, life and health. A professional with a proven track record of helping improve people's lives. Entrepreneurs, authors, professionals, etc., are welcome. Want to know credentials and experience in area of discussion. First read my website to see what my show is about. Make sure your idea fits with the purpose of my show. E-mail your idea for a show explaining how your show idea will help the LISTENERS. Give me a reason that I can't refuse as to why I should have you on my show.

Guest from Hell: A guest that gives two-second answers.

Contact: info@ryancgreene.com; 443-744-0778; http://www.ryancgreene.com; Ryan C Greene, host and producer. Best method: E-mail. No response? If I have booked them then please e-mail me again. If it's a query, I will get back to you when I see a fit in the show schedule.

Invited Back? Listener feedback and guests overall interaction, energy and performance.

Bio of Ryan C. Greene: Ryan's leadership development began at a very young age. His single mother raised him with his younger sister in the suburbs of Baltimore, Md., and Ryan became the man of the house quickly as a "latch-key kid" at the age of eight. He attributes his determination, commitment to succeed and never give up attitude to watching his mother sacrifice her life for the life of her kids. Watching his mother's fight through sickle cell anemia gave Ryan the determined resolve to be the one to make a difference in his family.

Today, Ryan is one of the most sought after speakers and trainers on the East Coast. In January 2006 he founded Bakari Book Publishers and published his first book, *Success Is in Your Hand: 19 Keys to Unlocking the Successful Person You Were Designed to Be*. His second book, *Success 101: 19 Keys to Success in College That Your Professor Won't Teach You* was released in September 2007 and *My Little Black Book of Leadership Lessons I Learned from My Ex-Girlfriends* was released in the spring of 2008.

Ryan graduated from Hampton University with a Bachelors of Science degree in Marketing. In 2003, he founded Maximum Leadership Concepts, whose mission is to educate, empower and equip today's leaders.

He resides in Baltimore with his wife, Leslie, his son, Jordan, and daughter Jayden.

The Small Business Big Ideas Show with David Cohen and Garth Riley on CKDO 1580/107.7 FM, Ontario, Canada, on Sunday at 9 AM (ET).

Theme: Small business help show ... interview/talk format.

Guest Profile: Authors, coaches, speakers, business experts, motivational, success, finance, sales, marketing, stress/wellness, local government, etc. I like someone fun, sincere, kind, easy to talk to, informative, motivational, real and topical ... in keeping with the vibe of the day. I want to know about their angle, experiences, what the message is, are they fun, well known, good references, topical, informative, etc.

Guest from Hell: Someone who is a "no show" is off my Christmas card list and someone who reads their answers or is a bland guest. Guests on air should have some "personality" for sure.

Contact: info@smallbusinessbigideas.com and or garthriley@rogers.com; 416-630-3527; http://www.smallbusinessbigideas.com; David Cohen. Best method: Phone or e-mail first, then a press kit ... or send a book, etc. No response? Keep trying. I have a career in coaching/training too ... so if I don't get back to you ... it's not personal ... it's just that I am busy and the message you are sending me isn't compelling enough for me to really take note.

Invited Back? That they have something compelling to say, that they champion the show and are appreciative about being a guest.

Bio of David Cohen: David has had a vibrant career in both radio advertising and promotional products marketing business for over 14 years. During the past 8 years, he has shifted his career and focus and embarked on launching a business in consulting, coaching and training. The result was the launch of The Technicolour Umbrella in 2002.

David prides himself on working and teaching at a variety of local government economic development agencies, specializing in small business start-up programs. He has trained with the Adler School towards obtaining a certificate in professional coaching and soon afterwards began working as a business advisor, coach and consultant with JVS and Rexdale Microskills.

David works as a business advisor, facilitator and coach at the Toronto Business Development Centre, the School for Promotional Marketing, and Essential Communications in Whitby. He has also worked with youth entrepreneurship programs with the BE Network, St. Stephen's Youth Enterprise Program, and does some work for Centennial College's Center for Entrepreneurship. David has worked one-on-one with over 200 start-ups and has taught marketing, selling, business start up, cold calling, and market research to over 1000 students. He is the originator, host and producer in charge of his radio show.

Small Business Power Hour with Top Dog Business Booster Eileen Proctor and Exhibit Expert Susan Ratliff on AM 1510 KFNN, Phoenix, Arizona, Friday Mornings 9–10 AM.

Theme: Issues and topics to help small businesses get to the next level of success.

Guest Profile: Experts on the topic of the day — see editorial. We welcome guests who can add interest and entertainment to a business topic. Expert knowledge and enthusiasm for the topic.

Guest from Hell: A slow-talking, monotone one-syllable answering guest.

Contact: susan@smallbusinesspowerhour.com or Eileen@smallbusinesspowerhour.com; Susan 602-437-3634; Eileen 602-867-3647; http://www.smallbusinesspowerhour.com; Eileen Proctor or Susan Ratliff. Best method: E-mail or phone. Provide a brief bio, including credentials that make them an expert in the topic. Ten questions they would like to discuss. The person should look at our website and editorial calendar of upcoming topics to see if they fit then contact us by any of those methods. No response? Call or e-mail. We try to respond to all inquiries in a timely manner.

Invited Back? We try not to repeat guests.

Listener Comments: "The Small Business Power Hour is really on the 'go!' The dynamics were terrific again and the subject matter ... was filled with solid content. Much thanks and remember... 'I got the power.'"— D. Hines, Phoenix, AZ

"I love your Friday show at 9:00 AM, the *Small Business Power Hour*. The hour goes by fast and contains a lot of top quality information for small business owners. I am a business broker so I have been telling all of my networking groups about this program."— J. Roth, Scottsdale, AZ

Bio of Susan Ratliff: Susan is an award-winning entrepreneur and author with 30 years' experience in sales and marketing. She started a home-based business in 1989 and learned her trade show talents from the trenches, selling personalized children's books on weekends at swap meets and craft fairs. As her knowledge of exhibiting evolved, she expanded her goals, sold the book business and started Exhibit Experts in 1994.

She is president of the company, which provides display products, service, resources and booth staff training that helps her clients increase profits, stand out from the competition and capitalize on marketing opportunities at tradeshows and events. Susan is author of *How to Be a Weekend Entrepreneur: Making Money at Craft Fairs and Trade Shows* (Marketing Methods Press 1991).

In 2004, Susan created the Women Entrepreneurs' Small Business Boot Camp, fueled by her desire to provide a forum for creating synergy, support and celebrating the successes of local women running companies with under 10 employees. Her goal was to gather experts who would teach no-nonsense, practical, tactical tips and techniques that could be easily and immediately implemented to improve and grow their business.

Her latest award was the 2005 Pioneer Award from NAWBO (National Association of Women Business Owners).

Bio of Eileen Proctor: An entrepreneurial, results-oriented professional with over 30 years of diverse business experience, Eileen has enjoyed successful tenures with a number of industry-leading corporations. Additionally, as owner of Graphic AdVentures, she developed compelling graphic and marketing campaigns that drove sales, profits and success for hundreds of small-to-medium sized businesses.

Fulfilling her passion and actualizing her vision of creating a successful business that improves the quality of life for dogs and the people that love them, Top Dog Eileen pioneered the dog daycare industry within the Valley of the Sun, launching award-winning It's A Ruff Life! in October 2000.

In response to persistent requests from small business owners and fledgling entrepreneurs, Eileen launched Top Dog Business Boosters in 2005 as a means of sharing the proven success strategies, programs and tools that have given her a "leg up" on the competition and positioned her as undisputed Leader of the pack.

Among her awards are the 2007 NAWBO Phoenix Pioneer of the Year Award and the 2006 Greater Phoenix Chamber of Commerce Small Businessperson of the Year Award.

SmallBizAmerica Radio with David Wolf, executive producer, aired on 75 Markets on Am Talk Station, Internet streaming internationally.

Theme: Small business and entrepreneurs.

Guest Profile: Leaders, experts, consultants and/or interesting entrepreneurs. Expertise, articulate, focused, real. Should have dynamic and modulating speaking style, but natural, real and spontaneous.

Guest from Hell: Someone that is reading answers from a pre-planned sheet, or someone that answers every possible question I could ask with the first answer!

Contact: david@smallbizamerica.com; 888-415-5990; toll free 877-798-2534; http://www.smallbizamerica.com; David Wolf. Best method: E-mail bio and press kits are good, no pitch. No response? E-mail or call.

Invited Back? Good info, serving the audience well, good vibes ... more to say.

Bio of David Wolf: Creator, host and executive producer, David is the "classic entrepreneur" who started in the music and audio production business in Chicago in the early 80s, then continued in Dallas in through the 90s. He has composed and produced music and audio content for a diversified base of advertising clients such as Texaco, Embassy Suites, Miller Brewing, P&G, Southwest Airlines, Pepsi, Frito-Lay, McDonald's, Shaklee International, GTE and many more.

He and wife/partner Phyllis' Crywolf Productions produced and recorded audio content for NBC, Universal Studios, Amblin Entertainment, Hit Entertainment (Barney the Dinosaur), TNT, The Discovery Channel, Walt Disney Television and more. In business, Wolf co-led the turnaround of Wolfe's Bagels, a regional commercial bakery located in Albuquerque, NM. He holds a Series 7 Securities License, and is a real estate investor. Wolf is also a commercially certified private pilot with 1000 hours.

Sound Investing with Paul Merriman, Tom Cock and Don McDonald on KVI 570 AM, Seattle, WA, and KPQ 560 AM, Wenatchee, and soon to be nationwide on Business Talk Radio Network. The program is archived online at http://www.soundinvesting.com

Theme: Retirement planning and investing issues/news.

Guest Profile: Authors, investment experts, retirement lifestyle–types. Engaging, energetic, well-spoken — someone with a passion for their point of view. Want their credentials, their story/angle.

Guest from Hell: Someone who gives one-word answers, or someone who goes on and on... Shy, quiet, meek types that are scared to even be on the radio.

Contact: eric@merrimanberkmannext.com; 206-838-1542; http://www.soundinvesting.com; Eric Paine, producer. Best method: E-mail. No response? I always respond to guests, whether or not I'm interested in having them on the show.

Invited Back? How interesting they are to my audience, audience feedback.

Bio of Paul Merriman: Paul is founder and director of Merriman Berkman Next, recognized as one of the nation's top experts on mutual fund investing.

He is publisher and editor of *FundAdvice.com*, a newsletter dedicated to investing in no-load mutual funds, and of an educational web site of the same name. In 2000, 2001 and 2002 *FundAdvice.com* was named in Forbes' "Best of the Web" issue.

Paul's newest book, *Live It Up Without Outliving Your Money: Ten Steps to a Perfect Retirement Portfolio* (Wiley 2005), has been on Amazon's top 25 "retirement planning" book list for over two years. He is also the author of *Investing for a Lifetime* and *Market Timing with No-Load Mutual Funds* (Irwin Professional Pub 1991).

Widely quoted in such national publications as *Money, U.S. News and World Report, Kiplinger's Personal Finance, USA Today, Barron's, Business Week, The Wall Street Journal, Investor's Business Daily* and *Forbes*, Paul has been a special guest on "Wall Street Week" with Louis Rukeyser, PBS' "Nightly Business News" with Paul Kangas, plus many financial talk shows on CBS, CNBC, and CNN. He has also produced four investing videos.

Paul has twice been a guest speaker at the annual psychology of investing conference at Harvard University. Recipient of a distinguished alumni award from Western Washington University's School of Economics, he is a founding member of the board of directors of Global HELP (www.Global-Help.org) and chairman of the board of directors of BITV (Bainbridge Island TV).

For speaking engagements and media inquires, Paul can be reached through his e-mail or his assistant's, Kara Weber, at kara@merrimanberkmannext.com or at 1-800-423-4893.

Bio of Tom Cock, Jr.: Tom plays a key role in the growth of Merriman Berkman Next and has been instrumental in making it one of the fastest growing private companies in Washington state, as ranked by the *Puget Sound Business Journal*. A well-known financial educator, he is publisher of one of the company's websites, www.401khelp.com and has written several articles including a feature in *Horizon Air* magazine.

Tom has been involved in business — either reporting on it or as a businessperson — since his youth. He has been in broadcasting for 30 years and was host of PBS's "Serious Money" for five years. Prior to joining the company in 1998, Tom had a long career in journalism including a stint as publisher of *The Bellingham Business Journal*.

Much of Tom's off-duty time is spent on area soccer fields where he plies his trade as a nationally licensed soccer coach and referee. tom@merrimanberkmannext.com

Bio of Don McDonald: Don is one of the nation's top professionals on money and investing. Don has hosted a nationally syndicated financial talk show for 14 years. Known for his frank advice to investors, he has also published a popular financial newsletter.

Don joined Merriman Berkman Next in 2005 as a speaker and co-host of Sound Investing. He also hosts the Merriman Berkman Next Investing and Retirement Cruises to Alaska.

Don owns a host of companies including PastPresent Gallery, Shareboards and tackamaps.

He resides in Celebration, Florida, with his wife Debie, and four children; don@merrimanberkmannext.com

Stu Taylor has three shows:
(1) *Equity Strategies* on Business Talk Radio Network airs on 33 radio stations nationally;

(2) *Equity Strategies* (different show) on Radio America Network airs on 26 radio stations nationally;

(3) *Stu Taylor on Business* on 1060 WBIX, Boston, reaches into Massachusetts, Rhode Island Connecticut, Maine, New Hampshire, Vermont, and Pittsburgh, Pa.

All shows streamed on Internet and archived.

Theme: Informational, educational, entertaining on topical issues of the day.

Guest Profile: Business and political. Ideal guests have a value proposition that is presented in an articulate manner to a sophisticated audience. Potential guest should have a history of communicating with the public. Among the prominent personalities who have been guests are Jack Welch, CEO of GE; Dick Morris; Andrea Mitchell; Doris Kearns Goodwin; George Foreman; Suzie Orman; F. Lee Bailey; Newt Gingrich, former Speaker of the House; Carly Fiorina, former CEO of Hewlett Packard; Bill Bradley; and Mitt Romney.

Guest from Hell: Guest from hell is one who is unprepared and unable to provide enough substance in answering questions.

Contact: office@StuTaylor.com; http://www.StuTaylor.com; 781-860-9548; Stu Taylor. Best method: Phone or Contact: telephone, e-mail, or snail mail. No response? Follow up by telephone.

Invited Back? Based on quality of first interview and additional information that has not been covered during the first interview.

Guest Comments: "I've been doing a monthly series of financial shows on Stu's programs for over a year now and my client base has grown remarkably throughout the country as a result. As an author and a professional investment manager, I've been around the talk show circuit, and I can say without reservation that he is the absolute best host for leading the discussion to the most important areas. My books sales have grown as a result of our unique programming." — Steve Selengut, Sanco Services

"I enjoyed my time with Stu Taylor. He was easy to talk to and did a great job of raising key issues for discussion. He provided an excellent opportunity for us to communicate the purpose and mission of iExalt. Stu and Business 1060/Radio America have been key participants in the success of iExalt." — Don Sapaugh, Chief Executive Officer. iExalt, Inc.

Bio of Stu Taylor: After starting as a sales training consultant with Teaching Systems Corp, Stu moved on to start his own very successful business. With more than 25 years as president and founder of Taylor Associates, Inc., he founded and operated the largest distributorship of commercial spin-off and movie-related fad merchandise in the United States and contributed to the success of several merchandising products, including Batman, The Simpsons, Ninja Turtles, Saturday Night Fever and Power Rangers.

In addition to his three shows, Stu has hosted the Baseball Hall of Fame inductions at Cooperstown, N.Y., has served as an analyst for the NHL Stanley Cup Finals, presided at the White House on Health Care Reform and broadcast live at the 104th Congress at the Capitol in Washington, D.C. He has also hosted radio shows with former Boston Red Sox star Rico Petrocelli ("The Home Team"), ex–Red Sox ace relief pitcher Dick Radatz ("Circle the Bases") and three-time world boxing champion "Dangerous" Dana Rosenblatt ("In This Corner"). Stu has also broadcasted scores of professional boxing matches with Rosenblatt for television, including DirecTV, Joe DeGuardia's Star Boxing, and Fox Sports Net's "Mohegan Sun Fight Night New England."

He is author of an autobiographical business book entitled *How to Turn Trends into Fortunes (Without Getting Left in the Dust)* (Carol Publishing Corporation 1993). Stu was once promoter for George Foreman, who wrote the forward.

Stu is a graduate of Northeastern University in Boston, and holds a degree in experimental psychology.

Taking Care of Business with Richard Soloman and Rick Frishman on WCWP FM, Long Island, NY, airing Thursday, 2–3 PM (ET) and web cast.

Theme: business self-help.

Guest Profile: Business authors and experts who are smart, good talkers and funny. We'd like to know their past interview experiences, credentials and sound of their voice.

Guest from Hell: One who shuts up and is dumb.

Contact: rick@rickfrishman.com; 516-620-2528 ext 110; http://www.tcbradio.com; http://www.rickfrishman.com; Richard Soloman at richsol@mindspring.com. Best method: E-mail first. No response? E-mail.

Invited Back? Their passion.

Bio of Rick Frishman: Founder of Planned Television Arts and among the leading book publicists in America, Rick has worked with many of the top book editors, literary agents and publishers in America, including Simon and Schuster, Random House, Wiley, Harper Collins, Pocket Books, Penguin Putnam, and Hyperion Books. He has worked with best-selling authors, including Mitch Albom, Bill Moyers, Stephen King, Caroline Kennedy, Howard Stern, President Jimmy Carter, Mark Victor Hansen, Nelson DeMille, John Grisham, Hugh Downs, Henry Kissinger, Jack Canfield, Alan Dershowitz, Arnold Palmer, and Harvey Mackay.

In addition to his work at PTA Rick has now taken on the new role of publisher at Morgan James Publishing in New York. David Hancock founded Morgan James in 2003 and in 2007 it published over 130 books. Morgan James only publishes non fiction books and looks for authors with a platform who believe in giving back. Morgan James gives a portion of every book sold to Habitat for Humanity. (http://www.morganjamespublishing.com)

Rick is the co-author of eight books, including national best-sellers *Guerrilla Publicity* (2002) and *Networking Magic* (2004), both published by Adams Media Corporation. He and media personality Robyn Freedman Spizman co-wrote the popular four-book series *Author 101* and recently teamed up for their highly acclaimed book entitled *Where's Your Wow? 16 Ways to Make Your Competitors Wish They Were You!* (McGraw Hill, March 2008).

Rick has a B.F.A. in acting and directing and a B.S. from Ithaca College School of Communications.

He and his wife Robbi live in Long Island with their three children, Adam, Rachel and Stephanie, and a cockapoo named Rusty.

The Tom O'Brien Show on TFNN, aired weekdays, 4–6 PM (ET) in Massachusetts, New Jersey, Florida, Colorado, and on the Internet at http://www.tfnn.com

Theme: Financial talk radio.

Guest Profile: CEOs, politicians, authors, investors, fund managers, market timers, bankers, etc. Someone who can provide value and insight to our listeners, whether it is in the financial market place or in any aspect of life. Work experience, and credentials needed.

Guest from Hell: Someone simply trying to sell themselves or their product while providing no value to the listener.

Contact: ob1@tfnn.com; 877-518-9190; http://www.tfnn.com; Tom O'Brien, Host. Best method: E-mail works best. No response? E-mail.

Invited Back? Quality of interview.

Bio of Tom O'Brien: Tom is founder, owner and CEO of Tiger Financial News Network, which produces his two radio shows, *The Tom O'Brien Show* and *The Opening Growl*, along with several other radio shows, and http://www.TFNN.com. Investors across the country and throughout the world have come to view Tom and his radio programs as the most dependable source of stock market news, information, and analysis. Listeners continue to tune in everyday to hear his views and his voice; radiating with confidence, wildly energetic, and incredibly accurate as a forecast of where stock prices are going — and what you should do about it.

Proudly calling themselves "Tigers," Tom's listeners call in daily for a chance to growl and ask questions about specific stock and option trades. What they get is an open, honest, and enlightening dialogue that serves to both answer their question and educate the audience. This educational approach is what sets *The Tom O'Brien Show* apart from so many others. Those that tune in each day get to take away with them practical tools that can be used immediately to improve their trading results. Many of today's financial talk radio hosts strive only to impress the audience with their own knowledge; Tom tries to help you get some of your own.

The audience finds in Tom's programs something they won't find anywhere else on financial talk radio; an education. This unique, educational aspect has helped to give Tom an audience that is extremely devoted and loyal. Tom's views are often quoted on http://www.forbes.com

Tom is author of *Timing the Trade—How Price and Volume Move Markets* (TFNN 2005), which has sold thousands of copies and is the textbook for his trading system bearing the same name. He also authors two newsletters, Market Insights, and The Gold Report, which does an in depth analysis of the gold market and gold stocks.

Tom's goal, and the goal of his audience, is that they will be even better traders tomorrow than they were today.

Traders Nation with Kurt Schemers, on the ABC Starguide Satellite System and syndicated on five radio stations and nearly 100 online affiliates. Trader's Nation is the only financial talk show pre-loaded in Apple's iTunes software, Real Media's European platform, and LePlayer's video on demand software. Additionally, Trader's Nation is embedded in several online financial software trading platforms.

Theme: Financial, individual stock movers, stock market analysis and news.

Guest Profile: Financial, industry, business, geo political, and social experts. Someone who is knowledgeable in their field. Presumed expert. Entertaining and energetic. Fast paced with clear and concise answers. I don't need to know more unless they are well known like Steve Forbes, Willie Nelson and Steve Doocey from Fox and Friends. I do some research on the topic but leave the rest as a surprise. This makes for a genuine, eventful interview.

Guest from Hell: Dull, boring, let me drag the answers from them. I also feel sorry for the nervous ones — I generally have techniques to calm them down to end with a good interview.

Contact: kurt.s@tradersnation.com; 623-465-0844; http://www.tradersnation.com; Kurt Schemers. Best method: We get pitched by all methods of approach — phone, e-mails, and the occasional direct-out-of-the-blue book mailer. No response? We always respond quickly and professionally. This may be one of the reasons why *Traders Nation* is so popular to book on. We always welcome phone calls and guest topics ideas.

Invited Back? Guests always want to come back because of our style of interview. In fact, many want a copy of their interview for their own media packets.

Bio of Kurt Schemers: Under the experience of Kurt, *Trader's Nation* has achieved phenomenal success over the last seven years. A seasoned and professional interviewer who's tackled nationally-recognized guests like country icon Willie Nelson and billionaire Steve Forbes, Kurt excels at developing a friendly rapport with his guests that help them look their best.

Book authors, economists, and financial editors frequent the program, in part, because of Schemers' strong reputation for delivering some of the best independent interview content available today.

Kurt has more than 10 years' experience in the U.S. financial markets, has completed over 1,000 interviews, and is an avid and insightful purveyor of current events.

Unlock Your Sales Potential with Debra Pearlman on WTBQ 1110 AM, Florida, New York, serving all of Orange County and Northern New Jersey, on Tuesdays 4–5 PM (ET).

Theme: Sales/business/motivation.

Guest Profile: Marketing experts/sales gurus/business consultants/CEOs. Guest who offers valuable information to my listeners, whether on ways to increase their business revenue, sales technique, marketing medias, etc. Want to know about their interview experience, credentials and sound of their voice, as well as any published works they have, speaking engagements, etc.

Guest from Hell: One who is interested in primarily conducting a personal commercial for themselves and offers little or no value to the program.

Contact: Debra@dpsalespro.com; 845-649-2727; http://www.dpsalespro.com; Debra Pearlman. Best method: E-mailing a bio and sending a press kit works best. No response? If for some reason a potential guest does hear back from me, they can e-mail me again. I have a standard "thanks, but no thanks" letter if I'm not interested or don't think they will be a good fit for my main theme.

Invited Back? The camaraderie and ease in conversing with the guest on the air. They should be able to have a conversation with me, sound natural, while offering valuable tips and information to the show.

Bio of Debra Pearlman: Debra has more than 20 years' experience in sales and business management, sales team development, professional speaking and marketing. Her company, DP Sales Pro, provides clients with assessments and recommendations that specifically address their needs. By partnering with clients, Debra gains an understanding of their product and/or services as well as their target market. This allows her to successfully implement processes ensuring sales goals and objectives are achieved.

Some of the major corporations Debra has worked with include: AmeriPride Services, MTA Long Island, Estee Lauder, Avon Products R&D, George Weston Bakeries (Arnold's Bread), Sandoz/Novartis, Metal Container Corp. (Anheuser-Busch Co.) and Decorative Product Source.

Debra holds a BA degree in business marketing/management from the University of Phoenix.

She resides in Blooming Grove, NY, with her husband and three children.

Where Wall Street Meets Main Street with Jack Warkenthien, on KTEK in Houston and KJSA in Dallas/Fort Worth, TX, Monday through Friday, 7–8 A.M. (CT).

Theme: Taking the mystery out of personal investing and running a business on "Main Street."

Guest Profile: Mostly national celebrities or personalities. I want to know why they're "subject matter experts" in the topic of discussion and what their "end game" is, because every guest has one. The sooner I know what it is, the easier it is for me to facilitate their "agenda." Also, I want to know that they know a little about a lot of different areas in case a caller takes us in a different direction.

Actually, there are 20 things I believe the "perfect guest" can do to be on the radio — early and often. In fact, I wrote a brief speech titled, "20 Tips in 20 Minutes: How to Be the Perfect Guest." The main ingredients are enthusiasm and passion for their particular topic and having something "fresh" and distinct to share with my very discriminating listeners.

Guest from Hell: Conversely, when a guest sounds like they've just recovered from "charisma bypass surgery" and make me nod off during the conversation, that's a bad thing. Also, when they break into "infomercial" mode, and feel they have to start "selling" to my audience, it's amazing how fast our producer can cut them off.

Contact: jwarkenthien@bizradio.com; http://www.bizradio.com; Stephanie Frishberg, producer/community outreach coordinator, at Stephanie@bizradio.com or 713-490-8705. Best method: E-mail. No response? Of course, e-mail or call. While we strive to always be timely in our correspondence, "stuff" happens on radio. If they have a strong pitch, they should continue pitching.

Invited Back? Feedback. We'll get phone calls, e-mails, text messages, etc. from parties that listened to the segment(s). The more feedback the better, regardless if it's positive or negative. The other main factor involves the timeliness of the information. If the topic is very much in the news — and continues to stay in focus — we'll invite the good ones back for a "curtain call."

Bio of Jack Warkenthien: When Jack is off the air, he's helping clients fill their sales "pipeline" by writing award-winning sales commercials and designing radio campaigns for clients who market to an affluent listener base, comprised of investors and business owners.

For almost a dozen years, Jack and NextStep Solutions (www.nextstep-solutions.com), which he founded, have been delivering personalized sales, marketing, service and leadership training to firms all over the world — with quantifiable and measurable results.

Believing that 85 percent of anyone's success in the world can be attributed to two things: relationship building and communication skills, they focus on delivering programs that address both needs.

After graduating from the University of Illinois, Champaign-Urbana in 1978, Jack began a decade-long career with IBM. He quickly established a stellar reputation as a "closer," leading the nation in new account sales — 53 systems in 52 weeks — *before* the advent of the PC. The most amazing part: he did it in only his *second* year on quota! It was the next year that he launched his professional speaking career, criss-crossing the country sharing sales strategies with other IBM professionals.

Jack wrote the book on sales! In fact, the most recent book he wrote, *Life's a Sales Call: How to Succeed in the World's Oldest Profession* (Next Step Solutions 2005), has been a best seller wherever Jack hangs his hat.

Women in Business Radio with Dr. Gayle Carson on http://www.wsradio.com. Gayle also broadcasts *Women in Business* for 30 minutes and *SOB (Spunky Old Broad) Radio*, for women over 50, for 30 minutes, both on WS Radio.

Theme: Successful women who are in business either as entrepreneurs or senior managers.

Guest Profile: Authors and non-authors who have run companies, departments or organizations that are for profit; attorneys, bank presidents, owners of companies that are home-based; senior managers from corporations. The companies can be large or small, private or public, home based on not, but the most important thing is to have them future focused. I look for a guest who is animated, excited and knowledgeable.

Guest from Hell: Someone who sounds scripted — doesn't listen to the questions I'm asking, and pushes her own agenda.

Contact: gayle@gaylecarson.com; speaker-coach@att.net gayle@spunkyoldbroad.com and devechtrealty@gmail.com; 305-534-8846; http://www.gaylecarson.com; Sherrin Ann Smith at sas56chevy@bellsouth.net. Best method: E-mail bio and pitch. No response? We always respond quickly.

Invited Back? What I want to know most about someone is what she has done in the past, present and future, what makes her unique and personal interests and hobbies. Don't want guests back too frequently, but if they are doing something new and different, of course.

Guest Comments: "You are a wonderful radio host — very easy to talk to! You made it enjoyable and showed impeccable customer service."— Elinor Stutz, CEO, Smooth Sale

"Your radio show was a lot of fun, but I wish I could have talked with you even more. Thank you for thinking of me."— Bernadette Martinelli, Jewel Caddy.com

Bio of Gayle Carson: Known as the "Wiz of Biz," Gayle is author of *Winning Ways: How to Get to the Top and Stay There* (Lane Pub 1988) and *How to be an S.O.B.— A Spunky Old Broad Who Kicks Butt* (Wun Publications 2005).

An entrepreneur from the age of 13, Gayle is celebrating her 47th year in business for herself. Throughout her career as the owner of a chain of career and technical training schools, head of one of Florida's top casting and talent agencies and convention services companies, directing seven divisions and several hundred people, she has practiced what she preached.

Gayle has been a speaker and consultant for over 25 years, and currently heads an Internet Information Marketing Association, is branding her Spunky Old Broad series, and heads a real estate investment group.

Work at Home Family Talk Radio with Sandra Weber on http://www.wahftalkradio.com

Theme: Help and information for people who work at home.

Guest Profile: Authors, specialists who work with home based entrepreneurs, entrepreneurs. We want something that makes them unique, a new way of doing business, helping business owners succeed. Guests should have a willingness to be interviewed and at least six months in their area of specialty.

Guest from Hell: Haven't found one yet.

Contact: junglemom9@yahoo.com, sandra@wahftalkradio.com; 207-689-8901; http://www.wahftalkradio.com; Sandra Weber. Best method: E-mail me with information and a link to your website. I go and look and see if it's something interesting. No response? If I miss you or accidentally delete you, e-mail again and put show idea or guest in the subject. I have triplets at home! I try to answer as soon as possible, but I'm human.

Invited Back? We are still on the first go round...

Bio of Sandra Weber: Originally from Texas and now living in Maine, Sandra has a BS in liberal arts, psychology concentration and 30 hours towards her Masters in counseling. She's taken courses in radio, marketing and advertising and hosted a radio show in a small AM station in Texas.

Work Matters with Nan Russell on http://www.webtalkradio.net

Theme: *Work Matters* sees itself as a catalyst for inspired and reflective thinking about what your work is and isn't. Part inspiration, part mentor, part real world workplace, this show will help you offer the best of who you are to the world, live your life's potential, and actualize your dreams. In the broadest sense of the show's vision "your work" is about becoming who you are capable of becoming. We talk about work, we talk about life, and we talk about you.

Guest Profile: Two interview segments: 1) author/expert; 2) real people living their work dreams. Passion for what they do; knowledgeable expert with an on-air presence; guests who are interested in making a difference; focused on the audience with an authentic style; real-world experiences, passion; articulate; thoughtful.

Guest from Hell: Sales pitch. Trying to sell and promote vs. inspire and motivate.

Contact: workmatters@nanrussell.com; 406-862-0820; http://www.webtalkradio.net; Nan Russell. Best method: E-mail query with background and information. No response? Follow-up e-mail; No phone calls please.

Invited Back? Response of audience; rapport with host; value of information.

Bio of Nan Russell: From minimum wage employee to vice president of a $4.4 billion dollar company, Nan spent 20 years in management and knows what it takes to survive and thrive in this what-have-you-done-for-me-today world. Her syndicated column, *Winning at Working* (http://www.winningatworking.com) reaches over five million readers.

Nan is author of *Hitting Your Stride: Your Work, Your Way* (Capital Books, 2008) and *Nibble Your Way to Success* (Capital Books, 2007).

A sought after speaker, living her life dream to work and write from the mountains of Montana, Nan has a B.A. from Stanford and an M.A. from the University of Michigan.

Work with Marty Nemko on KALW 91.7FM, an NPR affiliate in the San Francisco area and on http://www.martynemko.com/radio.shtm

Theme: Improving your work life and education — from cool careers to not-so-cool co-workers, from salary negotiation to procrastination, from racial issues to work/life balance.

Guest Profile: Authors and others who can offer something new and practical for listeners, especially if it's contrarian but well defensible. Someone who is smart and offering practical non-obvious advice. Also, I do a semi-regular series called the Genius Interviews: hour-long interviews of very smart, famous people of all stripes. Past guests have included Alan Dershowitz, Robert Reich, Richard Dawkins, and Craig Venter. Great content is key.

Guest from Hell: I don't like theoreticians, both because their theories almost invariably lack sufficient empirical validation and because they're long-winded and too abstract for radio. (And I say that as a former academic myself—Ph.D. from Berkeley.) I also eschew the endless torrent of old-wine-in new-bottles books and guests who clearly are motivated mainly by self-promotion; http://www.martynemko.com

Contact: mnemko@comcast.net; 510-655-2777; Marty Nemko. Best method: E-mail or U.S.-mailed book and press kit.

No response: No calls or e-mails. If I want someone, I'm not shy about picking up the phone. I find publicist calls annoying.

Invited Back? That's rare. Only if they are filled with fascinating information and stories, and I'm clear they have much more of the same to bring back on a return interview.

Bio of Marty Nemko: Known as "The Bay Area's Best Career Coach," Marty Nemko is among the nation's most sought-after experts on both career and education issues. He's been interviewed in hundreds of major media — from CNN to the *New York Times* to the *Los Angeles Times*. Marty is a columnist for Kiplinger.com

His latest book, *Cool Careers for Dummies* (For Dummies, revised third edition) was the #1 rated career guide in the *Readers Choice* poll and reached #2 on the *Wall Street Journal* national business bestseller list. His first book, *How to Get Your Child a Private School Education in a Public School* (Ten Speed Press 1989), was named one of the year's Ten Musts by the American School Board Association.

Marty holds a Ph.D. from UC Berkeley and subsequently taught there. Marty has worked as a professional pianist, New York City cab driver and community theatre actor and director.

Cars

"To inform, educate and entertain radio listeners and television and Internet viewers on all aspects of cars, trucks, SUV and motorcycle transportation."— Part of the Mission Statement of Bobby Likis Car Clinic

America on the Road with Mike Anson and Jack Nerad, nationally syndicated.

Theme: Automotive for the regular driver.

Guest Profile: Authors, automotive experts, automotive industry representatives.

Someone who is knowledgeable about the various aspects of the automotive and aftermarket field. Credentials and expertise important.

Guest from Hell: Someone who is plugging a product, who is looking for free publicity, but doesn't think he/she should be using paid advertising.

Contact: h-and-h@verizon.net; 888-750-6590; http://www.americaontheroad.com; Al Herskovitz. Best method: E-mail and press kit. No response? If they don't get a response, then they should consider themselves rejected.

Invited Back? Audience reaction.

Bios of Mike Anson and Jack Nerad: Mike is a veteran automotive journalist, having served as associate editor of *Car Life* magazine; road test editor of *Road and Track*; editor of *4-Wheel* and *Off Road* and editor of *Motor Trend*. He also has considerable experience in TV, having hosted and/or reported on automotive shows for KTLA, Los Angeles, TNN, ESPN and SpeedVision. Mike also is a competition race car driver.

Jack is an experienced automotive journalist having written for the *Chicago Daily News* and served as editor of *Motor Trend*. He also worked within the auto industry as public relations director for the Amati Division of Mazda and as publications director for the research firm J.D. Power and Associates. Jack is also the author of *Fatal Photographs* (Avon Books 1998) and *The Complete Idiot's Guide to Buying or Leasing a Car* (Alpha 1996).

Bobby Likis Car Clinic airing on 110 affiliates, including terrestrial radio, Sirius Satellite Radio, American Forces Radio, and Internet (originating from his all-digital, custom-designed studio in his service center). Rated among The Talkers 250.

Theme: Increasing consumer cache and cash. Programs are sheer "Infotainment," designed to inform and entertain consumers in the automotive lifestyle, including aftermarket products and services, new and used vehicle purchases, OEM (automaker) issues, safety, mobile technology, consumer buying and service advice, preventive maintenance, gas mileage, vehicle performance and repair, and, very importantly, automotive trends and "what's hot."

Guest Profile: Relevant, automotive subject-matter expertise (e.g., Rick Wagoner, president, General Motors); companies that impact automotive consumers, including alternative fuels (e.g., Tom Rooney, president, Insituform (repairing Alaskan pipeline); Tom Sluneka, executive director, Ethanol Promotion and Information Council; Joe Averkamp, vp, Sprint); industry insiders (automotive, safety, trends) (e.g., Mike Marshall, director, Emerging Automotive Technologies, J.D. Power and Associates; Megan Pollack, spokesperson, Consumer Electronics Show and "Watch the Road" Campaign).

The ideal guest is well versed in his/her critical subject matter; good on-air voice and presence; sticks to the subject or question, not sidelined; credentials, and most of all, good chemistry with Bobby.

Guest from Hell: Guest from Hell is under-informed; pompous; weak on-air presence; tries to dominate the interview.

Contact: Diane Somer at DSomer@CarClinicNetwork.com; withheld on request; http://www.CarClinicNetwork.com; Diane Somer. Best method: E-mail. No response? E-mail.

Invited Back? See Guest Profile. If they're the ideal guest, they're invited back.

Bio of Robert A. "Bobby" Likis: Bobby has worn every hat in the automotive industry: technician, race car driver and pit crew, automotive service center owner, industry consultant, and radio and TV talk-show host. Acknowledged by industry and consumers, Bobby "talks the walk" as he hosts nationally syndicated, automotive-oriented programs.

Bobby has been published in *Motor Age, BE Radio* and *AutoInc*; produces a monthly e-newsletter of automotive advice, trends, tips and technology; and authors a weekly newspaper article. The eyes and ears of automotive enthusiasts, he has broadcast his show live from Daytona, Charlotte and Saratoga race tracks; Consumer Electronics Show; Concours d'Elegance; Automotive Aftermarket Industry Week; Woodward Ave Dream Cruise and Mid-America's 10th Anniversary.

Bobby is president, CEO, and chief cheerleader of Car Clinic which has two subsidiaries: Car Clinic Service and Car Clinic Productions. CCS, celebrating its 35th anniversary, specializes in one-stop, full-service automotive maintenance, repair, inspection, information ... and newly trademarked Pre-Repair. Under CCP, Bobby produces nationally syndicated radio and television programming, which includes *Bobby Likis Car Clinic* and *Car Clinic Minute*.

He lives and thrives on Florida's beautiful Gulf Coast, where he enjoys the company of many friends, two daughters, four grandchildren (two sets of twins) and sweetheart.

Crime and Child Abuse

That I will see and cause our community's peace to be kept and preserved—and that—I will prevent to the best of my power—all offenses against that peace...—from the Police Officers Oath on the website of ***The Watering Hole***

Breaking the Conspiracy of Silence with Dr. Kathleen Brooks on http://www.ethicalife.com/showlist.asp

Theme: Recognizing, reacting responsibly and preventing child sexual abuse.

Guest Profile: People with experience in child sexual abuse, either personal or professional. A sincere person who has accomplished something noteworthy in the area of child sexual abuse. I get a bio from them that includes education, credentials, job experience and expertise in the field, publications.

Guest from Hell: I haven't had one—I don't even invite them on my show if they don't have good credentials or if I preview what they have written and don't think it's good enough.

Contact: KBrooks107@cox.net; 619-287-0793 or 888-300-8626; http://www.ethicalife.com. Best method: Call with a pitch, e-mail a bio and send a press kit. No response? E-mail or call.

Invited Back? Level of expertise and personal warmth and sincerity.

Bio of Kathleen Brooks: Raised in a small town in Upstate New York, Kathleen has a Bachelor's degree in music and did graduate piano study at the Eastman School of Music. She has played professionally, as well as taught and trained teachers in the Suzuki Piano Method. She was also a church organist and choir director and is an experienced accompanist.

Kathleen has a master's degree in education with an emphasis on early childhood and extensive teaching experience in both public and private schools from preschool through high school. Since completing her Ph.D. in psychology at International College, she has been in private practice and a consultant and mediator with corporations, including Chase Manhattan Bank in New York City and Parinello, Inc. in San

Diego. She maintains a private practice in San Diego, CA, where she specializes in integrating psychological and spiritual growth. She teaches Light Alchemy Meditation, is a Reiki Master and facilitates workshops.

As a survivor/thriver of child sexual abuse, she is actively involved in the prevention and healing of this global epidemic, both through her radio show and as a facilitator of Darkness to Light's training program, Stewards of Children, which educates adults about child sexual abuse.

Crime and Punishment with Mike McIntyre, syndicated by the Corus and Rawlco Radio Networks, aired in B.C., Alberta, Saskatchewan, Winnipeg and Montreal, Sundays 7–9 PM (CT).

Theme: Stories from the crime beat, courts, justice issues.

Guest Profile: Victims of crime, lawyers, judges, police officers, legal experts, even criminals. Someone with a strong opinion, ability to clearly express themselves in a fast, concise way and an interesting story to tell. Want credentials for sure, and where they stand on a certain issue. The sound of voice, past interview experiences isn't something I'd concern myself with.

Guest from Hell: Someone who waffles, takes too long to get to point and makes little to no sense.

Contact: Mike.mcintyre@freepress.mb.ca; 800-665-2202; http://www.mikeoncrime.com; Mike McIntyre. Best method: E-mail is the best method, something concise and to the point is always preferred. No response? A follow-up e-mail is always a good idea.

Invited Back? Good chemistry on the air, lively, animated discussion, and an ability to get people to respond.

Bio of Mike McIntyre: An award-winning journalist, national radio show host, author, webmaster, pundit, movie consultant and cruise director, Mike loves to keep busy.

Born and bred in Winnipeg, he is, at 32, the justice reporter for the Winnipeg Free Press since 1997. He operates his own website, which is updated several times a day and features the latest in local, national and international crime and justice news along with daily jury polls, a discussion forum and breaking news mailing list.

Mike has produced and hosted his show since February 2003, and in March 2006, the show was picked up by the Corus Radio Network and launched in 12 Canadian cities.

Mike also makes regular appearances with Charles Adler on his national Corus talk radio show and is also called upon frequently by talk show hosts across the country for his insight into crime and justice news and issues.

Mike is author of three Canadian true crime books, all published by Great Plains Publications: *Nowhere to Run: The Killing of Const. Dennis Strongquill* (2003), chronicles the tragic murder of a Manitoba RCMP officer. The book is in its third printing and was a national bestseller within 15 days. Film rights have been sold to a Calgary production company, Alberta Filmworks, and a feature movie is in development. *The Yuletide Bandit: A Seven-Year Search for a Serial Criminal* (2004), chronicles one man's daring crime spree, the desperate police search to catch him and the dramatic conclusion inside a Winnipeg massage parlor. Feature film rights have been sold to a Winnipeg production company. *To the Grave: Inside a Spectacular RCMP Sting* (2006), already a national bestseller in its third printing, chronicles the mysterious disappearance of Brandon teenager Erin Chorney and the incredible RCMP operation which uncovered the shocking truth.

Born and bred in Winnipeg, Mike graduated from River East Collegiate and completed his journalistic studies in the Creative Communications program at Red River College. He and wife, Chassity, are parents of Parker, 5, and Isabella, 2.

The couple hosted the inaugural "Crime and Punishment Caribbean Cruise" in January 2006 and hosted another tropical adventure in February 2007.

Las Vegas and the Mob with Dennis N. Griffin on Blog Talk Radio http://www.blogtalkradio.com/dennisngriffin

Theme: The Las Vegas reign of Chicago Outfit enforcer Tony Spilotro.

Guest Profile: Former lawmen, entertainers, mobsters, and media who plied their trade in Vegas during the Spilotro era. A credible individual with knowledge/experience of the topic to be discussed, a reputation for truthfulness, and ability to express themselves coherently.

Guest from Hell: Someone who won't stay on point, is on an ego trip, or proves to be a liar.

Contact: griff1945@hotmail.com; 702 454-8217; http://www.dennisngriffin.com; Denny Griffin. Best method: E-mail a bio. No response? I prefer a follow-up e-mail.

Invited Back? Their ability to provide factual information the audience found highly interesting, candor, and personality.

Bio of Denny Griffin: Denny began writing in 1994, following a 20-year career in investigations and law enforcement in New York State. That same year he and his wife moved to Las Vegas, but spend the summers in upstate New York.

Denny's first book, *The Morgue* (1st Books Library 1996), is a fictionalized account of an investigation he did of a medical examiner's office run amok. The facility was involved in illegally harvesting research tissue, keeping bodies that should have been buried or cremated and falsifying records to conceal its activities. Five more mystery/thrillers followed.

In 2001, Denny turned his attention to non-fiction, the last of which was *Policing Las Vegas* (Huntington

Press 2005). His crime books focus on the Vegas reign of Chicago Outfit enforcer Tony Spilotro. This is the same time period dramatized in the 1995 movie *Casino*, in which actor Joe Pesci played a character based on Spilotro.

His most recent book, *Cullotta—The Life of a Chicago Criminal, Las Vegas Mobster, and Government Witness* (Huntington Press 2007), was co-authored with Frank Cullotta, Spilotro's former lieutenant-turned-government witness. Frank was a technical consultant to the film and appeared in several scenes as a hit man.

Disabilities

"Remember ... Whatever we do, we do it for the Kids!"—Rose Moore

Disability Beat with Vicki Niswander on WEFT 90.1FM, Champaign, IL.
Theme: Disability issues.
Guest Profile: Authors, consultants, professors, service providers, parents and people with disabilities. Knowledge or experience in an area related to disability issues — someone with a story to tell, new or unusual information. Experiences and credentials pertaining to disability issues.
Guest from Hell: Someone who prepares something to read in response to interview questions. Or someone who does not fully answer questions that are asked.
Contact: disabilitybeat@gmail.com; 217-359-9338; http://www.disabilitybeat.com; Vicki Niswander. Best method: Call with pitch, e-mail a bio or send a press kit. No response? E-mail.
Invited Back? Breadth of knowledge in areas of interest.
Bio of Vicki Niswander: Vicki is a former teacher and consultant, and also the parent of an adult daughter with a disability. She's active in a variety of advocacy organizations, chairing several committees.

Vicki is also in a leadership role, serving on the programming committee at WEFT and on a local board of education.

Making Life Easier with Shelley Peterman Schwarz on http://www.MakingLifeEasier.com
Theme: Support for people living with chronic illness, disabilities, and age-related limitations.
Guest Profile: Authors, counselors, therapists, healthcare professionals, parents, people who can share their wisdom, lessons, and strategies for living with chronic illness. I look for people who have a positive attitude, tell personal stories and use them to teach lessons for surviving chronic illness.
Guest from Hell: I talk with my guests before the interview and those that raise "red flags" would never be on my show in the first place. (i.e., negative, dogmatic, pushy, rambles, etc.).
Contact: Shelley@MakingLifeEasier.com; 608-824-0402; http://www.MakingLifeEasier.com; Shelley Peterman Schwarz. Best method: Phone is preferred but people can contact me in ways that are easy for them. Always, follow-up with a call. I want a resume or vita and the topics the guest feels comfortable discussing (parenting, working/employment, grief, relationships, etc.). I also want a list of questions the guests would like me to ask during the interview. No response? Call or e-mail.
Invited Back? I would ask a guest back if we didn't finish talking about the topic, there was more ground to cover than we had time for, or the guest had a new book or topic to discuss.
Bio of Shelley Peterman Schwarz: Shelley graduated with honors from the University of Wisconsin-Milwaukee and was a teacher of the hearing impaired in the Madison (WI) Metropolitan School District for 13 years. In 1979, she learned that she had multiple sclerosis, but continued teaching until 1981 when the effects of the illness began to restrict her mobility. Since retiring because of her disability, she has been using her professional training and personal experiences to help others cope with life's "ups and downs."

Married and the mother of two adult children, Shelley is a motivational professional speaker and award-winning writer and author. She has published more than 350 essays, how-to's, service pieces, columns, and features and currently writes for newspapers and magazines reaching a readership of nearly two million. Her *Making Life Easier* tips have appeared in numerous publications including the *Wisconsin State Journal*, *Mature Lifestyles*, *Arthritis Today*, and *Inside MS*. She appears monthly on the noon news program on the Madison, WI CBS affiliate (WISC-TV3), presenting tips and demonstrating products to make life easier. She also appeared on the Discovery Channel's popular "Home Matters" program, in a segment on home accessibility modifications.

Shelley is author of *Memory Tips for Making Life Easier* (Attainment Company 2006), *Organizing Your IEPs* (Attainment Company 2005), *Parkinson's Disease: 300 Tips for Making Life Easier* (Demos Medical Publishing 2002, 2006), *Dressing Tips and Clothing Resources for Making Life Easier* (Attainment Company 2000), *Multiple Sclerosis: 300 Tips for Making Life Easier* (Demos Medical Publishing 1999, 2006), *Blooming Where You're Planted: Stories from the Heart* (Shelley Peterman Schwarz 1998), *250 Tips for Making Life with Arthritis Easier* (Longstreet Press 1997).

Her story "Judy's Birthday" won first prize in *A Second Chicken Soup for the Woman's Soul* contest and was published in the book of the same name.

The Rose Moore Show on KLAV 1230 AM, Saturday, 4–5 PM (PT). Shows are archived at http://www.adhdservices.org, http://www.therosemooreshow.com and http://www.klav1230am.com. Guests not solicited are charged $124 for a half-hour interview.

Theme: To find, address and solve the "unmet needs" of the learning disabled in the public school system. To have professionals talk about all sorts of disabilities that the parents, teachers and school administrators must know to help our children. We have expanded our audience to include "issues of the week" concerning all problems in the 50 states concerning school district mistakes that affect the disabled child or teen and give solutions to the problems through the experts that come on the show. In this segment we monitor and hold accountable the school districts and the trustees for the errors that they make. The new facet is called The Nevada [and other states] Stakeholders Educational Monitoring and Accountability Task Force. The Task Force is to monitor the goings on of the trustees and the school district when it comes to special needs kids not getting their services. The parents call in with the problem and the task force investigates it ... especially when all of a sudden the district and trustees decide to change the policy procedures and regulations to get them out of trouble. It gives the parents an avenue to investigate problems instead of having an "internal Investigation" of which they will not get an answer due to the "Privacy Act."

Guest Profile: Authors welcome — usually the ones with the most popular books; know what they are talking about; have numerous degrees behind their name and years and years of direct interaction with schools, parents and disabled kids. We look for expertise in the areas we are discussing. Specialties are all areas of a disability and the experts include psychologists, occupational therapists, reading specialists, teachers, principals, doctors, seasoned advocates, different races, and judges. What books and articles have they written? We ask for 15 questions from the person to be interviewed with their comments on each question and then I design the show around that so we can pull out of this person the pertinent information needed for the listeners to be informed. We also have an hour interview with the person on the phone as well before we commit to having them on the air. Anyone with a special event concerning any disability that would like us to "pre-record" to put on our show and our website, please call and discuss the cost at 866-361-2343 (toll Free) or 702-492-2343 PST.

Guest from Hell: I have no guests from Hell due to the fact that I am able to confront the guest when what they are saying is wrong. No holds barred when it comes to wrong information to the parents — I don't put up with wrong and inaccurate information. I keep them on the show and keep at them until they finally admit they are wrong.

Contact: therosemooreshow@hotmail.com; http://www.therosemooreshow.com; www.adhdservices.org; Rose Moore. Best method: Write to therosemooreshow@hotmail.com with their press kit (and picture) and what they feel is necessary for parents to know right away. This is a timely show on issues of the week concerning special education, including the law. We are willing to put people on that are "controversial" as well so we can get to the bottom of what they are talking about or pushing in their books and articles. No response? They should e-mail me right away. We always make sure we answer them immediately because we do not like to leave people hanging.

Invited Back? If we have not exhausted the topic we have them on again.

Guest Comment: "I had a great time on her show ... talking about a very serious issue."—Shirley Cheng, a blind and physically disabled poet and author of *Daring Quests of Mystics* (Lulu Press 2005), an autobiography, *The Revelation of a Star's Endless Shine: A Young Woman's Autobiography of a 20-Year Tale of Trials and Tribulations* (Lulu Press 2005), and *Dance with Your Heart: Tales and Poems That the Heart Tells* (Lulu Press 2004), http://www.shirleycheng.com

Bio of Rose Moore: Rose is a "Senior Master Level" Professional Disability Advocate working for the rights of all our disabled kids in grades K–12 in the public school system for over 24 years, making sure all public schools provide the services needed for our disabled kids mandated by law.

Her many accomplishments include a Governors Award for "Most Innovative Project concerning ADHD," a personal invitation from the White House to attend and speak at the White House Conference on School Safety, and co-founder and CEO of The National Association of Professional Child and Family Advocates. Rose is author of *Fundamentals of Special Education (K–12)* (an on-line class book through Seattle Pacific University) for teachers and administrators who want to become highly qualified — 5 credits.

She is also a Truancy Specialist, working with judges, attorney and parents in Truancy Court Matters and appearing in court on behalf of the child and parents.

The Yvonne Pierre Show on HYH Radio and Blog Talk Radio.

Theme: To empower parents with special needs children and women (in general).

Guest Profile: Authors, physiologists, motivational speakers, therapists, business owners, nonprofit, advocates, activists for women and/or the special needs community, and ordinary people. What we look for depends on the topic. If we are working on a show about Down syndrome, we see if the guest is creditable, informative, talkative, has passion for the topic, and has past interview experience. If we have an inspirational show with a parent of a special needs child, the most important thing is that the guest is not shy.

Guest from Hell: Ideal guests from hell would be someone who is unprepared to answer questions, lack of knowledge about the topic, no personality, fake, or rude.

Contact: YPierre@Zyonair.com; 404.246.2129; http://www.HYHRadio.com; http://www.myspace.com/hyhonline; Yvonne Pierre. Best method: E-mail. The best approach is to go to the website and click on the "Suggest a Guest" button or a direct e-mail that consists of a brief bio, contact information, website, and suggestive topic. A press kit would be ideal. No response? If we are interested in the guest being on the show usually we contact the guest within 48 hours. Resend the information within a week, just in case we did not receive it.

Invited Back? Guests are welcome back if they have a wealth of information and tips to share with the listeners, speak with passion, and a great dialogue with the host.

Bio of Yvonne Pierre: Yvonne is a mom with two boys ages 15 and 6 and lives in the Metro Atlanta area. Her youngest son was diagnosed with Down syndrome after birth. For the past few years she has been devoted to spreading special needs awareness and is passionate about helping others find their passion and peace. Yvonne is a member of the Down syndrome Association of Atlanta, Grassroots Advocacy group, and the Atlanta Press Club.

Yvonne is a survivor of two date rapes, molestation, overcoming the challenge of illiteracy, has overcome battles with weight, self-confidence, and homelessness, just to name a few obstacles. She is very passionate about motivating others. She decided to combine her two passions to uplift and inform.

Yvonne is the founder of HYH Online (www.hyhonline.com), HYH Radio (www.hyhradio.com), Zyonair's Unlimited LLC (www.zyonair.com), and Zyonair's Media Corporation. She is the writer, producer, director for the film *Chosen* (www.chosenthemovie.com) in development.

She received her dual associates degree in business and accounting in 1995 and is currently working towards her MBA.

Entertainment

"A lot of people want to know how to get a job talking about movies and television shows, as it just sounds like a dream vocation. Well, it is! It generally doesn't happen overnight." — Rick Forchuk, host of *Rick's Picks*

Barry Reisman Show on WNWR AM 1540, Philadelphia, Pa., broadcast weekdays, 9–10 AM and Sundays, 4–4:30 PM and on http://www.wnwr.com

Theme: Klezmer and other Jewish music plus some interviews.

Guest Profile: Entertainment celebrities, some authors. Someone who fits in with the Jewish entertainment format of the program. I want to know what they can add to my program and how they fit in with the format.

Guest from Hell: Someone who can't hold up their end of the conversation.

Contact: Radiobarry@aol.com; 888-228-5550; http://wnwr.com; Barry Reisman. Best method: A brief e-mail. No response? E-mail or call.

Invited Back? How well they do the first time.

Bio of Barry Reisman: Barry began his radio career in 1962 at WRNJ-FM, a "beautiful music" station in Atlantic City.

From 1963 to 1999, he would move from one station to another as stations were sold or changed format: WSLT in Ocean City, N.J., WMID in Atlantic City, WTEL, WQAL, and WIBF in Philadelphia, and WSSJ in Camden, N.J.

Celebrity Stars with Mike Kurban on All Talk Radio, http://www.alltalkradio.com

Theme: Celebrities.

Guest Profile: Celebrities, authors, health, and spiritual topics. We look for talent and experience and want to know if they have a website or MySpace.

All testimonials and pictures of guests are in Mike's museum in Las Vegas in the Celebrity room. Signed autographs by authors, pictures of celebrities signed by them as well as letters by many others saying how they had fun on the show. To see this rare museum that has had many write ups from top newspapers contact Mike by phone.

Guest from Hell: Don't have any problems for each guest has experience and is glad to be on the program.

Contact: thirdeyemike@cox.net; 702-457-1377; http://www.relationshipfever.com; Mike Kurban. Best method: Phone. Call me direct and tell me what you have and let me know the website. No response? They should call me for I return everyone's phone calls. E-mails can be deleted by mistake.

Invited Back? If they are considerate and know when to shut up when a commercial is about to be aired.

Bio of Mike Kurban: Mike is a nationally recognized speaker on relationships between men and women with more than 30 years experience as a consultant who reaches thousands of people each year with his proven seminars. Mike is one of America's foremost speakers on relationships and metaphysics, having authored more than 40 books on these topics. Mike is deeply committed to helping those who seek the perfect soul mate.

To read more about Mike, go to www.alltalkradio.net, scroll down to Celebrity News and hit the archives.

Dr. Blogstein's Radio Happy Hour on BlogTalk Radio.

Theme: Interview/comedy.

Guest Profile: Anyone (author, musician, newsmaker, politician, athlete, celebrity, internet celeb) with an interesting story to tell, controversial, humorous, quick wit, well spoken, engaging conversationalist. Credentials, back story.

Guest from Hell: One without a sense of humor. We do serious long form interviews but with sarcasm, comedy and witty jokes.

Contact: DrBlogstein@gmail.com; 201-683-6224; http://www.DrBlogstein.com; David "Dr. Blogstein" Brown. Best method: E-mail is always my favorite. No response? E-mail me again b/c chances are I missed the first e-mail. I always respond.

Invited Back? If they jive well with us and have something further to discuss.

Bio of Dr. Blogstein: Dr. Blogstein was born in Brooklyn, New York, and now lives in Hoboken, New Jersey — the birthplace of two of his passions: baseball and Frank Sinatra. If he were to relive anyone's life, Dr. Blogstein has always said he'd like to live in Old Blue Eyes' shoes.

In his spare time, Dr. B enjoys rooting for the New York Mets, watching quality TV such as "24" and "Lost," and reading good magazine articles. He is single and willing to sleep with any attractive female groupie.

DRC-FM Morning Show with Jerry Kristafer, Monday–Friday, 5–9 AM (ET) on WDRC-FM, Hartford, CT, airing in the entire state, southern MA and Long Island.

Theme: Hits of the 60s and 70s — topical issues.

Guest Profile: Lifestyle authors, celebs who are entertaining and topical. Since we're a music station, they have to sound entertaining and get to the point quickly. We don't have a lot of time. They should also have some street cred. Notable guests have included Conn. Sen. Joe Leiberman and Conn Gov. Jodi Rell.

Guest from Hell: Policy wonks. Enough of those to go around.

Contact: jerry.drcfm.com; 860-655-5464 (c) 860-243-1115 (station); http://www.drcfm.com; Jerry Kristafer. Best method: E-mail for most, phone for celeb/time sensitive. E-mail press release, send press kit, call after those are done if you want to be persistent. If we can't use it, there are other hosts in the building who might be interested. No response? Do what I do. E-mail again. Leave a message. We get a lot of e-mails so persistence is a virtue

Invited Back? Are they entertaining? Interesting? Shocking? Funny? Relevant to 30 Plus demo?

Bios of Marianne O'Hare (former cohost) and Jerry Kristafer: Between the two of them, the duo has a combined 70 years in radio. Marianne grew up in Rochester, NY, surrounded by five siblings and a variety of pets. During high school, she engaged in sports, sang with the chorus, performed in school plays and interned at the local rock station. She graduated Syracuse University with a degree in broadcast journalism but took leave after her sophomore year to work at the UN in New York City, dreaming of becoming a foreign correspondent.

But her appetite for live radio was ignited when she returned to Syracuse to finish school and work at a local station in Rochester. She began stringing regularly for ABC Radio Network and when a job opened in Hartford at one of the rock stations, she decided to take it to get closer to New York.

After marrying and giving birth to a daughter, she settled in Connecticut. She moved from station-to-station, and then her dream job showed up. Connecticut Radio Network offered a gig covering the arts throughout Connecticut and the region. It was something she could do while home with a newborn, and it opened up such an unexpected world of wonder. Connecticut is so rich in the Arts, she was constantly going to theatre openings, rock shows, art openings, and special events. It was like getting paid to have fun. That wonderful gig lasted 14 years. And, during that time she also began doing voice-overs for commercials in Connecticut and in New York. Things were good.

But like the commercial says, life comes at you fast. The SAG strike in New York brought voice-overs to a standstill. 9/11 happened. And changes in her personal life brought many of the good things to an end. During that time, she worked for *Hartford Magazine*, ARTfx Signs, and then Robertson Productions which does national media tours for authors. That brought her back to the world of radio as part of the DRC-FM Morning Show.

Jerry's 40 year radio career began at the age of 14 in South Jersey, where grew up on a farm in "Pig's Eye." After a year of college he hit the road, working at radio stations in Atlantic City, Indianapolis, and Pittsburgh (twice). In 1977 Jerry moved to Connecticut, spending four years on-the-air in New Haven.

In 1981 he was offered a job at "another" station in Hartford. Then exactly one year later, Jerry became the morning show host on WDRC-FM, a position he held for more than 15 years (including a number of years as the program director of both WDRC-AM and FM). In late 1997, he "left" the station (that's radio speak for "fired") and following an extended "vacation," was hired as morning show host and program director at a news/talk radio station in New Haven. Fast forward to January 2008, when 10 years after "leaving," Jerry accepted an offer to return to host the *DRC-FM Morning Show*.

He has two sons and three grandchildren.

In his spare time — what spare time?!

Entertainment and the Arts with Brenda Martin and John DiSanza on WTAN, AM 1340, AM 1350 and AM 1400, Clearwater, FL on Sundays, 7–8 PM (ET).

Theme: Promote relatively unsung heroes of the arts.

Guest Profile: Authors/playwrights/actors/musicians/artists, etc. Interesting conversationalist involved in arts. Credentials and subject matter most important.

Guest from Hell: Unenthusiastic — gives one word answers.

Contact: brenmar@entertainmentandthearts.com; http://www.entertainmentandthearts.com; http://www.tantalk1340.com; 727-239-6711; Brenda Martin. Best method: E-mail a pitch with related press info. No response? E-mail.

Invited Back? Fun to talk with — interesting topic.

Guest Comments: "You have the wonderful knack of making people feel comfortable and important while talking with you. And I really appreciate all the nice things you said about my books." — Betty Jo Tucker, editor and lead film critic for ReelTalkReviews.com and author of *Confessions of a Movie Addict* (Hats Off Books 2001), and *Susan Sarandon: A True Maverick* (Hats Off Books 2004). http://authorsden.com/bettyjotucker. See Betty Jo's show on page 73.

Bio of Brenda Martin: Brenda was born, raised and attended college in the cold, windy and snowy Midwest. She hated cold weather and, by age three, was already complaining to her parents: "my hair is cold." Her dream of living in a warmer climate finally became a reality when she and her husband, Mike, relocated to Tampa in 1989.

An actress who had also previously served as publicity rep for a local community theatre, Brenda was well aware of the difficulty creative artists had in gaining media exposure and in 2003, she and two fellow actors, Rich Aront and Ginny Fraebel, began producing and co-hosting their radio show to promote the many unsung heroes who are making a significant contribution to the arts. Brenda loves interviewing interesting guests, acting, writing and generally indulging her creative side.

Brenda's first children's book is *Freddie, Hector and Tish: The Treasure-Hunt Fish* (PublishAmerica 2008). www.brenmarcommunications.com/books.htm

Bio of John DiSanza: John is an actor, artist, author and veteran. A native New Yorker and a true renaissance man, John, his wife Susan, and their children, have lived in the Tampa Bay area since 1979.

John became a self-taught visual artist, in response to the incomprehensible destruction and chaos in his home town on September 11, 2001, and his art is featured in exhibitions all over Florida. In addition to his artistic accomplishments, John was awarded a Purple Heart while serving in Vietnam. His first book is *Johnnie Saigon No Band Played* (PublishAmerica 2007). http://www.livedart.com.

Everyday People's Entertainment Guide with Reggie McDaniel on WIXY radio in Champagne, Illinois, KLZ, 103.5 The Fox, and KTRS 550AM (St. Louis, Missouri).

Theme: Entertainment.

Guest Profile: Actors, directors, CIA agents, FBI informants, etc. Guests with entertainment value. Like to know their history.

Guest from Hell: One word answers.

Contact: rocknreggie@msn.com; 303-522-1603; http://www.reggiemcdaniel.com; Reggie. Best method: E-mail or phone. No response? E-mail or phone.

Invited Back? If I can get them again.

Bio of Reggie McDaniel: A retired Army sergeant from St. Louis, MO, Reggie never would have thought he would be on the radio. Then one day he called in to discuss unusual foods and good movies, and the rest is history.

A Fistful of Quarters (now ***Custom Made***) on WQSU Tuesday, 4–6 PM (ET) with Steve Urena and James McKay.

Theme: Entertainment talk show.

Guest Profile: Comedians, wrestlers, musicians, unusual walks of life. They have to be interesting, have some sort of notoriety and have entertaining stories to tell. I want to know about their past history and how they made their success, future exploits, and where can we see them next.

Guest from Hell: Somebody who is not into the show and is out for themselves and puts down the hosts.

Contact: Surena6189@msn.com; 973-580-7421; www.susqu.edu/wqsu-fm; Steve Urena. Best method: E-mailing me a press kit or a bio. No response? Call.

Invited Back? If they provide entertaining stories and crowd interest.

Bio of Steve Urena: An 18 year old student attending Susquehanna University, Steve has been interviewing people since he was 15.

Gary B. Duglin Talks with the Stars, nationally syndicated.

Theme: The show highlights some of the entertainment industry's biggest and brightest stars. I'm proud to say that the show has been called the best in celebrity conversation. I do not delve into any personal moments of the performer's private life, unless it is a topic that the star wants to discuss. Each hour of broadcast programming features a spectacular discussion with a celebrity from the world of motion pictures, television, music or theatre.

Guest Profile: The show focuses on the most recognized and respected names in show business, plus the most promising, up and coming stars. Gary then celebrates the lives and careers of those stars without any gossip or controversy. That is his pledge to each celebrity. I do a tremendous amount of research; so as my guests and I walk down memory lane together they are pleasantly surprised that I know so much about them. But since I never embarrass or offend anyone, they are glad to share their life experiences with me. It's all about having fun with the stars so that they are entirely comfortable while talking with me and so they will be pleased and happy afterwards. The stars trust me and I've never given any one of them a reason not to trust me. I am very proud of that fact. My show is designed to salute and pay tribute to the stars and that's what I do.

Guest from Hell: I'm delighted to say that I've never had a bad guest. My guests have all been wonderful. I begin each show with a special introduction to pay tribute to my guest and always end each program with a special thank you to the star. My words of praise have become somewhat of a trademark for me and are widely received by the stars and by the listeners.

Contact: PlanetRadio@Duglin.com; Withheld upon request; http://www.Duglin.com; Gary B. Duglin. Best method: Publicists, managers and other representatives, plus the stars themselves, are always welcome to contact me directly with a request. It is my great pleasure to hear from them. No response? All performers' e-mails (or those of their representatives) are answered in a timely fashion.

Invited Back? It's not a matter of inviting a star back. The show is a one-time celebration of each star's life and career who appears on the show. In recent years, I generally spend between three and four hours or more with each performer.

Guest Comments: "First of all, I will say to you what people sometimes say to me. Oh my God, have you done your homework. I salute you. I tip my cap to you. This is the best interview I've ever had. It was wonderful. It was remarkable. Just remarkable."—James Lipton, award-winning host of television's "Inside the Actors Studio." (Gary's show has been compared to that TV show.)

"Gary, I appreciate your affection. You're too good to me. My dear friend, it's been a great few hours with you. I've had a wonderful time. I embrace you and wish you good luck."—Tony Curtis, Academy Award nominated actor

Bio of Gary B. Duglin: Throughout his extensive broadcasting and entertainment career, the award-winning Gary B. Duglin has been involved with almost every facet of the world of radio including on-the-air programming, creative development, executive producing, station management, sales and operations. He has created and produced many radio programs including game shows and other original radio concepts in the talk format.

As a talk show host, news anchor and correspondent, Gary has been congratulated and applauded for broadcast conversations with a galaxy of show business stars and government luminaries. He has interviewed countless dignitaries and news makers throughout the entertainment world and the political arena.

Outside the walls of the radio studio, Gary's voice has been heard in scores of national television and radio commercials, motion pictures, and documentary presentations.

Gary is no stranger to personal appearances either; his include fund raising events for the President's Council on Physical Fitness and others. He also performed a live narration of Aaron Copland's *The Lincoln Portrait* to a standing ovation audience at Lincoln Center in New York City.

Gary made his mark in television as a writer for syndicated game shows hosted by Bob Eubanks of *The Newlywed Game* and *Card Sharks* fame, and Tom Kennedy from *Password Plus*, *Name That Tune*, *Split Second* and *You Don't Say*.

Gary has also contributed to the producing of a variety of network television series and specials, working with such celebrities as Dick Clark, Billy Crystal, Helen Hayes, Bob Hope, Ron Howard, Barry Manilow, Tony Randall and Betty White, among hundreds of others.

Holder Tonight with Peter Anthony Holder on CJAD 800 AM, Montreal, Canada.

Theme: Fun, little politics, mostly pop culture.

Guest Profile: Authors, professionals, celebrities. Just someone who is passionate about their topic or area of expertise. A sense of humor doesn't hurt either. If it's a professional then credentials are important. If they have a thick accent I would need to know. Lots of interview experience is not vital.

Guest from Hell: Can't expand on their thoughts.

Contact: peter@peteranthonyholder.com; 514-989-3834; http://www.peteranthonyholder.com; Peter Anthony Holder. Best method: E-mailing a press kit, but phone is fine. No response? They should e-mail me again.

Invited Back? How much fun they were. Do they engage in conversation as opposed to just answering questions?

Guest Comment: "Long-time radio personality Holder is a pleasure to work with ... and asks intelligent questions. He has interviewed a lot of very well-known guests—but he's also very open to non-famous authors."—Shel Horowitz, whose two latest books are *Grassroots Marketing for Authors and Publishers* (Infinity Publishing 2007) and *Grassroots Marketing—Getting Noticed in a Noisy World* (Chelsea Green Publishing Company 2000).

Bio of Peter Anthony Holder: Peter has vast experience in both television and radio, beginning in 1979 when he was a morning show producer. Since then, he's been a TV series writer and researcher, on-camera TV host, street reporter, announcer and freelance writer.

As for his radio show, Peter has been on-camera television host of "Soul Call" on CH since 2000. He also does freelance voice work on commercials and media visuals and also voice work dubbing for animated and live action films and television shows.

The Indie Music Showcase with Jeffrey S. Monks and Dean Graveel on The Monks Media Radio Network, http://www.monksmedia.com. Archives of all shows are at http://www.monksmedia.com/indie.php

Theme: Exposing independent music artists.

Guest Profile: Indie artists and music industry guests. Independent musicians with talent looking to expand their exposure. Important to us is their musical talent, biography, background and their goals in the music industry. We especially like the opportunity to get to know them personally rather than just listen to music. This is more of an intimate dialogue into their person along with exposing the listeners to their art. The listeners are also allowed to dialogue with the guests presenting a unique opportunity to really get to know these artists.

Guest from Hell: A guest with no real musical talent who is unable to speak well, carry on a conversation or express themselves in an intelligent manner. (We usually eliminate this via submissions review and pre booking conversations.)

Contact: jeff@monksmedia.com; 317-565-1416; http://www.monksmedia.com; Jeffrey S. Monks. Best method: E-mail. Submit biography, contact information and hard copy (CD) of their music. Send to: Indie Music Showcase, Attention Jeff Monks, 5751 Bruce Blvd., Noblesville, IN 46062. No response? E-mail or call.

Invited Back? Listener response and host's fondness of their appearance.

Bio of Jeff Monks: When Jeff decided to enter the world of internet radio broadcasting, he was well aware of the fact that many individuals claim to also be in the Internet radio business. His goal in forming the Monks Media Radio Network was to offer superior sound quality, programming, news and local event coverage. Many other groups, while they claim to also be an Internet radio broadcaster are small organizations, with little to no investment, programming and no operating expense. "Be assured that at the Monks Media Radio Network, our goal is quality first!" says Jeff.

Since January 10, 2005, 10 hours of daily programming have been added, a brand new easy to navigate website was launched, the broadcast schedule of sporting events and racing industry broadcasts was increased and a new interview program, *Mary's Menagerie* was added and attracted record numbers of regular listeners as a result. "I have listened to several Internet radio broadcasts from around the country who offer what appears to be similar programming to ours," says Jeff. "I maintain that NOBODY provides more content of meaning to the listeners than the Monks Media Radio Network, and none of these have invested in the ability to provide more than 20 simultaneous broadcasts, from anywhere to everywhere."

Jay Grayce Variety Show with Jay Grayce on TribecaRdaio.Net (now NY Talk Radio, http://www.nytalkradio.net), airing Monday at noon (ET). Jay is also co-host of the Rape Declaration Forum on WBAI 99.5 FM in New York City.

Theme: Variety.

Guest Profile: Musical guests, authors and inspiring guests. What I look in a guest is that they are talented and informed on what expertise they are going to share with my audience. What I look for in a guest is their bio, samples of their work and the ability to hold a conversation.

Guest from Hell: A guest from hell is one that gives me one word answers.

Contact: bmgjaygrayce@aol.com; 347-860-4617; http://www.myspace.com/jgrayce; http://www.jaygrayce.com; Jay Grayce. Best method: Phone. Potential guests should send an e-mail with their biography and sample of their work. No response? If I am not able to get in touch in a timely manner I suggest to e-mail again.

Invited Back? What determines me asking a guest back is if they were entertaining and or informative; also that my audience request them back.

Listener Comments: "I have listened to your show several times and find it enjoyable. What I like is that every show is different. But always filled with laughter, good music and inspiring information. Now how come most people don't know about your entertaining show? TibecaRadio.Net has great programming and YOU Jay Grayce have a gift."—Sandra

"Wow What a Fun and Interesting Show. I like the radio theater feel to it." GOOD STUFF—Larry

Bio of Jay Grayce: A native New Yorker, Jay has been a crisis counselor, advisor, teacher, published poet and author, dancer, back-up singer, artist, motivational workshop speaker and entrepreneur for well over 15 years.

She is a board member for NPO's on Women Rights, Media, Hospice and Animal Care, and has actively participated in the NYC Alliance Against Sexual Assault "SAY SO" Campaign, and has been featured in such periodicals as *Entrepreneur, Start Up* and *Life @Work*. She has also been featured on several television and radio shows.

Jay is soon to be author of *Thank God I Was Raped* which is from the Thank God I Book Series.

The Jiggy Jaguar Show with James "Jiggy Jaguar" Lowe on KJAG, an Internet station that is syndicated and podcast.

Theme: Multi-themed.

Guest Profile: Anyone with an interesting story to tell ... authors, athletes, odd guests (adult film, web celebrities, etc.). I look for something I may be interested in — for instance when I had John McCarthy from the Ultimate Fighting Championship on the program. I was interested in talking with a guy I had followed since UFC started. However, in another case, I had on Gia Darling and she is the most downloaded transsexual on the web. I figured that would be great shock to our regular listeners but also educate the new listeners to have the guest be more human than a freak show. I need in cases of bands, press kit and cd

70 Entertainment

or mp3 of their music. In authors' cases, a copy of the book. I hate going into a interview cold (not prepared) or going into it with little to work with.

Guest from Hell: The idea of a guest from hell would be a guest I have booked for 15–30 minutes and I cannot keep the interview going and they cannot keep it going for 10 minutes. I used to run into this with many unsigned artists. They just had not done much, so 15 was reaching at best.

Contact: kjagradio@kjagradio.com; 620-402-0878, 785-201-1055; www.jiggyjaguar.com; James Lowe. Best method: E-mail or phone. Call with a pitch, e-mail a bio and/or send a press kit. All of those work ... I get press releases and the pitch is so good I am nailed then. If a band sends me a cd and I like the cover or a song title, I am hooked. The ones that call the show ... they picked me — not just sending out millions of e-mails hoping for one or more returns. It shows they know the show and know what we are doing and are not turned off by one or two things we have done. It also shows they are in on the joke. We definitely are not what we seem on paper. No response? I try to respond ASAP ... however, if they cannot get me on e-mail, call me and hunt me down. Come on, with one TV program ... managing an online magazine ... one monthly radio show and one weekly radio show and a daily air shift on a local rock station, plus sleep, occasionally something slips through the cracks.

Invited Back? The key things for a guest to come back... First, did I or they have fun? For instance when I had Skip Hall (the oldest active mixed martial arts fighter) on the program. We had a blast talking and both hated to end the segment. Second key factor is something to push, for instance, if I have on an unsigned band and they never put out another cd but we had fun; what do we push when they come back on the program? Finally, questions. Did I get all of them asked the first time out or did afterward it generate more. I have talked to Veronica Monet (sex educator) and never will find out enough or have no need for further questions because her knowledge on everything is so deep.

Guest Comments: "Jiggy Jag gave us our first interview and he knew we had something because we were on his show. We now have a HUGE following." — Dirt, local heavy metal band

"Jiggy Jag is so untouchable on radio. It's like he is part of a radio mafia." — Christopher Schroeder, local artist

Bio of James "Jiggy Jaguar" Lowe: James grew up listening to radio and heard everyone from the local circus clown DJ's to the national talkshow hosts. He did much like everyone who starts radio — a "mock" show on a tape recorder, then eventually working in mainstream radio with a pop station. Got railroaded and ended up on Internet radio. With hard work and making the right connections and doing all he could to fight and scrap it back up the ladder, he became #1 rated Internet talk on several sites and eventually met different people in and out of the broadcast field. James ended up doing an internship and got a break on a local station plus did some community TV.

Jim Cates Show on www.cjonline.com/jimcates weekdays, 8–10 AM (CT).

Theme: General talk.

Guest Profile: Baby boomer topics. Majority of shows centered around baby boomer audience. Credentials important.

Guest from Hell: Someone coming on the show with no intention of having a conversation, just there to sell their book, product, etc.

Contact: jim.cates@cjonline.com; 785-295-1193; www.cjonline.com; Jim Cates. Best method: Snail mail or e-mail. No response? If I haven't responded the guest is not a good fit.

Invited Back? Feedback from listeners.

Bio of Jim Cates: Jim is a former Kansas State senator and Kansas state representative, who chaired the Kansas Lottery for four years. He served as the Kansas national term limits chairman for two years.

He's been a talk show host in Topeka, Kansas, for a decade.

The Jordan Rich Show on WBZ News Radio 1030, Boston, covering all of New England and 38 states in the late night hours.

Theme: Inspiration, education and entertainment with a positive spin, upbeat conversation deep into the night.

Guest profile: Authors including novelists, medical pros, pop culture icons, actors, musicians, comedians, local newsmakers. When it comes to guests, I'm always welcoming folks with fresh perspectives, lively personalities and credible portfolios. I investigate guests and their topics thoroughly. A well-written bio suffices. I do not need to hear previous interviews or pre-screen the guest. A spontaneous conversation is desirable.

Guest from Hell: A guest from hell? Of course, there's the grunter who answers in one or two word spurts, and the guest who finds it a chore to be up late on one of the most popular stations in the northeast. Energy is critical. Please be happy to be here.

Contact: radiospots@aol.com; 617-542-8251; http://www.jordanrich.com; Jordan Rich; Best method: E-mail is great, a press kit if one is available, and a copy of the author's book to me if that's the guest's reason for coming on the show. No response? E-mailing initially is wonderful. I don't mind a follow-up phone call. I try to get back to all requests, but it is sometimes difficult, so a second e-mail or call is fine. Please know to whom you are pitching — spell the name right, get the call letters right and know going in that it's a late night show. When someone begs to be on then balks at staying up late, I generally say thanks but there are others who will gladly take their place.

Invited Back? Guests who offer info on general

human interest topics and who sparkle with energy and enthusiasm are often invited back — mechanics, physicians, mediums, grammarians, storytellers, etc.

Guest Comments: "You are a total class act. Thank you so much for the wonderful interview." — Barbara Delinsky (best selling novelist)

"It was a pleasure. Thanks for a great interview. It is always a joy talking about my work with someone who has read it and prepared so well." — Gay Talese (celebrated author)

Bio of Jordan Rich: Jordan was born and raised in Boston and has been a fixture on radio and TV for nearly 30 years. A communications major at Curry College in Milton, he began his career at age 18 at WRKO in Boston. From 1978 to 1982, he worked as weather reporter, morning show sidekick and was eventually promoted to morning co-host. One of his favorite on-air assignments was hosting a Broadway music show called *Music Sunday* for a few years.

In 1982, Jordan signed on with WLLH-AM as a talk-show host and handled the weekend music shift at WSSH-FM. From 1983 to 1995, he was WSSH morning host. In 1996, Jordan signed on with WBZ News Radio 1030 as a fill-in talk host and eventually succeeded his longtime friend and mentor, the late Norm Nathan. Since then, Jordan has hosted the weekend late nights at WBZ, where he loves connecting with his listeners and callers from around the nation. Jordan's approach is simple — to be positive and supportive adding a gentle dose of humor and fun throughout the night.

He maintains a full schedule running his audio production and marketing firm Chart Productions.

Jordan and his wife, Wendy, have two children, Lindsay and Andrew.

Judy Carmichael's Jazz Inspired on Sirius Satellite and broadcast on over 170 stations throughout North America and abroad and on NPR's Sirius Satellite channel 134.

Theme: Jazz pianist Judy Carmichael talks with guests from her viewpoint as an artist about their creative process and how jazz inspires them.

Guest Profile: Professionally creative people from actors (Robert Redford, Blythe Danner) to writers (E.L. Doctorow) to architects (Frank Gehry) to astrophysicists (Neal deGrasse Tyson) and everything in between. One who's highly accomplished and interested in inspiring others and educating them on the joys of a creative life. The show is NOT about promoting the guest or their work, but rather understanding their talent, drive and art so that others can better appreciate it. By focusing on the guests' love of jazz, the listener gains new understanding to the music and a unique insight to the guests' work. I want people who are highly accomplished and serious about their work and either so celebrated that they don't need press but love the opportunity to discuss ideas, or not celebrated at all, but should be, and are thrilled to be given an arena to discuss their work and the meaning of inspiration.

Guest from Hell: One who is completely self-absorbed.

Contact: judy@judycarmichael.com; 631-725-2531; http://www.jazzinspired.com; Judy Carmichael. Best method: Sending press kit and sample of work. No response? E-mail me again in a month.

Invited Back? It would be many years before someone would be invited back. It hasn't happened yet.

Guest Comments: "*Judy Carmichael's Jazz Inspired* is an hour of intelligent, entertaining radio. Judy's warmth and humor engages her guests in fascinating, unexpected conversations and takes them places that seldom go in other interviews. I highly recommend *Judy Carmichael's Jazz Inspired* for a fascinating look at the creative process and jazz." — Tim Owens, Peabody Award Winning producer of National Public Radio's Jazz Profiles, http://www.npr.org/programs/jazzprofiles/about/owens.html

"I finally got around to hearing our entire interview on Jazz and Astrophysics. I think it is one of my best ever — magnified and strengthened by our on-air chemistry. Thank you again for your interest and your enthusiasm for what I do." — Neil deGrasse Tyson, astrophysicist, director of the Rose Center for Earth and Space at the Hayden Planetarium in NYC, http://research.amnh.org/~tyson/

Bio of Judy Carmichael: A Grammy nominated pianist, Judy is one of the world's leading interpreters of stride piano and swing. Count Basie nicknamed her "Stride," acknowledging the command with which she plays this technically and physically demanding jazz piano style. Another early fan, Sarah Vaughan, encouraged her to record her first ensemble album, which she did with members of the Basie band.

A native of California, Judy moved to New York in the early 80's and has maintained a busy concert schedule throughout the world ever since. She has toured for the United States Information Agency throughout India, Portugal, Brazil and Singapore. In 1992 she was the first jazz musician sponsored by the United States Government to tour China.

The musician that critics have referred to as "astounding, flawless and captivating" (*The New York Times*) has played in a variety of venues from Carnegie Hall with Skitch Henderson and the New York Pops, to the Peggy Guggenheim Museum in Venice (the first concert ever presented by the museum) to programs with Joel Grey, Michael Feinstein, Steve Ross and the Smothers Brothers. She has also done comic skits and performed her music on radio and TV. A favorite with fellow artists, Judy has done concerts for both Robert Redford and Rod Stewart.

Judy is one of a handful of musicians who approach jazz from a perspective of its entire history. Choosing to study jazz piano from its early roots on, she explores the music deeply, infusing it with a "fresh, dynamic interpretation of her own" (*Washington Post*). The National Endowment for the Arts rewarded Carmichael's knowledge of jazz piano with a major grant to present early jazz greats on film and to discuss the history and development of jazz piano with college students across the country.

Judy's Grammy-nominated recording "Two Handed Stride" teamed her with four giants of jazz from the Count Basie Orchestra. She has written two books on stride piano and numerous articles on the subject of jazz.

She has appeared frequently on Garrison Keillor's *A Prairie Home Companion,* and has been featured on National Public Radio's *Morning Edition, Entertainment Tonight* and CBS' *Sunday Morning* with Charles Kuralt and recently with Charles Osgood. Her recordings and music books are available at all major record stores, or by mail order through C&D Productions, P.O. Box 360 Sag Harbor, New York, 11963, 631-725-3603 and http://www.judycarmichael.com

The Kathleen Show with Kathleen Slattery-Moschkau, Sunday at 10 AM (ET) on 1670 AM The Pulse, WTDY, Madison, WI and Saturday at 2 PM (ET) on DC 700 am, Washington Business Radio, Washington, DC.

Theme: Life, health and entertainment.

Guest Profile: Authors, health professionals, filmmakers with credibility and a great presence — but also everyday folks with experiences that we can relate to, such as Chris Erickson, who did a segment on being a Lyme disease survivor. People who overcome adversity, and folks who achieve success. Kathleen also has financial experts on (David Bach, Dave Ramsey), life coaches — Martha Beck, fitness experts — Gunnar Peterson, and motivational speakers like Dan Clark. Want to know their past interview experiences, credentials, sound of their voice and potential topics.

Kathleen has many interests, as you will see from her guest page: http://www.thekathleenshow.com

Guest from Hell: Pompous, doesn't wrap it up or get to the point.

Contact: kslatts@mo-info.com; 608-441-5310; http://www.thekathleenshow.com; Kathleen Slattery-Moschkau or Karen Felber. Best method: Call with a pitch, e-mail a bio and send a press kit. No response? They should call or e-mail again.

Invited Back? If they connect with the host and the audience, and good timing of books, etc.

Bio of Kathleen Slattery-Moschkau: Kathleen is a mom, wife and former drug pusher (legally) turned filmmaker, whose road to the microphone was anything but a straight path.

Growing up in Ladysmith, Wisconsin, she was a collegiate racquetball player, who graduated with a political science degree from the University of Wisconsin and spent a decade working for the pharmaceutical industry as a drug sales representative. During this time, she documented both amusing and frightening incidents about the marketing tactics of Big Pharma. In an effort to raise public awareness, Kathleen wrote a screenplay based on these experiences and left her career in the pharmaceutical industry.

When her LA agent wanted her to dumb down the script into a generic Hollywood story to make it more appealing to the studios, Kathleen decided to take a leap of faith and make the film herself. She raised the funding within a month, cast Katherine Heigl (*Grey's Anatomy*) as the lead, and filmed in less than 16 days in and around Madison, Wisconsin. The independent feature film *Side Effects* was Kathleen's debut as a director and opened to unprecedented international press attention.

This was followed by her documentary *Money Talks: Profits Before Patient Safety*. Seen by the media as an expert in her field, Kathleen's credentials include interviews featured in *The New York Times, USA Today, CNN, The Economist, Atlantic Monthly, British Medical Journal, The Lancet* and *Financial Times,* as well as in The Associated Press, NPR and many other media outlets worldwide. Known for her warmth, humor and down-to-earth style, she has been invited to speak across the country about her inspirational journey and on various health, wellness, business and women's topics.

Kathleen is currently writing two other scripts and was selected by The MGH Institute of Health Professions, Inc. to produce a Continuing Medical Education documentary that will be used by medical professionals throughout the United States.

To schedule an interview or to book a talk with Kathleen, please contact her public relations director, Cari Reisinger at cari@hummingbirddistribution.com (209-736-6769). For more information about Kathleen's films visit http://www.sideeffectsthemovie.com and http://www.moneytalksthemovie.com

The Mark and Brian Program with Mark Thompson and Brian Phelps, airing on 95.5 KLOS in Los Angeles and 12 other western markets.

Theme: Entertainment, comedy, live music.

Guest Profile: Celebrities, musicians, who are quirky, energetic, funny and answer questions. Experiences, sound of voice, are they fun.

Guest from Hell: Someone who won't answer questions and says "read it in the book."

Contact: ted.lekas@citcomm.com; 310-840-4822; http://markandbrian.com; Ted Lekas. Best method: E-mail or mailing info. That's what I'll tell them if they call. No response? Call me.

Invited Back? Depends on the interview.

Bios of Mark Thompson and Brian Phelps: The duo was introduced in 1986 by a mutual friend who was working at radio station I-95 in Birmingham, Alabama, who felt that their personalities "might click." Deciding to heed the friend's advice, Mark and Brian each gathered bags of audio cassettes, locked themselves in a hotel room with coffee, junk food and a tape player and proceeded to sit through an entire evening listening to each other's work. Management at I-95 agreed to give the pair a chance. In no time, the radio team was racking up solid ratings. After a year at the station where they reached number one status, Mark and Brian left Birmingham in September 1987 and ventured west where as they say, "the rest was history!"

Built on the foundation of friendship, comedic timing and mutual respect, *The Mark and Brian Program* is currently in its 21st year on the air. Already two-time winners of *Billboard Magazine*'s "Air Personalities of the Year," Mark and Brian are also credited with achieving the radio industry's highest honor — The National Association Broadcasters' Marconi Award for "Air Personalities of the Year."

The duo won an Emmy Award for hosting an Andy Griffith TV Special which aired on the Fox network. And, they starred in their own NBC television show.

Movie Addict Headquarters with Betty Jo Tucker on BlogTalkRadio

Theme: Movie reviews and all things cinematic.

Guest Profile: Film-related personnel and movie critics. I like guests who are knowledgeable and have a good sense of humor. I like to see a summary of their background related to the topics they want to discuss. Film critic and author Diana Saenger was an ideal guest on my show dealing with the subject of classic films. Having recently set up a website about classic movies, she imparted important information about the topic and did so in an entertaining manner. She answered questions in a good-natured manner and projected an enthusiasm that was catching. I also appreciated the way she linked the show prominently on her classic film site.

Some of Betty's guests who came on during her horror movies series have been Barry Bostwick, one of the stars of *The Rocky Horror Picture Show,* and actress Rosemary Gore, who plays Alice Walker in *Fear of the Dark*, and whose latest movie is crime drama *Alibi.*

Guest from Hell: One who talks too little or talks too much.

Contact: reeltalk@comcast.net; 719-562-9740; http://blogtalkradio.com/movieaddictheadquarters; Betty Jo Tucker. Best method: By e-mailing a request including topics they want to discuss and a summary of their related background. No response? The guest should e-mail me.

Invited Back? If they are willing to come back and if the topic is one I think they would be informative and entertaining about while discussing.

Guest Comments: "Host Betty Jo Tucker's expertise and infectious love of movies makes *Movie Addict Headquarters* one of the easiest and most fun radio shows to be a guest on. My time on her show flew by, and it was totally enjoyable."— Diana Saenger, ClassicMovieGuide.com and author of *Everyone Wants My Job: The ABC's of Entertainment Writing* (Piccadilly Books 2000)

"I had a blast being a guest on Betty Jo's show. As a fellow film buff and radio host, I'm always glad to be a part of any great forum for movie discussion, and Betty Jo brings enough enthusiasm to the table to make her show great to listen to or take part in."— Adam J. Hakari, the Mad Movie Man of the University of Wisconsin at River Falls

Bio of Betty Jo Tucker: Betty Jo currently serves as editor/lead critic for *ReelTalk Movie Reviews* and writes film commentary for the *Colorado Senior Beacon*. She also writes movie reviews for *The Romance Club* and the *Omaha Family* newspaper. Her two radio shows are the *ReelTalk Movie Reviews Show* on the iWRN network and *Movie Addict Headquarters* on BlogTalkRadio.

Betty Jo's online course, "The Reel Deal: Writing about Movies," is offered through the Long Story Short School of Writing. She belongs to the Online Film Critics Society and is a founding member of the San Diego Film Critics' Society. She's written two movie-related books, *Confessions of a Movie Addict* and *Susan Sarandon: A True Maverick,* which received an Honorable Mention in the 2007 New York Book Festival.

The Movie Show with Joel Gibbs on the Lifestyle TalkRadio Network on Saturdays, 4–5 P.M. (ET)

Theme: Movie talk.

Guest Profile: Actors, producers, writers and directors, as well as authors of books related to the motion picture and entertainment industries. A fun, engaging conversational style with a great sense of humor. What makes their experience or product relevant to the movies and interesting to listeners. Some celebrities that have been on the show were Oliver Stone, Danny Glover, and Paul Sorvino.

Guest from Hell: Quiet, boring, one-sentence answers and dialogue — absent of the "get-it" factor.

Contact: voices@comcast.net; 215-750-1520; http://www.voicechoice.com; Joel Gibbs — Host/Executive Producer. Best method: Calling, e-mailing, sending press kit and product for review ... it's all cool. No response? E-mail ... call ... jump up and down.

Invited Back? I have fun ... the guest has fun ... the listeners have fun.

Bio of Joel Gibbs: Joel is a nationally-known writer, producer, and director of radio and TV spots and the voice talent in thousands of commercials featuring more than 100 celebrity impressions in his repertoire. For over 15 years, listeners have enjoyed Joel's unique brand of movietalk on radio stations in markets and cities all over the world.

His 60-second daily feature, "The Movie Show Minute," is heard on nearly 400 stations across America with all the latest buzz about the movie industry, showbiz gossip, what's hot on video, celebrity interviews, entertainment news and more.

Joel is one of the Academy Awards' annual emcees of "Oscar Night America" and a member of the prestigious Broadcast Film Critics Association. As producer, writer, and host of the TV talk show, *LiveWired* in Philadelphia, he earned a Cable Ace Award nomination and the Telly Award for America's "Best Talk Show." He also appears as a panelist on Comcast's Emmy award-winning program, "It's Your Call" as the show's resident movie and entertainment expert.

Joel's years of experience in broadcasting and production, along with his extensive knowledge of film, TV, music and the entertainment industry combine to make *The Movie Show*, one of the most unique and original talk shows on the air.

Mr. Media with Bob Andelman on Blog Talk Radio, http://www.blogtalkradio.com/mrmedia, also on iTunes and Odeo.

Theme: Celebrity/media newsmaker interviews.

Guest Profile: Actors, directors, authors, artists, bloggers, editors, media personalities from radio, TV, film, print, and web sites. Guests should have an interesting, topical angle on their area of the media and be good conversationalists. Their credentials are important, but mostly that they will be an interesting guest. A sense of humor helps.

Guest from Hell: That would be someone who makes it clear that they would rather be anywhere but in an interview at the time it is taking place. A good interview is a conversation, a give-and-take with contributions from both parties.

Contact: bob@andelman.com; 727-458-6475; http://www.mrmedia.com; Bob Andelman. Best method: A simple e-mail pitch is the best way to start. No response? Follow up with a second e-mail. You never know when something might have been lost to a spam folder.

Invited Back? If they give as good as they get the first time, they will always be welcome to return.

Bio of Bob Andelman, aka Mr. Media: Bob has been a professional journalist for more than 25 years and is the author or co-author of 10 books.

The Music Connection with Loyce Smallwood aired on KAHI AM 950, Auburn, CA.

Theme: Music.

Guest Profile: Musicians and community movers and shakers.

Guest from Hell: I don't have boring, one-dimensional, self-serving people.

Contact: loy@foothill.net; 530-906-4502; http://www.kahi.com/loyce'sblog; Loyce. Best method: E-mail a bio. No response? I always respond.

Invited Back? If they show up and show appreciation.

Loyce also hosts *The Golf Connection* (see page 264).

Bio of Loyce Smallwood: Loyce moved to the Gold Country in 1989 from the SF Bay area, with husband Jack and pets. Jack traveled and Loyce knew nobody so she decided to open (with no previous experience) The Turquoise Connection (Southwest jewelry, crafts, art) in Old Town Auburn.

A successful retailer for eight years, she moved on to real estate. In 2001, she decided to venture into the media and produce a local *Connections* program on access television. Again with no previous background, she started her radio venue with *The Health Connection*, *The Pet Connection*, *The Home Connection*, and *The Dining Connection* and eventually *Connections* and *The Golf Connection*.

"A small town is safe, clean and defined, but I have sought stimulation by creating my own productions and providing my own amusement/entertainment with the media," she says. "At long last, I have found my niche. I became addicted to golf a year ago and thus spawned *The Golf Connection*, acquiring the local golf club as my sponsor."

Now Showing with Bill Wilson on WDUN-AM 550, aired in metro Atlanta, Ga., and on the web; now off the air.

Theme: Entertainment.

Guest Profile: Fiction authors, actors, writers, directors, artists, musicians. Someone entertaining and enthusiastic, working in any entertainment field or medium. Credentials important.

Guest from Hell: Self-important, ethereal, ponderous, monosyllabic in response.

Contact: bill.wilson@jacobsmedia.net; 770-531-6512; http://www.wdun.com; Bill Wilson. Best method: E-mail or press kit, preferably. No response? E-mail or call.

Invited Back? Flow of conversation; is the guest enthusiastic and interesting; does his/her segment move well and hold attention?

Bio of Bill Wilson: Bill has been a producer in radio for 14 years. This is his fourth year hosting and producing *Now Showing*.

He holds a BA degree in speech and theater from Kutztown University, and reviews TV-on-DVD for www.wdun.com

Out and About with Richard G. with Richard Gerstner and Ann Smith (news, weather, phones) on WDVR-FM 89.7, Delaware Township 91.9, aired in Princeton, Lawrenceville, and Trenton, New Jersey. Richard also co-hosts *Juke Box Saturday Night* and once a month hosts the *All Night Diner*.

Theme: Topics from serious to silly.

Guest Profile: Authors, community leaders, entrepreneurs, entertainers, journalists, charity, etc. I look for guests that range from informative to entertaining. In some ways my radio show is an extension of a community based web site, http://www.mainstreetflemington.com, that I created. With that web site and the radio comes the responsibility and privilege to serve the community in whatever capacity I can. I basically check to see if they are legit.

Guest from Hell: I had one guest who froze up and no matter what I said or did the answers were yes and no and nothing more. Then there was the guest who was more concerned with promoting himself/herself rather than the subject matter at hand.

Contact: rlgerstner@embarqmail.com; 908-782-0027; http://www.wdvrfm.org; Richard Gerstner. Best method: Call with a pitch, e-mail a bio or send a press kit. Mostly I meet people at community functions or through associates. No response? Being a web designer, I am on the Internet more than most, so I respond to e-mails almost immediately. Of course if someone does not hear back from me they should just e-mail again or call. There is the chance that the e-mail got lost in cyberspace.

Invited Back? If the subject matter needs a follow-up. I also have monthly regulars, ask a nurse, ask a computer expert, two guys talking movies, etc.

Bio of Richard Gerstner: An artist for as long as he can remember, Richard's first showings were in kindergarten when he took in his drawings of the Sunday comic characters to Show and Tell. Since then, his life has been a balance of graphic design and fine art.

Starting out after the Army as a board artist in a printing company in Dayton, Ohio, he soon realized he needed to be in New York City. So he packed up his VW and drove to the Big Apple, taking the first job he could find as art editor for *TV Star Parade*, then ad agencies. Richard then took a position with *Newsweek*, and after 21 years as an associate editor decided to leave and jumped feet first into the web. That was 12 years ago and since then he has designed nearly 75 web sites and spent 18 months setting up the Princeton Packets web presence.

An illustrator, painter and photo silkscreener, Richard's last traveling show "Orphans of Viet Nam" was photosilkcreens he created from photos he took in Viet Nam in 1994. It opened in May of 1995 at the Senate Russell Building in Washington, D.C., with Hillary Clinton as the host and Kodak as his corporate sponsor.

He has exhibited in galleries and museums across the country and his work is in private collections in the United States, England, the Philippines and Japan.

Guest Comments: "What a wonderful opportunity to connect to our community in such a unique and friendly venue. Richard's show has given us exposure to many viewpoints and listeners who look to his radio show for insight into important community topics and issues of interest. He is masterful at identifying interesting community personalities and events that make people 'sit up, listen up' and take notice. We are extremely grateful!"— Dr. Lisa Brady, superintendent, Hunterdon Central Regional High School

"Richard's radio show reminds us of the roots of radio; bringing together a community in conversation about local events and concerns. It's an experience in the unpolished and unpretentious warmth that separates radio from its shiny shark-skinned suit cousin, TV."— Bill Tucker, journalist

Poppoff with Mary Jane Popp on KAHI AM 950 in northern California, airing daily M–F 10 AM–noon (PT).

Theme: Magazine format.

Guest Profile: You name it — as long as it has pizzaz. Practical information. If you disagree with something, give me a solution — not just griping. Basic info on topic and their read on it. Bio ... short and sweet. Past interviews if pertinent.

Guest from Hell: One with yes or no answers and no explanation ... monotone ... lacks energy and excitement.

Contact: poppoffwithmaryjane@hotmail.com; 916-929-7962; http://www.poppoff.com; "The Poppoff Report" on http://www.lamasbeauty.com; Mary Jane Popp. Best method: E-mail a pitch on one or two pages. Get me a number to call. No response? Try the e-mail again. It might not have reached me. Then call to ask if I like the topic or not. I will be honest.

Invited Back? Did you excite me to want to know more, or were you boring?

Bio of Mary Jane Popp: Mary Jane is a thinking, self-motivated woman whose skills and professionalism will take her rocketing into the new millennium. Her entertainment background has given her the ability to communicate with the masses, yet maintain a one-on-one relationship. She can give you the inside track on the famous and the infamous.

Her experience far surpasses her years. She has anchored the "Prime Time News" on two coasts and been a reporter on features, from bungee jumping to hurricanes. She has produced and anchored her own radio and TV talk programs, interviewing the likes of Ronald and Nancy Reagan to vitamin guru Earl Mindell ... from gossip columnist Liz Smith to fashion mogul Mr. Blackwell. She possesses the knack to influence and inspire others by delivering old material in a new and exciting fashion. She can be aggressive when called for. She can be a caring shoulder when needed. She can reach into the deepest psyche and separate truth from fiction.

Mary Jane has sung for major sports events, toured the U.S. as a speaker and entertainer, starred in several films, appeared in made for TV movies and has written, produced and voiced hundreds of radio and TV commercials.

Mary Jane is co-author of the nationally acclaimed book *Marilyn, Joe and Me* (Penmarin Books 2006) with June DiMaggio, niece of Joe DiMaggio.

Mary Jane has an MS and 43 hours toward a Ph.D. from Indiana University.

Pride Radio with Ryan and Caroline, Clear Channel's nationally syndicated radio talk show on FM stations across America, on HD radio nationwide, online and podcast.

Theme: Entertainment talk show covering movies, TV, Broadway, fashion, travel, relationships and lifestyle trends.

Guest Profile: Celebrities. Guests who are upbeat, fun, light, energetic, pop culture aware, irreverent, funny. What is their appeal to a national audience? Famous guests have included Queen Latifah, Hilary Duff, Alan Cumming, Joan Collins, Rufus Wainwright, Ellen Pompeo, Liza Minnelli, Robert Downey Jr., Amanda Bynes, and John Travolta.

Guest from Hell: Someone who gets political ... someone who gives short or one word answers ... someone who speaks quietly

Contact: RyanJay@clearchannel.com; Phone withheld upon request; http://www.RyanAndCaroline.com and http://wwwWeSeeMovies.com; Ryan Jay. Best method: E-mailing a pitch is best ... include a contact number for us to call if we're interested, or call Rebecca Rosoff at 212-424-6347. No response? A second e-mail is reasonable.

Invited Back? If they play well with the hosts of the show ... if they're funny, witty, entertaining, or uber famous.

Bios of Ryan and Caroline: Known as radio's "Will and Grace," Ryan and Caroline met during the summer of 2000 while working at VH1 in New York City and fast became best friends. Sharing a passion for film, they see more movies together than they do with anyone else.

In 2004 their friendship reached new heights as they created the incredibly popular movie review blog WeSeeMovies.com where sexy people the world over go to read their cheeky and fresh movie reviews. The duo also syndicates a weekly radio movie weekend preview segment.

Both have worked in television as producers of major pop culture programming for networks like MTV, VH1, Showtime, Bravo and even *The Jerry Springer Show* (don't hold it against them).

The Radio Host Show with "talk radio advocate" Francine Silverman on Blog Talk Radio, http://www.blogtalkradio.com/francine-silverman and Shelby Radio, http://www.shelbynradio.com

Theme: Talk radio shows.

Guest Profile: Talk radio hosts.

Guest from Hell: Someone who fails to show up, or arrives late, for the interview. I prepare for every show and I regard this as disrespect for the host's time.

Contact: franalive@optonline.net; http://www.blogtalkradio.com/francine-silverman; http://www.bookpromotionnewsletter.com; www.talkradioadvocate.com; Francine Silverman. Best method: E-mail.

No response? I respond to all e-mails. If I don't for any reason, e-mail again.

Invited Back? The show is too new at this point, but I foresee inviting back some good guests.

Guest Comment: "I really enjoyed the interview. Thanks for making it so easy."—Pat Montgomery, host of *Parents Rule!* (see page 173)

Bio of Francine Silverman: A lifelong New Yorker, Fran honed her writing skills as a newspaper reporter and freelance writer. She authored two travel guidebooks, *Catskills Alive* (2000 and 2003) and *Long Island Alive* (2003), both published by Hunter Publishing.

In 2003, Fran started *Book Promotion Newsletter* for authors of all genres. The bi-weekly ezine spawned *Book Marketing from A–Z* (Infinity Publishing 2005), containing the best marketing strategies of 325 subscribers. The 400-page paperback is in alphabetical order for ease of use, and received nearly 40 rave reviews from on-line reviewers.

In 2006, Fran started a publicity service and has gotten subscribers placed in the *Boston Herald*, *Oklahoman* and *Chicago Tribune* as well as on hundreds of Internet and terrestrial radio programs. She adopted the tag, "talk radio advocate," after starting her radio show.

Radio Rickshaw with John V, Don Fowler, Ian Covell, Di and Dan on http://rickshawboy.com/radiorickshaw

Theme: Theatre, arts, music and some tech.

Guest Profile: Independent musicians and theatre/TV/film professionals. Someone who is willing to hang out for a while and shoot the breeze. Someone who wants to let us know about him/her and not simply there for promotional purposes (though the promo does happen organically). Like to have an idea of their credentials, appearances, overall bio, what they like to drink.

Guest from Hell: Someone who tries too hard to be funny, rather than letting go and being real.

Contact: e-mail@rickshawboy.com; 407-965-2939; http://rickshawboy.com; John. Best method: E-mail. Bios and press kits are always welcome. No response? They should e-mail again or leave a message.

Invited Back? Did we or they have a good time, did they think it was fun?

Guest Comment: "This is the best interview I've ever done."—Mark L. Walberg, TV personality ("Antique Road Show," "Temptation Island")

Bio of John Valine: John's professional theatre career began when he was 16 years old in Houston, Texas, as a stagehand for STAGES Repertory Theatre. In Orlando, John became the technical director of the improv theatre Sak Comedy Lab. He also became vice president of Sak and an improv teacher.

His directing credits include Todd Kimbro's

"DeCaffeinated," "Caffeine Episode II," "Failure an Epic Adventure," "Equus: On Ice," Stephen Belber's "Tape" (*Orlando, FL*) and the award-winning "Farrago," which he co-wrote.

In 2001, John joined the theatrical acapella group Toxic Audio as their 6th member and technical director. With John's help, Toxic Audio went to New York in 2004 and became an off–Broadway sensation winning the Drama Desk award for "Most Unique Theatrical Experience," the same award that had been given previously to Cirque du Soleil.

John is the producer and co-host of *Radio Rickshaw* which is produced by his company Rickshaw Boy. The show is a weekly podcast about theatre, music, art and tech. John also produces podcasts *Heart of Darkness Comedy Podcast, Leaving L.A.* and *Toxic Audio unofficial Podcast*, all of which are part of the Rickshaw Boy family.

Bio of Don Fowler: Don is co-founder of Rickshaw Boy and *Radio Rickshaw* and John's creative partner since 2000.

Don has been working in the entertainment industry for the past 20 years in many capacities, but mostly as a performer. He has worked on productions for companies such as HBO, Nickelodeon and many more. He has also performed on stage in Florida, New York and California.

Red Bar Radio with Mike David and Dean Carlson on http://redbarradio.com

Theme: Comedy talk radio. The show is difficult to describe — we try not to stick to one formula. Each episode is unique, with an open-magazine style. We talk about whatever we think is funny at the time. We try to bring comedy into every situation. The show can be offensive, obnoxious, and silly — but that's what we're trying to give our audience — a chance to listen to something that is refreshing, funny, and down to earth. We find comedy in everything. The show sometimes goes over the line, but I think that's why people listen — they can take a break from their serious lives and experience things that they can't hear or say during reality. It's therapeutic to make fun of everything.

Guest Profile: Comedians, celebrities, musicians, authors. Most importantly is this guest going to be interesting? It's not always about the big names, but more of who can hold the most entertaining conversation. Are they fun?

For past guests, go to: http://redbarradio.com/forum/index.php?topic=229.0

Guest from Hell: Someone who doesn't want to be there. Gives one word answers. Someone who is only there to push their product or project.

Contact: mike@redbarradio.com; 312-576-1714; http://www.redbarradio.com; Mike David. Best method: E-mailing me their info with links to their site is fine. No response? If they really want to be on I would expect them to pursue me.

Invited Back? Most importantly the listeners have to like them.

Bio of Mike D: Mike D, along with comedian friends, harshly judge pop culture and make fun of everybody on *RBR*, created in 2003 by Mike and then co-host, Ron Galperin. Originally intended as a "goof" on Chicago radio, through word of mouth and links passed along on other websites, *Red Bar Radio* grew.

RBR is now one of the top rated comedy podcasts on the net. Local Chicago comedians help Mike co-host the show, rotating a different co-host for each episode.

Rick's Picks with Rick Forchuk on CKNW, Vancouver, airing in BC — Alberta — Saskatchewan — Quebec — along the Corus Radio Network.

Theme: Movie and television talk.

Guest Profile: TV people — actors, writers, those involved in network TV. Someone who is articulate, connected to radio and/or television and movies, and has an interesting viewpoint with a story to tell. Not interested in past interview experience, only what they bring to the microphone at this time.

Guest from Hell: Non-responsive, or one-word answers.

Contact: rick.forchuk@corusent.com; 604-340-1165 (cell); http://www.rickspicks.ca; Rick Forchuk. Best method: E-mail a bio, send a press kit, and a DVD if applicable. No response? I always respond, but if not, a second e-mail or phone call is always welcome.

Invited Back? If they were interesting, provocative, or fun, they are welcome back.

Bio of Rick Forchuk: Beginning as a freelance writer for such publications as the *Toronto Star Weekly*, Rick went on to become a daily television columnist for the Edmonton, Ottawa, and Winnipeg *Sun* newspapers for 20 years; a daily columnist for the *Victoria Times* columnist for four years; weekly columnist for *Fredericton Daily Gleaner*, and *Regina Leader Post* for 15 years. He was a regular movie/TV reviewer on both CBC Television network show "Midday" for five years and on CBC Radio (network) for 15.

Rick was a regular on *CKVU* (now *CityTV*) *Vancouver Show* for six years as movie/TV reviewer and had similar roles at various times at CFUN Vancouver and CJOR Vancouver. Along with being a movie/TV reviewer on his radio show, he's a regular movie/TV reviewer daily on CHED Edmonton, CHQR Calgary, CFAX Victoria, CKNW Vancouver, and weekly on AM 940 Montreal. Rick is also a weekly columnist for *TV Week Magazine*, Vancouver/Victoria since 1980.

He has a BA in media and mass communications, and an MBA with major in strategic management.

Sassy Sistah Radio Show with Cathryn Michael Murray on Blog Talk Radio, http://www.blogtalkradio.com/Sassy-Sistah-Magazin

Theme: Showcase positive talent in the entertainment business. We are a webzine online that focuses on eliminating the labels placed on models in the industry.

Guest Profile: Someone positive — doing something to achieve their goals. Go getters.

Guest from Hell: Someone who is negative and shows disrespect to others.

Contact: Cathryn_Michael2005@yahoo.com; 925-349-4275; http://www.cathrynmichael.com, http://www.sassysistah.com; http://www.myspace.com/sassysistahmagazine; Cathryn Murray. Best method: Someone should e-mail me a bio and tell me about themselves. No response? E-mail or call.

Invited Back? The way the audience relates to them.

Bio of Cathryn Michael: Cathryn is a model, actress, singer, writer and motivational speaker based in the San Francisco Bay Area. As a teen, Cathryn founded and managed "Global Teen Club International," an international organization comprised of ethnically diverse and socially aware teenagers. The program produced a monthly 'zine by and for young people. And a few years ago, Cathryn was selected as a "Noxzema Extraordinary Teen" and flown to New York City for the gala awards ceremony.

She has appeared in such ezines, newspapers and books around the world as *Teen Magazine, Sassy Magazine, Working Women Magazine, Diablo Magazine, Fast Cash for Kids* book (nationally published and still available in bookstores), *No More Frogs to Kiss* (still available in bookstores nationwide) by Joline Godfrey.

Full bio at http://www.cathrynmichael.com

Show Business 101 (How to Turn Your Hollywood Dream into a Career) with Barbara Niven on Big Media USA, http://www.bigmediausa.com/show.asp?sid=501 and available on the internet 24/7 and also on iTunes and podcast.

Theme: Interviews with experts in every aspect of show business, to help you learn how to turn your Hollywood dream into a career. Barbara's been living her dream of being an actress for over 20 years, and wants to inspire others and say that it is possible! She shares her secrets and business techniques, and says that you can have all the talent in the world, but if you don't know how the business actually works, and use it to your advantage, your odds go way down.

Guest Profile: Experts in every aspect of show business: Acting, writing, directing, kids in show biz, casting and auditions, producing and getting funded, promoting yourself and your project, film festivals, animation, careers below the line, entertainment tax tips, and everything in between. People who have been there, done that, and who can give a reality to those who are considering show business as a career.

Contact: barbara@barbaraniven.com; withheld upon request; http://www.barbaraniven.com; Barbara Niven. Best method: E-mail.

Note: For answers to questions and Barbara's bio, please see her other show, *Animal Rescue* on page 7.

Guest Comments: "First of all, Barbara Niven is one of my favorite people in the entire world. Beautiful, intelligent, talented, compassionate, and wonderfully insightful. I very much enjoyed my interview with her, it was relaxed and free-flowing and that's because she sets such a comfortable milieu. Hollywood sets the tone for the globe, and we'd have a radically different world if everybody in Hollywood was like Barbara."— Jack Barnard, master presentation and branding coach, media trainer and writer, http://www.speakerservices.com/products

"Barbara made me feel so comfortable on her show. She helped guide the conversation and we got to talk about the important reasons to rescue animals, as well as some heart warming stories. I started volunteering with animal rescues through fundraising with my photography. It all grew from there. We were able to touch on the importance of spaying/neutering and also give vital information on how people can help and what they can do if they find a stray dog. Barbara's love of animals really shows and I am so happy she has given animal rescue a place to get their message out."— Lori Fusaro, photographer, http://www.FusaroPhotography.com

Six Degrees with Anthony Brice and Dirty Dishes on Blog Talk Radio, http://www.blogtalkradio.com/six degrees

Theme: Everyone is connected somehow, someway just open dialogue to see where the connection lies. Genuine passion for what they do. Genuine desire to open the hearts and minds of listeners toward a higher purpose.

Guest Profile: All types, mainly entertainment professionals so far. We want to now their past interview experiences, credentials, and sound of their voice.

Guest from Hell: A guest that has a hidden agenda. One that does not articulate well or think about the greater good ... i.e., selfish.

Contact: anthonybrice@hotmail.com; 850-217-0445; http://www.myspace.com/anthonybrice; Anthony Brice. Best method: E-mail. No response? Call me and e-mail if I haven't responded in three business days.

Invited Back? If we had a good time doing the show they should be invited back.

Bio of Anthony M. Brice: Anthony is a retired master sergeant USAF, where he spent 17 years as buyer. He is the recipient of many awards, including the Air Force Meritorious Service Medal — 2004. He has an AAS surgical technology degree and is presently surgical technician, orthopedic surgery team leader — Baptist Hospital, Gulf Breeze Hospital in Florida. http://www.ebaptisthealthcare.org/Gulf BreezeHospital.

Anthony is also president of Cradle House Official Records. http://www.cradlehouse.com

Talk to Me ... Conversations with Creative, Unconventional People with Rita Schiano on Blog Talk Radio, http://www.blogtalkradio.com/rita

Theme: Entertainment.

Guest Profile: Authors, musicians, artists, poets, entrepreneurs, i.e., all types of CUPs (Creative, Unconventional People). People who have taken risks, stretched themselves, used their talents to attain their goals. Accomplishments, credentials, interesting story to tell, personality.

Guest from Hell: People who answer questions with a yes or no.

Contact: rita@ritaschiano.com; 508-347-7237; http://www.blogtalkradio.com/rita; http://www.rita schiano.com; Rita Schiano. Best method: E-mail a bio and/or press kit. No phone calls. No response? Response time is quite good. A second e-mail is preferable.

Invited Back? Engaging conversation, extended interests to pursue.

Guest Comments: "Rita did her homework, and as a result, I felt completely at ease discussing my acting career and producing aspirations. I was amazed how quickly the time went and, with her smart questioning, we probably could have gone on indefinitely!"— Gary Galone, actor "Law & Order," "Brotherhood," "Ashecliffe"

"It was an absolute pleasure being interviewed by Rita Schiano on BlogTalkRadio. Her questions were thoughtful, enthusiastic, and specific to me. It was obvious that Rita had done her homework — she'd read my book, gone to my website, and read my Blog. So we actually had a real conversation, and I feel that anyone listening had the opportunity to learn the truth about me, my book, and why they might want to read it."— Lisa Genova, author of *Still Alice* (iUni verse 2007)

Bio of Rita Schiano: Rita wanted to be a writer ever since Santa Claus gave her a Tom Thumb typewriter when she was six years old. Her first story, "My Mom Is Love a Bull," was an instant hit with the family. Years later, at the ripe old age of 11, Rita began writing "Girl from U.N.C.L.E." episodes after her then favorite television show was cancelled.

After college, Rita followed in her mother's footsteps and moved to New York City to pursue a career in music. She spent seven years performing at various clubs including the Red Parrot, Trax, Inner Circle, and Studio 54.

Fast forward to 1989.... Pursuing yet another dream, Rita opened an Italian-Japanese restaurant in Sturbridge, Massachusetts. She cooked, baked, and operated The Casual Café for 11 years and then sold it in 2000. During that time, Rita began writing late at night to relax after the long hours a restaurant demands. She went on to write her first novel, *Sweet Bitter Love* (Rising Tide Press 1997). In 2003, Rita bought back the rights to her novel and wrote the screenplay. She teamed up with Paul Gemme to create *T.I.M.E. Share, Inc.*, a sci-fi/drama written for television, and *G.E.O.P.S.*, a full-length movie screenplay. Her "truth-based" novel, *Painting the Invisible Man* (The Reed Edwards Company 2007) explores growing up in a family on the fringe of the Mafia. Rita is working on her third novel, *Sanctifying Grace*, scheduled for publication by The Reed Edwards Company in 2009.

Rita is a published songwriter and member of ASCAP. She co-wrote with Jamie Notarthomas two children's songs for KidsTerrain, Inc., *The Magic in Me* and *Tiny Acts of Kindness*.

The TV of Tomorrow Show LIVE with Tracy Swedlow on Blog Talk Radio, http://www.blogtalkra dio.com/itvt-tvoftomorrow

Theme: Interactive and multiplatform television of tomorrow.

Guest Profile: High-level executive guests (business, creatives, technologists, philosophers, cosmologists) who are doing something innovative, with intelligence and insight; nice person. I just want guests that know their topic.

Guest from Hell: Late, inarticulate, stupid, scatterbrained.

Contact: swedlow@itvt.com; 415-824-5806; http://www.itvt.com; http://www.thetvoftomorrowshow.com or http://www.blogtalkradio.com/itvt-tvoftomor row; Tracy Swedlow. Best method: E-mail or call. No response? They can call me.

Invited Back? If they are interesting.

Bio of Tracy Swedlow: Tracy is the CEO, publisher, and editor-in-chief of InteractiveTV Today [itvt], which she founded in early 1998. Her writing has appeared in such prestigious publications as the *New York Times*, the *San Francisco Examiner*, *PC World*, *Multimedia World* and *VR World*.

Covering such topics as virtual reality, e-mail communities, privacy and technology, online gravesite memorials, and interactive television, she has received awards from the Computer Press Association and the Western Regional Magazine Association.

Prior to founding [itvt] she was chief evangelist at eGroups.com (now Yahoo! Groups); new media editor at PC World; a producer and director for Telemorphix, a pioneering interactive TV company, and a video producer at Steve Michelson Productions in San Francisco.

Tracy has a Ph.D fellowship in directing at the University of California, Berkeley; a Masters degree in dramatic criticism from Northwestern University; a certificate in French and French literature from the

Université de Cannes; and a Bachelor of Arts degree in theater history from Tulane University.

Full bio at http://www.itvt.com/tsbiography.html

Ultrasonic Film with James Borsa and Lindsay Brown on CJUM 101.5 FM, Thursdays 10–11 PM, and rebroadcast on Sunday 7–8 AM, and Tuesday 6–7 AM

Theme: Winnipeg's only film talk radio show. Covers local Canadian production as well as Hollywood and international productions.

Guest Profile: Directors, actors, producers, festival staff (both local and foreign). I prefer them to be charismatic and talkative. I also would like them to be reliable and respectful. I prefer to know a little about them personally and just let that come out naturally in the interview. I would like to know a little about what they are promoting and that's about it. Among the notable actors and actresses interviewed were Jennifer Tilly (*Bullets over Broadway*), actor Djimon Hounsou (*Blood Diamond*), and actor Jake Busey (*Starship Troopers*). Directors on the show include David Cronenberg (*Eastern Promises*), Brian Helgeland (*A Knight's Tale*), and James Moll (Oscar winner—*The Last Days*).

Guest from Hell: When a guest gets pushy and disrespectful, someone who could care less about the interview and has an unrelenting ego. I've had guests who just refuse to answer simple questions and then change the topic suddenly without explanation. Very odd interviews sometimes...

Contact: jamesmgr@mts.net; none available; http://www.umfm.com; joining our facebook site *Ultrasonic Film* is a good idea; James Borsa, Lindsay Brown. Best method: If I've never heard of them, then e-mail is best; typically I find my show guests thru other areas in the city: Winnipeg Film Group, Catecomb Microcinema, local film festivals etc. Publicists have assisted me as well, or I seek them out because I want to talk to them. No response? I respond to all e-mails as well as Facebook comments. I'm on there daily. Typically a response will be returned within a day or two. If not I certainly wouldn't take offense to attempts to re-contact me.

Invited Back? The most frequent reason is if there are recurring events for them to promote, or if they are very charismatic and engaging and one interview just wasn't enough.

Guest Comments: "Wow, you have really done your homework, man!"—Oscar-winning Director James Moll, while being interviewed about his film *The Last Days*

"You seem to know my films better than I do!"—David DeCoteau, who had directed more than 60 low-budget films

Bios of James Borsa and Lindsay Brown: James has a Bachelor of Arts, with a film major, from the University of Manitoba. He is also a former video store manager and is the proud owner of over 5000 movies. An avid film buff, James has been hosting *Ultrasonic Film* for almost 10 years.

Lindsay teaches high school by day and is a relentless movie buff by night; she has also toiled in the video store industry and has a fierce, blunt and passionate take on her favorite films.

Environment

In Deborah Lindsay's view, the most important environmental steps to be taken are to drastically lower our fossil fuel usage and change the end of the Oil Story. "The survival of the human race depends on how we collectively proceed."

Healing the Earth Radio with Matt Soltys on CFRU, Guelph, Ontario.

Theme: Ecological and social.

Guest Profile: Many different guests—authors, indigenous people, activists, prisoners, community organizers, psychologists, scientists. An engaging speaker who is willing to say what they feel must be heard by others. Someone who wants to give back to the world with their work. I want to know as much as I can about their beliefs and opinions, so as to ensure they are not sexist, racist, classist, in denial about certain political realities, and so on. I want to spread the words of people who are underrepresented and challenging the status quo in an honorable way.

Guest from Hell: Someone who either doesn't have their thoughts together enough to keep listeners excited, or someone who speaks so much that I don't have an opportunity to ask a question.

Contact: healingtheearth@resist.ca; Withheld upon request; http://www.resistanceisfertile.ca; Matt Soltys. Best method: E-mailing with a bio is the best way to go. I like to establish a connection that is as personal as possible; we need not be too formal. No response? Please do e-mail back. Sometimes e-mail work can be overwhelming.

Invited Back? If they've got a lot more great stuff to say, or if their work becomes increasingly exciting.

Bio of Matt Soltys: Matt has been doing radio journalism on a weekly basis since October 2004. He began by co-hosting *Environment Radio*, and proceeded to produce *Healing the Earth* in June 2005, with the intent of highlighting more of the connections between ecological, social, and political issues. "I began http://www.resistanceisfertile.ca in February 2006, to spread the interviews via the web," recalls Matt. "Overall, my interviews have been played on dozens of radio stations across the continent, and tens of thousands of people have downloaded various interviews."

Matt has found his radio shows and the Internet have extended to print journalism as well as different kinds of community organizing. Not content to sit tight with journalism, which offers few tangible results, the relationships he has fostered through his radio show have led to speaking events, fundraising efforts, educational material for indigenous, anti-colonial, prisoner support, and ecological justice movements, networking between different groups of people working for change, and so on.

Besides producing *Healing the Earth*, Matt also works with The Appleseed Collective (www.appleseedcollective.org), a local food security organization, The Indigenous Peoples Solidarity Movement–Guelph (www.indigenoussolidarity.org), and The Guelph Free School (www.guelph.anarchistu.org). "I live off the grid in a forest near the Eramosa river and have been self-employed since 2005," he says.

Healthy Planet, Healthy Me! with Sherry Beall on KPFK, Los Angeles, Ca. and 98.7FM, Santa Barbara.

Theme: Environment and health.

Guest Profile: Investigative journalists, authors, experts. Someone who is passionate, articulate, knowledgeable and confident about their topic; and is also passionate about helping others and the planet. I'd like to know their past interview experiences, credentials and sound of their voice.

Guest from Hell: Shy, timid, nervous, very soft spoken, doesn't have many of the answers that they should in their area of expertise.

Contact: info@hphme.com; 818-988-4441; http://www.hphme.com; Sherry Beall or assistant. Best method: Mail press info, or send an e-mail. No response? E-mail; please; only call if it is a timely matter or if I've responded to their e-mail.

Invited Back? A good attitude, very knowledgeable about their topic, offering helpful information to the listeners, articulate and confident.

Bio of Sherry Beall: Sherry has always felt a deep connection to Mother Earth. Her radio show is her pet project and in 2008 it became the only radio show in Los Angeles to focus solely on environmental and health issues.

She is the creator, host and producer of her radio show (formerly—*A Right to Know*), which is currently in development for television.

With a passion to pave the way and make healthy alternatives for the home more convenient for others, Sherry has created yet another venture with this purpose in mind. Namely, At Home Naturally (http://www.athomenaturally.com).

A member of the Los Angeles Press Club, Sherry has been in the broadcast and film industry her entire adult life, starting out as a performer and voice-over talent before breaking into production. She is also a published journalist.

She was the first foreign exchange student with a double major to graduate from George Mason University, having studied in Paris her junior year. She holds a B.A. in theatre (dance) and French.

Full bio at http://www.hphme.com

Science in Action, podcast, with Jerry Kay. Also host of *EarthNews*, *Aquarium of the Air*, *Your Wetlands*.

Theme: Sustainable living, health, environment and culture.

Guest Profile: Authors, scientists, organic farmers, energy experts, entrepreneurs, etc. Knowledge and passion. Plus I expect someone who has thought about how to communicate. This is a learned skill and some people are dedicated to learning and practicing it. Want to know topics the interview might cover; brief bio, experience presenting to the public.

Guest from Hell: Has not given any thought to what might be asked ... not prepared with specific stories ... does not have any specific information such as statistics-background-perspective regarding topic.

Contact: Earthnewsradio@gmail.com; 415-479-5300; *EarthNews*, http://www.earthnewsradio.org; *Science in Action*, http://www.calacademy.org/podcasts; *Aquarium of the Air*, http://www.montereybayaquarium.org/news/audio_stories.asp; *Your Wetlands*, http://www.yourwetlands.org. Jerry Kay, Executive Producer. Best method: Brief e-mail is preferred. No response? A second e-mail followed by a phone call would be great.

Invited Back? Their preparation, knowledge and commitment.

Bio of Jerry Kay: Jerry has been a broadcast journalist for 35 years, including: public affairs director — KFRC Radio San Francisco, talk host — KCBS, host — EarthNews Radio heard on CBS nationally, host — Beyond Organic Sirius Satellite Radio, host of a variety of podcasts, founder — Teen Environmental Media Network, publisher — Environmental News Network.

Tomorrow Matters with Deborah and Spencer Lindsay, Sundays, 10–11 AM (PT), on KRXA 540 AM, aired in Monterey, Santa Cruz and San Benito Counties in California, and at http://www.deborahlindsay.com, http://www.KRXA540.com

Theme: Solutions to the environmental problems of today for a better tomorrow.

Guest Profile: Wide range; local and national activists, business people, authors, ngo's, government officials. The guest needs to be actively involved in a solution to some environmental problem ... they need to be able to offer my listeners a concrete thing to do to make a positive impact in the world, big or small. I try to get people who are active in education, as they tend to be more animated. All I want to know is what they're doing for the Earth and why ... this lets me know if there's a possibility of a good show.

Guest from Hell: Someone who answers in monosyllabic responses, and is a very slow speaker; who shows up late and doesn't call to inform you of their situation.

Contact: tomorrow@deborahlindsay.com; 831-419-7242; Deborah Lindsay. Best method: E-mail me with a bio. No response? Either e-mail or call ... but give me a couple of days to try to respond.

Invited Back? If the show is really exciting and dynamic, with lots of callers and I have a really good feeling of accomplishment after the interview, or we had lots of laughs. Also, if I know we hardly touched the tip of the iceberg with their information and I need to get them back in to continue the interview.

Guest Comment: "You really listen with interest and curiosity and ask great questions. You brought out the best in me. I look forward to our next time knowing I'm in good hands. And, I am enjoying tuning in when I can."— Hina Pendle, Ph.D., a founding principal of Us Partners, an organizational, development and transformation consultancy serving clients in a variety of industries, http://www.uspartners.com

Bio of Deborah Lindsay: Deborah is the Central Coast's premier green event planner, producer, and consultant. She offers her clients the benefits of comprehensive, local green event services. Deborah delivers expert local planning, production, green merchandise, event greening, and strategic consulting.

One of Deborah's many distinctions is that she supports her client base to become organizations that are committed to the practice of environmental responsibility She focuses on event opportunities that reflect these sustainable values. Deborah strives to combine the best local people, services and ideas to create an event in a way that promotes ecological stewardship.

Her clientele includes: Sustainable Monterey County, The Monterey Peninsula Sustainability Fair and Solar Home Tour, University of California Extension, and The Northern California Post Carbon Institute.

Food and Wine

> *"I know beyond a shadow of a doubt that good ingredients and the love of the cook make all the difference in the taste of a meal."*— Charli Vogt, host of *Beyond the Measuring Cup*

America's Dining and Travel Guide with Pierre Wolfe, aired on 84 stations in the U.S. through Business Talk Radio Network, on Sundays at 1 PM (MT). Pierre also hosts or co-hosts two Internet shows: *World Travel and Dining Show*, http://www.pierrewolfe.com, and *Talk Shoe*, http://www.talkshoe.com

Theme: Travel, food and wine.

Guest Profile: Editors and publishers of national magazines pertaining to food and travel; authors of cookbooks and travel guides. Well-versed in the areas described above; if they have a presence on radio. I want to know a little about their background.

Guest from Hell: Rarely have one; we talk ahead of time. But a guest from hell would be one who stutters or has long pauses. Whether they are guests or callers, I gently but firmly get rid of them.

Contact: Quorum10@aol.com; http://www.pierrewolfe.com; Pierre. Best method: Call with a pitch, send a press kit, and e-mail a bio and why you want to be on radio. If an author, send me your book. No response? It means I am not interested.

Invited Back? The way they handle themselves on the air and the way they describe and talk about the subject.

Bio of Pierre Wolfe: Born in Europe, Pierre immigrated to the United States in 1950, having served as a 16 year old with Allies in Africa and the Middle East. He received an honorable discharge as a second lieutenant. He began his broadcasting career in Colorado in 1956 on KFML Radio.

Pierre's culinary training began on the cruise ship *Caronia*, Cunard Cruise Line. He formally attended hotel management schools in Switzerland. Pierre was also owner of four award winning restaurants in Colorado. He is a Hall of Fame member of the Colorado Restaurant Association and is on the advisory board of various culinary organizations. Pierre has traveled the world with his wife, Jean, as broadcaster and guest chef on many of the leading cruise lines, including Crystal, Cunard, Seabourn, Windstar, and Radisson Seven Seas. He has broadcast live from all parts of the globe and from all continents with the exception of Antarctica and the Artic Circle.

Beyond the Measuring Cup with Charli Vogt aired on http://www.beyondthemeasuringcup.com

Theme: Food and health, which includes farming, locally grown food, the chemistry of cooking, food, growing food and eating, and healthful ways of preparing food. A look at things beyond the usual in food and health that can be derived by good food and good eating.

Guest Profile: Cookbook writers who focus on health, chefs, activists in the slow food and similar other organizations, sustainable and local farmers, artisan creators of good food (i.e., cheese makers, beer makers, and small companies that preserve traditional ways of preparing or growing food), as well as physicians and other healthcare providers well-versed in nutrition. Someone knowledgeable, who is able to explain concepts in easy to understand language. Enthusiasm for their topic. I'm looking for a wide range of topics. I introduce people to different ways of looking at health and food. The opinions of the interviewee do not have to be the same something I might suggest. In fact, I'm very interested in many different opinions and ideas that would promote tasty, healthy eating.

I would love to know the sound of their voice, a copy of their book if they have one, credentials ... not that interested in whether they have previous experience. If they are enthusiastic, I feel, that will come across.

Guest from Hell: Someone who answers questions with one word or sentence. Someone who is so invested in their own agenda that they would not consider the possibility that there could be a different opinion. Also someone who shows up late or doesn't come at all.

Contact: charli@beyondthemeasuringcup.com; 404-377-1257; http://www.Beyondthemeasuringcup.com; Charli Vogt. Best method: E-mail me with a bio or send a press kit (if this could be done electronically, that would be best). I would rather not be called until after we have decided to talk about an interview. No response? I do travel a fair amount. If they don't hear from me after about 3–4 days they are welcome to call or e-mail again. Sometimes I miss a call or e-mail.

Invited Back? If I have fun with the interview and I feel that quality information was shared.

Guest Comment: "Charli's interview was fun and one of the first ones where I wasn't interrupted in the middle of a point."—Tom Cowan, MD, holistic physician

Bio of Charli Vogt: Charli has taught extensively in the Atlanta metro area on a wide range of topics related to health, including aromatherapy, herbal therapy, healthy cooking, energy healing and mind/body medicine. With her advanced degrees in nursing and public health, she has an excellent vantage point to see the worlds of both alternative and conventional healing.

Because of her infectious enthusiasm and extensive knowledge, Charli is regularly invited back to groups who have enjoyed her presentations. Many people know Charli as a certified nurse midwife who for 10 years "caught" babies in the Atlanta Metro area. Since 1999 she has had a private practice in Decatur in mind/body medicine that includes aspects of all the things she knows about health and healing.

Charli is known as a great cook. Her love of cooking started early in her life on a dairy farm in Michigan where she showed her cows at the Fowlerville Fair and won the Grand Champion 4-H ribbon for her bread. Charli relates, "I love to cook and do anything you can do in a kitchen, baking bread, making soup, exploring ethnic foods, making herbal medicine, bath salts, massage oil, jelly, canning vegetables, and fruits ... basically anything that can be created in a kitchen. I first learned about fresh food from our vegetable garden and the fresh fruits grown in the area. My very first job was picking strawberries for a nearby farmer. We were paid seven cents a quart."

Charli extended her reach to the public when she started her radio program, *Beyond the Measuring Cup*, where she has interviewed a wide ranging group of people from pig and dairy farmers, to chefs, and activists in the slow food movement.

Culinary Confessions with Kim and Don on KXAM 1310, Phoenix, Arizona, soon to syndicate nationally.

Theme: Food and restaurant game show. We do food trivia, guess the movie bite (I record food quotes from movies), taste of music (we play a cut from a song and they guess the song with a food word in the title). We also have our mystery food of the day; we give hints as the show goes on. We give away lots of prizes. It's a lot of fun for the whole family.

Guest Profile: Chefs, cookbook authors, new food products. Someone who is topical and entertaining. Past interview experiences and credentials are important, sound of their voice less so. If they have had experience that is helpful, we can pull anyone out of their shell. We help our guests shine.

Guest from Hell: Guests with one word answers or whose English is difficult to decipher.

Contact: kim@kxam.com; 480-423-1310; http://www.kimanddon.com or http://www.culinaryconfessions.com; If you have a great kitchen tip or wish to contribute one, visit http://www.culinaryconfessions.com/tidbits-kitchenTips.html; Kim. Best method: Please send a press kit, review copies and e-mail. No response? Always feel free to e-mail again.

Invited Back? Guests are invited back if they have anything new to share (new book, experience etc.) or if the time slot was too short and we couldn't get enough, then we will book Part 2.

Bios of Kim Laurie and Donald Sandler: Kim was born and raised in New Jersey; her dad sat on the board of Restaurant Associates so her passion for food began at an early age. She got her BS in special education which brought her to Boston, where she practiced as a special needs teacher, owned her own crafts business and became a business broker.

Along with being a proud mom, in 1985 Kim found her dream job hosting two TV shows, an interview show and a cooking show with chefs from around the country. Kim got to cook and interview the best; Emeril Lagasse was no stranger on Kim's show. After 5 years, Kim pitched her idea for a radio show to Don, who owned a station in the Boston area. It was a match in many ways and she began hosting a popular daily morning magazine-style radio show featuring various topics including food, of course.

Donald grew up in the Boston area and was born with a passion for radio. He graduated from Emerson College with a BS in mass communications, and later got his degree in special education and taught for a short time.

Pursuing his dream of a radio career, he worked as a DJ, sports talk show host, and even hosted a reggae show. He also excelled in radio sales. When an opportunity arose, Don took a gamble and bought a defunct radio station that he started from scratch. He turned it into a successful talk station which he sold 10 years later after he moved to Arizona. Don is also the station manager at KXAM.

It was 1996 when the weather drove Kim and Don to Arizona. When they arrived in Scottsdale they saw so many restaurants. "How do you know what is good," they asked? This sparked the concept for *Dial to Dine*. Kim and Don bought radio time on Sundays at KXAM and sold their own advertising. The idea was, the listeners who have lived here a while would be the food critics. They would call in and make recommendations while new residents could call in for advice. Everyone loves to answer trivia, and with a friendly caring attitude, the listeners become part of the Culinary Confessions family. After 5 years it became a daily show and changed the name to *Culinary Confessions*. The show just celebrated 11 years on the air, the longest continually-running food and restaurant show in the Valley.

The Curious Cook on Tastebuds Food Show with Beci Falkenberg on 1620 AM Radio Sandy Springs, Tuesdays, 11 AM–12 PM (ET) http://www.radiosandysprings.com to listen or hear archived podcasts; now off the air.

Theme: Food and cooking.

Guest Profile: Cookbook authors, chefs, culinary experts, food writers and anyone with an interesting involvement with food. I look for articulate and interesting people in the food world who can entertain and inform about the world of food. I want to know about past interview experiences, credentials, sound of their voice and their background — why they have something unique and compelling to teach us about food, cooking, and dining.

Guest from Hell: A guest from hell would be one that is monotone, inarticulate, unprepared, or talks excessively instead of getting to the point.

Contact: becif@aol.com; 770-604-9806; http://radiosandysprings.com/tastebudsbeci.php; Beci Falkenberg. Best method: E-mail. No response? Call me.

Invited Back? A guest is invited back if they are knowledgeable, entertaining, easy to interview, and an authority in their field.

Bio of Beci Falkenberg: Beci grew up working in the family restaurant business, assisted in cooking schools, took specialized courses at major culinary schools, freelanced as a food and travel writer, and has hosted a weekly radio food show since Dec. 2005.

Deconstructing Dinner with Jon Steinman on CJLY, aired on 25 Canadian stations, 8 American, Podcast (http://www.cjly.net/deconstructingdinner/listenlive.htm)

Theme: The impacts our food choices have on ourselves, our communities and the planet.

Guest Profile: Authors, university research, corporate, food activists, environmentalists, health professionals, government, small business, farmers, unions.

We've never chosen a guest based on ability to speak or present. If we recognize that an individual retains important content for our program, we bring them on. It's for this reason we pre-record all interviews, so that any guests who may not be so comfortable on radio, can end up sounding great. It's often us who go out and research our guests, but when approached, we appreciate potential guests exhibiting adequate knowledge of our program and an agenda of what the guest is most interested to speak of.

Guest from Hell: While not so much a guest from hell, we do cringe when guests continually try to be politically correct. Our form of media provides a space for uncensored and objective opinion.

Contact: deconstructingdinner@cjly.net; 250-352-9600; http://www.cjly.net/deconstructingdinner; Jon Steinman. Best method: A pitch, a bio and a press kit are always the most efficient tools to get our attention, but links to this and other relevant information on the web is just as effective. No response? We are often more accommodating to persistent approaches from guests. Our program was founded upon the idea of being a voice for those with something to share in the realm of how our food choices impact ourselves, our communities and our planet. Both e-mail and phone are effective, but phone is often an easier way to get a more prompt response.

Invited Back? It's ultimately our content that determines whether we invite a guest back. We can admit that those guests who require little editing are often at the top of the list.

Guest Comments: "I just wanted you to know that I've received a wonderful response on our interview. I never listen to anything I've done (I find it too painful!), but I've had such wonderful comments on it. In fact, I just talked to a young woman from Vancouver who is visiting Seattle this weekend and coming to some of the Phinney EcoVillage events. Thanks again" — Cecile Andrews, author of *Slow Is Beautiful* (New Society Publishers 2006)

"It was incredible to understand what was happening when I realized the whole hour program was focused on me. It has been very helpful to me to hear how you describe and understand what I am trying to do. I am stunned at the amount of attention you gave to me, and have spread your creation to as many people as possible. Your program helped me to reflect on what it is I do and how it is received by the public." — Maria Solakofski, Guerrilla Gourmet

Bio of Jon Steinman: Getting his radio start as a CJLY technical operator and host for *Nelson Before Nine* in the winter of 2004/2005, Jon was opened up to the potential of radio as a powerful medium by which to disseminate information. After spending almost two years in the Niagara region of southern Ontario, and one year biking through and living in France, Jon arrived in British Columbia in 2004. Exposed to the world of food while studying at the University of Guelph, Jon believes food takes precedence over every facet of our lives, and that we owe it to this planet and each other to fully understand the implications of our food choices.

Jon is no stranger to publicly sharing his views on food and drink. While maintaining a column in St. Catharines, Ontario–based *PULSE Niagara*, Jon focused his writing on the exposition of independent and family-operated producers and retailers. After being re-published in two other southern Ontario publications, Jon extended his writing to Vernon, BC based *Off-Centre Magazine.*

He currently sits on the board of the Kootenay Country Store Co-operative. He has become involved in the creation of Community Food Matters—a coalition of Nelson-area residents who are inspired to foster a more food-secure community.

Dr. Tea! Show with Dr. Tea on http://www.healthy life.net

Theme: The importance of tea and how to incorporate it into your everyday day life through proper preparation of a cup of tea, *The Ultimate Tea Diet*, cooking with tea, frozen tea drinks, tea in beauty products and more.

Guest Profile: Anyone with a love of tea and can offer listeners breakthrough ways to explore a healthy mind, body and spirit. Knowledge of their respective profession and also share some thoughts about tea in their lives. A brief background on their subject of choice and contact info are needed.

Guest from Hell: Never have any. There is always something positive that comes out of every interview.

Contact: drtea@teagarden.com; 310-948-9779; http://www.teagarden.com; Angee Jenkins at angee@ ajenkinspr.com. Best method: E-mail. No response? Call Angee at that point at 661-297-0009.

Invited Back? Always asked back if there is a slot open for them and they e-mail us their request to do so.

Bio of Dr. Tea, a.k.a. Mark Ukra: Mark and his wife, Julie, bought the Tea Garden and Herbal Emporium in West Hollywood (founded in 1988), approximately a year ago. The doc, who comes from a family of Middle Eastern tea merchants dating back 400 years, still travels the globe to different tea houses and farms, bringing back specimens to share at his store.

Mark was dubbed "doctor" by a group of tea-tasting toddlers who once visited the Emporium, where he and his wife are dedicated to "bestowing knowledge" about tea's health benefits each day.

Dr. Tea calls the Emporium "similar to the Cheers bar but with tea," as health-minded barflies come for conversation, some slightly less caffeinated inner peace, or just a spot of tea-and-quiet. One-on-one or in the dozens, he hopes to provide this coffee-crazed city with just a little bit of Zen.

Ed Hitzel's Radio Show with Ed Hitzel, aired Saturday morning, 10 A.M. to 1 p.m., on NewsTalk WOND 1400 AM in Atlantic City, Cape May, Long Beach Sound in South Jersey, and WVLT 92.1 FM, Vineland, Cherry Hill, Wilmington, Delaware, and Philadelphia, Pa and on http://www.wond1400am. com and http://www.edhitzel.com

Theme: Restaurants, travel, hospitality.

Guest Profile: Representatives of the above industries with personality, confidence and accomplishments. Click "Radio Guests" at the top of the site for a sampling of current guests.

Guest from Hell: Someone who has nothing to say. Someone who cancels at the last minute; http:// www.edhitzel.com

Contact: edhitzel@earthlink.net; 609-909-9755; Ed Hitzel. Best method: E-mail. Make sure the tagline on the e-mail is explanatory and brief. The e-mail could be pithy and helpful, but if the tagline is vague or inaccurate, the person being mailed will move on or delete. No response? E-mail or call. Some things slip through the cracks, although e-mail is more efficient.

Invited Back? My reaction and audience reaction.

Bio of Ed Hitzel: Ed reviewed restaurants for *The Press* of Atlantic City for 16 years and publishes two publications and is seen on the NBC affiliate in Atlantic City.

Ed Hitzel's Restaurant Newsletter features honest restaurant reviews and restaurant news and is available by subscription.

Ed Hitzel's Restaurant Magazine, available free in restaurants throughout southern New Jersey and by subscription, features hundreds of capsule reviews of area restaurants, columnists and features.

Food Chain Radio with Michael Olson heard on radio stations throughout the U.S. and on http:// www.metrofarm.com/mf_affiliate_web.php

Theme: What's eating what up and down the food chain.

Guest Profile: Those who can tell good stories well. I look for conflict in the food chain, and for those who can do a good job of describing the elements of that conflict. I do not take a position on these conflicts, but I expect my guests to do so. I want to know if [guests] are real.

For past guests, go to http://metrofarm.com/mf_ Food_Chain_Radio.php

Guest from Hell: Someone who is afraid to speak their mind.

Contact: michaelo@metrofarm.com; http://www. metrofarm.com; 831-475-1080. Best method: E-mail a pitch no longer than one paragraph defining the story and their position on that story. No response? I try to respond to all pitches, though sometimes I do not, for one reason or another. If you have a good story and can tell it well, keep trying.

Invited Back? In the 548 editions of *The Food Chain*, I have invited only half dozen back, and they were special ... very special.

Bio of Michael Keith Olson: Michael is an agriculturalist and journalist. He has produced, written, and photographed news for the *San Francisco Chronicle* and *Examiner* newspapers, NBC, ABC, the Australian Broadcast Commission, and KQED Public Television.

He is the executive producer and host of his syndicated talk show and is currently president of the MO MultiMedia Group in Santa Cruz, California, where he lives with his family.

His father, Robert "Pat" Olson, served aboard the USS *Dale* from 1942 to 1945, and Michael's latest book is *Tales from a Tin Can: The USS Dale from Pearl Harbor to Tokyo Bay* (Zenith Press 2007) http://tincan.us/author-contact.php. His previous book, *Metro Farm: The Guide to Growing for Big Profit on a Small Parcel of Land* (Ts Books 2004), is a PMA Ben Franklin Book-of-the-Year award winner.

The Good Food Hour with John Ash and Steve Garner, Saturday from 11 AM to Noon (PT), on KSRO 1350 AM, Santa Rosa, CA.

Theme: Anything to do with food and wine.

Guest Profile: Authors, farmers, historians, ethnic home cooks, growers and producers. Someone who has a unique point of view or is doing something interesting in the food and wine world. Since we've been on the air for more than 20 years, food and wine authors who are visiting the San Francisco Bay area usually get booked with us if time allows. We are interested in those who have stories, have a point of view and something unique to share. Big list guests include national celebs like Jacques Pepin, Pam Anderson, James Peterson, Peter Reinhart, all winners of James Beard and/or IACP awards.

Guest from Hell: Someone who is only there to pump a book.

Contact: chefash1@aol.com; 707-544-2029; http://www.chefjohnash.com, http://www.ksro.com; http://www.sauvignonrepublic.com; John Ash. Best method: E-mail a press release if one is available or a brief pitch. No response? E-mail one more time.

Invited Back? New book or activity.

Bio of Chef John Ash: John first came to national prominence when he was selected by *Food and Wine* magazine as one of America's "Hot New Chefs." He founded his restaurant, John Ash and Company, in Northern California's wine country in 1980 and it continues to be critically acclaimed more than 28 years later.

Nationally renowned as a wine and food educator, John served for many years as the culinary director for Fetzer and Bonterra Vineyards. He is on the faculty of the Professional Wine Studies Program at the CIA Greystone. He is also the chair of a new program there for home cooks called The Sophisticated Palate. He travels widely teaching to both home and professional cooks.

His new winery venture, Sauvignon Republic Cellars, specializes in Sauvignon Blanc only, produced around the world.

John is author of *John Ash Cooking One-on-One: Private Lessons in Simple, Contemporary Food from a Master Teacher* (Clarkson Potter 2004), winner of the 2005 James Beard award; *From the Earth to the Table: John Ash's Wine Country Cuisine* (Chronicle Books 2007), a completely revised and updated version of *From the Earth to the Table* in 2007 and awarded the IACP awards for Best American Cookbook and the Julia Child Cookbook of the Year, and American Game Cooking (Addison Wesley Publishing Company 1993).

John writes periodically for the *Los Angeles Times/Tribune Syndicate* and is an occasional contributor to publications such as *Eating Well* and *Fine Cooking* magazines.

He was featured for two years on the Food Network and has co-hosted a live food and wine radio talk show on KSRO in Northern California for the past 21 years. A passionate voice on sustainable food issues, John has served on the Board of Overseers for the Chef's Collaborative and the Board of Advisors of Seafood Watch, an educational initiative for sustainable seafood by the Monterey Bay Aquarium.

In April of 2008, he was voted "Cooking School Teacher of the Year" by the International Association of Culinary Professionals at their annual gathering in New Orleans.

The Good Life with Guy Bower on KNSS 1330 AM, Wichita, KS aired Saturdays, 9–10:00 AM.

Theme: Food, wine and fun for your ears.

Guest Profile: Winemakers, cookbook authors, chefs, anyone on the cutting edge of food and wine production, education and enjoyment. Enthusiasm about subject, knowledge, and willingness to talk — yet aware of time constraints of a 1 hour program. Someone who is FUN to talk to and for my listeners to listen to, and conveys an interesting story. I like to establish a friendly relationship with a pre-interview chat. I determine by that how much time to allot and have a good idea of potential success of a future interview.

Guest from Hell: Opposite of number 1 above. Someone who is too busy to commit to an interview, or is a no-show on the day of the interview. (Most of my interviews are by phone and guests receive an e-mail/phone reminder two days prior.)

Contact: guy@goodlifeguy.com; 888-788-WINE; http://www.goodlifeguy.com; Guy Bower. Best method: E-mail topical info about the potential subject or send a press kit. Detailed press kit with good info and suggested questions is always a help … might not use the questions, but it shows forethought. No response? I respond if I am interested.

Invited Back? A good previous interview and a new story, a new wine, a new book published, etc.

Guest Comments: "I thoroughly enjoyed our interview — you are good, very good and your show is great fun!" — Melanie Barnard, cookbook author, food consultant

"Your uncomplicated manner of conducting your interview was a great help in putting me at ease and helped me to convey Gallo's message about our super-premium wines. I am in total agreement with your philosophy of food and wine enjoyment from the 'every-man' perspective. We wish you all the best!"—George Thoukis, Ph.D., V.P.—senior winemaster, E & J Gallo Winery

Bio of Guy Bower: Guy is a retired Air Force fighter pilot and currently a FedEx captain flying Airbus A300's. Throughout his military career, which involved many years living and traveling in Europe, he has been a dedicated food and wine enthusiast and home chef.

He regularly attends major national wine events, seminars and tastings as enthusiast, participant and also judges at the Annual Jerry Mead's New World International Wine Competition, and the Denver Food and Wine Fest. He has authored many articles on the enjoyment of food, wine and the "Good Life"—and is called on often to share his knowledge and enthusiasm with wine appreciation classes, waitstaff training, and educational tastings and seminars. He teaches a basic and advanced wine class at Wichita State University each semester.

The Good Life radio program began in Miami in 1988 on WKAT 1360AM. In 1990 a military move to Kansas brought the show to the Midwest.

In 1992, Guy founded the Wichita Chapter of the American Institute of Wine and Food and was chairman for the first three years. He was actively involved in starting the Midwest Winefest and the Midwest Beerfest in Wichita, and remains an integral part of both great events.

"Good Life Guy" truly lives the good life and enjoys sharing his enthusiasm through his radio program and wine education classes.

GrapeRadio with Brian Clark, Eric Anderson and Jay Selman. The show is a podcast and new shows are posted every Monday morning.

Theme: Wine education.

Guest Profile: Winemakers, vineyard owners, magazine editors, authors, restaurateurs, sommeliers, critics, etc. Great personality with a great personal story; most guests have gone through long struggles to get to where they are today and we love to hear about it. We want to know all about their credentials in winemaking; also geographic viticulture region they represent is very important since wine place and origin is a big factor in wine. Past interview experience is very important since it is very evident in the quality of their responses.

Guest from Hell: Foreign (French, Spanish, Italian, etc.) guests are often difficult since English is a second language. It usually adds hours to editing files.

Contact: brian@graperadio.com; 714-883-2720; http://www.graperadio.com; Brian Clark. Best method: E-mail or phone. We get it all; we receive over 25 requests a week for interviews. They all work equally well—it really boils down to what kind of story/angle we are looking for at the time and what would be the most interesting to our listeners. No response? I think they should keep trying if they feel it is important. We try to respond to most requests.

Invited Back? Feedback from listeners is the single biggest factor.

Guest Comments: "As a writer, I find it challenging to convey my enthusiasm for my subject matter (Pinot Noir). But the first time I sat down behind a mic at *GrapeRadio*, I felt this surge of pent-up passion come pouring out. It was an ebullient experience to say the least and now I am hooked. The friendly and unpretentious *GrapeRadio* gang welcomed me into their clubhouse and now they will have trouble shutting me up."—Prince of Pinot, http://www.princeofpinot.com

Bio of Brian Clark: A business owner and entrepreneur, Brian discovered his passion for wine on a trip to Napa in 1995. Over the last 10 years, his enthusiasm for wine has only increased. His preference includes mostly red wines from California (Napa and Paso Robles areas), Australia, Spain and France.

In 2004, *GrapeRadio* was founded to promote Brian's love of wine. In 2006, the show was selected as "Podcast of the Year" and is currently nominated for the coveted James Beard Award. *GrapeRadio* has been featured on CNN and Slate.com and in *The New York Times, Business Week, Food and Wine Magazine*.

Brian also spends a great deal of time volunteering in his local community. When called upon on serves the Orange County Sheriff's Department Search and Rescue Team. Additionally, Brian co-founded the charity Share Our Wine Foundation to raise money for abused and neglected children. He also serves as an Executive Board Member for the Child Guidance Center.

Grapevine Radio with Cliff Stepp and Jan Manni on KVEC 920AM, aired in San Luis Obispo County and Northern Santa Barbara County, Ca., Saturdays at noon and on http://www.grapevineradio.net; now off the air.

Theme: Interviews with winemakers, chefs and event organizers from the third largest and fastest growing wine region in California and thereby, the U.S. Guests who are fun and interesting and have credentials ... everything else is of minor importance.

Guest Profile: Winemakers, chefs, caterers, grape growers, micro brewers, olive oil and cheese and artisan bread producers.

Guest from Hell: Answers questions with yes or no or doesn't bring any wine to studio (LOL).

Contact: cliff@grapevineradio.net; 805-440-7129; http://www.grapevineradio.net. Best method: E-mail with a personal note. No response? E-mail or call.

Invited Back? Our booking commitments and if they have something truly new that's of interest to our listeners.

Bio of Cliff Stepp: Cliff has been a home winemaker since 1977. His work in marketing and advertising brought him into contact with San Luis Obispo's fledgling wine industry in the early eighties.

During the creation of a "touring and tasting map" of SLO County, a group of six Paso Robles wineries asked him for help in designing a cohesive marketing program financed with their pooled resources. Soon after the first print and TV campaign launched the group, it grew to 24 wineries. This was the beginning of the area's first wine industry trade association, the Paso Robles Vintners and Growers Association (now the Paso Robles Wine Country Alliance).

During this time Cliff created the first "Wine Tasting Passport" program in the state of California, helped launch the spring and fall wine events in Paso Robles, and conceived of the mileage marker signs now seen at nearly every tasting room in the County.

He has a long history in marketing and has created award winning campaigns for clients as diverse as restaurants, Proctor and Gamble, Valvoline, gourmet baked goods, recording artists and hardware stores.

Cliff is also credited with writing songs that were produced by B. B. King and a tune that was recorded by the Pure Prairie League and various bluegrass groups. He is often seen performing at winery events as a solo artist, trio or his full band, The Cliffnotes.

During the past 15 years he has hosted several different radio shows featuring wine makers, chefs and special event coordinators. Cliff was also the media coordinator and MC for the Winery Music Awards series of events in Paso Robles, which highlighted primarily local talent judged by major music industry figures.

Cliff is currently the resident Marketing Genius at S. Lombardi and Associates and heads up their Wine Marketing Services Division.

Bio of Jan Mann: She is a certified sommelier and owns The Wine Attic in Paso Robles, GA.

Judy a la Carte with Judy Gilliard on 1110 KFAB, Omaha, Neb.

Theme: Food and entertaining.

Guest Profile: Chefs, food writers, restaurateurs who are known for their food or entertaining expertise.

Guest from Hell: Someone who does not know their subject.

Contact: judy@judyalacarte.com; 402-884-2248; http://www.cookwithjudy.com and http://www.kfab.com/pages/judyalacarte-new.html; Judy Gilliard. Best method: E-mail a pitch, and two copies of latest cookbook, or feature, bio and/or press kit. No response? E-mail.

Invited Back? If they are engaging and know their subject, fast on their feet and have a sense of humor.

Bio of Judy Gilliard: Judy grew up in the restaurant business in Ventura, California. She is a graduate from the Santa Barbara School of Culinary Arts and Hotel Management. Her approachable style easily inspires the home cook to prepare quick and simple meals. Judy has authored ten cookbooks focusing on food for the healthy lifestyle, written a monthly feature about entertaining on emerils.com, and reaches thousands of people each week on her live radio show, *Judy a la Carte*. Broadcast on the Heritage Midwest radio station News Radio 1110 KFAB, *Judy a la Carte* reaches into five states via the airwaves and into homes around the world via the internet. In her radio show, television appearances, cooking classes, and speaking engagements, her main focus has always been and continues to be the pleasure of the table with friends and family.

Life Bites News with Bonnie Carroll on CRN-Radio; Bonnie does remote broadcasts from different travel destinations, so show is not scheduled on CRN.

Theme: Food/travel/lifestyle.

Guest Profile: Chefs/food writers/wine experts/travel specialists. Latest information on a specific topic. Someone with a passion for their field of expertise, and with the ability to be interesting on air. Expertise, experience, credentials, interesting data available for interview questions, do they speak English? Guests have included Shelley Kakuna, director of the Kannapali Beach Resort Association, Maui, Hawaii, and Patrick Terrail, chef, author, and former owner Ma Maison, Beverly Hills, CA.

Guest from Hell: A guest who cannot answer questions thoroughly and creates long lapses in the show, or someone who insists on trying to turn the interview into a commercial for their product or services.

Contact: writebc@aol.com; 805-845-4214; http://www.lifebitesnews.com; Bonnie Carroll. Best method: E-mails or a press kit. I will call them if it is a win-win. No response? E-mail me again, but I do respond.

Invited Back? Their easiness in answering questions, sense of humor, audience perception as likable and interesting. Just an enjoyable person to talk to.

Bio of Bonnie Carroll: Bonnie has been a food, beverage, travel and health writer for more than 20 years.

Mouthful (The Wine Country's Most Delicious Hour) with Michele Anna Jordan on KRCB-FM 90.9 and 91.1 FM in Sonoma County, California. Michele also hosts a music show, *Red Shoes Rodeo*, on alternating Friday nights and produces specials for the radio station.

Theme: Food, wine, agriculture and its preservation.

Guest Profile: People with good stories to tell. I look for authenticity, a good story, warmth, excitement, a lack of too much self-promotion, lack of salesmanship. I want someone genuinely interested in what they do, not just what they sell. I want to know their story and why they are telling it. Credentials within their field are good, too. Interview experience is not necessary. Media training is usually a bad thing. Recent guests included Alice Waters, Jacques Pepin and Julia Child, Mollie Katzen, and B. Smith.

Guest from Hell: The guest who gives one-word answers is the worst. I've had the occasional rude guest, too, which is a nightmare.

Contact: catsmilk@sonic.net or mouthful@micheleannajordan.com; 707-823-8154; http://www.krcb.org; Michele Anna Jordan. Best method: A short e-mail telling me who they are and when they will be in the area is best. Ask if I want anything else and I'll let them know. If this is a book tour, please send two copies before calling, if possible. It's nice to see the book first. No response? Check that the address is correct. If it is, send a second e-mail with a brief polite query explaining that you never know with e-mail, that you don't like to assume it's arrived and that you're just checking. I'd probably let it go at that unless you are very familiar with me.

Invited Back? Geography; topicality, more to tell. If the show moves along well and the guest is available, there is a good chance of being invited back.

Bio of Michele Anna Jordan: A second-generation Californian who has lived in the San Francisco Area her entire life, Michele possesses a unique blend of talents. A chef as well as a writer, she brings a solid culinary background to her work. During her 12 years as a working chef, she received numerous awards, yet in the early 1990s she changed her professional focus to her first love, writing.

Michele's first five books were published by Addison-Wesley Publishing Co. The first, *A Cook's Tour of Sonoma* (1990), received wide critical acclaim for its celebration of the agricultural bounty of Sonoma County. Her second book, *The New Cook's Tour of Sonoma* (2000), contains 150 new recipes, an in-depth look at Sonoma viticulture, and an exploration of both the region's history and its future. Her ninth book, *California Home Cooking* (Harvard Common Press 1997) was a finalist in the 1998 Julia Child Cookbook Awards and was voted Best Cookbook in the 1998 Small Press Awards.

Michele launched *Mouthful*, in 1995, which was nominated for a 1998, 2003 and 2004 James Beard Electronic Journalism Award.

Raw Inspirations Radio (also ***Visionary Culture Radio*** and ***Music of Awakening***), all hosted by Laura Fox. Schedule on Blog Talk Radio at http://web.me.com/lighteningblossom/site/visionary_culture_radio.html

Theme: Raw and living foods, conscious living, eco and sustainable technologies, sustainable solutions to global challenges, high vibrational living, personal activation and empowerment.

Guest Profile: Raw and living foods leaders, conscious entrepreneurs, people who are making a difference in the world — making a difference on conscious living, sustainability and global solutions from a high vibrational, positive viewpoint. People who are intelligent, thoughtful, heartful and wanting to bring greater clarity to issues of global awakening, ecological solutions and raw and living foods from a genuine, integrous, "dharmic" place of true world service. Radio experience and credentials are great and not necessarily necessary if the person is up to new things and thinking/working to bring change.

Guest from Hell: Argumentative, egotistical, wanting to sell their own agenda without consideration for the conversation.

Contact: laura@rawinspirations.com; Withheld upon request; http://www.rawspirit.com; http://www.rawinspirations.com; Laura Fox. Best method: E-mail only only only if there is some connection to raw foods, sustainable solutions to global challenges and the raw spirit festival. No response? If I don't answer e-mail once, a second one is okay but no more than that. Sometimes I get 600 e-mails.

Invited Back? Fun, upbeat to talk with, movement forward, positive feedback from listeners.

Bio of Laura Fox: Laura is the former director of sales and marketing for the Raw Spirit Festival, held in September or October in Sedona, Arizona.

A certified practitioner of traditional Thai Yoga massage and a Reiki master and originator of Manna touch healing, Laura is also a raw gourmet chef who regularly teaches classes on adding more raw food to the diet in gourmet ways. Her free monthly e-zine *Raw Inspirations* offers helpful hints, articles and interviews to help people achieve their raw and living foods goals. Her life is focused on service that soothes the spirit and brings a high vibration of health and well-being.

She is the author of *Return to Center, That Address Now Known* (1994–out of print), *Anchoring the New Dream of Earth: Visionary Stewardship for Planetary Transformation* (Audio CD 2005), and two e-books, *Dream It Now!* and *Raw Inspirations*.

She is producing a film, "Visionary Stewardship," with partners Jeffrey Hagerman and Martin Verigin, the creative forces behind Footage Entertainment. Laura enjoys writing esoteric-spiritual-transformative poetry and will be releasing her poems in an audio book with original music composed by collaborators.

Seattle Kitchen (now ***In the Kitchen with Tom and Thierry***) with Tom (Douglas) and Thierry (Rautureau) on KIRO 710 AM.

Theme: Food.

Guest Profile: Cooks and authors welcome, especially cookbook authors, food historians, food researchers and educators. Someone who can speak passionately and informatively about food and cooking. We often pre-interview.

Guest from Hell: Someone unable to elaborate or engage in a conversation.

Contact: thierry@rovers-seattle.com; withheld upon request; http://www.kiro710.com; http://www.tomdouglas.com/radio; Amy Pennington at amyp@tomdouglas.com. Best method: E-mailing their idea for a topic, along with a bio. No response? E-mail is best.

Invited Back? If everyone enjoyed themselves and if they bring a good topic to our attention.

Bio of Tom Douglas: Five of Seattle's most remarkable restaurants are owned and operated by Northwest chef Tom Douglas and his wife and business partner, Jackie Cross. The latest addition is Serious Pie.

A Delaware native, Tom started cooking at the Hotel DuPont in Wilmington, Delaware, before heading west to Seattle in 1977. From house building to wine selling to railroad car repair, he tried his hand at several jobs before making the obvious career choice of the restaurant business. Never having attended a culinary school, Tom's cooking knowledge has come mostly from dining out across America and Asia, using his "taste memory" to recreate and develop recipes in his own style.

He won the James Beard Association Award for Best Northwest Chef in 1994 and in 1996, his restaurant, The Palace Kitchen, was nominated by the James Beard Foundation as one of the country's best new restaurants.

Tom is author of several cookbooks, all published by Morrow Cookbooks: *Tom Douglas' Seattle Kitchen* (2000), named Best American Cookbook by the James Beard Foundation in 2001; *Tom's Big Dinners* (2003); and *I Love Crabcakes* (2006).

Bio of Thierry Rautureau: Hailing from the Muscadet region of France, Thierry is the James Beard Award–winning chef and owner of Rover's Restaurant since 1987. Raised on a farm, Thierry helped his mother prepare meals for the family. From an early age he learned to appreciate seasonal cooking and utilizing fresh, homegrown ingredients.

Known as the Chef in the Hat due to his ever-present fedora, Thierry began a cooking apprenticeship in Anjou, France, at age 14 and from there continued on a culinary Tour de France, training in the cities of Le Mont Saint Michel in Normandy, Chamonix in the French Alps, and Hendaye in the Pays Basque.

Table Talk with Jo McGarry on Saturday, 10–11 AM, on KHVH 830 AM, Honolulu. Podcasts are available at http://www.wineanddinehawaii.com

Theme: Lifestyle.

Guest Profile: Foodies, winemakers, chefs, restaurant owners. Lively, good subject knowledge, interesting topic. Guests have included Roy Yamaguchi, Elia Abroumad, and the chef for the Lakers basketball team.

Guest from Hell: Monosyllabic.

Contact: tabletalk@hawaii.rr.com; 808-783-1060; http://www.wineanddinehawaii.com; Jo. Best method: E-mail a bio or pitch. No response? E-mail.

Invited Back? Call-ins and e-mails determine how popular a subject or guest is.

Bio of Jo McGarry: Jo has been writing about food and wine for more than a decade in Hawaii. Former editor of *Gusto Magazine*, she began working as restaurant specialist for the *Honolulu Star Bulletin* in 2001 and writing a food column for *MidWeek* the same year. For seven years she hosted a daily radio show devoted to the pursuit of excellent food and wine and the promotion of local restaurants and chefs.

Local produce is a passion. She has been an advocate for farmers and for local produce for years through her radio work and writing both for local publications and mainland magazines. She is also known as "the voice of tailgating" bringing the pregame tailgate show to thousands of devoted UH fans during football season. Author of the successful *Hawaii Tailgate Cookbook* (Watermark Publishing 2004), Jo knows local food and the people who prepare it — as well as anyone in Hawaii.

She was born and raised in St. Andrews, Scotland, and spent her formative years in Edinburgh where she maintained a home until recently. She is a freelance writer, a musician, a single malt scotch enthusiast and a mom.

Her food columns in *MidWeek* (Wednesday) and *MidWeek* (weekend) and the *Honolulu Star Bulletin* reach more than 400,000 people each week. She lives in Honolulu with her husband, sportscaster Bobby Curran and their son Max.

The Urban Herbalist with Marguerite Dunne on 1110 AM, WTBQ.com, airing in Orange County, NY, and Northern New Jersey, on Saturdays at 7 AM (ET).

Theme: The medicinal use of herbs, scientific studies, health food stores 101, allopathic medicine countermoves, and all of the shenanigans in the alternative health industry.

Guest Profile: Industry experts and interesting authors. *The Urban Herbalist* is NOT an infomercial; no canned pitches. If someone can discuss a health issue or provide news, we can discuss it. Every guest has written a book or does represent a company, but the guest MUST be able to have a discussion, not recite a pre-written public relations paragraph. We do want to know their credentials. We also want the person to tell how the "average" listener can start using this information/product himself or herself at home. In other words, it's not about how someone has to see an expert.

Guest from Hell: A guest from hell sounds phony. One of our worst guests claimed she could discuss "all-natural" facial care, and in the middle of the show, pitched Botox treatments.

Contact: mdunne@hvc.rr.com; 845-534-8971; http://www.herbs-on-hudson.com; Marguerite Dunne. Best method: E-mail a bio, call with a pitch, send a press kit. No response? Do not call or e-mail.

Invited Back? Guests are invited back if they sound natural and well-informed.

Bio of Marguerite Dunne: While practicing as a

medicinal herbalist for the past 30 years, Marguerite also earned a BA in sociology/English, a double master's degree in education, and certification in herbology. She has lectured, written articles, and made media appearances.

This clinical herbalist has a consultation practice in Cornwall-on-Hudson, New York, and New York City. Marguerite is also profiled as the featured herbalist in the recently published book, *The New Healers* (Vista Publications) by Dr. Barbara Stevens Barnum.

Vegan Radio with Derek Goodwin, Megan Shackelford, and Scott Lahteine on ValleyFree Radio WXOJ-LP 103.3 FM in Northampton, MA, on alternate Thursdays at noon.

Theme: Vegan culture — news, interviews, music.

Guest Profile: We mostly interview interesting vegans, or vegan activists. Sometimes we have celebrities who are vegetarians or local people who are doing cool things that are environmentally sustainable. Mostly credentials are important.

Guest from Hell: Our show tries to have a sense of humor, so when people are too serious or have monotone voices and talk too much it is difficult, but we have never had anyone I would consider a guest from hell.

Contact: veganradio@mac.com; 413-320-1001; http://veganradio.com; Derek Goodwin. Best method: E-mail. No response? E-mail again, or, if it is time sensitive, then call.

Invited Back? If they are fun, or if they are our friends.

Listener Comments: "A few months ago, I typed 'animal rights' into iTunes and came up with your show. Having become vegan in recent months, and being surrounded by meat eaters as I am, it has been a wonderful support to have your friendly voices talk to me through my computer. It has been such a heart-warming relief, as I have often felt very lonely in my endeavors. Luckily, my partner has been a great support as well and has followed suit. By the way, I live in Australia, so you really are reaching out there."— Jane

"I just discovered your Vegan radio widget and Loooooove it! It's so great to be able to get great quality veggie radio any time I want. Melbourne is a pretty vegan friendly city, but we don't yet have a dedicated radio show. Keep up the great work." — Jenn

Bios of Megan Shackelford, Derek Goodwin and Scott Lahteine: Megan is from Oh Sweet Mama's Vegan Bakery; Derek is creator of Veganica and the Vegan Bus Project, and Scott is the resident renaissance geek.

Wine and Dine Radio with Lynn Krielow Chamberlain aired on iTunes Radio Talk Directory, Live 365, VinVillageRadio (www.vinvillage.com), http://WSRadio.com, www.broadcast.com and http://www.WineandDineRadio.com. Wine and Dine Moment is a short daily feature available to radio stations, affiliates, and media broadcasters.

Theme: News, facts, public policy, lifestyle and personal conversations about wine and food. *Wine and Dine Radio* supports the continuing education, appreciation, and healthy-use of wine, in addition to the economic, public affairs, and cultural impact of wine and grape growing on people and their communities worldwide.

Guest Profile: Winemakers, winegrowers, chefs, authors, public policy makers, newsmakers, trendsetters, fashionistas, politicians, educators, commentators, scientists, environmentalists, organic and biodynamic activists, attorneys, historians, travel hosts, auctioneers, columnists, brokers, culturalists, bloggers, photographers, architects, philosophers, economists, culturalists, health leaders, religious commentators, personal stories and journeys about wine and food that touch everyone's lives bringing the world community full-circle ... any subject that I can weave into a conversation about wine. I look for guests that bring the who, what, where, when, how and why of anything directly or remotely, subtly or overtly, of influence or interest, in or to, the world-wide wine consumer, with factual information, timely news, entertainment, inspiration, enlightenment, sensory perception, expert opinion ... that will appeal to as wide an audience as humanely tangible. A guest must have an honest, veritable resume or credential to be considered as a guest on *Wine and Dine Radio*.

To view the current week's guests, go to http://www.winefairy.com/guests.asp

Guest from Hell: Someone who does NOT speak into the phone receiver but instead, holds the receiver down at their chin, or wobbles the phone up and down so that their voice fades in and out. A guest who is timid in their voice delivery. Certain guests tend to monopolize the conversation and run on, thus not allowing for more information to be shared via shorter responses (and more questions). There is a specific group of people that tend to fall prey to this recurring issue but I won't divulge here.

Contact: lkc@WineFairy.com; 252-635-6325; http://www.WineFairy.com, http://www.WineandDineRadio.com or FoodTastesBetterWithWine.com although all domains lead to http://www.WineFairy.com; Lynn Krielow Chamberlain. Best method: Call with a pitch, e-mail a bio and send a press kit. No response? There is a time and place for every potential candidate. Perhaps the guest is over-exposed and I'm not interested. Perhaps the person delivering the query to me is too late: I need at least one to three months lead time for booking in advance. I do not interview PR/marketing/communication directors/agents as a general rule. I want the name behind the wine, the vineyard, the food, the book, etc.

Invited Back? I do not repeat very many guests.

There is just too much to learn and too many people throughout the world to hear their stories, their news, their opinion.

Guest Comments: "The time flew. I could go on for hours. Thank you very much ... that was great. Thank you very much. You're a very, very good host!"—Christy Campbell, British journalist and author of *The Botanist and the Vintner* (Algonquin Books 2006), winner of the 2005 Glenfiddich Food and Drink Award

"Lynn is a rare combination: a dedicated host with a relaxed attitude. She's extremely enthusiastic about her chosen subjects—mainly food, travel and wine. She'll prompt guests when necessary, and sit back and listen when they have a lot to say."—Becky Sue Epstein, senior editor, *Intermezzo Magazine*

Bio of Lynn Krielow Chamberlain: Lynn is a 31-year career wine professional with a Master of Science in oenology, 1981 OSU; a certified wine educator, 1985, Society of Wine Educators; member, Brother Knights of the Vine—North Carolina chapter, with experience in wine on-premise, off-premise, beverage wholesale, wine production, wine travel, wine journalism, wine radio, wine television, wine public relations, wine judge, and wine academia. She has sat the MW exam twice, with dissertation pass in 1995.

Lynn continues to write about wine for several small papers and maintains a license as a wine merchant in the state of North Carolina, where she resides.

Her radio career began in Arizona at a commercial classical station and USA Today SkyRadio with the introduction of *Food Tastes Better with Wine* audio feature broadcast in 1994. Upon moving to the east coast, she was asked to be a regular guest on local talk radio.

According to Lynn, *Wine and Dine Radio*, since 1999 on commercial radio stations, is the first Internet radio broadcast devoted to wine and food.

Gardening

Gestalt is a German word that means both "pattern" and "whole." The word is used in English to refer to a completed cycle, something that is finished. Felder Rushing sees the concept relating to gardening by how it takes into account the whole garden (or gardener—body, mind and spirit); uses an experiential approach to gardening; assesses what is happening in the present (the here-and-now); emphasizes self-awareness; encourages personal (garden) responsibility; acknowledges the integrity, sensitivity, and creativity of the gardener; recognizes that the gardener is central to the gardening process—From The Gestalt Gardener

Arbor Talk with Ken Six and Peter Felix on http://www.ArborTalk.com

Theme: Tree care in the urban forest.
Guest Profile: Authors, arborists, landscape professionals, scientists, celebrities, developers, CEOs, media, and the bublic. Enthusiastic, knowledgeable, and passionate about whatever it is that they are being interviewed for and not too long winded. Why they wrote the book, what was the feeling or need to do this.
Guest from Hell: The guest from hell is someone who answers a question with *one* word. Then you have to drag the second word from them.
Contact: kensix@TreeTV.com; 281-808-1202; http://www.TreeTV.com; www.arbortalk.com; Ken Six. Best method: Call with a pitch, e-mail a bio, send a press kit and then follow up. No response? E-mail or call.
Invited Back? The feeling and flow of the interview.

Bio of Ken Six: Ken was involved in Arboriculture (the science and art of caring for trees, shrubs and other woody plants in landscape settings) and was a tree care professional for more than 30 years, in Texas, Louisiana, Florida and California.

From 2003 to January 2009, Ken was a consulting arborist and president of TreeScapes by Six Inc., which provides tree care services. His areas of expertise were diagnosis, tree preservation, hazard tree assessment, inspection and assessment of trees on real estate, planning and management, bid evaluation, plant health care, tree appraisal, expert witness testimony and education and training.

Ken passed away in January 2009 and is survived by his with wife, Gloria, and their three children, Dezeray, 22, Kenneth, 16, and Tyler, 14.

Bio of Peter Felix: Peter has more than 20 years' experience in arboriculture. He is an ISA Certified Arborist and an innovator in plant health care for urban trees. His company, Tree Health Management, is a pioneer in the use of air-tools, compost teas, growth regulators and other treatments to recreate soil environments for optimum tree health and longevity.

Peter attended the State University of New York Agricultural College of Delhi.

Bob Tanem in the Garden with Bob Tanem on KSFO 560 in the San Francisco/Bay area.
Theme: Most anything garden.
Guest Profile: Anything about gardening (can include botanical gardens, etc.) or parks or unusual material that concerns landscaping, gardening, etc. Authors about gardening—new tools—organic fertilizers. I usually require their work (book, reports, etc). I usually have the engineer handle the voice problem.
Guest from Hell: A person so impressed with themselves that they cover their ignorance with a lot of botanical terms. I usually warn my guest that most people aren't interested in technical terms.

Contact: bobtanem@aol.com; Voice Mail 415-954-8611; http://www.bobtanem.com; Bob Tanem. Best method: E-mail. I'm always approachable. No response? If I don't respond, I'm not interested.

Invited Back? Former good interviews, exceptional writing, and like things.

Bio of Bob Tanem: At age 77, America's Happy Gardener is a retired retail nurseryman. Up until 1998, Bob owned and operated Tanem's Garden Centers in Belvedere and San Rafael/Santa Venetia. He bought Santa Venetia Nursery in 1961 on a whim and with no experience except the teachings and love for gardening that his grandmother and grandfather instilled in him.

His garden show has won the Garden Writers Association of America award of excellence nationwide for "on air talent." He has been honored with this award three times in the past five years. His radio show is one of the most listened to Sunday programs on KSFO radio in San Francisco, CA.

Since retirement Bob has volunteered to supervise an organic vegetable garden at New Beginnings in Novato. This is a program to feed and house the homeless while training them for employment. Homeward Bound is the parent organization.

He is a graduate of UC Berkeley.

Bob has authored five books on gardening, four published by Lone Pine Publishing and co-authored by Don Williamson: *Annuals for Northern California* (2002), *Perennials for Northern California* (2002), *Trees and Shrub Gardening for Northern California* (2003) and *Gardening Month by Month in Northern California* (2004). His first book, *Deer Resistant Planting*, was self published in 1993 and is still a hot seller.

Florida Gardening with Mark T. Govan on 970 WFLA, aired in Florida on Sunday mornings from 7–9 AM and simulcast on http://www.newsradio970wfla.com worldwide

Theme: Gardening, pest control, home improvement.

Guest Profile: Authors, inventors, people of interest, etc., or those who have specialty knowledge to share with my audience. Sound of voice does not matter.

Guest from Hell: Someone who does not know their subject matter, or one who prefers to argue with the host.

Contact: mark@a-b-c-pest.com; 727-546-8787; http://www.a-b-c-pest.com; Mark Govan. Best method: E-mail. Personal contact or a press kit. Authors may send a book for my review. No response? Call or e-mail.

Invited Back? Guest must be informative.

Bio of Mark Govan: Mark has more than 20 years of local central Florida pest control experience. He started ABC Pest Control, Inc. in 1985 and is a Florida state certified pest control operator in general household pest control and rodent control, lawn and ornamental pest control and termite control. Additionally, Mark is a certified arborist with the International Society of Arborists and a certified nursery professional. Mark carries the following product certifications. Certified in Firstline termite control, Termidor termite control, and the Sentricon Colony Elimination Systems, and is recipient of the "Top Choice Fire Ant Certification" for the use of Top Choice once a year fire ant control.

Mark opened ABC Tropical Plant Nursery, Inc. in 1990, located at the ABC Corporate Headquarters in Largo, FL. The nursery specializes in rare tropical flowering plants and trees, specifically in the Plumeria, the Hawaiian LEI flower.

From 1994 to 1997, Mark co-hosted "Gils Garden," a live television call-in gardening show with Gil Whitton. Next Mark joined Gil as his co-host of *Florida Gardening* on 970 WFLA AM. Mark and Gil worked together on *Florida Gardening* for nine years until Gil retired in 2003. Since then, Mark took over the *Florida Gardening* show and in March 2003 was joined by Stan De Freitas, "Mr. Green Thumb."

Garden Girls with Dr. Sue Hamilton and Beth Babbit on WNOX 100.3, Knoxville, TN, area and four other states.

Theme: Gardening.

Guest Profile: Gardeners, horticulture specialists/professionals, arborists, authors, naturalists, humanitarians and volunteers. Our show is about educating people and helping them with their gardening problems. We would like guest to be able to answer questions and share interesting and relevant information. We know most of our guests very well and invite them to the show knowing most of this information, i.e., prior interviews, credentials, sound of their voice, prior to the interviews.

Guest from Hell: Someone who is non-interactive or if this person is disrespectful to guests or makes them feel uncomfortable. The guest needs to use factual information, and offer practical advice.

Contact: ebabbit@utk.edu; withheld upon request; http://gardengirls.tennessee.edu; Beth Babbit. Best method: Calling, e-mail, press kits would be OK as long as we can talk to the person prior to booking. No response? Sure, we are both very busy people, keep trying a couple more times. But desperation does not look good either.

Invited Back? How they do on the air, how comfortable they are, how they sound, if they have more information to offer our listeners.

Bio of Beth Babbit: Beth grew up in Nashville TN, where she discovered her love for gardening from her mother and learned to admire its science from her father. She received her bachelor of science in horticulture from Auburn University in June 1997 and her Masters of Science in horticulture in 2000.

During college she worked in several different fields

of horticulture as a propagator, landscaper for the Robert Trent Jones Golf Trail and a student greenhouse worker. After college she worked for the Opryland Hotel as a senior gardener.

Beth was awarded an assistantship for graduate school at Auburn University to study the best management practices of various horticulture consumers and professionals. Following graduation she joined the University of Georgia Cooperative Extension as an area horticulture agent in the north Atlanta area where she served master gardeners, professional green industry and consumer audiences. This was followed by a position as an assistant manager of one of Pike's Family Nurseries retail stores.

Beth is the urban horticulture area extension specialist for the University of Tennessee Extension in Knoxville, TN.

Garden Mama with Nellie Neal (W, Th, Fri, Sat)/ SuperTalk Info Monday on WLBT, SuperTalk MS Network (8 stations weekdays)/ Weekend Gardening Network (20+ stations) aired in Mississippi, surrounding states, and live streaming on the Internet.

Theme: General interest (Monday)/gardening, environment, science (W, Th, Fri, Sat).

Guest Profile: Authors, spokespeople from non-profits and companies. A person who knows their material and is excited about it makes a great guest. If there's a smile in that voice, so much the better. Tell me what you want to be sure the audience learns about your subject, and something personal that will help the audience identify with you.

Nothing too personal, of course, but if the guest has a cookbook, it's interesting to know that his college degree is in philosophy and he races bicycles on the weekend. Such information can also help the listener remember the writer when shopping for the cookbook.

Guest from Hell: A bad guest is one who answers only "yes" or "no," but the real nightmare guest is one who thinks he/she is smarter than the audience. It's also a huge issue if the guest wants me to talk about a book or product that does not arrive before the interview.

Contact: mama@gardenmama.com; 601-613-1953; 982-0385; http://www.gardenmama.com, http://www.supertalkms.com; Nellie Neal. Best method: E-mail anything you like and put a "return read receipt" on it. No response? E-mail again, please. The in box stays full.

Invited Back? There's no set criteria, but audience reaction and timeliness of the subject certainly figure into it.

Bio of Nellie Neal: Nellie has been a radio talk show host for 15 years, all of it in commercial radio. Her primary beat is organic gardening, but she also does regular programs that cover news, human interest, and anything else that she thinks will be informative and amusing. Nellie is a published author, spouse, parent, and pet owner.

The Gardener with Dorothy Dobbie on CJOB 68, Winnipeg, Canada, on Sundays at 9 AM.

Theme: Gardening. I start with a 4 or 5 minute monologue on some topic and I have two things as an objective: the connect with the audience through personal observation and to provide information they likely don't have. In my mind, each show should have a little "wonder" factor.

Guest Profile: Local gardening and tree experts in summer. Solid knowledge base, relaxed manner, sense of humor, intelligence, how much they know about the topic at hand. More esoteric things in winter — we have even had the conductor of the Winnipeg Symphony Orchestra talking about gardens as a theme for music. We also have guests to talk about tea, gifts, lawns, etc.

Guest from Hell: One who freezes or, conversely, one who won't shut up.

Contact: mbgarden@mts.net; 204-940-2716 (my office); http://www.localgardener.net; Dorothy Dobbie. Best method: Call with a pitch, e-mail a bio, and/or send a press kit. No response? Call.

Invited Back? How well the audience responded and whether I feel there is more there to draw out.

Bio of Dorothy Dobbie: Dorothy is president and founder of Pegasus Publications Inc., the publisher of the local gardener magazines *Ontario Gardener, Manitoba Gardener* and *Alberta Gardener*. Pegasus, which has offices in Winnipeg and Toronto, also publishes *Smart Connections, Beautiful Communities, Canadian Trees,* and a half dozen other magazines and annuals.

Dorothy produces a weekly column during the summer months for the *Winnipeg Free Press* community newspapers and for the *Edmonton Examiner*. Her columns also appear in the *Calgary Herald* in spring. She's an avid garden photographer and takes most of the cover shots for the gardener magazines. She is a frequent guest garden speaker on television and for garden clubs and horticultural societies.

A former Member of Parliament (1988 to 1993) and Parliamentary Secretary in several portfolios, including Indian and northern affairs, consumer and corporate affairs and the environment. Dorothy co-chaired the Dobbie-Beaudoin Joint House-Senate Committee on the Renewal of Canada, which led to the Charlottetown Accord.

Dorothy and her husband Glenn have two grown daughters and four grandchildren.

The Gestalt Gardener with Felder Rushing on Mississippi Public Broadcasting (eight stations, covers portions of five states).

Theme: Highly southern garden chatter.

Guest Profile: Unusual or outstanding garden or environmental personalities. High commitment to topic, strong personality, sense of humor.

Website info with personal details — a guest needs to come across as "real people."

I interview LOTS of guests (coast to coast) for their quirky personalities, as well as their narrow topic expertise (worm growers, home-made salsa makers, backyard chicken people, clay eaters, cloud watchers, etc.).

Guest from Hell: Inability to chat informally (too structured), too shrill on topic (agenda-driven).

Contact: felder@felderrushing.net; http://www.felderrushing.net (click on Gestalt Gardener link); Felder. Best method: E-mail. I tend to select guests based on my own interests, but will accept simple e-mail pitches. No response? Never happens.

Invited Back? Ability to cover broad range of areas within topic.

Bio of Felder Rushing: Felder has been doing his live gardening show for 25 years. He is also a well-known lecturer (away from home 150 nights a year, 600,000 frequent flier miles), and author or co-author of 15 garden books and has written countless articles for newspapers and magazines, including *Garden Design, Horticulture, Landscape Architecture, Better Homes and Gardens, Fine Gardening, Organic Gardening*, and the *National Geographic*.

A 10th-generation American gardener, Felder's pioneer ancestors settled across the Southeast, bringing many plants with them. His overstuffed, quirky cottage garden has been featured on many TV programs and in magazines (including a cover of *Southern Living*), and includes a huge variety of weather-hardy plants along with a collection of folk art. There is no turf grass, just plants, yard art, and "people places."

He has also hosted a television program that was shown across the South.

The Mike Nowak Show on WCPT 820AM, Chicago, Illinois and streaming on http://www.wcpt820.com

Theme: Gardening and environmental issues. As I say, "Good gardeners are good environmentalists." I take questions and comments via phone. However, what I really like is get a guest expert in the studio and dig deeply into a particular subject. I ain't a genius, but I figure I'm smart enough and well-versed enough to ask good questions.

Guest Profile: There are a lot of people writing gardening books, so it has to be something special to catch my eye. I generally don't interview authors who focus on one plant. For instance, if you wrote "Great Hydrangeas for the Landscape" or something like that, you're probably not going to make the cut. It needs to be a little more comprehensive. On the other hand, the great thing about rules is that they're made to be broken. Since I have the attention span of a six year old, you never know what's going to draw my focus. The best guests are the ones who know their subject well, can tell a story and have a least a cursory familiarity with the medium. That is to say, for example, they understand that they will need to use headphones to hear the callers, they know how to use a microphone, and they know that there are time constraints. But the technical stuff is really my job. I want somebody who has something interesting to say that will keep my listeners from reaching for the radio dial. Above all, I want to know if they're entertaining. I don't care about the sound of their voice or their past interview experiences. In fact, I pride myself on getting guests to appear on my show who say they're terrified of being on the radio. Hey, we're talking about horticulturists here. I loosen them up, make them human, encourage them to paint a vivid word picture of their work, and have some fun.

Guest from Hell: I don't think that there really is such a person. Oh, sure, there are guests that are boring and long-winded and obtuse and smarmy. But a good show host can work around any of those types. You see, I'm the guy in charge. It's only two hours. It ain't rocket science. I should be able to do my job professionally after ten years on the air in a major market.

Contact: mike@mikenowak.net; http://www.mikenowak.net; Mike Nowak. Best method: Well, it's definitely going to have to be my e-mail, as I'm not sure I even have a phone number at my new station. And I'm sure not giving out my cell number to everybody in the world. Press kits are okay but anybody can put together a press kit. Well, that's not exactly true, as I've seen some mom and pop press kits that were pretty hilarious, in a bad way. It helps if I sense that they've taken even thirty seconds to look at my website and learn something about me and then personalize the message in some way. Ultimately, however, it boils down to whether they're book or expert interests me in the least. That's a crap shoot. No response? You're asking this question just to humiliate me, right? Look, I pretty much book my own shows and I have a zillion e-mails sitting in my inbox and in various folders. I always intend to get back to people but stuff happens. If you're not willing to send a follow up message, then you're obviously not that interested in promoting your topic. It's pretty simple. If you forgive me for not getting back to you, I'll forgive you for cluttering up my inbox. By the way, when I used to do some overnight radio (and I may again, you never know), I was always amazed that someone could spend five years putting a book together and then would be unwilling to do one 3 AM interview (on a 50,000-watt radio station!) because it was too early in the morning.

Invited Back? Did I have fun? Did they teach me something I didn't know? Did I like them? Did they seem self-serving? It's kind of a touchy-feely thing. Sometimes I can't tell you why I didn't invite somebody back. It's not a particularly scientific process.

Guest Comments: "Oh, man, you were TOTALLY channeling Garry Moore and Steve Allen with the "I've Got a Secret" opener with Kathy. How fun. Your segment with Kathy sounded like you were both just chatting and I was eavesdropping. Well, me and

5 million other people across the Midwest. Thanks so much for your support." — Diane Laux, Guild for the Blind

"Mike, I really enjoyed your new show. Thanks for all the support for the master gardener program as well as the rest of extension. It is going to be great to have you on the air consistently." — Elizabeth Bruhns, Cook County Extension

Bio of Mike Nowak: For a decade before hosting his show, Mike was host of WGN Radio's *Let's Talk Gardening*, and has appeared on WGN-TV Channel 9, CBS 2 Chicago and the DIY Network. He is also an award-winning columnist for *Chicagoland Gardening Magazine*. About that column he says, "I make up stuff and they pay me for it. Great gig."

Mike often says that his background in gardening is show business, which is pretty close to the truth. Although he is a master gardener and a certified treekeeper, trained by the Openlands Project, he is actually a professional writer, actor, director, radio host and speaker on gardening and the environment ... and a fervent amateur when it comes to growing things.

In 2002, Mike founded the Midwest Ecological Landscaping Association with landscape designer Connie Cunningham. The organization promotes environmentally responsible landscaping and horticultural practices among professionals and the public. Mike served as MELA's president for four years. He is vice president of the Chicago Recycling Coalition and on the board of the Lincoln Park Conservancy in Chicago. He recently joined the Speakers Network for Safe Lawns, a non-profit organization dedicated to promoting natural lawn care and grounds maintenance.

He speaks extensively about ecologically sound gardening everywhere from the mayor's landscaping awards program to the Chicago Botanic Garden to your neighborhood garden club. But he's going to try to inject humor whenever he can, so don't try to stop him.

Gay and Lesbian

Queer FM with Heather Kitching on CITR, airing in Greater Vancouver, Canada, airing Sunday, 6–8 P.M. (PT), and as a live Internet stream and downloadable podcast.

Theme: Queer current events and legal, political and social issues affecting the LGTB communities. Some arts coverage.

Guest Profile: Activists, lawyers, politicians and political organizers, queer journalists, health professionals, authors and artists. Someone with a timely topic to discuss related to lesbian, gay, bisexual or transgender issues. Someone who is well-informed, articulate and personable. I obviously would want to ensure that the person is sufficiently qualified to speak to the topic. And if English is their second language, I would like to ensure that they speak it well enough to express themselves easily and that their accent is not so strong as to make them incomprehensible. Beyond that, if the topic is sensitive in some way ... controversial ... deeply personal ... etc., I would like some sense of how the interviewee handles delicate or provocative questions; i.e.: does an activist for a severely oppressed minority group ever respond angrily to questions from interviewers who are members of the dominant culture? (If they do, it doesn't mean I won't interview them. I just want to be prepared.) To what extent does an author who's written a book about rape feel comfortable discussing her/his own experience of it? etc.

Guest from Hell: Those who are clearly unprepared to answer even obvious questions arising from their work or activities. Those who are monosyllabic, overly verbose, or just plain inarticulate.

Contact: queerfmradio@gmail.com; 604-924-4968; http://www.citr.ca; Heather Kitching. Best method: E-mail a media release with a brief personal note explaining why you think the person would be suitable for the show. No response? A follow up call is fine as I do sometimes forget to respond to things that looked genuinely interesting.

Invited Back? If they have a new project to discuss or if there is a new development in something they're working on, I'd certainly consider it unless they were completely dry, rude, or otherwise unpleasant to talk to.

Bio of Heather Kitching: Heather founded Queer FM in 1993 after leaving professional radio to work in music industry sales and marketing. She is a former activist with the December 9th Coalition (British Columbia's provincial queer lobby), a former board member of Egale (Canada's national queer lobby), and the former vice president of the organizing committee of the North American Conference on Bisexuality, Gender, and Sexual Diversity. When not hosting *Queer FM*, she works as an independent publicist for roots and world music artists. She also contributes queer news items to *Sirius Out Q* and *This Way Out*. And she's been a very-occasional-contributor to the Canadian Broadcasting Corporation.

This Way Out, The International Gay and Lesbian Radio Magazine, with Greg Gordon (and occasionally Lucia Chappelle), airing internationally on 150+ local stations, short wave, online, direct satellite to home and cable outlets.

Theme: LGBT news and culture.

Guest Profile: Writers/performers/newsmakers—anyone with appropriate credentials whose subject matter has an LGBT focus. Ability to convey ideas in a lucid and compelling manner, hopefully with humor as well. Credentials (i.e., what qualifies her/him to discuss the specific issue/s involved).

Guest from Hell: Unable to communicate clearly, no sense of humor, doesn't specifically address direct questions.

Contact: TWOradio@aol.com; 818-986-4106; http://www.thiswayout.org; Greg Gordon, coordinating producer. Best method: E-mail a brief pitch that I can distribute to our small volunteer group of producers to see if anyone's interested. No response? Please don't call or e-mail. It just means there was no interest among our volunteers to pursue the pitch.

Invited Back? Rarely invited back — again, it's not the guest, it's the subject matter (e.g., an LGBT-related new book, new film, new CD, a newsmaker).

Bios of Greg Gordon and Lucia Chappelle: Before starting his radio show in 1988, Greg served as the executive producer for *IMRU* (as an unpaid volunteer), the locally-produced GLBT program at KPFK-FM in Los Angeles.

He holds a Bachelor's Degree in radio-television production from U.C.L.A. and spent most of his professional life coordinating commercial operations at various Los Angeles radio and television stations, as both a radio talkshow producer/host and broadcast coordinator for a major advertising agency (the latter while handling his *This Way Out* duties as an unpaid volunteer).

In May 1995 Greg was able to leave his "day job" and began working full time on the show; he recently also worked part-time as an online news researcher and writer for the PlanetOut Web site.

Associate producer/co-host Lucia became a volunteer at KPFK-Los Angeles in 1973 and joined the collective that produced *IMRU* two years later. She was the "WomanTimes" editor for the national lesbian/gay newspaper *Coast to Coast Times* and served in the clergy of Metropolitan Community Church for 10 years before returning to KPFK as program director in 1987.

After leaving KPFK she worked and took classes at The Grantsmanship Center (which offers fundraising and development seminars to non-profits). In 1996, along with executive producer Greg Gordon and news director Cindy Friedman, she established the daily online text news service of *PlanetOut*, and later became the writer/producer/anchor of *PlanetOut*'s audio news service. Since leaving *PlanetOut* in 2001, she has worked as a freelance journalist for Free Speech Radio News.

Lucia holds one B.A. in speech-drama and one in theology, and did graduate work in religion and the arts with a major in film.

Health and Fitness

Rhythm. Harmony. Balance. Peace.
...and a radio show—from the website of Ilene Dillon, Full Power Living

Autism: Help, Hope and Healing with Teri Arranga (formerly Teri Small, if you do a Google search) on http://www.autismone.org/radio. Teri also hosts a program on the VoiceAmerica Health and Wellness Channel, www.health.voiceamerica.com, called *Autism One: A Conversation of Hope.*

Theme: Autism: help, hope, and healing.

Guest Profile: Doctors, researchers, parents, authors, advocates. Guests need to provide information towards recovery/optimal rehabilitation for persons on the autism spectrum. Information must be scientifically-sustainable. I need to know that the guest has safely and successfully helped/recovered children. I want to know about their scientific credibility/credentials/experience or, in the case of a parent, that they researched what they did and used appropriate medical oversight.

Guest from Hell: I research, select, and screen guests who participate in my show. An undesirable guest would be someone who provided inaccurate or ambiguous information.

Contact: smallmp@comcast.net; 714-680-0792; http://www.autismone.org/radio and http://www.autismone.org; Teri Arranga or Ed Arranga. Best method: Phone, but either is fine. People should e-mail information about their research and successful work helping children and families touched by an autism spectrum diagnosis. No response? E-mail or call. I am very busy, so I appreciate the persistence and patience of others.

Invited Back? I want to air interviews with those who have new research and those who continue to help children. I need to feel that the person has a true love of and selfless priority towards helping these children and their families.

Bio of Teri Arranga: Teri is the director of Autism One and general manager of Autism One Radio, as well as an Autism One Radio program host (*Autism: Help, Hope, and Healing*). She serves as project manager for the Autism Coalition for Treatment.

Teri is the editor of the U.S. and Canada edition of *The Autism File* magazine, www.autismfile.com. She is vice president of Medical Veritas International and commissioning editor of *Medical Veritas: The Journal of Medical Truth*, the journal of MVI. She has been involved with a number of media projects, including consulting for medical documentaries by award-winning filmmakers Lina Moreco of Canada and Gary Null of the United States, appearing in the award-winning documentary *Beautiful Son*, and consulting for the April 2007 *Discover* magazine article "Understanding Autism."

Teri was given honorable mention in *Spectrum* magazine's "Top 10 Faces of Autism" article of April 2006 and was subsequently invited to the advisory board of *Spectrum*. Teri has been an active advocate in the autism community for many years, including attending and broadcasting events in Washington, D.C.

Teri and Ed Arranga have two boys: Jarad, 13, Ian, 10.

The Balancing Point with John Nieters on KEST 1450 AM, San Francisco, CA.

Theme: Health from a multi-modality perspective (acupuncture, herbal, supplement, diet, exercise, qi gong). This is a call-in question and answer show, sometimes with guests, sometimes only my input.

Guest Profile: Any area of health, medicine, above topics. (Acupuncturists, facial care, Parkinsons prevention, dementia prevention, liver disease, etc.) Clear, helpful, health oriented, speak to lay audience, able to answer questions. Credentials are very important.

Guest from Hell: Negative about other systems than their own system or position, speak over the head of the audience, only "selling" their product or book.

Contact: jnieters@pacbell.net; 510-814-6900; http://johnnieters.com; Thea Thatcher at healthandwellness@pacbell.net. Best method: E-mail. Press kit 1st, e-mail bio 2nd, no calls. No response? E-mail.

Invited Back? Generally have not invited guests back. We have had sponsors who have been on the show more than one time and pay to sponsor the show

Guest Comments: "Talking to John on his health radio show is like chatting with your best buddy, only he's really articulate and brings out the best in you. His audience is really interested in the same variety of health topics you are passionate about. It's no wonder his morning show on KEST is so popular in the San Francisco Bay Area."—John Steinke, L.Ac., http://www.TangoNutrition.com

"I had fun doing the radio show. The host, John, made me feel very comfortable and confident. I got at least one client from the show. The show was a good length, an hour. I would definitely do it again."—Shelley Rosenfeld, Conscious Skin and Body Care, http://www.consciousskinandbody.com/

Bio of John Nieters: John is a licensed acupuncturist, nationally certified in acupuncture and herbal medicine. He is an assistant professor at both Five Branches Institute of Traditional Chinese Medicine and Academy of Chinese Culture and Health Sciences. He teaches six levels of courses in herbal medicine I, II, III, IV, V, and herb drug interactions.

His specialties are western nutrition, Chinese nutrition, Tai Chi Chuan and Qi Gong, Chinese martial arts and energetic arts, practice management ethics for medical professionals, Research Methodology I, II, III.

John also teaches continuing education classes for licensed acupuncturists and is a guest lecturer at several venues including Integrative Medicine Program at UC Berkeley.

He is creator and author of "The Vision Program" for life transformation.

John is a doctoral candidate at Zhejiang University in China.

Beyond Health with Dr. Raymond Francis, based in San Francisco and syndicated on KNTS, KKNT, WWNN, etc.

Theme: Health.

Guest Profile: Authors. Newsworthy with something different to say and articulate enough to say it well. What they have to say that's different and how well they can say it.

Guest from Hell: Someone who is poorly prepared and inarticulate or who doesn't know when to shut up.

Contact: mail@beyondhealth.com; 415-453-7588; http://www.beyondhealth.com; Marketing Manager. Best method: E-mail. Send press kit and copy of book. No response? We are all busy. One gentle reminder is in order.

Invited Back? How much new information they have to offer and how entertaining they are — how many calls we get from the audience.

Bio of Dr. Raymond Francis: Dr. Francis is an MIT-trained scientist and an internationally recognized leader in optimal health maintenance. He is the author of *Never Be Sick Again* (HCI 2002) and *Never Be Fat Again* (HCI 2007), and chairman of the Project to End Disease.

His radio show is in its 15th year of broadcasting.

Caregiving 101 with Starr and Bob Calo-oy on KKYX-680am, San Antonio, Texas, airing Saturday 8–9 AM (CT).

Theme: Caregiving.

Guest Profile: Caregivers, doctors, service providers, authors. Someone who has good advice or an uplifting message of victory overcoming difficult situations and who offers hope to a hurting or burned out caregiver. I need a bio, a website that I can explore and to know they are interesting enough to hold a listener audience without putting them to sleep and that they have a good sense of humor that they don't keep to themselves.

Guest from Hell: I've never had one nor do I expect to because my guests are well screened long before they come on.

Contact: starrcalo-oy@satx.rr.com; 210-521-8668; http://www.caregiversadvice.net; Starr Calo-oy. Best method: Phone or e-mail. No response? E-mail or call.

Invited Back? If the audience was helped with what they had to say and we had people call in during the hour for advice or to make comments.

Bios of Starr and Bob Calo-oy: Both born and raised in San Antonio and married for 27 years, from 1989 to 2006 Starr and Bob owned and operated a personal care home specializing in the care of terminally ill patients and victims of Alzheimer's disease and other forms of dementia in their San Antonio home. They also cared for the well-minded elderly who could no longer care for themselves at home.

The couple has also provided in-service training for doctors, nurses, the staffs of hospices and home health agencies, sharing tips and unique ideas for caring for people with dementia. Starr also gives private consultations to individuals on how to start and operate a successful personal care home as well as helping family caregivers set up their home for care.

She is a columnist for SAWorship.com as well as an occasional freelance writer for the *San Antonio Express-News*.

Starr and Bob are authors of *The Caring Caregivers Guide to Dealing with Guilt* (2004), *Hospice Care at Home/ A Guide to Caring for Your Dying Loved One at Home* (2006), *Caregiving Tips A–Z, Alzheimer's and Other Dementias* (2008) and *Caregiving Tips A–Z* (2008), all published by Orchard Publications. All of their books are available in Spanish.

Coping with Caregiving with Jacqueline Marcell on http://www.wsradio.com/CopingwithCaregiving, more than 700 archived interviews are available for free listening-on-demand: http://www.wsradio.com/internet-talk-radio.cfm/shows/Coping-with-Caregiving/archives/date.html

Theme: The challenges of caregiving and many issues related to health and aging.

Guest Profile: Caregiving, health, aging, long-term care insurance and long-term life planning.

We seek knowledgeable upbeat personalities who speak with passion about their topic.

Guest from Hell: Those who don't speak up, read their answers, don't follow directions.

Contact: j.marcell@cox.net; 949-975-1012; http://www.wsradio.com/CopingwithCaregiving. Best method: With a short and to-the-point e-mail. I will e-mail back instructions. No response? If I don't respond, I didn't get the e-mail — please e-mail again.

Invited Back? I don't repeat guests unless they help pay for the airtime.

Bio of Jacqueline Marcell: Jacqueline was so compelled by being the sole caregiver to her challenging elderly father and sweet but ailing mother (both with early Alzheimer's not properly diagnosed for a year), that she gave up her stalled career as a television executive to become an advocate for eldercare awareness and reform. Her passion resulted in her first (best-selling) book, *Elder Rage* (Impressive Press 2001); her radio show, media including TODAY and CNN, two Blogs; and over 150 keynotes — including replacing Maureen Reagan at the California Governor's Conference for Women.

Elder Rage is a Book-of-the-Month Club selection being considered for a film. Over 50 endorsements include: Hugh Downs, Regis Philbin, Johns Hopkins Memory Clinic and Duke University Center for Aging. It is also required text at numerous universities for courses in geriatric assessment and management.

Jacqueline is also a recent breast cancer survivor who advocates that everyone (*especially* caregivers) closely monitor their own health.

Create Abundance Now! with Roxanne Brown on BBS Radio, every other Monday at 1 PM.

Theme: Promotes healing, knowledge and transformational information and services.

Guest Profile: Guests who have knowledge about mind, energy and body healing and transformation that can be shared with the world. A guest with knowledge about their book or their methodologies. A guest that wishes to share their particular ideas, thoughts, beliefs and methodologies about healing or knowledge. We want to know their credentials, trainings, books to their credit, events upcoming if they have any.

There is a small fee for guests. This includes up to an hour interview, a link to their websites from Roxanne's website permanently and a link from the bbsradio info page which will remain there for the duration of the show.

Guest from Hell: A guest who is spouting unfounded truth and who is sharing information from a biased or bigoted view point. I do not allow negativity or anything derogatory on my show.

Contact: roxieb5@juno.com; 360-909-4460; http://www.createabundancenow.net; Roxanne Brown. Best method: E-mail or phone. Send press kit and/or e-mail bio and interest. No response? Always e-mail or phone, as I get busy from time to time.

Invited Back? Willingness to discuss information and make it understandable for all who listen.

Bio of Roxanne Brown: Roxanne is a certified master practitioner/coach/trainer of neuro-linguistic-programming, time line therapy and hypnosis.

Her career in hypnotherapy started in March of 2000. "My life has spanned from being an entrepreneur for over 20 years to a licensed massage therapist (in WA, OR and TX) since March of 1992 and licensed realtor WA 2003–2007," she says.

Roxanne has an Associates of Arts (psychology) degree from Clark College Vancouver WA 1983, a Bachelors of Clinical Hypnotherapy with American Pacific University (Honolulu HA) 2000 to 2003, Past and Present Life Regression Training, February 2003 in Newport Beach CA, and Neuro-Linguistic Programming (practitioner/master practitioner/trainers training level) 2006 and 2007.

"My studies have focused on the mind and the energies of the human life force and body since my early college years," she says.

Deborah "Doc" Watson airs live Monday through Friday from 5–7 PM (ET) on http://www.HealthRadio.net

Theme: My show is about health and healing with a natural perspective. However, whether we are discussing the latest medical treatment, the possible effects of GMO foods, the benefits of vitamins and herbs or how remote prayer can assist healing; all have a place on the show. Armed with the information we impart, listeners can be empowered to take back responsibility for their own health and make that connection between body, mind and spirit.

Guest Profile: The guests that grace our show can come from all areas of the health industry. Scientists, health advocates, health practitioners from both allopathy and naturopathy express differing views giving the audience a better understanding of what is available for a more integrative approach to health care. Authors must write about issues that impact our health. Being articulate and having a grasp of the subject is always important in a guest but having a sense of humor plays a key role in keeping the audience engaged. Having knowledge of the guest's credentials, affiliations, and accomplishments assists me in delving into the subject matter and putting my guest at ease during the interview process. My ideal guest not only brings an issue to light, but provides action that listeners can take as both advocates for themselves and on behalf of others.

Guest from Hell: A guest from hell is one who gives you monosyllabic answers to your questions so you have to drag the information out of them. Or one who drones on and puts me in a coma before I have a chance to ask my next question.

Contact: info@docwatson.com; http://www.deborahdocwatson.com; 480-897-1476; Tim Disa Jr. at guest@healthradio.net. Best method: I am pretty approachable, but these days it is best if potential guests contact me via e-mail and attach a bio and/or press kit. If there is a book, sending an advance copy for review is also recommended. No response? If there is no response after a reasonable amount of time follow up with an e-mail or a phone call is always appropriate.

Invited Back? When a guest gets invited back it means: I was impressed with the guest's performance and I thought the interview went well, we connected on several levels during our conversation, we had humorous episodes during the interview (even when the subject was of a serious nature) or the subject was important but the time expired before we had adequately explored it.

Guest Comments: "I LOVED being on your show yesterday!!"—Peggy Collins, speaker, trainer and author of *Help Is Not a Four-Letter Word* (McGraw-Hill 2006). http://www.helpisnotafourletterword.com

"Thank you for having me as a guest on last Friday's radio show. I think we were successful in disseminating some good and much needed information about diabetes to an audience that really needs it. You're a very good host; within minutes you had me relaxed and pontificating about my favorite subject as if we had done a hundred radio shows together. The show notes that I used were from my diabetes 101 show, which is just an introduction to the subject.

"Thank you for the plugs for my book; you were very generous."—Thomas Smith, author of *Insulin: Our Silent Killer* (T. Smith 2000), http://www.healingmatters.com

Bio of Deborah "Doc" Watson: Deborah has been on the air for 12 years serving up her style of health talk as only she can with a careful blend of entertainment, critical information, and razor sharp wit. She is an entertainer, lecturer, business woman, author, and nutritional consultant specializing in personal health and wellness programs, making that connection between body, mind and spirit.

Deborah is in the forefront of the natural healing world as an innovative professional that understands education to be the most important ingredient when regaining your health and making informed choices about your health care and your life.

With over 18 years' experience in the natural health field and her dozen years as a radio talk show host, Deborah has become a Dynamo. She's a member of "Who's Who Worldwide" for outstanding leadership and achievement in her chosen profession.

Dr. Fred Bell's Health, Science and Energy Show with Dr. Fred on http://www.bbsradio.com

Theme: I cover all topics relating to health; I often do political topics, as global warming, government cover ups and bring in the intelligence community discussions including remote viewing, which I have done since I was a teenager.

Guest Profile: Research folks, specialists, doctors, inventors, and people with good exciting knowledge. Science and energy topics guests are scientists, astronauts specialists, and these topics often cross pollinate with the health topic. Integrity, outgoing and knowing their topics, along with self-confidence projected vocally, are all vital. I would like a history of their experience.

Guest from Hell: A substance abuser while on the substance. Horribly overbearing people that do not know what they are there for.

Contact: fredbell@pyradyne.com; 949-499-5940; http://www.pyradyne.com; http://www.raysoftruthtv.com; Mikelle Williams at Mikelle@pyradyne.com. Best method: E-mail a bio, call with a pitch, send a press kit. No response? Yes, e-mail or call, I am usually overwhelmed.

Invited Back? Amount of interest and excitement in their interview.

Listener Comments: "Your guest for Sat Evening April 28 was great and so were you. Love your show! You are like no other. What he said about music following the golden mean is also true in Art."—Marcia McMahon, host of *Peaceful Planet Show* (see page 150), whose latest book is *With Love from Diana, Queen of Hearts* (Eternal Rose Pub 2005). http://www.DianaSpeaksToTheWorld.com

"I really enjoy your shows. I burn them on CD and listen to them as I commute between Seattle and Spokane weekly. Great stuff. I burn them for friends as well. You can tell Fred Bell he has more than 13 listeners for certain. Keep up the good work."—Daniel

Bio of Fred Bell: Because Fred began his career in the intelligence community, he "was able to go inside the minds and spirits for misdirected souls that live, breathe, and spread hatred," he explains. "To me, this was the best grounding zone, before I was able to reach back again into stars. I remember after my first 20 years of working with the United States government, the huge switch in energy and consciousness I felt when I first became a contactee. This of course occurred after an interim period, whereby I studied with various Tibetan and Eastern masters."

His next and final step was to become part of and helped form one of the largest media networks in the world. In August of 2005, Fred joined a fledgling Internet radio group called www.BBSradio.com. Here, he worked continuously building a worldwide audience and was able to secure a hotline into the NSA intelligence community, as well as with, and introduce many world-renowned personalities. His show quickly became one of the largest world wide Internet programs.

The Dr. Meg Jordan Show with Meg Jordan, Ph.D., RN on Health Radio Network, airing Sundays, 2–4 PM (ET).

Theme: Integrative health and wellness, nutrition, fitness, medicine — all with a social and cultural commentary. Dr. Meg is a medical anthropologist and behavioral medicine specialist. She covers health topics from a lively perspective that brings in social and political commentary.

Guest Profile: Authors, leaders, doctors, scientists, researchers, natural health product formulators. We are looking for expertise on topic, able to cite research, familiarity with media commentary, good communication skills, able to engage in a conversation and not lecture. I'd like to know the guest's credentials and the PR agency to screen them for communication skills.

Guest from Hell: Impossible accent, nonstop monologue, monotone, boring, hidden religious agenda that sudden inflames — I've had them all.

Contact: meg@healthradio.net, mail@megjordan.com; 415-785-7987; http://www.megjordan.com; http://www.healthradio.net; Samantha Sowassey, program director. Best method: E-mail Meg at maggijordan@comcast.net. No response? YES YES please e-mail again — just got lost in the pile.

Invited Back? If they had something vitally new, useful and interesting to share — something that enhanced the lives of listeners.

Guest Comments: "I just love doing the show with you, as always." — Shari Lieberman, http://www.drshari.net

"Thank you so much for having me on the show. I thoroughly enjoyed it! I also appreciate you sharing your story with me and your viewers. It is important to have people hear that smart, vibrant women are having midwives. (I had a midwife for my last 6 children.) Thanks for everything you do." — Robin Elise Weiss, LCCE, About.com Pregnancy/Birth, http://pregnancy.about.com

Bio of Meg Jordan, Ph.D., RN: Meg has motivated millions to live healthier, more fulfilling lives. Author, speaker, international health journalist, registered nurse and a clinical medical anthropologist, she is one of the most recognized names in health and wellness reporting. Her syndicated columns, television reports, and special media projects cover health, wellness, integrative medicine, indigenous healing traditions and cultural trends. In fall 2007 Meg began teaching Health and Human Nature at San Francisco State University from a global perspective.

As former director of Integrative Practice of the Health Medicine Institute in northern California, she specializes in behavioral medicine interventions.

Her doctoral research focused on the collaborative attempts among practitioners to combine medical modalities within integrative settings. She was a core faculty member of a new media venture with Deepak Chopra entitled MyPotential, and was a founding correspondent on iVillage, covering Global Health for women. Her syndicated columns on health and wellness are distributed to over 17 major newspapers and magazines worldwide, including the most respected newspaper in India, *The Hindu*. She is a former health reporter for FOX-TV and has been a regular media commentator for CNN.

The latest of her five books is *The Fitness Instinct* (Rodale Books 1999), acclaimed as "the most original thinking in fitness in 20 years."

Fitness and Nutrition Radio with Dave DePew on http://www.FitnessandNutritionRadio.com and *Primary Network:* Dave DePew Network; http://www.DaveDePewNetwork.com. New shows on the Dave DePew Network are Grip Strength Radio, http://www.gripstrengthradio.com, with Jedd Johnson, jedd.diesel@gmail.com (one podcast per month) and *Natural Body Building Radio* with John Hansen, prou96@aol.com (one show per week). Dave always has new shows in the works. See www.davedepewnetwork.com

Theme: Fitness and nutrition.

Guest Profile: Authors welcome; top fitness and nutrition professionals, competitive athletes, sports scientists and doctors. We prefer to interview guests who have a strong level of expertise in one or more areas in fitness or nutrition. Our topics are broad with this show, but we prefer to have very specific show topics we can direct our listeners to in our archives. We only want guests who have a service or product that goes with their topic in order that we might help our listeners get the solution to their fitness and nutrition needs. Past interview experience is very important. Canned questions are welcome, but we want the guest to be willing to field additional questions.

Guest from Hell: Any person who keeps plugging their site or product out of context. We can do a very good job of promoting the product and providing questions that provide appropriate placement for product mentions without the guest making unnecessary plugs.

102 Health and Fitness

Contact person: Dave DePew dave@davedepew.com; 888-376-1315. Best method: First e-mail a pitch. If we accept the pitch we will request a media kit along with a copy of the book or the product to be mentioned in the interview. No response? The squeaky wheel gets the grease. All e-mails and calls are welcome.

Invited Back? Response from listeners and the willingness of the guest to provide straight-forward information. Guests who only provide a tease of information with answers like "It's in my book," will not be asked back. In some cases bad interviews will not be archived.

Guest Comment: "My experience working with Dave DePew has been GREAT! Dave allowed me the opportunity to reach more people and sell more books with a single podcast than I was able to do on other more 'traditional' radio shows. The fantastic thing about doing a podcast is that it stays out for a long time so I and my books can continually help people months and even years later."—Joe Cannon, MS, CSCS, NSCA-CPT, author of *Nutritional Supplements: What Works and Why. A Review from A to Zinc and Beyond* (Infinity Publishing 2006), http://www.Joe-Cannon.com

Bio of Dave DePew: Dave, MFT, LSN is an experienced San Diego–based personal trainer, weight loss specialist, licensed sports nutritionist, strength coach, and natural bodybuilder. One of the nation's most highly sought after transformation and performance enhancement specialists, his reputation throughout San Diego for producing amazing results with his clients is well known.

He picked up his first barbell at the age of 8 years old and started personal training in 1991.

Having attained a wide variety of certifications and specializations from more than a dozen nationally recognized organizations, he operates an online fitness and nutrition radio network and is a contributor to many of the best online fitness and nutrition websites. He's also on many expert panels and helps to consult with many of the industry's top health and fitness companies.

Dave's life's mission is to motivate and teach others how to lead a more healthy and fit lifestyle and to wage a war against obesity. His objectives are to educate and empower, to expose the sources of fitness and weight loss deception, and to assist in changing the lives of people everywhere.

Dave lives in San Diego County with his wife, Brandi, sons Kyle and Aidan, and daughter Katelyn.

Fitness Business Radio with Tom Perkins on http://www.fitnessbusinessradio.com

Theme: Business and personal growth for health clubs, fitness professionals, manufacturers, suppliers, certifying organizations, associations, etc.

Guest Profile: Well-known personalities in the fitness industry and or famous authors outside of the fitness industry. We want great content and to know how the contact will be of benefit to our listeners.

Guest from Hell: Lateness, on a cell phone with bad reception, only concerned with getting their info out but not offering content to the listeners as part of their marketing funnel.

Contact: info@fitnessbusinessradio.com; thecoach@fitnessbusinessradio.com; 800-801-4423/603-502-9755; http://www.fitnessbusinessradio.com; Tom Perkins. Best method: E-mail. Calling with a pitch, e-mailing a bio and sending a press kit is welcome. No response? Please try back if no response within 72 business hours.

Invited Back? Really if the interview went well (and most do), its timing and subject matter. I tend to re-interview someone after 90 days, but in some circumstances sooner.

Bio of Tom Perkins: Tom is a business coach/consultant, personal trainer, and fitness nutritionist. As a successful business owner with experience working with dozens of Fortune 500 companies, he brings a unique perspective to the fitness industry. With 17 years of experience, he understands the intricacies of the fitness industry and is an expert in the process of building a rewarding and profitable fitness enterprise.

Tom's passion for the fitness industry is governed by two philosophies: bring the mind and the body will follow and stay focused until the miracle happens. Tom prides himself on his ability to inspire people. He holds certifications from NESTA as a certified personal trainer and a certified fitness nutritionist in addition to a degree in business management/accounting.

Full Power Living with Ilene L. Dillon, M.S.W. on World Talk Radio http://www.worldtalkradio.com (Studio A).

Theme: Awakening to power and importance of human emotions.

Guest Profile: Individual, author or expert in area of show's focus and any area of life. Interesting topic, fit with our themes, enthusiasm, knowledgeable, responsible, clear communicator. Their topic, involvement with it, past interview experiences, credentials, ability to present themselves and their ideas coherently, level of enthusiasm, acquaintance with the theme of our show, how to contact them (and when) and when they are available.

Guest from Hell: In the *Electric Kool-Aid Acid Test*, the leader of the Merry Pranksters (a hippie group that moved around the U.S. on a converted bus) had a saying: "You're either on the bus, or you're off the bus." We don't have guests from hell—they would be the ones that don't really fit our show; and they're off the bus.

Contact: Ilene@emotionalpro.com; 510-665-1973 Toll Free: 866-385-5769 ext 801; http://www.emotionalpro.com; Ilene L. Dillon. Best method: I prefer an e-mail inquiry. Attachments of bios, descriptive information, pictures, etc. are fine. Once we speak and agree on a show appearance, press kit and book (if any) to be sent directly to my office. No response? We try to respond right away. If we miss our target, a second e-mail is the step of choice.

Invited Back? Qualifications listed in (1) above. More than one book or product. Good emotional and verbal exchange; positive presence on air.

Guest Comments: "I was very impressed how thoroughly Ilene prepared for our interview by reading my book and crafting excellent questions for me. She really 'got' what I was about and helped me communicate effectively to her audience to deliver a rich, meaningful show that I'm proud to be part of. Thanks Ilene!"—David Steele, MA, LMFT, Founder of Relationship Coaching Institute and author of *Conscious Dating: Finding the Love of Your Life in Today's World* (RCN Press 2006) and *Conscious Dating: How to Find the Love of Your Life* (RCN Press 2007), http://www.relationshipcoachinginstitute.com/faculty/DavidSteele.htm

"Ilene Dillon is a fantastic interviewer. She not only thoughtfully reviews what she requests from an interviewee, Ilene is wise, warm, and witty. Since she always has her audience interests as heart, everyone has a great time. I highly recommend Ilene and her fun, enlightening show."—Doris Helge, Ph.D., author of *Joy on the Job* (Shimoda Publishing, Dec 2006) and *Transforming Pain into Power* (Shimoda Publishing 1998), http://www.joyonthejob.info

Bio of Ilene Dillon: Ilene is author of 12 books, a teacher's manual on emotional literacy, and a professional multi-media training course on anger mastery. Holder of two professional psychotherapy licenses and a lifetime junior college teaching credential, she has maintained a private practice in California for over 35 years, and has been featured in publications such as *The San Francisco Chronicle, Care Notes, Feel.com, The Marin Independent Journal, Excellence* and *Woman's Day*. A professional member of The National Speakers Association, Ilene has spoken and appeared on the media in the U.S., China and Australia.

Ilene's clients include California colleges and probations officers, Dallas Presbyterian Hospital, American Family Cruises, California Council for Self-Esteem, California Personnel and Guidance Association and Adelaide, Australia's C.O.P.E. She has presented to Beijing's China Rehabilitation Research Institute, women's conferences and federal and state penitentiary inmates. Since 2004 Ilene has been creator/host of Internet radio's Full Power Living (aired over www.worldtalkradio.com), which is dedicated to awakening the world to the power and potential of human emotion. Ilene leads audiences to renew and build "Foundations—for Life!"

All of Ilene books are focused on emotions, including *99 Tips for Mastering Fear, Exploring Anger with Your Child, Bouncing Back from Jealousy (Self-made Madness)*, and co-author of *Happiness Is a Decision of the Heart*.

Heal Yourself Talk Radio with Rebbekah White on http://www.healyourselftalk.com

Theme: Health Related issues, healing mind, body and spirit

Guest Profile: Anyone who has a story to share about healing, whether mind, body or spirit; authors who have written books about healing with the mind, body or spirit or who have products that they know work for healing and want to help others improve their health and well being. Rebbekah likes to view potential guest speakers' website, but if they do not have a website that is not a problem. She requires a copy of their book or product to look over before she will do an interview. Rebbekah is very easygoing; she likes her guest speakers to feel like they are sitting in her living room just having a normal conversation with a friend. *Heal Yourself Talk Radio*'s daily motto is: Desire it, Believe it, Accept it, & Receive it.

For information on past guests go to: http://www.healyourselftalk.com

Guest from Hell: "I have had the pleasure to not really have a guest speaker that is hard to deal with; on the rare occasion it has happened it only made the show better. However, I do not want guest speakers to entirely take over the show and only promote their products during the entire interview process; should this happen the show will not air on the site or be included in any promotional materials. All guest speakers do get many chances, through my own lead, to share where my listeners can receive more information, including saying their website address etc. I do this for a reason; the more you show your own expertise the more people will want what you have to offer and it doesn't come across as just a sales pitch. *Heal Yourself Talk Radio* was created to share information and to give the world a place to come and learn more about how they can create a better life through healing their mind, body and spirit."

Contact: Rebbekah@healyourselftalk.com; 419-318-0895; http://www.healyourselftalk.com. Best method: I prefer potential guests to e-mail me any information they have on themselves, their website, a press kit is great if they have one but not required. Not all potential guests will be asked to be on the show; if I feel the topic does not fit in with *HYTR* I will not have the guest on the show.

Invited Back? On many occasions guest speakers are invited back; it all depends on the topic and if Rebbekah feels that her audience would enjoy more information from the guest speaker.

Bio of Rebbekah White: Rebbekah is a 35 year old mom to 3 boys ages 13, 11 and 5 and has been married to her high school sweetheart for 16 years. She has been dealing with depression now for almost 12 years.

"Because of my own personal journey I have for

the past year felt a strong urging to start an Internet talk radio show to offer guidance and help for those who are looking for ways to heal their mind, body and soul no matter what the source of pain is," she says. "It was a long hard decision to make but with guidance from friends and advisors I realized I had to make the first step." Her radio show was born.

About eight years ago, Rebbekah started Support for Moms, now under new ownership. "I wanted to spread the word to people who deal with physical and emotional difficulties that they are not alone," she says. "Over the past two years I have received several e-mails from women I have never met before thanking me for sharing my story on depression."

Among her guests are people she has known. Yet, until starting her show, she "never knew the pain they were dealing with. Now these same people want to share their experiences with others in an effort to help those who may be facing similar situations learn that they are not alone and that they can heal."

Listener Comment: "This podcast has been and continues to be a vital part of my self-healing process. The fact that I have been through many difficult and traumatic events allows me to recognize how overtly essential, in today's society, Rebbekah White's *HYTR* podcast is.

"Sharing my experiences was a healing event for me, even given the fact that it has been ten years since their occurrence. Not only have I found it beneficial to be a speaker but in listening to other speakers and being given the opportunity to present questions that are actually addressed by Jack N. Singer, Ph.D., licensed clinical psychologist, I cannot relate to you how very important and impactful *HYTR* has been for me." — Ginger Marks, Clearwater, FL, http://www.documeant.com

"I have come to know of Rebbekah White's work, as I've come to know about Rebecca personally, through an online business network, www.ryze.com. Rebbekah is a thoughtful, caring, and very enterprising woman. She's deeply committed to helping others find the path to healing, in whatever form that may need to take for each individual. Her internet radio show, *Heal Yourself Talk Radio — HYTR —* has taken off from the moment she launched. Rebbekah has offered topics of interest to the betterment of each and every one of us, wherever we may be on our path to emotional, physical, and professional success.

"Rebbekah White is a savvy businesswoman and a credit to the international community which she serves — women, and men, around the world through the amazing reach of the internet." — Linda Alexander, author, http://www.authorsden.com/lindajalexander

The Healing Sounds Show with Jonathan Goldman on http://www.healthylife.net aired the second Wednesday of each month at noon (ET).

Theme: Sound healing.

Guest Profile: People involved in the therapeutic and transformational uses of sound. Musicians, authors, scientists, healers. Someone who is or has contributed to the field of sound healing — could be an author or a musician or a practioner. Also someone who is focused on positively shifting the consciousness of people on this planet. Thus far, because I know so many people in this field, I've been familiar to some degree with all my guests, so I know their validity as well as having some resonance with them. When this stops occurring, I'll have a brief chat with them beforehand to see what they're like and if necessary, I'll be prepared to do a lot of talking.

Guest from Hell: Someone who is not very talkative — answering in one or two word sentences.

Contact: jonathangoldman@healingsounds.com; 303-443-8181; http://www.healingsounds.com; Jonathan Goldman. Best method: E-mail a bio. No response? E-mail again — e-mails can get lost in cyberspace all too easily.

Invited Back? If the show is interesting and exciting. If the hour ends and it seems like we've only just touched upon the subject.

Bio of Jonathan Goldman: Jonathan is an international authority on sound healing and a pioneer in the field of harmonics. He is the author of *Healing Sounds* (Healing Arts Press 2002); *Shifting Frequencies* (Light Technology Publications 1998); *The Lost Chord* (Spirit Music 1999); *Tantra of Sound* (Hampton Roads Publishing Co. 2005), co-authored with his wife, Andi Goldman, which won the 2006 Visionary Award for Best Alternative Health Book, and his latest, *The 7 Secrets of Sound Healing*.

Jonathan presents Healing Sounds Seminars throughout the world. He is the director of the Sound Healers Association and president of Spirit Music, Inc., in Boulder, Colorado. A Grammy nominee, Jonathan has created numerous best-selling, award-winning recordings, including *The Divine Name* (with Gregg Braden); *Reiki Chants; Ultimate Om; The Lost Chord;* and *Chakra Chants,* winner of the Visionary Award for Best Healing-Meditation Album. He is also a lecturing member of the International Society for Music and Medicine.

The Health and Beauty Revolution Show with Patty Kovacs on WS Radio.

Theme: Life is too short. Create a healthy, beautiful life.

Guest Profile: *New York Times* best-selling authors, renowned physicians, surgeons, lifestyle experts and authors. Impeccable qualifications that make a guest/author an expert in his/her field. An engaging and passionate audio presentation of the material. Knowledge that is cutting edge or extremely well presented with absolute confidence. Credibility of their material. Period. Truth and genuine delivery always send the message.

Her more prominent guests have included Suzanne

Somers, Arianna Huffington, Denise Wattley and Dan Millman.

Guest from Hell: Cold delivery. Indifferent tonality in voice. Interrupting me, the host, all too often. Disrespectful attitude. I have worked with such top publicists that I've never really had them. I hear them on radio and cringe.

Contact: pattykov@san.rr.com; 619-807-2174 and 858-792-9819; http://www.wsradio.com/healthandbeautyrevolution; Patty Kovacs Executive Producer/Host. Best method: E-mailing a terrific one-sheet and press kit. Phone calls do it also. Samples mailed to me from a client have actually opened interest when otherwise I might have passed them over. No response? My byline on my e-mail address says it all. I totally respect my (potential) guests and expect the same. It is a busy world. If I don't respond in a timely manner, e-mail me again. Kindness and respect go a long way.

Invited Back? I am inundated with top publicists contacting me so a repeat all boils down to either my personal interest, topics of interest to current affairs, or the station's request that a client/guest has purchased advertising.

Guest Comments: "Thanks for helping me get out the message that there's wonderful medical help for people suffering with bipolar disorder." — Sean Astin, son of Patty Duke Astin, actor, Rudy, Fox-TV's 24, activist for bipolar disorder

"What a terrific interview, Patty. You really know your material." — John Connolly, CEO, Castle Connolly Medical, LTD.

Bio of Patty Kovacs: A marketing, public relations, and strategic business consultant, Patty has led in the promotion and business development of medical and integrative health centers, spas and fitness facilities, having developed such operations from inception to completion. Patty also heads her own PR and event management firm.

From President George Bush's broccoli bouquet presentation on the White House lawn, to Mr. Blackwell's runway antics, Patty has created PR that is "out of the box" and right on target. Her interview style engages the guest with fun, smarts, enthusiasm, and passion for the topic at hand. She was PR director and integral to the founding of the San Diego chapter of the President's Council for Physical Fitness and Health. Today Patty is a featured writer and business development/event planning expert for national publications (pen name: Patty Kovacevich). Patty introduced (2) physicians to Suzanne Somers, both of whom she included in her last (2) best selling books.

Health in 30 with Barbara Ficarra, RN, BSN, MPA on WRCR-AM 1300 airing in Rockland County, New York, Friday, 5:30–6 P.M. and streaming live at http://www.Healthin30.com — click the WRCR logo to listen live. http://www.wrcr.com

Theme: Health show. Thirty-minute live health show that focuses on education, wellness and prevention and at times listeners call-in with questions.

Guest Profile: Physicians, *NY Times* writer and author, *NY Times* best selling authors, nurse practitioners, nutritionists, authors, etc. I look for a guest who has passion, enthusiasm and heart. One who tells a story. Past interview experience is not that important; for many of the expert guests on *Health in 30* this has been their first interview. Credentials are important, knowledge of topic, passion are all important. Sound of voice?—if someone is monotone with no enthusiasm that doesn't make for the BEST guest, the best sounding voices are filled with energy, passion, enthusiasm and heart. Guests have included Nancy H. Nielsen, MD, president-elect of the American Medical Association (AMA), and Boomer Esiason, the former football quarterback and founder of the Boomer Esiason Foundation, established to fight cystic fibrosis.

Guest from Hell: One who doesn't answer your question or someone who is monotone and stilted is a poor guest.

Contact: B.Ficarra@Healthin30.com; withheld upon request; http://www.Healthin30.com; Barbara Ficarra. Best method: The best way is by e-mail. Either e-mailing me at B.Ficarra@Healthin30.com or presently there is a "Speak Out" logo on the homepage where experts can go and send me their info. Sending a bio is a definite. No response? Absolutely e-mail! I respond to all (mostly all) e-mails in a timely manner; however, if one unintentionally gets overlooked I would hope the guest would contact me again. So yes, they can be persistent—another e-mail.

Invited Back? Guests who are passionate and "tell a story" during the interview and the guests who are invited back.

Listener Comment: "Love your radio show, the format and the variety of topics and speakers."—from a nurse listener

Bio of Barbara Ficarra: Barbara is an award-winning journalist, media broadcaster, creator/executive producer/host of her show. She is also founder and editor-in-chief of the Healthin30.com website, which is dedicated to the responsible sharing of information from leaders in the healthcare industry. The highlight of the website is the "Speak Out" logo, where all medical communicators can go to sign-up to be a guest on the *Health in 30* show and/or write for the website. Healthin30.com is geared to the general public to obtain vital health information as well as the health care professional.

Barbara is the medical/health correspondent and executive producer for Web/TV, and is the creator/host/executive producer of "Nurses in Motion" for Web/TV. The program delves into the complex issues surrounding the nursing and medical profession. The American College of Emergency Physicians (ACEP) awarded Barbara the prestigious Journalism Award of

Excellence for Coverage of Emergency Medicine, given for outstanding coverage of an emergency medicine issue. The program, "Ins and Outs of the ER," covered what to expect in the ER and the challenges of crowding and waiting on the *Health in 30* radio show.

Health Matters with Rachel Rockafellow on Yellowstone Public Radio, Billings, Mt., aired monthly in Montana and Wyoming.

Theme: Health topics.

Guest Profile: Experts in an area of health or health-related theme that would be of interest to our local listeners. I like to interview local people. If there is something that is a national issue, then I need a local person on with them to relate to our listeners.

Guest from Hell: One who is very nervous and lacks confidence or pushes their products more than what will benefit the listeners.

Contact: healthmatters.rachel@gmail.com; withheld upon request; http://www.ypradio.org then click on Health Matters; Rachel Rockafellow or producer Ken Siebert. Best method: E-mail. No response? I usually respond fairly quickly. If I don't, it must be that I'm out of town or something.

Invited Back? If there is more information to cover than we have time for.

Bio of Rachel Rockafellow: Rachel is a registered nurse and an adjunct assistant professor at Montana State University College of Nursing. She also works at Bozeman Urological Associates as one of the three certified continence nurses in Montana, as well as other health-related outreach such as CPR instruction, adult community education, and consultation. Rachel is the author of a monthly health education column appearing in the women's magazine *Balance*, which is published by the *Bozeman Daily Chronicle*. She is a member of the Bozeman Women's Activity Group, enjoying weekly outdoor adventures like hiking, biking, back country skiing, and canoeing.

Rachel lives in Bozeman with her husband Dave and their dog Annie.

Full bio at http://www.ypradio.org/programs/local/health_matters.html

Health Matters with Dr. G with Gloria Gilbere, N.D., and D.A.Hom., Ph.D., CWR on http://www.gloriagilbere.com and http://www.healthylife.net; now off the air.

Theme: Natural health, environmental health, and rejuvenation.

Guest Profile: Authors, physicians, natural product manufacturers, victims of disorders. One that will share new natural health information and validation for victims of chemically-induced immune system disorders and disorders that are misdiagnosed, undiagnosed or viewed with suspicion and hostility in a conventional medical setting because their disorder is invisible or their testing incorrectly shows "everything is within normal range"). It is important that their voice projects and they speak clearly. They must have specific experience within the scope of topic being discussed and passionate about their subject matter.

Guest from Hell: One who has never experienced the illness or disease we are discussing yet has an opinion about everything and nothing is the correct solution except their specific point of reference.

Contact: drgilbere@verizon.net; 208-255-5252; http://www.gloriagilbere.com; Dr. Gloria Gilbere. Best method: By sending a press kit or e-mailing, not calling. No response? As a practicing practitioner who also maintains a heavy travel schedule to teach and lecture, it is best they e-mail as a reminder if they have not received a reply within 30 days.

Invited Back? When the information provided is so valuable and well presented that a one-hour program simply cannot capture all that needs to be said to educate and alert the audience.

Guest Comments: "For five years Dr. Gilbere has been an invaluable asset to the readers of *Total Health Magazine*. Her dynamic energy and commitment to guide others to health, particularly those being poisoned by their own bodies, enables thousands of readers and listeners of her talk show to bring their health into homeostasis each year.—L. Hurd, Publisher, *Total Health Magazine*

"Truly a professional's professional. Her 'on the air' energy is contagious, just as it is when she teaches, consults or delivers a presentation. She knows her material and engages her audience with her candidness about her own health challenges and what it took to overcome them and then maintain her exuberant health and energy."—G. Dutson, D.C. test committee member, Nat'l Board of Chiropractic Examiners

Bio of Gloria Gilbere: Gloria is a traditional naturopath, homeopath doctor of natural health, Eco-Ergonomist, and Wholistic Rejuvenist—renowned for her certificated skin and body rejuvenation programs.

She is internationally respected as a natural health researcher and medical journalist, environment health consultant, and an authoritative influence in the discovery of the causes, effects, and non-drug solutions for fibromyalgia, chronic fatigue, digestive disorders, chemically-induced immune system disorders, and for her Wholistic Skin and Body Rejuvenation programs.

Gloria is associate editor at *Total Health Magazine* and author of six books: *I Was Poisoned by My Body* (Lucky Press 2005), *Invisible Illnesses* (Freedom Press 2005), *Pain/Inflammation Matters* (Lucky Press 2002), *Wholistic Skin and Body Rejuvenation Program* (a series of four books currently available only to students taking the programs), *Natures' Prescription Milk* (Freedom Press 2002) and *Colon Cleansing* (E-Guide)—currently under revision.

Healthy Lifestyles with Barbara Mendez on http://www.lifestylenutrients.net, Tribeca Radio (now NY Talk Radio, www.nytalkradio.net)

Theme: Health related topics and alternative medicine.

Guest Profile: Anyone in the health and/or alternative medicine field. Informative, interesting, with an ability to speak fluently about topic. Good personality, fun. What their background in alternative medicine is, their credentials, experience on the air.

Guest from Hell: Someone that gives one word answers and makes me chase down responses.

Contact: barbara@lifestylenutrients.net; 212-465-7551; http://www.lifestylenutrients.net. Best method: E-mailing me with their pitch and bio is fine. No response? E-mail me again. Sometimes I get swamped but never rude.

Invited Back? How interesting topic was, how fluent they were in topic, how well we communicated with one another and whether or not I had fun interviewing them. If I feel I could have continued talking for another hour, it's likely I will invite them back.

Bio of Barbara Mendez, R.Ph.: Barbara is a registered pharmacist and the president of Lifestyle Nutrients, a nutritional consulting practice she developed in 1999. She studied pharmacy at St. John's University and in 1989 earned a Bachelor of Science in pharmacy. Barbara studied nutrition with the Designs for Health Institute in Boulder, Colorado, and with the American Academy of Nutrition, receiving her certificate in nutritional counseling. She is currently in the process of studying for her master's degree in nutrition. Barbara is also a certified Hatha Yoga instructor and in 2002 developed the Lifestyle Nutrients Workshop Series, which combines yoga and nutrition to target specific health concerns including: weight management, stress management and using alternative therapies to transition through menopause. These workshops have helped hundreds of people achieve their health goals through the integration of nutrition and yoga. In December 2004, Barbara was invited to be the director of nutrition for the Fratellone Group for Integrative Cardiology and Medicine, counseling each patient on proper diet and supplement use for the management, treatment and prevention of heart disease, as well as many other health concerns, including cancer, neurological disorders, diabetes and immune dysfunction. She is the author of the monthly newsletter, *Healthy Lifestyle News* and in 2006 she became the in-house nutritionist for the Harvard Club of New York City.

Healthy Talk Radio with America's Wellness Doctor, Julian Whitaker, M.D, and Deborah Watson, syndicated and on the Internet.

Theme: Lifestyles of wellness seekers.

Guest Profile: Credentialed guests with newsworthy topics. Someone who has a nickel word vocabulary (can communicate in understandable terms).

Guest from Hell: Someone whose refrain is "it's in my book."

Contact: questions@healthytalkradio.com; 727-572.0400; http://www.healthytalkradio.com; Deborah Watson. Best method: Snail mail only. Need guest CV/bio plus topic material, mailing address: Healthy Talk Radio, 311 112th Ave. NE, St. Petersburg, FL 33716. No response? Call.

Invited Back? Newsworthy information.

Guest Comment: "I had my interview with Deborah this morning and it went extremely well. Can't believe how quickly the time flew by! I had so much more to say, which is a good sign. She was wonderful. I think I was very informative and fairly relaxed. Deborah is very friendly and has a wealth of information on pain management and alternative health. Also I found her sound engineer Ray to be quite warm and helpful." — Sigrid Macdonald, author of *Getting Hip: Recovery from a Total Hip Replacement* (AuthorHouse 2004) and Editor, http://damourroad.blogspot.com

For Deborah Watson's bio, see her show, *Deborah "Doc" Watson*, on page 99.

Bio of Julian Whitaker, MD: America's Wellness Doctor, Dr. Whitaker is a pioneer in complementary medicine. After graduating from Dartmouth College, obtaining a medical degree from Emory University, and completing a general surgical residency, he became interested in nutrition and other therapies not taught in medical school. In 1979, he opened the Whitaker Wellness Institute and began utilizing nutrition, supplements, and other unconventional therapies to treat and even reverse serious health problems. Today, Whitaker Wellness, located in Newport Beach, California, is the largest and most comprehensive clinic of its kind in the U.S. Dr. Whitaker is also a respected educator and outspoken advocate of integrative therapies. He is the author of *Health and Healing*, a popular monthly newsletter that has reached millions of households since 1991, and has written 13 books, including *Reversing Diabetes* (Grand Central Publishing 2001), *Reversing Heart Disease* (Grand Central Publishing 2002), *Reversing Hypertension* (Grand Central Publishing 2001) and *Dr. Whitaker's Guide to Natural Healing* (Prima Health 2001). He is also a tireless spokesman for medical freedom and founder of the Whitaker Health Freedom Foundation.

Healthy Woman with Jewel on KSFR, 101.1 FM, Santa Fe, NM, aired from Santa Fe Community College.

Theme: Health, services, providers.

Guest Profile: Health advocates, conference speakers, community leaders, consumers, personal testimonials. Desired: Friendly, good self image, confident (not cocky) sense of humor, "a real person," acquainted with area resources, informed, articulate, and when guests connect with their listening audience. Make an impact that makes a significant difference in their lives. Important are past interview experiences, credentials and sound of their voice. Is their "focus" linked to the needs of the community, and the appropriateness of their message?

Guest from Hell: Very limited public persona, oral communication skills weak, does not "flow" with the interview process/subject matter ... not the right person for the interview.

Contact: Siete@sisna.com; 505-690-4837; http://www.ksfr.org; Jewel; Best method: E-mail or phone, bio, press kit. No response? E-mail preferred.

Invited Back? If they fulfill requirements in Guest Profile.

Bio of Jewel Cabeza De Vaca: Born and raised in Santa Fe, Jewel is single parent with two adult children, and has a BA in public administration. She is bilingual, public speaker, events organizer, leadership skills/training, facilitator, health activist/advocate, lobbyist, and has more than 16 years radio experience.

Herb Talk Live with Wendy Wilson on WBCQ, WWCR Shortwave Networks, GCN Genesis Communications Network (www.gcnlive.com), and American Voice Radio, a podcast and satellite network, www.theamericanvoice.com

Theme: Natural health solutions using organic herbs and natural therapies.

Guest Profile: MDs, vets, chiropractors, herbalists, authors, psychiatrists and any professional using natural therapies in their practice. Someone with information that will empower the listener with better health.

Guest from Hell: Someone who cannot stay on topic and brings political or other agendas not formatted for the topic and show. Guests who talk over the heads of the listener are not good communicators.

Contact: wwilson@thepowerherbs.com; 704-875-8010 x9; http://www.thepowerherbs.com; Wendy Wilson or Jane Greene at 704-875-8010 x8. Best method: Call or e-mail with a short paragraph of their topic. Topic should touch on self-help for the listener or empower listener with some information to improve or protect health. If I'm interested I will request bio or press kit. A trusted referral is helpful as well. No response? Please call.

Invited Back? Quality of information that is communicated effectively to the audience.

Bio of Wendy Wilson: Wendy is a vitalist, aka an herbalist. She believes in the "original medicine" to balance and restore the body. For more than a decade, she has studied and enlightened people to the healing power of herbs and natural therapies. A graduate of the University of North Carolina (Charlotte), Wendy is a student of the martial arts, and an herbalist for Apothecary Herbs, Inc. located in Huntersville, North Carolina. http://www.thepowerherbs.com

After college, Wendy started her family while working in the medical field as a physician's personal assistant. She became aware of the healing power of herbs and natural therapies when her infant son became seriously ill and modern medicine had no solutions. She turned to a natural healer for help. Her child made a full recovery and Wendy's journey towards becoming an herbalist began. She enrolled at the School of Natural Healing in Springville, Utah, in the Master Herbalist Program.

In 1999, Wendy wrote a "how to" book called *The Power Herbs: 13 Herbs Every Medicine Cabinet Should Have* (Morris Publishing). She wanted to reveal the herb secrets she had learned from her traditional training and practical experience. There is a high demand for knowledge on how to use herbs and natural therapies effectively and the book shows you how.

In 2000 Wendy founded Apothecary Herbs, Inc., which manufactures professional strength immune boosting and body cleansing formulas. She also enjoys writing her health column for various newsletters, including *International Forecaster* and *Health Quest* and producing her nationally syndicated talk radio show.

In Short Order with Sue Vogan on http://www.highway2health.net

Theme: Health.

Guest Profile: Physicians, scientists, researchers, advocates, expert authors, etc. We like to know the guest's background. I pre-interview for voice, research credentials, and never look at past interviews.

Guest from Hell: The one that is short on responses (i.e., complicated question and response is "yes"), who freezes or rambles on and on.

Contact: TVogan45791@suddenlink.net; 252-566-9559; http://www.highway2health.net; Sue Vogan. Best method: E-mail. Press kit/book combo; e-mail a show idea/guest. For writers — their written articles/books. No response? Person should call — "This is _____ and I sent you a pitch ___ weeks ago. I am calling to follow up, do you have a couple minutes?"

Invited Back? Feedback from listeners and number of calls received during the show.

Guest Comments: "Sue Vogan interviewed me for her radio show. She was totally professional and prepared all the questions in advance. It gave me time to think about responses and I was not caught off guard. She thoroughly researched the area of interest and did a great job." — Lesley Ann Fein, MD, MPH, rheumatologist

"It was a pleasure. Let me know if you need me again." — Dr. Daniel Cameron, NY, LymeProject.com

Bio of Sue Vogan: Sue is a published author of *NCO: No Compassion Observed* (Bedside Books 2006), and two books under a pen name, journalist (*The Public Health Alert* and other publications), radio show host, assistant publisher at Balumond Press (http://www.freddyrocks.com), and Lyme disease advocate.

Married for 11 years (Tim), mother of two (Phillip and Michael) and grandmother of two (Courtney Rose and Katlyn Marie). "Having Lyme disease since 1997, it has been difficult to find avenues to get the word out about the disease, treatments, and problems associated with the disease. The radio show, the book, and the articles are excellent means of communication for me."

Insights with Michelle Caporale on Ask 1 Radio Network, formerly *The Mix Talk*, http://www.themixtalk.com, or http://ask1radio.com

Theme: Intuitive Info/Readings, enlightening subjects for self growth. Knowledge based programs.

Guest Profile: Guests who are well versed in the Intuitive field. Yes, some are authors. Self help. Well speaking manners. Someone who is very well educated in their field. Interesting content that will attract listeners as well as information that I feel is helpful.

Past interview experiences, credentials and sound of voice are important. I research all my guests and listen to archived interviews. I buy their books if they are authors. When they accept my invitations, I speak to them in depth prior to the show.

Guest from Hell: A guest who is rude, speaks over the host. Does not deliver information in a professional courteous way. Someone who is arrogant and self centered, as this is not what I/we are about. A guest who claims to be educated in a field in which they are not.

Contact: mcaporale1@tampabay.rr.com; 727-804-5958; http://www.michellecaporale.com and http://www.themixtalk.com; Michelle Caporale. Best method: E-mailing bio. Contact will continue from that point. No response? No need to call or e-mail. I always respond. I take my show very seriously.

Invited Back? Availability, how that interview went. Were they beneficial to the listening audience? Did we get a great response, etc.?

Bio of Michelle Caporale: Michelle had her first experience communicating with spirits at the early age of 11 when her departed great grandmother appeared in her room to "talk." With a desire to learn more about her abilities, Michelle studied under Dr. Paul Daniele, Ph.D., D.D., P.C., the president of the College of Metaphysical Studies in Clearwater, Florida. She earned a degree as a spirit medium and another as an intuitive practitioner. Dr. Daniele is quoted as saying, "Michelle possesses an unwavering sense of confidence and determination that is shared by all who know her. As a psychic reader, I consider her head and shoulders above most psychics that I have come in contact with and I would highly recommend and support her in any endeavor due to her work ethic, intelligence, psychic ability and above all her innate spirituality." Michelle is multi-gifted, which means as soon as she connects with an individual, she immediately taps into the ability that is best suited in obtaining the most accurate information. Her gifts include mediumship (spirit communicator), clairaudience (clear hearing), clairsentience (clear feeling), clairvoyance (clear seeing), and psychometry (reading the energy attached to objects and photos). Her delivery exudes confidence, and her compassionate humor is her calling card. After delivering approximately 10,000 readings over the course of her career, she feels honored knowing that she is able to deliver messages that help heal and console her clients, and if they laugh or chuckle along the way, well, that is a bonus.

Living on Purpose with Lynn Thompson is heard on http://www.WomensRadio.com, http://www.RadioEarNetwork.com and http://www.rabble.ca/rpn/lop. After three years as a volunteer host and producer of the show at CHLY Radio Malaspina on Vancouver Island, Canada, Lynn "graduated" the live show from CHLY to focus on web-based radio venues. Lynn charges a guest fee, which includes the interview preparation, recording and editing of the interview, airing on the three websites listed, an audio link for the guest's website, and a CD copy if requested. A flat rate of $100 is suggested. Transcription at additional cost. Customized recording and production services negotiable.

Theme: A thoughtful, nourishing blend of ideas, conversation and music offered in a spirit of health and well-being.

Guest Profile: Authors, healers, musicians, doctors, life coaches, spokespeople for current events and organizations, actors, artists, and scientists. Whether new to radio or a well-seasoned speaker, someone who is open to sharing thoughtful conversation about their interests and experiences with enough spontaneity to appeal to both women and men, young and older. A person who is passionately living their life with a sense of purpose, and willing to share their inspiration with perspective on the challenging chapters of their lives. Even if they are off the wall in their ideas, guests are welcome if they have a genuine and grounded sincerity that will translate into helpful information and inspiration for the listener and are knowledgeable about their subject and articulate in conversation.

Guest from Hell: Someone who is incommunicative, indecisive or pushy prior to the interview. Someone who is unable to have a satisfying conversation either by hardly speaking, by speaking quietly, or by launching into a monologue with little opportunity for dialogue and exchange of ideas.

Contact: livingonpurpose@chly.ca (alternative: livingonpurposelynn@gmail.com); 888-878-4935; http://www.livingonpurposelynn.com and http://www.rabble.ca/rpn/lop; Lynn Thompson, producer and host. Best method: An initial e-mail is welcomed to introduce the author (or proposed guest), to say why they would be great guests for *Living on Purpose*, what topics they want to focus on and how they found out about the show. Once we establish if and when an interview will follow, then an author (or someone with material essential to prepare for the interview) is requested to send the material by mail along with written reviews and suggested interview questions if available. (Although I generally compile my own questions and points of reference for each interview, it is helpful to know the questions with which they are familiar.) No response? Should the person e-mail or call you? They should send a follow-up e-mail, and if there's still no response, call. I generally respond fairly promptly to all inquiries one way or another.

Invited Back? Occasionally a guest is invited back if the conversation needs to be continued in further directions. On the "live" show one local psychic medium was welcomed back due to a busy call-in show and listener request.

Guest Comments: "I found your questions to be probing and interesting, and your style to be warm and engaging. You are living proof that one doesn't need to be cutting at someone's jugular in order to feel their pulse."— Dr. Laura Schlessinger

"I'm grateful to know things went as well on your end as they seemed to do on mine, Lynn. It was a thoroughly enjoyable interview. Thank you so much!"— Ilene Dillon, host of *Full Power Living*, page 102.

Bio of Lynn Thompson: Lynn has been the producer and host of *Living on Purpose* since August 2004. She continues to add to her extensive experience in recording and editing material for broadcast. Prior to her radio life, she was a self-employed creative photographer for 18 years. Lynn was born in Toronto, Ontario, Canada, and has been living in British Columbia, Canada, since 1978, mostly on Vancouver Island. Lynn holds a B.A. in philosophy and is a full-time student of life.

"The New You" Radio Show with Cher Ewing and Jeff Cadwell on Blog Talk Radio, http://www.blogtalkradio.com/thewlscoaches

Theme: Empowering the weight loss surgery patient.

Guest Profile: Authors, psychotherapists, surgeons, nutritionists, support group leaders, and patient advocates. Somebody who provides resources and or motivation for our listening audience. Credentials important.

Guest from Hell: A silent guest; one who doesn't contribute to the conversation.

Contact: info@thewlscoaches.com; 214-534-7455; http://www.TheWLSCoaches.com; Cher Ewing. Best method: E-mail a bio, call with a pitch, send a press kit. No response? E-mail.

Invited Back? If we are not able to conclude the interview; i.e. ran out of time

Bios of Cher Ewing and Jeff Cadwell: Cher is a certified health and wellness coach specializing in weight loss surgery. As a coach, she helps clients going through the weight loss process gain personal empowerment as they lose weight.

Jeff is a professionally certified life coach who specializes in motivating people through their weight loss surgery journey. He works with people who already have a measure of success in their lives, but who want to bridge the gap between where they are and where they want to be. His passion is the empowerment of individuals to live more robust lives — mind, body and soul.

Both Cher and Jeff run a "WLS" support group, contribute "Health and Wellness" articles exclusively for *Avid Living* and *WLS Lifestyles* magazine, host teleseminars and maintain a private practice in Dallas, Texas.

No Bones About It with Dr. Alvin Stein on WWNN, South Florida.

Theme: Advanced medicine for pain reduction; discussing various treatments that I use in my practice to treat pain patients in an effort to reduce or eliminate their pain

Guest Profile: Physicians or health care persons who can enhance the theme and give my audience a better understanding of the problems and the available treatments. Someone who speaks well and can articulate a clear concept to my audience and who can lend more credibility to the concepts that I endorse. We want to know their past interview experiences, credentials and sound of their voice.

Guest from Hell: Someone who rambles and is mumbling and can not answer questions that might challenge his opinions

Contact: nobones@aol.com; 954-581-8585; http://www.proloshot.com; Alvin Stein, MD. Best method: E-mail or phone. Start with e-mail or press kit and go further with references and personal conversation. No response? E-mail or call. I will give an up or down opinion as to whether I want them on my show.

Invited Back? Listener feedback and if they complemented my concept of practice of medicine.

Bio of Dr. Alvin Stein: Dr. Stein graduated from Rosalind Franklin University of Medicine and Science/The Chicago Medical School in 1961 and did his orthopedic surgery residency training at Hospital for Joint Diseases in NY and at the New York Medical College Program at Flower 5th Ave Hospital, Metropolitan Hospital in NY and the Hospital for Crippled Children in Newark, NJ. He has been in private practice since 1966 and practicing in Florida since 1973. Dr. Alvin Stein has been a board certified orthopedic surgeon for over 35 years and has done various types of orthopedic procedures. These include general orthopedic, surgery fracture care, spinal surgery, arthroscopic surgery, surgery of the foot, skeletomuscular pain therapy.

These forms of treatment have often left patients less than fully cured and often in chronic pain. By using the techniques of neural therapy and prolotherapy, combined with chelation therapy detoxification and nutritional supplementation, Dr. Stein has been able to significantly reduce patients' pain and disability safely, without further need for surgery. Free of narcotics and other dangerous medications, natural healing is possible with the proper treatment plan and knowledgeable guidance available under Dr. Stein's care. Certified by the American Academy of Pain

Management, Dr. Stein has combined the best of both the western and eastern healing philosophies, offering his patients a balanced approach to their health and well being. So if you are sick and tired of feeling sick and tired, there is an answer. There is someone who cares.

Nutrition and Health with Dr. Susan Mitchell on AM 580 WDBO, Orlando, FL, and http://www.wdbo.com

Theme: Hottest topics in the nutrition health world.

Guest Profile: Guest with credentials (author, doctor, etc.) or someone that has a background on the show topic. Guests coincide with the theme of the show, which we try to determine months ahead of time. We do welcome ideas and show suggestions from our listeners. Please provide a bio, with credentials if you are interested in becoming a guest on Dr. Mitchell's podcast.

Guest from Hell: Our guest interviews are pre-taped. We spend time researching, reviewing and talking over the fine details with the guest before the taping.

Contact: drmitchell@susanmitchell.org; 407-629-1101 (Dr. Susan Mitchell's office number, but please contact Terri Spitz — preferred method for media); http://www.wdbo.com, click on Nutrition and Health Center; Website and Free Ezine: http://www.susanmitchell.org; Terri Spitz /publicist. Best method: Terri Spitz Publicity, Inc. If you have an idea for a show topic and feel you would be a good candidate to be interviewed, please e-mail pitch or press material to Terrispitz@earthlink.net, 407-718-8297, then office 407-880-8297. No response? E-mail Terri Spitz, Dr. Mitchell's publicist. Allow a few days, before an e-mail response.

Invited Back? It depends on the nature of future show topics.

Bio of Dr. Susan Mitchell: Thousands of faithful listeners tune in to hear Dr. Mitchell's radio and Internet segments on WDBO where she's been the nutrition expert for over 10 years or read her blog on ThirdAge.com. Dr. Mitchell is a candid and energetic advocate of nutrition education. Her innovative approach to eating well and feeling better is changing lifestyles at work and in homes across the country. An award-winning registered dietitian, Dr. Mitchell serves on the health and medical advisory board of *Family Circle* magazine. She is co-author of three books — *Fat Is Not Your Fate* (Fireside 2004), *I'd Kill for a Cookie* (Plume 1998) and *Eat to Stay Young* (Kensington 2000), as well as a contributing author to Macmillan Reference USA's *Nutrition and Well-Being A to Z* (2004). A reliable source to the media, Dr. Mitchell has appeared on *The Today Show, CNN,* the TV *Food Network* and the *Daily Buzz.* She is also quoted extensively in *Reader's Digest, Time, Redbook, Fitness,* and *Cooking Light.*

Distinguishing Dr. Mitchell's work is her ability to integrate sound nutrition and fitness into busy lifestyles to achieve better health, increased energy and creativity. She serves as the nutrition expert for SuperTarget, Nutrihand.com and ThirdAge.com. A licensed nutritionist, registered dietitian, and Fellow of the American Dietetic Association, Dr. Mitchell earned her Ph.D. from the University of Tennessee (Go Volunteers!) and taught nutrition and health science at the University of Central Florida for over 8 years. She loves cats, loves to cook and freely admits to being a chocoholic and says that in realistic amounts most any food can be part of a healthy diet.

The Patient's Voice with Rosemary Roberts on http://www.thepatientsvoice.com

Theme: Healthcare; advocacy and education.

Guest Profile: Patient advocates, patients who have become advocates, healthcare professionals, nutritionalists, progressives, naturalists. There should be an honest and frank dialog with information that real people can use in their real lives. What motivates them to tell their story, and why that story should matter to others.

Guest from Hell: A) someone more concerned about sounding like an intellectual than delivering a purposeful message, and B) someone intent on discounting anything outside of mainstream medicine; alternative therapies.

Contact: rosemary@thepatientsvoice.com; 916-652-5309; http://www.thepatientsvoice.com; Rosemary Roberts. Best method: Contact: bios are great and support your knowledge and experience of a topic, but a bio without a clear message of what you can bring to listeners is useless. I respect honesty, integrity and the ability of someone to stand in their own shoes. Answers to issues are often difficult to come by, but that shouldn't stop the dialog about that issue. No response? I typically answer e-mails within the first day or two. If I don't, it usually means I'm just really busy at that time. I'd appreciate a follow-up e-mail, but don't mind if someone wants to call.

Invited Back? Energy: engaging.

Listener Comment: "What a calling answered by you with your show. Truly a gift of service to those in need. Simply stated, thank you for all that you do as an advocate for all of us. When the white coats, scrubs, and stethoscopes come off we are all consumers of healthcare!"—Shelly Anderson, RN

Guest Comment: "Rosemary Roberts' true professionalism and caring nature puts her at the top of the list for radio show hosts."—Jeff Elliott, Normal, Illinois

Bio of Rosemary Roberts: The founder of GirlOnPoint, a creative services firm specializing in custom medical and business content for education, advertising and marketing efforts, Rosemary's experience and voice have long been an advocate for consumers.

A freelance writer first published in 1993, Rosemary was the writer for "California's Emerging Healthcare Advocate: You!," a consumer's guide to choosing a healthcare plan — their rights and responsibilities, which won a 2002 Cappi award, honorable mention in the category of Best Public Relations Tool, Brochure. A twice published book author (Fair Winds Press), Rosemary is also featured twice in the inspirational anthology, *The Miracle of Sons* (Penguin Putman 2003).

With over 20 years' experience in the medical field as a clinical manager, patient educator, clerical coordinator and creator of policy in the area of patient advocacy — including access programs for the non–English speaking patient and the non-insured, Rosemary lends her unique style and communication skills to her role as the producer and host of her radio program centered around today's healthcare consumer. Her passion as a lecturer to high-risk teens, beginning in the early 80s, and her dedication to the promotion of timely and effective emergency medical information for at-risk individuals and seniors within the assisted living environment today, encompass a career of advocacy dedicated to the inspiration and education of consumers through collaborative efforts with both grassroots America and the corporate world.

The Peter K Show on Blog Talk Radio, www.blogtalkradio.com/peterk

Theme: Health success.

Guest Profile: Authors, medical, health specialists who are sharp, fun, engaging, interesting. What makes them or their message unique. What is their #1 contribution? A prominent guest has been John St. Augustine, executive producer of *Oprah*.

Guest from Hell: Quiet, slow, monotone.

Contact: peterk@peterkfitness.com; 877-364-7383; http://www.peterkfitness.com; Peter K. Best method: E-mail. No response? E-mail follow-up.

Invited Back? Fun segment full of take home info.

Bio of Peter K: A fit lifestyle expert, Peter is a speaker, author, nutritionist, and physical therapist. His own challenge with weight and losing 60 pounds 18 years ago has led to the development of this complete approach to living a healthier and success oriented life. "5 Minutes to Fitness+" guides people away from diets, ineffective exercises, and gimmicks, and towards real health solutions."

His organization, Peter K Fitness (http://www.peterkfitness.com) offers innovative health interventions through live seminar events, consulting, and health coaching, for individuals, businesses, and organizations to help people take control of their health, life and happiness.

The Positive Mind with Armand DiMele, aired weekdays on WBAI-99.5 FM, New York City

Theme: Popular psychology — presenting ideas and concepts that help people develop a greater understanding of themselves, and others as well.

Guest Profile: Authors, psychologists, scientists. Someone who can speak clearly and logically and has something to say that is novel. I look for credentials and their belief system,

Guest from Hell: One who freezes on the mike.

Contact: armand@thepositivemind.com; 212-757-4488; http://www.thepositivemind.com; Armand DiMele. Best method: Call with a pitch, e-mail a bio and send a press kit. No response? Sure, e-mail me a second time.

Invited Back? Successful exchange with host and dynamic presentation of material.

Bio of Armand F. DiMele, R-C.S.W., C.R.C., B.C.D.: Scientist, teacher and supervisor, Armand has conducted workshops, lectures, classes and training seminars on understanding human functioning at learning and health care institutions throughout the United States and Europe. In addition to producing and hosting his radio show, he is the founder of the DiMele Center for Psychotherapy, Counseling and Research in New York City.

Armand is a board certified diplomate in clinical social work, a certified rehabilitation specialist and a registered graduate education supervisor. He is chairman of the Foundation for Positive Psychology, president of Tudor Health Equities, past-president of both The New York Institute for the Dynamic Psychotherapies and The Institute for the Study of Human Energies.

He has served as instructor at Hunter College, Adelphi University, and at the New School for Social Research. His research findings on the nature of anxiety have been featured on numerous radio and television programs including a recent CBS — TV news special focused on new remedies for depression.

Armand has also served as psychology expert for the R.K.O. radio network and co-chairman of the Mental Health Division of Pratt Institute's Health and Nutrition Certification Program. He is a Fellow of Great Britain's Royal Society of Health.

His background in the social sciences includes learning and memory research at the Albert Einstein College of Medicine and extensive training in both traditional and contemporary modalities of psychotherapy and healing.

Armand is known for his pioneering therapeutic treatment of multiple personality dysfunction, and his unique understanding of the causes of human fragmentation and unity. He teaches strategies for fusing feelings and knowledge.

Problems and Solutions with Cathy Blythe on KFOR 1240 AM, Lincoln, NE, and 900 AM KJSK, Columbus, NE.

Theme: Information you can use to make your life better. Lots of health and lifestyle topics.

Guest Profile: Authors welcome. Mix of local guests and national authors. I am very selective about which ones. No controversial subjects, no religion, no politics, no divisive issues. It's a listener friendly format, non-combative in nature. One who has the book that he or she wrote close at hand so during the breaks I might guide him or her to the direction I am going next. I also appreciate the guest knowing my name, what town I'm in and calling me by name. Past interviews and credentials are good. I sort of take my chances on the sound of the voice. I always read every author's book (at least speed read :-) before an interview. It makes me a better interviewer and it certainly gains their respect and gratitude.

Guest from Hell: Someone who constantly promotes their book or service blatantly about every other sentence. I am happy to do that for them multiple times during the interview. Also, short answers can be a nightmare in a longer format like we have.

Contact: cathy@threeeagles.com; 402-325-7747; http://www.KFOR1240.com or www.problemsandsolutions.net; Cathy Blythe. Best method: Definitely e-mail press kits are welcome. I prefer not to receive phone calls. No response? Please e-mail me again.

Invited Back? Just basically how well the interview went ... although no matter how well it goes, there are many topics that I would only want to do once a year.

Guest Comments: "As an author and media personality I have had the opportunity to be interviewed by outstanding broadcasting professionals and journalists. Cathy Blythe is by far the most prepared, insightful, and passionate that I have had the pleasure to work with. Not once, but twice, and for interviews lasting an hour each on her program.

"She spent the time to read my book from cover to cover and a year later to review the book once more in preparation for our second interview. Instead of the questions provided by my PR firm, she developed lines of questioning that were unique (and I have heard them all!). I believe that her approach brought out the best in me." — Debra Fine, author of *The Fine Art of Small Talk* (Hyperion 2005)

"We need more shows like yours on the dial. It was an honor and we had a bunch of people download the free 10 energy plan so that shows that it made a difference." — Jon Gordon, known as the "Energy Addict" and author of *Energy Addict—101 Physical Mental and Spiritual Ways to Energize Your Life* (Perigee Trade 2004)

Bio of Cathy Blythe: Born and raised in Lincoln, Cathy attended Kearney State College and was focused on becoming an elementary education teacher. She then took what turned out to be a permanent detour into the world of radio when she was hired at KFOR as a receptionist in 1972.

She's been co-host of the KFOR *Morning Show* since 1982. In 1991 she began hosting her current show, which has won top awards from the Nebraska Broadcasters Association and the Associated Press for service to the community.

In 2002, Cathy was named National Personality of the Year, receiving the prestigious Marconi Award from the National Association of Broadcasters. In 2005, Cathy and her morning show co-host Ward Jacobson were named National Personalities of the Year and each received a Marconi at ceremonies in Philadelphia. The Marconi Award is the highest honor in broadcasting.

Psychiatry Today with Dr. Scot with Dr. Scot Bay on Radio Sandy Springs, 1620 AM, Sandy Springs, GA, and Jefferson, GA and on http://www.radiosandysprings.com

Theme: Help listeners with mental illness, stress, emotional problems, reducing stigma and misinformation about mental illness.

Guest Profile: Mental health professionals. Someone with experience, qualifications, credibility, and an area of specialization or expertise that they have a passion for. Training, credentials, work experience, and special subjects of interest/expertise are important.

Guest from Hell: Someone who is arrogant, overbearing, pedantic, talks too much, or is too anxious to be able to communicate their thoughts and ideas.

Contact: drscot@radiosandysprings.com; 404-943-1620 or 866-356-0789; http://www.radiosandysprings.com; Dr. Scot Bay. Best method: Via e-mail, with whatever information they wanted to include, but especially what topic they are interested in discussing on the show. No response? If they don't hear back from me within 3 days, they should call the station and leave a message.

Invited Back? If the guest and I had a good rapport, and if the information presented was of value to the audience

Bio of Scot Bay, MD: Dr. Bay is board certified in psychiatry and belongs to a group practice in Roswell, GA, called Northwest Behavioral Medicine. He majored in psychology at the University of Rochester and attended medical school at New York Medical College. He completed his residency in psychiatry at St. Vincent's Hospital in New York City. He was clinical director of an outpatient clinic at St. Vincent's Hospital in Harrison, New York, until 1995 when he moved to Columbus, GA, where he was in private practice and was an assistant medical director at the Bradley Center of St. Francis. He moved to the Atlanta area in August of 1998.

Dr. Bay specializes in the evaluation and management of mood and anxiety disorders. He has lectured all over the Southeast regarding practical and innovative uses of psychiatric medications, and also participates in clinical research regarding novel uses for current medications as well as potential new medications.

Dr. Bay is concerned with helping Radio Sandy Springs listeners cope better with stress, and feel well emotionally.

He also strives to reduce the stigma in the general public regarding mental illness and psychiatric treatment by debunking myths, discussing news stories relating to mental health issues, and giving a balanced explanation of media reports on the latest developments in medical research. Listeners to *Psychiatry Today* will hear useful tips on how to reduce the impact of stress on their lives and how to achieve better emotional well being.

The Real World of Autism with Chantal on http://www.autismone.org/radio aired in both English and in French on Autism One Radio

Theme: Autism.

Guest Profile: Authors, anything to do with autism, transition to adult life for those on the autism spectrum, positive aspects and strategies to help transition to adulthood. Someone who has something positive and constructive or encouraging to say about helping people on the spectrum. Need to know: Sound of their voice and past interview experiences, how to correctly pronounce their name, how they preferred to be called, any specific questions/answers they would like to cover or not discuss.

Guest from Hell: A person who talks non-stop, not allowing a conversation to occur during the interview. A person who is complicated, i.e., keeps changing the interview time, or needs constant communication before the interview.

Contact: sicilekira@yahoo.com; withheld upon request; http://www.chantalsicile-kira.com; Chantal Sicile-Kira. Best method: E-mailing with a pitch and or press kit the best. No phone calls to start, please. No response? E-mail me again. 99 percent of the time I respond right away, but sometimes I am on a writing deadline and then I forget.

Invited Back? Whether or not they were enthusiastic, and interesting and had a good conversation going.

Bio of Chantal Sicile-Kira: Chantal is an international speaker, award-winning author, and advocate who has been involved with autism spectrum disorders for over 20 years as a parent and a professional on both sides of the Atlantic.

She is author of *Autism Life Skills: From Communication and Safety to Self Esteem and More: 10 Essential Abilities Every Child on the Spectrum Deserves and Needs to Learn* (Penguin 2008), *Adolescents on the Autism Spectrum* (Perigee Trade 2006), awarded the 2006 San Diego Book Award for "Best in Health/Fitness" and *Autism Spectrum Disorders* (foreword by Temple Grandin, Ph.D.) (Perigee Trade 2004), recipient of the 2005 Autism Society of America's Outstanding Literary Work of the Year Award, and nominated for the 2005 PEN/Martha Albrand Award for First Nonfiction. The UK edition was the winner of the 2003 San Diego Book Award for Best in Health.

Chantal is the founder of Autism: Making a Difference, which provides consultation services. She served on the Taskforce on Transitional Services and Supports reporting to the California Legislative Blue Ribbon Commission on Autism.

Chantal was born into a large French family and was brought up bilingual and bicultural in Ohio, New York and California. Family pasttimes included cooking frog legs for breakfast over an open fire during summers spent camping in Louisville, Kentucky.

Chantal received her BA in social eecology from the University of California at Irvine (UCI). Her first practical experience with autism was at Fairview State Hospital, teaching self-help and community living skills to severely developmentally disabled and autistic adolescents in preparation for their de-institutionalization. Then, as a case manager for Orange County Regional Center for the Developmentally Disabled, Chantal provided information and resources to families.

Little did Chantal know that years later, these work experiences would prove invaluable when her son Jeremy (now a teenager) was born and eventually diagnosed with autism in Paris, France, where the only treatment on offer was psychoanalysis. Chantal's struggle to find appropriate treatment for him led them to move to England, where they became one of the first families in the UK to run a Lovaas-type (based on applied behavior analysis) home program.

Chantal also writes for various publications and her family was highlighted in *Newsweek* and featured in the MTV documentary *True Life* series.

Spencer Power Hour with Dr. John Spencer Ellis aired Tuesdays, 4–5 PM, PST on http://www.SpencerPowerHour.com

Theme: Fitness, wellness, personal development.

Guest Profile: All fitness, nutrition, and life coaching, healthy living experts. Proper education, book, video or program to talk about. Past interview experiences, credentials, sound of their voice — I want to know it all.

Guest from Hell: Non-responsive.

Contact: john@johnspencerellis.com; 877-573-6474; http://www.SpencerPowerHour.com and http://www.JohnSpencerEllis.com; Dr. John Spencer Ellis. Best method: E-mail a pitch and a link. No response? E-mail.

Invited Back? My personal experience.

Bio of John Spencer Ellis: Each week, over one million people around the world enjoy a fitness program created by John, CEO of NESTA (National Exercise and Sports Trainers Association), and the

Spencer Institute for Life Coaching. These two professional associations have 45,000 members in 35 countries.

John is also the CEO of the Get America Fit Foundation and on the Advisory Boards of the National Health, Wellness and Prevention Congress, Exercise TV, Select Comfort (Sleep Number Bed), Conference for Healthy Living, Irvine Valley College, Life and Leisure Television and Health Journal Television. In addition, he is a Fellow of the National Board of Fitness Examiners. He is the author of *How Badly Do You Want It?— Your Ultimate Guide to Optimal Fitness* (Endurance Plus Publishing 1998) and a contributor to "Power of Champions."

He created Adventure Boot Camp, the largest fitness boot camp program in the world. His TriActive America signature series of outdoor exercise equipment is used worldwide. His fitness programs are implemented in the top resorts, spas and health clubs.

John held the post of fitness editor for *OC Flair* magazine, and has been featured on ABC, NBC, CBS, PBS, FOX, SPIKE, ESPN and BRAVO. He is a host for *The Fit Show*, and the producer and host of *The OC Body* TV show and *The Spencer Power Hour* radio program. John is a Nautilus sponsored athlete and Fitness Apparel Council Member. He stars in the workout DVDs *Playground Boot Camp* and *Kung-Fu Fitness*. He created fitness programs used by Cirque du Soleil and the U.S. Secret Service, and consults the UFC (Ultimate Fighting Championships).

John has been continuing his professional education since 1987, and holds bachelors degrees in business and health science, an MBA, and a doctorate in education. He also completed doctoral level studies in naturopathy. He has 15 certifications, including massage therapy, plyometrics, self-defense, fitness kick boxing, fitness boxing, water fitness, exercise rehabilitation, golf conditioning, Pilates, personal training, clinical hypnotherapy, sports hypnosis, PACE circuit training and yoga. He holds a 2nd degree black belt in kung-fu, has completed the Ironman triathlon, and finished 5th at the U.S. National Biathlon Championships. His medical training includes a license in radiological technology, a medical assisting certification, and training in McKenzie rehabilitation. John was nominated for the California Community College Distinguished Alumni Award.

Turn On Your Inner Light with Debbie Mandel on WGBB 1240, airing in Long Island and Western Queens NY and on http://www.turnonyourinnerlight.com

Theme: Stress management.

Guest Profile: Authors, physicians, psychologists, leaders in their field as well as pioneers. Knowledge, experience, fresh tips and the ability to speak in radio bytes create a good guest, someone who delights and instructs within the context of dialogue. I want to read their book and look at their website.

Guest from Hell: Plugs his book or product in every other sentence, delivers a monologue and confuses the audience.

Contact: debbie@busybeegroup.com; 516-371-3325; http://www.turnonyourinnerlight.com; Debbie Mandel. Best method: E-mail a press release and a link to the website. No response? Send another e-mail. If I don't respond, then I'm overwhelmed and not interested. People don't like to say no to guests.

Invited Back? The quality of the interview, how much we covered about the topic and the timeliness of the content.

Bio of Debbie Mandel, M.A.: Debbie is a motivational speaker, stress management expert and author of *Changing Habits: The Caregivers' Total Workout* (Catholic Book Publishing Company 2005) and *Turn On Your Inner Light: Fitness for Body, Mind and Soul* (Busy Bee Group 2003).

Debbie took care of two parents with Alzheimer's, while she worked and raised three children. Debbie is determined not only to survive, but to really live. She is an enthusiastic believer in the mantra of living life longer, fuller and with a sense of humor.

Debbie graduated summa cum laude, Phi Beta Kappa from Brooklyn College and received her graduate degree from New York University. After a first career as an English professor, she has embraced mind/body fitness and devoted years to studying stress-management. However, her best credential is what her workshop participants have bestowed upon her: "Sunshine Girl."

Vibrant Living with Diane Brandon on www.webtalkradio.net; Diane also hosts *Vibrantly Green with Diane Brandon* on http://ecology.com/radio

Theme: Improving all aspects of one's life (personal growth, health, career, healthy children, etc.).

Guest Profile: Experts on the above topics — preferably authors — show is theme-specific, so guests just looking to promote themselves as celebrities are not used. Someone who is an expert in their field and can speak articulately about a topic (that suits my show) and feels passionately about it. Someone who can address concepts and issues without self-promotion, is pleasant/warm, and can engage in dialogue, rather than just delivering a monologue. I'd like to know their body of work and expertise, past media experience, and preferably the opportunity to read their work (books), as well as how original their work is.

Guest from Hell: Someone who is monosyllabic, speaks in a monotone, or is noncommunicative — or self-promoting. Equally someone who either gives interminably long answers or overly terse ones.

Contact: diane@dianebrandon.com; 901-752-5052; http://www.dianebrandon.com and http://www.dianebrandon.net; Diane Brandon. Best method:

E-mailing me about their work and/or mailing me their book. No response? Another e-mail after a reasonable amount of time.

Invited Back? How well I feel they did and whether they fit a future topic.

Bio of Diane Brandon: Diane is eclectic — a rare combination of artist and intellectual. A professional performer — actor and singer — she has also studied the mind and consciousness, foreign languages, intuition, and creativity — as well as being the author of *Invisible Blueprints* (Insight Publishing 2005).

Diane has an A.B. from Duke University, did graduate work at the University of North Carolina, and went to a language institute in Geneva. She has worked as a corporate manager (the first female one in marketing there), translated international maritime regulations, owned a performing arts store, spoken to groups, taught voice, acting, and intuition, and delivered corporate seminars. She's an intuition expert, which she felt compelled to study because it came out of the blue for her. (Diane has always wanted to understand the deeper meaning and inner workings of things.) The result of her quest is a thorough understanding of intuition, how it presents itself, how it works, and how to develop it.

Diane's expertise in personal growth came from her integrative intuitive counseling work, in which she increasingly found herself helping people find more fulfillment in their lives — to raves from her clients. This intimate view and facilitation of people improving their lives led to the theme of her talk show: providing a range of tools, information, and resources to improve all aspects of one's life. A true product of her hometown, New Orleans, Diane loves people and life — and her irrepressible humor can't help but creep in whenever she's talking to others. Listeners will be the beneficiaries of her avid mind, insatiable curiosity, extensive knowledge, conviviality, and passionate interest in things.

Wake Up America with Tina Volpe on Global Talk Radio, http://www.globaltalkradio.com

Theme: Health, animal rights, vegetarianism.

Guest Profile: Physicians, authors, movement leaders. Someone who is knowledgeable about health, animal welfare, and can help "Wake Up" America to dietary disasters in our country today. Just want to know that they are educated about their subject.

Guest from Hell: Someone who will not answer questions, and rambles about things not related.

Contact: books@fastfoodcraze.com; 605-990-0200; http://www.fastfoodcraze.com; Kevin Dawson or Tina Volpe. Best method: E-mail. Press kit works best, with book. No response? I respond timely.

Invited Back? Whether they authored another book, or have new information to share.

Bio of Tina Volpe: Tina was raised in Lake View Terrace, California, a northern horsy suburb of Los Angeles. Her childhood home had many farm animals, most of which were eventually slaughtered for food for the family. She endured many serious emotional blows as the pigs, cows and chickens were hung from trees while she was at school. This had a lifetime effect on her.

As a result of her love for, and interaction with, animals, Volpe became a vegetarian over three decades ago. Over the past seven years, she has been studying the farm industry and the effects its business decisions and resulting procedures have on animals. Volpe also realized that the fast food giants are a large cause of this suffering. This research convinced her that while advocacy and activist groups have made advances in informing the public about farm industry carelessness, that more efforts are needed because animals are still suffering at the hand of businesses.

Tina is author of *The Fast Food Craze, Wreaking Havoc on Our Bodies and Our Animals* (Canyon Publishing 2005). She is a health researcher, 32 year vegetarian, speaker, educator/consultant, television guest appearing all over the country, and published columnist. She is now affiliated with PCRM (Physicians Committee for Responsible Medicine) as a "heart health" speaker, and SPEAK, as a humane educator. Tina lives in Northern Arizona.

The Wellness Roadshow: Searching for Whole Being with Catherine Bradford on Contact Talk Radio.

Theme: Raising consciousness around well being through conversation.

Guest Profile: As you can imagine, well being covers a huge gamut, thus allowing me a great abundance of varied guests. Experts in their fields, authors, normal people who have a story to tell, many come to the show to share their inspiration, knowledge and wisdom. Anyone who offers knowledge and wisdom through their work, life experience, and can share with our listeners in a manner that excites and inspires. It is important that I determine prior to the interview that the guest will appeal to the vast majority of people. It is not my intention to race off into one "point of view" that isolates rather than joins together the audience.

Guest from Hell: Someone whose ego blocks their ability to transfer their knowledge and wisdom to our listeners.

Contact: wellnessroadshow@hotmail.com; 425-698-9896; http://www.contacttalkradio.com/hosts/bradford.htm; Catherine Bradford. Best method: Most of my guests initiate contact by e-mail, introducing themselves and their subject matter (telling about their books, sending bio pages). I can usually arrange a quick pre interview and tell if the guest is good for the show. Always important to send review copies of books. No response? I'm usually pretty punctual about responding; however I have "not" written back to a couple of inquires that were not good fits.

Invited Back? If they have a great deal to share that cannot be crammed into one hour of interviewing.

Guest Comments: "Being on Catherine's radio program, *The Wellness Roadshow*, was a fabulous experience. She immediately put me at ease with her friendly and insightful manner. Without 'scripted' questions our conversation was authentic and organic in its flow and presentation. I had several people tell me, after listening to the program, how powerful and inspirational they found it. We need more radio programs like this — and more hosts like Catherine willing to open up a natural dialogue about important and relatable topics that make people feel uplifted." — Melissa Wadsworth, http://www.melissawadsworth.com, Seattle

"I would like to share with you my interview experience, being a guest on Catherine Bradford's *Wellness Roadshow*. My wife Marilyn and I felt Catherine's love and strength right from the very beginning. After getting stuck in traffic and arriving late to Catherine's live radio interview, we found her calmly waiting on the porch of the radio station when we arrived. At that point, the show was already in motion so with gentleness and good humor, Catherine quickly ushered us into the control booth and without skipping a beat, light-heartedly jumped right into the interview. I have done over 50 radio, TV and magazine interviews and I can say without a doubt, it is rare that a show host does their homework as thoroughly as Catherine did in preparing for our interview. Not only did she read my book — she spent hours reading our extensive web site. It became clear after spending time with Catherine that she did not do this just for the sake of the interview. She did it because she genuinely cares and gets excited about the people she interviews.

"Catherine is a master networker. After we completed a lively, in-depth interview, she sat Marilyn and I down and excitedly brainstormed with us about the possible friends, acquaintances and radio colleagues that might be interested in our work and what we had to say. We were left in awe of Catherine and felt like we made a friend." — Jerry Wennstrom — artist, author of *The Inspired Heart* (Sentient Publications 2002) and subject of Sentient Publications and Parabola video, *In the Hands of Alchemy*. http://www.handsofalchemy.com/

Bio of Catherine Bradford: Catherine's personal journey with wellness began as a young child when she found herself relating to people through her intuition, compassion and deep sense of authentic connection. It came as no surprise when she chose a career in medicine and during her 20s worked supporting people in ways that exceeded normal medical traditions.

After many years devoted to raising her children, she returned to her passion for healing. During the past 12 years she grew from a private practice in medically based esthetics to founding a unique center for healing which she directed for many years. Always striving to create connection she began *The Wellness Roadshow: Searching for Whole Being*. Her goal is simple — to raise consciousness through conversation. Her desire is to bridge global communities, bringing the common pieces of "being" in this world into a light that promotes wellness and peace for all.

What's Ailing America? with Rebecca Carley, MD, on Republic Broadcasting, http://republicbroadcasting.org airing Saturdays 3–5 PM (ET).

Theme: A combination of what is making Americans sick (for ex, vaccines, pesticides, aspartame, etc.) and what can be done to heal problems caused by these toxins.

Guest Profile: Healers and those investigating what is poisoning us. Someone with cutting edge info to share with listeners who want the truth. What is their info, how did they get it, documentation.

Guest from Hell: A disinformer, who has 95 percent truth but 5 percent lies (like someone who states that vaccines cause autism, but it is because of the mercury).

Contact: drcarley@gmail.com; 828-294-0662; http://www.drcarley.com; Dr Carley. Best method: Call and tell me what they have to offer; I will request a bio if I am interested. No response? I get hundreds of e-mails a day; that is why I prefer calls.

Invited Back? Since all my shows are archived and can be listened to as long as the Internet is up, I would have them back if they have additional info to share, or if we did not have time to cover everything.

Guest Comment: "After having Dr. Carley on my show many times, I was a guest on her show. She was very well informed, very respectful doing the interview. She promoted me and my work several times on the show. I highly recommend tuning her in." — Meria Heller, producer/host of *The Meria Show* (see page 195).

"Dr. Rebecca Carley was a delight. She is a very professional and sensitive host towards the topic and her guest. It is clear that Dr. Carley is devoted to revealing truth at whatever cost." — Wendy Wilson, host of *Herb Talk Live* (see page 108).

Bio of Dr. Rebecca (Roczen) Carley: Dr. Carley received her Bachelor's degree in diagnostic ultrasound, attended medical school (and received the Samuel L. Kountz Award for clinical excellence in surgery at graduation), and trained to be a general surgeon at State University of New York at Downstate Medical Center in Brooklyn. Dr. Carley also worked as an attending emergency room physician at Kings County Medical Center in Brooklyn (which is the primary training affiliate for downstate students), and is the largest hospital (and busiest trauma center) in the United States.

Dr. Carley left the practice of general surgery and "allopathic" medicine after realizing that no one was actually being healed of their diseases, and she started researching "alternative" medicine while taking time off to start a family.

After her only child was brain damaged as a result of inoculations he received, Dr. Carley learned how to reverse the damage with homeopathy and other natural supplements, and subsequently realized that inoculations of disease are causing the corruption in the immune system which leads to all autoimmune diseases and cancer. Dr. Carley has developed the Hippocrates Protocol which has successfully reversed all autoimmune diseases (including autism) and cancer in over 2,000 clients (including pets) over the past nine years. She has written the definitive paper explaining the mechanism whereby inoculations with disease are causing VIDS (Vaccine Induced Diseases), which has been featured in multiple publications all over the world and is available under the title "Inoculations: the True Weapons of Mass Destruction" on her website at www.drcarley.com. She has offered a $10,000 reward for any vaccine promoter to come on her Internet radio show and refute the documents she has authored. No one has stepped forward to do so. Dr. Carley has been qualified in court as an expert witness in VIDS, Legal Abuse Syndrome, vaccinology, and child abuse.

Dr. Carley no longer "practices medicine," but instead teaches clients nationally and internationally how to reverse their diseases using the Hippocrates Protocol she developed. She also goes into the hospital as a patient advocate for clients who are not satisfied with the care their loved ones are receiving.

Besides being a guest on over 200 radio and television shows, for over 9 years Dr. Carley had her own weekly public access television show in Long Island, followed by her weekly Internet radio show, both entitled *What's Ailing America*.

Your Doctor Said What? with Terrie Wurzbacher, D.O. on www.blogtalkradio.com/yourdoctorsaidwhat

Theme: Discussing doctor-patient communication issues.

Guest Profile: Anyone — patient or provider who has comments or complaints about doctor-patient communication. Someone who has a sense of humor or is vibrant and can keep a conversation going to maintain the audience's attention. Comments (even if complaints are able to be discussed and are not just venting). Sound of their voice; past interview experiences; attitude are paramount.

Guest from Hell: Someone who just complains and does not want to discuss an issue; always has a "yes but," someone who answers "yes" or "no" and never says anything else

Contact: ermadness@mindspring.com; Withheld upon request; http://www.yourdoctorsaidwhat.com http://www.yourdoctorsaidwhatblogs.com; Terrie Wurzbacher. Best method: E-mail me with a bio and a pitch. No response? Person should re-e-mail me, wait a day, if no response then they should call in case I didn't get the e-mail or the subject line led to it being deleted because I couldn't tell what it was.

Invited Back? If things go smoothly and they stay on the topic of doctor patient communication.

Bio of Dr. Terrie Wurzbacher: Terrie is a retired Naval officer and an emergency physician. She spent 29½ years in the Navy and devoted much of her time trying to teach interns and medical students the fine "art" of communicating with patients. She does not claim to be an expert in that field, but knows that once she realized that she was not getting the point across to her patients, and began to concentrate on ways to help them understand, she was way ahead of most of her peers. There are great doctors out there and some of that greatness is based on technical skill. However, the majority of the great doctors are great because they make the patient a big part of the entire game plan. Terrie has always aspired to be that kind of doctor. She knows she's not great but hopes that patients will help their own doctors get to "great."

Perhaps a more important qualification for authoring materials about doctor-patient communication is that she's been a patient herself. Although she is very fortunate to have had excellent health, she has had to visit the doctor for several things and has had a sampling of pretty poor physicians and also wonderful ones. So, she does have the "credentials" to talk about doctor-patient communication.

She is a graduate of the University of Vermont and the College of Osteopathic Medicine and Surgery in Des Moines, Iowa. She joined the Navy in the early 1970s and served on active duty from 1975 until 2004.

Terrie is board certified in emergency medicine, and now works in disability medicine.

Your Health Matters with Dr. Craig M. Wax on 89.7 WGLS-FM, aired in southern NJ, Philadelphia, northern DE.

Theme: Health and wellness.

Guest Profile: Physicians, authors, health experts. We have interviewed many experts and authors over the years form Nobel Prize–winning authors to famous diet advocates.

We interview health experts on health and wellness topics. Guests must provide credible health information in a well-spoken manner. We are most concerned with their information, history, credentials and credibility. It is also nice if they are not boring as hell.

Guest from Hell: We have interviewed these guests from hell in the past. They hawk their book or product after every sentence. "In my book, The Title, I reveal..."

Contact: health@healthisnumberone.com; 856-863-WGLS; http://wgls.rowan.edu; Dr. Craig M. Wax or Derek Jones, Asst. station mgr. Best method: E-mail a bio and send a press kit. No response? E-mail or call.

Invited Back? If the show goes well, they can be invited for an update show or a different topic.

Bio of Craig Wax, DO: Dr. Wax is a board certified family physician in private practice in Mullica Hill, New Jersey. He is also the executive producer and host of *Your Health Matters* on radio. Dr. Wax created and maintains the web health info site http://www.HealthIsNumberOne.com. His practice experience ranges from pediatrics to geriatrics, and he also has experience as a speaker in family medicine, prevention, health promotion, diabetes, hypertension, coronary artery disease, cerebrovascular accident (CVA), back pain, depression, anxiety, asthma, and infectious diseases.

Dr. Wax is on the speaker panels for GlaxoSmith-Kline, Aventis, Reliant, Pfizer Pharmaceuticals, and Novartis. He has also served as a consultant at AstraZeneca. Dr. Wax has many publications in medical journals, such as *Medical Economics* and is often quoted in the local newspapers on matters of local health importance.

History

"History graduates are able to think critically, write effectively, and assess the dynamics of the world around them. History graduates learn how to become life-long learners, capable of success in a wide variety of fields. No matter what the future holds, there will always be jobs for people with these abilities. Woodrow Wilson, W.E.B. Dubois, Katharine Hepburn, Lee Iacocca, Kareem Abdul-Jabbar, Antonin Scalia, Larry David, Wolf Blitzer and Conan O'Brien have this much in common—all were history majors!"—from the Department of History, University of East Carolina University, where Dr. Gerald J. Prokopowicz is a history professor.

Civil War Talk Radio with Gerald J. Prokopowicz on http://www.modavox.com, click "network"; originates from Greenville, NC, aired by *World Talk Radio*.

Theme: The history of the Civil War.

Guest Profile: Professional historians, novelists, artists, collectors, re-enactors, filmmakers or anyone else who has produced something worthwhile in connection with Civil War history. Published scholarly work, or its equivalent, on some historical aspect of the Civil War. What they have published, created, or otherwise done that would be of interest to the audience. A brief phone conversation to confirm that they can communicate audibly is useful.

Guest from Hell: *Civil War Talk Radio* wouldn't invite such a guest. The most difficult guests have been those who tended to give brief, one-word answers. The worst voice ever on *CWTR* was my own, when I had laryngitis.

Contact: prokopowiczg@ecu.edu; 252-328-1027; http://www.modavox.com; Gerald J. Prokopowicz. Best method: E-mail. Have the publisher make contact. If my university library does not have a copy of your book for me to read before the interview, ask the publisher to send one. No response? Lack of response within a month would normally indicate that the proposed guest is not appropriate for the show.

Invited Back? *Civil War Talk Radio* tries to invite a new guest each week.

Bio of Gerald J. Prokopowicz: Gerald is a history professor at East Carolina University, where he specializes in public history and the Civil War era. He received his undergraduate and law degrees from the University of Michigan, and practiced law for several years in Chicago. He received his Ph.D. from Harvard University, and served for nine years as the Lincoln Scholar at the Lincoln Museum in Fort Wayne, Indiana, where he co-wrote the award winning permanent exhibit "Abraham Lincoln and the American Experiment," and edited the quarterly bulletin *Lincoln Lore*. His books include *All for the Regiment: The Army of the Ohio, 1861–62* (2001) and *Did Lincoln Own Slaves?* (2008).

The Oopa Loopa Cafe with Rick Osmon (aka "Oz") on Blog Talk Radio, http://blogtalkradio.com/oopa-loopa-cafe

Theme: Pre-Columbian contact / diffusion theory / ancient site preservation.

Guest Profile: Authors, researchers, scientists, educators, lecturers—all with the central theme of Columbus was a latecomer. The guest should have something to say within theme, should (ideally) have something in print, blog, or video, should be reasonably articulate, and above all, should be capable of responding to my questions and to callers with both knowledge and aplomb. All those things come into play, but I usually am more concerned about the message they are promoting and how clearly they convey that message. Credentials and titles are "nice to have" attributes for my audience, but the theme and message along with the delivery are the key factors.

Guest from Hell: That's one I have not yet experienced, so I can only tell you what I think it would be: One who is confrontational and abrasive as a matter of course, who is less concerned with facts than with his or her own dogmatic opinions, or one who is prone to language unsuitable for a family audience.

Contact: oz@oopaloopacafe.com; 812-259-1102; http://www.oopaloopacafe.com; Rick Osmon. Best method: Any means of initiating contact will be met with respect and consideration. After I first read their work, conduct a pre-interview, or receive recommendations from listeners, I'll try to set up an interview or roundtable discussion, depending on what we all determine is the best forum for that particular material or message. Part of arranging and promoting the segment is providing to the listeners (in the show's e-mail newsletter) any bio or other appropriate materials, so it's all part of the process. No response? Guests, potential guests, and listeners find that I am very responsive to all communications, but should something slip through the cracks, please try again.

Invited Back? Many things influence that determination, including listener feedback, total listener count, related news or interviews, and phase of the moon.

Guest Comments: "Anytime we have an opportunity to get this information and our ideas out there to hopefully inspire others that's a great thing! Thanks for the platform to preach, Rick!"—Scott F. Wolter P.G., geologist/petrographer and president, American Petrographic Services Inc.

"Thank you Rick. I enjoyed that talk immensely. Will be happy to share again."—Crichton E. M. Miller, author of *The Golden Thread of Time* (Pendulum Publishing 2000); http://www.crichtonmiller.com

Bio of Rick ("Oz") Osmon: Born a few years before Sputnik, Rick has had a lifelong interest in lost cities, vanished civilizations, odd and out-of-place artifacts, and many equally esoteric subjects. Raised on a cattle and grain farm in Southern Indiana that had a working blacksmith shop and was heavily laden with points and other stone artifacts, Rick attended the U.S. Air Force Academy, received an Associate of Science in laser and electro-optics technology from Vincennes University, studied industrial, vocational, and technical education at Indiana State University, had a career as a civilian engineer for the U.S. Navy, and saw much of the world.

Now married to Pat and working as a consultant in the field of industrial controls and security, Rick pursues his esoteric interests and avocations that include not only his internet radio talk show but also shooting sports, sport aviation, reading, camping, strategy gaming, cuddling grandchildren, and fishing.

Labor

"To educate the community about the role, significance and contributions of unions in our society, and to promote labor education in the schools."—From the Mission Statement of The Institute for Labor Studies on *The Heartland Labor Forum* website

The Heartland Labor Forum with Judy Ancel, coordinator with volunteer hosts, on KKFI 90.1FM Community Radio aired in Kansas City, Missouri, metro area.

Theme: Workplace, labor and political economy.

Guest Profile: Union and workplace leaders and activists, authors of books and articles on our theme, professionals. Ability to tell a story or to make a complicated idea understandable to a diverse audience. Experience in successfully taking on the system. Why guest is qualified to speak on the topic proposed, something of their background to tell listeners.

Guest from Hell: Doesn't want to have a conversation, doesn't respond to the questions but goes on and on without taking a breath.

Contact: ancelj@umkc.edu; 816-235-1470; http://www.heartlandlaborforum.org; Judy Ancel. Best method: E-mail with idea for the show, bio information and qualifications. No response? Do not e-mail or call.

Invited Back? Many things, whether we want to follow up on the topic, a new book, how engaging guest is.

Bio of Judy Ancel: Judy is director of The Institute for Labor Studies at UMKC (University of Missouri-Kansas City), a joint project of UMKC and Longview Community College. The university sponsors the show, produced by volunteers from Kansas City area unions and unorganized workplaces. "We decide our schedule collectively in meetings once every two months," explains Judy.

The Labor Show with Greg Giorgio on WRPI-FM, Troy, N.Y. covering a 70 mile radius in Eastern N.Y., mainly in the Capital District, Tri-Cities area, with reach into southwestern Vermont and western Massachusetts.

Theme: Labor news, economic news affecting working folks, local union and labor struggles coverage and general news and features built to educate and inform workers of their issues and how to fight back.

Guest Profile: Guests are normally activists and experts on labor issues from the union movement and NGOs involved in labor and human rights. Also labor leaders and rank and file activists and union members involved in struggles against oppressive employers, bad government economic policies and anti-sweatshop activists to name a few. Everyone from Congressman (now Senator) Bernie Sanders to AFL-CIO v.p. Rich Trumpka, Father Roy Bourgeois, Arundahti Roy, to Amirul Haque Amin of the National Garment Workers Federation of Bangladesh. The best guests are the committed activists who know their issues, tell their stories and voice their concerns without being too preachy or condescending. Humor helps, too. I don't need to know much about the guest in most cases. For pre-recorded interviews, their voice quality is a concern.

Guest from Hell: The guest who speaks in run-on sentences or cannot seem to get to the point of the question in the first place. Guests who are not really prepared to answer the important questions.

Contact: ggblackcat27@yahoo.com; 518-861-5627; http://www.upstate-ny-iww.org; Greg Giorgio—host, producer. Best method: Usually a phone call or e-mail is fine but a press kit rocks. No response? Best case is for the guest to call me.

Invited Back? Two things. Relevance of the issues they are involved with and their general competency and enthusiasm.

Bio of Greg Giorgio: Greg is a labor and community activist who has been involved with the labor movement for over 20 years. He has nearly 35 years on-air experience in various radio and television gigs and over 20 years experience as a freelance writer on various topics, including labor, wine and food. He started a similar radio program to *The Labor Show* in 1994, which was an inter-union project and then went on the air at WRPI in March of 1997.

Law and Law Enforcement

The Dailey and Stearn Law Show with Brian Dailey and Todd Stearn airing Saturday, 3–4 PM (ET) on 760 WJR, www.wjr.com or on http://www.thelawshow.com

Theme: Legal advice.

Guest Profile: Lawyers, judges, legislators and other people involved with law. Some relevance with the law and/or interesting legal issues. Provide interesting information for guests.

Guest from Hell: A guest that won't talk or who has nothing interesting to add.

Contact: Todd@thelawshow.com; 1-866-66-LAWYER; http:www.thelawshow.com; Todd Stearn. Best method: E-mailing or telephoning with a topic that I believe our guests may want to hear. No response? E-mail or call.

Invited Back? Whether they added something to the show.

Bios of Brian Dailey and Todd J. Stearn: The Dailey and Stearn Law Firm provides legal services to the people and businesses of the State of Michigan.

Brian is a graduate of the University of Iowa and Thomas M. Cooley Law School (J.D. 1987) and was admitted to the bar in Michigan, Iowa and Illinois. He specializes in litigation, personal injury, malpractice and criminal law.

Todd is a graduate of the University of Michigan and Indiana University (J.D. 1994), and was admitted to the bar in Michigan. His specialties include criminal law, automobile negligence litigation and malpractice.

The Expert Witness with Mike Levine and Mark Marshall on WBAI, New York City, and WJFF-FM.

Theme: Court-qualified experts and whistleblowers, comment on law enforcement, intelligence gathering and covert operations in the news.

Guest Profile: Law enforcement and covert operations, whistleblowers, court-qualified experts, authors, journalists with real expertise in the areas they cover. We want to know their past interview experiences, credentials and sound of their voice.

Guest from Hell: A fake expert and/or a conspiracy theorist rehashing someone else's conspiracy theory ... any phony.

Contact: Expert53@aol.com; 845-687-9642, 845-853-8196; Expertwitnessradio.org and policetrialexpert.com; Mike Levine or Mark Marshall. Best method: E-mail — who you are, what your story is, and how you corroborate it.... No response? We always respond promptly.

Invited Back? Listener reaction — and — our instinct

Bio of Michael Levine: With more than 40 years of intensive hands-on, award-winning experience on the streets and in the courtrooms, Michael has acquired the vast insider's knowledge and razor sharp eye for details that are vital to expert testimony. The details that underlie and support his resume have stood up to the rigorous cross-examination of some of the best prosecutors and attorneys in the nation. One of the most decorated supervisory agents in the history of the Drug Enforcement Administration, Michael has also served with great distinction with the U.S. Customs Service, BATF, IRS (Criminal Investigations Division) and the FBI/DEA Task Force. Trained and licensed as a police instructor by DEA, his career in police training, now numbering more than 30 years, continues to this day. Michael's expert testimony (as regards all areas of expertise listed) has been accepted on more then 300 occasions in federal and state courts (both criminal and civil) in 17 states as well as Puerto Rico.

He is a widely published, highly skilled professional writer, well known for the effectiveness of his reports and affidavits. His training and experience as a supervisory officer, inspector of operations and police instructor, combined with his insider's anatomical knowledge of law enforcement operations, make him an invaluable asset in a number of important services. As a trial consultant and expert witness commencing with his DOJ retirement in 1990, Michael has reviewed and commented upon in excess of 200 full case files, relating to both civil and criminal matters, and involving a wide array of areas of expertise. This involves exhaustive and lengthy reviews of the investigative and law enforcement practices of many local and federal agencies, including but not limited to FBI, DEA, Customs, Homeland Security, BATF, IMNS and more than 30 local, state and city police agencies throughout the U.S. This ongoing experience keeps Michael current and up-to-date on policies, procedures and standards of U.S law enforcement. A licensed private investigator, Michael is also active as a law enforcement instructor, journalist and investigative researcher. He maintains an extensive and continually updated database of information that relates to each area of his expertise. An important part of this database involves direct contact with more than 200 court-qualified law enforcement experts worldwide ... colleagues with whom he consults on a case-by-case basis. Michael has appeared as a guest/expert on dozens of nationally televised shows, including "60 Minutes," "Good Morning America," "Today Show," "Early Show," "MacNeil-Lehrer News Hour," "20/20" and many others.

The Power of Attorney with Marsha Kazarosian on podcast.

Theme: Legal talk show with guest commentators on rising issues.

Guest Profile: Commentator to discuss or provide first hand knowledge of rising legal issues and innovative cases. Background, such as would be offered on a resume, accomplishments, what their position is on an issue that will be discussed on the air, what their experience is with the issue discussed, most recent interviews (with whom, in what forum, and topic).

Guest from Hell: Those without the attributes specified above.

Contact: marsha@kazarosian.com; 978-372-7748 (office) or 978-994-1184 (cell); http://www.kazarosian.com; Marsha Kazarosian. Best method: Send a press kit, e-mail a bio and/or call with a pitch. No response? E-mail or call. With spam folders, many important e-mails are lost inadvertently. Don't give up.

Invited Back? Their ability to generate interest on the issue discussed, their animation and personality on the show, their knowledge of the subject and their ability to field questions, and viewer feedback.

Listener Comment: "Another noteworthy Podcast in this genre is by private practice trial lawyer Marsha Kazarosian. The Massachusetts-based Kazarosian explores everything from sexual harassment in the workplace to the way that media is influencing her job. One recent broadcast included an interview with an NBC producer on how Hollywood shows like "Ally McBeal" and "CSI" affect the U.S. justice system." — Eriq Gardner, *Corporate Counsel Magazine* (November, 2005)

Bio of Marsha V. Kazarosian: In 2006, Marsha was the cover story for SuperLawyers MA, and was chosen by her peers as one of the top 50 female lawyers and one of the top 100 lawyers in the Commonwealth. In 2007, she was also chosen by Superlawyers New England as one of the top trial attorneys in New England. She has been named one of the top ten lawyers in Massachusetts by *Massachusetts Lawyers Weekly* and has built a national practice representing clients in high profile cases.

In 1999, Marsha and her associate, Janet E. Dutcher, Esq., won a verdict in excess of a million dollars in a gender discrimination case against the Haverhill Country Club, the first case of its kind ever to go to trial in the country. It has become the landmark case in the nation for gender discrimination in a country club/public accommodations setting.

Marsha first gained national attention in 1990 when she represented one of the defendant boys charged with murder in the Pamela Smart case, one of the first fully televised trials on broadcast television. She is past president of the Massachusetts Academy of Trial Attorneys, Essex County Bar Association, and currently sits on the Board of Delegates of the Massachusetts Bar Association.

The Watering Hole with Lieutenant Raymond E. Foster, LAPD (ret.), MPA, on Blog Talk Radio, www.blogtalkradio.com/lawenforcement

Theme: Conversations with cops about life and work.

Guest Profile: The guests must be current, former or retired law enforcement, or provide a unique and interesting product/service for law enforcement. Most of the police guests are authors. The format of the show is a "conversation" so it's someone comfortable with just "talking" about their job, experiences, etc. Primarily credentials — are they a subject matter expert about the topic?

Guest from Hell: They pitch instead of talk.

Contact: editor@police-writers.com; 909-599-7530; http://www.police-writers.com; Lt. Raymond E. Foster. Best method: E-mail "I want to be on your show — here's why." No response? If I don't respond in 24 hours I am dead or out of town. They can always make follow-up phone calls.

Invited Back? Audience reaction.

Bio of Lt. Raymond E. Foster: Raymond was with the Los Angeles Police Department from 1980 to 2003, and a lieutenant, 1997–2003.

He has an MPA in Public Financial Management from California State University, Fullerton, Ca., graduating with a 4.0 GPA (member Phi Kappa Phi) — 2003.

Raymond is author of *Police Technology* (Prentice Hall, July 2004) and editor of the *Hi Tech Criminal Justice Newsletter*, 2003 to present.

He is, or has been, an instructor at California State University, in Fullerton and Fresno, and at Union Institute and University. He is owner and president of Hi Tech Criminal Justice, whose mission is to provide online resources for criminal justice practitioners.

He is also the founding board chair of Connection House, which provides transitional housing, independent living skills and educational opportunities for emancipated foster youth.

Men and Women

Cosmolicious with Diana on Cosmo Radio Sirius XM, www.sirius.com/cosmoradio, weekdays 2–5 PM (ET). Diana also hosts her own show, *The Diana Falzone Show* on Paltalk.com which focuses on dating and relationships.

Theme: Based on *Cosmopolitan* magazine. Her show is dedicated to more than girls, comedy, sports, and music. Diana talks about pop culture, politics, and current events.

Guest Profile: Authors, psychologists, celebrities, sex experts, relationship experts, hypnotherapists, musicians, models. A person who is comfortable in front of a mic and who can be concise, interesting and, most importantly, provide information to the listener. I also want someone who has a clear speaking voice. If someone mumbles or speaks too quietly they will not make a good guest. Past interview experiences only make me more confident the guest will feel at home in the studio and credentials for experts are required.

Guest from Hell: Someone who clams up and does not talk. Another problem is when a guest does not realize that it's a national show and talks specifically about New York and the city's culture. It alienates our listeners.

Contact: dfalzone@siriusradio.com; withheld upon request; http://www.dianafalzone.com and devoreanddiana.com; Diana Falzone; Preferred method of contact: The best approach is via e-mail with a bio and link to a website. No response? We get so busy preparing a live show every day that sometimes things slip our minds.

Invited Back? If a person was late, cancelled multiple times or was a diva, they are not invited back. However, if they were friendly and professional, most of the time they are invited again.

Bio of Diana Falzone: Diana was the first female personality on Maxim Radio, where she co-hosted *DeVore and Diana*. She is also an advice columnist for Military.com where she does a weekly column. Diana can also be seen as a relationship expert on *The Morning Show with Mike and Juliet*. Her voice can be heard on Sirius's Octane Channel, ABC Radio, and the soon to be released video game, "Grand Theft Auto."

She is the official spokesmodel for "Hard Rider NYC." Diana has been featured in *Maxim* and is number 5 of the most viewed models. Diana has hosted for MTV as a red carpet correspondent, Fuse as the host of "Tip of Your Tongue" and a commentator for the "F-List," the CW news as the entertainment anchor for the KXVO nightly news, AMC as a commentator for "Date Night," Vh1's "Best Night Ever" and NYC-TV as the host of "That's So New York" and "The City that Never Sleeps." While still in her teens, Diana appeared as a lead in an off–Broadway show, *Valentino the Musical*, several regional productions, and worked with the USO of Metropolitan New York. She graduated from the New School University with her BA in psychology in 2005. Diana is a member of the Friar's Club and the Society of Memorial Sloan Kettering Cancer Center. Diana is represented by the William Morris Agency.

The Divorced Fathers Network Radio Program
with Steve Ashley and Rocky Snyder on KSCO AM 1080, Santa Cruz, CA, aired from Sacramento to Bakersfield and the Central Coast.

Theme: Educational to teach divorced parents how to work together to raise their kids.

Guest Profile: Authors, experts (judges, attorneys, psychologists), divorced parents and kids, etc. Guests are a mix of men and women. At least 50 percent of the listeners are women and probable 30 percent of guests are women. I want guests who have personal experience and who are passionate about their subjects. I want my guests to feel strongly about their subject and to be able to speak concisely about the subject. John Gray and Dr. Warren Farrell have been among the more prominent guests.

Guest from Hell: Authors who have written books on subjects that have been covered already, yet these authors view themselves as above the rest and some even write books on subjects they have no personal experience with.

Contact: Steveal8@aol.com and steve@divorcedfathers.com; 831-335-5855; divorcedfathersnetwork.com; Steve Ashley. Best method: E-mail or phone. I like to get a press kit and an e-mail works well too. No response? E-mail or call.

Invited Back? If the show was exciting, the guest enjoyed him/herself, and listening audience was engaged and phone in and there was more to the subject that was not covered due to lack of time.

Bio of Steve Ashley: Founder of the Divorced Fathers Network in Santa Cruz, California, Steven has assisted thousands of men and women in creating cooperative relationships with their former spouses. Steven speaks on behalf of fathers and their important contributions as co-parents. He is often a featured guest on radio shows and is frequently mentioned in the media.

Military

"Our Life. Our Family. Our Soldier."—The motto of *Army Wife Talk Radio*

Army Wife Talk Radio with Tara Crooks on Mondays at http://www.ArmyWifeTalkRadio.com as well as on itunes, and many other podcast directories. Also Aired: http://armywifetalkradiocast.blogspot.com

Theme: *Army Wife Talk Radio* is the Internet talk radio show designed specifically for army wives by army wives: We feature information, special reports, empowerment, inspiration, stories and interviews that affect you

Guest Profile: Any type guests are welcome — authors, coaches, military spouses, musicians, etc. Our stipulations are that they or their product/creation must have some relation to the military. (i.e., they are military wives, the book is about military, offering something specific to the military, etc.). Personality is key to our success, so guests must be personable and have fun.

See what our listeners, sponsors, and guests are saying by visiting http://www.armywifetalkradio.com/applause.shtml

Guest from Hell: A guest who does nothing but answer the question, has no conversation within the interview. A guest who has not educated themselves on the military. A guest who does not respond to e-mails or confirmations. A late guest or a no-show guest. A guest who only participates to "advertise."

Contact: info@armywifetalkradio.com *or* tara@armywifetalkradio.com; 1-888-866-5041; http://www.ArmyWifeTalkRadio.com; http://www.TaraCrooks.com; Tara Crooks. Best method: E-mail. Do not call with a pitch. Fill out the "be a guest on AWTR" form via the website, or send us a press release from your publisher. You will need to submit a full biographical and credentials profile to tara@armywifetalkradio.com; these need to include your full name, title/position, full contact information (including the number of the line you will be using to call in) and any pertinent information regarding your affiliation with the military.

A set of 5–8 questions pertaining to your subject topic must be submitted 10 days prior to your interview. We have found our guests are experts in their field and so having them submit some "prepared" questions helps us to better navigate the interview. The questions you have prepared will be used as a guide and are not definitive. No response? All responses should be within 48 hours unless noted otherwise. If you do not hear back chances are we did not get your e-mail, which is why we request you fill out the form on the website. You can do a follow-up call if you wish. Even if we do not think your topic/product/service is applicable we will still send you a response to your e-mail.

Invited Back? Personality, applicability of product/service, ease of communication, and listener response.

Guest Comment: "I had a great time being on your show... Thanks so much for having me. You do an awesome job and what a fabulous resource." — Susan Mitchell, Ph.D., RD, FADA, co-author of *Fat Is Not Your Fate* (Simon and Schuster 2005), *Eat to Stay Young* (Kensington 2000), and *I'd Kill for a Cookie* (Penguin 1997). Fellow of the American Dietetic Assoc. (See Susan's show, *Nutrition and Health*, on page 111.)

Bio of Tara Crooks: Tara, or "Household 6" in the Crooks' family, is best known for her ability to motivate and empower others. She holds a Bachelor of Business Administration in human resource management but mocks the applicability it has to what she feels she was "born" to do.

Tara's journey with the military began in 1998 when she and her husband PCS'd to their first duty station, Fort Hood, TX. Tara started her original home business, which she has since sold, The Candle Coop, in 2001 to be able to raise her daughter in a more stable environment, given her husband's career choice. She is married to her wonderful husband, Kevin (U.S. Army), and has two beautiful little girls, Wrena and Chloe.

Their family, including two dogs and a cat, is all snuggled in their cozy home in Richmond Hill, GA.

The Captain's America with retired fire-rescue captain Matt Bruce on Live 365, Net Talk World, weekends on Accent Radio.

Theme: American, conservative, military support, politics.

Guest Profile: Anyone who fits the above mentioned. Honesty above all and who they are and what they stand for. Guests have included DOD/DVIDS military guests from Iraq, Afghanistan and around the World serving America. Various state officials such as former FL Gov. Jeb Bush, Pres. George W Bush, VP Dick Cheney, local and county officials, Cong. Vern Buchanan and veterans from all across America, including some of my brother IAFF FF's.

Guest from Hell: Someone who tried to dominate the conversation instead of sticking to the prearranged question and answer script on the topics agreed to be discussed.

Contact: thecaptainsamerica@verizon.net; 941-907-2126; http://thecaptainsamerica.com. Best method: Press Kit or Bio works. No response? E-mail or call — usually I'm able to answer right away.

Invited Back? Calls and e-mail requests.

Bio of Matt Bruce: A retired fire captain, Matt is a two-time combat wounded Vietnam vet with a son currently serving in the U.S. Marine Corps.

He's been to Ground Zero and did what he could to help with his fire department; he also helped FEMA in Katrina in Louisiana and Mississippi as well as Charley in Florida.

Matt is now a CERT team member in Manatee County and a disaster response team member for the American Red Cross.

Career Call with Ted Daywalt aired on 1620 AM, Sandy Springs, Ga., 3–4 PM, Sunday, and simulcast on Internet at http://www.radiosandysprings.com

Theme: Career talk show with military emphasis for transitioning military and veterans.

Guest Profile: Economists, human resource personnel, veterans who have transitioned to civilian jobs, career coaches, recruiters, veteran service organizations, etc. Also employers who want to reach transitioning military and veterans as candidates for employment. Experience in HR/Recruiting or military person who has been successful in civilian career? Definitely want a good voice. I ask for their bio to use as a guide, and I look for individuals who have had an interesting career.

Guest from Hell: A guest who will not give complete answers or too short of an answer

Contact: tdaywalt@vetjobs.com; 877-838-5627; http://www.vetjobs.com; Ted Daywalt. Best method: Send me an e-mail with why they want to be on the show. No response? Call.

Invited Back? How well they do during the show and if we get good comments about their participation from listeners.

Bio of Ted Daywalt: For the last eight years, Ted has been the CEO and president of VetJobs, the leading military related job board on the Internet. As a four year recipient of the WEDDLE's User's Choice Award, VetJobs is ranked as one of the top 14 job boards out of 40,000 sites on the Internet.

Following seven years of active Navy military service as a Surface Warfare Naval Officer and Intelligence Officer, and completing his MBA, Ted entered private industry in 1980 as a plant manager in the steel industry, and later was a regional manager for a steel company in Cleveland, Ohio, with responsibility for three plants and trading operations. He returned to Atlanta in 1982 and joined a major electric utility as its economic development field officer and directed international sales and training.

His career includes experience as the founder of an import company, as the Southeastern senior sales manager for a U.S. based multinational chemical conglomerate, as the general manager (North America) for a European based chemical conglomerate, CEO of a biomedical waste incineration firm, and president of TAMB Associates Inc, a third party recruiting firm with national offices. Ted has been active in the recruiting and staffing industry since 1994.

Ted earned a BS from Florida State University (1971), an MA in international relations from the University of Southern California (1977) and an MBA from the Goizueta Business School, Emory University (1980).

Nautical

Nautical Talk Radio with Capt Lou on 95.9 FM WATD, Marshfield, Massachusetts, broadcast Sundays, 11 AM–noon EST in the Boston area and Cape Cod. The most recent shows can be heard anytime during the week at http://www.nauticaltalk.com

Theme: Anything that happens on the ocean or affects the ocean.

Guest Profile: Almost every show features a guest — celebrities, law enforcement officials, legislators, people involved in boating accidents, historians, authors, fishermen, treasure hunters and sailors. About one-fourth of the guests are authors. Specialties are nautical stories, survival at sea, naval stories, coast guard stories, maritime history, cruising or sailing destinations, recreational boating stories, commercial fishing stories, treasure hunting, shipwrecks and weather related stories. Someone who designed an innovative nautical product, a boat builder, an author of a nautical book, someone who survived at sea, someone who rescued someone at sea, a marine environmentalist, a politician trying to regulate fishing or matters of the sea, or someone participating in a record breaking event or competition.

Celebrity guests have included Billy Joel, Florence Henderson, Jonathan Edwards, Sebastian Junger, and Linda Greenlaw. Political guests have included presidential candidate Mitt Romney, Senator Ted Kennedy, Congressmen Barney Frank and William Delahunt. CEOs have included Irwin Jacobs (Genmar Corp) and Roger Berkowitz (Legal Seafood). Coast Guard admirals Nimmick and Sullivan have been guests. Professional baseball and football players who have boats and America's Cup sailing champions too.

Guest from Hell: No such thing as a guest from hell. It is up to the host (the interviewer) to make all guests comfortable by easing them into a conversation.

Contact: NauticalTalk@aol.com; 781-925-3939; http://www.NauticalTalk.com; http://www.959watd.com; Capt Lou. Best method: E-mail or phone. If they are authors, I must receive a copy of their book prior to interview. No response? They sent it to the wrong address or for some unknown reason I didn't receive it. I respond to all e-mails usually within 3 business days.

Invited Back? If they have more than one story to tell

Bio of Capt Lou: When he's not on the air, Captain Lou (Gainor) works as a real estate agent or is sailing the seas. He owns a 36-foot cruiser, G-Force, docked at Metropolitan Yacht Club in Braintree, Mass. He has cruised from Maine to Florida, but his favorite destinations remain close to home: Boston Harbor and Cape Cod. Lou was an active member of the Coast Guard Auxiliary from 1980 to 2005. Capt Lou's show was named winner of the Mass/ Rhode Island Associated Press "Best Talk Show" and Boston's Achievement in Radio "Best Interview" Award.

New Age

"We are not human beings having a spiritual experience. We are spiritual beings having a human experience." — By Pierre Teilhard de Chardin, favorite saying of Carole Matthews, host of The Messengerfiles

Ageless Lifestyles: Cutting Edge Thinking on Being Youthful at Every Age with Dr. Michael Brickey on Web Talk Radio http://webtalkradio.net and syndicated to libraries nationwide.

Theme: What it takes to live longer, healthier, and happier. The program takes a holistic approach in addressing anti-aging psychology, alternative medicine, medicine, fitness, nutrition, health, and wellness. The emphasis is on innovative thinking and practices that have solid data and results.

Guest Profile: Cutting edge anti-aging experts in aging psychology, medicine, alternative medicine, fitness, nutrition, health, and wellness. Guests with an ability to explain ideas to audience and give practical advice. The most important question is what they are likely to talk about. I also check to make sure they don't have flakey ideas. Credentials are usually easily gleaned from the Internet or book publicity. A copy of the book is helpful but not required.

Guest from Hell: Pedantic or trying too hard to push a product or book.

Contact: DrBrickey@DrBrickey.com; 614-237-4556; http://www.DrBrickey.com http://www.Anti-Aging-Speaker.com; http://agelesslifestyles.com; Michael Brickey, Ph.D. Best method: I usually find them but prospective guests are welcome to send an e-mail and follow-up with a phone call. No response? A follow-up e-mail or phone call is appropriate.

Invited Back? The quality of the program, response to the program, and whether there is more to say

Bio of Dr. Michael Brickey: America's preeminent anti-aging psychologist, Michael's award winning book, *Defy Aging* (New Resources Press 2000), was featured on *Oprah*, CNN, and the Voice of America. His second award-winning book, *52 Baby Steps to Grow Young* (New Resources Press 2005), gives two-page-a-week steps for being more youthful at every age. His also publishes *Defy Aging Newsletter*, offered free to subscribers.

His unique *Reverse Aging* hypnosis CDs help people relax and become ageless. He has appeared on more than 20 TV programs and 100 radio programs.

Michael is an ABPP Board Certified Psychologist and Fellow of the American Psychological Association.

All Things That Matter with Philip Harris on Passionate Voices Internet Radio. Phil also has a show on BlogTalkRadio with the same name and criteria, only he is the contact. sundiskhermit@yahoo.com, http://www.blogtalkradio.com/pharris

Theme: Major issues affecting all of us.

Guest Profile: People addressing important issues, including authors, healers, philosophers, environmentalists. Someone who has depth on topics — I do not just want authors to promote books — I want to know what they have to say and why — social/spiritual issues are a big plus. I just want to be sure that they have something to say that is important to all of us and that they know what they are talking about.

Guest from Hell: Someone who needs constant prompting and where I have to lead the whole conversation.

Contact: Sundiskhermit@yahoo.com; 207-549-5339; http://www.internetvoicesradio.com; Lillian Cauldwell at Lillian@authorsden.com. Best method: E-mail why and what they have to say makes a damn bit of difference. No response? Call or e-mail. My shows are booked three months in advance — I keep a file for future guests and a reminder is good.

Invited Back? If we had fun and if the topic needed more coverage.

Guest Comments: "Thanks, Phil — it amazes me how comfortable you make me feel." — Joyce Anthony, author of *Storm* (Star Publish 2007), http://joyceanthony.tripod.com/

"I thoroughly enjoyed it! I came out of the office saying ... that was so much fun!" — Lisa Saper-Bloom, healing arts specialist and author of *Peaceful Mind, Thinner Body: A Woman's Week-by-Week Guide to Emotional Weight Loss* (Wheatmark 2007) http://www.nothingbinding.com/writer/lisa-saper-bloom.html

Bio of Philip F. Harris: Being knowledgeable in the areas of secret societies, occult and religious studies, Phil has been a student of mystical studies and a member of several "fraternal" organizations for over 25 years. He is co-author of the novel *Waking God* (Star Publish 2006), coined a "spiritual thriller." He is author of a novel, *A Maine Christmas Carol* (Cambridge Books 2007, and two non-fiction books, *Jesus Taught It, Too: The Early Roots of the Law of Attraction* (Avatar Publications 2007) and *Raping Louisiana: A Diary of Deceit* (Cambridge Books 2007).

Phil has contributed to UPI's, "Religion and Spirituality" web site and is listed as an "Expert Author" and writer for "Ezine Articles.com" and writes for AC Media.com. He is a nationally syndicated and featured writer for The American Chronicle and has a blog called All Things That Matter.

More information concerning his work can be found on:http://dickens111.tripod.com,www.wakinggod.com., http://www.americanchronicle.com, http://philipharris.blogspot.com, http://ezinarticles.com and http://www.nothingbinding.com .

Another Reality Show with Golden Hawk aired on 1320 WARL, Providence, Rhode Island.

Theme: Spiritual programming opening hearts and minds.

Guest Profile: Authors, healers, personal stories of enlightenment. I look for authenticity in their belief structure and how they live their lives. I look for people who reflect their message in their personal lives, people who walk their talk. I look for a genuine desire to share Universal Truth with my audience.

Guest from Hell: A guest from hell is someone who puts sales as a number 1 priority, instead of passion.

Contact: GoldenHawkFeather@yahoo.com; 203-847-787; http://www.AnotherRealityShow.com; Golden Hawk. Best method: E-mail or phone. Preferably send me a press kit, but I am open to e-mail and phone connections as well. No response? I am open to a person connecting with me in any form that works for them. I honor persistence and personal drive.

Invited Back? The chemistry I feel and also how

my guest feels after the show will determine whether they will return.

Bio of Golden Hawk: Golden Hawk comes to us from the Heyoke Path — the path of Truth. Empathic her whole life, she began counseling people in 1996, and further developed her keen intuition. In 1999, she became certified by the National Guild of Hypnotists (NGH) in hypnotherapy. In 2001 training as an EMF Balancer. True to her Native American name she studied the medicine ways of the Cherokee in 2002, earning status as a Kolaimni practitioner. 2002 also brought her to the understanding of Christ Consciousness, so she added this templating to her many skills and talents. Rounding out her work and her Being, in 2003 she achieved her Reiki Mastership status. Continuing her pursuit to understand life, and share this understanding with others, she focuses on her radio show called *Another Reality Show*.

Ask the Psychic with Danielle Daoust on Ask 1 Network, www.ask1radio.com and iTunes.

Theme: Answering questions about being psychic, spirits, guides, angels.

Guest Profile: Psychics, mediums, astrologers. Knowledge and experience in the field.

Guest from Hell: Someone who doesn't talk ... has to be probed ... also anyone who would be disrespectful of the work or the audience.

Contact: danielle@globalpsychics.com; 519-681-7779; http://globalpsychics.com; Danielle Daoust. Best method: E-mail. No response? E-mail, then call.

Invited Back? Audience reception, ease of communication.

Bio of Danielle Daoust: Although gifted with a keen intuition and clairvoyance from childhood, Danielle did not focus on these talents until later in life. For some 20 years she held mainstream management and consulting positions, first with Imperial Oil Ltd, later with Systemhouse (one of Canada's pioneers of the computer age).

Soon after she turned 40, she found herself challenging all that she had believed about herself and her world and decided to give up her business career to pursue a more spiritual life. This began her transition to a career as a psychic reader and teacher, developing and refining her natural talents for seeing beyond the present. Beginning with a handful of loyal subscribers, word of mouth soon brought many who sought and benefited from her wisdom and counsel.

Full bio at http://globalpsychics.com/about-global-psychics/danielle-daoust.shtml

Between Two Worlds Radio with Derrick Whiteskycloud on BBS Radio http://www.bbsradio.com Tuesdays, 8 PM (PT).

Theme: To learn and share all facets of spiritual and paranormal and alternative health information. It is all about our spiritual journey.

Guest Profile: Listed on the bbsradio topic information. I look for the most unusual type of guest that not everyone knows from media. But I do make exceptions that are already in the media. I like to find the people that like to tell their story, what they've witnessed in the paranormal field. Or those who are dealing with an illness that can be healed and sharing alternative ways to get back into a healthy society. Also I do my one night per month psychic mediumship readings on radio. It has to be their energy that feels good to me which is positive. Also their story that can lead into an even more interest coming up next, you know? (A cliffhanger) something that can keep you on the edge of your seat. Then there is the human interest of alternative health that everyone keeps on searching out the better results to cures and not band-aides.

Guest from Hell: Satan? Fire and Brimstone. OUCH.

Contact: whiteskycloud@yahoo.com; 604-818-8375; http://www.bbsradio.com/between2worlds/between_two_worlds.php; Derrick Whiteskycloud. Best method: Call with a pitch, e-mail a bio, send a press kit ... please. No response? It does get difficult to return all calls back to people all at once. Just be patient and they will get a response.

Invited Back? They have to be able to keep the public interested. When we get calls requesting are guests to return back and saying to us we need to add more online time for these guests. Then you know they will be returning back to the show. I do have many guests now that have returned 4–5 times. Time is never enough through the interviews.

Guest Comment: "Derrick always makes me and the public feel welcome and comfortable. I have known him a long time as a friend and work associate. We always have very positive feedback about the show from all over the world, and besides that, we have fun. That seems to be lacking in this world with folks focusing on gloom and doom, so we just have fun and try to help people as best we can."—Joanne Giroux, herbalist and healer, http://www.wildwomanherbs.com

Listener Comment: "This is an essential show—could you extend it to 90 minutes? I am always learning new related stuff here (guests, herbs, etc.) that I cannot find on any other radio talk shows."—Remi-Yves Breton, Montreal, Canada

Bio of Derrick Whiteskycloud: Originally from Brandon, Manitoba, Derrick Whiteskycloud was drawn to the traditions of his Métis and Algonquin-Ojibway ancestry when he was 13 years old. In the years between his roots in Manitoba and his current home in Surrey, British Columbia, he travelled extensively across Canada developing and sharing his gifts as a spiritual counselor, teacher, psychic, medium, and artist.

Derrick's approach to counseling, mediumship, and healing incorporates techniques from both traditional practices and alternative methodologies. In practice, his work draws from the Great Spirit, his spirit guides, celestial beings, E.T.'s, and other spiritual guides as determined by the needs of the individual, and incorporates elements of sound and song, drumming, sacred ceremonies, healing energy, crystals, and Wing Chi. His overall philosophy of healing is that knowledge should be open and accessible to everyone and, as such, he offers workshops in hands-on healing energy, Wing Chi, psychic mediumship, past life regressions, spirit guides, animal totems, drum making, soul retrieval (traditional blanket ceremony), and shamanic journeys.

Derrick's healing gift also extends into the realm of the expressive arts. His self-published book, *Spiritual Journeys with Whiteskycloud, Spiritual Wisdom and Poetry* (Dancingfirewolf 2002), is a collection of channelled writings, stories, poetry, and illustrations. He is also working on his second book, *Spiritual Awakenings*.

He is also a prolific artist. His artwork, which emphasizes historical and cultural themes and spiritual symbolism, materializes in a range of mediums including smudge bowls, dancing fans and staffs, jewelry, shields, beaded feathers and wings, dream catchers, mandelas, medicine pouches, crystal healing wands, carved horn pieces, deerskin drums, rattles, and works on canvas. His most recent work, a wall mural titled the *Spirit of Batoche,* is on display at the Métis Family Services Cultural Building in Surrey, British Columbia.

Derrick is also known for his gifts for entertaining through traditional song, inspirational storytelling, and drumming. He has previously hosted *Between Two Worlds: A Talk Show About Your Spiritual Journey*, on 1410 CFUN in Vancouver and can be heard on the *Jimmy Lowery Show Radio Program*, http://www.apsrradio.com.

Beyond Reality with Shelley Kaehr, Ph.D. on Global Talk Radio http://www.globaltalkradio.com.

Theme: Paranormal/alternative healing

Guest Profile: Authors, leaders in the field of alternative healing. Entertaining experts in the field of alternative healing who enjoy teaching people about positive alternatives to health and wellness. Credentials—books written, celebrity endorsements. I prefer published authors and people who already have celebrity status in their field.

Guest from Hell: Cannot keep talking or gives me one or two word answers to a question.

Contact: shelley@shelleykaehr.com; 469-556-HEAL(4325); http://www.shelleykaehr.com; Shelley Kaehr, Ph.D. Best method: E-mail please. Thank you. I normally only book a guest if I read and enjoyed their book. If you e-mail me and I am interested I will request a sample book. Otherwise, don't send it blind. I know materials writers send cost money and I don't want to take away from a guest who is not right for the show. If I think you're right for the show, I will request more info. No response? E-mail me again ... might have been lost in cyberspace...

Invited Back? Fun, fun, fun. Are we having a good time talking? If so, you can always come back.

Guest Comments: "An important contribution to the field of regression therapy."—Brian Weiss, MD, author of *Many Lives, Many Masters* (One Spirit / Simon and Schuster/ Warner Books 2002)

"I commend Shelley for her commitment to the spirit of honest inquiry."—Raymond Moody, MD, author of *Life After Life* (HarperOne 2001)

Bio of Shelley Kaehr, Ph.D.: Shelley is author of 15 books in the mind-body arena and has been working in the field of human potential for over 20 years. Her work has been critically acclaimed and she has traveled and lectured all over the world.

Blog Talk Radio's Holistic Integrative Energy Medicine, http://www.blogtalkradio.com/BrentAtwater

Theme: Alternative medicine answers and holistic solutions to traditional health questions about facilitating you and your pet's health and wellbeing.

Guest Profile: Documented, evidence-based established educators, researchers, traditional and integrative medical professionals and alternative practitioners. Authenticity, with the ability to relate to the target market base with clarity, ability to educate, and to help expand the listener's awareness.

Guest from Hell: A person who is more interested in personal promotion, rather than expanding and helping others.

Contact: Brent@BrentAtwater.com; 910-692-5206; http://www.BrentAtwater.com; Brent Atwater. Best method: E-mail. I search for my guests. No response? E-mail.

Invited Back? Listener response.

Bio of B. Brent Atwater: Brent is an energy medicine specialist: a medical intuitive and distance energy healer. She is the author and illustrator of her Just Plain Love Books (http://www.Justplainlovebooks.com) whose titles include: *How to Overcome Your Health Problems, Positive Actions to Help Survive Your Cancer* and healing books for children: *Cancer Kids—God's Special Children* and *The Heavenly Express for MY Daddy*. For pets there's *I'm Home Again: A Dog's Love Story* about pet reincarnation, all published by Booksurge a division of Amazon.com

Brent states, "I'm trained by God/the Universe, certified by client results, documented by traditional medicine and scientific research."

As a gifted child, Brent was tested by J. B. Rhine from Duke at age 5, for her intuitive abilities. When her dog fell and became paralyzed she discovered her incredible gifts.

Brent could look inside Friend's body and actually see his organs and systems and could accurately determine the causes, location, extent, and severity of his physical problem. When she focused her healing energy his spinal cord nerves, spinal cord discs and vertebrae, and his pulmonary functions were restored.

After her hand was caught in a lawn mower's blades, she learned to stop bleeding and pain, to regenerate bones, tissue and nerve cells. When she held her hands over a client's tremors, they stopped. When she directed her energy with independent client cases, epileptic seizures stopped or shortened, brain damaged, injured or paralyzed nerves were restored to function and able to feel sensation, wounds were healed. Brent's energy work is transformative healing.

Breaking Through with Georgiann on http://www.georgiann.com, Wednesday at 8 PM (ET)

Theme: Self-help, environmental or green living, spirituality, metaphysics, health and wellness.

Guest Profile: Authors, celebrities, doctors, gurus, organizations. The preferred guest has a fascinating topic and exudes enthusiasm. A talkative and informative guest results in the best interview. Want credentials, biography, and an audio air check if available.

Guest from Hell: Answers questions with short sentences (doesn't elaborate), doesn't speak clearly, uses a cell phone or a cordless phone with poor reception or interference.

Contact: info@kirico.com; 336-659-0111; http://www.kirico.com and http://www.georgiann.com; Office representative. Best method: E-mail. A press kit is preferred — including a promotional photo, biography, resume of experience, credentials, a copy of their book (if the guest is an author), a demo or air check, and a list of past appearances. No response? If there is not a response within seven business days, send the e-mail again or call.

Invited Back? The audience response, statistics of show, and the effort the guest puts forth to promote their appearance.

Guest Comments: "Georgiann is a true gift to radio. Her enlightening and thought provoking shows contribute to the spiritual education of society in a truly remarkable and soul touching way." — Pamela Aaralyn, Divine Dimensions, LLC

"Georgiann is a natural host with a broad understanding of topics. Her show, *Breaking Through* gave me the opportunity to convey my message of how to live a more intuitive and fulfilling life with an audience I had not previously reached." — Kimmie Rose Zapf, author, speaker, intuitive

Bio of Georgiann Kiricoples: Georgiann's management career began in 1984 working as an assistant manager in a woman's clothing store in Winston Salem, NC. She had a natural flair for management and within months was promoted and relocated to Greenville, SC, to manage her own store. Shortly after, she was chosen to troubleshoot locations within her district.

Her career took an unexpected turn in 1993 as she took the plunge into the world of entertainment and accepted a position to travel with one of the most sought after psychic radio personalities. Her experience stretched from the top ten radio market such as NYC (WPLJ) and San Francisco (KSOL), to smaller markets including Richmond (WRVQ) and Omaha (Sweet 98).

Armed with diverse knowledge, in 1996 she decided to combine her management and marketing skills in retail and small business with her experience in the entertainment industry to create her company, Kirico Management. Her new found love of radio propelled her to expand into the music industry where she managed and consulted artists and musicians across the United States.

Georgiann is a consultant with over 23 years' experience and one of the highest rated business advisors on the Internet.

Bridging Heaven and Earth with Allan, aired on over 150 cities on cable TV (see http://www.heaventoearth.com/stations.html) and on the Internet on YouTube and Google video.

Theme: A spiritual talk show that focuses on oneness, joy, compassion, inclusion, the infinite, and love.

Guest Profile: Individuals who experience, manifest and dedicate their lives to oneness, joy, compassion, inclusion, the infinite, and love, whether they do it through the written word, music, art, experiential recognitions, etc. This is usually evident from their books, press packets, websites, etc. All interviews are done in-studio in Santa Barbara, CA. For past guests, go to http://www.heaventoearth.com/guests.html

Guest from Hell: Fortunately, Bridging hasn't really had one.

Contact: info@HeavenToEarth.com; 805-687-2053; http://www.HeavenToEarth.com; Allan or Bianca. Best method: E-mail or phone. We are open to collaborations with anyone who is manifesting oneness, joy, compassion, inclusion, the infinite, and love ... so any way they think would best present that to us is wonderful. No response? Yes, that would be fine, but we make every effort to answer every contact, whether e-mail or calls, in a reasonable timeframe. We try to respond to everyone as we'd want to be responded to.

Invited Back? That all those concerned doing and viewing the specific show have the experience of oneness, joy, compassion, inclusion, the infinite, and love.

Guest Comment: "Allan is an inspired, dedicated and ceaseless voice for the power of love.... He is a pioneer in bringing new thought to the public by engaging his guests with dignity and encouraging all of us to walk together as one." — Harold W. Becker, president and founder, The Love Foundation, Inc., http://www.thelovefoundation.com

Bio of Allan Silberhartz: Allan is a master spiritual teacher, a mystic, and a healer, who has been on a spiritual path since childhood. He has written songs and screenplays, and has produced CDs and DVDs.

Allan never really resonated with any particular religion and, from early on, his spiritual experiences transcended traditional religious affiliations. He graduated from the Wharton School at the University of Pennsylvania and from the National Law Center at George Washington University. He later lived on a commune in Maryland where he had an experience that he felt could only be described or defined as love, or oneness, or God.

It was a complete fulfillment, and he had since experienced it regularly. With a great passion and joy for love and oneness, Allan started a non-profit, educational Foundation and his talk show is "dedicated to the Oneness."

Since the collaboration between Bridging and Google Video/YouTube that allows his shows available 24/7 on the Internet, people from all over the globe have contacted Allan to talk about their experiences of "awakening" after watching the program.

The show is also involved in the International Art Project. After announcing the project, more than 100 art pieces began arriving at the Bridging offices from talented artists of all stripes. "The Art Project is now in its 'second wave' and, again, the response is extraordinary," says Allan.

Allan's "Oneness" energy makes everyone feel unconditional Love and Joy in his presence. He was appointed as a "Love Ambassador" by The Love Foundation (http://www.TheLoveFoundation.com) and was given the "Lifting Up the World with a Oneness-Heart" Award by Sri Chinmoy and his worldwide service organization. Allan is truly a Renaissance Man.

Brightlights Pathfinders with Tassy Hill on BBS Radio, http://www.bbsradio.com, on Thursday at 9 PM (ET).

Theme: One's callings.

Guest Profile: Guests in their simple raw forms are what I look for, the real in truth ... what one lives by and yearns for. Expertise in the consistency of the knowledge of their calling with charisma and etiquette of honor. I feel from the energy and their spirit within giving one a chance to evolve in their callings.

Guest from Hell: Not original work, being in other words indecisiveness of one's original work.

Contact: Hillustrations11@aol.com, Brightlightspath@aol.com; (Cell) 704-906-3004; Cathy "Tassy Hill" Cook. Best method: Call with a pitch, e-mail a bio, send a press kit, or word of mouth. I prefer a Press Kit and Bio. No response? Call.

Invited Back? Enthusiasm! Ambience.

Bio of Cathy "Tassy" Hill Cook: "Tassy" was born and raised on the out-skirts of Charlotte, North Carolina. She is spirit led by the Holy Ghost. She broadcasts from her home in Charlotte, opening her show with "hello, you are on the air. Welcome to BrightLightsPathfinders with Cathy Cook as your Host."

Tassy is a teacher, published writer, photographer, mother of three, and creator of all arts in the field using many mediums. "I feel the words of beyond, and am a prayer warrior," she says. "I believe in all positive spiritualities.... Negativity feeds me into doing even greater positivity. I am a Bright Lights PathFinders Way."

Calling All Angels with Debara and Devona on Fox KZNU 1450 am, airing in Utah/Nevada on Saturday 8–9 AM (MT). Debara also hosts Calling All Angels, Monday, 6–7 PM (ET) on WARL 1320 am, airing in Rhode Island and Massachusetts; now off the air.

Theme: Miracles, stories of hope, angels, messages for callers.

Guest Profile: Everyday people, scientists, archaeologists. We want to know the guest's past interview experiences, credentials and sound of their voice.

Guest from Hell: Never had one.

Contact: Debara@Callinallangels.com; 435-467-3075; http://www.Callinallangels.com; For Calling All Angels show only: Donelle Carter at donniellec@yahoo.com. Best method: E-mail or phone. No response? Due to e-mails. Leave message again.

Invited Back? Audience.

Guest Comment: "Debara Bruhn is a glorious spirit guide to humankind of all ages ... she illuminates the world with her ability to radiate love ... with her work with Vision Quest she brings all people to a place of peace and healing. Debara is a clairvoyant with a multitude of talents including communicating with angels and hearing their messages of miracles she so joyfully shares. She is a beautiful songwriter, musician and sings like a bird. Debara's radio show, *Calling All Angels*, showcases angels, music, crystal/rainbow children and many wonderful guests within the healing genre. She is an amazing soul!" — Deborah Beauvais, owner, Empowered Connections, and host of *Love by Intuition Show* (see page 222)

Bio of Debara Bruhn: Debara is a clairvoyant with a multitude of talents including communicating with angels and hearing their messages of miracles she so joyfully shares. She is a songwriter, musician and sings like a bird.

She grew up in with a family who encouraged her intuitive gifts as a child. At the age of four she recalls the family dinner table as a fun time. Her father would set a plate for her "invisible," friends at the dinner table.

The Candia Sanders Hour on Contact Talk Radio. http://www.contacttalkradio.com/hosts/candiasanders.htm; now off the air.

Theme: Intuitive informational format with callers asking pertinent questions relating to health, abundance, relationships.

Guest profile: Callers and occasional spiritual authors. Someone who is out of the box with ideas and information; someone who is willing to reach beyond the day to day normal. The right idea combined with well written thoughts, written numerous songs and is currently waiting for one of her favorites to be released.

Guest from Hell: Someone who is so pushy, over-the-top, the person who talks over you with information with self-righteous indignation.

Contact: candiasanders@yahoo.com; 360-608-9555; http://www.candiasanders.com; Candia Sanders. Best method: The best way for contact is a quick explanation via e-mail with a possible excerpt from their book. It really is a great window into their perspective as well as learning about the writing abilities of the potential interviewee. No response? If time has elapsed, please resend me another e-mail for consideration. It could be that my travel schedule has conflicted, not my interest in the potential interview.

Invited Back? The invitation is based on listeners' feedback as well as a good rapport between the two of us.

Bio of Candia Sanders: Candia has been intuitive her entire life, having done readings for the past 25 years. Due to her own injury in 1993, it took her down the path of discovery into alternative medicine and other forms of healing.

In 1999 a local paper mill dumped illegal toxins into the air, resulting in 64 school children going to the hospital. Candia was home when this occurred, altering her health for two years. During that time she learned to see inside the body, allowing energetic manipulations and energy work to the distressed areas, thus clearing herself of the toxins and heavy chemicals, as well as realigning her physical structure. "After that I realized I could do the same for others, looking into their physical distress, then taking it to the next level of emotional imbalances and the root of the cause," she says. "Since that time I have worked on thousands of people with great results. I travel and teach, host 'playshops,' work with clients on a weekly basis, have a radio show, and am currently finishing several books and stories that I have compiled over the years. I can be contacted for consultations and sessions to explore the deeper levels of the experiences in your life.

Client Comments: "Candia is a gifted and compassionate psychic with whom I have had several meaningful readings. Through Candia's insights, I have gained greater understanding into my relationships, abilities, and purpose in life. She has even helped me connect with my own psychic abilities. Candia's readings are fascinating, life-affirming, and inspiring. She has accessed many past life connections for me and healed me remotely. I have always been truly impressed by — and thankful for — her profound empathy and ability to help and heal." — Mary Simmons, high school teacher, Bothell, WA

"Her Spirit embraces her with healing light and that light she sends into the world to help soothe our pain. Her warm personality and wonderful smile greets every stranger as a close friend. I'm blessed to know her and be a part of her life." — Stuart Davis, Stuart, Florida

Connect with Jeanne White on 95.9FM WATD, Marshfield, MA, airing Saturday, 10:30–11:00 AM (ET). There is generally a small guest fee for the half-hour. Non-profits pay half.

Theme: Sharing resources, information and knowledge on how to enhance your business, personal and spiritual experience.

Guest Profile: Authors. I have had artists, inventor, TV cable host, exchange student programs. I look for interest in the guest. If I am interested I think my listening audience will be also. I want someone who has something to offer my audience. I like to have a bio and some questions from the potential guests. I like to meet them a half hour before the show to get to know them and what is the comfort level for them. I want them to feel comfortable on the show. I have had very interesting guests on the show.

Guest from Hell: I am not sure since I have not encountered one. I do not believe there is a guest from hell.

Contact: Jeanne@ConnectShow.com and JWhite7033@comcast.net; 781-326-4902; http://www.959watd.com/Saturday.asp and http://www.TheConnectShow.com; Jeanne White. Best method: E-mail. I like to have a bio and then talk with them. No response? If for some reason I do not respond they can call or e-mail.

Invited Back? If they ask to come back on the show. If they have some further information for the listening audience. Will depend on the schedule of the guest and what is the reason to come back on the show.

Guest Comment: "I just wanted to thank you Jeanne for having me as a guest on your show, *Connect*. I really enjoyed myself and you made it one of the most pleasant experiences I have ever had. Not to mention the publicity and help it gave my business. You made me feel comfortable and did a wonderful job interviewing me.

"It is great to know that in this world filled with bla bla on the airwaves there is a show such as *Connect* and a host such as yourself who help people and bring good programming to the airwaves. Your show is one of the finer things in life and I look forward to listening to it to get information and to hear some great guests. Of course, my favorite part is listening to you work with your guests to bring out some cool stuff.

"I could go on and on but I guess what I just should say is that I look forward to working with you in the future and was honored to be part of a radio show that is as good as yours. I am hoping that others will want to have the experience I have had so we can all share and bare instead of selling and telling. Keep up the good work." — LauRA Sheridan, aka RaRa, host of TV cable show, "Ra! Ra! with LauRA Sheridan"

Bio of Jeanne White: Jeanne is a native of Boston, Massachusetts, with a Bachelor's degree from Simmons College. She received her paralegal certification from Aquinas College in 1996, and attended the University of Massachusetts, Boston, where she received the Frank J. Manning Gerontology Certificate in 2003. As an adjunct to that education she became a certified Shine Counselor working with the elderly population helping them make educated insurance decisions.

She holds a seat on the board of directors for the Southwest Boston Community Development Corporation (CDC).

Jeanne worked for John Hancock Financial Services in various capacities and was a human resource consultant for several years.

Jeanne is a true entrepreneur who is always looking for ways to broaden her horizons.

In addition to her radio show, she is involved with an online greeting card company called "I Love Cards." She is also the production assistant for "Ra! Ra! with LauRa Sheridan Show," a monthly cable TV program that teaches people how to live a happier life.

Connecting the Light with Mike Quinsey on BBS Radio Station.

Theme: New Age and spiritual subjects.

Guest Profile: Author or practitioner. Personal experience of their subject. Sound of their voice is important.

Guest from Hell: One without good background knowledge of their subject.

Contact: michael@brookwood96.orangehome.co.uk; 01233 637607 England; http://www.treeofthegoldenlight.com; Mike Quinsey. Best method: E-mail a bio. No response? E-mail again.

Invited Back? Good speaker and plenty of material for another interview.

Bio of Mike Quinsey: Mike Quinsey has been told that he is a young looking lad of 69, which he attributes to healthy living and an ongoing interest in life. He has two sons, Alan and Colin, who have both done him proud. "My wife Cathy keeps me on my toes, and I am lucky enough to be married to an excellent cook," he says. "To her credit, she tolerates my interests which take up a lot of my spare time, which is mainly reading, and since I retired in December 1999 I have moved more into the computer world, giving me the opportunity to circulate my articles and enjoy the multitude of websites available."

Mike has always found himself in electrical or mechanical companies, in sales or service, and had his share of management positions, spending his last 30 years as a sales representative.

"I found my spiritual path in the late 70s through the Atlantean Society, ran my own branch soon after, during which time I started a section called the Universal Network that supported Tuella and her work with Ashtar," says Mike. "I then started Galacticom Europa to cover the messages from Ashtar through Carole Hall. In conjunction with all of this, I produced my own magazine called the *Messenger*. During this period I had my most convincing UFO sighting, one of several all told. After these activities had ran their course, I returned to giving talks, until the mid 90s when I became editor for a local magazine called *Quest*, which is devoted to spiritual growth and enlightenment.

"My affinity is with ancient Egypt and Atlantis, having found the readings of Edgar Cayce of considerable help. I am told I was a high priest in Egypt, but have no waking memory of this or any other incarnation."

Conscious Healing with Sherry Anshara, airs Wednesday at 5:00 PM (MT) on http://www.achieveradio.com

Theme: Consciousness.

Guest Profile: Scientists, doctors, healthcare professionals, conscious intuitives, counselors, addiction experts, empowering women, cellular research, "out of the box" experts in their field, pre and post natal experts and researchers, physicists, science meets spiritual experts, and other spiritual authorities. I would also like to interview any politicians who may be open to alternative methods for healing emotional and physical issues outside the box of allopathic medicine. Most important — that they know their topic. I want a copy of their book (if they have one).

Guest from Hell: One who can't articulate their message in "real" terminology that the average person can understand.

Contact: sherryanshara@quantumpathic.com; 480 609-0874; http://www.quantumpathic.com. Best method: E-mail. Do not call unless we've established an initial contact. No response? The person should re-e-mail us.

Invited Back? The success of the show and if there is a connection with the host.

Guest Comment: "Sherry was a phenomenal host. She seemed to be on the same wavelength as I was and we both had very similar experiences in the medical field even though we came at them from vastly different perspectives. She made me feel more at home than any of the other folks I've been interviewed by and in so doing we were able to have a much more casual but informative conversation which, I believe, benefited the listeners even more. She has very open-minded and accepting way about her that makes it very easy for a doctor to understand where she's coming from and not be intimidated by her non-traditional approach. She is the ultimate complement to traditional medicine. I loved being on her show and hope to see her soon when I go to Phoenix in July." — Terrie Wurzbacher, host of *Your Doctor Said What?* (see page 118)

Bio of Sherry Anshara: Sherry is founder of QuantumPathic Center of Consciousness and creator of QuantumPathic Cellular Therapy. She has her medical intuitive practice in Scottsdale, AZ.

Sherry is author of *The Age of Inheritance: The Activation of the 13 Chakras* (QuantumPathicsm Press 2004).

Conversations from Beyond with Lenny Feldsott on Achieve Radio, http://www.achieveradio.com

Theme: Readings and special guests.

Guest Profile: Guests that read or have something interesting to say regarding metaphysical matters. I really look for people that do readings or have something to say about spirit.

Guest from Hell: A guest from hell would not have any stage presence, coughed, chewed gum or just only wanted to talk about themselves. I usually interview guests before a show and/or have them give me a mini reading so I can see how they work and deliver messages. I really don't emphasize accuracy as much as presence and delivery style as not every reading is great.

Contact: Lenny@lennyf.com; 626-864-7076; http://www.lennyf.com; Lenny Feldsott. Best method: Call with a pitch, e-mail a bio and send a press kit, but they will have to talk to me and go through my process. No response? They should call or resend to be sure they didn't get lost in the shuffle.

Invited Back? If I enjoyed working with them.

Client Comments: "I want to reiterate to you that yesterday's session was a life changing experience for me.... You were completely accurate on so many things. I made a commitment to be open to the intuitive thoughts and impressions that come to me and to stay open to messages that my spirit guide is trying to get across to me.... I thanked God all day for allowing us to communicate."—Barb

"You have changed my life tremendously and I thank you so much.... I went over so much of what you said and I have been totally amazed ever since." I have always had a terrible fear of death all of my life that I would get very upset and scared at the thought if I dwelled on it. Ever since my husband passed away, I have felt differently. I have been through the worst experience of my entire life but, now, from all the signs he has sent me and especially since our reading, I am no longer afraid at all. I will look forward to the day that I can be with him again whenever it's my turn. Right now, I have to take care of my kids and myself. You have a special gift and I am happy I had the chance to meet you. Hopefully I can have another reading sometime in the future and looking forward to receiving the meditation tapes."—Debi

Bio of Lenny Feldsott: Lenny Feldsott is a spiritual medium, gifted in clairvoyance, clairsentience, and clairaudience. "I try to help people to understand their paths through life," he says. "I have an uncanny record for accuracy in my readings.... Spirit is my guide in this channeling work with the after-life." He has worked on radio, television and for the Pasadena Police Department reviewing cold case files. Lenny is a member of the Spiritualist Church of Revelation in Monrovia, California.

Conversations of the Quantum Age with Marlene Caldes aired on InnerVoice Network.com, womensradio.com and various links to author sites.

Theme: Body, mind and spirit.

Guest Profile: Authors, innovators, body. Mind and spirit educators, metaphysicians and personal growth/health experts of our times for general audiences. Guests that are making a contribution to humankind in an impactful and positive manner. Guests who are talking about health, personal development, spirituality and life enhancing techniques and tools for better living, better health, better human understanding. I look for the paradigm breakers, those authors who have broken through the language barrier of buzz words and medieval values and present even the most ancient principles with clarity, ease and grace. I want to know that they are articulate, speak English well and have established their expertise through seminars, books, public speaking, etc.

Guest from Hell: The guest that belittles and assassinates the subconscious of their listeners with critical, unsupportive statements and ideas with the intention to incite. That includes religious fanatics, all organized religion proponents.

Contact: marcaldes@aol.com; 415 381-0287 Canada: 888 922-7070; InnerVoiceNetwork.com; Marlene Caldes or Carol Blembe/ofc asst. Best method: Most publishers send us a press kit with two copies of the author's book. One for host, one for staff. E-mail requests are answered the same way should the subject interest us. We request two books and press kit. We request that they send a short, succinct e-mail with pertinent information about the proposed guest, the book, the situation, why that person is an authority (if it's about an issue), and the topic that is important to cover. No response? If a guest e-mails me and I don't respond it is likely that the subject has already been covered by one of our other programs or doesn't meet my criteria for interest. I normally do not respond by e-mail quickly that I want to pass. Sometimes I hold the e-mail for future consideration.

Invited Back? We enjoy bringing back guests who are constantly growing, writing and speaking on their area of expertise. We will do follow up interviews for guests who have a great deal to offer beyond our ordinary 30 minute timeframe.

Guest Testimonials: "It is a privilege, thank you"—Deepak Chopra, whose book, *How to Know God* (Running Press Book Publishers 2001), was winner of the 2000 Quantum Age Book award

"Marlene, thank you for the enlightening interview! Continue to spread the word"—Carol Bowman, author of *Children's Pat Lives* (Bantam 1998).

Bio of Marlene Fern Caldes: Executive director of InnerVoice Network, Marlene is a broadcast and

Internet radio host, entrepreneur, author, artist, activist, practicing intuitive, feng shui and space clearing specialist.

She works with highly successful Fortune 500 Executives and CEOs, internationally known designers and artists, radio, book and television celebrities, everyday working people and stay at home caregivers. She has helped over 30,000 individuals worldwide.

Marlene is the creator of the IntentionMap method of personal success. She is intimately familiar with the intangible effects of energy and intention on our daily lives. She has been in private practice for more than three decades.

Widely known as "Our Psychic Friend," Marlene is on the Bay area's top rated Renel in the Morning radio show on 98.1 KISS FM currently, since 1997—10 years.

A Bay Area resident since 1972, Marlene is a graduate of St. John's Preparatory School, San Juan, Puerto Rico, and attended Emerson College, Boston, Massachusetts, focusing on mass communications, and the Academy of Art College in San Francisco (1981–84).

In 1974, she established the InnerVoice Network, a life enhancement company. It is the foundation of her private practice, radio and media presentations, seminars, and website, callmarlene.com. In 1996 she developed her newest service, SacredSpace Energy Clearing based on her feng shui, vastu, and ancient Hawaiian traditions expertise.

With 30+ years experience, Marlene knows that you get a better life when you get the bigger picture. She is passionate about sharing information that enhances the lives of people everywhere.

When she's not in front of a microphone in the studio, seminar audience or working with clients individually, Marlene enjoys time with her family, her husband Carl, her son, Alex, the mountains, creeks and trails of Mill Valley, Marin County, inventing gourmet recipes, brainstorming infinite possibilities, and rendering pastel aura portraits of friends and renowned individuals.

Creative Health and Spirit with Linda Mackenzie on http://www.HealthyLife.net, airing live Tuesdays, 8–9 AM (PT) and again at 8 PM.

Theme: Mind-body-spirit topics.

Guest Profile: Credentialed mind-body-natural health authors. No sensationalism, little controversy, positive uplifting subjects and well articulated and understandable speech. Who they are, what they did and what they are doing.

Guest from Hell: One who rattles on and on and on and forgets there is an interviewer in the conversation.

Contact: linda@lindamackenzie.net; 800-555-5453; http://www.healthylife.net; http://www.lindamackenzie.net; Linda Mackenzie. Best method: Send a book and press kit to CHSR Radio, P.O. Box 385, Manhattan Beach, CA 90267. No response? Do not e-mail or call. The only contact I want is by snail mail.

Invited Back? Content, courtesy, warmth and respect.

Bio of Linda Mackenzie: Linda is a doctoral clinical hypnotherapist candidate, award-winning author, feature writer, lecturer, psychic, and president of Creative Health and Spirit, a media and publishing company. A former telecommunications engineering analyst, she has held managerial positions in sales and marketing; owned one of the first used PC stores in America; owned a data communications consulting company that serviced government and Fortune 1000 companies and owned a dietary supplement manufacturing and distribution company.

Linda is author of *Inner Insights—The Book of Charts* (Creative Health and Spirit 1999), recipient of a 1998 COVR award for Best Metaphysical Book; *How to Self-Publish and Market Your Personal Growth Book* (Crossing Press 1999) and *Help Yourself Heal with Self-hypnosis* (Sterling Publishing 2000) and producer of the "Help Yourself Heal" Series of 17 audio-visualization tapes and CDs.

In 2002, Linda founded and owns one of the first all-positive talk and music Internet radio stations in America, HealthyLife.Net. A member of the National Association of Broadcasters, the station's 45 (and growing) seasoned TV, film, radio and national lecturer hosts reach an average audience of 837,000 a month in 99 countries (83 percent in 1,240 cities in all 50 states in the U.S.) and is simulcast on nine other private, public, PDA and Smartphone Internet networks.

Dimensions of Light with Anna Robles on Blog Talk Radio, http://www.blogtalkradio.com/DOL-Radio

Theme: Law of attraction through spirituality.

Guest Profile: Clients — Students taking my manifesting course — Those who have had success with the law of attraction in their lives. Someone who is ready to take charge of their life. I would like to know where they are on their path to manifesting, if they have had success. If they are taking my course, I want to have their feedback. I want to know what methods they are using for the manifesting.

Guest from Hell: Someone who calls while sitting in front of their computer where we get feedback. Really, I am lucky to have awesome guests. I have never encountered a bad guest.

Contact: Anael32@sbcglobal.net; 361-290-8661; http://www.dimensionsoflight.com/; Eileen Koch Agency, my PR Agent at 310-441-1000. I am under Anna Robles for www.Dimensionsoflight.com. Best method: E-mail and/or press kit. We will then make our decision based on this information. No response? I always respond to every e-mail. Kelly is also helping me to respond. We do our best to stay current with all e-mails and phone calls.

Invited Back? Usually the response from my listeners, and those in the chat room.

Bio of Anna Robles: When she was a little girl, Anna would have visions about things and receive messages for others. However, she didn't realize that she was communicating with angels. Since then, Anna had many experiences with psychic phenomena. By the time she was a young adult, she began doing psychic readings for friends and family. Then 12 years ago a great tragedy changed the course of her life. As her relationships and finances fell apart, she lost all sense of inner peace. "I doubted what role I had to play in this world," she recalls.

"But I clung to the knowledge that I still had my power of clarity and I prayed for true spiritual guidance. One day I was awakened by a strange light in my bedroom door. I saw an image of an angel who came to me and said, 'You must help others understand how to connect to God.'"

One week passed and Anna found herself drawn to people who had taken the path of true spiritual calling. One day she went for a reading and the lady told her that she needed to use her gifts of clairvoyance to help others. Although Anna loved helping people, she didn't know how to start. "She showed me, and has become a close personal friend over the past decade," says Anna. "Today, I am doing my life's work. I attract wonderful people into my life, loving relationships, financial success, and true inner peace. This is what I want for you. This is my role. To gently guide you to the universal truth of who you are.

"I want to share something with you — something very important:
- You deserve to live your dreams — to truly know the wonder that is you.
- When you believe you can make anything happen in your life, it will happen.
- All you need is someone to help bring out your own beautiful spirit.
- Seek and you shall find God within."

For the last 12 years Anna has supported herself as a spiritual, psychic medium that helps people reach their enlightenment stage.

Divine Awakening with William Constantine on Nowlive.com, http://www.williamconstantine.com, Widgets via Myspace Pages and other websites.

Theme: Transformational, spirituality, self help, paranormal.

Guest Profile: Authors, metaphysicians, holistic practitioners, ghost hunters, and many more. I look for a guest who is knowledgeable in their field, has something to offer the listeners, and is of course personable. They need to focus on being a guest and relaxing — it's really about enjoying getting your message across. Potential guests should have an angle or a hook. A website link, a review copy of their material, i.e., a book or CD. If they have a list of questions they are familiar with answering they can feel free to submit them for review.

Guest from Hell: It's the host's job to know about the guest, approve the guest, and know how to direct the show in a positive, professional manner. In my opinion, there is no guest from hell because everyone has something to bring to the table.

Contact: Cheryl@williamconstantine.com; 518-642-8009; http://www.williamconstantine.com/radio and http://www.nowlive.com/desktop/default.aspx?id=100236852; Cheryl or William. Best method: Send a pitch in an e-mail — Who you are, what is your message, why Divine Awakening? Send along a press kit too as it helps for the show introduction. Finally, mail me several promotional copies of your material for use in contests and other exciting events where the gift will be the prize. No response? We respond quickly with regards to guest inquiries so if you haven't received a reply odds are you ended up in the SPAM folder. Please send another e-mail or feel free to call.

Invited Back? The overall success of the first appearance and how they were received by the listenership.

Guest Comment: "My books, movies, and television work have given me the opportunity to be on countless radio shows and the privilege of meeting a few dedicated, enlightened professionals in the process. William Constantine is committed to his guests' messages and his listeners' well being. This is a powerful combination that makes all the difference." — Jim Stovall, author of *The Ultimate Gift* (David C. Cook distribution 2007), http://jimstovall.com

"William Constantine is an honest and sincere host and a very talented psychic. When he interviews someone, he puts them at ease with his genuine and friendly style, he makes his guests feel like they are talking to a trusted friend. William is not afraid to talk about his own personal life experiences in order to illustrate a concept that he is bringing to light. When listening to William talk on his radio show Divine Awakening, it is apparent that he is very open to celestial inspiration and is ready and willing to share that gift with others in order to guide them on their spiritual path." — Mickie Mueller, spiritual illustrator, http://www.mickiemuellerart.com

Bio of William Constantine: Born an Indigo Child of the Star Child Evolution, William has ascended into the ninth dimension of consciousness — which is also considered Full Christ Consciousness. He continues to raise his vibration and consciousness level aiming for the thirteenth dimension which is Universal Consciousness.

William has survived a life fraught with every possible personal challenge available to the human experience: the foster care system, enduring a 2½ year molestation, the tragic loss of his grandparents, the loss of his birth mother to AIDS, being homeless for a duration more than once, divorce/separation, and so much more. All of this by the age of 26.

William is far from throwing himself a pity party!

Instead, he seems to be empowered by these experiences — and devotes his life to sharing his message of love and healing to the world.

With his message of unity — "We are all one. There is nothing that separates us — except whatever illusion we choose to create. We are all GOD and thus we are all love. Love is all there is; anything else is an illusion."

As a psychic, William has been included in the, Akashic Who's Who of Psychics and Mediums, as well as *The Best Psychic Medium Directory*. He has made astoundingly accurate predictions; the release of John Mark Karr, OJ Simpson's acquittal, Michael Jackson's vindication, that both an African American and a woman would run for presidency (made in '06), and countless others.

He is the author of the widely popular column, "Insights into the Afterlife," within the pages of *Taps Paramagazine* — the official magazine for Sci-Fi's *Ghost Hunters*.

William has lectured at numerous Metaphysical and Whole Health Expos and filmed two online courses for The Learning Annex. It has been through his writings and teachings he has been dubbed a living luminary.

Divine Manifesting with Christy Whitman and Rebecca Grado on http://www.bbsradio.com; now off the air.

Theme: Manifesting using the universal laws.

Guest Profile: Authors, speakers, experts in manifesting and spirituality. Someone who has been working with the universal laws and can give insight to the listeners on how to apply them. Someone who is to the point and relevant. Expertise, credentials, sound of their voice.

Guest from Hell: Someone who stammers over their words and goes on and on and on with no relevance for the topic.

Contact: christy@christywhitman.com; 610-883-7345; http://www.bbsradio.com/hosts/divinemanifesting/; http://www.christywhitman.com; Christy Whitman. Best method: E-mail me with a pitch and bio first. No response? Follow up with another e-mail.

Invited Back? Good show, informative and upbeat.

Bio of Christy Whitman: Founder of magnetizewhatyoudesire.com and divinemanifesting.com, Christy is the best-selling author of *Perfect Pictures*, which helps people free themselves from the idea that they must always be infallible, and *Why Did She Choose Suicide?* both published in 2003 by GMA Publishing.

She is a respected businesswoman, who has spent the majority of her professional life in sales and marketing and been the recipient of awards from every company for which she has worked.

A well-known public speaker, Christy runs women's empowerment workshops and seminars, and is building a platform that is centered on women who are ready to let go of female competition in their lives. She also speaks in high schools and colleges on the topic of suicide prevention.

She is a graduate of Arizona State University, and holds a Bachelor of Science in organizational communication. Christy has engaged in a meditative spiritual practice for many years and is a graduate of Light Body and Theta, which is a healing modality transforming a person's beliefs, and healing at the soul level.

Christy is a Certified Law of Attraction coach and has helped hundreds of her clients create their ideal bodies, find their ideal partners, and create more success in their lives. She speaks at the Learning Annex in Manhattan, San Diego, Los Angeles, and San Francisco on "How to Attract Anything and Anyone by Using the Law of Attraction."

Bio of Rebecca Grado: Rebecca is a licensed marriage and family therapist in the San Francisco Bay Area. She holds a Master of Science degree in counseling, and a Bachelor of Arts degree in clinical psychology. For over twenty years, she has maintained a thriving private practice and has helped many women access their power and potential through the techniques taught in this book. Rebecca takes a unique, holistic approach to healing and promoting well-being. She blends traditional psychotherapy with spiritual practices in a way that recognizes and honors her clients' essential nature and higher purpose.

Rebecca also leads several meditation groups — both intensive and ongoing — and is connected to a rapidly developing platform of individuals who are seeking self-empowerment and greater freedom in their lives. She is also the clinical director and supervisor for MFT interns at Awakening: A Center for Exploring Living and Dying. She has been guiding MFT interns for many years, as they navigate through the journey of self-discovery as clinicians. To augment her spiritual approach to mental health, Rebecca has completed extensive coursework at the Berkeley Psychic Institute, and is a graduate of their Clairvoyant Training Program. Rebecca is also a graduate and certified teacher of Light Body, an intense meditation program that focuses on harmonizing and balancing energy centers, as well as creating emotional flow and physical vitality. A respected teacher of both Light Body and energetic healing, in addition to her psychotherapy practice, Rebecca is a font of information and assistance for a variety of alternative-healthcare practitioners.

The Dr. Anne Marie Evers Show on Contact Talk Radio, aired in Seattle over Radio Station 106.9 FM HD CHANNEL 3. Dr. Anne also co-hosts shows with Greg Norman of WARL 1320 A.M. Providence, Rhode Island.

Theme: Positive affirmations and giving hope to people worldwide.

Guest Profile: Positive, uplifting guests. I look for a guest that has a very interesting and newsworthy topic. He or she must be positive and uplifting and have good, solid knowledge to share with my listeners. I feel the most important information I need to know about the guest is their credentials and how their voice sounds over the radio.

Guest from Hell: My idea of a guest from hell is one that speaks in a very low monotone voice so I have to strain to hear every word. Another guest from hell would be one that hogs the conversation and does not let the interviewer get a word in edge wise and when I ask him or her a question they respond always with the tag ... and my website is ... my e-mail is ... and my phone number is ... etc.

Contact: annemarieevers@shaw.ca; http://www.annemarieevers.com; http://stores.lulu.com/affirmations8; 604-988-9907. Best method: E-mail (phone is fine too). I would prefer to have them send me a press kit and if they don't have one, then send me their bio and their website information. No response? I would ask him or her to please e-mail me again or call me directly at 1-604-988-9907 as I have a very busy practice and sometimes I find it hard answering all my e-mails in a very short period of time quite challenging.

Invited Back? I invite a guest back when I feel their information and delivery is excellent and that my listeners really and truly enjoyed the interview. My e-mails give me a great deal of feedback about my guests.

Bio of Dr. Anne Marie Evers: Dr. Anne has been passionately involved in the personal growth field for many years as an ordained minister, Doctor of Divinity, motivational speaker, affirmations coach, teacher, columnist and producer and host of her radio show.

Her four "Affirmation" books, all published by Affirmations-International Publishing, are: *Affirmations: Your Passport to Happiness* (2007 7th edition), *Affirmations: Your Passport to Lasting Loving Relationships* (2002), *Affirmations: Your Passport to Prosperity/Money* (2003), *Affirm and Learn Enhancement Program for Children* (2003).

She is also co-author of the best-selling series, *Wake Up and Live the Life You Love* (Global Partnership 2006) with Drs. Deepak Chopra and Wayne Dyer.

Dynamic Transformations Where Intuition and Inspiration Collide with Mark Patterson on Blog Talk Radio on http://www.blogtalkradio/dynamic-transformations on Wednesdays, 7–8 PM (MT) and 9–10 PM (ET), and on Independent Production of Evolution Revolution at http://www.evolutionrevolutionradio.com and http://www.DulcineasDivinevision.com; his show was previously on Sedona Talk Radio (STR).

Theme: We offer live readings on air to help guests with their problems or unanswered questions. Every now and then I throw in my writing or work. "God's Life as You," "She Wants Your Shiva" (What women really want from men) or I'll do a "new thought" message, i.e., Michael Beckwith.

Guest Profile: Psychics, astrologers, mediums who have authenticity, sincerity, and a desire to be of service to humanity. Want to know — Who were they referred by? What is their web site like? What is their bio like? What others have said? Do they "show up" on time?

Guest from Hell: One who is non-responsive to questions. Meaning there are a lot of pauses, I am not sure, etc. I also don't like guests who e-mail you a set interview with their questions. It has to be live, spontaneous, etc.

Contact: celestialovertones@hotmail.com; 941-375-8940; http://www.thegodtone.com; http://www.blogtalkradio.com/dynamictransformations; Mark Patterson. Best method: E-mailing me a bio and a web page works best. No response? I always reply within 24 hours. However, they can call me.

Invited Back? Audience participation and response determines if a guest comes back or not.

Guest Comment: "Mark Patterson is a really good host on a very new talk radio station and I thoroughly enjoyed working with him. Both author-friendly and media savvy, Mark not only makes a great effort to promote each one of his upcoming broadcasts with flyers and reminders before the program, he takes great pride in promoting each one of his guests when he does. It shows too because during my guest appearance on *Dynamic Transformations*, the chatroom as well as the phone lines were just the way every guest hopes they'll be ... jammed and jumping. Mark's a credit to STR but even more importantly, he's a really nice guy." — Marguerite Manning, author of *Cosmic Karma, Understanding Your Contract with the Universe* (Llewellyn Publications 2007), http://www.margueritemanning.com

Bio of Mark Patterson: Mark is an internationally acclaimed Sound Healer in Venice, Florida, who received his ability to heal others through sound in a near death experience. He has experienced the angelic realms since childhood and his intuitive abilities are very accurate.

He attended undergraduate and graduate school at New Mexico State University in Las Cruces, New Mexico (psychology and communications).

He is the author of *A Mystic's Way* (Writer's Showcase Press 2003) and *You Are God* (Writers Club Press 2000). Mark's Documentary DVD/CD, "The Sound of Stillness," is a remarkable story of his uncanny abilities with sound.

Currently, Mark is working on two audio programs, "She Wants Your Shiva" (Being Spiritual while Remaining Masculine) and "God's Life as You."

Mark resides in Venice, Florida, with his wife Tiffany and two sons, Richie and Austin.

Earth Angel with Carol Guy on Blog Talk Radio, http://www.blogtalkradio.com/earth-angel

Theme: Angels and other spiritual teaching.

Guest Profile: Angel counselors, spiritual teachers,

healers, life coaches. I look at the person's work and what they do. If I enjoy and believe in their teaching then I ask them to be a guest. I want people who I believe teach truth and honesty. I teach about angels. I hear, see, and feel them. I am guided to most of my guests and their work. All my guests are teachers of spirituality or authors. I study their work first. I also exchange e-mails and phone calls before I invite a guest to my show to see if we are going to be a good fit in conversation.

Guest from Hell: I have had one and I learned from this. Someone who thinks they know it all and tries to overpower the host.

Contact: cdgl059@aol.com; 2354-289-7106; http://www.carolguy.conm and http://www.anauthenticlife.com; Carol Guy. Best method: Phone. No response? I feel that if someone takes the time to e-mail me then I will get back with them as soon as I can. They can e-mail me if I hadn't responded back to them; e-mails do go to spam and I didn't see it.

Invited Back? I will invite a guest back if we had fun teaching and sharing ideals that will help people.

Guest Comments: "I've been on many shows and you are a natural! I can tell that you love it. Thank you for having me on the show. It was a joy."— Peggy McColl, goal coach and author of *Your Destiny Switch* (Hay House 2007), http://www.destinyswitch.com

"I had a great time on the show, it was really a lot of fun. I feel honored that you asked me."— Tony Masiello, psychic, medium and author of an e-book, *Whispers of the Universe*, http://www.universalinsight.com

Bio of Carol Guy: Carol is an angelic counselor and life fitness coach with an extensive background in metaphysical studies and physical fitness. A former personal trainer, helping people with a physical transformation, she finds that in her life of yo-yo dieting and endless weight loss programs that something was missing in relation to a healthy body. She is gifted in clairvoyance, clairaudience, clairsentience, and claircognizance. She communicates with angels, fairies, nature spirits, animals, and deceased loved ones.

Carol is the author of *A Healthy Mind Leads to a Healthy Body* (iUniverse 2007) that talks about fitness and *Coming Out of the Spiritual Closet: Being an Earth Angel* (CreateSpace 2007) that tells of her journey with angels.

Earth Harmony Divinations with Elizabeth Peter on BBS Radio, http://www.bbsradio.com Station 1 every second Friday of the month at 11 AM to 12 PM (PT) 2–3 PM (ET).

Theme: Topics vary from abundance consciousness, divination methods, BaZi and Tarot readings, interviews with intuitives, seekers and other light beings. (BaZi is not about fortune telling—it is about empowering individuals. Through a good understanding of their strengths and weaknesses and with a thorough knowledge of challenges that are likely to take place, BaZi enables an individual to take charge of their destiny, to be pro-active in overcoming challenges and to effectively fulfill their life potential).

Guest Profile: Brings light and positive outlook with an encouraging tone and good timing/exchange while talking. Subject matter is well researched, they know what they are talking about, genuine interest, ethical conduct.

Guest from Hell: Hogging time, negative, combative—not staying on the subject.

Contact: elizabeth@redlotus.org; 503-697-6909; 1-800-720-5592; http://www.redlotus.org; Elizabeth Peter. Best method: E-mail or phone. E-mail me a subject synopsis and short bio. No response? I will respond with a yes or no.

Invited Back? Time and interest in the same subject.

Listener Comments: "Your subject on the history of the Tarot (No. 3 show) was very interesting, I learned so much."— Wendy Parker, Denver, CO

"I love the format of your show: you begin and end with a positive affirmation. I also love your topics — I will tune in every time."— Sheryl Nairn, Santa Maria, CA

Bio of Elizabeth Peter: Elizabeth is an expert BaZi consultant and clairvoyant life coach.

"Life's changes are the greatest opportunities for spiritual growth," she says. "Fear can keep us from accepting change." Elizabeth has spent close to 25 years helping people reach success in their lives. She offers effective coaching expertise coupled with the deep knowledge of the Ancient Art of Chinese method of Destiny Analysis, BaZi for short: "BaZi helps us make informed decisions in life."

From an early age, Elizabeth felt different, but did her best to fit in and keep her abilities and sensitivities well hidden. From a working-class home in a humble town of Hungary, she journeyed at the age 19 through countries of Austria, Switzerland, Germany, France, learning the languages and the culture wherever she lived. Her life path led her to the United States, and became her second home for the past 30 years.

Full bio at http://www.redlotus.org

Embracing Mother Earth with Tazz Powers and Paula Nunes, airs Thursdays on KKUP 91.5FM in Santa Clara, California (South Bay) and on Blog Talk Radio, www.blogtalkradio.com/tazzandpaula

Theme: We want to present the credible edge in science, religion and culture. We want to inform you about the real unknown—the world of genuine scientific mysteries and possibilities that the general media ignores.

Guest Profile: Authors, counselors, healers, shamans, scientists, plus many more. We want guests who can keep our listeners interested (well versed in their subject and have upbeat, clear and loud voices).

Guest from Hell: One who we interview for one hour, but only has 10 minutes worth of material. One who we can barely hear and have to ask repeatedly to speak up.

Contact: info@tazzandpaulashow.com; 916-797-1033 or 408-554-9000; http://www.tazzandpaulashow.com; Paula or Tazz. Best method: E-mail. Their bio should cover their experiences and credentials. Past interviews are helpful. If the guest is an author, we like a copy of their latest book. Sending a press kit is great. No response? If we don't e-mail you back in a reasonable time, give us a call.

Invited Back? Good response from our listeners.

Guest Comments: "Tazz and Paula form a dynamic team that works brilliantly to showcase the very best that their Guests have to offer. Through their innate ability to ask relevant questions, they're able to probe deeply into a subject matter while, at the same time, openly sharing their own human reactions to what is being revealed in the discussion. By deliberately keeping it casual and low-key, they effectively invite their listeners to eavesdrop on some fascinating conversations among three friends who are sharing informally and even intimately about some very important topics."—Chuck

"I have been interviewed many times, by many people, but today's interview with the two of you was the best by far! I hope I have the opportunity to be on your show again."—Peggy Black

Bios of Tazz and Paula: The Tazz and Paula cohost combo began in 1989 in Cupertino, California, when a mutual media friend urged them to meet. Paula invited Tazz's TV camera crew and radio taping devices into the BOOK JUNCTION (Paula's bookstore) every Saturday afternoon, where they simultaneously taped live TV and radio programs with guest authors from around the world along with audience participation. The television videos were also played for the greater Bay Area Community channels, while KEST, 1450 AM, aired the audio portion.

After a year, circumstances took Tazz and Paula in separate directions, but they met again in 1995 and resumed their love of live dual-host community radio programming on KKUP. Presently, Tazz and Paula are in the last throws of completing their long time vision, which is an international talk show *Community* with "LIVE" audio broadcasting 24/7 on the Internet. The community consists of individuals who host their own talk show from their computer at an affordable rate. The growth of the community excels as each program host brings their listeners to the website.

Going Global for Spirit with Elaine Ireland on BBS Radio, http://www.bbsradio.com on Wednesday, 7:55–8:55 PM (CT); now off the air.

Theme: Spirit/metaphysical lessons of life and sharing one's experiences with the world.

Guest Profile: Knowledgeable, caring, willing to share their experiences in a straightforward and open manner. I look for ease of communication and knowledge in my guest.

I want to know where their experiences are based, what they intend to do with their knowledge and what is their motivation for wanting to be on the show. Credentials and sound of their voice is good as well.

Guest from Hell: My idea of the guest from hell is one that is stiff and unresponsive. Arrogance and a "better than thou attitude" is not welcome.

Contact: eionly@aol.com; elaine@elaineirelandpsychic.com; 512-922-4723; http://www.elaineirelandpsychic.com; Elaine Ireland. Best method: Phone. Please approach me with an introductory phone call or e-mail and give me the option of requesting a promo kit that includes a bio. No response? If I do not respond in a reasonable amount of time to that first e-mail or phone call I would appreciate another contact attempt.

Invited Back? A guest is welcomed back if the audience has responded positively and I "feel" that they are coming from a solid space and we, as a team, can share their experiences well.

Bio of Elaine Ireland: Elaine believes that life gives us many choices and that we have the freedom of will. But, because we are all part of the whole we have an interconnectedness that gives us responsibility for our choices. It is the balance between our individual free will and our responsibility to the interconnection that often brings challenges to our lives.

With that in mind, for the 40+ years that she has been doing Tarot and psychic readings, she has been blessed with clients that have shared many challenges with her. As a teacher of three levels of Tarot and ongoing psychic development classes, she uses her experience and knowledge to help guide you towards a path that can be helpful with your spiritual growth.

Before coming to BBSRadio, Elaine hosted a show on VoiceAmerica.com.

GoofyGoddess Radio with Licia Berry on Blog Talk Radio, www.blogtalkradio.com/goofygoddess

Theme: Life and spirituality.

Guest Profile: Authors, teachers, visionaries, interesting and intelligent people who are living their passion in the world. I am attracted to guests that are intelligent, joyful and doing inspiring work in the world ... their messages are positive, uplifting and empowering. I would need to feel very confident about their body of work; I read and research all of my guests, and if what they do is a good fit for me, I invite them on.

Guest from Hell: Gosh, I've never had one of these.... I am very discerning about who I choose for a guest; their work and walk in the world must resonate deeply with me before I would let them on my show.

Contact: licia@liciaberry.com; 719-657-0424; http://www.liciaberry.com; http://www.goofygoddess.com; http://www.berrytrip.us; Licia Berry. Best method: E-mail is the best way to reach me for guest spot approaches; I work on the phone a lot in my practice, so it is hard to reach me by phone. I value my privacy very much, so calling would be a sure way NOT to get on my show. No response? E-mail me again.... I check e-mail all day long, so there is no reason I would be delayed in getting back to them unless I didn't get their e-mail in the first place. Again, don't call.

Invited Back? If we have a good time, and if I feel the segment was engaging and thought provoking.

Bio of Licia Berry: Licia is a reverend, teacher, energy facilitator, and wise woman, a/k/a The Goofy Goddess. She is a recognized WiseWoman, soul-tender and bridger of worlds, who teaches others to reclaim their joy and purpose in their lives through her writing, art and spiritual teaching practice. Called a "True Human" by her indigenous contemporaries, she joyfully stretches to the spirit realm while having her feet firmly on the ground; her most passionate message is to love ourselves unconditionally.

A translator for the angelic realm, Licia's message to the world is one of joy, play, and affirmation of our power as creators. Finding the angels (aka Divine Comedians) to be harmonious playmates, she delights in the respectful and straight-forward wisdom that is offered from that realm. Through tele-classes, playshops and private practice, she assists others to wake up to their most joyful life. Licia feels that the path of wisdom is to embrace what we are rather than to resist it. She says, "It is only through acceptance and love that we find ourselves already on the path."

Licia and her husband have two growing sons and a blissed-out cat in the boonies of Colorado.

Happy Hour Radio with Sandi C. Shore on BBS Radio, http://www.bbsradio.com/HappyHourRadio, Thursdays, 7–8 PM (PT); now off the air.

Theme: Metaphysics and standup comedy. "Don't you think we take life too seriously?"

Guest Profile: Authors, psychologists, metaphysicians? Animal intuitives, ... science, topical ... nothing mainstream. Subject knowledge and new and interesting topics are important. I want to know their credentials and track record.

Guest from Hell: Someone who talks over the show host and doesn't listen.

Contact: Sandi@sandishore.com; 760-271-0277; http://www.sandishore.com; Sandi Shore. Best method: E-mail a bio. No response? E-mail again.

Invited Back? I'll ask them.

Guest Comment: "That was the BEST radio show I ever did! Thanks, Sandi! You are a great host and I would do your show every week — if you'd let me." — Stewart Swerdlow, http://www.expansions.com

Bio of Sandi Shore: Sandi grew up around "lots of amazing comedians." Her home-away-from-home was The Comedy Store in Hollywood, where she has been teaching classes since 1992. She now lives in La Jolla.

Sandi's father is the legendary Sammy Shore, her mother is Mitzi Shore who owns both the La Jolla and Hollywood locations, and her brother, Pauly Shore, is an actor, director and producer.

"I am Sandi Cee Shore," says Sandi. "What does that tell you? My parents definitely had a sense of humor and I can appreciate that."

The Heart and Home Healing Show with Faith Ranoli on http://www.HealthyLife.net

Theme: Real estate, spiritual — designed to teach people how to heal their lives and their homes.

Guest Profile: Real estate related as well as guests who support health of spirit and home. Their work reflects the value of the show, real estate education or healing of heart and home. Their body of work, what makes them an expert in their field and how well they convey that information to my listeners.

Guest from Hell: One who is not prepared and doesn't give details of their work.

Contact: FaithRanoli@aol.com; 303-797-0884; http://www.HeartAndHomeHealing.com; Faith Ranoli. Best method: Either calling or e-mailing with a pitch or media kit. No response? Follow up with a call.

Invited Back? The information they provide.

Bio of Faith Ranoli: Faith's vision is to help heal the planet, one person and one home at a time.

She offers a range of workshops, heart and soul healing sessions, consultations, and books — each with a transformative, holistic point-of-view.

One of the few holistic home inspectors in the United States, Faith is an Earth acupuncturist and a student of geobiology. She believes that everything is connected, energetically — feelings, bodies, pets, homes, the Earth, water, even inanimate objects such as furniture, rocks, and TVs.

With more than 35 years in the construction industry, Faith counsels homeowners and realtors on how to find the best home inspector. As a house psychic, she works with energy fields and emotional blocks to help homeowners discover the soul of their home.

Faith holds a Ph.D. in metaphysical studies and is a certified heart and soul practitioner and graduate of the Institute of Multidimensional Cellular Healing.

Full bio at http://www.heartandhomehealing.com

Intuitive Living with the Rev. Therese Inzerillo (interfaith minister and holistic health practitioner) on http://www.intuitivelivingministry.org/radiopage, Monday at 6 PM (MT) and on Tuesday at 4 PM (MT) on Achieve Radio, www.achieveradio.com/intuitive

Theme: Spiritual, holistic and inspirational guidance to help you live an empowered, enlightened life.

Guest Profile: Top authors, leaders and teachers in the arena of spirituality, interfaith, peace, multicultural, holistic health, self-empowerment, self-realization, evolution of consciousness and inspiration.

Someone who authentically is about "service" and helping to uplift the consciousness of the planet with the knowledge they have to share. Credentials, background and their message are primary.

Guest from Hell: A guest that totally dominates the conversation, talks a hundred miles a minute, never comes up for air and will not allow for the flow of conversation between parties. Also, anyone who would be rude or inconsiderate to others' points of view.

Contact: intuitiveliving@qwest.net; 602-995-7360; http://www.intuitivelivingministry.org and http://www.namastecenterllc.com; Rev. Therese Inzerillo. Best method: E-mail a bio or info to intuitiveliving@qwest.net or mail a press kit to 1311 E. Helena, Phoenix, AZ 85022. No response? Send a second request via e-mail or call.

Invited Back? Rapport is key… Also if their message is evolving and there is new information to impart.

Guest Comment: "Being interviewed by the Rev. Therese Inzerillo for her talk show, *Intuitive Living*, was a delight. Her inquisitive, present style allowed the space for fresh, authentic conversation. And isn't that what people are hungry for? Conversation that matters, conversation about the best in human nature and the conditions that allow for its emergence." — Joan Borysenko, Ph.D., *New York Times* best selling author, http://www.joanborysenko.com

Bio of the Rev. Therese Inzerillo: Therese has studied spirituality, world religions, metaphysics and holistic healing for the past 22 years. Her passion is to use her gifts of healing, speaking and intuition to uplift, inspire and enlighten individuals in their quest to live healthy, balanced lives, embrace their divinity and learn to use their intuition to enhance their relationship with spirit. She believes that when one follows their intuition, which is their innate inner wisdom, it is the voice of God guiding them to their highest good.

She is a graduate of the University of Missouri in Kansas City where she earned her degree in paralegal studies. After working for many years in the legal field, Therese followed her heart's desire and became a youth minister, serving as director of Youth and Family Ministry for Unity Church of Overland Park, Kansas. Although as director she served nearly 300 youth per week, she held a special gift and passion of working with teenagers.

The Reverend Therese was ordained as a minister in the International Interfaith Ministry of the Alliance of Divine Love, which promotes the philosophy of "many paths to God" and is respectful of all spiritual traditions. Her "Intuitive Living Ministry" is an international interfaith "ministry without walls" which reaches out to create bridges of understanding, compassion and world peace to people around the world by sharing spiritual truth, wisdom and divine love.

Therese resides in Phoenix, Arizona, where is the founder and director of The Namaste Center, LLC, which offers one-on-one sessions for holistic therapies, spiritual/life coaching, intuitive readings, classes, workshops, conferences, and various private and group ceremonies, including Native American Medicine Wheel ceremonies, weddings, memorials (for humans and animals), christenings, house blessings and other rites of passage. (Telephone sessions are available for coaching and readings.)

She is currently working on her first book, *The Namaste Way*, soon to be released.

Just Energy Radio with Dr. Rita Louise on http://www.justenergyradio.com

Theme: Alternative health, paranormal, New Age, spirituality.

Guest Profile: Authors of books on spirituality; spiritualists, mediums, holistic health practitioners, New Age specialists. Someone with an interesting message to share. One that will lift, inspire or share resources or new thoughts with listeners. Credentials, book titles, past experience (especially lecturing/speaking).

Guest from Hell: Someone with nothing to say or, someone who wants a monolog vs. a conversation.

Contact: rita@soulhealer.com; 972-475-3393; Dr. Rita Louise. Best method: E-mailing with a pitch/bio. Web page URL also really important. No response? Don't e-mail or call. This probably means that we are either not interested, or are not scheduling at that point in time but will keep their information on file.

Invited Back? If they have more excellent information than one show can handle.

Bio of Dr. Rita Louise: At the age of 12, Rita Louise, Ph.D., became fascinated with the concept of extrasensory perception (ESP) and that passion has lasted a lifetime. After years of intense study and in-depth research into the fields of health and wellness, psychology, philosophy and the esoteric arts and sciences, she has emerged as a leading voice in the fields of holistic health and mind/body healing.

Founder of the Institute of Applied Energetics, Dr. Rita is the host of *Just Energy Radio* and the author of the books *Avoiding the Cosmic 2 x 4* (SoulHealer Press 2004), and *The Power Within* (BookSurge Publishing 2002).

A 20-year veteran in the Human Potential Field, it is her unique gift as a medical intuitive and clairvoyant that illuminates and enlivens her work. Her unique insights bridge the worlds of science, spirit and culture and are changing the way the world views physical, mental and emotional wellbeing. Most importantly, she helps individuals reclaim their most valuable asset — their health.

Knowing Spirit Radio with Reverend Cherise Thorne and Angela Thorne on Blog Talk Radio, http://www.blogtalkradio.com/knowingspiritradio and on Live 365, http://www.live365.com/stations/reverendthorne, the show is called *Healing Your Soul Radio*.

Theme: Talks on soul healing, guidance and how to attain enlightenment. Reviews the best new literature in self-development to deliver as wide a range of thinking as possible.

Guest Profile: Spiritual teachers, healers, New Age authors, energy workers who will share their teachings of healing and add insight and techniques on how to help others heal themselves.

Guest from Hell: Some one who is only interested in pitching their new book or publisher and truly is not interested in educating my listeners.

Contact: knowingspirit@gmail.com; 773-831-4496; http://www.knowingspirit.org; Reverend Cherise Thorne. Best method: E-mailing a bio and phone follow up works very well. No response? E-mail or call.

Invited Back? If they were positive and open to engaging in an educational and uplifting dialogue.

Bio of the Reverend Cherise Thorne: The Rev. Cherise is a licensed ordained minister, spiritual teacher, healer, and the spiritual preceptor of the Temple of Knowing Spirit, an interfaith spiritual center located near Chicago, where she is a proud member of the Chicago Healers Network and offers weekly sacred gatherings and meditations, blessings of liberation, spiritual counseling, and classes.

After a profound awakening and transformation, she began dedicating herself to assisting others to open their hearts and uplift their minds. As a gifted healer and spiritual teacher, the Reverend Cherise channels divine universal energy to offer the blessing of liberation, healing through the Infinite Goddess for the purpose of re-patterning or resolving karma. She is the co-founder of New Dawn Ascension Foundation and The New Dawn School of Enlightenment, established to facilitate the spiritual evolution of all peoples drawn to the teachings of healing and unity of ALL THAT IS.

Along with clinical hypnotherapy and crisis intervention counseling she has studied many healing arts, including ancient goddess wisdom and divination, therapeutic touch, Reiki, shamanic healing, cranial-sacral therapy, healing touch, astrology, Kriya yoga, Hatha yoga, magnified healing, and Zen Shiatsu massage therapy.

Lanto's Lantern with Suzanna Axisa on Contact Talk Radio, http://www.contacttalkradio.com

Theme: Putting together a spiritual toolkit so that each spiritual seeker can step into their own mastery.

Guest Profile: Expert practitioners in the various modalities (astrology, Reiki, Aura Soma, crystals, heart healing, numerology, etc.). Someone who is very knowledgeable about their field, but who can help the listeners share their passion for their subject and get them the help they need in a concise, approachable and easily digestible way. Their professional credentials; their personal credentials (how generous they are with sharing their knowledge and their complete belief in what they do), are they concise in their answers and do they listen well; do they have a good radio voice and can we work together well?

Guest from Hell: I've not had one so I don't think I can answer that with any degree of objectivity.

Contact: suzanna@axisalighthouseintuition.com; (Italy) 0461 861 564; http://www.axisalighthouseintuition.com; Suzanna Axisa. Best method: They should contact me by making a targeted approach and sending a brief e-mail explaining what they do, preferably with their website so I can do some research about them on my own. I am increasingly getting recommendations from other guests about potential guests, which works very well for me. Above all they should listen to my show and look at my website so that they know the sort of work I do before approaching me. No response? It's either because the approach is a round robin so I'm not interested, or I'm travelling and either have no Internet access or don't have the time to check my e-mails. If the approach is a personal one (e.g. directed only at me) then it is worth sending me another e-mail and I will reply as soon as I can, even if the answer is in the negative.

Invited Back? The response from the listeners. If we have a lot of call-ins and there is excitement in the chatroom during the program I know that this guest is right for the listeners.

Guest Comment: "Suzanna Axisa is more than just a gifted metaphysician and one of my favorite people. She's also a great Internet radio talk show host who never fails to be as genuinely invested in her guest's work as she is passionately immersed in her own. As an author and frequent guest on her radio program, I love working with Suzanna almost as much as I feel blessed knowing her. Not just because of the fun we always seem to have on *Lanto's Lantern*, but because of the generous spirit she never fails to display when making her guests feel welcome and her listeners feel important."—Marguerite Manning, author *Cosmic Karma: Understanding Your Contract with the Universe* (Llewellyn Publications 2007), http://www.margueritemanning.com

Bio of Suzanna Axisa: We all have a lighthouse in our lives—someone to guide us through the storms and act as the beacon to show us the way through the fog, the rocks and the waves to safety.

Born to a 15-year-old schizophrenic mother and violent father, Suzanna's childhood allowed her to experience the whole range of storms as a "guest" of numerous state homes and private families. She escaped to university at the age of 19 and spent the next 20 years of her life alternating between trying to make sense of and denying her childhood.

At the age of 40 a heart attack brought her face to face with the decision to live or die. Determined not to die before she had led the life she knew was waiting for her, she set out on her road to recovery and the realization of how wonderful life can be when we honour our gifts.

A change management specialist with companies and charities in the UK and Italy for over 20 years, Suzanna now works with individuals who want to change some aspect of, or simply move forward with their lives, because her personal path to healing makes her uniquely equipped to help. Everyone who knows that a life of joy and abundance is theirs for the taking; all they need is a lighthouse to guide them.

She teaches workshops on how to develop your intuition and become your own master in Europe, Asia and Scandinavia and is writing a book about how to use the spiritual map that is each soul's birthright to abundance.

Life Beyond Reason with Margo Carrera on http://www.WIBMNews.com

Theme: Become inspired by those who are tapping into their intuition and creating change in the world.

Guest Profile: Our guests are those who are tapping into their spirit to celebrate life, to inspire, to unfold new way of thought, to bring forth new technology that is making a difference in our world today. A person who has gone beyond the defined. Someone who is presenting new thought, new technology, or new healing modalities. I choose to know what their view is on life. What are they bringing forth that has never been spoken about in the mainstream circles and then have them tell us how they came about their new insights.

Guest from Hell: Someone who doesn't fit the criteria for my show.

Contact: MargoCarrera@aol.com; 760-436-3004; http://www.WholisticHealth.net; http://www.LifeBeyondReason.com; Margo Carrera. Best method: E-mail a bio and a short paragraph on what they wish to share about themselves. No response? Call, if I don't respond their e-mail probably got lost in cyberspace or spam mail.

Invited Back? If they have something new to share.

Guest Comments: "Thank you sooooo much Margo. The show really turned out well. I had no idea how good it was until I listened to it. I felt so connected talking with you."—Susan Wight, U.S. Director of Education for Venus Sequence Program

"You asked questions that no one had ever asked before."—World spiritual teacher, Mirabai Devi

Bio of Margo Carrera: Margo is a transformational coach known for her ability to permanently shift old patterns of thought and behavior that has lasted lifetimes to restore personal freedom and integrity of the true self. She is also known for her spiritual work with the Great Council of the Grandmothers. She shares their messages with women all over the World.

She is the visionary founder of Encinitas Integrated Wellness Center, where traditional healers, alternative healers, and medical doctors work together to restore health and vitality to their patients.

Lights On! with Nancy Lee on http://www.NancyLee.net, http://www.HealthyLife.net; http://www.Penquinradio.com, and http://www.Earthlink.net

Theme: Inspirational, motivational, consciousness-raising; evolutionary radio.

Guest Profile: Authors, speakers, healers, teachers, experts in the body-mind-spirit arena. The ideal guest knows their material well, but can be flexible in subject matter, is not afraid to be real, and has a positive outlook. This includes showing mutual respect for the audience, for self, and for the host. Would like to know their past interview experiences, credentials and sound of their voice.

Guest from Hell: The guest from hell is an extremist in one of two ways: The first gives very short "yes-no" answers. The other speaks on top of the host, doesn't answer the questions asked, and inserts their prepared speech into any question. To have a question ignored or dismissed without addressing even the refusal to do so is a big red flag. It all boils down to professionalism, being courteous and kind, and realizing that the show platform is a gift given to promote your book. There is a two way conversation that is the interview, not the stage for a monologue.

Contact: lightson@nancylee.net; 970-472-9104; http://www.NancyLee.net; Nancy Lee. Best method: Send a press kit, then follow with a phone call and e-mail. No response? Persistence works.

Invited Back? If we have a need to continue the conversation, or if there is new material coming.

Guest Comment: "Nancy is a bright spirit—a shining star in the constellation of internet radio. She has a deep understanding of spiritual truth and draws the best out of her knowledgeable guests. Her interviews will lift you out of the doldrums and leave you soaring in skies of spirit!" Richard Salva, minister, Past Life Expert, author of *Soul Journey from Lincoln to Lindbergh* (Crystar Press 2006).

Bio of Nancy Lee: Nancy is an internationally known media personality, author, spiritual intuitive counselor, medium, teacher, and keynote speaker, and was most recently inducted into the Colorado Association of Psychotherapists.

Nancy, BA, DD, is the CEO and founder of Visionary Communications, Inc., a multi-media company, and the creator and host of her radio show, on since 1997.

She is the author of *Voices of Light: Conversations on the New Spirituality* (Chrysalis Books 2003) (http://www.Swedenborg.com), a compilation of 14 of her best interviews from her show when it was on KCOL Colorado for seven years, and *Awakening the Mystic: Adventures in Living from the Heart* (AuthorHouse 2006). She has a BA in English literature and is an Honorary Doctor of Divinity from ULC.

She lives in Fort Collins, Colorado.

Live Your Purpose Radio with Michelle Vandepas on Blog Talk Radio, http://www.blogtalkradio.com/LiveyourPurpose

Theme: Inspiration and spiritual self-help.

Guest Profile: Self improvement, spiritual, coaches etc. Personal experiences to draw from. Able to engage in conversation — not having to stick to a script. Why are they doing what they are doing? Everyone has a story, what is yours?

Guest from Hell: Someone who wants to promote themselves, but only talks about themselves and keeps plugging whatever they have to sell relentlessly. I'll plug your book and your site or whatever, please guest, keep it interesting so people care about what you have to offer

Contact: michelle@divinepurposeunleashed.com; 719-527-1404; http:divinepurposeunleashed.com; Michelle. Best method: Phone or e-mail. I love getting a personal e-mail or a phone call. The press kit is candy. Do we have a connection? Are you friendly? Approachable?. No response? I should respond so if I don't it's because it slipped through or I got busy and forgot. Please e-mail or call again.

Invited Back? If I had fun and it was an easy interview. If we got to explore and inspire.

Guest Comments: "That was such fun to be on your podcast. I think you did a really professional job — so much so that I started to think 'Is this an interview or a chat with an old friend?' Thanks for having me on. I enjoyed every minute."— Corinne Edwards, TV interviewer, http://personal-growth-with-corinne-edwards.com

"Thanks so much again, Michelle, for the interview — I had a great time talking with you about the wide range of subjects we covered (whew!), and (in my humble opinion) it was the best interview I've done yet."— Adam Kayce, http://monkatwork.com

Bio of Michelle Vandepas: Michelle is living her divine purpose by gently nudging others to theirs. She is a leader who inspires others to action. Along with her radio show, she has a blog and is a speaker.

Michelle is author of *Marketing for the Holistic Practitioner* (Conscious Destiny 2003), produced a documentary on creativity and was president of a medical manufacturing company. She's also owned a restaurant, a homeopathic laboratory and a computer store. Her focus in the corporate world combined with entrepreneurial experience allows her to resonate and connect with business audiences. Michelle loves to discuss personal development and the role of spirituality and conscious living in the workplace.

Manifest Change Now with Elaine Maroulakos Edelson on Contact Talk Radio, Wednesdays, at 5 PM (PT) and 106.9 hd3 Seattle Satellite radio in 200 countries; now off the air.

Theme: Conscious awareness, well-being, personal growth.

Guest Profile: Metaphysical and change-agent authors, celebs, entertainers and those who've undergone miracle changes. Someone who has faced fear and overcome personal odds to achieve a dream. Want to know their past interview experiences, credentials, sound of their voice plus what they did to overcome fear.

Guest from Hell: Someone who doesn't listen and who shows lack of gratitude.

Contact: Aum1133@msn.com; 928-284-3716; http://www.manifestchangenow.com, http://www.thewholecosmos.com http://www.minutestomanifesting.com and http://www.contacttalkradio.com/hosts/edelson.htm; Elaine Maroulakos Edelson. Best method: E-mail first — in three sentences who they are and how they manifested a change. No response? E-mail again — timing is key and we can't control cyberspace.

Invited Back? Rapport with host and information imparted.

Bio of Elaine Maroulakos Edelson: A modern mystic, Elaine has spent 20 years as a spiritual, intuitive counselor to 74 countries. She's a professional intuitive/empathy, astrologer, energy worker, and is certified in applied kinesiology (muscle testing aka contact reflex).

Elaine is author of an e-book, *Minutes to Manifesting: How to See It, Get It, Keep It* (2007), showing how to create the life of your dreams with simple techniques.

Manifesting Miracles in Your Life with Christina Marino, airing Mondays 2–3 PM (PT) on Contact Talk Radio.

Theme: Health and wellness, self help, metaphysics.

Guest Profile: Authors of health, wellness, self help, and metaphysical topics (psychics, mediums, angel readers, intuitives). Someone who is enthusiastic and passionate about their subject matter and someone who has an interesting topic and timely topics. Credentials, past interview experience and what their topic is.

Guest from Hell: Someone who does not respond right away, no humor and talks over the host.

Contact: Christinamarino@aol.com; 818-505-9511; http://www.contacttalkradio.com/hosts/christinamarino.htm; http://www.alternativehealthcareconcepts.com; Christina Marino. Best method: They should send me a press kit through e-mail. No response? The person should e-mail me. If I don't respond, they should follow up with another e-mail in a week.

Invited Back? Personality, knowledge, pleasantness and professionalism.

Bio of Christina Marino: Christina has dedicated her life to understanding and applying the kinds of natural healing techniques perfected only by an expert few. Those lucky enough to receive treatment at Alternative Health Care Concepts remark that Christina's treatments are highly effective right away and, better yet, the health benefits stay with them over time.

With certification and training far beyond the norm, Christina has made it her life's goal to surpass standard natural healing techniques to provide her patients with a level of care and expertise that goes straight to the heart of what ails you.

A vegetarian for over 20 years and in private practice since 1994, Christina's early interest in dietary and nutritional therapies led her to pursue studies in the Oriental healing arts of Chinese herbal medicine and acupuncture. Licensed by the State Acupuncture Committee and with a "Diplomate Acupuncture" from the National Commission for the Certification of Acupuncturists, Christina received her Masters degree in traditional Oriental medicine from Emperor's College of Traditional Medicine in Santa Monica. She also completed program of study under the nation's top homeopath doctors at Hahneman's College of Homeopathy. From there, Christina moved on to a three year shamanic program through the Foundation of Shamanic Studies to learn from the well known Michael Hamer and Alicia Gates, then trained with indigenous shamans in the Peruvian Amazon. She is currently finishing a four year program in Hands on Healing with the well-respected Barbara Brennan School of Healing.

Marketing as a Spiritual Practice with Andrea Adler on Sedona Talk Radio aired once a month on http://www.sedonatalkradio.com; now off the air.

Theme: Marketing as a spiritual path introduces innovative, and inspired approaches to marketing one's business. Based on holistic PR principles, Andrea Adler engages her guests and her audience with provocative topics and solutions that stimulate new insights, new ways to create an outreach that will make your business, profitable and sustainable.

Guest Profile: All of the above plus authenticity, integrity and passion, and the ability to articulate their message in a cohesive way. I want to know that they have a desire to learn and keep learning. A guest who thinks they know everything is not interesting to me or to my audience. I want to know that they are experts in their field and that they are relevant to the show.

Guest from Hell: One who tries to sell their product or service instead of educating my audience.

Contact: andrea@HolisticPR.com; 505-983-7777; http://www.HolisticPR.com; Andrea Adler. Best method: Phone or e-mail. No response? Absolutely — call or e-mail again. Persistence is a virtue.

Invited Back? The clarity in which their information is delivered, the amount of information they have to share and their enthusiasm in which they share it.

Guest Comment: "Andrea Adler intuits your needs before you state them. Many consultants and radio interviewers give good advice but Andrea Adler's 'Great Advice' comes from her true insight into the global centric vision which is her client's real offering. Her extraordinary ability to listen provides a space for transformational messages for those who want to bring their gifts to humanity. The high frequency energy is than grounded in practical specific suggestions. Truly an "Initiation into Magnetism!" — Victoria Friedman, co-founder, Vistar Foundation

Bio of Andrea Adler: Andrea is the founder of HolisticPR.com, an international speaker, workshop presenter, and consultant. She is the author of *Creating an Abundant Practice* (Adler 20030) and *The Science of Spiritual Marketing: Initiation into Magnetism* (Prasad Publishing 2007).

Andrea specializes in educating entrepreneurs, small and large business owners, and students on the relevance of spirituality in business. She teaches a practical philosophy of consciousness that demonstrates how to integrate spiritual practice and psychological self-inquiry into a concrete and fundamental transformation of people's lives and their marketing approaches.

She lives in Santa Fe, New Mexico.

Mastering Ourselves with Keith and Sharmai Amber airs Monday thru Friday, 7–8 PM (PT) 10–11 PM (ET), Saturday, 7–9 PM (PT), and 10 PM to 12 AM (ET) in 250 markets nationwide through all major cable TV companies through CRN on http://www.crni.net/default1.aspx?date=6/29/2007andeid=265554 andpid=1 (or go to http://www.crni.net and click "List of Shows"). We also have live streaming through CRN and archives are available through TalkZone at http://www.talkzone.com/show.asp?sid=587; now off the air.

Theme: As listeners seek lifestyle changes and a better quality of life, the hosts offer them a spiritual compass to guide their way. Topics range from spirituality in the workplace, tips on effective childrearing, how to tap your own intuition, reading omens in your life to understanding karma as it applies to your life. Also covered are current events, politics, war on terror, world events all from a spiritual perspective. The show is helping humanity wake-up, one show at a time with sound answers to life's tough questions.

Guest Profile: Guests who can bring listeners tools that they can use in everyday life. Service oriented and interested in getting substance out to our audience. What value they have to give to the audience.

Guest from Hell: Over-active ego with more interest in showing what they know or wanting the center of attention.

Contact: ambers@masteringourselves.com; http://www.masteringourselves.com; Andrea Yamazaki Station Manager, KEST AM 1450, 1-415-978-5378, aya mazaki@juno.com. Best method: E-mail a pitch. No response? Do not e-mail or call. We review every e-mail. Not many get responded to. All are considered.

Invited Back? Good chemistry with hosts and more substance to share with audience.

Guest Comments: "I've been on nearly 300 radio

programs in the last year and Sharmai and Keith stand out for their personal interest and deep understanding of the topics they discuss, their rapport, commitment to serve their audience and dedication to personal growth and practical spirituality. Their message has very broad appeal. They are both delightful interviewers — with their friendly and personal style, they take their listeners on a journey through their wide-ranging questions, deep inquiry, personal sharing and insight." — Judith Wright, author of *There Must Be More Than This* (Broadway 2003), barbb@wrightlearning.com

"THANK YOU for the very positive interview! There were two things you did that I really appreciated, and that most hosts do NOT do: 1) You read my book beforehand and took a genuine interest in it, 2) You talked with me for a few minutes TWICE before the interview. That makes a winning combination! You also asked really good questions ... thanks again for the great interview" — Brooks Peterson, Ph.D., author of *Cultural Intelligence: A Guide to Working with People from Other Cultures* (Intercultural Press 2004) peterson@AcrossCultures.net

Bios of Sharmai and Keith Amber: Sharmai began her spiritual journey at age 11. At 26 a fire was ignited within her with a voice that kept repeating, "There is something I'm here to do." In search of her destiny, Sharmai and her first husband, David, moved to Portland, Seattle, and finally Mount Shasta where her spiritual studies intensified in earnest. Through a most unusual source, Sharmai was privileged to be in the presence of numerous ethereal light-beings who spoke, or channeled, through her husband David and their friend Katrina. Sharmai is the author of *The Melding* (Sambershar 1999) and *Steps to Enlightenment* (Mastering Ourselves LLC 2008).

Keith began his spiritual path at the age of nine with the realization that he was winning almost every game he played by running over the competition with the use of his willpower. This pattern soon began to fill him with disgust. At the same time, he became obsessed with who he really was at a deeper level. He began to question the purpose of his life and wonder what his direction was. He searched for answers: what is God? And, what is God's purpose for him? This was also the beginning of the life-long process of taming his inflated ego to live a more spiritual life.

He first managed one of the largest health spas in Reno, Nevada, then left to begin a full time practice as a psychic soul healer. Keith is the author of three Wisdom Toning Series CD's entitled: *Your Inner Child*, *The Mirror* and *Stay Centered in God in the Middle of Chaos*.

There was an instant connection between Keith and Sharmai when they met in 1989. They started working together, leading spiritual groups and designing workshops in Seattle and Minnesota.

The Messengerfiles with Carole Matthews on 560 CFOS, Owen Sound Ontario, and on http://www.carolematthewsintuitve.com

Theme: Informative "Now Age" topics.

Guest Profile: Authors, feng shui experts, astrologers, past life regressionists, dream analysis, etc. Enthusiasm about their purpose and of course good energy. Past interview experiences, credentials, sound of their voice, but I also like to go with the flow ... it has worked so far.

Guest from Hell: One word answers and egotistical ... so far haven't attracted that problem.

Contact: messengerfiles@hotmail.com; 519-538-1516; http://www.carolematthewsintuitive.com; http://www.mycollingwood.ca, *Tomorrow Today*; Carole. Best method: E-mailing a bio seems to be the easiest. Skype is being set up but e-mail best. No response? Oh please.

Invited Back? The above ... enthusiasm and being real.

Bio of Carole Matthews: Carole touches the lives of people everywhere, whether in a private session or broadcast to thousands over national media. Her message is one of hope, clarity and spiritual enlightenment. It is a message that few will forget.

Carole's inner strength and witty sense of humor comes from her own life: her roots in both Winnipeg and Keswick, Ontario, the challenge of two near fatal car accidents, and the joys of her three children and six grandchildren and her Bichon dog/friend Tuffy.

Carole has recently found balance with a coast to coast life style — alternating between her loyal clientele in both British Columbia and Ontario. Being a Sagittarius it is very difficult to keep her in one place.

As an intuitive medium Carole does not speak for people; rather, she opens the door to let the communication between loved ones flow. Through her, many have discovered their guardian angels — those gentle spirits who once loved us dearly and continue to guide us and guard us and therefore help to shape our lives. Carole unlocks the barriers that may prevent people from realizing their potential over personal, career, health and spiritual challenges.

Strength — passion — affirmation — these are some of the many gifts Carole leaves with her audience. Thousands have heard Carole through broadcast media such as *Jane Hawtin Live*, *The Erin Davis Show*, daytime television show and radio broadcasts on 640AM and CFRB, and numerous speaking engagements.

Metaphysical World and Beyond with Nancy Wallace on http://www.AchieveRadio.com and http://www.bbsradio.com

Theme: Interview different guests and do readings.

Guest Profile: Any and all guests. People who are knowledgeable in their field. Someone who is interesting to interview. Mostly interested in the sound of their voice.

Guest from Hell: One that does not cooperate. And doesn't talk.

Contact: nwallace77@hotmail.com; 630-941-6816; http://www.nancyspsychicresources.com; Nancy Wallace. Best method: Phone. No response? A phone call would be great.

Invited Back? If they are interesting and there is more to talk about.

Bio of Nancy Wallace: Owner and founder of Psychic Resources Unlimited, Nancy reads tarot cards. (If you see Nancy's cards you will wonder how she read them — most of the pictures are missing and they have grooves in the sides from the way she shuffles.) The cards displayed on her website are a few cards from Nancy's deck she has used for 26 years. They show the wear from all of the love that has been demonstrated to her thousands of clients across the U.S.

Her gift goes back to childhood when she could see things happen before they happened. With her compassion for people, she is a delight to have at any party/event or to have her do a reading for you. Nancy's 30-minute readings are either in person or by phone and recorded upon request.

She also does psychic pet readings, noting that pets are easier to read than a person because pets have their own psychic abilities (without the hang-ups of anyone telling them they can't). Nancy has grown from having a home-based business through a 500-square feet office within one year to a 3,500-square feet office. She has also produced two TV talk shows and a radio talk show.

Nancy is the founder of a 501c, a not for profit organization called A Child's Miracle Mind, whose motto is "For every hurt there is a helper."

Nancy hosted her own show broadcast from Zion, Illinois for ten years called *Psychic R U*.

The Michael Gogger Show on Blog Talk Radio, http://www.blogtalkradio.com/Michael-Gogger

Theme: Free Psychic readings and highlighting metaphysical world.

Guest Profile: Anything, or people making a difference in the world. Someone that can leave a footprint on the souls of my listening audience. I want to know whether or not they are sincere and I like to know what they are doing with their gifts, books, do they fundraise, do they teach, do they give back to the universe? I would rather a great teacher than a movie star.

Guest from Hell: Guest from hell would be a know-it-all and full of ego.

Contact: michael_gogger1@yahoo.com; 518-694-0120; http://www.michaelgogger.com; http://www.myspace.com/michaelgogger; Michael Gogger. Best method: E-mail me a bio; me and my staff will check it out and if they are what they say they are and I like them I will l have them on my show. Will also take calls. No response? Please e-mail me to make sure that their initial letter did arrive.

Invited Back? Their willingness to come back and their enjoyment of what I do. Traffic, exposure and if my listening audience wants them back.

Guest Comment: "Michael Gogger is more than an intuitive and a psychic. He is a warm-hearted man who gives freely of his time and energy to everyone: whether it be an interview guest or someone who calls in to his radio show. And oh, by the way, he absolutely nailed the current key issues in my life during the psychic reading he did for me on the air." — Richard Salva, author of *Soul Journey from Lincoln to Lindbergh* (Crystar Press 2006), and host of http://www.LincolnReincarnation.com

"When Michael started my reading by telling me he saw an Anthony or Tony and a Lucinda or Lucy around me, I thought he was nuts. I asked everyone in my family — no one recognized the names belonging to anyone in my family. Then he told me about a new man in my life who would give me something of sentimental value — this man already had, a bracelet of his grandmother's. Then Michael told me he saw my new man giving me a ring. Two weeks later, at a wedding reception of a friend, my man asked me to marry him and did give me a ring. Those names popped into my head and I asked him if they rang a bell with him. Wouldn't you know — Tony is his cousin and Lucy is his aunt.

"Michael is so scary accurate, he gave me goosebumps when he did my reading. And everything so far has come true." — Jayne Hitchcock, cybercrime expert and author of *Net Crimes and Misdemeanors* (Information Today, 2nd edition 2006), http://www.netcrimes.net/order.html, netcrimes.net/netcrimesblog.html

Bio of Michael Gogger: Michael is "first and foremost a family man," married for 35 years with two children and two grandchildren.

He lives in quaint sleepy village in upstate NY and is "world renowned." "I only ask that people respect my private life. I am available by phone from anywhere in the world."

A psychic medium, Michael became aware of his special gifts and developed his abilities over the past 40 years, 10 of which he has done professionally — as an intuitive consultant, entertainer, fundraiser for good causes and a radio host personality. "I have an accuracy of 98 percent with my readings," he says.

In addition to his radio shows, Michael does free group chat room shows. "An e-mail will be sent to everyone in my group membership advising of group shows and the radio show," he says. "I will also send out a mass pm to my paltalk messenger friends list, stating that a radio show or chat room show is beginning. My group chat room shows will be announced around my work and home life."

"If you have an event that is a fundraiser and benefits disabled children or educational programs, I offer my fundraising services for free," says Michael. "I have the capability of doing long distance readings via the computer, telephone, or radio with the capacity of doing non stop readings." More information is on his website.

My Spiritual Healer with Kriss Van Hook on Achieve Radio, http://www.achieveradio.com

Theme: Positive talk, spiritual growth.

Guest Profile: Authors, spiritual teachers/healers, self help speakers, metaphysical practitioners with a desire to help others through knowledge. My primary concern is the intent of the guests in regards to what information they want to share and teach. I find it helpful for "flow" of the show to clarify the guest's intent.

Guest from Hell: Someone who responds "Yes," "No" or with another repeated answer and does not expand on their information.

Contact: Kriss@myspiritualhealer.net; http://www.myspiritualhealer.net; Kriss Van Hook. Best method: It is most helpful to e-mail me a bio and I will respond with request for a press kit if the show schedule has an opening and I believe the listeners would be interested. No response? Please feel free to follow up via e-mail. Your original e-mail may have been "lost" in the quantity ... and a second e-mail helps me focus action with that potential guest.

Invited Back? The guest's energy, quality and quantity of information. If the show seemed too short, I may schedule a encore presentation. Or if the guest is an expert in various areas and communicates well, they will be higher on the "call back" list.

Guest Comments: "2007 was the first year I had done radio interviews so I was somewhat green. Kriss immediately put me at ease, and made me feel like I was talking to a friend I had known for years. She was instantly able to zero in on the points I was trying to get across, and was able to intelligently discuss those points with callers all while having fun, something that is important to me."—David Weber, http://www.therishis.com

"Being on Kriss's show *My Spiritual Healer* was such a delight! It was a very professional, yet relaxed experience from pre to post interview. Kriss's interviewing style is very fluid and easy going. I loved the fact she read my book prior to the interview and infused her own personal experiences into the interview questions, which, I believe, made the interview a rich listening experience for the audience. I would highly recommend Kriss; she is a top-notch interviewer."—Khama Anku, author of *Spiritual Physique—The Three Phases of Spiritual Fitness* (Spiritual Physique Publishing), http://www.spiritualphysique.com

Bio of Kriss Van Hook: Born in Long Beach, California, Kriss spent a major part of her childhood in hospitals, clinics and doctor offices with a poor immune system, asthma and allergies; she was unable to learn social skills and became an isolated and independent child.

Without any friends or guests to her home, Kriss was unaware that she was being raised in an unusual house. Her home was haunted and had spurts of poltergeist and apparitional activity. Kriss was able to tap into their energies, locate their "zone" and identify their "emotional imprint."

At 14, Kriss and her mother moved to Ohio where she spent 10 years completing her primary and collegiate education. During this time, her mother became "born again" and took Kriss to a lot of "teen Christian" functions. "It was during this period in my life that I really became aware that I didn't have the same belief system that others did. Prior to moving, I had never really thought that there was any confusion or conflict about what happens when we die, how we should live, etc. I was startled and needed to know if anyone else had similar beliefs and experience to mine." Kriss tried to find others who were psychic or enlightened but had little success in the Bible belt and a LOT of questions.

In her mid-20s, Kriss moved to Phoenix, Arizona, and "found" a "guided meditation" instructor. It is through this meditation class that Kriss found other beings with similar beliefs and was able to ask questions without fear of persecution.

Realizing that many people have become enlightened but are unaware of community resources, Kriss uses her website to help those individuals find an easier route to enlightenment by providing a listing of practitioners, teachers, intuitives and calendar of events.

Myth or Logic Radio with Tom Murasso and Cheryl Dobbins on Talk Shoe Radio.

Theme: Where science meets spirituality.

Guest Profile: Authors, coaches, and professionals in the self-development field who are well-versed in their field of study and enjoy helping people. Biography, topics of discussion, past, present and future works (books, courses, etc.).

Guest from Hell: Those who are not talkative.

Contact: borntomanifest@gmail.com; 509-471-7303; http://www.talkshoe.com/tc/59174; http://www.borntomanifest.com; Tom Murasso. Best method: Press kit or short e-mail with their website. No response? E-mail.

Invited Back? Number of downloads of the show they participated in.

Guest Comment: "I had very much enjoyed my first appearance on Tom's program, and your comments indicated that it has become a major favorite on everyone's list."—David Wilcock, http://www.divinecosmos.com

Listener Comment: "The *Myth or Logic Show* was truly explosive and interactive. In the chat room they had tons of people who were loving and inquisitive people. The whole experience was quite healing, rewarding and loving."—Brent

Bio of Tom Murasso: Tom is a Law of Attraction

trainer, personal coach, EFT practitioner, certified hypnotherapist, musician and author of several books on the power of the mind including *Born to Manifest: Law of Attraction Tools and Techniques* (Lulu 2007).

Tom's background as a certified hypnotherapist and student of the esoteric arts has contributed to his expertise in teaching people the amazing power of the mind and its use to consciously attract what they desire.

News for the Soul with Nicole Whitney aired on select stations in the U.S., on shortwave, on MANY Internet radio stations and affiliates ... and on http://www.newsforthesoul.com in the permanently available free radio show archives.

Theme: Life changing talk radio from the uplifting to the unexplained ... self empowerment.

Guest Profile: Anything that pertains in any way to the above mentioned theme. Someone with a valuable message of empowerment ... even our paid guests must be prescreened for our criteria of coming from the heart and living a life on purpose before they can register to join us on any broadcast. Are they authentic, on purpose and coming from a good intentioned place ... and what do they have to offer our audience in the way of making a positive difference. Her prominent guests have included Deepak Chopra and Stuart Wilde.

Guest from Hell: Bill — "fine." Someone who doesn't talk, i.e., host — "so Bill how did you feel about blabbedby blab bla?"; http://www.newsforthesoul.com

Contact: nicole@newsforthesoul.com; 604-780 NEWS [6397]; Nicole Whitney. Best method: E-mail is best but we have over a two year waiting list for guests. This is why we created the sponsored guest opportunities — the paid spots. Those enable us to continue offering our ENTIRE radio show archive free and it enables a potential guest to jump to the front of the line — a win win win for everyone involved. No response? We receive thousands of e-mails daily. And we have over a two year waiting list for guests. Having said that, e-mail is the best line of communication and it wouldn't hurt to resend once or twice — but unfortunately we are not able to guarantee any response due to the sheer volume of these requests we receive.

Invited Back? Amount of new things to offer that are of value — and audience feedback.

Guest Comments (from paid/sponsored guests): "I checked the stats to our website (I get pretty detailed stats) and discovered that over 40 percent of our visitors since the show first aired were directly from your site. THAT was pretty impressive, especially considering that most of our visitors come from Google pay per click searches. We get close to 3k visitors a month. So that says a lot for Google's efforts, but says even more about the results we just experienced from your show.... I just signed up another surprise vision quester — he's coming out tomorrow to join another quester who's been planning this for several months now. Talk about amazing results (I've never had anyone sign up one day and come out the next to do a quest. Usually, they give themselves at least two weeks or more to plan)." — Virgina Levy, http://www.mastersofsedona.com

"I admit I was a bit nervous before the interview; however, once we began our conversation I relaxed as you charmingly led me through the process. This opportunity has allowed me to see first hand just how life changing your radio show is for people. While listening, I know people's lives are touched in a way I had never before imagined, mine included." — Bethany Staffieri, http://www.concentricrings.org

Bio of Nicole Whitney: Radio producer, host, journalist, artist, musician, vocalist, writer and single mom of two children, Nicole is a true explorer in her own life as well as on the air, perpetually investigating the "reality" of our world.

She was inspired to create a more empowering form of media service in January 1998, after the growing concern of many over the amount of negativity in mainstream news.

In its early beginnings, NFTS was a positive news newspaper which grew rapidly, evolving into various formats over the years. But after 9-11, Nicole stepped fully into the world of live talk radio shows as well as "webcasting" on the Internet and has not looked back. And *NFTS*'s popularity skyrocketed, now receiving hundreds of thousands of visitors every month from 93 countries around the world.

Originally airing on CFUN in BC, *NFTS* has been a journey more than a career for Nicole who has partaken in extensive personal development and consciousness study, including all levels at remote viewing technologies with former CIA remote viewer Dr. David Morehouse, extensive training with Peak Potentials in Vancouver including four years at Success Tracks Training, Enlightened Warrior Training Camp, Enlightened Wizard Training Camp and much more.

Now That's What I'm Talking About! with Louise Aveni on Sedona Talk Radio, http://www.sedonatalkradio.com in Arizona; now off the air.

Theme: Positive talk radio.

Guest Profile: Extremely diverse. Authors, doctors on health care, psychologists, UFO abductees, spiritual activists, etc. I look for an interesting subject, well spoken, able to share something of value to listeners. Past interview experiences, credentials, sound of their voice are important. In addition, I do extensive research prior to interviews. I read their books if they are an author, I ask them for 10 questions they'd like me to ask so I stay on task with their agenda and I formulate my own questions so as to keep a nice flow going. I also talk with them several times prior to the show and explain the process.

Guest from Hell: Don't know. Never had one. But I would say that it would be a challenge to have someone who is very negative, rambles on and preaches and doesn't let the interviewer get a word in edgewise.

Contact: laveni50@yahoo.com; 941-822-0206; http://www.sedonaangels.com or http://www.louiseaveni.com; Louise Aveni. Best method: E-mail, please. I ask those interested in becoming a guest to e-mail me from my web site at http://www.sedonaangels.com. No response? That hasn't happened as I always get back to inquiries as soon as possible, as that is how I operate.

Invited Back? If they're wonderful speakers and their subject is fascinating and can't be told in one hour.

Guest Comments: "I was honored to be Louise's first guest. The show went off without a hitch and I couldn't believe that she hasn't been doing this for years! My business has increased and I've sold more books as a result of her show. Very grateful!"— Frank Kinslow, author of *Beyond Happiness* (The Peppertree Press 2006).

"I enjoyed being a guest on Louise's show and having the opportunity to share what I know as both a physician and a patient about what's wrong with today's health care system and offer some plausible solutions. Great opportunity to let people know about my book."— Dr. R. Garth Kirkwood — author of *Equal Health Care for All* (Triad Publishing Group 2007)

Bio of Louise Rose Aveni: A native of Boston, Massachusetts, Louise has dabbled in fictional writing for many years. It wasn't until her bout with cancer in the mid 80s that she found her true literary voice. Simultaneously, as her spirituality awakened, a long time curiosity with the idea of life on other planets and inter-dimensional realms gave rise to a renewed passion to explore the possibilities in earnest.

No longer concerned with how she would be perceived in her pursuit of obtaining answers to her own core questions, Louise penned her first novel, *LUPO—Conversations with an E.T.* (The Peppertree Press 2007), the first of a trilogy series with *HYBRID—The Conversation Continues* (TRIAD Publishing Group 2008). *KRYSTAL—A New Beginning* is scheduled for a 2009 release. Louise has written a children's book, *There's an Angel in My Closet,* and for the teen set, *The Prophecies of Jake Littlefeather* also slated for a 2009 release.

A keynote speaker, Louise travels around the country with other authors of like mind, such as Jim Sparks (The Keepers) and Sheldan Nidle.

She is a resident of Sarasota, Florida and Sedona, Arizona.

Peaceful Planet Show with Marcia McMahon, M.A. on http://www.bbsradio.com Sundays 12:00–1:00 P.M. (PT)

Theme: Angels, psychics/music of the angels, ascension, ancient mysteries.

Guest Profile: World renowned experts in all fields metaphysical, UFO, creative music talent, psychic readers, healers, ascension experts, Holy Grail and other art/history experts, etc. Title of the book they wrote, and area of research with credentials and or other extraordinary gifts from spirit.

Guest from Hell: Someone who thinks they know it all on a topic and won't work with you on helping an audience understand their field. Someone who is opposed to metaphysical truth, or opposed to angels, divine guidance.

Contact: marciadi2002@yahoo.com; 217-391-6701; 877-876-5227 call in toll free to BBS line 1 for those wanting a reading or to speak to our guests (not for inquires about being a guest on the show; you may e-mail Don our producer at donald@bbsradio.com for that); http://www.dianaspeakstotheworld.com; Marcia McMahon, M.A. Best method: E-mail with biography and request to be on the show; and send the book on once e-mail is confirmed. No response? E-mail again

Invited Back? Flow of the conversation, expertise of subject and command of emotions with guests who call in.

Guest Comments: "If Princess Diana were alive, would the people of the world listen to what she has to say about our current world situation? Definitely! Diana is speaking through channel Marcia McMahon. The world needs to hear what Diana has to say. Diana speaks in my channeled messages and often mentions Marcia and their conversations."— Robert Murray, author of *The Stars Still Shine: An Afterlife Journey* (Aura Publishing 2000). http://www.thestarsstillshine.com/

"How we loved Diana. We could identify with her as our very own princess as she seemed part of the world and not some lofty Royal that was untouchable. We watched her as she blossomed into a peace ambassador and celebrated with her all of her successes. We indeed grieved for her when we received the news that this inspiring life was cut short.

"Now Marcia McMahon, Diana's channel, is pulling back the curtain between our two worlds so we can see that even on the other side Diana is still working for world peace.

"As Marcia brings forth Diana's messages that she gives to us in love, we find that her special friend, Dodi, is with her and they work together in this joint effort.... We thank Marcia for her dedication to assist in this effort. The world will not find the peace that we all hunger for if these problems are not resolved."— Carolyn Evers, author *Conversations with Caeser* (Cosmic Connections 2003); htttp://www.healingmysteries.com/

Bio of Marcia McMahon: An accomplished artist and author, Marcia has her art in numerous private collections throughout the U.S., Europe, and Canada. She was recently named in Who's Who in America 2002 and for 2003 for her accomplishments.

Marcia has an MA from Case Western Reserve University and The Cleveland Institute of Art.

Her art is inspired directly by Princess Diana, and she channels her energy as she paints. Princess Diana rests peacefully here on the Oval Island at Althorp, the estate of her brother Earl Spencer. Marcia's other Diana Galleries can be found elsewhere on this site. Diana Gallery Index, http://www.dianaspeakstotheworld.com

Marcia's newest release, *With Love from Diana, Queen of Hearts; Messages from Heaven for a New Age of Peace* (Eternal Rose Pub 2005), highlights messages from Princess Diana that can if implemented save the world more terror, particularly the United States and countries in the Middle East. Princess Diana in life knew most of the world's leaders, and it should not come as a surprise that she chose her channel to assist our planet as it transforms to ascension.

Marcia gives powerful lectures and readings of Diana's messages. She brings her artwork to accompany the reading of Diana's words. Marcia also does radio and TV interviews.

Quantum Health with Pete Muran, MD, and Sandy Muran, Ph.D. in holistic nutrition, on KVEC, aired on the Central Coast, California, on Saturdays 1–1:30 PM (PT).

Theme: Education/integrated medicine.

Guest Profile: Local and national health practitioners who are leaders in integrative medicine. We look for someone who is articulate in their field of expertise, expresses excitement, has an interest in educating the community in addition to promoting their book, product, etc. A sense of humor is a plus. We would like from them: Their background (CV), areas of expertise, 15 media questions that communicate the message they wish to convey.

Guest from Hell: The guest from hell gives limited answers, speaks in a monotone and has no sense of humor.

Contact: symuran@earthlink.net; 805-548-0987; http://www.longevityhealthcare.com (Longevity Healthcare Center is the Central Coast holistic, complementary and alternative medicine health care center serving all of San Luis Obispo County and adjacent communities); Sandy Muran. Best method: E-mail a bio, send a press kit to 1241 Johnson Ave., #354, San Luis Obispo, CA. Follow up via e-mail. No response? E-mails are answered within reasonable time ... a week. Please, no phone calls.

Invited Back? Guests are invited back based on their ability to stay current in their area of expertise and, therefore, have additional information to share with the audience.

Bio of Peter J. Muran, MD, MBA: Dr. Muran entered medical practice as an emergency room physician. Throughout his eight years in emergency medicine caring for the most critical conditions, he never lost his desire to provide care that effectively considered all aspects of the individual's well being.

He was drawn away from emergency medicine to practice in the most innovative areas of health care — in-home geriatric care and hospice care. These experiences cemented his belief that optimal health care could only be achieved through consideration of the physical, emotional and spiritual facets of the individual.

The advanced science of Dr. Muran's training in Western medicine does not frequently address all the important aspects of the individual. Thus Dr. Muran developed an expertise in complementary techniques that draws upon the innovations of other cultures and experiences in health.

Dr. Muran has become a recognized expert in the treatment of candidiasis, natural hormone replacement therapy and the use of chelation for cardiac disease. He creates a partnership between traditional primary care and alternative and complementary medical practices. The intent of his medical care is to seek out the most effective, least invasive and most natural means of promoting optimal health.

The Robert Scott Bell Show on Talk Radio Network, and nationally syndicated on about 90 stations in the U.S. that focus on the theme, "The Power to Heal Is Yours" (the title of his book in progress).

Theme: Natural health, alternative medicine, the politics of healing.

Guest Profile: Authors, doctors, politicians who have passion, integrity, knowledge and confidence. Their past interview experiences, credentials, and sound of their voice are important. His prominent guests have included Dr. Bruce Lipton (cellular biologist), Aaron Russo (Filmmaker, Libertarian presidential candidate), John Stossell (ABC Network, *20/20* television host), Jane Seymour (actor), and Ed Begley (actor, environmentalist).

Guest from Hell: Lifeless, lacking passion and conviction.

Contact: rsb@talkradionetwork.com; 888-383-3733; http://www.rsbell.com, http://www.talkradionetwork.com http://robertscottbell.blogspot.com; Don Naylor, producer at don@talkradionetwork.com. Best method: E-mail to the producer. No response? It may mean that there is no interest.

Invited Back? It's up to the host.

Bio of Robert Scott Bell: Robert is a homeopathic practitioner with a passion for health and healing. He personally overcame numerous chronic diseases using natural healing principles and has dedicated his life to revealing the healing power within all of us.

He previously hosted the *Jump-Start Your Heart Radio Show* in Atlanta, GA, and *Passion for Health Television Show* in Mt. Shasta, CA.

Robert is author of *The Last Word — FDA and GMP's* (Breakthroughs in Health and Science 2006).

SAGE: Spirit, Angels and Guides Entertainment with Sher Emerick and Laura Sharp, on 1150AM

KKNW from Seattle, and streaming live on http://www.SageRadioShow.com and http://www.1150kknw.com; on hiatus while developing TV show.

Theme: SAGE is a sacred space for gifted metaphysical professionals and practitioners to share their stories and wisdom with listeners and callers from our worldwide audience.

Guest Profile: Scholars and practitioners in the metaphysical field. Skilled and experienced in metaphysical practice or studies and the ability to relate to hosts and callers with warmth and humor. Our purpose is to provide a platform for gifted practitioners who would like to expand their practice and share their gifts with a very broad audience. We would like to know prior experience in practice and/or study and potential guest's ability to converse easily, speak effectively and provide meaningful insight to callers.

Guest from Hell: A non-stop talker who spews information rather than converses with hosts and callers.

Contact: satorisevenproductions@comcast.net; 425-463-8128; http://www.SageRadioShow.com; Sher Emerick. Best method: E-mail is best — either with website/bio or press kit. No response? E-mail again. We try to respond within two business days.

Invited Back? A meaningful and mutually enjoyable interchange between guest, hosts and callers.

Guest Comments: "It has been a delight and an honor to be a guest on *SAGE Radio Show*. The hosts have been wonderfully warm and professional. They not only incorporated my suggested talking points, they creatively engaged in the discussion with their own curiosity and comments. The *SAGE Radio Show* offered ample opportunity to promote my products and websites, plus we had great fun with callers." — Mary Lee LaBay, prolific author and founder of Awareness Engineering

"Great show and great callers! You two were so easy to work with!" — Dr. Joe Dispenza, author of *Evolve Your Brain* (HCI 2007)

Bios of Sher Emerick and Laura Sharp: Master's of divinity Sher is based in Seattle, Washington. Having lived and worked on four continents, she's a natural explorer and finds her bliss in guiding others to their Satori moments: those "aha!" moments of discovering one's life purpose, wholeness and greatest joy. Sher's conversational style and her engaging qualities of compassion, clear intuitive insight and gentle humor provide the safety for her radio listeners and beloved clients to open their hearts and lives to new, empowering possibilities.

Laura, master's in counseling psychology, is based in San Francisco, California. Her international childhood influenced her inclusive nature, expanded her insight and clarity and is now a clear and direct channel of spiritual information and energy. Her work is a tremendous gift, especially in times of transition and personal change. For her radio listeners and her cherished clients, Laura is a safe and compassionate presence, a teacher, and literally a conduit that hooks one up with their own innate knowing and wisdom. Her work is extraordinary and deeply transformative.

Soul Connections with Kimberly Marooney, Ph.D., on Wednesday 5:30–6:00 PM (PT) on Internet Voices Radio. Kimberly is also host of *Angel-Love* at www.blogtalkradio.com/angel-love

Theme: When we take the time to connect with our souls, and then connect from one soul to another soul, something extraordinary happens. We create an opening for inspired, impassioned creativity to occur.

Guest Profile: Authors, musicians, people who have created something worthwhile from a mind-body-spirit connection. Someone who has personally experienced soul inspired creativity and wants to help others through sharing the realizations gained. What have they done with the realizations gained from their soul experience? Write a book, create an event or product, help people in some way? I want to see their website and product. Past interviews are helpful.

Guest from Hell: Don't know, I've never had one. Possibly someone who is not connected with themselves and has no idea what that even means.

Contact: Kimberly@KimberlyMarooney.com; 831-419-3200; http://www.KimberlyMarooney.com; http://www.internetvoicesradio.com/arch-kimberly.htm. Kimberly Marooney. Best method: E-mail a request with a short bio and pitch. If we connect, I'll ask for more. No response? E-mail again or call.

Invited Back? Did we connect from a soul level? Did they have something worthwhile to share?

Guest Comments: "As someone who has been a guest on hundreds of radio shows, my experience with Kimberly Marooney, host of Soul Connections, was by far, one of the most enjoyable. Kimberly genuinely cares about her guests. She is engaging, connected and a delight to talk with.

"Kimberly asks questions that allow for her guests to convey their message in a very relaxed and natural way. She is a delightful host and one I will remember always." — Kathleen Gage, author of *The Law of Achievement* (Maxwell Publishing 2006), http://www.kathleengage.com

"Kimberly Marooney, host of *Soul Connections* on www.internetvoicesradio.com brings inspiration and hope to listeners who are seeking a deeper connection with their spirit and the universe. As a recent guest expert on her show speaking about ways to transform fear, her easy style and faith-filled comments made the interview inspirational and uplifting. Listeners are always in for a treat when Kimberly airs." — Lorraine Cohen, business coach and life strategist, motivational speaker, radio show host. http://www.powerfull-living.biz (see page 52).

Bio of Kimberly Marooney: Kimberly has been described as a pioneer in the field of angelology and spiritual transformation. A gifted author, mystic, workshop leader, spiritual counselor and radio host, she has helped hundreds of thousands of people worldwide open to God's love, heal and move forward on their life paths.

The turning point in Kimberly's life came during her tenure as vice president of a financial planning practice when a devastating illness forced her to resign. Near death, Kimberly turned to God in a deep and passion prayer of surrender. In response, the heavenly host descended to cradle Kimberly in love and invite her to co-create a bridge to spirit.

Over the next few years, the angels infused her with the energetic essence of God while she wrote her first book, *Angel Blessings*. Kimberly shares this essence by connecting others with the aspects of God's love they most need through her books, workshops, and private healing sessions. This extensive background in mysticism earned Kimberly one of the first Master's degrees in angelology and a Doctorate in spiritual psychology. A respected author, her three internationally acclaimed books for self-transformation follow the angel's path to the soul: *Angel Blessings: Cards of Sacred Guidance and Inspiration* (Merrill West Publishing 1995); *Your Guardian Angel in a Box* (Fair Winds Press 2003) and *Angel Love Cards of Divine Devotion, Faith and Grace* (Fair Winds Press 2004).

Soul Journeys Live with Jennifer Longmore on Contact Talk Radio and WARM 106.9 HD3 radio in Washington.

Theme: Spiritual growth and development.

Guest Profile: Authors, psychics, spiritual leaders, healers, astrologers, metaphysicians. Someone who is an expert in their field who can provide deep insight into a particular area of spirituality; one who also embodies compassion, confidence, commitment to their work, personable with a great sense of humor. Credibility, testimonials, evidence to support a thriving practice and commitment to the work.

Guest from Hell: One who is unprepared, unpredictable, unfriendly, projecting a spiritual superiority and clearly not presenting what they claim to be an expert in.

Contact: Jennifer2@souljourneys.ca; http://www.souljourneys.ca; 905-646-9168; Jennifer Longmore. Best method: E-mail and sending a press kit. No response? Sometimes e-mails get lost in cyberspace. I would prefer another e-mail before a phone call.

Invited Back? The same criteria as in question (1).

Guest Comment: "I want to thank you with all of my heart and soul for the work that ... you do for the world ... your Light shines so brightly you can't help but to illuminate that which is deeply hidden within the subconscious minds of all you work with. Your level of integrity and honesty is amazing. I trust in you completely ... thank you, thank you, thank you.— Kathy Karlander, author of *Discovering the Essence of Your Soul* (iUniverse 2006) and host of *Sacred Insights* on Contact Talk Radio."

Listener Comment: "Thank you for being an Earth Angel and shining your light through you show."— Karen Anderson, host of *Divine Journeys* on Blog Talk Radio.

Bio of Jennifer Longmore: Jennifer is an international healer, speaker, teacher, and founder of the Soul Journeys School for Spiritual Studies and the Soul Journeys Method.

After a serious car accident, Jennifer was introduced to Reiki, which became pivotal in healing her physical pain from the accident. It also introduced her to the ower of healing energy and the mind-body-soul connection. She wanted to help others and set out to learn Reiki, Integrated Energy Therapy, Akashic Record Consultations as well as other healing methods.

She shares her expertise with thousands of people around the globe each year as an Akashic Record Teacher-Consultant, Direct Channel, Medical Intuitive, and Light Worker in helping people permanently shift the limiting beliefs and patterns that prevent them from being who they really are.

Spirit Connections with Donna and Dudley Voll on Achieve Radio, http://www.achieveradio.com

Theme: Spiritual. We have experts in all areas of spirituality sharing insights, quantum science, dreams, meditation, motivation, healing methods, mediumship, self awareness.

Guest Profile: Authors, teachers, psychologists, doctors, mediums, healers, and more. Someone who can link their topic in connection to spiritual view.

Guest from Hell: Someone unwilling to talk and open up to the audience.

Contact: spirit_connections@alltel.net; 706-894-1582; for spirit connections info at www.angelstoguideyou.com; Donna Voll, host/producer. Best method: E-mail or phone. Need a media kit, points on how their topic would work for our show, a review copy of their book. They should check out our program archives to hear the content we look for. No response? Try again, I am often very busy, and reminders help get on the interview list.

Invited Back? If they are well informed, and if their topic can be expanded. We often have returning guests going more indepth on topic.

Bio of Donna Voll: Donna is an ordained minister, certified clairvoyant, and an intuitive spiritual counselor. Her earliest clairvoyant visions came during childhood. Though difficult to comprehend, her mother helped Donna use prayer to keep her visions directed to the Higher Spheres. As she matured, she experienced premonitions and prophecies that confirmed her spiritual gifts.

By the time she became a mother of three young children, the visions became more prevalent. She began a course of study into spiritual development, which allowed the clairvoyant visions to become focused and the messages to become clear. She also understood the need for prayer and meditation to truly hear her Higher Self and the connection from the Great Source, Holy Spirit.

Donna received her degree in early childhood education, served as a pre-school teacher, and has written and illustrated two children's stories: *Tell Me ... Could Bad Things Happen to Me?* (Goldenwords 2002), deals with how to cope with grief and fears. The second book (as yet unpublished), *What's a MuchMore?*, written in collaboration with her husband, is a story about children learning to appreciate themselves and others.

Bio of Dudley Voll: The Rev. Dudley J. Voll is an ordained minister and a certified spiritual healer. Along with his wife, Donna, Dudley teaches spiritual philosophy and development classes that stress the understanding of natural law: how it is an intricate part of our everyday life, and an individual's personal responsibility. He has spent the last 25 years studying the comparative nature of religions. Dudley has Vision Quested with elder Mary Thunder, taken wilderness survival with Tom Brown, Jr., hiked the Appalachian Trail, and studied Yoga and T'ai Chi.

Full bios at http://www.angelstoguideyou.com

Spirit Is Speaking with Salvatore Candeloro on Blog Talk Radio, http://www.blogtalkradio.com/salvatore. He also hosts the show *Pets Are Speaking.*

Theme: Sharing experiences of spirit/God communications, or pet communications from people's current living pets.

Guest Profile: This show promotes my gift of communications. I prefer guests who can share a spiritual story that I can pull out a clear message or lesson that the experience represents. Since they only share personal stories and the guests are call-ins there is no time to screen.

Guest from Hell: A guest that might share an experience that is so far removed from my work and that I cannot make any sense of or turn into a benefit for the listeners.

Contact: Salvatorelight@aol.com; 561-588-8623; http://Broadenyourvisions.com; Salvatore. Best method: E-mail or phone. No response? E-mail or call. That is up to them.

Invited Back? If a guest has some valuable life experiences that had strong spiritual content, I would ask them to call in again.

Bio of Salvatore Candeloro: Salvatore has been a professional medium for 18 years. "I get visions and messages about life and people's lives from the Spirit side," he says. "I do not limit the messages from family only. I go directly to God and allow the perfect message for me or the person to come through."

He has taught adult education classes in spiritual development in New Jersey and Florida in numerous schools for many years. Salvatore is an ordained minister and worked as a guest minister for a church in Old Greenwich, CT. He does readings both in person and over the phone. Pet communications is another branch of his work. He goes to the pet's owner's home or can also do it over the phone.

Spiritual Hollywood with Kate Romero on BBS Radio, http://www.bbsradio.com/bbc/spiritual_hollywood.php

Theme: Raising consciousness through positive media.

Guest Profile: Various guests with purpose/passion and sanity. Bio/platforms also.

Guest from Hell: One who doesn't believe what they are saying.

Contact: guardianangelmgt@sbcglobal.net; Withheld upon request; http://www.GuardianAngelManagement.com; Kate. Best method: E-mail with press kit. No response? Do not e-mail or call.

Invited Back? Fun.

Guest Comment: "Thank you so much for a great interview. It was REALLY fun and inspiring to be a guest on your show. You do a wonderful job of it! I look forward to continuing our dialogue and synchronistic adventure! Peace and Many Blessings." — Derek Rydall, author of *There's No Business Like Soul Business* (Michael Wiese Productions 2007)

Bio of Kate Romero: Kate is president-CEO of Guardian Angel Enterprises as a progressive talent manager with a focus on consciousness; she represents Interventionist Jeff Van Vonderen of the Emmy Nominated A&E hit show "Intervention."

Out of a deep love for facilitating the restoring of a client to their true nature, Kate is also a Quantum Leap Life Coach, co-creator of Quantum Hypnotherapy, and a non-denominational ordained minister.

Born in Detroit, Michigan Kate lived on an 80-acre farm in Morehard, Kentucky, with her parents and siblings. After becoming very physically fit from farm life, Kate applied her strength and unique abilities to things that seemed to come natural to her. She later achieved awards in track and field, skeet shooting, and holds a world title in arm wrestling. Kate is an avid player of ping pong, chess, and billiards.

When Kate was very young she knew her purpose was "to raise consciousness."

It is Kate's wish to write as many books as possible for those who suffer from being told there is no hope. She is the author of the upcoming book *Huckleberry Memoirs: An Extraordinary Journey*, http://www.HuckleberryMemoirs.com

Terry Nazon Talks Astrology with Terry Nazon on http://www.themixtalk.com

Theme: Astrology and spiritual topics.

Guest Profile: Psychics and spiritual advisors who have an interesting personality and I want to know what they have to talk about.

Guest from Hell: Someone who doesn't talk.

Contact: Terry@terrynazon.com; 954-214-6005; http://www.terrynazon.com; Terry Nazon. Best method: E-mail. No response? E-mail again.

Invited Back? Their vibe.

Bio of Terry Nazon: Terry is a professional celebrity astrologer and psychic to the stars. For more than 16 years, she has been practicing as a professional astrologer and consulting clients professionally and was voted among the top 10 astrologers by Time Warners Books — Top Best Astrologers in America.

Developer and owner of several psychic hotlines, Vision Quest, heart and Soul Psychics, Terry has also published *Vision Quest*, a printed astrological newsletter and horoscope column since 1997. Her horoscopes and columns are seen all over the world and have been published in many magazines, and used for hundreds of web sites worldwide providing online content.

Terry has an accuracy rate of 99 percent and a repeat clientele of 100 percent. Many of her articles, horoscope columns, and predictions have been published in national and international magazines, and Terry's top trademarked logos have become household words and become so popular that others commonly use it: Sexstrology Prediction Addiction, and "Get Names, Dates, Times, and Places!" "She is the standard today that everyone wishes to copy," says Tom Bushnell, editor.

A Time to Heal with the Rev. Claudia McNeely on http://www.talkshoe.com

Theme: Healing in body, mind and spirit.

Guest Profile: Alternative healers, Law of Attraction, creating reality, vibrational tools, metaphysics, New Age, etc. Interesting subject that is of benefit to my listeners. Someone who can teach my listeners something new and healing and are knowledgeable about what they want to speak about.

Guest from Hell: One who doesn't talk.

Contact: claudia@askclaudia.com; 903-576-9068; http://www.askclaudia.com; Rev. Claudia McNeely. Best method: E-mailing bio, phone, link to website or press kit. No response? E-mail again or call.

Invited Back? Knowledge. The ability to share interesting information. Listener's interest and response.

Guest Comment: "I really appreciated your 'down to earth — get to the point' style and how you are so responsive to your listener's call-in questions. I received a lot of good feedback. I look forward to being on your show again." — Dr. Earl B Hall, http://www.AtlantisHealthCenters.com

Bio of the Rev. Claudia McNeely DD: Claudia is a gifted and caring psychic healer. As a medical intuitive, she can psychically "see" problems in your physical body and help you to release them.

A minister and Doctor of Divinity and certified in hypnotherapy, Reiki, One Brain, and Iridology, Claudia attended classes in bio energetic synchronization technique, healing touch, radionics, radiathesia, numerous alternative healing techniques, psychic development, past lives and much more. She has seriously studied feng shui, meditation, psychotherapy, transpersonal psychology, ascension techniques, herbs, crystals, Native American spirituality, shamanism, wicca, and candle magick.

The Truth About Life with Stephen Hawley Martin on http://www.WebTalkRadio.net

Theme: New science, metaphysics, body-mind-spirit, health.

Guest Profile: Authors, psychologists, psychics. Witty, articulate, gives clear, pithy answers. Fun. Want their credentials and topic of expertise. Edgar Evans Cayce, son of the world renowned psychic, Edgar Cayce (1877–1945), has been a guest.

You can check his recent guests on his website.

Guest from Hell: One who talks a lot and doesn't say anything.

Contact: Use contact form at website; 804-281-5685; http://www.shmartin.com; Stephen Hawley Martin. Best method: Website contact form — E-mail bio, topic of expertise, sample questions. No response? Send another e-mail. I will say yes or no thanks.

Invited Back? If they are witty, articulate, give clear, pithy answers. Fun.

Bio of Stephen Hawley Martin: Stephen was editor-in-chief of his college yearbook, an all-conference center on the varsity football team and cartoonist for the college newspaper.

After graduation, he went to work for an advertising agency and in just 18 months was handling that firm's largest account, USAirways.

Six years later he went into business with his brother, David, and The Martin Agency was formed. Named the hottest ad agency in the country by *Adweek*, the firm grew to $500 million in billings and today boasts such clients as GEICO auto insurance (gecko and caveman), UPS package delivery and Wal-Mart.

Stephen sold his interest in the agency in order to devote his full energy to writing books and to the pursuit of his passion for digging into and unraveling life's mysteries. He now defines his life mission as being "to delight, enlighten and entertain seekers by revealing the truth about life on earth."

Three books by Stephen have won top industry awards, all published by Oaklea Press. *In My Father's House* (2004), a thriller, won the Writer's Digest Book Award for Fiction, and First Prize for Fiction from *Independent Publisher* magazine. *Death in Advertising* (1997), a whodunit, also won the Writer's Digest Book Award, making Martin the only two-time winner of that prize. In October 2007, it was announced that his nonfiction title, *A Witch in the Family* (2006) — already an award-winning finalist in the USA Book News national book awards — had captured an unprecedented third Writer's Digest Book Award for Martin. In it, he offers a theory to explain what was behind the witch hysteria in 1692 Salem, and he writes about how growing up knowing of this injustice affected his worldview and his attitude toward individuals and institutions in positions of power and authority.

In pursuit of his mission and his passion for digging into life's mysteries, Stephen began his radio show with the goal of determining why and how life works and how it can work for the benefit of each of us.

Stephen and his wife have three school age children and live in central Virginia.

Truth from the Source with Dr Ann West on KKCR and KAQA, Kauai and aired throughout Hawaii; www.kkcr.org

Theme: Discussions on the environment, metaphysics, alternative healing.

Guest Profile: Quantum physicists, researchers in alternative medicine, authors willing to make a difference for the better. Well informed, upbeat, cutting edge personality and enthusiastic about the material and their credentials. Her prominent guests have included Dr. Wayne Dyer, Deepak Chopra, Jean-Michel Cousteau, Dr. Dean Ornish and Dan Millman.

Guest from Hell: When it's all about themselves or low energy.

Contact: drannwest@mac.com; http://www.drannwest.com; 808-828-0370; Ann West. Best method: E-mail me a breakdown of the issue their book is dealing with. If the topic is useful to my audience I will ask for a review copy to be sent to me. No response? E-mail is better but only after at least two weeks.

Invited Back? How informed they were and how easy to get along with they are.

Guest Comments: "Dr. Ann listens compassionately, speaks intelligently and has the amazing capacity to understand with her heart. She touched lives with her talent for deep communication, and her courage to explore all arenas of the spirit, including the places in us where the 'shadow' resides. In this way she not only delivers teachings, but healing as well." — Kenny and Julia Loggins (musicians and authors)

"Ann has found the courage to launch out beyond the familiar and fearlessly explore uncharted territory. The good news is that she has charted it for us that our lives may be easier for it." — Alan Cohen, author of *I Had It All the Time* (Alan Cohen Publications 2004).

Bio of Dr. Ann West: For the past 10 years, Ann's show has successfully brought many leading authorities and international authors on air to discuss cutting edge environmental, health and spiritual issues that are rarely discussed on other talk shows.

Ann's mission is to inform the public about alternative ways to live a healthier, more conscious life style and create a healthier environment by becoming a part of the global solution and not part of the problem.

Turning of the Wheel with Chris Flisher on Contact Talk Radio, http://www.contacttalkradio.com/hosts/chrisflisher.htm

Theme: Astrology — art — adventure.

Guest Profile: Astrologers, New Age visionaries, artists. The show focuses on astrology so my typical guest is well-versed in astrology. I look for knowledge and good radio presence, i.e., quick thinking. References, past experiences, tapes of past appearances, etc.

Guest from Hell: An ill-informed guest or unprepared guest is the worst. They must be able to think quickly and provide educational information that serves the listener.

Contact: chris@chrisflisher.com; 508-517-0969; http://www.chrisflisher.com; Chris Flisher. Best method: E-mailing is the best way to open the door and start a dialog. No response? If I don't respond within a week, call.

Invited Back? The number of callers, my rapport with the guest, and the success with the topic and format.

Bio of Chris Flisher: As a former talk show host on two nationally-syndicated talk shows, Chris' approach to guests and callers alike is one of openness and engaging enlightenment. Every effort is made to educate listeners on the complexities of planetary alignments, current transits, and zodiacal characteristics of one's natal charts in plain simple language.

Chris has been a student of astrology ever since he had his first chart done at age 20. At the time, a perfect stranger asked him his astrology coordinates (birth date/place/time) and within a few days he had the most amazingly accurate account of himself that he had ever read; delivered by a person who had no previous knowledge of him. He was immediately hooked. He has spent the rest of his time researching, understanding, and practicing astrology.

Visible by Numbers with Alison Baughman on BBS Radio, http://www.BBSRADIO.com

Theme: Numerology and spiritual philosophy.

Guest Profile: Not limited to any particular genre. Most often I interview mediums and psychics. My show is not entirely devoted to interviewing guests, but, rather, I bring on guests 2 times a month. Because numerology validates spiritual philosophy, generally I enjoy a guest who is open to numerology. Genuine passion for their work and desire to be of service to others is a plus. I am also interested in ordinary people with an extraordinary story to tell so I do not limit my guests to notables within the spiritual field. I look for sincerity of intent, passion in their work and a desire to help others. I like to look at a bio of course but I do prefer to speak to the potential guest to get a "feel" for their personality to see if we are a compatible fit energetically.

Guest from Hell: Ego.

Contact: alynch@ptd.net; 717-859-3772; http://www.visiblebynumbers.com; Alison Baughman. Best method: Phone. No response? Calling is best as I get many e-mails daily and sometimes I do get behind in priority. I am a reader myself so you can imagine the volume.

Invited Back? I will not invite a guest back if they promise a caller something and do not follow through on it (which has happened).

Guest Comment: "It was a pleasure to be a guest on *Visible by Numbers* with Alsion Baughman. She was an in-depth interviewer who really did her homework. Alison was totally familiar with my books and graciously gave them a really great plug. She gave good information and allowed me to answer her questions without interruption. I said to her as I will say here that I'd be happy to be a guest on her program anytime." — Rita Berkowitz, http://www.theSpiritArtist.com

Bio of Alison Baughman: Alison has often been questioned about her path to becoming a Numerologist and she can trace it to her childhood. "My mother was a teacher and she taught me at a very early age, the value of a good book," says Alison. "I spent my summers walking to the local public library and was an avid reader of the biographies of famous philosophers, scientists, humanitarians and the like. I suppose even at an early age, I was questioning how a person achieves their destiny.

"On one of those trips to the library, I discovered my first numerology book. Little did I know at the time that this numerology book held the answers I was seeking. As I got older, I began to seriously study the subject of numerology. I read extensively, studied the theories of numerology, took numerology workshops and eventually began doing numerology readings. Soon it became evident that somehow I instinctively knew the nuances of numerology without being told, as if I was being divinely led to it."

Walking with Spirit with Monique Chapman on Achieve Radio, http://www.achieveradio.com, Tuesdays, 5–7 PM (PT)

Theme: Personal growth, metaphysical, spiritual.

Guest Profile: Authors of books on the following subjects: Spiritual, metaphysical, personal growth, alternative healing. Someone who can position themselves as "the" expert in their field. Show excitement and sound upbeat. A pre-show interview is required 90 percent of the time. Past media experiences and credentials.

Guest from Hell: Someone who tries to take over my job as host. Someone giving one word answers.

Contact: Moniquechapman@comcast.net; 510 659-9178; http://www.moniquechapman.com; http://www.healing-visions.com; Monique Chapman. Best method: Send a letter of inquiry and a dynamic pitch. If I am interested I will ask then to send a press kit including bio and a review copy of their book. Once the book is reviewed, if I am interested in taking the next step, potential guests are contacted for a screening interview. If all goes well, I invite them to be a guest on the show, and will provide them with a copy of the protocols. If they agree to the protocols we set a show date. No response? If I do not respond in 30 days, a phone call is acceptable. Getting 200 pitches a week can take some time to get through.

Invited Back? Guests are invited back if I feel that they brought life to the show. They shared their topic without trying to turn it into an infomercial. For my audience the "connection" is made if I have many call-ins during the show. Also the level of respect the guest gives me. It is amazing how many guests want to exert their own agenda while on the air. And of course they will have followed the protocols for the show to the letter.

Guest Comments: "You are an excellent host. Your questions reflected your knowledge of my work." — Gregg Braden, author of *The Divine Matrix* (Hay House 2006), http://www.greggbraden.com

"I love being on *Walking with Spirit*. Monique asks great thought provoking questions and I love her conversational style. The audience response was great during the show and afterward." — Cynthia Sue Larson, author of *Aura Advantage: How the Colors in Your Aura Can Help You Attain What You Desire and Attract Success* (Lightworker Publishing 2006), http://realityshifters.com

Bio of Monique Chapman: Monique is a personal growth expert, radio personality, and author of *Getting Your M and M's — The Men and Money Book: How to Tap into Universal Source Energy to Reclaim Your Power and Create Meaningful Relationships and Abundance* (Sirrah Publishing 2006).

Monique uses her skills of intuition to help you wake up, gain clarity and insight to create the life of your dreams. She founded and produces the award winning Walking with Spirit radio show which celebrated its 5th year in August 2007. She has a thriving practice as an intuitive that assists people in becoming who they were meant to be in this lifetime.

Wellness, Wholeness and Wisdom with Parthenia S. Izzard, CNHP and psychologist, on Achieve Radio, www.achieveradio.com

Theme: Alternative medicine, related products and issues, and with the experts.

Guest Profile: Authors, practitioners, celebrities, manufacturers of holistic products, and resort spas (local, national, and international). A warm friendly conversationalist with a sense of humor. I ask them to send me their bio. When I talk to them and/or go to their web site I can pretty much tell their radio experience. I really like to get a chance to talk with them to get a feel for how they talk.

Guest from Hell: Ohh, I wouldn't call them that. Some are just inexperienced and nervous. They tend to give one word responses and do not really use the opportunity to sell themselves, their book, product or service.

Contact: consult@amtherapies.com; 610-658-0135 and 866-472-6094; http://www.amtherapies.com. Best method: Phone. In order of preference: press kit, bio, or pitch. No response? Either e-mail or phone is okay but I think the telephone is more reliable. I do not sit in front of a computer all day.

Invited Back? The flow and tenor of the interview exchange. I also take into consideration audience response.

Bio of Parthenia Izzard: Parthenia is founder and president of Alternative Medicine Therapies. As a child she wanted to be a healing energy in the lives of those with whom she comes in contact. For as long a she can remember her life has revolved around alternative ways of enhancing her health and the health of those around her.

She has spent her adult life devouring books on acupressure, herbology, psychology, nutrition, vegetarianism, yoga, and meditation. Some years after marriage to John, and while in the dissertation phase of her Ph.D. in clinical and health psychology (ABD), Parthenia decided to become a certified Natural Healthcare Practitioner (CNHP) and Pennsylvania state certified psychologist. She studied nutrition, iridology, kinesiology, bodyworks, body systems, and energy medicine at the Delaware Valley Naturopathic Medical Association in Pennsylvania (accredited by the American Naturopathic Medical Association).

She is also a college professor (teaching psychology) at CTU Online and does psychological evaluations for Therapy Sources, Inc.

Full bio at http://www.amtherapies.com/about.html

When Pigs Fly with Andrew Feder on BBS Radio, http://www.bbsradio.com

Theme: Politics, ET, UFOs, religion and spirituality.

Guest Profile: See theme — authors, bloggers etc. Someone who is interesting and unique has something to say about his or her subject without any holding back.

Pre-interview for chemistry and their ambiance and demeanor plus obvious information regarding his/her subject.

Guest from Hell: Duh ... dull... boring ... when talking about his or her subject without any enthusiasm and/or real substance.

Contact: flyingpigs@artlover.com; 702-364-8727; http://www.AndrewFeder.com http://www.AndrewtheHeretic.com; Andrew Feder. Best method: First send e-mail w/ bio and information and pitch. No response? Re-e-mail follow-up in a month.

Invited Back? If I like what they were trying to convey and there was good chemistry.

Bio of Andrew Feder: Andrew was born in Hollywood, California, looking like a cross between a Nordic and Asian baby. His father would later sarcastically say that he was adopted from Korea.

He grew up in a dysfunctional Jewish family in San Fernando Valley and later studied at San Diego State University.

He then went for one year to the University of Haifa in Israel where he lived on a kibbutz and met his ex-wife. (He has three children from this marriage.) In Israel he studied Kabbalah (Jewish mystics) under guidance of the renowned holy man known as The Moah. (He continued studying the Kabbalah after returning home.) During his religious studies, he was quite pious as an orthodox observant Jew.

He completed his studies at UC Davis in viticulture and enology.

In the late nineties, Andrew drove a cab and a limo during hiatus while working as an assistant director in the film industry. At the end of the nineties, he moved to Las Vegas from Los Angeles which, for one year, he was (and hates to admit it) a damn telemarketer selling long distance, and for the past six years he's been a graphic artist.

During his college years, Andrew wrote several editorials and short stories. Much later, during the so-called mid-life crisis, he evolved in his development to include writing both novels and poems along with subsequent screenplays.

When people first see Andrew they are commonly surprised by his lack of aging and youthful appearance. In the other words, they think that he is ten years (sometimes more) younger then his actual age. His response: Well, we do come out in the daytime.

Windows to Wellness with Linda Woods on 98.9 FM, Nashville, TN, http://www.radiofreenashville.org. My radio program is approximately one hour in length (with three short breaks) and is pre-recorded. During those breaks, I air public service announcements, guest event information, and reflective music. That's a lot of air time and exposure for your message. I usually record by phone in the afternoon, between Thursday and Sunday at a time convenient to my guest. Some shows are pre-recorded in my studio if the guest is visiting Nashville, TN. Since the program airs on a non-profit station, there is no fee for the interview. However, as an independent producer, I charge $75 to edit your show (so that you'll end up with a perfect interview with no hiccups or glitches) and I charge an additional $25 to cover bandwidth charges on iTunes. To date, my podcast has had over 15,000 downloads. Your interview will remain on my podcast and streaming all over the world for over one year.

Theme: Healing, Self-help and empowerment.

Guest Profile: Anyone who is passionate and knowledgeable about their topic, and interested in motivating and empowering others. Anyone who has an uplifting message to share. I'm not concerned with credentials, as much as I am the message. It helps if they can convey their story, how they found their path, what challenges they have overcome, and how they are now helping others. What matters is what's in their heart. It's also nice to hear their voice — since it creates a powerful impression. I can tell a lot about a person from their voice.

Guest from Hell: Someone who feels that they (alone) have all the answers. Someone who pontificates and speaks so rapidly that I don't get a chance to ask a question. Or, the opposite extreme, someone who is vague or avoids answering question. Someone who talks at me, and not with me.

Contact: lindawoods1@bellsouth.net; 615-781-1551; Linda Woods. Best method: E-mail a bio and send a link to your website or a past radio interview. Please no phone calls initially. No response? They should e-mail me again. Sometimes I may miss one along the way.

Invited Back? All of my programs are pre-recorded and I often re-air programs. If a past guest has an event coming up in the Nashville area, I sometimes re-air their original program and change the event information. If their topic is timely and people can benefit, I will invite them back; however, I usually wait at least six months before airing the topic again.

Bio of Linda Woods: Linda is a former stand-up comic who performed self-deprecating humor, until she realized the toll it took on her health. When she joked about being overweight, the cells in her body responded by staying that way. After all, they were famous (the punchline of her joke) and the center of her focus. Now, Linda's changed her act, and shares her humor based on one main predominant thought, "I am whole, complete and perfect, just the way I am — and my cells love it."

Having experienced more than 30 different alternative healing therapies for herself and writing about them as a guest columnist in the *Franklin Review Appeal* newspaper, she is now working on a book about how "natural healing" has changed her life and how those cells inside her body have taken on a complete life of their own.

Former accountant and glorified bean counter, Linda now finds balance the holistic way, using muscle testing and meditation, light therapy and love, flower essences and feng shui.

As a committed vegetarian for the last 20 years, Linda founded EarthSave Nashville, a chapter of an international non-profit organization that helps people move toward a healthier diet.

Guest Comments: "I felt very comfortable and I that I was able to talk about my practice and what I do and what I'd like to say, better than in any other setting that I've had. You have a way of drawing out the pertinent information, focusing on that and making your interviewee very comfortable in the process." —

J. David Forbes, MD, http://www.NashvilleIntegratedMedicine.com

"I've had the opportunity to work with a lot of folks over the years, giving lectures, teaching people and also giving interviews, and I must admit that your probing questions, and your ability to grasp precisely what we were doing and what I was attempting to tell people, really impressed me. I think it helped me answer the questions in a way that was hopefully much more effective for everybody.... So, having the ability to tell folks about that is extremely important to me, but more importantly, having someone who is able to bring out those questions, and be able to understand where we were going with it, was extremely appreciated. So very much, I wanted to thank you for everything you've done. And let me just reassure you, that by reaching folks in this manner, I think you are going to be able to help a lot of people over the years." — Joe Culbertson, Doctor of Chiropractic, http://www.spinetuner.com

For more testimonials, visit http://www.windowstowellness.com/GuestTestimonials.html

Wings of Love with Allie Cheslick on http://www.nowlive.com, airing Monday, Friday and Saturday, 2 PM (ET) and 11 AM (PT), Blog Talk Radio at www.blogtalkradio.com/wingsofloveshow, and on iTunes.

Theme: Metaphysical, paranormal, psychics, mediums, spiritual and religious energy, consciousness and the subconscious.

Guest Profile: Authors, mediums, parapsychologists, psychologists, New Age musicians, New Age authors (as found on hayhouse.com, well known for having authors and mediums as guests). We look for quality guests with a following and someone whose background falls within the scope of the show. Our guests must have experience within their modality /field of expertise. We like to know about past interviews, credentials and what current projects they are involved with.

Guest from Hell: A guest from hell is one that cannot carry on a conversation or is really not comfortable taking calls and answering questions.

Contact: Allie@AllieCheslick.com / Cristina@AllieCheslick.com; 518-280-6363; http://www.AllieCheslick.com; Claudio, Cristina or Allie. Best method: They can e-mail a bio and or/press kit preferably as the initial contact. They can call with a pitch however the initial preference of contact is through e-mail or postal mail. No response? We usually attempt to respond to e-mails within a 24–48 hour turn around time. If by chance your e-mail is not responded to, please e-mail again or you can certainly call and leave a message for us.

Invited Back? If the guest, number one had an enjoyable time on the show and has expressed an interest in coming back and number two, how appealing and in synergy the guest is with the listening audience.

Bio of Allie Cheslick: Allie is an angelic medium,

life coach, spiritual teacher and radio show host who has delivered very profound messages and highly accurate details in her readings. Allie's love and her gift from God truly shines through in her readings. Allie's blessing is one she shares openly and lovingly with those that seek her out.

Allie uses her gifts to bring emotional and spiritual healing to those whose lives she touches and has been actively helping others since 1987. She offers a variety of services including telephone, instant messenger, gallery readings and works with various charities and agencies.

Testimonials, show schedules, upcoming guests and services offered can be found on Allie's website. Allie works with the ascended masters, angels, spirit guides as well as connecting to loved ones crossed over.

You Are What You Love with Vaishali on Contact Talk Radio, http://www.contacttalkradio.com and a second show on http://www.worldtalkradio.com

Theme: Self growth, spirituality.

Guest Profile: Very wide from medical professionals, writers, psychics, fitness experts, paranormal experts, channelers, palm readers, anyone who offers wisdom and insight. Radio friendly personality, authenticity, service to my listening audience. Past experience is not important. If they are engaging, know their field of expertise and are fun.

Guest from Hell: Dull personality, or pushy and arrogant, or someone who takes a long time to respond to questions.

Contact: v@purplev.com; HM (239) 514-7193, Cell (409) 354-9021; http://www.purplev.com and http://www.purplehazepress.com. Best method: Call with a pitch, e-mail a bio, send a press kit. E-mail is usually easiest. No response? Absolutely call or e-mail. I try to read each and every guest's book personally or seek them out to experience their work if they do not have a book. That takes time, lots and lots of time. But that is what it takes to create the best, most meaningful interview. If I have not gotten back to someone, it does not mean I am not interested ... it means I'm buried and working to get to them as I can.

Invited Back? How much fun they were, and if the listening audience in the chat room responded enthusiastically.

Guest Comments: "Vaishali's radio show is a one of a kind that should be heard worldwide. I say this because it is the only program I know that allows its guests to express their deepest most feelings on matters of urgency to us all. I'm thankful that her amazing gift to inspire and bring out the best in her guests has found its way onto the airways. I know it will inspire, enlighten and hopefully elevate a world much in need of what she's presenting."—Allan Jay Friedman, producer, songwriter

"Working with Vaishali was an interviewee's dream: She gave me a clear orientation to the show format and to the technical aspects of communicating with both the audience and with her. The experience of the interview was totally comfortable throughout. It gave me a chance to present important material in a very informal and fun way. Her intelligence and wit put everyone at ease. I'd highly recommend interviewing with Vaishali and would gladly do it again."—Dr. Stuart C. Marmorstein, co-author of *A Healthier You!* (Office of Disease Prevention and Health 2005), http://www.drstuart.net

Bio of Vaishali: Vaishali is part stand-up comic, part spiritual teacher and full time soul stripper. She attended San Francisco State University where she graduated magna cum laude with degrees from both the religion and philosophy department, as well as the radio and television department. Her adult life has been devoted to the learning and sharing of esoteric wisdom. She has been teaching and providing self-emergence individual consultations since the early 90s.

Vaishali has been enormously influenced by 18th century mystic Emanuel Swedenborg, whose brilliant wisdom is the central core of her spiritual practice, and the remarkable Sir Oscar Wilde, which is where she says she gets her invincible sense of humor. "What life has taught me," Vaishali will tell you, "is 'if you can't beat 'em laugh at 'em.'"

Vaishali has survived a life fraught with every possible personal challenge available to a human experience: the violent death of a loved one, lying and cheating significant others, a messy and painful divorce, financial devastation due to life threatening illness and injuries complete with years of physical agony. These experiences have shaped her book, *You Are What You Love* (Purple Haze Press 2006), with honest heartfelt and deeply insightful knowledge on how to understand the purpose behind human life on Earth.

Pronounced "Why-shaw-lee," Vaishali has worn only the color purple — exclusively, for over a decade as her spiritual uniform of choice. She currently resides in Florida and continues with her life purpose of spiritual teaching and providing individual self-emersion consulting, as well as working on her next book.

Outdoor Life

"I can't remember a day in the outdoors I didn't like."—Jim Slinsky's favorite quotation

Big Outdoors with Chip Hart and Rick Combs on 700WLW AM, Cincinnati, Ohio, Saturday, 5–5:30 AM (ET), aired in 32 states.

Theme: Fishing, hunting, conservation, outdoors legislation.

Guest Profile: Fishing and hunting experts, authors, fish and wildlife administrators, destination representatives, guides, outfitters. We look for the ability to communicate concisely and paint the picture. We want to know that they have expertise and knowledge about the subject and can communicate it.

Guest from Hell: The guest from hell that bores a rock.

Contact: Chip@hartproductions.com; rcombs@cinci.rr.com; 877-797-7900; 513-260-7213; http://www.bigoutdoors.net; http://www.hartproductions.com; Chip Hart. Best method: We wish for people to contact us by e-mail providing a bio with interview references. A mere phone conversation following can determine their capability. Humorous personality preferred. No response? Don't concern yourself with this. We respond to everything.

Invited Back? We invite guests back that pass muster and represent subject matter that changes with time.

Bio of Chip Hart: Chip has been producer of sportsmen/boat shows in Cincinnati and Columbus since 1977.

He is also creator and host of 700WLW Big Outdoors (1995).

Outdoor Talk Network with Jim Slinsky aired on more than 50 stations nationally.

Theme: Anything to do with the outdoors.

Guest Profile: Smart, clever, articulate and involved. Articulate, knows the issues. Want to know their area of expertise.

Guest from Hell: Slow talker with little knowledge.

Contact: slinskyj@ptd.net; 570-325-5560; http://www.outdoortalknetwork.com; Jim Slinsky. Best method: e-mail. Send me a press kit or announcement. No response? E-mail or call.

Invited Back? A great show.

Bio of Jim Slinsky: An avid hunter and fisherman for almost 50 years, Jim was taught by his father to shoot and fish before he ever started school. Equally capable with a fly rod, baitcasting, spinning gear, bow, rifle, shotgun and handgun, he believes variety is the key to the total outdoor experience. Freshwater, saltwater, small game, big game, Jim enjoys it all and is in the field every chance he gets. He passionately writes about many of his experiences and the issues that sportsmen face in our ever-changing world.

Jim is an amateur rod and gun builder, precision handloader, former English setter dog breeder, multi-species fisherman, former college professor, active conservationist and staunch supporter of individual freedoms. His favorite modified quotation is, "I can't remember a day in the outdoors I didn't like." Every show is dedicated to his father, the late, great, Jim Slinsky Sr. "His hunting and fishing plans always included me." The show is Jim's full-time endeavor.

The Outdoors Experience with Steve Sarley heard live Saturdays 8–9 AM (CT) on New Choice for Intelligent talk — WIND AM-560. The Chicago-based show can be heard in Illinois, Wisconsin, Indiana and Michigan.

Theme: Hunting, fishing and other outdoor sports.

Guest Profile: Professional outdoorspeople and also people who have a passion for the outdoors but are primarily known for other careers like politics or professional sports.

Expertise in their field and a passion for it that easily comes over the airwaves. The sound of their voice doesn't matter and it is my job to make them sound good during the interview, so past interviews mean nothing to me.

Guest from Hell: One that answers questions with a "yes" or "no," or who wants to be argumentative.

Contact: sarfishing@yahoo.com; 847-791-0132; http://www.oexperience.com; Steve Sarley. Best method: E-mail a bio and/or information about their new work. I want their bio and a copy of their publication well in advance. No response? E-mail or call. I always respond.

Invited Back? Topics left uncovered, new information to discuss and audience feedback.

Bio of Steve Sarley: Prior to hosting his current show, Steve was host for 3½ years of CLTV's *The Great Outdoors* on Thursday, 8:30–9 PM. CLTV is a Tribune Company station and is the local news sister station to WGN.

He is a weekly outdoors columnist for the *Northwest Herald*, *Kane County Chronicle* and *Lake County Journal*, monthly columnist for *MidWest Outdoors Magazine* and bi-monthly columnist for *Illinois Outdoor News Magazine*.

Paranormal

Paranormal — Phenomena which seem to defy the known laws of science. — from the Paranormal Dictionary on **Eastern Paranormal**'s website (which produces *A Glimpse Through the Veil*)

As You Wish Talk Radio with James Gilliland on BBS Radio, http://www.bbsradio.com; also picked up by many stations to fill dead air; it is offered free.

Theme: Cutting edge authors, physicists, UFOs, NDEs, geared towards the awakening and healing of humanity and the Earth.

Guest Profile: All the above. Guests have included J.J. Hurtak, Nick Begich, Meceal Ledwith. Integrity, service oriented, outside the box. Past interview experiences, credentials, sound of their voice, but most important — their intent.

Guest from Hell: Full of themselves and misinformation.

Contact: ufojames@gorge.net; 509-395-2092; http://www.eceti.org; James Gilliland. Best method: Bio, press kit, or just e-mail. No response? Real busy — e-mail again.

Invited Back? Performance.

Guest Comment: "James certainly is a very genial and courteous host. He allows the guest ample time to state his/her own views and he supplements with comments pertinent to the general discussion. I felt very comfortable on his program." — Brad Steiger, whose newest book is *Shadow World* (Anomalist Books 2007), http://www.bradandsherry.com

Bio of James Gilliland: James was raised in a small desert town, spending most of his time in nature. From high school through work, his experiences have been very diverse, ranging from studying prelaw and pre-dental to working in the construction and real estate industries to managing multi-million dollar projects.

After a near death experience brought about by drowning, he could no longer continue business as usual. His eyes were fully opened, and he saw the lack of love and joy in his life and his work. Success through material acquisition — "the American dream" — was now seen for its emptiness. He realized that the temporary joy and pleasure possessions and outer appearances brought were not the goal and began his inward journey. After experiencing the pure unconditional love and joy, "BLISS," of connecting directly to the source during his near death experience, all that mattered was to reconnect and maintain that contact.

This began a spiritual journey and 20 year quest which included six years of yoga, The Inner Christ Ministry, and the Tibetan foundation where he was certified as being an intuitive visionary of the highest consciousness and energy. He has studied with other yogis, lamas, master teachers and continuously has been taught from within through his extensive practicing of meditation. He is a teacher, spiritual counselor, energetic healer, and author of *Becoming Gods (1 and 2)*, published in 1997 and 1998 by Self-Mastery Earth Institute.

James has lived a semi-reclusive life since 1986 at the Sattva Sanctuary, a 70-acre mountain retreat located at the base of Mt. Adams in Trout Lake, Washington.

Celtic Seers with Sally Painter and Melissa Alvarez on Blog Talk Radio, http://blogtalkradio.com/Celtic Seers. Melissa has two other shows, *Friesian Ink Radio* (see page 11), and *The Readers Roundtable* (see page 30).

Theme: To discuss all things of a paranormal or metaphysical nature. Free clairvoyant readings will be offered at times.

Guest Profile: Someone who is knowledgeable about their new age, paranormal or metaphysical topic and who is interesting and engaging during conversation.

Guests are invited on once a month.

Guest from Hell: One who doesn't know their topic.

Contact: radio@celticseers.com; Withheld upon request; http://apsychichaven.com, http://melissaa.com, http://sallymidnightnews.blogspot.com, http://apsychichaven.com; Sally Painter or Melissa Alvarez. Best method: E-mail a brief bio, the topic they'd like to discuss and what they feel they can offer our guests. They can contact us through the show's e-mail or via our individual e-mails listed on our websites. No response? E-mail questions again.

Invited Back? How well they were prepared for unexpected questions and how they present themselves to the public — lively and knowledgeable will be invited back before dull, boring and without a clue.

Bios of Melissa Alvarez and Sally Painter: Do you ever wonder about the paranormal? Have you had experiences with ghosts or haunting? Have you ever wanted to talk one on one with a seer? Have you had clairvoyant readings in the past that left you feeling nervous or confused? If any of these things apply to you, then you've come to the right place.

Melissa, an internationally renowned clairvoyant advisor, and Sally, seer and paranormal expert, team up to discuss all things physical. Each show they will answer your most pressing questions, discuss your experiences and do co-readings for those who call in.

Dark Matters Radio with Don Ecker on PBRN (The Patriot Brigade Talk Radio Network), http://www.patriotbrigaderadio.com, now off the air.

Theme: Those subjects that run (under) mainstream media (in other words — paranormal subjects, *which of course, do run under the mainstream radar*).

Guest Profile: Authors, researchers, investigators who know their subject inside and out. Credentials and background in their subject are important.

Guest from Hell: A bullsh*t artist, and they end up paying.

Contact: decker0726@yahoo.com; Withheld upon request; http://www.darkmattersradio.com; Don Ecker. Best method: E-mailing me describing what they would like to talk about. No response? E-mail.

Invited Back? I decide.

Bio of Don Ecker: Don is a writer/researcher/commentator currently living in the Los Angeles area. Serving as director of research and media liaison for *UFO Magazine*, he is an internationally renowned investigator of the UFO phenomenon. A former law enforcement officer and criminal investigator with over 10 years' experience, he brings legitimacy to a field that has for years suffered being painted with a fringe brush.

He has written numerous articles for the definitive UFO publication, *UFO Magazine*, as well as articles for international publications, the United Kingdom's *Fortean Times*, *Omni*, the *Compuserve System*, and the *ParaNet Computer Data Base*. He has appeared numerous times on the "Larry King Live" talk show on CNN, and has been utilized repeatedly as an expert commentator and technical adviser by NBC's "Hard Copy."

Don became interested in the UFO question in

1966, when he and others were witness to a sighting of the enigma. "It was unlike anything I had ever seen before, and I realized then that there was much more to this than the authorities were letting on."

With a year of college under his belt, he enlisted in the United States Army and was selected for the elite Army Security Agency, where he volunteered for Special Operations. Don served in Southeast Asia for 26 months, was wounded twice, decorated and then returned to the U.S.

In 1986, while a member of his hometown police department's SWAT Team, he was wounded, which led to his retirement. While recuperating, he started to research and write on the UFO mystery. As a criminal investigator in 1982, he had been leading an investigation of several cattle mutilations, which Don later discovered were somehow connected to the UFO mystery.

Don hosted his own weekly national radio talk show, *UFOs Tonite!*, on Cable Radio Network for five years, and most recently *Strange Daze* five nights a week on the Liberty Works Radio Network.

Darkness on the Edge of Town Paranormal Radio Show with Dave Schrader and Tim Dennis on http://www.DarknessRadio.com

Theme: Paranormal radio.

Guest Profile: People with a background with paranormal, authors of fiction and non-fiction aimed at the field of the paranormal. Strong speaking abilities. Interesting stories. Want to know their basic history, what is so important about their story.

Guest from Hell: Weak speaker and defensive when questioned about their theories and ideas.

Contact: Dave@DarknessRadio.com; 612-388-3283; http://www.DarknessRadio.com; David Schrader. Best method: By e-mailing and sending a bio and pic of themselves and any links they may have to websites. No response? Follow up with a second e-mail.

Invited Back? Strength of first interview, popularity with listeners.

Bio of David Schrader: He is a contributing writer to *TAPS Paramagazine* and now he hopes to explore and learn with you each week as we delve deeper into the Darkness on the Edge of Town.

Ghostly Talk with Doug, Scott and Bonnie aired on many Internet streaming stations as well as on several smaller community traditional airwave-based radio stations. List of known affiliates is on the website on the Affiliates page.

Theme: Talk format focused on the paranormal.

Guest Profile: Authors, researchers, musicians and hobbyists that have something to say about anything paranormal or "fringe" science. Ghosts, Bigfoot, UFOs, ancient mysteries, conspiracy theories, and prophesy are examples of popular topics. Guests who have ideas or comments that make the co-hosts — and therefore the audience — think, wonder, and learn are the most enjoyable. Some playful banter to help provide comedic relief while presenting tough topics is preferred, but not required. We only want a general familiarity with the guest's topic (book/DVD/organization/website/etc.) before the show. Past interviews, credentials, voice quality is unimportant if their topic is exciting. We see it as our job to guide guests past hurdles such as inexperience and nervousness so they have an enjoyable time telling us about themselves and their topic.

Guest from Hell: Guests who respond with one word or short sentence answers make their segment seem three times longer than their allotted time.

Contact: ghostlytalk@ghostlytalk.com; http://www.ghostlytalk.com; Withheld upon request; Co-host Doug Semig: doug@ghostlytalk.com; Co-host Scott Lambert: scottl@ghostlytalk.com. Best method: An e-mail is all it takes. If we're interested, we e-mail back and exchange phone numbers. No response? Please e-mail again about two weeks later. We do get overwhelmed sometimes.

Invited Back? Three things help determine if we want a guest to repeat: 1) the guest has to make us think and learn; 2) we must have fun talking to the guest; and 3) the guest must have fun talking to us.

Guest Comment: "*Ghostly Talk* is an excellent program. The hosts go out of their way to promote guests and treat them with respect. They also care about their listeners and provide valuable website content for visitors. Doing a guest spot on *Ghostly Talk* is an enjoyable experience that brings many additional visitors to my website and exposes my paranormal research to a large and diverse audience." — Bill Knell, http://www.UFOguy.com

"Being a guest on *Ghostly Talk* is very exciting. Doug and Scott are very down to earth when they interview people and keep an open mind to the paranormal and let every body view their feelings." — John Zaffis, http://www.johnzaffis.com, http://www.johnzaffisparanormalmuseum.com, http://www.prsne.com, http://www.shadowsofthedark.com

Bio of Doug Semig: Doug has been interested in paranormal topics ever since checking out a book about witchcraft from his elementary school library. Among all the books he has read about paranormal subjects, his favorite topics are out of body experiences, Edgar Cayce, ESP, prophesy, and ghosts.

While surfing the Internet in 2001, he was happy to learn that other folks actually went prowling about cemeteries and haunted places looking for ghosts. Since then, he has been an avid ghost hunter. Doug had done terrestrial radio before at WTWR, the station at the University of Detroit. He received his Bachelor's degree in management sciences and information systems from the University of Detroit. Upon meeting Scott L on ghost hunts, Doug suggested doing an internet talk show about ghost hunting.

The premier of *Ghostly Talk* in February 2002

streamed to a total listening audience of one (1) computer, though two (2) people were listening. Doug continues to ghost hunt and co-host his show from Fraser, Michigan, a suburb of Detroit.

Bio of Scott Lambert: Born and raised in the suburbs of Detroit, MI, Scott became interested in the paranormal as a young child when he bought his first book *Haunted Houses* by Larry Kettelkamp at a garage sale for $.25. Intrigued and frightened by this book, Scott developed an adolescent interest in the paranormal that rooted itself firmly into the little boy's mind through the present day: "For a while, with college going on and being a professional musician, I didn't have time to really pursue the paranormal field as extensively as I wanted to," he recalls.

However, after Scott graduated from Wayne State University with a major in operational logistics and minor in information systems development, he had time to pursue his passion.

How did he get into radio though?

"Honestly, I have wanted to do radio for a very long time," he says. "I had some downtime from playing music about 5 years ago, and it was something that went through my mind a lot. Unfortunately, I had no contacts at the time to break in and try to pursue it. When I met Doug after doing a lot of ghost hunting and talking about the paranormal, he asked if I wanted to try to do an Internet talk show on the subject(s)/ I jumped at the opportunity."

In addition to being one of the creators of the show, Scott is the webmaster/caretaker for the now defunct speed metal band Holy Terror.

A Glimpse Through the Veil with Gabreael aired on Planet Paranormal.

Theme: Paranormal and metaphysical.

Guest Profile: Paranormal, esoteric, and metaphysical. We look for people we would like to listen to. We also try to mix in current events. Their interest and credentials.

Guest from Hell: A quiet one that simply answers yes or no to every question.

Contact: radioguest@easternparanormal.com; Paranormal is currently working on my website, but here is my current one — http://www.easternparanormal.com/Paranormal_Radio_Show_A_Gli.html; Unpublished upon request; Gabreael or Darla at darla@easternparanormal.com. Best method: E-mail. Press kits are great, bios are nice and even simply an informative e-mail stating their case (haunted homeowners and such would not have a press kit). No response? E-mail.

Invited Back? My audience downloads.

Guest Comment: "Having had my own radio shows and a frequent, repeat guest on radio and television, I enjoy the time spent with host Gabreael on *A Glimpse through the Veil*.

"Gabreael is a fresh voice asking questions the audience wants answered just in case their calls or e-mails are not answered. Gabreael is genuinely interested in your expertise, knows just enough on your subject matter to carry on a conversation and she allows you to talk. Gabreael keeps her show upbeat and the pace allows the audience to be entertained with the type of information they want to listen to."—Dana Haynes, astrologer, http://www.AstrologyWorldNews.com, dana@astrologyworldnews.com

Bio of Gabreael: Gabreael is the founder of Eastern Paranormal, bringing over 20 years of paranormal research to the table. Gabreael is a noted author, psychic researcher, photographer, radio host, and a natural born clairvoyant. Her co-authored book, *The Book of Thomas: A Guide for Life and the Afterlife* (Cork Hill Press 2003), was on Amazon's New Age best seller list in 2004.

Haunted Voices Radio with Todd Bates on http://www.hauntedvoicesradio.com, live 3–4 times a week (Archives 24/7).

Theme: Bringing paranormal to the world.

Guest Profile: Ghosts, haunted locations, UFO research, OBE, NDE, astral projection, demonology, religion. *Haunted Voices Radio* takes a different approach to our shows; we allow the guest to speak more on subjects that most will not allow on their programs.

We want to know their past interview experiences and credentials — voice is unimportant. We just want to get the information out to the community regardless of how one voice sounds.

Guest from Hell: A guest that is forced to be "carried" by the host due to lack of knowledge or nervousness

Contact: host@hauntedvoicesradio.com; 618-215-2136; www.hauntedvoicesradio.com; Producer Stephen Wren at producer@hauntedvoicesradio.com. Best method: E-mail via show's producer. You can also call with a pitch and/or send a press kit. It would be nice to have as much information about the guest prior to the interview as this will help it flow much more smoothly. I enjoy talking to each guest prior to the interview but they mostly are screened through the producer prior to being scheduled. No response? Yes, by all means they should e-mail or call. I receive a lot of e-mail and do my best to keep up and I do not mind, nor am I bothered with phone calls from guests in anyway. I learn just as much from them as the community does for the most part and that is what makes it a great and unique interview.

Invited Back? If the guest brings education to the community, feedback from our audience, as well as their attitude and mood during the interview.

Bio of Todd Bates: Chances are you'll find him in an abandoned home, walls yellow with age and doors teetering dangerously on their hinges. Maybe there was a murder in the home or perhaps a fire. Whatever the case, Todd is intent on one thing: hearing the voices of the dead.

Electronic Voice Phenomena, or EVP, as it is known in the industry, is the collection of disembodied voices via digital or analog recording devices. For Todd, it is a way of life. After years of investigating these mysterious phenomena, he decided to create a website dedicated to EVP research and education.

With the help of audio editing software, he has collected some of the most impressive samples of the phenomena available today.

Todd's radio experience began with Dr. Ed Craft of Magick Mind Radio and following that, he met up with and decided to co-host with Dr. Jimmy Lowery of APSR Radio. Todd was then given the opportunity to host his own show on the BBS Radio Network.

He then went on to podcasting his pre-recorded information and shows before starting up and recording live, the *Haunted Voices Radio*.

Journeys with Rebecca with Rebecca Jernigan, airing Saturday, 7–8 PM (PT) on Internet, Satellite Terrestrial Radio, podcast, simulcast.

Theme: Metaphysical, paranormal, consciousness.

Guest Profile: Alternative thoughts and actions for the New Age — Must have knowledge and practical application of topics to assist people in becoming aware and enlightened. Someone who can provide the audience with information in a clear manner and who will bring their information with humor, uplifting, and useful way. I prefer their voice (over past interviews and credentials) and a book if an author.

Guest from Hell: Combative, argumentative — a know-it-all — will not listen or continually talks even when asked a question.

Contact: mailbag@journeyswithrebecca.com; 888-958-2768; http://www.journeyswithrebecca.com; Rebecca Jernigan. Best method: E-mail and press kit. No response? They should send a second e-mail one week.

Invited Back? Content — delivery — If there was not enough time on a show to share valuable information to the audience.

Guest Comment: "Rebecca is a deep soul with a profound understanding of spiritual truths. She is an ideal host who draws the best out of her guests. I thoroughly enjoyed being on *Journeys with Rebecca*." — Richard Salva, author of *Soul Journey from Lincoln to Lindbergh* (Crystar Press 2006). http://www.LincolnReincarnation.com

Bio of Rebecca Jernigan: Rebecca's enhanced Psi abilities were discovered at age four growing up on a Midwest farm. Psi (pronounced *sigh*) is a term commonly used by parapsychologists to refer to both ESP and psychokinesis taken together. While learning how to gently care for animals and nurture gardens, her innate psychic abilities continued to flourish naturally. As a young adult, Rebecca expanded her knowledge and practices of psi by undertaking a wide range of intense studies in a variety of metaphysical subjects.

Counter to the skeptical society of 1988, Rebecca's strong and capable use of clairvoyance, mediumship and channeling allowed her the confidence to open her own practice as a professional psychic reader/consult. As her business grew, so did her thirst for more knowledge, leading her to explore and excel in the fascinating and socially beneficial fields of hypnosis, divine healing, meditation and Reiki (Rebecca is a master/teacher in 5 Reiki disciplines).

Using what she has branded as intuitive diagnostics, it is common for Rebecca to consult with high level executives, CEOs and CFOs, providing clear and guiding insight on a clairvoyant level for issues concerning large financial decisions, business negotiations, restructuring of human resources and operations and exact personnel issues.

Rebecca has also been called to apply her psi abilities behind the scenes in high profile, Hollywood entertainment cases. Most recently, the psychic work she performed for a Hollywood executive producing team's lawsuit against a major television network resulted in a complete victory for the executive producers in an astounding and record-breaking four days.

On the other end of the criminal justice arena, Rebecca discreetly assists those who have been victimized in crimes as well as their family members and legal counsel. Earlier in 2006, Rebecca consulted long-distance on a week-old missing persons case in New Orleans without knowing the name or age of the abducted victim. Her information once again proved exact and the case was resolved within an amazing 24 hours.

Rebecca was one of the first psychics on television to host not only one, but two television series, "Psychic Voyages" and "Psychic Impressions." When the internet proved a viable medium for reaching audiences worldwide, she turned her attentions to her current show.

She is author of *Tarot: The Intuitive Approach* and the first in a new line of meditation audio CDs.

Full bio at http://www.ghostradiox.com/people_rebecca_jernigan.asp

Kevin Smith Show with Kevin Smith, syndicated in 70 Countries

Theme: Paranormal/strange and unexplained.

Guest Profile: Paranormal/strange and unexplained. The essential qualities I look for in a guest are freshness, and verifiability. If everything the guest is going to talk about is internalized (i.e., psychic or channeled information), we cannot check the information or verify its accuracy. That won't fly here. I do not care if a guest has "credentials." But if the guest claims credentials, I must be able to verify them. I am interested in knowing the following: a.) what is your topic? b.) what is your point? Once we hear your views, so what? c.) how does the listener benefit? d.) why is this different than what we already know?

Guest from Hell: A guest that knows less about a

topic than I do is a guest from hell. A guest who is not a conversationalist is a guest from hell. A guest who is a know-it-all is a guest from hell. A guest who insists on bringing up partisan politics or religious dogma is a guest from hell.

Contact: host@kevinsmithshow.com?subject=Suggestion; http://kevinsmithshow.com. Best method: Here is how to approach me: a.) Send me an e-mail that states plainly that you want to be a guest. State what your topic would be, and why you think my audience would benefit from hearing what you have to say; b.) It's okay to send me a link to your web site. However, don't expect I will have time to devour its content; c.) If I invite you to be a guest on the show, send me a media kit and e-mail me your photo. No response? I get from 30 to 500 e-mails daily. Depending upon the amount of e-mails I have received on the day your e-mail arrives, I may or may not respond. If I do not send you a letter saying that I am not interested, assume I am interested and send another e-mail.

Invited Back? Guests are invited back if they know their topic inside and out, and are good conversationalists. Audience reaction to the guest is also a great factor in my decision.

Guest Comment: "As a nuclear physicist with a very strong interest in flying saucers and Roswell, I have done many hundreds of radio shows to discuss my books, answer questions, etc. Often the hosts don't know much about the subject. I have enjoyed my appearances on the *Kevin Smith Show* because he is very knowledgeable and asks sensible questions. The number of hits on my website www.stantonfriedman.com always goes up when I am a guest on his show." — Stanton T. Friedman, the flying saucer physicist

"I found and find Kevin Smith's show engaging, and he packs some pretty decent punches. I like the tough questions and the digging for the med/sci police approach. Ken, as you know, is a former cop too. This allows him to pursue his guests with real decent questions." — Derrel Sims, UFO researcher, http://www.alienhunter.org

Bio of Kevin Smith: Kevin has spent his life in law enforcement, having worked as a deputy sheriff, a city police officer, an international police officer, a diplomatic observer, and an international police commander. He started this talk show while he was stationed in Kosovo in 2000.

Matthew and Friends with Suzanne (Suzy) Ward on BBS Radio/Station 2; now off the air.

Theme: Spiritual enlightenment/guidance; extraterrestrial life.

Guest Profile: Authors of pertinent books; channels; people who have had extraordinary "paranormal" experiences. A knowledgeable, articulate person with genuine interest in light service; a sense of humor is an asset. All their pertinent experiences; if authors, I need review copies of their books. I always talk with guests prior to their appearance on my program.

Guest from Hell: The opposite of that.

Contact: suzy@matthewbooks.com; Withheld upon request; http://www.matthewbooks.com; Suzy Ward. Best method: E-mail a bio that includes phone number. No response? Please resend e-mail.

Invited Back? First interview.

Bio of Suzy Ward: The evening of April 17, 1980, Suzanne (Suzy) Ward was packing for her next day's business trip when she received the call from Panama that changed her life: Her 17-year-old son Matthew had died after a vehicle crash that day.

The loss of a child has such an immeasurable impact upon the family that Suzy's preoccupation with Matthew's death would not be considered quite unusual. The direction she took in trying to cope with her grief, however, might be considered that. She called a medium with whom she had become friendly three years before, when they had lived in the same city, and asked about her son. The medium told her that he was in "deep rest"; she would receive an unmistakable sign when he was ready to send her a message, and when that time came, she would be led to a trustworthy medium.

The sign came almost nine months later in her first dream about Matthew since his death, and in the months that followed, she learned first of a medium in Virginia, then one in Maryland, and later another, in Delaware. None of them knew each other and none asked Suzy anything except her son's name. Yet all accurately described Matthew's physical appearance and personality; they told her the cause of his death and the ease of his transition. They talked about his new interests and activities, sometimes with a progress report on educational pursuits or piano lessons. And they gave her explicit information about her own life, even details that she alone knew. They could tell her all of these things because they were merely passing on to her what Matthew was telling them — the love between him and his mother was the inseparable bond that enabled him to be aware of her comings and goings.

Still, she could not help but doubt that Matthew ever would talk with her directly.

But it *did happen*! in early February 1994, almost 14 years after his death, when he started speaking to his mother. It was not simply her longing for this moment that created it — something definitely extraordinary was happening. It wasn't long before Matthew started talking about the books she was meant to prepare. Finally, he told her that her primary mission of this lifetime was to publish that information about life beyond Earth and the celestial advice and guidance urgently needed during this era of unprecedented planetary changes. Finally, he answered her question about why he had died at such a young age: He had to, so he could send her that information.

And thus began The Matthew Books: *Revelations for a New Era: A Matthew Book with Suzanne Ward* (Xlibris Corporation 2001), *Matthew, Tell Me About Hea-*

ven: A Matthew Book with Suzanne Ward* (Xlibris Corporation 2002), The last three, published by Matthew Books, are *Matthew Tell Me About Heaven: A Firsthand Description of the Afterlife* (2002); *Illuminations for a New Era: Understanding These Turbulent Times* (2003) and *Voices of the Universe: Your Voice Affects the Universe Let It Be Love* (2004).

P.O.R.T.A.L. Paranormal Talk Radio with Tuesday Miles and Angela Thomas on Sundays, 7–9 PM (ET) and 6–8 PM (CT) on AOL Radio ... MSN Radio ... Tricom ... BBS Radio ... Aussie Chat radio ... Live 365.com ... Satellite radio UK.

To view a list of countries and cities we broadcast to go to http://www.portaltalkradio.com/SHOW INFO.html

Theme: Paranormal, ghosts, hauntings, psychics, supernatural events.

Guest Profile: Authors re: the paranormal, credential psychic mediums, paranormal investigators. Movie stars that have worked in either a movie RE: ghosts etc. Parapsychologists. We look for guests that have gone an extra mile for their research or work. Although we do support those who are also beginning their careers. We look for dedication in their work ... documentation of their work ... published either by web site, or public information. We try to speak with them a couple of weeks prior to the interview; if they have a new book out we try to read the book beforehand or at least research their work; we also create a one page profile for the guest on our website.

Guest from Hell: A guest who is unprepared to answer questions during the interview or gives the short Yes or No replies.

Contact: Portaltalkradio@aol.com; Angela Thomas — Oct13baby@aol.com; Tuesday Miles — TuesdayMiles2@aol.com; 636-278-2272 (Angela Thomas); http://www.portaltalkradio.com; Tuesday Miles: http://www.TuesdayMiles.faithweb.com; Angela Thomas: http://www.Oct13baby.com; Either Tuesday Miles or Angela Thomas. Best method: Usually we receive e-mails; they can send their press kit, word of mouth, someone recommending a guest, or we approach them. No response? We have a rule with the show — we believe in politeness, we respond to all e-mails within 24 hours, even if we can not use them on the show.

Invited Back? If we feel we were not able to cover all of the guest's information, or the guest was willing to really participate with the interview we invite them back to continue with the interview.

Guest Comments: "With Tuesday's insight and experience in the paranormal, her radio show is not just informative, but also very enjoyable. Like sitting down with an old friend, her easy going and smooth interview style creates an atmosphere whereas the allotted time always passes far too quickly."— Debra Pickman, co-owner, founder and administrator, The SallieHouse, http://www.thesalliehouse.com

Bio of Tuesday Miles: Tuesday was born in the 60s in the flower power years, raised with both parents and her older sister. "Growing up I guess they thought I was odd (I didn't); I thought I was just a normal kid," she recounts. "I do recall seeing ghosts when I was little. I was always going into my parent's bedroom at night, waking them up, telling them that there was something in my room (they never believed me). Over the years I had visitations, but not enough to say I was haunted. It wasn't until my Mom died that Spirits really made themselves known to me. I was hit all at once. I first started to feel them. Then to see them. Then to hear them. I hated it because I didn't understand any of it. I thought I was being attacked by some sort of demon energies. I was scared to death. After about a year had gone by, finally giving up on the fact these abilities weren't gonna go away, and for me to stop praying for it to go away, I finally gave up fighting it. Took off my sandals, put on my working boots and got tough, and took my power back.

"'I have had enough of being afraid,' I yelled at the top of my lungs, sounding like I was completely crazy. 'This is my house, and I will not put up with any more chaos!' It was then that I finally felt I had some control over this."

Tuesday has spent the last eight years developing her abilities as a psychic medium. ("I don't call them gifts," she says. "Not yet anyways.")

Bio of Angela Thomas: Psychic-clairvoyant, medium and radio host, Angela was born in Warner Robins, Georgia. After living many years along the Mississippi Gulf Coast and New Orleans, Louisiana, she relocated to the St. Louis, Missouri, area after hurricane Katrina.

Angela has gained a reputation for her psychic abilities through private session and instruction throughout the United States and abroad. Her psychic sessions are sought after from peers in the psychic arena, and beyond. Angela developed a method utilizing the tarot, and various psychic development exercises that she uses, and teaches to others. Her classes are available both online and within the local community.

Angela is author of as yet unpublished books: *Developing Your Psychic Abilities: The Fast Track Guide to Expanding Your Gifts,* and *Three-dimensional Tarot: The Art of Gathering Information.*

The Sasquatch Experience with Sean Forker, Melissa Hovey, and James Baker on BlogTalkRadio, http://www.blogtalkradio.com/sasquatchexperience, aired Sundays at 9 PM (ET).

Theme: Paranormal, science. Subject: Sasquatch/Bigfoot.

Guest Profile: Authors, anthropologists, biologists, field researchers, documentarians, filmmakers. As the producer, I look for people who are interesting, honest, passionate and hard working. It helps the booking process when a potential guest makes themselves stand out with their own work. We interview people from all walks of life, but the common thread that connects is that they all are investigators that spend a great deal of time researching this mystery. To us, it doesn't matter if they have a Ph.D. or a GED — as long as they are out there trying to uncover the facts. Ideally the person inquiring does have some past experience with media interviews. Voice quality only matters if they are inaudible. You can sound like a total geek and we will still book you, as long as you can talk the game. We accept all comers that are serious about the research. Preferably the guest would have some field work experience.

Guest from Hell: We had a guest on the show once who would only answer a question with, "It's in the book. If people want the answer — they have to buy the book." The entire time we had him on the show, all he did was complain about how he was screwed by Hollywood. In the archives to this day you may be able to hear me banging my head off the wall. Worst guest we ever had in the two years we have been on air.

Contact: sasquatchexperience@gmail.com; Call in Live: 1-347-996-5814; http://sasquatchexperience.blogspot.com; Sean Forker, producer/host (moderator). Best method: We take e-mail pitches, bios, and press kits. Those with books and DVDs are encouraged to send us a copy for review. No response? I always tell people if I do not respond in more than three days, start e-mailing the heck out of me. Many times the role in this is reversed, as the host badgers the potential guest to get them on the show. It's fair game for a potential guest to do the same.

Invited Back? The listeners. Also a lot depends on the quality of the guest's material and if they have anything new to offer. Listeners do not want the same selection of material beat to death. That is the hardest part about this particular research.

Bio of Sean Forker: An active researcher of the Sasquatch since age 10, Sean's serious field investigations began in his late teens, and helped shape his understanding of the wilderness and the way it works.

At the age of 22, he is highly regarded in the field of Sasquatch research due to his logical reasoning and equal treatment of all researchers. In 2005 he founded the American Bigfoot Society and was president from 2005 to 2006. In 2006 the group was reorganized and Sean was named chairman, a position he holds for life. He joined the Pennsylvania Bigfoot Society in 2005 and is an active member. In 2007, Sean was accepted into the Alliance of Independent Bigfoot Researchers, a national research organization made of some of the elite members of the Sasquatch research field.

From February to December 2006, Sean joined the *"X" Zone Radio Show* (see page 169), in a monthly segment entitled "The Sightings of Sasquatch/ Bigfoot."

When the wildly popular radio show, *Bigfoot Central*, went off the air, Henry May and Sean Forker created their current show.

In October 2007, Sean Forker teamed with Eric Altman to form Anomalis Entertainment.

Sean has a burning passion for the entertainment business, the paranormal, and the mystery we know as Bigfoot. It is with that passion that he will continue his work for many years to come.

Sean is a resident of Williamsport, Pennsylvania, located in the picturesque Susquehanna River Valley. He and his wife of six years, Laura, raise two children.

UFO Radio with Sam Willey on http://www.podomatic.com and http://www.ufo-radio.net; now off the air.

Theme: Paranormal (primarily UFOs).

Guest Profile: Authors, film directors, researchers, scientists, radio hosts. Anyone with anything interesting to say regarding the paranormal is welcome to share their views on the show as long as they are deemed as a credible source of information. The general public are also urged to participate and share their experiences. I always look for past appearances they have done on other radio shows. I am willing to give everyone a chance who has something of interest to say as long as they can be understood by me and my audience.

Guest from Hell: I have had my fair share of bad guest encounters. The guest from hell when it comes to the paranormal is someone who has obviously fabricated a story and attempts to pass off his fabrication as the truth.

Contact: sam.willey@btinternet.com; 0191-645-2498; http://www.ufo-radio.net; Sam Willey. Best method: I usually contact those whom I wish to have on the show but as for contacting me I usually just like an e-mail explaining what the guest would like to talk about, any past experience, their field of expertise and from there I will reply to the potential guest with any questions I have about them. No response? I am very efficient when it comes to e-mailing and I respond to everyone. It is very rare that anyone has to wait over a week for a response; however, in this very unlikely event I urge the potential guest to make contact again.

Invited Back? A number of factors affect this. For one, if there is a strong listener response such as receiving a number of e-mails with regards to a particular program I may welcome the guest back on the show. Other factors include how interesting the person is and how easy I can understand the guest; for example, if a guest has a slow voice with signs of fatigue it is unlikely I will invite them back on the show. However, if they keep your interest during the show and explain things in full detail it is more likely I will make contact with that guest again.

Bio of Sam Willey: Sam is a 16 year old with a keen interest in the UFO subject, sparked in 2003 when he and two friends witnessed a triangular shaped craft silently float over his home in the North East of England near the city of Sunderland. Ever since the occurrence Sam has been dedicated to researching UFOs and seeking for some truth to what he saw.

His main research began back in September of 2005 when he began alienationsam.com and since then the site has developed dramatically into a vast library of UFO information, which collects all the latest UFO news. He never forgets those amazing incidents from years ago which need to be remembered such as the Roswell 1947 UFO crash.

The Unexplained World with Edward Shanahan and Annette on Blog Talk Radio http://www.blogtalkradio.com/tuw and archived on over 20 podcast sites.

Theme: Supernatural, spiritual, paranormal, unexplained, conspiracies, UFOs.

Guest Profile: Authors, psychics, paranormal investigators, and spiritual individuals who have a passion for or story to tell about their self and their subject of interest. I do request to talk to them first.

Guest from Hell: Individual who has nothing to say or is lost when it comes to having a discussion.

Contact: edwardlshanahan@comcast.net; 312-208-8333; http://www.blogtalkradio.com/tuw http://theunexplainedworld.com; Edward Shanahan. Best method: Send me an e-mail and inform me what you're about. No response? E-mail me again after about a week.

Invited Back? The feeling I get from the overall guest interview.

Bio of Edward Shanahan and Annette: Edward is a spiritual observer and psychic reader.

Annette is a high priestess and reader.

The Vike Report with Brian Vike on http://jancikradionetwork.com/innerstreamsradio/show/vike_report/index.html

Theme: Eyewitnesses to a UFO or alien abduction.

Guest Profile: Pretty much anyone with an amazing UFO or missing time/abduction experience. I look for someone who can relate their sighting or experience well. But mainly I look for an interesting event which I know my listeners will enjoy listening to, or relate to. I always call the guests ahead of time to talk with each of them; this allows me to check each person out the best I can. Most of the folks who come on the show are everyday folks like me. One does not have to be an expert in anything; if they have had a good UFO sighting, they are more than welcome on the show.

Guest from Hell: Someone who talks complete nonsense and cannot back up what he or she is talking about. Or a guest where you have to drag everything out of them.

Contact: hbccufo@telus.net; 250-845-2180; http://www.hbccufo.org; Brian Vike — Director of HBCC UFO Research. Best method: E-mail or phone, People can approach me very easily; I am an easy-going guy. If someone has written a book, done a DVD, etc., over what they have seen, they are welcome to join me on the show. They can pop me off an e-mail and I will call them up, or they are welcome to call me. But my radio show is for folks who have experienced something unusual. No response? Well usually I reply the same day or at the latest the following day. But if for some unknown reason something goes wrong as it does from time to time, I would suggest that they please write or call me again.

Invited Back? I do bring guests back onto the show — this is when they have a lot more to add to their ongoing experiences and are willing to relate the information to me and the listeners.

Bio of Brian Vike: Brian is an independent UFO investigator/researcher and director of HBCC UFO Research. He started HBCC UFO Research back in mid 2000 as he's always had a fascination with the UFO topic.

He works out of a small town called Houston in the northwestern part of British Columbia, Canada, where he receives hundreds upon hundreds of UFO sighting reports each year.

Long ago he was a member of the Royal Astronomical Society of Canada and of the American Association of Variable Star Observers. He also used to volunteer at the Vancouver Planetarium. He has been featured in UFO documentaries, on countless radio shows and in the newspapers. "I must say, I would have never imagined the UFO topic could ever keep me as busy as it does, but I do enjoy the subject very much," says Brian.

Brian is married with two grown kids and is grandfather of the light of his life, his 6-year-old granddaughter.

The "X" Zone Radio Show with Rob McConnell, aired worldwide on satellite, radio (am/fm/short wave) and audio/video streaming. The only radio show produced in Canada that is syndicated internationally (by the TalkStar Network), *"X" Zone Radio Show* is broadcast Monday–Friday 10 PM to 2 AM (ET) and then repeated in its entirety from 2 AM–6 AM (ET), and again from 10 AM–2 PM (ET).

Theme: The paranormal, parapsychology, New Age, spirituality.

Guest Profile: Roughly 50 percent are authors who write about paranormal and parapsychology topics; the guest is at http://www.xzone-radio.com/guests.htm. Someone who believes in what they are talking about, just not looking for an international audience to sell their wares to. Sincerity, honesty and who believes in what they are saying. Expertise, knowledge of topic, experiences, credentials.

Guest from Hell: Unfortunately, I cannot answer this. We have never had one.

Contact: xzone@xzone-radio.com; 905-575-5916; http://www.xzoneradio.com and http://www.xzonetv.com; Rob McConnell, host and executive producer. Best method: If an author, send a copy of the book or DVD to *The "X" Zone Radio Show*, 54 Tivoli Drive, Hamilton, Ontario, Canada, L9C 2E4 along with press release and press kit, or send an e-mail to xzone@xzone-radio.com. No response? E-mail or call — but this does not happen.

Invited Back? The manner in which the guest responds to my questions, their credibility, their knowledge of the subject on which they talk.

Guest Comments: "This was my first time on the radio and I had a thoroughly enjoyable experience with Rob. I was honored to have been asked to be on his show and would love to come back in the future. The topics that end up on his show are fascinating. A good show to listen to for supernatural, paranormal, and current trend issues. Thanks Rob." — Rona Anderson, paranormal investigator, Paranormal Explorers, http://www.paranormalexplorers.com

"It's great to have the X-Zone and Rob McConnell back. He's a well-informed interviewer, who asks both interesting and often thought provoking questions, and doesn't simply accept the 'true believers' perspectives without questioning them. It is an essential attitude if we are to understand anything about these phenomena which we call paranormal — one simply cannot be all-believing or all-disbelieving, as both perspectives eliminates the main way we learn, by asking questions.

"Thanks again for having me on the show, Rob, and I look forward to many more such experiences in the X-Zone." — Loyd Auerbach, author and paranormal researcher, http://www.mindreader.com

Bio of Rob McConnell: A well-known Canadian radio and TV personality, Rob has worked both in front of and behind the cameras on the popular Canadian TV Show "Creepy Canada" as a consultant to the producers and as an expert in parapsychology on the upcoming Canadian paranormal reality TV show "Proof."

Referred to by members of the media as one of Canada's leading paranormal experts, he first broadcast the show in 1993 on Hamilton's AM 900 CHML with Bill Kelly and it had its first airing on TalkStar Radio Network in 2004. (TalkStar has corporate offices in Oregon with studios/master control/satellite platform in White Springs, Florida and is now the flagship of both TalkStar and StarTV Networks).

Rob's media career includes hosting The "X" Zone at 1220 CHSC in St. Catharines; CJBK in London, Ontario; CKTB in St. Catharines — where he was also the executive producer of Talk Programming and Promotions Director; and CFBU in St. Catharines. After leaving CFBU, Rob's syndicated show was done from his own studio on the LWRN before the TalkStar Radio Network.

Rob is also the publisher of *The "X" Chronicles Newspaper* and the inventor and developer of "The 'X' Game" (1997).

"The 'X' Zone TV Show" is simulcast from Rob's Hamilton, Ontario, broadcast studio. Television stations in the international markets as well as satellite providers have already taken the opportunity of signing *The "X" Zone Radio* / TV Show. "The 'X' Zone TV Show" will also be available on the Internet through WIFI.

Rob resides in Hamilton, Ontario, with his wife Laura, who is the senior producer of *The "X" Zone Radio Show*.

Parents and Children

Chit Chat with Kat on All Talk Radio, http://www.alltalkradio.net; now off the air.

Theme: Teens.

Guest Profile: Anything that is teen related. Someone that is willing to talk about themselves and what they have experience in their life as a teen. I want to know if they are willing talk about themselves.

Guest from Hell: I don't think that there is a guest from hell because they are talking about themselves and it is a learning experience for me and my listeners.

Contact: chitchatwithkat@yahoo.com; 702-309-6127; http://www.alltalkradio.net/chitchatwithkat; Katrina. Best method: E-mailing a bio and sending a press kit. No response? E-mail or Call. Most of the time I will give them a reasonable amount of time.

Invited Back? If they want to come back on.

Bio of Katrina Carson: Katrina is 17 and was 13 when she started working. "I was inspired to do my show by *Coffee with Caryll*, who is my grandmother. She told me that I could do anything I want to; it might not be easy but I can do it. She also told me that teens are out there and they want to have people hear them but they do not know where to go to do so. That is why I started my show.

Creating a Family: Talk About Infertility and Adoption with Dawn Davenport on http://www.findingyourchild.com

Theme: Infertility and adoption.

Guest Profile: Infertility professional, adoption professionals, authors of infertility, adoption or parenting books. Knowledge of the topic and expertise are paramount.

Guest from Hell: A guest who either goes into a monologue or one who answers in monosyllables.

Contact: dawn@findingyourchild.com; withheld upon request; http://www.findingyourchild.com; www.creatingafamily.com; Dawn Davenport. Best method: E-mail. No response? E-mail me one more time.

Invited Back? Determinants are the knowledge of the subject and their ability to present the information in an easy to understand style.

Bio of Dawn Davenport: Dawn is a writer, attorney, researcher, radio host, and speaker specializing in adoption and infertility. Her book, *The Complete Book of International Adoption: A Step by Step Guide to Finding Your Child* (Random House/Broadway 2006)

and internet radio show help families through infertility and adoption.

She has published on adoption in national and regional publications, including *Conceive Magazine*, the *Christian Science Monitor,* and *USA Today*. She is interviewed frequently about adoption, including numerous times on National Public Radio. Her research has been featured on CBS News *60 Minutes* and *People Magazine*.

Dawn has served as a background consultant to CBS News *60 Minutes* and ABC News *Primetime Live* on adoption issues. She loves to speak at infertility and adoption conferences to help others on their journey to find their child. Perhaps most important, she is a mom of four by birth and adoption and cares passionately about this issue.

Friend of the Family Susan H. Turben, Ph.D., hopes to be on NPR affiliate WCPN 90.3 FM, Cleveland, Ohio, http://www.wcpn.org, http://www.friendofthefamilyradio.com

Theme: Early childhood, family issues.

Guest Profile: Authors, teachers, parents, directors of fine art facilities, directors of activity facilities. Someone who is involved in family life. Interests and value to our theme.

Guest from Hell: Someone who is negative or talks too much, or too little.

Contact: assistant@turben.com; 216-593-2134; http://www.friendofthefamilyradio.com; www.turben.com; Carol Lorek, assistant to Susan Turben. Best method: E-mail a bio with a reason why they're interested. No response? Yes, a follow up phone call would be appreciated.

Invited Back? How fun the show was — how well it went.

Bio of Susan Turben: When was the last time you heard of a doctor making a house call? If the doctor is Susan Turben, Ph.D., nationally known child development specialist, the answer is probably just yesterday. That's because Susan (as she prefers to be called) believes that the only way to get to the root of a family's issues and concerns is to observe its members in their natural surroundings — in their home, on a playground, or even at the local McDonald's.

But making house calls is only one of the many attributes that makes Susan very different and, at times, more controversial than your average child development expert. Aside from being a family counselor and child advocate, she is also a mother of five, grandmother of ten, a researcher, and a teacher. She understands the modern day, non-traditional families. Her family practice takes her (on a daily basis) into the lives of families. Susan takes a direct personal approach, incorporating family stories and collaborating with parents so that practical child-rearing methods allow families to decide for themselves how to raise their children.

As head of Turben Developmental Services Foundation, a Beachwood, Ohio, firm providing child development and parenting services for adults and their young children, Susan has developed a national reputation for offering straight-forward, street-wise advice.

Working with disadvantaged, disenfranchised groups, particularly working poor families and African American groups, she is the doctor who makes house calls with Human Services and Juvenile and Domestic Courts, and serves on Abuse and Neglect Advisory and Welfare-to-Work Boards. Susan regularly receives referrals from preschool, childcare, and early intervention programs to assist with families who are dealing with issues and concerns, which affect their children's future.

Susan got her start at Head Start in Albany, New York, and in 1974 received a grant for the Handicapped Children Early Education Program (HCEEP), to start the first infant stimulation program in the capital district of New York State. During the next 10 years, she designed, implemented, and evaluated more than 10 programs to serve families with infants and toddlers.

A lecturer at colleges and universities throughout Ohio, she is sought out as an "expert" by such major media outlets as CBS, Dateline Cleveland, Morning Exchange, Cleveland Live Web site, and Women Professionals in Ohio.

Growing Up with Dr. Jerry Brodlie, child psychologist, on the Business Talk Radio Network, airing Sundays, 1–2 PM (ET).

Theme: A discussion format that explores the challenges, rewards and nuances of parenting and most all aspects of the childhood experience.

Guest Profile: Authors, educators, physicians, legislators, celebrities, psychologists, specialists in childhood disorders — anyone dealing with parenting and children. Solid base of knowledge. Ability to express their thoughts clearly and succinctly. A sense of humor. Credentials. Experience with subject. Among his prominent guests were former Connecticut senator Lowell Weicker, Jr., and Miriam Arond, editor-in-chief of *Child* magazine.

Guest from Hell: Hard core book or program sellers.

Contact: jbrodlie@lifestyletalkradio.com, dprescott@lifestyletalkradio.com; http://www.lifestyletalkradio.com; 203-254-9245; Doug Prescott. Best method: Call, e-mail, press kit. No response? E-mail or call.

Invited Back? Subject relevance. On-air style. Contribution to our listening audience.

Bio of Dr. Jerome F. Brodlie: Dr. Brodlie is chairman, Department of Psychology, Greenwich Hospital, Greenwich, CT, Yale New Haven Health. He has an M.S. and Ph.D. from Columbia University and did his internship at Long Island Medical Center/Hillside Hospital.

He is in private practice in Greenwich, CT, and on the editorial board of *Child* magazine.

In addition, Dr. Brodlie is a consultant, Department of Education, Cayman Islands, consulting psychologist in the public and private schools in Fairfield County, CT, and a consultant regarding Post Traumatic Stress in children for both the U.S. Department of State, U.N. tsunami relief, U.S. Gulf Coast hurricane relief and Cayman Islands hurricane relief.

In addition to *Child* magazine, he has been published in *Seventeen Magazine* and *Business Week*.

Just One More Book! with Mark Blevis and Andrea Ross, a podcast, published each Monday, Wednesday, Friday and Saturday and distributed over the Internet using syndication feeds for playback on portable media players and personal computers; http://feeds.feedburner.com/justonemorebook

Theme: To promote and celebrate literacy and great children's books (mainly picture books).

Guest Profile: Our guests include children's book authors, illustrators, publishers, editors, promoters and enthusiasts, as well as professionals and volunteers who work to promote literacy and the enjoyment of children's books. We look for: excellence and innovation in children's book writing and illustration; strong opinions; unusual paths to their fields; interesting combinations of careers; dedication to volunteer organizations; and, expertise and innovation related to literacy and promotion of children's books. In the case of authors, illustrators and other talented people who create children's books, we like to be very familiar with and impressed by a good selection of their work. In the case of literacy and literature experts and enthusiasts, we like to be familiar with their work and achievements.

Guest from Hell: We've never had a guest from hell — perhaps because we only schedule interviews with polite, passionate and positive individuals. A mumbler or a rambler would not be fun to edit, but Mark is an excellent editor, so the published interview would sound great nonetheless.

Contact: JustOneMoreBook@gmail.com; 613-762-9704; http://www.JustOneMoreBook.com; Mark Blevis and Andrea Ross. Best method: The best way to initiate communication is by sending a friendly e-mail that presents a brief introduction and a reference to a website that highlights achievements and biographical information. It's ideal if the person who approaches us is familiar with our show, and podcasting in general, and understands how their project fits in with our community, i.e., picture books, types of authors. No response? If we do not respond to the initial e-mail within a week, it's possible that we did not receive the e-mail so you may want to e-mail us a second time. After our initial reply, it may be a while before we contact you to schedule an interview as we usually have a lengthy list of potential guests.

Invited Back? We generally only feature each guest once. However, we did run a nine part series in which we followed an author/illustrator through the creation and publication of one of his books. Future documentary series may examine other fascinating areas of children's books and literacy.

Guest Comment: "It's just so nice to hear you guys review books as thoroughly and as thoughtfully and as humorously and as cheerfully as you do — and to have mine picked up by you is just a thrill." — Scott Magoon, art director, Houghton Mifflin Company, and illustrator of *The Luck of the Loch Ness Monster* by A.W. Flaherty (Houghton Mifflin 2007), http://www.scottmagoon.com/ScottMagoonsWebsite.html

Bios of Andrea Ross and Mark Blevis: Andrea and Mark are co-creators of the children's book podcasts *Just One More Book!* and *Swimming in Literary Soup*. Through these podcasts and their websites, Andrea and Mark are building a lively, interactive community that links children's book authors, illustrators, readers, librarians and publishers.

Andrea lives in the heart of Canada's capital with her husband, two daughters and a ridiculously large number of children's books.

Mark has been a prolific podcaster since April 2005. Besides producing his own hobby podcasts (*Electric Sky, Growing Enthusiasm* and *Just One More Book!*), Mark provides audio production, consulting, voice overs and theme music through his audio production company, Third Storey Inc. As co-producer of the Canadian Podcast Buffet and co-founder/co-organizer of the annual Podcasters Across Borders conference, he has become a leader in the new media community and a columnist for *Podcast User Magazine*. When not producing podcasts, Mark can be found folding laundry — while listening to podcasts.

The Kevin and Trudie Show with husband-and-wife team Kevin Holden and Trudie Mason on CJAD 800, Montreal, Quebec.

Theme: Family matters, workplace issues, current events and entertainment.

Guest Profile: Any and all as long as they are interesting. Someone who is knowledgeable about his/her field, can communicate in layman's terms, is enthusiastic about the topic and is genuinely interested in helping the listeners understand. Credentials including educational and work background, then past interview experiences.

Guest from Hell: Someone who is only interested in peddling his/her book, i.e., someone whose answer to every question is "I cover that in my book." In other words, someone who wants to say nothing, offer no advice or insight during an interview for fear that "giving away" information on the radio will hurt book sales. Sorry, but our obligation to our listeners is not to help you sell your book — it is to make sure our listeners get something they can use or relate to out of the interview.

Contact: kevin.holden@cjad.com trudie.mason@cjad.com; 514-989-3858; http://www.cjad.com; Either of the show hosts or producer Yolande Ramsey at yolande.ramsey@cjad.com. Best method: E-mail us your pitch, including information about the book/project and your credentials. If we want a media kit or copy of the book, we'll request it. No response? Assume that we have seen your pitch and have decided not to contact you for an interview. If you must follow-up, do it by e-mail. However, we get many pitches and only respond if we are interested in an interview.

Invited Back? Whether they can supply useful information to our listeners in an engaging, passionate or entertaining way.

Bios of Kevin Holden and Trudie Mason: Both Kevin and Trudie are graduates of Concordia University in Montreal — Kevin has a degree in communications and has worked as a sound technician, master control producer, radio advertising copywriter and talk show host for 20 years.

Trudie has a degree in journalism and has worked as a radio reporter, newscaster, editorialist and talk show host in Montreal for more than 20 years. She is also a part-time radio news instructor at her alma mater, Concordia University.

Kevin and Trudie have shared on-air hosting duties for ten years and have two children.

Mom Talk Radio with Maria Bailey on WJBW 1000 AM, south Florida, and on iTunes and http://www.momtalkradio.com/shows

Theme: Issues important to moms.

Guest Profile: Authors, Drs., parenting experts, other experts. Someone with information that would help moms with children, work, relationships, health, etc. We usually require their bio and some general information about their book or a copy of the book and their website.

Guest from Hell: One that is not relevant to moms at all and that is not passionate about what they are talking about.

Contact: info@momtalkradio.com; 954-943-2322; http://www.momtalkradio.com; Laura Motsett at laura@bsmmedia.com. Best method: E-mailing a bio or sending a press kit or book copy would be the best way. No response? Please e-mail again. The quantity of e-mails we receive each day is very large. We try to respond to everyone but sometimes we can't. If the subject is a good fit we will be back in touch.

Invited Back? We have a long list of guests that want to be on, so it usually takes quite a while to repeat a guest.

Bio of Maria Bailey: Maria has long had a passion for helping mothers find the answers they need to become better parents. Her passion for business and desire to help moms juggle the tasks of motherhood led her to create BSM Media and its media properties, BlueSuitMom.com, and *Mom Talk Radio*.

In 1999, Maria launched *Mom Talk Radio* long before podcasting, iPods or online radio became hip. In fact, it was the first terrestrial radio show designed exclusively for moms and has been syndicated in several markets over the years and recognized in O*prah "O" Magazine*, *Women's Day*, *USA Today* and *Parenting* magazine. In 2006, *American Baby* and *Parents* named *Mom Talk Radio* one of the best mom podcasts.

Maria is host of "The Balancing Act" on Lifetime TV, co-founder of BlueSuitMom.com, co-founder of Newbaby.com and producer of Mom Talk Moments for Nestle's Verybestbaby.com. Formerly she was the work/life balance expert on "Simplify Your Life" which aired on The Fine Living Network. Maria can be heard everyday as the co-host of the *Real Life Hour of Good Day* with Doug Stephan, www.dougstephan.com which airs in 350 cities across America with an audience of 3.2 million listeners.

Inc. Magazine named Maria Bailey "One of America's Best Work/Life Resources."

She is the author of *The Women's Home-Based Business Book of Answers* (Random House 2001), *Marketing to Moms: Getting Your Piece of the Trillion Dollar Market* (Prima 2002) and *Trillion Dollar Moms: Marketing to a New Generation of Mothers* (Dearborn, 2005).

Maria resides in South Florida with her husband and four children.

Parents Rule! with Pat Montgomery on Thursday, 2–3 PM (ET) on 1620 AM, Sandy Spring, Ga., and live and archived at http://www.radiosandysprings.com

Theme: Anything to do with issues faced by parents, want to be parents, or grandparents.

Guest Profile: Parents, doctors, nurses, authors, therapists, schools, basically anyone who can help support parents. I look for someone who has a passion to help parents or children. Someone with a new idea or an innovative way of looking at something is great. It is not necessary that I agree with them and controversial ideas are also welcome. A short bio needs to be submitted so I know how best to introduce them.

Guest from Hell: Someone who freezes and speaks in monotone or short statements, forcing me to do all the talking.

Contact: mqei@mindspring.com; 770-945-7373 office; 770-891-8473 cell; http://www.parentsrulewithpat.com; Pat Montgomery. Best method: Phone a pitch, e-mail a bio or send a press kit. No response? I try to get back to a person in reasonable period of time. If I don't, they are welcome to call or e-mail again. I will tell them up front if I don't think they will be a fit for the show.

Invited Back? If someone has multiple topics and I think the interview is interesting to my audience, I welcome a guest back.

Guest Comments: "Thanks again for having me (and my family) on your show. It was a lot of fun!!" — Christie G. Crowder, life enrichment professional and author of *Your Big Sister's Guide to Surviving College*

(Wyatt-MacKenzie Publishing 2007), http://www.christiecrowder.com

"Thank you for the opportunity to join you on *Parents Rule!* Your warmth and insightful questions really made the show. It was such a pleasure to chat with you."—G. Wright Bates, Jr., M.D., Atlanta Center for Reproductive Medicine

Bio of Pat Montgomery: Pat is an entrepreneur, speaker, trainer, registered nurse, grandmother of 10 and author of *Now You Know What I Know: Parenting Wisdom of a Grandmother* (AuthorHouse 2005).

She and her husband own a consulting company in the railroad industry.

Pat is also active in city government in Suwanee, Ga., helping to create the city plan up to 2030.

Work at Home Moms Talk Radio with Kelly McCausey on http://www.wahmtalkradio.com and as a Podcast

Theme: Work at home moms or those who want to work from home; business topics, etc.

Guest Profile: Work at home moms, Internet marketing experts. We like to feature moms who are successfully working from home and we also bring interesting and entertaining home based business experts to the show. We interview a lot of moms who have never been on radio before so experience really isn't important.

Guest from Hell: Someone who doesn't talk at all or who only wants to talk about themselves like they were God's Gift to moms.

Contact: kelly@kellymccausey.com; 517-977-0103; http://www.wahmtalkradio.com; Kelly McCausey. Best method: In order to be considered as a guest on the show please first listen to the show. Then write down your topic ideas and share how you believe that your idea will benefit or entertain our listeners. If you really want to speed things up you can even create a list of suggested questions. E-mail everything along with your bio, website information and daytime telephone number to: kelly@kellymccausey.com. No response? They can always e-mail again. My VA usually responds to all inquiries within 24 hours, unless on a weekend (then she responds the following Monday).

Invited Back? If you're lively and provide great information, I'll usually think of you again.

Guest Comments: "Thanks so much, Kelly, for the fabulous opportunity to be on the show. It was a great experience for me and a ton of fun. I really appreciated the increase in traffic to my site, but most of all it gave me a great boost of confidence. It gave me that 'credibility' edge I think I needed to help me step out of my comfort zone as I interact with other moms in business."—Annette Yen

"I wanted to take a minute (or ten) and write to you about being a guest on your show. Wow. I've benefited in many ways from appearing on *WAHM Talk Radio*. It was the best possible way to be introduced to the WAHM community. I was worried that the WAHMs were going to be too 'Mary Poppins' to accept someone with my brash personality and sense of humor. What I found, thanks to your show, was that in the WAHM community there's room for everyone ... even me! I never would have known that had I not been a guest on your show. There are other great things that have come from it as well, but goodness knows I don't have four hours to write the next great novel on how amazing *WAHM Talk Radio* is and how it can change your business (and personal) life for the better!"—Jennifer Gniadecki, Marketing Curve

Bio of Kelly McCausey: Internet radio changed Kelly's business and it ended up changing her life.

In early 2002, Kelly turned to the Internet to help earn extra money through providing web and graphic design services. She wasn't making enough money at her full time job to make ends meet. As a single mom, Kelly wanted to earn more without sacrificing the amount of time she had to be home with her son.

In 2003, she first learned about Internet radio and became so enamored with it that she looked for ways to incorporate audio with her existing websites, choosing to launch a short audio newsletter for her work at home mom directory website, USAWAHM.com. The newsletter was only five minutes a week and quickly grew a listenership. This got her thinking seriously about how to bring more audio content to the web for other Moms like her.

With the sponsorship of InternetBasedMoms.com, Kelly launched her show in 2003 on a shoestring budget. When podcasting exploded in fall of 2004, she jumped onto the podcast wave, further growing her listenership and increasing her excitement about audio on the web.

Kelly believes that more moms should launch internet radio programs and podcasts on a wide range of family friendly topics. She created a tutorial that shows how it can be done and has formed the Mom's Radio Network, a network of programs to help to co-promote one another's shows.

Politics

Action Point with Cynthia Black on 1480 KPHX, Phoenix, AZ, Sunday, noon to 2 PM (MT).

Theme: "Solution politics: We attack problems, not people."

Guest Profile: Authors, journalists, linguists, pollsters, environmentalists, cultural leaders, activists, media critics, intelligence and national security analysts. Specialist or expert in field with command of topic. Solutions-oriented approach to area of interest or expertise. I want to know whatever is necessary to establish credibility and give good impression of interview skills.

Guest from Hell: Monotonous delivery or tone of

voice. Unable to expand on lead of idea or wandering ideas.

Contact: actionpointonline@cox.net; 602-502-6753; http://www.actionpointonline.com; Cynthia Black, host and producer. Best method: E-mailing with a pitch, bio and a link to an audio file of interview or clip. No response? E-mail or call.

Invited Back? Audience interest. Ability to present depth and detail in fairly short clips is especially appealing.

Bio of Cynthia Black: An artist since the 60s, Cynthia's populist politics have informed her choices.

Not content to stick with the arts, she went to the opposite end of the process by starting many businesses — her most satisfying work in mediation. So why radio? "The important message today is political and the important art is restoration of representative democracy, because legislation affecting every artist, business person or family, is being fixed at the top by special interest money.... Creating a processes for reversing that circumstance is now for me the only art — or business — worth doing."

AM South Florida with Russ Morley on WFTL, 6–9 AM (ET), airing in Ft. Lauderdale, Miami, and West Palm Beach.

Theme: News/current events.

Guest Profile: Commentary, opinion, expertise on topical issues and events. Guests should be upbeat, concise, and able to tie into the copy with minimal personal sell. Past interview experiences, credential and the sound of their voice are all important.

Guest from Hell: One who constantly touts their book or website rather than directly answers questions.

Contact: russm@jamescrystal.com; Withheld upon request; http://85owftl.com; Robin Garrett at live 85palmbeach@gmail.com. Best method: E-mail with ideas and creds. No response? E-mail again. It may have gotten lost.

Invited Back? Interaction skills, ability to make a point or offer a comment in limited time. Do they sound upbeat and awake at 6 AM, and dependability on agreed time?

Bio of Russ Morley: Looks like Brad Pitt, funnier than Jeff Foxworthy, smarter than Warren Buffett.

The Andrew Carter Show on CJAD 800, Montreal, Canada, airing weekdays, 5:30–9 AM (ET).

Theme: News, entertainment, information, wake-up.

Guest Profile: Authors, politicians, sports, actor, celebrities, etc. Compelling story to tell. Topical. Bright. That they have an ability to tell their story in the context of a 3–4 minute interview.

Guest from Hell: One word answers.

Contact: andrew.carter@cjad.com; 514-697-0367; http://www.cjad.com; Andrea Elias at 514-989-3813 aelias@cjad.com. Best method: E-mail with press kit. No response? Follow with a phone call.

Invited Back? If they are bright and interesting.

Bio of Andrew Carter: Andrew hosts the number one radio show in Montreal. He has been in Montreal radio for 25 years, and is active in supporting many Montreal charities. He has taught in the journalism department at Montreal's Concordia University, is a former champion curler, loves to play golf and is married with two children.

Battle Line with Alan Nathan, nationally syndicated from Radio America Network.

Theme: Aggressive centrism. Alan's show begins with his mantra "We want the Republicans out of our bedrooms, the Democrats out of our wallets, and both out of our First and Second Amendment rights." (He additionally challenges the Libertarians.)

Guest Profile: Political leaders, pundits, reporters, authors, activists and occasional celebs. Would like energy, animation, substance and credentials.

Guest from Hell: One who turns out not to be as promoted.

Contact: alan@alannathan.com; 703-719-0101; 703-899-3148; 703-302-1000 (ext. 251); http://www.alannathan.com; Alan Nathan. Best method: E-mail or phone. E-mail pitch and one-sheet bio. No response? Call.

Invited Back? If they're able to take it as well as give it.

Guest Comments: "One of the most unusual talk shows in the business because he is a radical moderate. It terrified me the first time I was on because within 30 seconds I realized I was playing in a very difficult sport..." — Michael Harrison, editor and publisher, *Talkers Magazine*

"Cut Throat Talk, No Holds Barred Debate. Right meets left and the sparks fly." — Alan Gottlieb, president, KITZ 1400 Port Orchard-Seattle, Washington; KGTK 920 Olympia-Seattle, Washington; KBNP 1410 Portland, Oregon; KSBN 1230 Spokane, Washington

Bio of Alan Nathan: Alan's been called the "centrist with teeth," whose show moves at about 125 mph. *Talkers Magazine* rated *Battle Line* among the Top 100 Talk Hosts in America for 2002, 2003 and 2005. As an Achievement in Radio award nominated talk host and former national television correspondent, Alan has gone toe-to-toe with national leaders, columnists and extremists from all corridors of public argument.

As an eyewitness on 9-11, Alan was the first member of the media to report the attack on the Pentagon. He has been on Fox News and CNN multiple times and lectures at live events. He's a regular columnist with *Front Page Magazine* and is often a guest columnist in *The Washington Examiner* and *The Washington Times*.

Alan began as a DJ at 1480 WPWC Radio in Dumfries, VA, and a year later started a talk show entitled *Profile and Comment with Alan Nathan*. Soon after, he created a public access television show version of "Profile and Comment" and was hired by legendary Pulitzer Prize winning columnist/reporter Jack Anderson, the host of "The Insiders with Jack Anderson" on the Financial News Network. Seven months later, FNN was sold and hundreds, including Alan, lost their jobs.

In 1998, he began an independent centrist radio show entitled *Spanking the Left and Right* on WZHF 1390 AM in Washington, D.C. Later that year he went to Radio America and became the nationally syndicated weekend host of *Battling the Left and Right*. He's been host of *Battle Line* for more than nine years.

Full bio at http://www.alannathan.com/biography.htm

Behind the News with Doug Henwood on WBAI, 99.5 FM, New York, Thursdays, 5–6 PM, and archived to the web.

Theme: Economics and politics, broadly defined, NYC to the world.

Guest Profile: Authors, pundits, academics, think-tankers, and the occasional stripper. (Doug explains how strippers fit in with the theme of the show: "One is that sex work is, after all, work for pay (and porn is a business), and I do a lot about working conditions, pay, boss-employee relations, etc. And two, I sometimes do stuff that isn't strictly economics or politics. I've had on a few novelists, a composer, and a music historian too. I'd die of boredom if it was all econ.") People who talk well, know what they're talking about, can clarify the complex, and have a sense of humor. Usually some idea of their expertise, and if possible, some exposure to their speaking style (other interviews, phone pre-interview, etc.).

Guest from Hell: People who drone on and on, never getting to a point, and not letting me ask another question, and people who give one- or two-sentence answers.

Contact: dhenwood@panix.com; 212-219-0010; http://www.leftbusinessobserver.com/Radio.html; Doug Henwood. Best method: Best is e-mail with a pitch or a review copy of book. No response? It usually means I'm not interested, so please give up.

Invited Back? If they're good at the qualities described in (1) above.

Bio of Doug Henwood: At Yale, where Doug graduated with a B.A. in English, he was briefly a conservative and a member of the Party of the Right, which maneuvered his election as secretary of the Political Union, but he quickly came to his senses (though he is, as they say around the POR, a member for life at least).

From 1976 to 1979, Doug did graduate work in English at the University of Virginia, concentrating on British and American poetry and critical theory, fulfilling all requirements for a Ph.D. except for that great stumbling block, a dissertation. After two years working as a copywriter and under-assistant promotion man for a medical publisher in New York, Doug revived the idea of writing his dissertation, which was to be an examination of the varieties of narcissism in American poetry from Emerson through Whitman to Stevens. The dissertation was never written. But in the course of boning up on the theory and history of the U.S. political economy, Doug got more deeply interested in economic matters and less so in literary ones, supplementing a decent base of undergraduate training with extensive self-teaching. After 5 years of contemplation, convinced that the 1980s experiment with free-market economics was a financial and social disaster and that much "left" writing on economics was usually dry and dated, Doug decided that there was room for a newsletter addressing both these deficiencies. He founded *Left Business Observer* in 1986, which covers economics and politics in the broadest sense. Doug is also a contributing editor of *The Nation*.

His book *Wall Street* (Verso 1997) went out of print in 2005 and is now available for free download. His social atlas of the U.S. (in the Pluto atlas series), is *The State of the USA* (Simon and Schuster 1994) and his latest effort is *After the New Economy* (The New Press 2003). He's now in the early stages of a book on the current American ruling class, whoever that might be.

Beneath the Surface with Suzi Weissman on KPFK, Los Angeles.

Theme: Public affairs — international, national, local.

Guest Profile: I have authors (generally of non-fiction books on politics, history or culture), policy wonks, experts, politicians and performers (and more!) on the show. I do want the guests to be experts in their area, but sometimes I interview journalists who have covered stories of interest. Articulate, knowledgeable, dynamic. Credentials above all.

Guest from Hell: One who doesn't listen to questions, doesn't allow host to ask questions (speaking non-stop), monotone answers, extremely short answers, trivial or superficial grasp of subject.

Contact: sweissman@igc.org; 818-985-2711 x252 (producer); http://www.kpfk.org and http://www.suziweissman.com; Alan Minsky. Best method: E-mail, follow up on phone. For authors, send a press kit and book, e-mail bio, reviews of work. No response? By all means try again.

Invited Back? Profound knowledge of subject matter, good radio experience, expert on current hot topic in the news.

Listener Comments: "KPFK's coverage of last fall's election was always interesting and its lineup of informed afternoon talk hosts (including print journalists Jon Wiener, Joe Domanick and Suzi Weissman) offers a bracing antidote to the usual topic-of-the-day talk show drone."—*Los Angeles Times*, May 21, 2001

"The jewel in the crown is drive-time public affairs: Cooper's daily show, plus *Radio Nation*, his weekly collaboration with *The Nation* magazine (he also writes a column for *L.A. Weekly*); Jon Wiener's, Suzi Weissman's and Joe Domanick's early-evening drive-time shows."—*L.A. Weekly*

Bio of Suzi Weissman: Suzi is professor and chair of politics at Saint Mary's College of California and sits on the editorial boards of *Critique* and *Against the Current*. Author *Victor Serge: The Course Is Set on Hope* (Verso, 2001), Suzi edited *Victor Serge: Russia Twenty Years After* (Humanities, 1996), and *The Ideas of Victor Serge* (Critique Books, 1997), as well as many articles on the Soviet Union and Russia. Her emphasis is on working class and left dissent. She is on the National Workers' Rights Board, composed of 50–75 national leaders who intervene with employers and the public to help resolve situations that threaten workers' rights.

Suzi has broadcast drive-time public affairs programs on KPFK for more than two decades. During the years of turmoil and disintegration of the Soviet Union, she hosted many special programs and live broadcasts from participants in the political turmoil. Her radio programs from 1986 to 2001 are a featured archive at the Hoover Institution for War and Peace at Stanford University. (Began as host of *Portraits of USSR* and *Read All About It*; later *The New World Disorder* before it morphed into *Beneath the Surface*.)

The Big Sauce Radio Show with Dean (Big Sauce), podcast (Dean is planning to join Break the Matrix, http://www.breakthematrix.com)

Theme: Political, social and economic talk.

Guest Profile: Psychologists, investors, real estate professionals, politicos. Interesting perspectives, easy to talk with, unique experiences. Past interview experiences, credentials, sound of voice and what makes them believe they would be entertaining as a guest.

Guest from Hell: Doesn't offer any anecdotal experience, must be led to expand of topics, runs off on imperceptible tangents.

Contact: dean@bigsauceradio.com; 786-312-9063; http://www.big-sauce.com; Dean. Best method: E-mailing a bio and/or sending a press kit. No response? Follow up e-mail is best.

Invited Back? Smoothness of conversation, feedback from listeners, enjoyment of the interview.

Guest Comment: "Dean is a great podcaster. He's a lot of fun, a good conversationalist, we're always laughing during the discussions and sharing some heavy insights. Santoro's years as a club DJ and MC have really honed his skills as a crowd-pleasing conversationalist."—Ted Terbolizard, running for the United States House of Representatives in 2008 and 2010, for California's 4th Congressional District. http://www.terbocongress.org

Bio of Dean "Big Sauce" Santoro: Originally from Waterbury, Connecticut, and now living in Miami Beach, Dean's life journey has been anything but ordinary. From the stock market to the supermarket, Dean's widespread knowledge and experiences are entertaining, insightful, educational, and at times, just plain hilarious.

Performing was in his blood since birth. His dad was a keyboard player for a funk and soul band in the 60's and 70's. Dean's first "gig" occurred when he was in just the seventh grade. He introduced a song as "guest DJ" at a school dance and the flame was ignited. He spent the majority of the 80's and 90's performing at nightclubs and private events, while simultaneously writing, voicing, and producing commercials for local Hartford and New Haven radio stations.

He has a Bachelor's degree in computer science and an MBA in management, which he obtained while working in the corporate world as a technology manager and consultant, primarily in the insurance industry in Hartford. Eventually he founded his own technology consulting firm in the mid 90s. As an added bonus, he was as an adjunct professor teaching technology classes at a local community college. In 2004 he sold his company and he and his wife moved to Miami a short time later—where his radio show was born.

Dean is a technology manager for a worldwide retailer and is embarking upon his first congressional run in Miami's District 21 in 2008.

Bill Dwight Show with Bill Dwight airs on WHMP, AM 1240/1400/1600, Northampton, MA, heard from Hartford, CT, to Brattleboro, VT.

Theme: Left Wing Talk

Guest Profile: Local, regional and national political personalities who are informed and articulate with a sense of humor, and have credentials and perspective.

Guest from Hell: Two word answerer or a filibusterer.

Contact: bdwight@whmp.com; 413-586-7400; http://www.whmp.com/page.php?category_id=193andjock_id=291; Bill Dwight or Chris Collins at collins@whmp.com. Best method: E-mail bio. No response? E-mail or call.

Invited Back? We hit it off or they give good counter-point.

Guest Comments: "You're good. Call me anytime. I'll come on again."—Janeane Garofalo, comedian, political firebrand

"Thanks. I appreciate all the time. You know your stuff. I'm used to short breaks with people who go for the lurid stuff."—Paul Rieckhoff, veterans advocate, author

Bio of Bill Dwight: Bill is a left wing commentator, former city councilor, middle-aged video clerk and writer.

The Bill Handel Show on KFI-AM 640, Los Angeles, Ca., aired in Southern California, Orange, Riverside, Ventura, and San Diego counties and on http://www.kfiam640.com. Rated #19 in the 2008 Talkers Heavy Hundred. Bill's other show, *Handel on the Law*, does not book guests.

Theme: Daily news based show, focusing on relevant issues and information presented in an entertaining way.

Guest Profile: Authors welcome. Must be extremely well-spoken, NOT boring, and willing to answer any and all questions from the host. We do NOT provide questions beforehand. A wide variety of specialties, depending on the subject being discussed. NO psychics ... Bill hates them, and they should know so before they even call to ask if they can be a guest.

We want an honest, well spoken person who is knowledgeable and able to debate well ... and someone who isn't afraid to be asked tough questions. What's important too are their credentials and I want to know the sound of their voice and how well they present their topic or issue.

Guest from Hell: Someone who asks for questions beforehand and someone who is schooled by the "media prep" people that tell them to mention their book every few seconds (nothing turns off a listener or a host more).

Contact: michellekube@clearchannel.com; 818-566-6425; http://www.kfiam640.com; Michelle Kube. Best method: E-mail first ... if we're interested we'll contact them. No response? If they don't get a response in a day or two, they can call.

Invited Back? If they're compelling and ABOVE ALL HONEST.

Guest Comment: "Bill Handel is a great interviewer ... for the listener. His cut-to-the-chase, rapid fire questions keep listeners on the edge of their seats and keeps me as the interviewee on my toes. Bill is a lawyer by training. So trying to redirect a difficult question that I'd rather not answer never goes well. He dislikes obvious questions with obvious answers. Forget about well rehearsed responses. He always makes me think. Be prepared for very good questions on topics peripheral to your main theme. Bill is a brilliant mind and a brilliant entertainer. As such, his questions range from perceptive to humorous. While some interviewers will try their best to make you comfortable, Bill assumes you can hold your own if you are discussing a topic on which you claim to be an expert. On the rare time I've been foolish enough to opine on a subject I did not have well thought out, he has left me with the scar to show for it. But no one is more appreciative than Bill when you provide honest, insightful and pithy analysis of a topic."— Jim Keany, MD, http://www.jim.md

Bio of Bill Handel: Bill was born in Brazil in 1951 and at the age of five immigrated to the United States with his parents. He grew up in the San Fernando Valley, learned English without the benefit of a bilingual education program and became one of the world's leading reproductive law experts.

In 1989, Bill began doing a Saturday morning legal advice show on KFI AM 640, *Handel on the Law*, a unique combination of "marginal legal advice" and outrageous Handel remarks. He gets joy out of repeating "you have absolutely no case."

It didn't take long for KFI to realize that this politically incorrect, self-proclaimed "Latino Jew" had the tell-it-like-it-is attitude listeners were looking for and gave Handel the coveted weekday morning show time slot. He was soon host of the top-rated morning show in the market and *Handel on the Law* was syndicated nationally.

In 2005, he was named Major Market Personality of the Year at the NAB Marconi Radio Awards and News/Talk Personality of the Year by Radio and Records.

The Bob Frantz Show on WTAM 1100, Cleveland, OH, airing mid-days 9 AM–noon (ET).

Theme: News talk.

Guest Profile: Elected officials, societal leaders, professors, athletes, etc. I look for guests who will inform my listeners. In other words, people who are smarter than I am, or who know more than I do. I have no use for guests who wish to use their appearance on my program solely for self promotion. This is why I avoid authors and others who have products to sell. Mostly want to know their credentials and their ability to articulate and respond to serious questions. The smartest man in the world does me no good if he's quiet or short in his responses. I need someone who knows how to reach out to lay people and make himself understandable.

Guest from Hell: A guest from hell is someone like the Reverend Al Sharpton; that is, a guest who wants to filibuster through the entire interview, rather than answering real questions. A guest who, when you try to get a word in edgewise, to advance the discussion, accuses you of interrupting them and not letting them speak.

Contact: bob@wtam.com; 440-309-3008; http://www.wtam.com/pages/bfrantz.html; Myself or my producer, Dave Ramos, at 216-520-2600. Best method: E-mailing bios and subject matter/expertise on an issue. No response? I can't usually reply to every e-mail or pitch. A non-reply should indicate to the potential guest a lack of interest on my part.

Invited Back? Their performance and the subject matter discussed. If a story has a shelf life, a guest may outlive his usefulness and not be invited back. If a story is evergreen, and a guest is entertaining and adds to the show, then he is going in my rolodex.

Bio of Bob Frantz: Bob began his broadcasting

career in 1996 at WOBL Radio in Oberlin, Ohio, where he worked as a sideline reporter, color commentator and play-by-play voice for the station's high school football and basketball broadcasts. While at WOBL, he created a high school sports talk show that launched his career into talk radio.

Bob continued his broadcasting career at Newsradio WTAM 1100 when he was hired in 1998 as talk show host, anchor and reporter.

After two successful years, he left WTAM to move to San Francisco where he hosted the afternoon drive show on the Ticket (KTCT). During his time, he was also the sideline reporter for the Oakland Raiders Radio Network. Bob then moved to Orlando to do afternoon drive on ESPN Radio AM-1080 before moving back to Northern Ohio in 2003 to take over morning drive on Newsradio 1370 WSPD in Toledo, where the morning ratings quadrupled in a little over two years. In March 2006, he returned to Newsradio — WTAM 1100.

He and his wife Jean have two children, 5-year-old Jaiden and 3-year-old Jaret.

The Brad Show with Brad Friedman on IBC Radio Network.

Theme: Live talk show where politics, media, civil rights including elections, social issues and more, are discussed.

Guest Profile: Members of Congress, state representatives, informed citizens who are leaders in their area of expertise, authors, lawyers, military members, activists — interesting people working to preserve democracy and able to discuss important and current events as they unfold. I want to know as much as possible about the guest. *The Brad Show* really is an extension of The Brad Blog where host Brad Friedman is an investigative journalist/blogger. Brad takes the little details about his guests and fits them into the big picture without losing site of the real issue.

Guest from Hell: Because Brad Friedman is so good at what he does it's highly doubtful there is such a thing on *The Brad Show*. However, more difficult guests might be those who have only a one-word response to Brad's probing, or a guest who is unable to cogently put forth his or her argument and position without attacking or becoming irrational, although sometimes that's interesting, sometimes not — it all depends.

Contact: Brad@BradShow.com; Withheld upon request; http://www.bradshow.com and http://www.bradblog.com; Brad Friedman. Best method: E-mailing a pitch is just fine that addresses why topic would be of interest to *The Brad Show* listeners. Sending a copy of a new book or DVD is also fine. Always good to include a bio and press kit. No response? Not possible, but follow up by e-mail is perfectly acceptable.

Invited Back? Current events, knowledge of the topic, ability to articulate their opinions rationally, and they got to be interesting.

Guest Comments: "You are a true American hero"— Robert F. Kennedy, Jr.

"Among the heroes that I mentioned today was Brad Friedman, and I really do mean that ... and you got a round of applause from the Detroit audience, you are well known here, my friend."— Tony Trupiano, host *Tony Trupiano Show*, 2006 candidate for U.S. House of Representatives, speaking about a "Downing Street Memo" Town Hall Forum he hosted with John Conyers

Bio of Brad Friedman: Brad is an investigative blogger/journalist and founder of the popular progressive website The Brad Blog (http://www.BradBlog.com) where he has broken innumerable explosive stories since 2004 on everything from the disastrous election irregularities of 2004/2006 and the current e-voting meltown, to the alarming string of ongoing corruption of the Bush Administration and their cronies in Congress and the corporate mainstream media. He discussed his reporting on ABC News, CNN and CourtTV, he's a contributor at Huffington Post, and has written for Harvard's Neiman Foundation of Journalism, *Mother Jones*, *Editor and Publisher*, Salon.com, *ComputerWorld*, *Columbus FreePress*, *Hustler* and TruthOut.org

Brad is a popular guest presence on radio programs left, right and middle and has guest hosted for Peter B. Collins, Mike Malloy, and The Young Turks. He is co-founder of VelvetRevolution.us, an umbrella organization on everything from election and media reform to the war in Iraq. In the summer of 2005 he brought his radio show to Camp Casey in Crawford, TX, where he broadcast more than 50 exclusive live hours of radio over two weeks in a special "Operation Noble Cause" edition of the radio program. "Brad's work is more than just good reading — his insight, his diligence, and his staying power make him one of the most informative progressive voices in the alternative media.

Talk show host Randi Rhodes, who was interviewed by Brad during special coverage at Camp Casey, had this to say — "I just wanted to say thank you for your blog. I love it! It's a go-to place for me every day. And I hope anybody who's listening to this understands that you can get great information from Brad. And he is committed and it's hard work ... and it's only about a thousand degrees and he's sitting here looking fresh as a daisy and I don't know how he does it."

Highlights from those broadcasts can be heard at http://www.BradShow.com

The Breakfast Show with Ray Gibson on KGUM-AM Agana (aka Hagatna), Guam, airing Monday–Friday, 6–10 AM (UTC/GMT — coordinated universal time/Greenwich mean time).

Theme: Current events.

Guest Profile: Guests who are upbeat and warm.

Guest from Hell: Vitamin peddlars.

Contact: rgibson@k57.com; 671-477-5700 ext:

290; http://www.k57.com; www.radiopacific.com/k57; Bob Gaeth. Best method: E-mail. Send press kit and product sample. No response? E-mail or call.

Invited Back? Telephone calls during the interview.

Bio of Ray Gibson: Ray is director of radio operations at KGUM.

BullDog and the Rude Awakening Show with BullDog, John Smith, The Dude, Phone Girl and Bug on WOCM-FM, Ocean City, MD, airing weekday, 6–10 AM, and Pearl 98.1FM, St. Maarten, Netherlands Antilles.

Theme: Various. It's very topical to what's going on today. No topic is off limits.

Guest Profile: One of the great things about the show is that there is no "profile" for a guest or for the show itself. I have a wide variety of guests from A-List celebrities, B-list celebrities, *New York Times* best selling authors, leading representatives from all medical fields, politicians, artists, athletes, psychologists, alternative medicine experts, adult film stars, business leaders ... etc. Someone who has a genuine passion about their subject. A person with a good attitude and a willingness to "go with the flow" of the interview. I either want to know EVERYTHING about the interviewee or NOTHING. I do extensive research on upcoming interviews to inform myself on their topic so I can ask intelligent questions that would benefit the listeners. On the other hand, I also enjoy going into some interviews with no information and an open mind. I always try to make the interview about the guest for the benefit of the listeners.

Guest from Hell: Anyone who sends a form with questions and scripted answers. Why bother?

Contact: bulldog@irieradio.com; 410-723-3683; http://www.irieradio.com and http://www.bulldogradio.com; Director Tanya Anderson at Tanya.anderson@irieradio.com. Best method: Call with a pitch, e-mail a bio and send a press kit. No response? Of course, mail or call — otherwise their chances are ZERO!

Invited Back? Attitude is number 1. Obviously the second most important thing is how relevant the subject matter is at the time.

Guest Comments: "Bulldog is a living legend; someone I've followed since his mysterious beginnings in the Caribbean. I became a fan there, then a regular guest, even guest hosted — often driving across the island at unholy hours just to hang out, goof around with Bulldog and his crew on air — and do station plugs for the local supermarket. And I'm on the new show at every opportunity. He's a Monster of Talk Radio." — Anthony Bourdain, author, chef, TV show host

"Bulldog has the ONLY radio show, other than my own, that makes me laugh. Radio people are usually jerks off the air, but not Bulldog., he is always himself. Bulldog abides!" — Mancow Muller, Syndicated Radio Show Host (see page 194)

Bio of BullDog: BullDog grew up Chicago and was introduced to the radio business at 16 by a friend who was working at WLUP. After spending a few seconds in the studio there was no doubt that this is what he wanted to do.

After hanging around the station and doing gopher work, he realized he needed a real job and for 18 years worked as a runner, then broker, on the trading floor of the Chicago Mercantile Exchange, where he is still a member. In 1998, he retired and moved to the Caribbean island of St. Maarten.

Although he had no intention of working, he accepted a job on a morning show on Laser101, which remained #1 for six years. Upon evaluating the island's educational system, he and his wife decided to return to the states for the sake of their two young children (Nikki is now 14 and Jack, 11) and moved to Houston.

In 2004, he received a call from an acquaintance, Leighton Moore, who he met through a mutual friend, Mancow Muller, asking if he'd like to do a morning show on his station, WOCM.

"After a nanosecond of thought I was on a plane to Ocean City and have been there ever since," says BullDog. "I have the greatest job in the world doing something I truly love doing and working for one of the last independently owned and operated stations. WOCM was called 'one of the best radio stations in the world' by *The Washington Post* and I couldn't agree more."

Canadian Voices with Zoe Creighton on Kootenay Coop Radio, CJLY in Nelson, BC, Canada, broadcast on 30 stations across Canada and podcast.

Theme: 50 minute talks by thought-provoking Canadians, one speaker per program, background provided by host.

Guest Profile: Speakers on topics of human rights, design, education, media analysis, climate change, spirituality, art, politics. First of all, when "curating" each season, we look for a diverse spectrum of speakers. This diversity is based on gender, ethnicity, geographical location, academic/non-academic, known/unknown, and subject matter. All speakers are selected based on their commitment (tacit or otherwise) to issues embraced by the campus and community radio sector in Canada ... the list is lengthy, but can be broadly encompassed by the word "progressive."

Just to clarify, on *CDN Voices*, they are not guests, so much as speakers — I don't interview them, I just introduce them, and provide some context for listeners, on the subject of their talk. Speakers are authors, artists, activists and academics. Each speaker must have a prepared, 50ish minute talk, and be a good, clear speaker.

A mixture of well-known, internationally famous (Stephen Lewis; Adrienne Clarkson; Jane Jacobs, Bruce Mau) and lesser known speakers.

I research the backgrounds of the speakers heavily, and ensure they fit into above diversity criteria ... we don't care much about credentials, just credibility, and the sound of their voice

Guest from Hell: We air lectures that we review first, as the program is not live, so this is not applicable to our show.

Contact: zoe@canadianvoices.org; 250-352-9600; http://www.canadianvoices.org; Zoe Creighton. Best method: E-mailing a bio, with an idea of when they have spoken, or their willingness to have us produce a lecture of theirs and record it. No response? They should e-mail again.

Invited Back? We have yet to have a repeat speaker, but are considering it for season 3, based on a new topic discussed by a previously well-received speaker.

Bio of Zoe Creighton: Zoe is founder of Kootenay Coop Radio, Nelson, BC, 1996. She served as board chair from 1996 to 1999, station manager from 1999 to 2003 and radio producer from 2000 to the present.

In addition to *Canadian Voices*, Zoe is involved in the *Kootenay Artists and Craftspeople* compilation CD (2000), *Rural Vocations* documentary series (2002), and *Dig Your Roots/Roots* compilation (2004) — http://www.digyourroots.ca

Capitol Talk with Calvin and Jon Iszard on WBCB 1490, aired in New Jersey and Eastern PA, Monday through Friday 1–2 PM (ET); now off the air.

Theme: Politics, current affairs and humor.

Guest Profile: All types welcome — politicos and non-pros. Topical, fun to talk to and interested in good talk radio. Don't need to know their credentials or past interview experiences. Just send me their promo and I will do the rest.

Guest from Hell: One that freezes and is so nervous that they can't remember exactly what they do.

Contact: calvin@wbcb1490.com; 1-888-wbcb (1490); http://www.calviniszard.com; Calvin. Best method: Call me and do your "elevator" speech. No response? Keep on calling — I don't make a full career out of this gig.

Invited Back? If they showed up the first time.

Guest Comment: "[Calvin] was certainly a friendly host and did make me feel very comfortable.... I do recall Cal congratulating me on becoming Mayor and giving me his best wishes for success." — Jack Ball, mayor, Ewing Township

Bio of Calvin Iszard: Calvin has had a very successful broadcasting and public relations career in major and small markets and has produced award-winning broadcasts.

He is currently chief spokesperson for Capitol Benefit Solutions, LLD in Trenton, NJ, and Atlanta, GA.

He previously held positions as one of New Jersey's most respected publishers of *New Jersey Reporter* and *New Jersey Heritage*. Among his positions in the TV field, he was manager of corporate TV at Bell Atlantic/Verizon and vice president of programming at WWAC-TV, Atlantic City, NJ.

Calvin holds a Master of Arts in institutional public relations, Glassboro State College.

The CBS Weekend Roundup, with contributions from Sam Litzinger, syndicated by Westwood One. He also contributes to *Sound Sessions* from Smithsonian Folkways (focusing on music), on WAMU 88.5 FM, American University Radio, and XM's Politics from the nation's capital.

Theme: General interest.

Guest Profile: I interview everyone from politicians to policy experts to authors of all genres. I look for knowledge of subject, willingness to engage in a genuine conversation.

Expertise is tops for me. My job is to handle the interview, so I don't worry much about their abilities there. I want to know if they can sustain an interesting conversation for at least ten minutes. Among his notable on-air interviews: those with singer Tony Bennett, the Dalai Lama, big band leader Artie Shaw, U.S. Poet Laureate Ted Kooser, author Maya Angelou, Lemmy from the British hard rock band Motorhead (Sam's sure Lemmy remembers nothing of the interview) and a Florida man whose company specializes in removing alligators from swimming pools.

Guest from Hell: One who never pauses and tries to pass off opinion as fact.

Contact: sam@samlitzinger.com; Withheld upon request; http:www.samlitzinger.com; Sam Litzinger. Best method: E-mailing a pitch is always good; press kits are always appreciated but not necessary. For authors, I would like a copy of the book because I do read it. No response? A follow-up call is fine.

Invited Back? Relevance of topic, response from listeners.

Guest Comments: "Thanks for the sound from the interview, and thanks so much for inviting me to come on. The program was excellent; kudos to all of you, and particularly Sam, for raising awareness on the important issue of domestic violence in the Muslim community." — Mazna Hussain, staff attorney/New Voices Fellow, Tahirih Justice Center

"That was such a great chat — we loved your questions and could have gone on for, oh, several more hours. At least. It was great fun." — Will Schwalbe, co-author, *Send: The Essential Guide to E-mail for Office and Home* (Knopf 2007)

Bio of Sam Litzinger: Sam has been a broadcaster for 35 years (which disproves his claim that he's only 29 years old), doing everything from reporting to anchoring to interviewing to managing. He's worked for various media outlets, including CBS News, the Mutual Broadcasting System, NBC Radio, the Associated Press, NPR and the BBC. He's been an anchor, talk show host and foreign correspondent, reporting from Great Britain, Poland, Israel and France, among other places. He delights in talking to anyone about everything. Sam's earned many broadcasting honors, including an Edward R. Murrow award for a series on race relations in the United States. He has a master's degree in comparative philosophy (be sure to ask him for his opinion on Kant's categorical imperative) and keeps threatening to finish his doctorate someday VERY soon.

In his spare time, Sam reads (*The Washington Post*, of course), writes, collects old stuff, has long conversations with his beagle (named Ella Fitzgerald), somewhat shorter conversations with his wife and he plays the same four or five blues songs on his guitar until his neighbors ask him to please, please stop.

Charlotte's Morning News Weekend with Don Russell on WBT, Charlotte, NC.
Theme: Everything you need to get your day started.
Guest Profile: Local, national and international newsmakers. Interesting, topical, good talker. (Authors are the worst ... they can't talk.)
Guest from Hell: One that doesn't listen to the question and is there to ramble about their cause. Also, something I learned about the third day I was in radio: never ask a question that requires a "yes or no" answer. You'll be talking to yourself for a half hour. I don't care what they sound like (if you heard my voice you'd understand why). I do care about their credentials.
Contact: drussell@wbt.com; 704-374-3500; http://www.wbt.com; Doug Thompson. Best method: E-mailing a pitch. By the way, mailing us product never hurts. No response? If we didn't respond it's because we didn't think it was compelling enough, i.e.: you probably suck.
Invited Back? If they entertained ME. I know my audience better than anyone. They listen to me because they like me. If they entertained me, they entertained the audience.
Guest Comment: "Don Russell's show is great. He always manages to stay right on top of the big news that is happening right then. Don makes sure his listeners wake up to what is really going on their world." — Dan Gainor, director, Business and Media Institute, http://www.businessandmedia.org
Bio of Don Russell: Don has been in the radio business for 37 years. "I've been on WBT for 34 and the only Democrat currently on talk radio in the South (I think)," he says. "I'm a pillar of the community. Smart, funny, knowledgeable, topical (Read OJ's new book? *If I Stole It*) and in demand for a variety of functions because of my notoriety. Married to the same woman for over 25 years. I'm the luckiest man on earth."

The Chuck Morse Show airs on 1110 WCCM-AM in Lawrence, Merrimack Valley, Massachusetts, southern New Hampshire, Monday through Friday, 10–noon (ET), http://www.chuckmorseshow.com
Theme: News, culture, health, money.
Guest Profile: Newsmakers, authors, who are either a principal player in a news story or someone who can competently comment on the story. I want to know their train of thought and a general sense regarding philosophy and approach.
Guest from Hell: Someone who is boring because they speak in euphemisms and abstractions.
Contact: emorse@1110wccmam.com; chuckmorse @gis.net; 617-271-5044; Chuck Morse. Best method: E-mail. No response? Do not call or e-mail.
Invited Back? If they are interesting, there is chemistry, and there are calls.
Bio of Chuck Morse: Chuck is a veteran radio talk show host, author, published columnist, and business owner who ran for Congress against Barney Frank in 2004.

He was once named a "Hot 100" upcoming talk show host by *Talkers Magazine*.

CHUM Radio Ottawa has a variety of news-oriented talk programs which deal with timely issues, with Lowell Green, Steve Madely (see page 193), Rob Snow, Nick at Night, Daniel Proussalidis, Ron Corbett, and John Counsell. Ottawa Ontario Canada.
Theme: Various.
Guest Profile: Authors, political figures, researchers, controversial writers. Well spoken, well researched. We want to know past interview experiences, credentials, sound of their voice.
Guest from Hell: One-word answers (like these).
Contact: Steve Winogron at steve.winogron@chumottawa.com; 613-789-2486 ext 4219; http://www.cfra.com; Steve Winogron, News Director/Asst. Program Director. Best method: Sending press kit or e-mail. No response? It means we are not going to be able to use that guest. One reminder e-mail is okay, but more would be considered pestering.
Invited Back? Caller reaction, flow on the air, credibility, entertainment value (not boring speaker).
Bio of Steve Winogron: Steve is the CHUM Ottawa news director and CFRA assistant program director.

A Community Affair with Julia Giacoboni on Rowan Radio 89.7 WGLS FM, airing Monday at 5 PM (ET).
Theme: Centers around community events, non profit organizations worldwide, helpful books, inspiring stories.
Guest Profile: The extraordinary average person ... people who have made great strides in their towns, overcome obstacles, written books, and do great volunteer work. Someone who is excited to talk about their book or organization. I love to speak to people who have tons to say and are very upbeat.
Guest from Hell: It's never a pleasure to interview someone who is in a rush and speeds through answers. I like to take our time through the interview and go off on tangents, explaining things along the way.

Contact: Giacob23@students.rowan.edu (personal) Any other inquiries forward to WGLS@rowan.edu; 856-863-9457; http://www.wgls.rowan.edu; Julia Giacoboni. Best method: E-mails with a press kit are the best. No response? Give me a call. That's best … sometimes my e-mail box gets full.

Invited Back? If I know more will be going on with their book or organization, they are more than welcome to come back. Usually if I am in a crunch, they are on my first to call list.

Bio of Julia Giacoboni: Julia is public affairs director at a college radio station. She is a junior studying communications and public relations and has been doing *A Community Affair* for the past year. While the station runs on a campus, listeners are from the South Jersey and Philadelphia area and are in their 40s. "I try my best to cater to them," she says.

I've received thank yous and compliments from many of my guests, including The Nutrition Twins, young adult author Megan McCafferty (*Sloppy Firsts, Second Helpings*), Werner Berger (oldest man to have climbed Mt. Everest) and independent film director Ali Selim (*Sweet Land*) to name a few. I've had the pleasure of interviewing representatives from organizations across the country as well, including Habitat for Humanity, Gilda's Club, Big Brother Big Sister, and various other service, support, and awareness groups.

Connecting the Dots with Frosty Wooldridge on http://www.republicbroadcasting.org aired in Denver, CO; now off the air.

Theme: Connecting the dots for Americans concerning immigration-driven overpopulation of the United States

Guest Profile: Governors of states, Congressmen, Ph.D.s, M.D.s and leaders in the field of overpopulation, authors and activists. I look for a knowledgeable, articulate person who educates, inspires and activates listeners.

Guest from Hell: One that can't speak very well and doesn't know the subject.

Contact: frostyw@juno.com; 303-666-6186; http://www.frostywooldridge.com; Frosty Wooldridge. Best method: E-mail me with what they do, what they want to talk about, who they represent. I ask for a bio and 10 talking points which usually gives me all I need to work with the guest. No response? I always respond to e-mails. But if one slips into cyberspace, e-mail again if I haven't responded.

Invited Back? If they have more to say and the audience responded.

Bio of Frosty Wooldridge: Frosty possesses a unique view of the world, cultures and families in that he has bicycled around the globe 100,000 miles, on six continents and six times across the United States in the past 30 years. In 2005, he bicycled 3,500 miles from the Arctic Circle, Norway to Athens, Greece. In 2006, he motorcycled 20,000 miles through 48 states on the 21st Century Paul Revere Ride.

Frosty is author of hundreds of articles (regularly) for 17 national and two international magazines; his many guest editorials are published in such top national newspapers as the *Rocky Mountain News, Denver Post, Albany Herald,* and *Las Vegas Tribune.*

His books are *Handbook for Touring Bicyclists* (Falcon 1996), *Strike Three! Take Your Base* (Tandem Library 2001), and the remainder published by Authorhouse: *Immigration's Unarmed Invasion: Deadly Consequences* (2004), *Bicycling Around the World* (2005), *Motorcycle Adventure to Alaska: Into the Wind — A Teen Novel, An Extreme Encounter: Antarctica* (2005), *Bicycling the Continental Divide: Slice of Heaven, Taste of Hell* (2007).

Frosty holds a BA, journalism/advertising from Michigan State University and graduated Grand Valley State University with a BA in English with a teaching certificate.

The Dark Side with the Rev. Damien Darko on The Free World Radio Network (Internet-based).

Theme: Politics with a liberal slant.

Guest Profile: Authors, pundits, political activists, etc. Someone who is passionate about their topic, whether I agree with it or not. I want to know their past involvement within the topic of their choice and if they are plugging anything.

Guest from Hell: Someone who only gives single word answers and/or doesn't expand on their thought without prompting.

Contact: revdarko@freeworldradionetwork.net; Withheld upon request; http://www.freeworldradionetwork.net; Damien Darko. Best method: By e-mailing me a pitch or topic they would like to discuss, along with a reason why they would be a good guest for that topic. No response? I generally answer all e-mails sent to me within 48 hours. If a request or inquiry is sent to me and I don't respond, the best bet is to resend the inquiry.

Invited Back? If the audience seemed to enjoy the interview, and if the guest enjoyed it.

Bio of Damien Darko: Damien describes himself as "just a regular guy who got tired of the combination of right-wing spin on standard talk radio and the lack of a voice for the 'everyman.'" He found that blogging was great but that it lacked the "voice" of real-time interaction. "I found a venue that allowed me to host my show via the Internet, which means I can discuss issues without the imposed control of a corporate owner," he says.

Born in Hartford, CT, and now living in Tennessee, Damien has traveled for most of his life. He is a legally ordained minister within the Universal Life Church, though an avowed atheist. "To me, right and wrong have nothing to do with a higher power, just common sense," he says. "This is a view I put forth on my show."

The Dave Elswick Show on KARN 102.9FM and 920AM, Little Rock, Arkansas. Rated among the Talkers 250.

Theme: Topical, live call-ins.

Guest Profile: Topical guests. For instance, I had Dr. Mao, Doctor to the Stars. I also have political authors, Hollywood stars, etc. Lively, interested in their material, communicates well with host and callers. Want to know the subject and why should they talk about it.

Guest from Hell: Boring, acts as if they don't really want to be on the air. No energy.

Contact: DaveElswick@citcomm.com; 501-401-0343; http://www.karnnewsradio.com; Dave Elswick, program director and afternoon host. Best method: E-mail the bio kit. Tell me why I should give up air time to the guest. No response? Normally I will let the pitch person know if I'm interested or not very quickly. I know my audience.

Invited Back? Calls and is it compelling.

Bio of Dave Elswick: Dave has been in broadcasting for 39 years, 20 of them in talk radio.

Before arriving at KARN eight years ago, he was at WMAQ, Chicago, WIBC, Indianapolis, and WCCO in Minneapolis.

Deace in the Afternoon with Steve Deace on 1040 WHO, Des Moines, Iowa, airing daily 4–7 PM (CT).

Theme: General talk show. We do everything: sports, culture, current events, theology, politics, etc.

Guest Profile: All types who are interesting, articulate, and must know something I don't know. Credentials and experience would come first for me, tone of voice second.

Guest from Hell: Boring, pretentious, and stale.

Contact: stevedeace@whoradio.com; 515-284-1040; http://www.whoradio.com/pages/stevedeace.html; Steve Deace. Best method: E-mail and snail mail are fine. No response? A follow up e-mail would be fine.

Invited Back? Audience reaction.

Bio of Steve Deace: Steve and his wife, Amy, have three young children: Ana, Zoe, and Noah.

The Dom Giordano Show on WPHT, The Big Talker 1210, Philadelphia, PA, aired weeknights 9 PM–12 AM (ET), and Saturday 1 PM–4 PM (ET). Rated among The Talkers 250.

Theme: Headline news, local stories, sports, religion, music, movies.

Guest Profile: National and local newsmakers, authors, celebrities. Someone with an enthusiastic personality who can articulate a point. He/she must not be afraid of debate.

Are they relevant or current in the news; can they make their topic global?

Guest from Hell: Someone who mumbles, is a lowtalker, gets upset if opposing point of view is offered.

Contact: renee.downey@cbsradio.com; domg@thebigtalker1210.com; 610-668-5814 or Dom's cell 215-906-0438; http://www.thebigtalker1210.com; Renee Downey, producer. Best method: E-mail or phone. Sending a press kit is probably the best. No response? I usually forward everything to Dom to see if there is interest. If he likes it, I will be in contact.

Invited Back? Entertaining and informative would be good reasons.

Bio of Dom Giordano: Born and raised in South Philly, Dom's local flavor makes him one of the region's best-connected media personalities. He began his unique path to broadcasting as a high school teacher in the Delaware Valley, where he received widespread media coverage for his innovative teaching and motivational techniques with his students. He was hired at WWDB Radio in 1987, becoming the country's first teacher-turned-talk show host.

Dom is a frequent guest commentator on the Fox News Channel, CNN's "Talkback Live," Court TV, "It's Your Call" on Comcast's CN8, NBC-10 News, and WHYY-TV 12 News Programs. He also writes columns for newspapers throughout the region, including *The Philadelphia Inquirer*.

Dom lives in Germantown with his wife Rosemary, and their two sons, Luke and DJ.

Evening Edition with Mark Haim on KOPN, aired in Columbia/Jefferson City, MO.

Theme: Interviews regarding war and peace, sustainability, environment, energy, human rights, politics and related issues.

Guest Profile: Activists, researchers, scholars, etc. involved with the sorts of issues listed above. Someone well informed, articulate and thinking outside the box. Most important is for guests to know what they're talking about and to have their views grounded in reality and solid data.

Guest from Hell: Someone inarticulate, irrational, and/or unwilling to be responsive to the questions being asked.

Contact: mhaim@riseup.net; 573-875-0539; http://www.kopn.org; http://kopn.org/a/showrss3.php?n=../aa/rss/Evening_Edition.xml); Mark Haim. Best method: E-mailing, no calls please. No response? I will reply if I'm interested, and, if possible let them know if I'm not. No follow-up is needed.

Invited Back? If the topic covered warrants more attention and the guest did a good job of covering the topic in an informative and accessible fashion.

Bio of Mark Haim: Active in progressive concerns all his adult life, Mark is a full time social change activist, serving as director of Mid-Missouri Peaceworks, a grassroots, membership-based organization in Columbia, MO.

Face the Tribune (now ***Veterans in Politics***) with Steve William Sanson on All Talk Radio. The show is produced by Las Vegas Tribune Media and airs Saturday at 2:05 PM (PT).

Theme: Correcting a wrong, political corruption, election debates, and information on a wide range of topics.

Guest Profile: Politicians, authors, military veterans, everybody. All interviews are conducted in-studio at 2350 South Jones Blvd, Las Vegas, NV (n/e corner of Jones and Sahaha). Motivation and something to talk about. Biography and their topic of expertise.

Guest from Hell: Exciting.

Contact: stevewsanson@cs.com; 702-283-8088; http://www.alltalkradio.net; http://www.SteveSanson.com; Steve William Sanson. Best method: E-mail a bio. No response? E-mail or call.

Invited Back? Performance and more to say or something different that has taken place.

Bio of Steve Sanson: Steve has a strong commitment to our country and to this community (Las Vegas, Nev.). His leadership and service in the United States Marine Corps during his service in Saudi Arabia for operation Desert Storm earned him the distinguished Certificate of Commendation from the United States Marine Corps.

Within Clark County, Steve is the past chaplain for the Henderson Veterans of Foreign Wars and the Las Vegas Marine Corps League. He has made numerous appearances at funerals for our fallen serviceman, parades, and community functions and testified in the State Legislature on various veteran issues. He is also director for Veterans in Politics International, Inc.

Steve is author of *How to Collect on Your Bad Debt Accounts* (Aggressive Collections 2005), an instructor for National Business Institute on collections law and a commentary writer for the *Las Vegas Tribune* with his own column "The Veteran's View."

Active in the Republican Party and a member of several Republican coalitions, he has been elected to the Clark County Republican Party — Executive Board and designated chaplain. He was a candidate for Las Vegas City Council Ward 6 in 2005 and Clark County public administrator in 2006.

First News with Bob Steel on KARN, Little Rock, Arkansas.

Theme: News talk, live interviews.

Guest Profile: Newsmakers, authors, etc. with a good voice, short summary answers (less is more), unafraid of any question(s). Courteous. It's always a crap shoot but if they've been featured often on network radio and television, that's a big plus and it says they're good.

Guest from Hell: Nervous, yes/no answers, crutch words like "and uh" ... and the worst for a show as tight as mine — a windbag.

Contact: bob.steel@citcomm.com; 501-401-0254; http://www.karnnewsradio.com; Producer John Payner at john.payne@citcomm.com. Best method: Best approach is to send an e-mail to the producer (not me) but I like to be copied on the pitch. No response? Do not e-mail or call — it means we didn't want them.

Invited Back? Their performance during the interview.

Bio of Bob Steel: Bob most recently served as a media relations consultant for the state's second largest advertising agency. (He owns and operates a public relations firm where he does media, presentation, and crisis communication skills training along with event management.)

He is a veteran television news director with 16 years in news management and almost 30 years experience as a broadcast journalist in the Little Rock market.

Bob was news director of television station KATV, the ABC affiliate in Little Rock. Channel 7 was the top-rated station for news during his entire 7-year tenure and at one point during his tenure attained the distinction of being the highest rated ABC affiliate for local news in America. His news department captured 11 regional Emmys and won over 25 first place Associated Press awards for its coverage efforts. He's a native of Little Rock and a Vietnam era veteran of the United States Air Force where he served four years as an audio-visual specialist attaining the rank of Staff Sergeant.

He and his wife, Sherry, live in North Little Rock and have three children and one grandchild.

Full bio at http://www.karnnewsradio.com

Fix Your Conflicts! with Doug Noll on World Talk Radio, Monday at 11 AM (PT) (http://www.worldtalkradio.com) and re-played Wednesday at 1 PM on Voice America Radio (http://www.voiceamerica.com). Doug hosts another radio show, *The Doug Noll Show*, on The Advice Radio Network live Thursday at 8 PM (PT). All of his shows are archived at his website http://www.lawyertopeacemaker.com/radio

Theme: Everyday peacemaking and conflict resolution.

Guest Profile: Authors, mediators, experts in all fields around human conflict, peacemaking, mediation, and peace building. Since conflicts, fights and disputes involve every aspect of living, I really cover the waterfront, i.e., law, business, personal growth, health. Most authors are writing books to solve problems revolving around conflicts of some kind of another, so I am really open to looking at any author. People that inspire or teach listeners about the skills of everyday peacemaking. I want to know that they demonstrated competence and expertise and deep passion for their work and life mission.

Guest from Hell: A person that has nothing to say of importance to my listeners or to me.

Contact: radio@lawyertopeacemaker.com; 800-785-4487; http://www.lawyertopeacemaker.com; Doug Noll. Best method: E-mail with a pdf press kit or just e-mail with a brief description of who and why? No response? Try again. The e-mail might have ended up in a spam folder.

Invited Back? How much fun we had together and how interesting the conversation was.

Bio of Doug Noll: Doug is a peacemaker and mediator, specializing in difficult, complex, and intractable conflicts. He graduated from Dartmouth College, earned his law degree at University of the Pacific McGeorge School of Law where he was a member of the law review, and earned his M.A. in peacemaking and conflict studies from Fresno Pacific University.

Doug is a Fellow of the International Academy of Mediators, a Fellow of the American College of Civil Trial Mediators and on the American Arbitration Association panel of mediators and arbitrators. He is an author of *Sex, Politics and Religion at the Office: The New Competitive Advantage* (Auberry Press 2006), with John Boogaert, and *Peacemaking: Practicing at the Intersection of Law and Human Conflict* (Cascadia 2002) and, numerous articles on peacemaking, restorative justice, conflict resolution and mediation, and is a mediator trainer, lecturer and continuing education panelist. As a lawyer, Doug is AV rated by Martindale Hubbell and has been voted as one of the Best Lawyers in America since 2005, by bestlawyers.com.

Doug is also a second degree black belt in Chinese kung fu, has taught tai chi for over 10 years, is a certified pranic healer, a Level III ski instructor, instrument-rated private pilot with multi-engine and helicopter ratings, Irish fiddle and harp player, whitewater kayaker and rafter, and Spey casting steelhead fly fisherman.

The Flipside Show (now *Eagle and Child*) with Don Crawford on the American Forces Network, www.afneurope.net

Theme: Defending America's founding principles; America as world's greatest nation.

Guest Profile: Political writers, authors, commentators, and elected officials. Established expertise in government, national security, American history, social ethics, or politics; energetic and fun interactive attitude; articulate. Scroll down on website for upcoming and recent guests.

Guest from Hell: Monotone, non-conversational monologue, self-promoting.

Contact: flipsidedon@yahoo.com; 512-627-5450 (cell); http://www.flipsideshow.com; Don Crawford. Best method: E-mail. I want two copies of their book or published article on the topic they wish to discuss; if no book or article exists, I want their credentials and media experience and a phone number at which I can reach them so I that I can evaluate their voice and "air presence." If not book or article, I would rather have a personal note explaining what and why they want to do on the air along with their credentials rather than a mass-produced press kit. No response? Do not e-mail or call unless I responded to their initial e-mail.

Invited Back? See Guest Profile and Guest from Hell.

Bio of Don Crawford: Don hosted the first radio talk show ever carried by the Armed Forces Radio Network, heard in 71 nations by a listening audience of some 22 million. He has also hosted talk shows for stations in Austin, TX, and Los Angeles, CA, and for a statewide network in Texas.

Don's academic work includes non-degree graduate work in philosophy at the University of Texas and the University of California, Santa Barbara, and Master's Degree course work in International Human Rights Law and Christian Apologetics at Simon Greenleaf School of Law and at the Inter-national Institute of Human Rights in Strasbourg, France.

Don also did his M.A. course work in family and child counseling at Michigan State University and received his degree in Biblical studies from Abilene Christian University. He has trained social agency staffs in sexual counseling for H.U.D; under Title IV grants he has trained parents and teachers of various school districts in conflict resolution, parenting and listening skills; and has developed modules for and trained personnel of crisis, drug, and suicide hotlines in listening and crisis intervention skills. On the management staff for Specialized Administrative Services, Inc. (SASI), he develops and delivers professional training seminars to business, government, and business institutions.

Don is a motivational speaker who conducts workshops and seminars on politics, ethics, faith and reason, and listening skills for universities and business and service organizations across America.

He and his wife now reside in the Austin, TX, area.

Focus580 (50 minutes) and *The Afternoon Magazine* (45 minutes) with David Inge; Celeste Quinn on WILL AM, an NPR affiliate, covering two thirds of Illinois, the western half of Indiana, and southern Wisconsin.

Theme: Newsworthy topics.

Guest Profile: Intelligent, knowledgeable individuals. Guest actually wants to do the interview and is "giving" in responding to hosts questions. Credentials such as cv and know if guest has radio experience.

Guest from Hell: Provides only short answer, is cranky.

Contact: hwillmsn@ad.illinois.edu; 217-244-2608; http://www.will.illinois.edu/focus580; Harriet Williamson. Best method: E-mail or press kit. No response? Call if have not responded to e-mail.

Invited Back? Treat listeners with respect, are giving in their interview, add to the knowledge of a topic.

Bio of Harriett Williamson: Harriett has been producer of *The Afternoon Magazine* for 11 years and of *Focus* for 6 years.

Free Forum with Terry McNally on KPFK 90.7 FM, Los Angeles, 98.7 FM, Santa Barbara, CA, and streamed on the Internet.

Theme: A world that just might work. We can do better. I want to find out how.

Guest Profile: Eclectic. I only choose about 50 guests a year — so the level of prominence, credibility, etc., is quite high. We explore the lives, work and ideas of highly credible and articulate individuals I suspect hold pieces of the puzzle of a world that just might work. We look at new, innovative and provocative approaches to business, environment, health, science, politics and media. It's all based on the fact that I believe we can do better and I want to find out how. I want to know why they might be right for my show as described above, evidence that they are credible and articulate; past interview experiences can be helpful.

Prominent guests have included Al Franken, Ken Burns, Roger Ebert, Arianna Huffington, Kevin Phillips, Cornel West, Eric Schlosser, Robert Reich, Andrew Weil, Noam Chomsky, Greg Palast, Paul Krugman, Robert Scheer, and Bill Maher.

Guest from Hell: Self-promoter, doesn't listen, unable to truly engage in a dialogue with me.

Contact: temcnally@mac.com; http://www.kpfk.org; 310-476-4999; www.terrymcnally.net; Terrence McNally, host/producer. Best method: E-mail press kit or mail a book and press kit. No response? E-mail again.

Invited Back? Quality of their work, quality of our conversation.

Guest Comments: "McNally asks the surprising questions." — Norman Lear, writer, producer

"Terrence's deep understanding of issues is rare in our fast-paced, chattering media environment." — Tom Hayden, activist, legislator, author, *Street Wars* (New Press 2006)

Bio of Terrence McNally: Terrence talks with people he thinks have pieces of the puzzle of "a world that just might work." His interviews appear in print at AlterNet.org (www.alternet.org/authors/5358) and he is in demand as a speaker, writer, consultant, and coach to public agencies, non-profits, foundations, and corporations, on strategic communications as well as issues of social responsibility and environmental sustainability.

A writer, producer, and director of documentaries including BBC's Earth Summit special "Greenbucks," he co-wrote and produced Julie Brown's *Goddess in Progress* (Homecoming Queen's Got a Gun; I Like 'em Big and Stupid"), voted #4 mini-album of the year in the Village Voice 1985 National Music Critics Poll. Having acted in more than 100 films and television shows, Terrence co-wrote and co-produced the musical comedy feature *Earth Girls Are Easy* (Geena Davis, Jim Carrey, Jeff Goldblum), now being developed as a Broadway musical. A Harvard graduate, where he won its highest academic award, Terrence's address to the 20th Reunion of the class of 1969 was featured on CBS's "Sunday Morning."

Free Range Thought with Adam Rougberg and Robert Johnstreet on WKNY, www.1490wkny.com, Kingston, NY, covering a 20 mile radius. Adam "Radmanx" Rougberg has another radio program on Vassar College radio, WVKR 91.3 FM, on Wednesday 1–2 PM (ET) — at http://www.radioactivelunch.com. The program features live music with socio political satire and has a 40+ radius from Poughkeepsie, NY, and streams on the Internet. The same information is true for all for the questions save the station info.

Theme: Human rights based accountability/politics/community + sustainability, arts and music.

Guest Profile: International human rights lawyers, Congress persons, citizen activists, veterans, human rights workers, local business owners and community members with expertise in their respective field. We like to be approached informally with an idea.

Guest from Hell: Disrespectful and inappropriate language.

Contact: adam@freerangethought.com; robert@freerangethought.com; 845-430-8673; http://www.freerangethought.com; Adam Roufberg. Best method: E-mail. No response? Indeed. I always respond to guests one way or another except when I am overly swamped — or that occasion when things get lost or too backlogged.

Invited Back? Congeniality and knowledge base.

Bio of Adam Roufberg: Adam is an educator, physicist, musician, radio journalist, program director, and producer of *Free Range Thought* and *Radio Active Lunch* (http://www.radioactivelunch.com).

He is founder of Natural Philosophers International — an organization dedicated to the human spirit and human rights via the natural sciences and arts.

Freedom Works!/The Paul Molloy Show with Paul Molloy on WTAN Radio, Tampa Bay, FL.

Theme: Talk, guest interviews, politics, current events, entertainment.

Guest Profile: Authors and political and news experts. Someone knowledgeable on the subject at hand — typically it's political. A background on their expertise as it relates to the interview topic.

Guest from Hell: Somebody that sounds amateurish or just plain dull.

Contact: pmolloy@tampabay.rr.com; 727-725-3035; http://www.thefreedomworks.webs.com/index.htm; Paul Molloy. Best method: Any method can work — calling with pitch, e-mailing a bio, sending a press kit — but I would like to talk with a potential guest before the interview to make sure we both understand what we'll be talking about. No response? I try to respond on a timely basis, but they are welcome to e-mail me again or phone me.

Invited Back? How interesting and forthright they are.

Bio of Paul Malloy: Paul has been hosting his show since 2004 and a radio broadcaster off and on for more than 30 years at stations in Chicago, Milwaukee and Tampa Bay, FL. He is employed by a management consulting firm.

Paul graduated Marquette University with an A.B. degree in journalism and minor in speech.

Howard Monroe and the Morning Show on 1490/WTCS and 1370/WVLY, Wheeling/Moundsville and 1490/WTCS, Fairmont/Morgantown, West Virginia, airing 7–10 AM (ET), www.talkradio1370.com

Theme: Politics, pop culture.

Guest Profile: Knowledge of subject. Ability to have fun with the interview, engage in a give and take with the host.

Guest from Hell: Guest who is more concerned with selling his book than with providing compelling conversation.

Contact: radiomonroe@wvly.net; 304-233-9859; http://www.Howardmonroe.net; Howard Monroe. Best method: An e-mail overview should be sent. If it intrigues me I'll e-mail back with a request for more info. No response? A follow up e-mail is ok.

Invited Back? Was the current interview entertaining? Did it provide new insights or information? Was there a rapport with the host? Did the guest "feel" like he was part of the show?

It Takes a Village with Carla C. Kjellberg, syndicated throughout Minnesota by the Minnesota News Network, www.villagetalkradio.com

Theme: How to change the world one community at a time.

Guest Profile: People who follow their calling and do something to change the world one community at a time. Like — Amy Berman, founder of the Mother Bear Project (upset about the children dying in Africa of AIDS started making teddy bears so they would not die without feeling loved); Sami Rasouli, Iraqi born American citizen (who after 20 years living in the USA left for Iraq to rebuild his country and helped found Iraqi Peacemakers). People who can inspire others to be involved in their project or to start their own. I just want to know that they have something to talk about and that they are not afraid to have a conversation. Experience doesn't matter — as long as they have a good story to tell.

Guest from Hell: Any guest who just talks about a problem and not something that can correct the problem. The show is about answers.

Contact: ckjellberg@kjellberg-law.com; 952-591-9444; http://www.villagetalkradio.com; Carla C. Kjellberg. Best method: E-mail or phone; e-mail is easiest. Send a pitch by e-mail — include a description of what they do to save the world one community at a time or their community building event and their contact information. No response? Once I receive a pitch I e-mail it to my producer. If you do not hear from him within two weeks e-mail me again.

Invited Back? If they were an interesting interview of course — and if what they are doing needs updating to our audience.

Guest Comment: "Thanks again for the great interview. Your thoughtful questions and your deep understanding of the book's message made it a wonderful experience for me."—Nancy Manahan and Becky Bohan, authors of *Living Consciously, Dying Gracefully: A Journey with Cancer and Beyond*, available at http://www.nanbec.com

Listener Comment: "Thank you for interviewing one of my favorite authors, Nancy Manahan. Once again, I was so impressed with the intriguing questions you asked and your generous promotion of her book. Afterwards, the first thing Nancy said to me was, "Carla really got it." She felt it was the best interview she has had thus far and she so enjoyed talking with you."—Linda Strommer, agent for independent authors

Bio of Carla C. Kjellberg: Carla was born in Chicago, attended college in northern Wisconsin and law school in Philadelphia. She started her legal career as a clerk for Judge Miles Lord, as a federal law clerk in Minneapolis. She turned down an offer from a big money law firm to work at MPIRG (Minnesota Public Interest Research Group) to practice environmental and consumer law.

Carla started her own firm in 1997 and for the past 20 years has provided legal services for clients in difficult family situations.

She has always been involved in her community politically and as a volunteer. In 2004 she felt that she needed to do more to save the world. In response she created her radio show to change the dialogue and help us all focus on how we can make a difference.

The Jeff Farias Show aired 6–9 PM (ET) on the Nova M Radio Network.

Theme: Liberal talk.

Guest Profile: Authors, activists and political pundits with passion, insight and information not available in the mainstream media. Need to know: Their credentials and viewpoint.

Guest from Hell: A guest whose voice-mail answers the phone when we are on air.

Contact: jeff@jefffarias.com; 602-577-3837; http://www.thejefffariasshow.com; Jeff. Best method: E-mailing is the best format as I am harder to track down by phone. No response? Re-send an e-mail. If I'm not interested I'll reply to the second attempt.

Invited Back? Their topic and its relevance.

Bio of Jeff Farias: Jeff is director of programming and production at Nova M Radio. He has served as a Democratic Party district chair for LD-14 AZ and is currently 1st vice-chair. He is founding member and served on the executive committee of local DFA chapter, DFA-MC.

He spent nine years in NYC working as a broadcast producer on Madison Avenue and on the documentary series "The Eagle and the Bear." This 52 part program examined U.S.-Soviet relations as seen through the prism of the Cold War and aired weekly on the A&E network.

Shortly after the Berlin Wall fell, the series was cancelled and Jeff became a full time touring musician. Having appeared on more than 30 recordings, Jeff started his own recording studio, Gecko Park, in Phoenix. He has produced more than a dozen albums for local Valley acts and was a founder and partner in a small Indie label, Rustic Records, specializing in Roots/Americana music. For fun, Jeff sometimes plays bass in a cowboy band at Rawhide Western Theme Park.

Jeff holds a B.A. in organizational behavior and management from Brown University.

The Jeff Katz Show on www.jeffkatzshow.com. Rated #93 in 2008 Talkers Heavy Hundred.

Theme: Driven by current events, mixture of issues and lifestyle.

Guest profile: Guests must be relevant to the issues discussed. A guest must bring some vital information to the discussion. The listeners must be able to learn something from that guest which they did not know before the guest was on the show. I want to know the background of the guest vis a vis their credentials to be on the show. I need to know what they have done that qualifies them for a guest appearance and what they will be able to bring to the listeners.

Guest from Hell: Worst guest would be the guest who believes they have a right to be on the show without any understanding of what the show is about.

Contact: radiokatz.aol.com; 704-374-3500; http://www.radiokatz.com. Best method: Don't call me with a pitch. Send me an e-mail. You may also send a press kit through the regular mail. No response? Guest could send a follow up e-mail. Don't call.

Invited Back? Guests who are invited back are those who have brought some great kernel of information to the show.

Bio of Jeff Katz: Jeff is a native of Philadelphia where he cut his teeth in politics at the tender age of 12. He worked as a police officer in Philadelphia's rough and tumble public housing projects before trading in his badge for a microphone.

Jeff has hosted award winning talk shows in Philadelphia, Las Vegas, Boston, San Francisco and since August 2006 at WBT.

He appears regularly on CNN and Fox News and writes for the *Jewish World Review*'s Political Mavens website. He sits on the board of directors of the American Jewish Committee and the Republican Jewish Coalition, as well as Jews Against Anti-Christian Defamation. In addition he has served as the vice-chairman of the California State Council on Developmental Disabilities and as a court appointed special advocate for children in the superior court system.

Jeff has won awards as Best Talk Show Host and for Best Radio Program. The Claremont Institute awarded him a Lincoln Fellowship and the Second Amendment Foundation presented him with their highest honor, the James Madison Award.

Jeff, his wife and three children have recently relocated from the Napa Valley in California to South Charlotte.

Jefferson City's Morning News with Jay Kersting on 1240 KLIK, Jefferson City, Missouri.

Theme: News oriented.

Guest Profile: Newsmakers and experts. Timely and topical guests that can take issues in the news and bring the information to the local listener. Or guests who can let my listeners know why their area of expertise is important to them. Tell me WHY they are important to the Jefferson City radio listener... And what makes them an expert in their field.

Guest from Hell: One who won't talk. Or worse yet, arrogant guests who talk down to me and my audience.

Contact: jay.kersting@cumulus.com; 573-644-2655 (cell); http://www.klik1240.com; Jay Kersting. Best method: Press kits and e-mails are the best start. Calling me directly FIRST is not always the best, due to other job related activities. Always OK to schedule a time to talk on the phone ... in other words, ask if this is a good time or if we can talk later. No response? Often times the SPAM filter catches e-mails that I want to see and don't. Follow up with a phone call if you think I missed something important.

Invited Back? Also helps that they have new reasons to be brought back on the show.

Guest Comments: "Why Should I Listen to Jay's Show?

"This is NOT your parents' version of talk radio. Whether you are 25 or 75, you will hear the difference. Opinions on topics will often surprise listeners and the variety of topics discussed could surprise you as well. Politics, sports, entertainment, family, media critique and where all of those topics cross. If you disagree with him, CALL!!! E-mail!!"—Bernard Goldberg, TV news reporter, winner of seven Emmys and author of three *New York Times* bestsellers about the media, *Bias* (Harper Paperbacks 2003), *Arrogance* (Grand Central Publishing 2004), and *100 People Who Are Screwing Up America—and Al Franken* (HarperCollins 2005), http://www.bernardgoldberg.com

Bio of Jay Kersting: Jay joined News Talk 1240 KLIK as host of Jefferson City's Morning News in January 2007 after a run at WNOX in Knoxville, Tennessee. While at WNOX, Jay was the traffic reporter and a weekend show host. A 2003 graduate of the University of Tennessee, Jay got his feet wet working in sports radio as a reporter, show host and stringer covering Tennessee football and basketball for networks like ABC, ESPN, Sporting News Radio and Fox Sports Radio.

Jay is also no stranger to the world of politics, having covered city councils, county commissions, school boards, state and local elections as well as covering the visits of two U.S. presidents, last time serving as co-anchor of President George W. Bush's visit to Knoxville, Tennessee, in 2004. Other highlights of his career include taking media flights in a KC-135 Stratotanker with the 134th Air Refueling Group of the Tennessee Air National Guard in 2003 and a flight in a B-17 Bomber with World War II veterans on Labor Day 2004.

Jay and his wife, the former Kathleen Shelton, have two sons, Alex and Ben.

Jim Bohannon Show, and his two other shows are aired on 300 radio stations nationwide by Westwood One Radio. Rated #22 in the 2008 Talkers Heavy Hundred. Jim is also host of *America in the Morning* news magazine, http://www.jimbotalk.net/America-in-the-Morning.php and *America This Week* feature magazine. Tom Delach is producer of both shows. aitm@jimbotalk.net

Theme: General interest: politics/entertainment/sports/whatever. We once did an hour on whether the toilet paper should hang over the front or the back.

Guest Profile: All types of guests (very few novelists unless relatable to a topical theme.) In a guest, I look for someone articulate and interesting. They can have either a point of view or information to impart. We want to know what a guest wishes to talk about.

Guest from Hell: A guest from hell is one who is inarticulate and/or not interesting. One who can't easily be understood (thick accent, etc.).

Contact: jim_bohannon@westwoodone.com; 202-457-7978; http://www.jimbotalk.net; John Stolnis at john_stolnis@westwoodone.com 202-457-7974; E-mail first. No response? Followup contacts aren't necessary. If we're interested we'll get back to you.

Invited Back? We invite them back if we liked them the first time and we have a desire to have them back. But a guest can be great and never be invited back if there's not a lot of general interest in their expertise.

Bio of Jim Bohannon: Jim is a veteran talk host and news anchor who has won numerous awards and is a member of the Radio Hall of Fame. He's broadcast from Moscow, Paris, Tokyo, national conventions, and taken calls from astronauts while they were in orbit.

Guest Comment: "Jim Bohannon is one of the best — and smartest — interviewers in the business. His questions are piercing, but he's not playing hardball. He's truly interested in what his guests have to say." — Prill Boyle, author of *Defying Gravity* (Emmis Books 2005), http://www.prillboyle.com

KnightTime Radio Show with Sheryl Youngblood, Ph.D., on WWCR, Nashville, Tenn, aired in North America, Mexico, Europe, Australia, Japan, and Africa; now off the air.

Theme: Politics, lifestyles, community action, spirituality, family, truck drivers.

Guest Profile: Songwriters, authors, psychologists, counselor, directors of organizations, truck drivers, executives. A topic that supports our themes; people who have overcome difficulties; people who are taking a stand for a cause. Credentials and current activities

Guest from Hell: People who answer questions with just "yes" or "no."

Contact: truckerdoc@hotmail.com; 570-357-9131; http://www.truckerdoc.com; Sheryl Youngblood. Best method: E-mail a bio or press kit; people can telephone, but sometimes it's difficult to get me. No response? Absolutely, e-mail or call — contact me a second time.

Invited Back? Good flow of conversations; heavy interest in the subject.

Guest Comment: "Focused on how Bush actions affect trucking industry. Much tighter focus than I'm used to, but I managed to fill about 20 or so minutes with discussion of some regs. (like increasing no. of hours a trucker can drive) ... and some other stuff. She plugged book well."— Walter Brasch, whose latest book is *Sinking the Ship of State: The Presidency of George W. Bush* (BookSurge Publishing 2007), http://www.walterbrasch.com

Bio of Sheryl Youngblood: Sheryl is an Industrial/organizational psychologist, former professor, researcher, and talk show host.

Laurie and Olga Show with Laurie Macdonald and Olga Gazdovic on CJAD 800 AM, aired in Montreal and surrounding area.

Theme: Light talk.

Guest Profile: Everyone. Generally, someone who is at ease with themselves, who has a specific message to relay to the audience, light and interesting cocktail conversation. I'd like to know the least amount of information as possible. My interview style is to chat with someone like I would when meeting them at a party. No inside edge.

Guest from Hell: Probably a guest who is not comfortable talking on the air who answers with yes and no answers!

Contact: laurie.macdonald@cjad.com; olga.gazdovic@cjad.com; 514-989-2523; http://www.cjad.com; Laurie Macdonald. Best method: E-mail is probably the best approach. No response? A follow-up e-mail would be a good idea.

Invited Back? The relationship we acquire is critical (the chemistry).

The Lee Rodgers Show on KSFO, broadcast in the San Francisco Bay Area and at http://www.ksfo.com, weekdays from 5–9 AM (PT). Rated #73 in the 2008 Talkers Heavy Hundred.

Theme: Entertaining, compelling conservative politics.

Guest Profile: Political analysts/commentators. Someone with someone interesting to say and who can say it articulately and passionately. They must be media savvy.

Guest from Hell: Someone who gives monotone, one-word answers to open-ended questions.

Contact: sheri.yee@citcomm.com; 415-954-8661; http://www.ksfo.com; Producer Sheri Yee. Best method: E-mail a pitch with an angle that appeals to our conservative audience, accompanied by a bio, press kit, etc. No response? They can follow-up, and the worst I'll do is say no, thank you.

Invited Back? If they are entertaining and/or compelling, they'll be back.

Bio of Lee Rodgers: "I represent the spirit of free enterprise. I'm a no-holds-barred capitalist," says Lee in his characteristically brash, up-front style. Known as the "open-line king" during the 10 years he was a host on KGO Radio in San Francisco, he is a passionate believer in the American Dream. "It's almost impossible for anybody to begin life in lower circumstances than I did (admittedly without racial handicap)," he says. "I figure that if you observe the wisdom in the words deferred gratification, and are willing to work your butt off, this society, with all its faults, offers you the opportunity to succeed. That's the starting point."

Lee has always been primed to succeed though born and raised in poverty near Memphis, Tennessee, and having lost part of a leg at age 13 working in the timber industry. A self-described part-time coach, referee, catalyst and provocateur, he began his broadcasting career at WIND in 1963 as a disc jockey and sportscaster, followed by stints with radio stations in St. Louis, Miami and Chicago.

Certainly Rodgers' show is spirited. Throwing out lines like "A conservative is a liberal who got mugged last night," and "It's my mission in my life to educate the heathen."

Full bio at http://www.ksfo.com/showdj.asp?djid=2254

The Leslie Marshall Show with Leslie Marshall, nationally syndicated, airing 7–10 PM EST and 4–7 PM PST.

Theme: Politics/social issues.

Guest Profile: Politicians, experts, authors: a) name recognition, b) expertise on the topic/news of the day that is being talked about by America. Our guests are either political, or regarding a specific item in the news, i.e., Iraq, immigration, the recent Michael Vick scandal, 2008 presidential candidates, etc. Host is a liberal Democrat, but has both liberal and conservative guests. Don't care about the sound of their voice. I care about their credentials and their opinion and what they are pushing/selling (book, idea, organization, etc.) I don't care what other shows they have been on.

Guest from Hell: Someone who is late, rude and doesn't know how to "play the game."

Contact: Producer Mark Grimaldi at mgrimaldi@entercom.com; 310-266-9476; http://www.lesliemarshall.us; for the show, Mark Grimaldi. For other — Agent: Eliot Ephraim 312-321-9700 or publicist, Wendy Guarisco 407-355-4205. Best method: Please contact either my producer via e-mail, or my agent or publicist via phone. No response? NEVER call/e-mail the host in my case at least. Contact my producer. If he wants to book you, he will contact you. If you bug him, he won't.

Invited Back? If they make the phones ring, or if they intrigue me, make me smile/laugh.

Bio of Leslie Marshall: Leslie has been a radio talk host for over 19 years and a pundit on national television for the past five. She became the youngest person ever to be nationally syndicated on radio when she replaced Tom Snyder on the ABC Satellite Radio Network in 1992. She was also the first woman to host an issues-oriented program nationwide.

Originally from Boston, Leslie earned her undergraduate degree from Northeastern University and her Master's in broadcast journalism from Emerson College.

She started her broadcasting career as a radio news reporter in Boston. Hoping to branch out into television, Leslie took her news skills to Miami, Florida, where she did news, traffic, weather and even disc jockey work. One night, when hosting an overnight nostalgic music program, Leslie did a special "Remembrance" hour in which veterans called in with their experiences. It was that night that Leslie was discovered by a program director at the talk station across town. He phoned her, and told she might have missed her calling.

After years of anchoring, reporting and hosting music programs, Leslie decided to give talk radio a try; and after one show, she was hooked. Leslie started her talk radio career at WNWS in Miami where she remained for three years.

She then moved to mid-days at WGR in Buffalo, followed by mid-days at KPRC in Houston; all the while, the network was watching. In 1992, Leslie was asked to replace Tom Snyder on the ABC Satellite Radio Network. Her program ran for three years on over 200 stations nationwide.

When the network disbanded, Leslie went to work for WLS/FM in Chicago, hosting an afternoon drive talk show. (She would later return to Chicago to work evenings on WLS AM and co-host *Beyond the Beltway* on WGR TV.) After the OJ Simpson trial ended, Leslie decided she needed a change of pace and followed her heart to San Francisco to marry her love of nearly eight years. Leslie then joined the great line-up at KGO radio in San Francisco and also hosted a mid-day show on KHTK/Hot Talk in Sacramento. On television she hosted "Bay Talk" on KRON T.V., the local NBC affiliate.

When Leslie's husband was offered a job opportunity in Los Angeles, she joined him. There, she hosted weekend talk shows on KFI, KLSX and KABC radio and was finally signed to KLAC, KFI's sister station at its inception. When KLAC flipped formats, Leslie decided to stay in LA with her husband.

Leslie is on television each week on the Fox News Channel and on CNBC's *Kudlow and Company*. (She most recently was seen debating Ann Coulter.) She is also an actress who has appeared on such shows as "Desperate Housewives," "NYPD Blue," "Seventh Heaven," and "General Hospital."

Leslie lives in the Los Angeles area with her spouse and their cat.

Liberalpro with Tim Gatto on Blog Talk Radio

Theme: Progressive News and Political Talk. A progressive voice and great ideas. Preferably with credentials and past experience, www.blogtalkradio.com/stations/headingleft/liberalpro

Guest Profile: Congressional candidates, book authors, movement principals.

Guest from Hell: One that won't talk or has to be prompted.

Contact: Timgatto@hotmail.com; 864-349-1271; http://www.liberalpro.blogspot.com; Tim Gatto. Best method: Sending me an e-mail and describing their pitch. No response? E-mail or call.

Invited Back? The amount of information that is put out and the listeners that are brought in.

Bio of Tim Gatto: Tim served in the Army for 20 years and has been writing on progressive websites for more than three years.

His 340 page e-book, *Kimchee Kronicles*, is available at http://www.ed-thelen.org/gatto_00-04.html

Liberty Watch with Charles Heller airs on AM 690, KVOI, Tucson, AM 930 KAPR Douglas, and AM 1100 KFNX, Phoenix, AZ, and streamed live on the Internet. He also hosts *America Armed and Free*.

Theme: So that government remains servant, not master; indepth review of things with a muzzle, nozzle, or blade.

Guest Profile: People who are intellectually honest and knowledgeable of topic. Could not care less who they have been interviewed by or what their voice sounds like. Want to know their bona fides — school, work or life experience in the topic area, and something about their hobbies or interests — what makes them tick.

Guest from Hell: People who are unfamiliar with their own work and cannot answer a simple question directly.

Contact: charles@libertywatchradio.com; 520 870-2700; http://www.libertywatchradio.com/bookings. Best method: E-mail. A well written one to two page press release is most effective. No response? E-mail again, then call

Invited Back? Intellectual honesty, knowledge of topic, passion for topic, presentation.

Bio of Charles Heller: Charles hails from Chicago and studied journalism at Northern Illinois University. He relocated to Arizona in 1978.

He is radio advertising salesman and owner of the *Liberty Watch* studio, and producer of his shows. He is also a state-certified concealed weapons instructor.

He is married and father of two grown children.

Lighting the Fires of Liberty with Michael Badnarik on GCNLIVE, www.gcnlive.com and dozens of micro-re-broadcasters. The show, airing weekdays 9–11 PM (CT), originates in Austin, Texas but also attracts international listeners.

Theme: LIBERTY! The explicit purpose is to teach people about their rights, and make them passionate about freedom.

Guest Profile: Patriots, economists, psychologists, authors, and occasionally victims of an abusive government system. Someone who has lots of passion, and at least a little expertise, in their given field. Any good conversationalist will work. I talk with each of my guests beforehand, so I know what their speech patterns are like, and whether they sound credible about their topic. Again, I've only had one that sounded coherent during the interview, but couldn't answer questions on the air. Apparently "stage fright" overcame him and his demeanor changed significantly. Afterwards he was excited and wanted to do another program because "I didn't get a chance to say everything I wanted."

Guest from Hell: Someone who won't (or can't) answer the question. Fortunately, I've only had one that drove me crazy. Guests who give long-winded answers are more frustrating to deal with, but I'm willing to interrupt them if necessary.

Contact: scholar@ConstitutionPreservation.org; 512-461-0995; http://www.WTPRN.com — http://mp3.wtprn.com/Badnarik07.html (archive files) — http://www.ConstitutionPreservation.org; Michael Badnarik. Best method: Phone. I haven't achieved enough notoriety to have people approaching me. I usually spend several hours each day contacting people I'd like to interview. Occasionally I'm forced to do a program without a guest, focusing on some particular topic that I've researched enough to speak authoritatively. Fortunately my listening audience is large enough and responsive enough that I can ask for callers and get immediate input. No response? E-mail or call. I get a little over 100 e-mail messages a day, so I can typically filter through the important messages in an hour or two. Unfortunately, some get forgotten, so I'm always open to a gentle reminder.

Invited Back? If their topic was interesting to my listeners. The two factors I use to determine this are how easy it is to converse with them on the air, and the volume of phone calls we get during the program. If I get several e-mail messages begging me to have that guest again, I will make it happen. My goal is to teach them about their individual rights, but if nobody is listening, it doesn't matter how clever and informative my guest and I think we are.

Guest Comment: "Two hours as co-host. Very

congenial. Asked solid questions; gave a lot of opportunity for me to go where I wanted to go, do what I wanted to do. Was obviously prepared for the show; extremely knowledgeable about many things, especially constitutional issues. A lot of call-ins from throughout the country; all guests were respectful and asked good questions. Two hours of enjoyment."—Walter Brasch, whose latest book is *Sinking the Ship of State: The Presidency of George W. Bush* (BookSurge Publishing 2007). http://www.walterbrasch.com

Bio of Michael Badnarik: Michael is a constitutional scholar, author and teacher. He's a longtime political activist and privacy advocate. He has developed computer programs to simulate nuclear power plants and the Stealth bomber. Michael was a Libertarian candidate for Texas House of Representatives (Austin area) in 2000 and 2002 and the Libertarian Party's nominee for president of the United States in 2004. He also ran as a Libertarian in Texas' Congressional District 10 in the 2006 general election.

He now devotes his time to hosting his daily radio talk-show, lecturing, and teaching an eight-hour class on the Constitution and Bill of Rights. His book, *Good to Be King* (Writers' Collective 2004), is used as the text for that class. One way or another, he is determined to change the course of American politics in the direction of world peace.

The Lionel Show, nationally syndicated by Air America Radio. Rated #31 on 2008 Talkers Heavy Hundred.

Theme: Politics, music, humor, ideas, pop culture, memetics, numismatics, name it — Lionel will tackle the issue.

Guest Profile: Newsmakers, authors, celebrities, historians, experts of all sorts, informed by personal experience, first person accounts, professional experience. Also good are guests who can give a lively presentation of ideas based on their research. What other shows they've been on is good to know. But more important is why they are qualified to talk about the topic.

Guest from Hell: Someone who has not even read their own book. Self-help does not work well for our show, nor personal stories of recovery or discovery.

Contact: thelionelshow@gmail.com; Withheld upon request; http://www.lionelonline.com; producer Alex Goldmark at agoldmark@airamerica.com. Best method: E-mail. Sending a press kit is great. No response? A second e-mail is helpful a week or more later. But after that, no need to clutter the inbox.

Invited Back? On a case by case basis.

Bio of Lionel: What's with the name "Lionel?" No last name? Nope. Mononymous, like God. Get over it. The name actually comes from Al Pacino's character in the 1973 film classic *Scarecrow*. Why? "Ben-Hur" was taken. Born Hiawatha Lipschitz, Lionel has been performing talk radio for 18 years (85 dog years). Don't even try labeling him or his ideology as such is for naught: He's the quintessence of sui generis. Carol Channing scares him. He implores and entreats his listeners to critically think and analyze, to parse topics and peel the layers of the issue onion. The barbate Lionel loathes trite shibboleths, playbook and bumper sticker labels as well as leprosy.

Lionel started as a mere caller whilst in law school in his home town of Tampa (cf. Tampa Bay) and was given his own show in 1988 on 970 WFLA — a weekend show (Sunday, no less). For reasons yet to be fathomed, he then jumped to middays, then afternoon drive in less than a year. The rest is ... well, you know the line. Lionel was a prosecutor and criminal defense trial lawyer, so when a legal issue needs dissecting, whom better to consult? Lionel hosted his own show on Court TV and has appeared as a guest on virtually every news commentary show. Then again, who hasn't? He never wears sandals with socks. He's a proud polyglot, sesquipedalian and accomplished manualist. Rachael Ray is the Antichrist. Lionel's wit and biting humor are nonpareil. He has often said that he'd rather be the editorial cartoon than the editorial.

He emphasizes the absurd and recondite and there's a lot to emphasize. Talk radio is supposed to be fun, last time Lionel checked; that's why he never listens to it. He's the Harold Stassen of talk radio. For revamped, rejuvenated, retrofitted and reinvented talk radio, Lionel is where to go. He has consistently been the Number One rated talk host during his time period in New York (no joke). New affiliates grow like yeast. Lionel redefines talk radio. He'll make you think, whether you want to or not. You will learn. He hates magicians and comedians. And, oh yes, mimes.

Madely in the Morning with Steve Madely from 6 AM–9 AM on 580 CFRA Radio, Ottawa, ON, Canada.

Theme: News talk.

Guest Profile: Newsmakers, journalists, non-fiction news/issues authors. Opinion backed by factual argument. Past interviews, appearances, clippings, reviews are usually helpful in establishing credibility and level of potential audience interest.

Guest from Hell: One who avoids direct answers, trying to "steer" interview.

Contact: Mornings@CFRA.com; 613-789-2486 ext 4235; http://www.cfra.com. Best method: E-mail only. No response? Volume of requests makes replies impossible. If there is no response, it means "thanks anyway."

Invited Back? Did they answer my questions or tease the audience with half answers, indirect answers, or book plugs? And, of course, were they interesting?

Bio of Steve Madely: Steve started his career as a broadcaster in 1964 while attending high school in Oakville, Ontario. After a number of radio and television positions in southern Ontario, Steve came to Ottawa as part of the founding management team for

CFGO Radio in 1972. He joined CFRA in 1981 as news director, later moving to station manager. He returned to the air on CFRA in 1993 as host of *Power of the People*— quickly building a #1 audience with the 9–Noon talk show. In 1994 *Madely in the Morning* Ottawa's premier news talk breakfast show, made its debut.

A valuable member of Ottawa's community for more than 30 years, Steve co-hosts the annual Ottawa Cancer Centre Telethon, is an Honorary Life Rotarian for his work with the Easter Seal Society, and is a past board member for the Children's Aid Foundation, The Regional Cancer Centre Foundation, and The Roberts Smart Centre.

Mancow, syndicated by TRN FM to 40+ markets from S.F. to Houston to Missoula MT. #14 in 2008 Talkers' Heavy Hundred.

Theme: Free thinking talk, libertarian.

Guest Profile: Celebs, authors, in the news, every aspect or everything. Someone with a story that can generate a phone call. Are they interesting?

Guest from Hell: Someone who reads prepared answers.

Contact: mancow@mancow.com; 630-280-9700 (Dustin assistant); http://www.mancow.com; Dustin Rhoades; dtrhoades@comcast.net. Best method: Phone. No response? E-mail or call.

Invited Back? If they get reaction from the listeners.

Bio of Erich "Mancow" Muller: Erich was a child model and actor, appearing in ads for Lee Jeans and Wal-Mart, and playing "the cute kid" in dozens of off–Broadway plays, including long runs of *On Golden Pond* and *The Crucible*. He earned Bachelors degrees in public relations and theater at Central Missouri State University in Warrensburg, MO, and that's where he started working in radio, at KOKO-AM.

From small-town Missouri to Kansas City, then to Chicago by way of California, Mancow has always drawn big ratings, and often drawn controversy. "My show is not for kids," says Mancow. "The whole world can't be aimed at seven-year-olds. Parents tell me, 'Well, my kid listens to you anyway.' I tell them it's sad that they can't control a child."

When he's not being "offensive," Mancow's show has often featured outrageous publicity stunts. He once had live cows delivered to competitors' radio shows, and in another instance draped a "Welcome to Chicago" banner over an arrival gate at the San Francisco International Airport.

Mancow's most infamous bit came in 1993, a few days after celebrity stylist Christophe had given President Bill Clinton a $200 haircut aboard Air Force One at L.A. International Airport. It had been widely (and incorrectly) reported that other landings and take-offs at the airport had been restricted while Christophe perfected Clinton's coiffure, so Mancow, then working at a San Francisco station, concocted this stunt cum political statement: Mancow and his then-sidekick Chuy "Chewy" Gomez drove onto the Bay Bridge, the double-decked freeway that connects San Francisco to Oakland. Then, at the height of the morning rush hour, they stopped the radio station's van in traffic while Gomez got a haircut. The traffic jam was enormous, and while the haircut only took a few minutes, traffic was clogged on the bridge for the rest of the morning and into the afternoon. The radio station was sued, and ended up paying more than a million dollars. Mancow became nationally famous, and locally both beloved and despised.

The Mark Reardon Show on KMOX, St. Louis, MO.

Theme: Mix of politics, pop culture, entertainment.

Guest Profile: Various — rarely fiction authors. I'm partial to more libertarian or conservative leaning guests. I'm not opposed to having someone on from the other side, but they'd better be good and able to debate. Qualities desired — Good sound credentials — energetic ... informative ... entertaining.

Guest from Hell: Dull.

Contact: mark.reardon@cbsradio.com; 314-621-2345; http://www.kmox.com; Rachel Doyle at Rachel.Doyle@cbsradio.com. Best method: E-mail producer. No response? No — that means we're not interested.

Invited Back? If I like 'em they get invited back.

Bio of Mark Reardon: A 20-year radio veteran, Mark was born and raised in the suburbs of Chicago, but moved to St. Louis in 1979 and spent the next 17 years in Missouri. His prior assignments included KFRU in Columbia, Missouri, the former KSD-AM in St. Louis and WTMJ in Milwaukee.

Mike is a graduate of the University of Missouri Journalism School. His passions include politics, hunting and fishing, going to the movies and his two children.

The Media Lizzy Show with Elizabeth "Media Lizzy" Blackney on BlogTalkRadio. She anchors Heading Right Radio Shows, which includes *Media Lizzy*. See http://blogtalkradio.com/channels/headingrightradio

Theme: Politics, foreign affairs.

Guest Profile: Authors, political consultants, pollsters, candidates, media personalities with a quick wit and challenging point of view. Credentials, their objective for the interview, and interesting details or anecdotes are essential. Her prominent guests have included the former governor of Virginia Jim Gilmore, Austrian scholar Hannes Artens, emerging Republican strategist Shawn Fago of California, Noam Chomsky, Howard Zinn, Naomi Klein, John Pilger, Barbara Ehrenreich, Greg Palast, Benjamin Barber, and Lawrence Lessig.

Guest from Hell: One with nothing to say, or with bad manners.

Contact: eliz@medializzy.com; Withheld upon request; http://medializzy.com; Elizabeth Blackney. Best method: E-mail first, always. Any other pitch is likely to be forgotten or overlooked. No response? We read every e-mail, and always try to respond quickly. Generally, if we don't reach out — it is because we aren't interested in booking the guest.

Invited Back? Manners, etiquette, my listeners' interest, and my gut instinct.

Bio of Elizabeth "Media Lizzy" Blackney: Elizabeth defines the 21st century Gen Xer. Part professional, part entrepreneur and part activist combined with a knack for seeing around corners; she is a publisher, author, streaming radio talk show host, blogger, and above all things — a mother. She brings a fresh, next generation perspective to every venture.

After leaving the three-ring circus of electoral politics in 2006, she developed a plan to broaden the literary voices of her generation. She encourages debate wherever she lands, and her coverage of foreign affairs, military affairs and American politics at the federal level is informed by more than a dozen years of working closely with newsmakers, industry icons and opinion leaders. She is author of *Sex Lies and Politricks* (2007) and *Unwitnessed Events: Diary of a Political Affair* (Spring 2008).

Media Matters with Robert McChesney on WILL-AM, Urbana, IL — reaching East-Central Illinois, as well as webcast live online. Also archived online (podcast).

Theme: Analysis and critique of media systems and institutions.

Guest Profile: Authors/film-makers/activists focused on media/communication and/or U.S. public policy. Education/academia and the relationship between media and public policy are also of interest. The host is in conversation with a variety of guests. Listeners may call with comments or questions. Able to speak in a non-technical and engaging manner for our broad audience. Responsive to listener calls. Format is 53 minutes, usually live, so we're looking for in-depth coverage rather than sound-bites. Primarily credentials [position, book-length publications, former positions]. Details of current book, or similar hook for interview at this point in time.

Guest from Hell: Arrogant or dismissive of listener questions. Difficult to draw out — remember this is an hour-long interview, so overly short answers can make it difficult to fill the time.

Contact: andrew@funferal.org; withheld upon request; http://will.illinois.edu/am/mediamatters; Andrew Ó Baoill (producer). Best method: E-mail. No response? Generally not a good idea to e-mail or call. We get more pitches from PR agents/authors than we can accommodate, and don't always have time to respond to all pitches.

Invited Back? New book/film, or specialist knowledge of a public policy issue that's back in the news (e.g. FCC regulations, certain foreign policy areas).

Bio of Robert W. McChesney: Robert is the Gutgsell Endowed Professor in the Department of Communication at the University of Illinois at Urbana-Champaign. He is the president and co-founder of Free Press, a national media reform organization.

The Meria Show with Meria Heller on http://www.meria.net

Theme: Breaking free of the matrix of mass media.

Guest Profile: Authors, producers and people in the news who are personable, knowledgeable and good speakers. Specialties are natural health, liberal/progressive politics, environment, veganism, spiritual subjects. I look for a guest who knows his/her material, speaks well, has a bit of a sense of humor about his/her work and knows what I and my show is about. I want to know they are understandable when they speak, what their politics are, and, in the field of health whether or not they are vegetarian. If not, I'm not interested. Credentials aren't important; you can be the new kid on the block if your work has merit, and betters the world somehow. Please check the website and show before submitting materials that may not fit in with the genre of the show.

Guest from Hell: Someone who doesn't show for their scheduled interview. Sometimes they get a second chance, most times never. There are tons of people desperate to get on the show.

Contact: Meria@Meria.net; withheld upon request; http://www.meria.net; Meria. Best method: E-mail/Snail mail; no phone inquiries or pitches, please. Check the site. If your material fits, send it. If it doesn't, it will go into the garbage. E-mail is best, giving website info. If you have a good CD, movie, a review copy must be sent to: Meria Enterprises, P.O. Box 879, Payson, AZ 85547. Do not send long drawn-out pitches, simplify it. A press kit is also welcome. No response? They should e-mail me if they don't hear from me within two days.

Invited Back? Their knowledge of their material and listeners' requests.

Listener Comments: "In the world of corporate 'sound bite' media, Meria Heller goes beyond that for a more detailed discussion and look at national and world events that are of importance to listeners."— J. Stevens, IL

"Like I always tell everyone, Meria Heller has the best, most interesting guests on her show. Meria's show is always thought-provoking, and despite the serious content, also makes me laugh. I can't imagine not having the independent Meria Heller show to listen to keep me informed on what really matters: life from the perspective of honesty and truth and democracy and a connection to our home, planet Earth."— Darren, Canada

Bio of Meria Heller: Meria has produced/hosted

her own show for 10 years, two on a Phoenix station, and eight on the Web.

Well read, self taught, an environmentalist, vegetarian and spiritual, Meria is not religious and does not touch religion at all on the show. "I am pretty radical in my political views," she says. "I actually believe the Bill of Rights and Constitution should always stand in the USA."

The Midwatch with Stan Waggoner on WEFT, Champaign, IL.
Theme: Political talk.
Guest Profile: Politicians, economists, professors. relevance to current events. Liberal leaning philosophy. Credentials, and past interviews with me.
Guest from Hell: One that only gives yes or no answers to questions.
Contact: swag312@consolidated.net; 217-254-4432; http://www.WEFT.org; Stan Waggoner. Best method: Whatever is convenient to them. I prefer e-mail. No response? E-mail or call. I get a lot of e-mails so something in the subject line that gets my attention is important.
Invited Back? Ease of talking to, and ability to express their views in a way I feel my audience will understand.
Guest Comment: "Stan knew the subject well and asked appropriate questions to make the interview interesting to us and to the listening public." — Jim Ennes, author of *Assault on the Liberty* (Reintree Press 2002) and webmaster of http://www.ussliberty.org
Bio of Stan Waggoner: Stan is in the financial industry and works with ING and other companies when not hosting his show.

The Morning Show with Gregory Berg (and *The WGTD Radio Theater* with Michael Ullstrup and Steve Brown), on WGTD Public Radio 91.1 FM, weekdays at 8:10 AM (ET), aired in Kenosha, Racine and Lake Geneva, WI, and streamed live at http://www.wgtd.org
Theme: Eclectic themes. There is no specific theme other than having guests who are able to answer a thoughtful and in-depth question in an intellectual and provocative manner.
Guest Profile: Authors of fiction and non-fiction; state and national politicians; actors in television, motion pictures, and radio; leaders in the medical field; inventors. A person who is smart, articulate, and "gets to the point." What life experiences have led them to where and who they are right now. And, can they truly carry on an intelligent conversation.
Guest from Hell: Someone who does not listen to the question and is just on their own "talking points."
Contact: stevenmbrown@hotmail.com; 262-813-0144; http://www.wgtd.org and http://www.thegiverplay.com; Dr. Steven Brown. Best method: E-mail me a bio, a book to read, a press release, and a press kit, as long as it's not some template that everyone uses. No response? E-mail me back. Harass me with a phone call is totally fine.
Invited Back? Is their next book a blockbuster, in terms of content, content, and content? And, would I like to have lunch with that person and just "chat."
Guest Comment: "I thoroughly enjoyed my interview with Greg Berg about greening religious communities and about a collection of sermons by various faith leaders on the environment that I had recently edited. I was very comfortable with the physical arrangement and the introduction. I did not feel as if I was being grilled or probed. I felt like we were in conversation. Greg's questions and comments were natural responses to the last thing I was saying. He introduced new directions with ease. He even drew out of me some new things I had not planned on saying. At the end, I had a sense of satisfaction that I had gotten across what I wanted to convey and did not get derailed with extraneous or irrelevant things. I would be more than pleased to do it again" — David Rhoads, professor of New Testament at the Lutheran School of Theology in Chicago — http://www.lstc.edu/people/faculty/individual/rhoads.html
Bio of Steven Brown: Steve is a public news producer and anchor, who specializes in taking in-depth looks at important community issues. He also anchors the local news segments during *All Things Considered*, on Monday, Wednesday, and Fridays.

Steve resides in the Town of Salem and is a fulltime professor of educational law at Northeastern Illinois University. He also volunteers his time to serve as producer/artistic director for the WGTD Radio Theatre. Steve has worked in both radio and television news in several markets around the country. He is also a producer of stage plays, and has written over 25 screenplays and radio dramas.

My Point Radio with David Odeen and Jenn Adlam on Blog Talk Radio, www.blogtalkradio.com/mypoint
Theme: Conservative based social commentary.
Guest Profile: Authors, psychologists, politcos, and fellow like-minded thinkers. Someone passionate about the subject on hand. Not afraid to discuss the issue. Friendly authors. Any detail info is good. They must be excited to be with you.
Guest from Hell: Dull, and not friendly. Will not talk on a talk show.
Contact: dtodeen@gmail.com; 651-270-9704; http://www.mypointradio.net and http://www.screwliberals.com; David Odeen. Best method: E-mail and press kit. No response? Call or e-mail, but I always respond quickly
Invited Back? Knowledge and ideas. Ability to be friendly.
Bios of David Odeen and Jenn Adlam: Just a couple of Americans concerned about our country and looking for leaders to lead it. We are both average Americans with average educations.

Mytalkshow with Mantalk on Blog Talk Radio at http://www.blogtalkradio.com/mytalkshow. Jerry also hosts *Jerry's Shopping Show* at http://blogtalkradio.com/shoppingbroker

Theme: We the people with freedom of speech. I talk about our freedom of speech and freedom of religion and all the freedoms that we do have. I talk about what is going on in the news and all over the world to bring it down to the way that we may think of it. Then ask people for their side of the story.

Guest Profile: All. A person that feels that we should have our freedom of speech among other things. All I can know about them.

Guest from Hell: Someone that just does not care about anything.

Contact: mytalkshow@gmail.com; 989-642-9157; http://a1personalsopper.blogspot.com; Jerry Spencer. Best method: Any. The way I am you can approach me as you choose to and I take it from there. No response? E-mail or call.

Invited Back? A person with a good heart and can speak their mind without hurting others.

Bio of Jerry Spencer: Jerry comes from an Army family; his uncle was in World War II, his dad was in V.N. and his son was in Iraq. "So I do know how it feels to have people at war and hoping they will come back; for me they all did, thank God," says Jerry. "I have been all over the world and loved it," he says. "So I try to share things with people when I can. On *Mytalkshow* I hope to help people to know that we can lose our freedoms if we do not speak out to keep them."

New Dimensions with Michael Toms. Guest hosts include Justine Willis Toms, Craig Hamilton, and Tarra Christoff. The show airs on 300 public and community stations around the U.S., throughout Australia on the ABC (Australian Broadcasting Corporation), Canada, New Zealand, NDIR (New Dimensions Internet Radio), iTunes, and is heard on http://www.newdimensions.org

Theme: Personal and social change.

Guest Profile: People who are coming up with positive solutions to the pressing questions of our times which include health and healing, sustainable living, spirituality, personal and social change, the arts, and environment. Someone who is grounded in solutions and has an understanding of the challenges we are facing today in many fields. Want to know their credentials, life experience, and if they have arranged their thoughts into a coherent whole.

Guest from Hell: Someone who is talking about a good idea, but has not been tested in the field.

Contact: justine@newdimensions.org; 707-468-5215 x14; http://www.newdimensions.org; Justine Toms. Best method: Press kit and book are preferred first contact. Then e-mail asking if we received package. No response? No, just e-mail us again. We receive over 400 program ideas for every one we produce. It is a swamp of requests.

Invited Back? If our listeners respond enthusiastically to them.

Guest Comments: "*New Dimensions* disseminates ideas, images and stories so that people catch the threads of imagination and weave them into their own lives that supports them to live a better life. *New Dimensions* is a great resource for anyone with an open mind and an open heart."—Michael Meade, renowned storyteller, drummer, scholar of mythology and author of *Ends of Time, the Roots of Eternity: Tales of Myth, Nature, and Culture* (Mosaic Multicultural Foundation 2007).

"One of the reasons I respect *New Dimensions* so much is because in an age where media is becoming increasingly owned by smaller and smaller number of mega-media corporations, it is important that the story, which doesn't make the national news, gets out. *New Dimensions* offers the voice of America at the grassroots. It's a voice that is several clicks ahead of where America is, as represented in the mass media. *New Dimensions* offers an approach to life that is open, inclusive, and compassionate. It digs below the surface, moving beyond sound bytes into the real stuff of life, faith, intellect, and of art."—Eric Elnes, Minister and author of *Asphalt Jesus: Finding a New Christian Faith Along the Highways of America* (Jossey-Bass 2007).

Bio of Justine Willis Toms: Justine is the co-founder and co-president New Dimensions Media and World Broadcasting Network and New Dimensions Radio, projects of New Dimensions Foundation. Her keen interest in non-traditional education and innovative learning techniques has helped to create the natural ambiance and engaging style of the show's broadcast programming and cassette tapes.

She serves as editor-in-chief of the *New Dimensions Newsletter*, a national publication based on the work of New Dimensions Radio, which reaches 30,000 readers nationwide.

She is co-author with her husband Michael Toms of *True Work: Doing What You Love and Loving What You Do* (Harmony/Bell Tower 1999) and author of *Small Pleasures: Finding Grace in a Chaotic World* (Hampton Roads 2008).

New World Order Disorder with Dr. Gianni Hayes on The American Voice, http://www.theamericanvoice.com on Wednesdays, 8–10 ET; also aired on FM stations, ipods, cell phones, satellite, and short wave. Gianni also hosts *Hotspots and Hotshots* on Saturdays, 5–6 PM EST, http://www.themicroeffect.com

Theme: Politics, religion, current events; mainly authors.

Guest Profile: Experts in their fields: science, politics, religion, conspiracies, and celebrities, including Bernard Goldberg (author, TV correspondent); Terri Schiavo's parents; and Mel Gibson's father and his chef. Knowledgeable, articulate expert who is passionate about his/her subject, and has preferably — but not necessarily — written a book or article(s) on his/her subject matter. Why they claim they are experts on the subject matter; the gravity of their research and documentation; how well they speak on the phone; how well they write in their e-mails; if there is passion in their voices for their subject matter; if they have anyone who can vouch for their credibility

Guest from Hell: Arrogant, cantankerous guest who demeans the hosts or the host's callers; one who doesn't like to be questioned or challenged; one who is not prepared for the interview.

Contact: ndhayes@worldnet.att.net; info@thenaz.com; 410-543-0448. Best method: Contact me by e-mail with bio; explain who you are, why you're the expert; request to send a book or articles to me and support materials on yourself and topic; send a press kit as well, if available. No response? Contact me again. I'm incredibly busy.

Invited Back? How they treated the host and callers; if they did a good job of making their point; if they weren't really "off the wall," if they were polite and willing to answer all types of questions; if they are reputable

Bio of Gianni DeVincent Hayes: Gianni is author of 14 books of fiction and non-fiction, a freelance writer and lecturer who holds a Ph.D. summa cum laude in English, creative writing and world/comparative literature studies from the University of Maryland College Park. She has also earned two Masters degrees. Gianni is an international speaker, as well as a former professor and college department chair. She has been honored with countless awards, endowments and tributes.

Among the biographies she has written are *Zambelli's the First Family of Fireworks* (Paul S. Eriksson 2003) and *The Last of the Wallendas* (New Horizon Press) on the famous Flying Wallenda family; Among her novels are *Jacob's Demon* (Cambridge Books 2005) about the current politics and the Apocalypse, and *Lucifer's Legion* (Write Words 2006) on cloning humans, *22 Friar Street* (Flower Valley Press) illustrating a teenagers coping with racial, educational, cultural, and age difference.

Gianni has appeared in many newspapers and magazines and on more than 60 radio and TV stations as a guest.

Nightside Project with Ethan Millard and Alex Kirry on KSL Newsradio 102.7 FM and 1160 AM, Salt Lake City, UT.

Theme: Talk.

Guest Profile: Pop culture, trends, relationships, interview experiences, credentials, and sound of their voice.

Guest from Hell: Irrelevant.

Contact: nightside.ksl.com; 801-575-7651; http://www.nightsideproject.com. Best method: E-mail. No response? More e-mail.

Invited Back? Chemistry and sense of humor if applicable.

Bio of Ethan Millard: Ethan Millard is founder of SLCSpin.com, one of Utah's premier political websites. Ethan is known for edgy, confrontational political commentary. A longtime political observer, Ethan studied contemporary East European history at the University of Utah and Central European University.

Bio of Alex Kirry: Alex Kirry graduated with a degree in broadcast journalism but doesn't consider himself a journalist because he thinks they are "way too full of themselves and smart." Alex started out in sports radio and still loves to school the *Nightside* staff in sports trivia and general knowledge. He has had jobs in radio ranging from reporter and producer, to part time donut guy and his current position as UFO expert. Alex split time growing up in Texas and the Greater Seattle area, both of which he loves. With a background in comedy writing, acting and being a general clown, Alex is a natural fit to the *Nightside* team. Also, the fact that he can't agree with Ethan on anything makes him a local hero.

NightSide with Dan Rea on WBZ Radio, Boston, airing Monday through Friday 8 PM to Midnight.

Theme: Politics, law, current events.

Guest Profile: Opinion leaders, authors, major and minor politicians. Interesting people, interesting topics, Why they would be a good guest.

Guest from Hell: A guest, unable or unwilling, to answer questions directly.

Contact: http://www.djrea@boston.cbs.com; 617-787-7033 and 617-787-7395; http://www.WBZ 1030.com; Dan Rea, Host and Rick Radzik, Executive Producer. Best method: Call with a pitch, e-mail a bio, send a press kit. No response? E-mail or call.

Invited Back? Their performance.

Bio of Dan Rea: Dan came to WBZ from its sister TV station WBZ-TV Channel 4 where he was a general assignment reporter since August 1976. Truly a "Boston-based" reporter, Dan was born, bred and educated in Boston and is a graduate of the Boston University Law School.

Since 1977, Dan worked primarily as a reporter for the station's evening newscasts, with an emphasis on live reports, local and national politics, and breaking news stories. In 1996, he moved to the morning shift in order to spend more time with his family.

Dan has received honors from the Massachusetts Bar Association, the Massachusetts Criminal Defense Lawyers Association and The New England Academy of Television Arts and Sciences. He has also been nominated for nine Emmy Awards. He won an Emmy in 1982 for Breaking News Story ("Sonoma Street Bust") and in 1986 for Outstanding News Reporting ("Cardinal Bernard Law at the Auschwitz Concentration Camp").

The Norm Jones Show on WTCM NewsTalk 580, Traverse City Michigan, aired weekdays, 10–11:20 AM (ET).

Theme: We cover current events or anything of interest. Lately it's been global warming, war on terror, illegal immigrants and NAFTA. Anything that is anti-big government.

Guest Profile: A guest needs to be knowledgeable. A good talker? Sure. About 10 percent of guests are from outside our listener area. It's very hard to define what guest(s) strikes my fancy. Strong conservative values or issues. I also tend to like celebrities (past or present). A strong bio with strong credentials (even if you have to embellish)

Guest from Hell: One who is obviously on my show to sell something. Let *me* sell your product or web site. Keep the message simple and conserve words. If I want a follow-up or more, I'll ask.

Contact: norm@wtcmradio.com; Withheld upon request; http://www.wtcmradio.com; Norm Jones. Best method: Pitch an interview with an e-mail, not a phone call. Save the press kit and/or book. That way you can send it 3 times over a period of a month. It always gets the second "look." No response? PLEASE don't follow up an e-mail with a phone call.

Invited Back? A guest will be asked back as long as your topic is still topical or interesting. It's different things to different hosts.

Guest Comment: "I have been on *The Norm Jones Show* several times. Always enjoyable." — Lee Boyland, author of *The Rings of Allah* (AuthorHouse 2004) *and Behold, an Ashen Horse* (Booklocker 2007), http://www.LeeBoylandBooks.com.

Bio of Norm Jones: Norm is a 30-year radio veteran, having worked in Grand Rapids and Traverse City, Michigan, and St. Petersburg, Florida.

One Hour of Hope with Doug Clifford aired on The Sky 943, North Central Florida.

Theme: Generally progressive politics.

Guest Profile: Mostly authors. Wellspoken guest with a well-informed point of view and credentials.

Among his most prominent authors has been Daniel Ellsberg of Pentagon Papers fame.

Guest from Hell: One who says "Ya Know" or "uh" every few seconds.

Contact: Dougcl7@hotmail.com; 352-337-9729; http://www.THESKY973.COM; Doug Clifford. Best method: E-mail or send a press kit. No phone calls please. No response? E-mail again.

Invited Back? Rarely do repeats.

Bio of Doug Clifford: Doug has been doing radio news/interviews in Gainesville/Ocala, Florida, for the past 16 years and has also done radio in Phoenix, Arizona, and Little Rock, Arkansas.

The Pamela Furr Show on WVNN, Huntsville, AL.

Theme: From politics to sex and the city and everything in between.

Guest Profile: All — any and everybody. Someone who is relevant, lively and informed.

Want to know their interview experiences, credentials, sound of their voice and more.

Guest from Hell: Someone who only gives yes and no answers; 615-512-2603 (cell phone); 256-830-8300 (station main number).

Contact: pamela.furr@cumulus.com; http://www.wvnn.com; Pamela Furr. Best method: E-mailing a pitch/bio, etc. No response? If I have not responded to the e-mail, please don't call. If I haven't responded, that means I'm not interested at that time. It doesn't mean you shouldn't continue to pitch guests. Keep 'em coming. Even the same guest. If it's timely and useful, you'll get booked.

Invited Back? If the interview went well, and if their topic is something relevant. I'll always know I'll invite a guest back if I've realized we've run out of time and there's so much more that I want to know.

Bio of Pamela Furr: Nobody loves radio more than Pamela. Since hitting the airwaves as a DJ at 14 years old, it's been her lifelong obsession to poke, prod, ponder and puruse every topic from politics and philosophy to religion and sex in the city.

This ballsy redhead has quite a diverse (some would say schizophrenic) career history, having done everything from writing chart topping gospel songs to singing backup on albums for the likes of Garth Brooks and Dolly Parton. She was the assignment editor for Channel 4 News, Nashville, Tennessee's NBC affiliate. She's been a disc jockey for nearly every genre of music except gangsta rap and Hungarian bluegrass, and she's been the producer for the number one radio talk show in Nashville.

While on a 2002 vacation in New York City, Pamela had the chance to visit with and watch one of her role models, Sean Hannity, in action. That experience brought her lifelong dream of being a radio talk show host to the surface once again. As soon as she returned to Nashville, she set that dream into motion by convincing her bosses to give her a shot at a weekend show of her own. Her impressive guests included such diverse personalities as country icon Naomi Judd, controversial Reverend Fred Phelps, KISS member Gene Simmons, the late Colonel David Hackworth, and then Tennessee governor–elect Phil Bredesen.

In October 2004, Pamela moved to Springfield, Illinois, where she was given the chance to go from weekly talk show queen to daily talk show diva. With a cosmopolitan figuratively in one hand and a microphone in the other, Pamela brought her southern charm to this midwestern capitol city and took the town by storm. She was the winner of Springfield's favorite conservative for 2005 by the readers of the *Illinois Times* and voted one of Springfield's favorite talk show hosts in 2006.

She cares about her country, her God and her friends. She cares about truth, justice and honesty. She cares about being informed, and wants you to be as well. She may make you laugh, and she may make you cry. But she will make you think. And THAT may be what she cares about the most.

The Party Line with Dave Palmer on WATH (AM), Athens, Ohio, weekdays, 9–10 AM (ET)

Guest Days: Tuesday–Thursday [Mondays and Fridays reserved for open topics call-in and talk ("Free For Alls")]

Theme: All manner of topics. Informational, classy. Talk and Call-In. My show also features a "Friends and Neighbors" series whereby many locals are also guests. We have just finished a series entitled Southeast Ohio's 20 Most Beloved People. We are not controversial, per se. Rather, we are informative, educational, interesting, etc. I guess we do steer away from "freaky" or odd stuff.

Guest Profile: All manner of guests — in studio and via telephone. Full hour only, no partials. Need to know if their knowledge will benefit or be of interest to my audience. Past interview experiences and credentials are important. Prominent guests have included Jessie Jackson, Michael Feldman, Ohio Governors Voinovich, Taft and Strickland, Jack Nicholson, President Ronald Reagan, Rodney King, Vice President Gore, Greg Kinnear, Dr. Joyce Brothers, numerous congressmen and senators, Steve Allen, Sgt. Stacey Koon (LAPD), Jack Jones, Arnold Schwarzenegger, Woody Hayes, Michael Jordan, Dr. Joyce Brothers, Hank Aaron, George Steinbrenner, Liza Minnelli, along with hundreds of authors, health professionals and educators.

Guest from Hell: Someone who wants to run the show and is constantly wanting to sell their book or service.

Contact: palmerd@wxtq.com; 740-593-6651 (office) or 740-541-9284 (cell); http://www.970wath.com; Dave Palmer or Angie Marks (angie@wxtq.com), who handles the calendar. Best method: E-mail or phone. No response? We're all busy. But you know the expression, "Persistence pays off." People are welcome to contact me any way they can or want.

Invited Back? Rarely happens — certainly not for a couple of years

Bio of Dave Palmer: Dave has owned radio stations for 35 years and is president of WATH and WXTQ. He also has had a career in public office, show business, sports, and broadcast leadership (NAB).

Though a native of Worthington, Dave moved from Honolulu in 1973 to purchase the stations along with his father — radio pioneer Fred Palmer, who began in radio in 1928 and was the only person from "management" inducted into the NAB's Radio Hall of Fame. The old principles of serving the public interest are etched deeply into Dave's operating and programming philosophy.

After brief but promising careers as a professional musician and a tech theater designer, Dave fell into broadcasting by accident (some would say *destiny*) where he worked for (KGMB, KIMN, WCOL) or has been consultant to (KCBQ, KFRC, KHJ, KOMA) some of the nation's great stations. He also served in the U.S. Army, owned WRAP in Norfolk (VA), was an Ohio University's E.W. Scripps School of Journalism faculty member and is General Manager of the Copperheads Baseball organization — a collegiate wooden-bat summer all star team supported by MLB.

He and wife Patricia have three children and three grandchildren.

ProAmerica Radio (now **Border Patrol Auxiliary Radio**) with Carl Braun on WS Radio, http://www.wsradio.com

Theme: Conservative talk.

Guest Profile: Authors, experts on immigration and national security. Their qualifications and level of expertise are important.

Guest from Hell: Bleeding heart liberal.

Contact: Carl@carl.braun.btaux.org; 619-575-6577; Carl Braun. Best method: E-mail with pitch. No response? I respond within 24 hours to all e-mails.

Invited Back? Conversational ability and knowledge.

Bio of Carl Braun: Carl is an executive recruiter and formerly the host of the ABC Radio talk show *The Soapbox*. He has 20 years of broadcasting experience and has authored four books including his latest fictional works (under the name C. Frederick Braun): *Border War* (Lulu 2007), *Above All Else* (Lulu 2008), and *Two Seconds* (Lulu 2005), his first fictional work.

One of the Founders of the Minuteman movement in California, Carl has been partly responsible for creating one of the largest Border Watch/Pro Border Security Operations in the U.S. Not the kind of guy to sit back and wait for someone else to do the job, he has logged more than 2,000 hours of Border Watch duty on the U.S. Mexican Border and currently leads the CA MSAR Search and Rescue Team. He has been featured on many of the major news venues nationally and globally and was recently one of the subjects in an art exhibit at the Orange County Museum of Modern Art in a video piece called "Paradise" — now on a world tour.

Carl is a motivational speaker and has received critical acclaim for his presentation "Border Insecurity."

Quinn and Rose, The War Room, America's Morning Show with Jim Quinn and Rose, aired on 920 AM, WHJJ and 14 affiliates (see http://www.warroom.com for list of affiliates), also Pittsburgh, PA and XM Chan. 165. Rated #54 on 2008 Talkers Heavy Hundred.

Theme: Conservative talk radio.
Guest Profile: Political mostly. Want their credentials and bullet points reflecting subject of books, articles, etc.
Guest from Hell: Needs to be coached or gives just a yes/no answer.
Contact: rose@warroom.com; withheld upon request; http://www.warroom.com; Rose or Tracee. Best method: E-mail. No response? E-mail again
Invited Back? How interesting and enthusiastic they are
Bios of Quinn and Rose: Jim Quinn is one of the nation's most successful radio broadcasters. He has been in "the business" since the 1960s, on the radio in markets like New York City, Buffalo. Cleveland, and, most notoriously, Pittsburgh. While his early days were spent spinning records, he found his voice as a conservative commentator in the 1990s.

It was then that Rose joined the show as his producer and sidekick becoming one of America's first female conservatives on the air. Since then their loyal audience has grown into more than just listeners, they are supporters.

Radio Free Volusia with Greg Lake on WELE AM 1380, Daytona Beach, FL, airing Monday–Friday, 6–9 AM (ET); now off the air.
Theme: Interactive political call-in talkshow.
Guest Profile: Politicians, Authors, Political Activists Those who are both knowledgeable of the topic to be discussed and can expound extemporaniously on the topic. Those who are happy to field questions from the callers and the hosts. First, I want to know their level of expertise to speak to the topic. Second, their background that gives them the ability to authoritatively address the issues.
Guest from Hell: Those who are poorly prepared to delve into the specifics of a topic or those that give very brief responses, i.e. one or two word answers.
Contact: greg@wele1380.com; 386-672-4123; http://radiofreevolusia.com; Greg Lake. Best method: E-mail. As a program director and show host I simply don't have time to take those types of calls. I request that they either e-mail me the pitch/bio or mail a press kit.... But I prefer e-mail. No response? I do not have time to respond to every request. If you don't get a response from me, that probably means that it's not a "good fit" for the show or maybe I just wasn't interested in the guest or the topic.
Invited Back? Mostly my gut-feeling but listener feedback is always an integral part of my decision.
Bio of Greg Lake: Originally from the suburbs of Washington, D.C., Greg moved to Florida in the late '70's to attend college in St. Augustine, where he met and married his wife, Kathy.

He started his radio career at WKGR FM 98.7 (Ft. Pierce, FL) as part-time weekends until the station was sold. He followed the rest of the "KGR airstaff" to Ft. Meyers and did overnights at WAKS-FM 103.7 until it was sold. Once again, the entire airstaff came back to the east coast of Florida to WZZR-FM 92.7 in Port St. Lucie where Greg continued his overnight show *The Dead Zone* until the winter of 1994 when he was given the morning drive slot. He stayed until the spring of 1996 when he was fired for sagging ratings. Within 6 months of the launch of the *Howard Stern Show* in the fall of 1995 on rival WBGG, Greg's ratings were cut in half.

Greg moved to Daytona Beach and started his own advertising agency Alternative Advertising and Production. After four years in the ad business, Greg was offered and accepted the production director post at WELE-AM 1380 in Ormond Beach. After a year, he traded in his production director duties for program director stripes. During the controversial 2000 presidential election, Greg launched his new morning call-in talk show.

The Right Perspective with Frank and John aired on shortwave and the Internet.
Theme: Politics.
Guest Profile: What we want to know about potential guests are: what are their politics, experiences in the field that they are talking about, and if they have written any books on the subject. Where they've appeared before, and who interviewed them. We want to know their political beliefs and actions in conjunction to any statements that they may have made. Interesting and provocative.
Guest from Hell: One who doesn't want to carry on a conversation and is oblivious to questions.
Contact: Frank@therightperspective.com; John@therightprespective.com; 718-761-9357; http://www.therightperspective.com; Frank or John. Best method: E-mail. No response? Call or e-mail.
Invited Back? How interesting they are and if they didn't complete their topic or book.
Bios of Frank and John: Armed with a knowledge of current and historical events, Frank and John were early callers to talk radio and Frank became known as "the greatest caller in the history of talk radio," and John was dubbed "talk radio's one-man swat team." In fact, listeners soon began asking "Did Frank of Queens or John of Staten Island call yet?" Of course, some hosts didn't like the fact that listeners would be more interested in a caller than the host, and they like it even less now that the best-known callers to talk radio have become hosts.

At first, Frank and John only knew of each other but had never spoken directly. Eventually, they were invited to appear as guests on a number of shows, including one of the founders of talk radio, Barry Farber. On one of these occasions with John as Barry Farber's in-studio guest, Frank called the show giving John his first opportunity to speak directly with him and tell Frank he had been a fan of his for years. They stayed in close contact and became best of friends.

Frank and John have co-hosted their show for

nearly eight years. The only thing you'll hear on this show is good old fashioned, God fearing, butt-kicking Americanism.

The Roth Show with Dr. Laurie Roth, nationally syndicated by the National/USA Radio Network, http://www.usaradio.com

Theme: Cutting edge issues, headlines, security, issues that reflect right and wrong, not just party lines

Guest Profile: National security, immigration, military, whistle blowers, investigators, others who say it like it is! etc.... Honesty regarding the issue, warmth and professionalism. Want to know the issue they represent, what is their passion and commitment to the problem. Book is optional.

Guest from Hell: Arrogance, manipulative, only interested in a political party, club or association.

Contact: comments@therothshow.com; 877-999-ROTH; http://www.therothshow.com; Laurie Roth. Best method: E-mail. No response? I usually respond within three days.

Invited Back? 99 percent of all my guests are invited back. I'm most comfortable if they can flow, visit, show an understanding regarding the subjects we are discussing.

Guest Comments: "Doing hundreds of radio and television interviews a year is rather tedious to say the least. Not so when I get an invite to do the Dr. Laurie Roth show. Her grasp of the subject matter and her way of delivering the questions makes for one great interview. She makes her guests look good. And for this, I'm always extremely thankful. How nice it would be for her voice to resonate from coast-to-coast. As it is said, we need to have Laurie keep-on-keeping-on. It's not only good for the soul but good for America."—Dr. Harvey Kushner, author and terrorism analyst

"Dr. Laurie Roth has the courage to attack big issues head on—open borders and immigration, Iran building nuclear weapons, the survival of Israel, our huge trade deficit with China, a federal budget deficit that is not reserving for future Social Security or Medicare liabilities. These are questions Laurie's audience knows will be debated truthfully and courageously, letting the facts fall squarely right where they belong. Laurie is an experienced radio host whose loyal audience knows the only thing not welcome on Laurie's show is a lie."—Dr. Jerry Corsi, best-selling author, FBI trainer and educator

Bio of Laurie Roth: Laurie has a Ph.D. in counseling and a black belt in Tae Kwon Do. If she can't reason with you, you had better duck before the roundhouse kick sends you flying. She is the proverbial "pastor's daughter" when it comes to her sense of adventure and her independent thinking. However, underneath her sharp wit, loony antics, and twisted views, you will find a woman with an uncommon gentle nature, a daily walk with God, and a unique talent for finding success against all odds.

She is a singer/songwriter with five CDs to her credit, one track which landed her in Billboard's top 40 ranks and on the cover of *Cash Box Magazine*. She plays the piano, keyboard, and violin and has a voice that can penetrate your very soul.

She was the host and co-producer for the popular PBS show, *CD Highway*, which was broadcast on 155 stations across the country. She has hosted successful talk shows on radio stations from Boston to L.A. with no shortage of callers.

Laurie is also an accomplished author, cartoonist, and artist. She has spent time in Japan and Australia and loves to travel. She is equally at home on horseback or motorcycle and enjoys scuba diving. She loves to watch NASCAR Nextel Cup Racing and has always liked vintage cars. Her favorite food is ... well ... just a hamburger, but with the works.

Laurie is happily married and resides in Washington State.

The Scooter McGee Show on 1310 KFKA, Greeley, Colorado, airing Monday–Friday, 9 PM–midnight (MT).

Theme: Variety—A cross between Tom Snyder and Art Bell. Considering the show is bracketed between Michael Savage and Neil Boortz, it is refreshingly progressive, with an open mic format and an emphasis on conspiracy, collusion and non-transparency of government. We talk about topics other shows in the [progressive talk] format won't even touch, and ask the questions listeners would if they were sitting in my chair.

Guest Profile: The guests are driven by the headlines of the day and of the past as well as what might be from the future. I look for guests that are able to take the bad news of the day and create solutions for tomorrow. Credentials are first and foremost. Everything else is just window dressing, and I can paint pictures within my own medium. Scotter's most prominent guests have included G.O.P. presidential candidate John Cox, Dane Alexander, author of the book, *MAYA*, and Greeley Mayor Ed Clark.

Guest from Hell: It would be a guest that cannot defend a position they claim to be an "authority" in

Contact: Scooter@1310KFKA.COM; 720-275-0708; http://www.scootermcgee.com; Scooter McGee. Best method: E-mail or phone. I can be contacted in any format comfortable to the guest (we do live in the 21st century now). No response? Of course I can be reached by phone if e-mail fails.

Invited Back? Interaction/energy/passion/out-of-the-box solutions.

Bio of Scooter McGee: Scooter attributes the apparent [instant] popularity for his show to more than four years of hard work developing a huge podcast and Internet radio audience before being offered his own show on broadcast radio in late April, 2007.

His *Conspiracy Keepers* and the *New World Order Report* shows, broadcast by U.S. Progressive Liberty

Airwaves Network on their We the People radio station — Live365 and the accompanying podcasts — absolutely topped the talk, political and government genres at Live365 and placed the station into the top 700 of over 35,000 stations on Live365 listened to by early April of 2007.

Before coming to KFKA, Scooter had more than three million listeners a month downloading his daily Podcasts, and much of that audience has followed him to his new show, listening to it via the Internet, as evidenced by his getting call-ins from all over the United States.

The Sean Leslie Show on CKNW aired in Vancouver, Lower Mainland, Sunday 3–5 PM (PT)

Theme: Mostly current affairs, pop culture, whatever grabs me. Regarding current affairs, the more local the better, as local issues tend to get the most calls ... but we certainly talk about international news a fair whack. I try to limit international topics to once a weekend, but if it's a good topic in and of itself, I'd be glad to talk about it.

Guest Profile: We'll talk to anyone, but authors are always welcome. The ability to boil down complex ideas for radio listeners who may be doing something else while listening — willingness to take calls from listeners. Background information on the topic/book/idea, whatever — the more background I have, the better I can prepare for an interview.

Guest from Hell: Short talkers! Nothing worse then setting aside 30 minutes for a guest who speaks in 2 word sentences ... arrogance ... it always comes through on air ... and guests who act like they're doing us a favor by coming on.

Contact: sleslie@cknw.com; 250-385-8622; http://www.cknw.com; Sean Leslie. Best method: E-mailing is the best, then maybe a phone call a little later. I'm also a working reporter, so am on the phone all day. No response? E-mail or call

Invited Back? Response from listeners ... lots of calls, etc.

Bio of Sean Leslie: Sean has been with CKNW for 6 years as reporter/desker, now legislative bureau chief and talk show host. He previously worked at CJCI in Prince George where he was the news director.

He now lives in Victoria, BC, with his wife and two daughters.

Shakedown Street with Brian Wolf on Free World Radio Network.

Theme: Progressive politics, news and commentary, special guests.

Guest Profile: Authors, professors (Juan Cole), presidential candidates, actors, musicians, writers, producers, directors (Bill Mumy). Someone who is passionate, knowledgeable and can talk with confidence. I research them on the Internet first. Voice isn't as important as confidence, knowledge and the ability to talk.

Guest from Hell: Ask question that leaves lots of possible answers; instead get a yes or no, and then dead silence.

Contact: brian@freeworldradionetwork.net; 253-222-7901; http://www.freeworldradionetwork.net; Brian Wolf. Best method: E-mail a bio, send a press kit and/or call with a pitch. No response? E-mail or call.

Invited Back? If they want to come back, they can.

Guest Comment: "Brian ... treats his guests well and keeps the show moving along nicely. It was a pleasure to be on the air with him and I look forward to having the opportunity to do it again in the future." — Frank McEnulty, 2008 presidential candidate, http://www.frankforpresident.org

Bio of Brian Wolf: Born and raised in southwest Pennsylvania during the height of the Steelers era, Brian joined the U.S. Army and volunteered for Infantry and Airborne. He was sent in 1978 to be a speed bump in Germany should the Russians invade.

After the Army he held several jobs while putting himself through college. Then in a brilliant stroke of insight, he decided to dump everything he had just learned and spent the next several years following The Grateful Dead from city to city. This only added to his education as he learned as much or more on tour than he did in school. On July 4 weekend 1988 he met a Deadhead girl at a speedway in Maine where the Dead were playing that weekend, and a year later they were married.

Following their honeymoon, the couple moved from Cape Cod to San Francisco, arriving July 31, 1989, less than 2 months before the 1989 Loma Prieta earthquake.

During this time Brian also met Keith McHenry and joined in with Food Not Bombs, feeding the homeless and trying to avoid getting arrested for doing so.

Ordained during this time, he later earned his Doctor of Divinity. Brian is an atheist, considers himself a secular Buddhist and is the pastor of the NW Branch of the Universal Life Church of the Outcast.

In 1999 Brian and his wife moved north to about 50 miles SE of Seattle where he lives to this day.

Brian is a strong advocate for free speech, the Second Amendment, and reminding the politicians in D.C. that they work for us and not the other way around.

They serve at the pleasure of the people. Remember that: We the people!

Situation Awareness with Hans Meyer on the Free World Radio Network.

Theme: Progressive politics.

Guest Profile: Progressive/liberal authors and bloggers. Someone who shares a similar political outlook OR someone with an opposing viewpoint and who is willing to debate the issues. Interested in their credentials and life experiences.

Guest from Hell: A guest who gives one word

answers to questions. Also, a guest who will not participate with the pre-show preparation (suggestions for questions, etc.).

Contact: Hans@FreeWorldRadioNetwork.net; 850.567.9854 (cellular); http://FreeWorldRadioNetwork.net; Hans Meyer. Best method: E-mail a pitch, and include a bio and/or press kit. No response? I never ignore a potential guest's e-mail. This is a "golden rule" issue for me. However, if the potential guest feels that a "reasonable time" has passed a follow-up e-mail is acceptable.

Invited Back? As a courtesy, during the broadcast all guests are invited back. The real determining factor would be the guest's interest(s) in a future broadcast topic.

Guest Comment: "Hans Meyer, host of *Situation Awareness* at Free World Radio Network, contacted me after reading an opinion piece that I had written for OpEdNews.com. The article was about uniting Liberals, moderate Democrats and Progressives to work together to make sure that Democrats win the White House and both houses of Congress, and therefore have the votes necessary to ensure they can undo the damage done by the Bush administration over the last 7 years. Hans is a great host, and he asked the right questions. I was prepared to go over specific points about why moderate Democrats and Progressives were so at odds in relation to the failures of the new Congress to pursue investigations into a variety of issues from the Bush administration falsifying intelligence before the Iraq war, to bypassing the FISA courts, and Hans guided the discussion perfectly through my prepared points. All in all, it was a very interesting discussion." — Dr. John Moffett, Internet broadcast pioneer and editor of http://www.Factinista.org

Bio of Hans Meyer: A life-long resident of Florida, Hans has been active throughout the years in political, educational, professional and civic organizations. This includes serving as president and executive director of the Florida Young Democrats, officer in Phi Rho Pi, chair for the Florida Jaycees Governmental Affairs Leadership Seminar, a founding officer and president and executive director of the North Florida Association of Networking Professionals, and serving on the board of directors of the Network and Systems Professional Association. He has published articles on 49-Reasons and OpEdNews.com.

Hans' career in computers and computer networks spans over 22 years, from MS-DOS 3.x to Vista, from Novell to VINES to Server 2003. He is a certified (and certifiable) Webmaster, and a professionally-trained bartender.

Sound Off Connecticut with Jim Vicevich on WTIC 1080, aired in southern New England.

Theme: Politics, culture, talk.

Guest Profile: Our guests must be knowledgeable, and experienced spokespeople. Want to know their background. Regular guest: Heritage Foundation Peter Brookes (*Sound Off* guest host), *National Review*'s Jim Geragthy, Powerlineblog.com's John Hinderaker, Democratic strategist Peter Fenn, Vets for Freedom founder Pete Hegseth, Iraqi War veteran Melissa Weaver (Sgt, CTANG, Ret), Center For National Policy Scott Bates, Col. Ralph Peters, psychologist Kathleen Cairns.

Guest from Hell: Folks who do not know their subject matter or recite talking points.

Contact: jim.vicevich@cbsradio.com; 860-677-6700 x369; http://radiovice.blogspot.com; www.radioviceonline.com; Jim Vicevich. Best method: E-mail and press kit. No response? E-mail or call.

Invited Back? Their knowledge and speaking ability.

Soundingboard with John Divinski on 97.9 FM–98 the Beach, Port Elgin, Ontario, weekdays 10–11 AM (ET), and middays 11 AM–2 PM (ET).

Theme: My show is all over the map. For instance, the next few days will be all political shows with candidates in our provincial election coming up. Yet every Friday I do an hour of trivia. In essence, I have a show that discusses the pressing issues of the day along with the occasional light entertainment shows as well.

Guest Profile: All types of guests. I have had psychics on, pet psychics, but cabinet ministers in our government as well, along with local mayors and councillors. Sometimes I don't have any guests at all and just wing it with myself and my callers. Someone who can speak well when expressing themselves and shows some personality. I don't need the sound of their voice but would like their credentials and any news releases about them or their subject.

Guest from Hell: Dull, boring, and sounds like they don't want to be there. If they don't want to be there, I'm more than happy to oblige.

Contact: johndivinski@98thebeach.ca; 519-832-9800; http://www.98thebeach.ca; John Divinski. Best method: E-mailing a bio is good. Sending a press kit is good. Calling with a pitch is bad. No response? E-mail or call.

Invited Back? If it works the first time and that doesn't necessarily mean lots of calls from listeners. Just need someone entertaining.

Bio of John Divinski: John has been in the radio business for more than 40 years, and doing talk radio since 1973. "I don't suffer fools lightly," he says. He is also the news director of the radio station and a newspaper columnist "so some guests might get a double whack ... once on radio and once in a newspaper (*Seaway News* in Cornwall, Ontario)."

Speak Up with the Rev. Zernial M Bogan, Robert Walker Sr., and Imani Bazzell on WEFT 90.1 FM, Champaign, IL.

Theme: Public affairs.

Guest Profile: Community leaders, gov. officials,

laypersons, clergy, doctors, lawyers, etc., with intelligence and knowledge of subject. What we want to know about potential guests if they are sincere about what they believe.

Guest from Hell: A person that does not respect the opinions of others or respect the on air mannerisms.

Contact: ZERNIALB@AOL.COM; 217-417-2035; http://weft.org; Rev Zernial M Bogan. Best method: Call with a pitch, e-mail a bio or send a press kit. No response? E-mail or call. I may have gotten distracted.

Invited Back? Their behavior, subject matter, and respect.

Bio of the Rev. Zernial M. Bogan: The Rev. Bogan is associate minister at Salem Baptist Church Champaign, IL, vice pres. of the Champaign County Black Chamber of Commerce, owner and operator of L and Z Cleaning and Construction, and more...

The Steve Gill Show, syndicated nationwide. Rated among The Talkers 250 for 2008.

Theme: Conservative talk.

Guest Profile: Political pundits, newsmakers, authors, commentators, politicians, actors, country music stars, news of the day interviews etc. We primarily look for a current and interesting topic — something that our listeners will have an interest in ... a guest needs to be engaging and knowledgeable on their topic in order to be deemed as a good interview.

We want to know background info, who has interviewed them prior and on what topic, what credentials do they have to speak on the subject and mostly I trust my sources for guests ... if the person representing them has merit and a track record with me then likely the guest will be acceptable. Noteworthy guests have included Mitt Romney, Bill Clinton, Newt Gingrich, Condi Rice, Charlie Daniels, Montgomery Gentry, John Rich, Fred Thompson, Mike Huckabee, TN Gov. Phil Bredesen.

Guest from Hell: Someone who has no intelligence in regards to their topic and who has no "on air" personality.

Contact: noelle@gillreport.com, steve@gillreport.com; 615-778-8767; http://www.gillreport.com; Noelle Federico, exec. producer. Best method: The best way to get to me is via e-mail with the pitch and then I will ask for more information if I would like it. No response? They can call me to follow-up or send a second e-mail ... mostly if I don't respond it is because we are not interested.

Invited Back? If they were a good interview and if they are an on-going source for something topical.

Bio of Steve Gill: Attracting the civic minded, politically inclined or general interest audience, Steve has a familiar native voice that people from all walks of life can understand. A graduate of the University of Tennessee, he has become a force in talk radio. Steve has been named one of the most influential radio talk show hosts in Tennessee.

In addition to *Talkers Magazine*, *Business Tennessee* named Steve among the 100 Most Powerful People in Tennessee, and the *Nashville Post* business magazine has twice recognized Steve as the most powerful media personality in middle Tennessee.

Steve is the political and news analyst for WKRN-TV Channel 2 in Nashville and has also made frequent appearances as a commentator on CNN, FOX News Channel and MSNBC. He's also a regular guest host for the nationally syndicated *G. Gordon Liddy Show* (see page 298).

The Steve Yuhas Show on AM 500 KOGO, Sunday, 4–7 PM (PT), airing in southern California: San Diego, Orange County, Los Angeles, Ventura, Santa Barbara, the desert communities and beyond as the signal has bounce up the CA coast as far north as San Luis Obispo.

Theme: Political and community issues of the day — current events. Steve hosts what has been dubbed "uniquely conservative talk radio" in a media market that is saturated with conservative talk show hosts. Yet while the program has what you would expect from a conservative talk program, Steve has also made himself overtly independent from being a follower and listeners formed what they called "Steve Yuhas Liberals" because they "can't help but listen."

Guest Profile: The program has had authors from every stripe on the air — so long as a guest has something that interests Steve and will interest his very diverse audience, they are welcome on the air. Not all political books get on the air and many non-political books get air time. It is all about the book and the level of interest in the author, the story and the ability of the guest to keep our audience interested. A guest must be able to keep the attention of our listeners. We've found that sometimes the most popular people do not make the best guests and there are occasions when a guest that might have been mediocre carried the day to make a great program.

I want to know how to pronounce their name, I want to be sure that they stick to the topic they are there to talk about and I want to make sure that there is interest in their ideas.

Further, I want to know that the guest knows and understands not only the host, but also the demographic that we cover and the enormous geography of our coverage area.

Generally speaking I want to know that a person will make good radio: informative, entertaining, accurate and polite — we do not need guests to shock our audience — we need guests that will inform us.

Guest from Hell: A guest from hell is one that misses their call-time, doesn't know the name or demographics of our program or who generally looked for the airtime, got it under the pretense that they were experienced and ended up interrupting, not listening to our callers or generally believed that they were more important than the audience. We serve at the pleasure of the audience and if they are unhappy with a guest we have to recover from it and if we have to recover — which we will — that person will never receive air-time again.

Contact: steve@steveyuhas.com; 619-384-9650; http://www.steveyuhas.com; Shane Scott. Best method: The best approach is a personal one by e-mail. Short, sweet with an addressee in the e-mail. Everyone wants air time to sell their book or be a guest on a program, and that is a good thing, but if someone can't take the time to address the pitch to our host or if they just send out mass e-mails — they get deleted. There is nothing interesting about mass e-mails that take too long to come to the point and contain nothing that makes their product interesting to our audience. If they can't take the effort to read up on the program and look at our huge coverage area and make the pitch specific to it — the e-mail never makes it beyond the inbox. No response? If a person that wants to be a guest on the program e-mails the show and they do not hear back it is because there was something about their e-mail that made it not interesting to our listeners. There is nothing personal in a non-response, but it is like a pocket veto — we do not, frankly cannot, respond to every single e-mail that comes requesting time on the air. There should be no follow up — if they sent it and it did not get returned we got it and if we got it and didn't respond the author can assume we are not currently interested, but we do keep them for use in possible future programs.

Invited Back? Something new. If a guest is made for good radio: that is to say if they pleased our listeners and if listeners gave feedback through e-mail or our online message system and it was positive they will be invited back for their next project or if there is something that they would make a good guest on that dealt with their first appearance. When they won't come back: if they strayed into the world of shock jock radio and assumed that all of our listeners were exactly the same — they are not, but one thing they are is opinionated and if they like a guest they will tell us; more importantly though if they do not like one they will scream it at us.

Bio of Steve Yuhas: A disabled and honorably discharged former Marine and soldier, Steve is Jewish and happens to be gay — a unique combination in someone on radio.

He has a Bachelor's degree in government and a Master of Science in homeland security studies from the first civilian university to offer such a degree. He is certified by various agencies including the Department of Homeland Security on threat assessment and was trained in Israel in counter-terrorism. His Master's thesis was on the definition of terrorism and the United Nations.

After the military, he was fired from his job as columnist in a large gay newspaper, being called "too conservative" by the publisher. After that he guest hosted the *Roger Hedgecock Show*, the anchor of the station, and from there he took off as his own host after an op-ed he wrote appeared questioning the wisdom of gay pride parades.

A target of some radical gay groups, Steve is often called a breath of fresh air and in a *San Francisco Chronicle* opinion piece it was said that he at least "makes us [gays] think about our positions on issues."

StraitTalks with James Strait on WNJC1360 and http://www.wnjc1360.com, Wednesday, 7–8 P.M., aired in Philadelphia, southern New Jersey, northern Delaware and WIFI 1460, Burlington, NJ, www.wifi 1460am.com and live Internet stream.

Theme: Conversations with Americans who have led meaningful lives.

Guest Profile: A knowledge or connection to the topic of interest, sincerity, honesty, reliability, availability. They span the spectrum of politcos from presidential candidates to county commissioners, authors, grassroots activists, private investigators, Hollywood producers, directors, actors, actresses ... but my favorite guest is an average American who has done something meaningful and extraordinary. Experience and credentials are important under many circumstances; however, I frequently know little about the guest other than what they do or their connection to a story. I like the challenge of having to think on my feet.

Guest from Hell: Just about any politician.

Contact: jim@straittalks.com; 610-847-8658/ 267-987-3256 cell; http://www.straittalks.com; James Strait. Best method: Calling with pitch, e-mailing a bio and/or sending a press kit. No response? E-mail or call.

Invited Back? It is subjective for the largest part. If I like them, if we had fun, or if they are a pivotal element in an ongoing story then a return visit may be in the future.

Guest Comment: "James is an astute observer of life ... his off the cuff analysis and commentary can bring pause to any dialogue."— Mary Ann Gould, Founder Coalition for Voting Integrity, host of *Voice of the Voters* radio

Bio of James Strait: James is just a thoughtful babyboomer.

Talk It Over with Terry Spence on C-FAX, Victoria BC weekdays at 11:00 AM. Terry also hosts the *C-FAX Travel Show*, Sunday at 3:00 PM.

Theme: General talk show. I cover pretty much everything.

Guest Profile: Someone who is topical and interesting, what they have to say and where they can be contacted.

Guest from Hell: Someone who answers every question with "that's covered in my book, available for only $29.95."

Contact: tspence@cfax1070.com; 250-920-4602; Terry Spence. Best method: E-mail.

Bio of Terry Spence: Terry is the general manager of C-FAX 1070; http://www.cfax1070.com; Terry

Spence. Best method: E-mail. No response? It's a pretty good signal that the topic wasn't of interest

Invited Back? Either there are new developments in the topics covered or there is a new book, etc.

The Things That Matter Most with Rick Davis and Lael Arrington on KSEV, KVCE, Houston, Dallas, TX.

Theme: Conversation (not debate) about what we believe and why we believe it; not politics but the values and beliefs that drive politics.

Guest Profile: Scientists, professors, movie producers, businessmen, dramatic spiritual journeys, web entrepreneurs who are able to well articulate what they believe and why they believe it; thoughtful, humorous, nuanced, willing to be engaged in a conversation with a person from another perspective without being aggressive or interrupting; good story teller of a dramatic life story/journey. What interesting take they have on what they believe or why they believe it. If they are a fit with the other guests archived on the "Listen to shows" page of our website. Ideal guests included skeptic Michael Shermer and *Time* magazine humor columnist Joel Stein.

Guest from Hell: Too vague or abstract, someone who is cliched, simplistic or not reflective, hasn't really thought their beliefs through; disrespectful. Mocking *#@%$!! Interrupting *$@*%and!!!

Contact: info@thethingsthatmattermost.org; Withheld upon request; http://www.thethingsthatmattermost.org; producer Lindsay Loughlin. Best method: E-mail pitch. No response? Do not e-mail again.

Invited Back? Terrific expertise, engaging personality, new book or project.

Bio of Rick Davis: Rick is the founder and CEO of CCG Venture Partners, a venture capital firm that gives the lion's share of its earnings to such charities as Mercy Ships (floating hospital-ships to poor nations) and Desire Street Ministries (inner city).

The journey to success in his professional life has been easier than his journey to confidence in his spiritual life. Starting at age 18, Rick began to experience what he today calls "existential despair"— depression and anxiety caused by an inability to determine any ultimate meaning or purpose to life. His 12-year struggle ended suddenly and completely when he came to faith in Jesus. Since that time, Rick has had a passion to explore and assess the rational aspects and evidences (scientific and other) of various faith systems.

Bio of Lael Arrington: Lael has a Master's in the history of ideas from the University of Texas (Dallas) and speaks as both an educator and a pastor's wife. She is author of *Worldproofing Your Kids* (Crossway Books 1997), *Pilgrim's Progress Today* (NavPress Publishing Group 2002) and *Godsight: Renewing the Eyes of Our Hearts* (Crossway Books 2005).

Her writing has been featured in *Focus on the Family* and *World* magazines, and she has appeared on *Family Life Today with Dennis Rainey*, *At Home Live*, *Moody's Morning Show* and Janet Parshall's *America*.

Lael and her husband, Jack, have one grown son.

Full bios at http://www.thethingsthatmattermost.org

The Todd Feinburg Show, syndicated by Worldview Broadcasting Corporation and aired on Sunday, 1–4 PM (ET). Rated among The Talkers 250 for 2008.

Theme: Current events/issues.

Guest Profile: Political analysts, middle east experts, military analysts. Good knowledge, good entertainment value. Want their background information and an interview sample.

Guest from Hell: People who communicate like college professors.

Contact: kim@toddtalk.com; Withheld upon request; http://www.toddtalk.com; Kim Henderson. Best method: Very short e-mail. No response? Send follow up e-mail.

Invited Back? If they're fun and informative.

Bio of Todd Feinburg: Todd spent ten years working at radio stations around New England before joining WRKO in 2003, and has been named three times to *Talkers Magazine*'s 100 Most Important Talk Hosts in America.

A graduate of Tufts University with a degree in political science, he worked at his college radio station as a newscaster, disc jockey, and general manager. Afterward, he was an international chemical trader with Sobin Chemical in Boston, focusing on trade with China. From 1985 through 1996, he owned and managed fine dining Italian restaurants in Marblehead and Sudbury, MA.

Todd has made a focus of gaining a better understanding of the Middle East, and in 2002 joined seven other radio talk hosts on a diplomatic tour of Saudi Arabia organized by the embassy in Washington. In the fall of 2005, he spent six weeks as a substitute middle school social studies teacher in an urban Boston area school. The first-hand experience was enlightening. "Everything you think is wrong with education is true," he says, "but its much worse than that."

Todd lives with his wife, Rosalie, on the north shore of Boston.

Full bio at http://toddtalk.com/bio.asp

The Tom Becka Show on KFAB, Omaha, Neb. Rated among The Talkers 250 for 2008.

Theme: The hot issues of the day with honesty, integrity, and a sense of humor.

Guest Profile: Guests who are relevant to the topics in the news delivered in an interesting manner. Whatever credentials they feel are relevant we want to know.

Guest from Hell: A person with no personality. A dull person more focused on facts and figures than relaying the story in an entertaining way.

Contact: Becka@kfab.com; 402-561-2001; http://www.kfab.com; http://www.TomBecka.com; Tom Becka. Best method: E-mail or send a press kit. No response? Don't call. I don't have a lot of guests. But as long as it's not obsessive they can e-mail me as much as they'd like.

Invited Back? The need for the topic and the chemistry between the guest and host.

Bio of Tom Becka: Tom has a strong background in both show business and advertising sales. His first book, *There's No Business Without the Show* (Orpheum Brothers Press 2008), shows salespeople how to use more show business techniques in a sales presentation.

Trevor Carey Show on Newstalk 710 KNUS, Denver, Colorado aired Saturdays 5–8 PM (MT). Trevor also co-hosts AM Colorado with George Gray on Newstalk 1310 KFKA, Ft. Collins, Greeley, Colorado. Phone: 877-353-1310. Website: http://1310KFKA.com, airing Monday through Friday 5–9 AM (MT). All other information is the same.

Theme: Current events and topics. Project the voice ... someone who lets me know talking points.

Guest Profile: Compelling. Basic info and background ... talking points from them.

Guest from Hell: Boring tone or delivery ... topic might be compelling, but they can kill it with their delivery.

Contact: trevorcareywork@aol.com; Withheld upon request; http://www.trevorcareyshow.com (up soon); http://trevorcarey.com/trevorcarey-home.php; Luciana Lamb at lucinanalamb22@msn.com. Best method: E-mail ... subject line should say "interview" (Topic). No response? E-mail back.

Invited Back? If they were interesting.

Bio of Trevor Carey: Trevor gained recognition as national director of promotion for Sony Music's Relativity Recordings in NYC. He was national director of promotions and drove the promotion team that launched Bone-Thugs and Harmony's single "Tha Crossroads" to #1 on Billboard. Their full length CDs went on to sell more than 10 million. By creating and implementing strategies for Sony Music to get rap music to cross over to pop music, Trevor learned how to increase market share and airplay.

In 1999, he started his own venture entitled DOM: detections of music, which acquired the contract to program for OnRadio.com programming, the online music stations for Quincy Jones–owned Vibe and Spin magazine's online radio stations.

Trevor walked away from every client after coming to a "crossroads" in his life. The problem was that he could no longer promote violent/sexual hip-hop to other people's kids, while trying to keep his own kids away from it. The *Trevor Carey Show* was the birth-child of that decision.

Trey Ware Morning Show on KTSA, San Antonio, TX.

Theme: News-talk-information.

Guest Profile: News makers of the day. We want someone who can, and will say what we can't, and say it with *passion*.

Guest from Hell: Think tank.

Contact: Dmurphy@bmpradio.com; 210-528-5145; http://www.treyware.com; Dawn Murphy. Best method: E-mail. No response? E-mail again with a better idea.

Invited Back? Were they interesting?

Bio of Trey Ware: Trey has more than 30 years' experience in radio. His father is well-known radio personality Ricci Ware, and Trey was always at his side while his father was on the air. At age 13, Trey became the "youngest DJ in America."

Trey and wife Nancy have two children, Justin and Rebekah.

Trey is a life-long resident of San Antonio.

The Uncooperative Radio Show with Brian Bonner on http://uncooperativeradio.com

Theme: Independent conservative talk radio.

Guest Profile: Authors, politicians. Usually the guests are conservative minded or non political, or on history, Islam, or the military. However, if the book was interesting and written by a liberal I would have them on the show and I would invite any politician on my show of any party affiliation as long as they can keep the discussion civil. I just have not gone out of my way to bring a liberal guest on and none have asked. I have to like their book and good information, or believe in their politics. Guests should have experience, credentials, or I've read the book and want to help promote it.

Guest from Hell: I have never had one, so I cannot imagine.

Contact: brianbonner90@gmail.com; 406-498-9541; http://uncooperative radio.com; http://coalitionagainstillegalimmigration; http://www.circle-b.com; and more; Brian Bonner. Best method: Call or e-mail bio or press kit. No response? E-mail or call.

Invited Back? My interest in having a guest back is based on timing. I would have all my guests back, but have not done so yet.

Bio of Brian Bonner: Among the variety of jobs Brian has held were senior electronic technician, heavy construction laborer, bartender, ambulance driver, dishwasher and cab driver. In 1995, when he was injured in an auto accident and permanently disabled, his wife received her Bachelors in nursing and the couple moved from Long Island to Tallahassee, Florida. After living off the land for three years, they packed and hit the road. Susan got a nursing job in Denver Colorado as a travel nurse. The Bonners stayed there for three months where people showed Brian what real four-wheeling was all about. That began their journeys throughout the south, southwest and northwest until settling in Montana.

Brian and his wife, Susan, share their home with their dog, Shorsha.

Vannah and Collins (now ***WHMP Morning News with Chris Collins***) on WHMP 1240-1400-1600, aired in Franklin, Hampshire and Hampden counties in western Massachusetts.

Theme: News and political analysis.

Guest Profile: Authors, political figures, college professors. Sense of humor, a passion for what they do, willingness to answer any question no matter how bizarre. Credentials mostly. The rest will work itself out.

A prominent guest was Burton Hersh, author of *Bobby and J. Edgar: The Historic Face-Off Between the Kennedys and J. Edgar Hoover That Transformed America* (Carroll and Graf 2007), an interview described by the host as "Absolutely riveting."

Guest from Hell: Someone who is terrified of being interviewed or someone who believes they are the only ones who should be heard in an interview.

Contact: collins@whmp.com; 413-586-7400; http://www.whmp.com; Chris Collins. Best method: E-mails and press kits work. If they have a book, sending an advance copy won't hurt. It's no guarantee that they'll get on, because the book will have to be a topic of interest to my listeners. No response? Follow up e-mails are fine. Calls are not preferred, but I won't hold it against anyone if they call.

Invited back? See Guest Profile.

Bio of Chris Collins: Chris is a native of Greenfield, MA, who graduated in 1992 from Emerson College with a B.S. in mass communication. He began his broadcast career in 1986 at a small Greenfield station, and worked in print journalism before becoming news director of WHAI in 1997. In 2001, he was promoted to the position of director of news and programming for WHMP Radio. He also writes a weekly political column for the *Greenfield Recorder*, and is a contributing local sports columnist/reporter for both the *Valley Advocate* and the *Recorder*.

Visibility 9-11 with Michael Wolsey, podcast, and various low power AM and FM stations around the country.

Theme: Dedicated to exposing the fraud of the official story of September 11, 2001. *Visibility 9-11* explores the many facets of the 9-11 attacks which contradict the government's official story, the massive cover-up which is currently underway, the failure of the mainstream media in America to ask real questions, and the aftermath of 9-11 including the un–Constitutional wars and the taking of liberty here at home. This broadcast examines the big picture of what is taking place in America today and how September 11th fits into the scheme of things. Forget "conspiracy theory!" The government's own story about what happened is itself a "conspiracy theory!" Learn for yourself why people are talking about what is becoming known as the "alternative conspiracy theory."

Guest Profile: 9-11 activists, researchers and students, authors, videographers, former politicians, anyone related to 9-11 research that is both knowledgeable and credible.

Knowledge and credibility of a guest who is presented as an expert is important for issues relating to evidence. Honesty and sincerity is important for those relating to activism.

I want to know past interviews and programs they have appeared on. I want to know about any books they have written and/or articles published. Credentials are important as well as careful and dedicated research.

Guest from Hell: Someone who answers questions in one or two sentence answers. Someone who is nervous and not presenting professionally.

Contact: michael@visibility911.com; 970-576-6431; http://www.visibility911.com; Michael Wolsey. Best method: Phone or e-mail is fine. I would prefer a call from someone wanting to appear on my program. No response? E-mail or call.

Invited Back? Guests are invited back if they continue their work that got them on my program in the first place.

Guest Comments: "This program is well produced and offers information, analysis and viewpoints that are badly needed in our age of corporate controlled media. The most important feature of this great program is that it emphasizes the need for truth about the events of 9/11, a need that affects all people."— Kevin Ryan, http://www.ultruth.com

"Hey Michael, I saw your bulletin about your interview with us and we listened to it. We thought it was awesome. We got to cover a lot of topics, it was great, and you played a lot of our songs too and they sounded great. Thank you so much, you did a fantastic job." — Three Shoes Posse, http://www.threeshoesposse.com

Bio of Michael Wolsey: Michael was first exposed to anomalies of the September 11th attacks in 2002, but rejected claims that 9-11 was an "inside job" for nearly a year. During this time, he learned about the USA PATRIOT Act and more about 9-11 and gradually began to see why people were questioning the "official story" of what happened on that dreadful day. He studied 9-11 for a year, and in August of 2004 helped form the Colorado 9-11 Visibility Project, http://www.colorado911visibility.org. "My sincere thanks to all those who have helped," he says.

Shortly after getting involved in 9-11 research, Michael met George Flynn, host of the *Words of Freedom* radio show. "It turned out that George is very '9-11 Hip' and he often asked me to be a guest on his show to talk about 9-11 and our efforts in Colorado," says Michael. "I had never been on the radio before and was nervous at first but I had to do it to get 9-11 truth out there. I had barely settled into this role when, one day, George asked me to sit in for him as a guest host. My first reaction would probably be akin to that of a "deer in the headlights" look, but I accepted the challenge of making the show happen. In the weeks and months that followed, George had several work related events, and again, asked me to guest host his show. It was great experience and really helped to grow our group and get public exposure for 9-11 truth. This got my feet wet in the broadcasting arena, so when I heard of podcasting, I was very interested in learning more about it."

Y Talk Radio with Bea Fields and Roger DeWitt on Blog Talk Radio, www.blogtalkradio.com/y-talk

Theme: Talk, interviews, news and stories for Generation Y and those people who lead them.

Guest Profile: Generation Y (young men and women born after 1977) who are making a significant contribution to their communities or getting solid business results. We also interview traditionalists, Baby Boomers and Gen Xers who are leading Gen Y or who are performing solid research around the topic of this young leader. We look for someone who is a Generation Y young adult who is creating change or making a big impact in their business, community or political system, someone who has very interesting stories about Generation Y (this could be a parent or a community volunteer) or someone who has conducted extensive, solid research on Generation Y to share. We also look for people who have some type of celebrity status around Generation Y that will draw in listeners. We usually get our guests from our close network OR we have heard them on the radio, and they are articulate and have an upbeat, cool, great voice and carry themselves off well in an interview (poised and polished). We don't necessarily look for MBAs or Ph.D.s, but we do look for people who have been in their current business or volunteer effort for at least one year. We also love interviewing book authors, because they do add credibility to the show.

Guest from Hell: Someone who talks on and on about themselves, says nothing or does not truly answer the question. We have also had someone who did not show up (is interesting leading a talk show on the fly when a guest does not show).

Contact: bea@millennialleaders.com; 910-692-6118; http://millennialleaders.com; Bea Fields. Best method: Send a press kit and an audio of a recent radio interview (last 6 months), or ask someone we know or they know to refer them. A second or third person testimonial usually grabs our attention. No response? We are really good about responding in 24 hours to e-mail unless our spam filter grabs the incoming mail. If they have not heard from us within 24 hours, they can contact Bea Fields.

Invited Back? If we have fun and if we are inspired, they get invited back. And, of course, if we attract a large listening audience for that show, the guest gets invited back.

Guest Comment: "I had a blast on *Y Talk Radio*. Bea Fields and Roger DeWitt make for a lively and interesting interview. And ... the cool thing is that within two weeks of the interview, I had two people who heard the call contact me for a consultation and are now clients!"—Adam Gilbert, founder of http://www.mybodytutor.com

Bio of Bea Fields: Bea is an executive coach, president of Bea Fields Companies, Inc and the founder of Five Star Leader Coaching and Training. She specializes in leadership and team coaching for high growth companies, non-profit organizations and medium-sized businesses. She is co-author of *Millennial Leaders: Success Stories from Today's Most Brilliant Generation Y Leaders* (Morgan James Publishing 2007) (http://MillennialLeaders.com) and *Edge: A Leadership Story* (Morgan Games Publishing 2008) (http://EdgeBook.com).

Bea has a Bachelor of Science degree from the University of Alabama and holds several important certifications, including a certificate in leadership coaching from Georgetown University.

Bio of Roger DeWitt: As a business and life coach, Roger comes to the coaching table with many years of business experience both as an entrepreneur and in organizations and more than 20 years of experience as a successful and working actor. Approximately 50 percent of his clients are business and community leaders and professionals from a variety of backgrounds and 50 percent are working performers and creative professionals.

His expertise in presentation skills and voice combined with his business savvy make Roger an exceptional marketing, prospecting and sales coach.

He continues to live his second passion as an actor on television, film and the Broadway stage. Around the country on tour and on Broadway, Roger has been in such shows as *The Phantom of the Opera, Jekyll and Hyde, Ragtime, The Woman in White* and on TV in shows like "The Snorks," "The Jetsons," "Law and Order" and "Rescue Me."

Roger has a BA in psychology from Loyola Marymount University and is a certified graduate of Coach University. He holds the designation of Associate Certified Coach (ACC) with the International Coach Federation. For more information on Roger Dewitt, visit. http://coachingnyc.com/

You Are the Guest with Bill Grady. Podcast.

Theme: News and politics.

Guest Profile: We look for the average person who has something to say and a story to tell. Usually those people fall into one of 3 categories; smart, funny, or crazy. The show features people from the United States and around the world who give their opinions on everything from the Iraq War, political corruption and conspiracies, to who they think the next president of the United States will be. Our guests submit an e-mail to our show with an explanation of why they would make a good guest. Most days you can also find out more about them from their own websites or blogs as most of our guests have them too.

Guest from Hell: The guest from hell can be the person who gives you really short answers, but those people are rare. Mostly they are the ramblers, who will give you a 6 minute monologue that sometimes will jump from topic to topic and will end up nowhere near the original question.

Contact: producers@youaretheguest.com; billgrady@youaretheguest.com; withheld upon request; http://www.youaretheguest.com; Bill Grady. Best method: They just need to send us an e-mail at the address listed at our website, and tell why they would make a good guest. No response? Neither call nor e-mail. It is a "don't call us, we'll call you" policy.

Invited Back? When we have invited guests back it is because they will have more things to say instead of a rehash of the past show, and they contributed to the show by demonstrating a good presentation of themselves and good content.

Bio of Bill Grady: Bill started as a radio announcer in 1979 at age 18, but later decided to drop his on-air aspirations and join a radio station's advertising sales staff in 1982. From that point on Bill's radio career was spent behind the scenes; first as a manager of a 100,000 watt FM station and later as a regional manager for a broadcasting group.

Bill has over 25 years of broadcasting, marketing and advertising creation, sales, and management experience, and his articles on sales and advertising have been published internationally. He is also a past president of the Iowa Broadcasters Association.

In 2005, his podcast received international praise from France's *Le Monde,* which wrote that Bill's news and political opinion talk show based in a small Iowa town of 25,000 people was "very original" and gave it a "10 out of 10" rating.

The show was also featured in January 2008 by USA WEEKEND, which had invited three celebrities to name their favorite podcasts. Well-known radio host Alan Colmes singled out the show, saying "I've always thought that anybody can be made to sound interesting, and, thus, be a good guest. This podcast proves my point—everybody has a story worth telling."

Your Call with Sandip Roy and Rose Aguilar on KALW 91.7, San Francisco, CA.

Theme: Politics and culture, transforming consumers into citizens.

Guest Profile: Authors, activists, people with firsthand experience of national issues, journalists, filmmakers and politicians. Personal experience of an issue of national importance or a savvy interpreter of political or cultural questions. Credentials, how their voice sounds, whether they can listen and tell stories are all important.

Guest from Hell: A blowhard with no stories. An Ideologue who disrespects people who live the policy debates.

Contact: Feedback@YourCallRadio.org; 415-841-4121; http://www.yourcallradio.org; Ben Temchine, Senior Producer. Best method: E-mail. If I don't know you, will you be in town? Is your topic connected to the news? Send an e-mail laying that out, but be succinct. No response? If I don't respond, call once. If I still don't respond, more calls won't make a difference. I will either pitch it or I won't, and they will either like it or they won't.

Invited Back? Do they tell interesting stories? Do they understand what we're trying to accomplish with the show and do they help us achieve it? Can they string a coherent sentence together?

Bios of Rose Aquilar, Sandip Roy and Ben Temchine: Rose is a San Francisco–based journalist who is writing a book about her road trip through the "red states."

Sandip is a faculty member in the School of Electrical Engineering and Computer Science at Washington State University.

Ben is a graduate of the U.S. Berkeley Journalism School and a returned Peace Corps volunteer.

Real Estate

The Future of Real Estate with Darryl Baskin at 12:30 P.M. on News/Talk 740 KRMG, aired in Tulsa, OK and northeast Oklahoma.

Theme: Real estate.

Guest Profile: Real estate related issues/ investment, insurance, repair, etc. Important qualities are clear concise message with sound bite points, credentials, their motive for requesting the interview, voice quality.

Guest from Hell: Rambler without a point or useful message. Poor voice quality or speech pattern.

Contact: Darryl@darrylbaskin.com; 918-258-2600; http://darrylbaskin.com/radio_shows; Anne Carlisle at anne@experttalkproductions.com. Best method: E-mail an interview content sample—a list of questions they are qualified to answer. No response? I will reply with an acknowledgement of receipt and respond further if I am interested in an interview. Please do not resubmit after a receipt confirmation for six months.

Invited Back? Value of content presented to my audience.

Guest Comments: "Many people have a preconceived notion about mobile homes, and almost no idea that you can really make great money investing in this off the beaten path investment vehicle. I enjoyed the interview with Darryl; he had a great style and did a super job getting my topic out in a way that is not only informative, it was fun as well."—Doug Ottersberg, doug@mobilehomemillionaire.com

"I contacted Darryl Baskin per his request regarding being interviewed on his show. At the time I contacted him, he had found out earlier that day he did not have a guest for his show the next morning. He asked me if I could be a guest the next morning at 6 am MST. Of course, I was more than happy to help him in this short time. We talked and I was able to give him an angle to discuss regarding real estate that had not ever been discussed on his show before. We did the interview the next morning. Darryl continued to address new items that had not been addressed before from a consumer's perspective. It was a great interview and I would interview with Darryl again."—Dr. Taffy Wagner, author of *Debt Dilemma* (2005), *Homebuyer's Helper—How to Have and Hold on to Your House* (2006), and *Discharged into Debt* (for military troops) (2005), all published by JTW Publishing, http://www.paidoff.net

Bio of Darryl Baskin: Darryl's innovative marketing approach has made his Team Tulsa's best known real estate group. Specializing in high-tech service, he provides his home sellers an unmatched marketing program and meets the needs of his clients faster than expected. He has sold and closed over 2500 properties.

J.T. Foxx Show on 560 WIND aired in Illinois, Wisconsin, Michigan, and Indiana.

Theme: Real estate, wealth, success, politics, current events.

Guest Profile: Authors, real estate mavens, politicians with passion, sense of humor, and are informative. I just want a good idea and a good angle for the show. Some of J.T.'s well-known guests have been Senator John McCain, George Ross, Robert Kiyosaki, Bob Proctor, the Rev. Jesse Jackson, Scott Scheel, and Donald Trump.

Guest from Hell: Boring and rambling.

Contact: Jt@jtfoxxshow.com; Withheld upon request; http://www.jtfoxxshow.com; J.T. Foxx. Best method: E-mail. No response? E-mail and persistence.

Invited Back? If they made great radio.

Bio of J. T. Foxx: At 27 years old, J.T. is known as the Real Estate Phenom and founder and president of Foxxonomics: The New Generation of Wealth and Success. Although a popular weekend radio personality, his day job and true passion is being a local Illinois and surrounding states real estate investor. In fact, J.T. spends 80 percent of his time managing his investments and purchasing great deals well below market value.

J.T. has invested in hundreds of properties, closing over $40 million in real estate, all with no money, no credit and no experience in the last 4 years—in a hot market. Before that he was a broker, then broke and came to Chicago with nothing more than the clothes on his back and his rusted Ford pickup with 250,000 miles. At one point J.T. was so broke that he slept on an office couch, ate Ramen noodles, and drank Kool-Aid everyday—not to mention showing up at the gym.

Unlike most so-called "millionaire maker gurus" who spend a lot of their time selling books and tapes and no longer invest in deals themselves anymore, J.T. has decided to reach out to those who really want to succeed and take their lives to the next level and show them the real way.

The Real Estate Guys with Corey Smith and Charlie Earp on WVOC AM 560, Columbia, S.C., www.wroc.com

Theme: Real estate.

Guest Profile: Someone who can get to the point in small sound bits. Sound of their voice is very important. Experience in knowing how to get their story across in very understandable, quick answers with intelligence. Their presence in the interview—not a nervous type personality.

Guest from Hell: Someone who tells you how to build a clock when all you wanted is the time or someone that answers with yes and no. We also have a problem with a guest that is more interested in selling their products than providing good usable information to our listeners.

Contact: charles.therealestateguys.org; 803-798-0555; www.therealestateguys.org; Jerry Fowler. Best method: E-mail with a bio and press kit. No response? I respond to all inquires.

Invited Back? The ease of the interview. Knowledge of their subject. It is terrible when we know more than the so-called expert.

Bios of Charles Earp and Corey Smith: Charles is a native of Lexington and deeply involved in the local community. He has a background in appraisal and home inspection, so he is well versed in all aspects of buying/selling homes. His professional career has taken him around the world; living abroad has instilled an understanding of many cultures. Whether buying or selling a home Charles will provide you with the highest level of integrity and service in a real estate transaction.

Corey is a hardworking motivated agent. He draws on his wide base of experience in many aspects of real estate to keep you and your property on the cutting edge of the market. When it is time to invest, Corey's years of experience managing investment home projects and portfolios will ensure that you get maximum return on your investments. His approach and techniques are proven and will add dollars to your bottom line.

Real Estate, Real Advice with Juli Doty, syndicated by Business Talk Radio Network in 32 major U.S. markets and 160 countries by Armed Forces Radio Network and others.

Theme: Real advice on everything real estate.

Guest Profile: I use guests on approximately 1 out of 4 shows and they must focus on some specialty area of real estate. I am seeking guests who will answer direct questions and give my listeners the details (in short form) that they want in order to improve their real estate, or their life through real estate. I enjoy guests of many styles. Knowledge of material is paramount.

Guest from Hell: I am not interested in arrogance or high pressure.

Contact: juli@julidoty.com; 509-662-7600; http://www.kpq.com; Juli Doty. Best method: E-mail or press kit to 100 Malaga Highway, Wenatchee, WA 98801. No response? If I do not respond, please re-e-mail. I do answer e-mails but hate the phone interrupting me.

Invited Back? Guests are invited back when they have a sense of play and valuable information.

Bio of Juli Doty: In addition to being a radio host, Juli is a real estate investor, broker, designer, buyer, seller; seminar trainer; public speaker who loves, really loves, to tell her listeners the absolute truth and details about how to improve life with real estate. She has bought, fixed and flipped many homes for herself and has helped thousands of clients with transactions.

Real Talk "With the Experts" with Dave Burke on 630 KHOW, Denver's Talk Station, airing Saturdays, 4–7 PM (MT), from Fort Collins to Pueblo, Colorado.

Theme: Business, real estate, mortgages and money.

Guest Profile: Experts in the above fields. Ability to contribute effectively to subject matter. Past interview experiences, credentials and sound of voice are important.

Guest from Hell: Gives one-word response — freezes up.

Contact: dave@realityfinancial.net; 877-291-8373; http:www.gorealtalk.com; Dave Burke. Best method: E-mail. No response? Do not phone or e-mail.

Invited Back? Feedback from listeners and staff.

Bio of Dave Burke: Dave is known in the real estate business for his ability to bring the best people together to educate listeners and clients in all of the elements of real estate, from analyzing the market and economy to understanding your credit and finances.

He has been around real estate basically his whole life. His father, one of the largest masonry contractors in the world, founded the earthquake institute in Southern California after the 1972 earth quake, where he developed structural systems with young Dave at his side.

In the late 1980s, Dave was hired as a consultant to help a large furniture operation increase its struggling sales numbers. Dave made an impact in the first 30 days and increased sales from approximately 40K per month to 500K per month. Dave then moved to Denver to work for Oakwood homes, where he exceeded 400 million a year in loans, selling hundreds of homes per month.

In 2004, Dave had his first taste of radio when he was invited to be on the air with *Straight Talk with the Judge*, a real estate, mortgage and legal talk show. He was then asked to do his own show on radio 760. It was at this time that Dave started Reality Financial. In June of 2007, he launched his current show.

The Townstone Financial Show with David Hochberg on AM 560, WIND, aired Saturdays, 1–3 PM in Chicagoland and surrounding areas.

Theme: Educating the listeners about the ins and outs of the ever changing Chicagoland real estate market.

Guest Profile: Politicians and realtors/developers. Show is more of an informational call-in show and we do not have guests unless it is a politician talking about legislation that will affect lending or real estate rules in the great state of Illinois. Want to know their position on the topic we are going to be talking about.

Guest from Hell: Somebody that takes three minutes to explain how to cook a three minute egg. No personality. Cannot connect to the audience.

Contact: Davidh@townstone.com; 312-896-2111; http://www.townstone.com; David Hochberg. Best method: E-mail. No response? E-mail.

Invited Back? If they were interested, they connected with audience and my ears were not bleeding by the time they leave the studio

Bio of David Hochberg: President of Townstone Financial, David started the firm because he wanted to build a mortgage brokerage company where the customer comes first. He does this by managing your mortgage as an asset that is part of your larger financial portfolio. He constantly monitors your mortgage so he can recommend the best products for his borrowers fiscal and economic needs for today — and into the future.

David has been in the mortgage business for more than seven years. For 12 years prior to that, he marketed scrap iron and metal to steel mills throughout the Midwest.

David earned a business degree with an emphasis in marketing at Northern Illinois University in 1988 and lives in the northern suburbs of Chicago with his wife, two daughters and golden retriever.

Your Home — Your Money Mortgage and Real Estate Radio with Bill Quigley and Art Blanchet on WTDY, Madison, Wisconsin, Saturdays at 9 AM (CT)

Theme: Unwinding real estate hype and giving clear advice and counsel

Guest Profile: Real estate industry professionals as well as scam victims (occasionally). We look for energy, a tale to tell, knowledge, experts, integrity, message, business sense. For locals — willingness to share or invite database of clients to both their interview and the ensuing podcasts. Fame or fortune secondary or negligible (i.e., authorship or radio/TV appearances)

Guest from Hell: Dull. Longwinded, monosyllabic answers. Hidden agenda.

Contact: ranchexit@gmail.com; 608-217-3252; http://www.yourhome-yourmoney.com; Art Blanchet. Best method: E-mail. Basic "hello, this is what I do and I want to network with you" type of approach. If a kit is available, I'll request one. No response? After a reasonable time, e-mail.

Invited Back? Personality and business-sharing cooperation. Reciprocal opportunities and personal tie-ins. Networking relationships.

Bios of Art Blanchet and Bill Quigley: Art's real estate career spans two decades; Bill's is longer. He served as a mortgage broker, real estate developer's sales manager, and worked for a large top 10 lender.

Regional

Aboriginal Connections with Moneca Sinclaire and/or Rhonda Cameron on UMFM 101.5, aired from the University of Manitoba; now off the air.

Theme: A talk show with a feature presentation and community announcements. The feature presentation can be anything that has an Aboriginal (First Nations, Metis and Inuit) view point or perspective from an Aboriginal artists, musicians, student talking about their experience at University of Manitoba, to poets citing a poem, to guest lectures in a colloquia series. The guest speakers are mostly Aboriginal and non–Aboriginal allies. The community announcements are events happening around Manitoba and other provinces, the majority of the community announcements are events in Winnipeg.

Guest Profile: Aboriginal authors, non–Aboriginal ally authors who write about Aboriginal concerns, musicians, professors, Reverends, local community people. Someone who is willing to talk about Aboriginal issues from their own experience and perspective. Want to talk about the issues without cloaking them in jargon, use language that is understandable to the non-academic. Credentials and if they have conducted a telephone interview or radio interview. Understand more than just their own topic.

Guest from Hell: Constantly asking, "Can you explain what you mean by that, I am not sure what you're asking me?" And they are speaking from a cell phone on their way to another meeting?

Contact: cjum@cjum.com; 204-474-7027; http://www.umfm.com; Jared McKetiak, Station Manager. Best method: Calling with a pitch, e-mailing a bio, sending a press kit are all fine. I have had people send a press release, bio's, send me a sample of their book and/or music. No response? Generally, I get back to guests as soon as they contact me and if I am overbooked when they are in town then I will let them know that I am not able to accommodate their time frame. And if for some reason I don't get in touch it is because I haven't received the e-mail (most cases it is an e-mail cyberspace losing thing happening)

Invited Back? Able to tell their story using humor and to talk as if we're sitting at the kitchen table and having tea.

Guest Comment: "Moneca was friendly, on topic and easy to work with. I've been interviewed by some of the best on radio, TV and in print. Moneca made me feel comfortable and also kept me on topic and knew when to push for more information."—Fred Shore, Professor at University of Manitoba who specializes in Métis history and political issues of the Inuit, First Nations and Métis people

Bio of Moneca Sinclaire: Moneca is a volunteer host at UMFM Aboriginal connections. She is employed full time, a part-time graduate student, and a full time parent. She has lived in Manitoba most of her life, but moved to Toronto for three years to study at Ontario Institute in Studies in Education (OISE).

Caribbean Crossroads with Marlon A. Hill, Esq. on 1080 WTPS AM, Miami, FL, on hiatus. Marlon does a commentary on Saturdays at 4 PM (ET) on 880thebiz.com. His show will most likely return as a podcast.

Theme: A crossroads of politics, arts/culture and community affairs.

Guest Profile: Community personalities. Dynamic personalities who are intimate with their issue, subject matter, or what they advocate for. Like to know their life experience, their story.

Guest from Hell: A person who lacks communicative skills

Contact: info@marlonhill.com; 305-244-4456; http://www.marlonhill.com. Best method: Call with a pitch, e-mail a bio, send a press kit. No response? Potential guests should always follow up. The more information and passion, the better.

Invited Back? The visceral response from the audience post-show and whether the host felt that the information or theme was conveyed to the audience.

Bio of Marlon A. Hill: Born in Kingston, Jamaica, and a past student of St. George's College (http://www.stgcfl.org) in Kingston, Marlon is a founding partner and corporate attorney with the law firm of Delancyhill, P.A. (http://www.delancyhill.com) in South Florida. He migrated to Florida in 1985.

Marlon has been recognized by numerous regional and local publications as one of the "outstanding members of the emerging generation of South Florida business and professional leaders."

A graduate of Florida State University, he is one of the Inaugural Fellows in the Dade Community Foundation's Miami Fellows Initiative (http://www.miamifellows.org). Professionally, he is a member, advisor/mentor, or an official of numerous businesses, and community-based and cultural organizations.

Marlon is married to Carla Hill, a programs manager with the National Foundation for the Advancement in the Arts (NFAA) (http://www.nfaa.org) and resides in South Miami-Dade County.

Eight Forty-Eight with Richard Steele/Alison Cuddy on WBEZ, Chicago, a weekday morning magazine, aired 9–10 A.M. (CT).

Theme: Focuses on topics and personalities related to Chicago.

Guest Profile: Anyone who originates from Chicago region or focuses on a subject related to the area. We look for people who are knowledgeable about the subject matter at hand, who can speak clearly, concisely and conversationally, and convey information in a way that is compelling to our listeners. We want to know why they are uniquely qualified to discuss a particular topic, and whether they can do so in a compelling manner.

We prefer guests who are available to join us in studio.

Guest from Hell: Someone who is late, particularly for a live appearance, or not reachable by phone at the time of a scheduled interview. A guest who gives long, unfocused answers to interview questions or terse, uninformative responses.

Contact: 848@chicagopublicradio.org; 312-948-4657; http://www.chicagopublicradio.org/848; Aurora Aguilar. Best method: An e-mail pitch is the best way to ensure a response. Please include all time sensitive information toward the top of the e-mail. No response? Neither call nor e-mail. If the person doesn't receive a response, which is unlikely, it's because we were not interested.

Invited Back? We invite compelling guests to return when they have something new and substantive to tell our listeners. We've also maintained relationships with out of town guests who are accommodating and flexible with their schedules and are willing to travel to be interviewed in remote studios.

Bio of Richard Steele: Richard Steele is host Monday–Thursday of *Eight Forty-Eight* and Alison Cuddy is the Friday host.

Richard joins the CPR's staff in 1987, where he has hosted such former programs as *The Richard Steele Show*, *A Richard Steele Friday*, *Page Two* and *Performance Space*.

Prior to that, he hosted many successful Chicago radio programs, including *The Morning Connection* on WVAZ 102.7 FM and *Late Night*, a talk and music forum on WGCI 1390 AM. He has hosted popular shows on WBMX 102.7 and WVON 1450 AM, and became "The Real Steele" on WGRT (950 AM) AM, where he progressed to program director shortly after the station's transition to WJPC 950 AM.

Richard attended Harold Washington College in Chicago.

Originally from Brooklyn, New York, Richard lives in Chicago. He and wife, Jera, have two children and three grandchildren.

Bio of Alison Cuddy: Alison is also senior producer of *Chicago Matters*, the year-long series examining various topics of broad interest to the region. After joining the staff of CPR in 2001, she became associate producer for the daily, nationally-syndicated program *Odyssey*.

Alison previously worked in the immigration department of ThoughtWorks, Inc. in Chicago, and was an adjunct professor at DePaul University as well as a teaching fellow at the University of Pittsburgh.

She holds an M.A. in English from the University of Pittsburgh and a B.F.A. in cinema studies from Concordia University in Montreal.

Originally from Winnipeg, Manitoba, Alison lives in Chicago.

Former host Steve Edwards is the acting program director of Chicago Public Radio.

Eye on Toledo with Larry Bertok or Maggie Thurber on NewsTalk 1370 WSPD, Toledo, OH.

Theme: Focus on local news/events/politics.

Guest Profile: All kinds of guests having to do with local issues/events. Interesting — knows how to have a conversation — provides more than just a one/two-word answer. Knowledge of the subject matter. If a political person, their history — votes, statements, positions, etc.

Guest from Hell: Someone who answers in one/two-word sentences.

Contact: Maggie@wspd.com; 419-276-1346; http://www.wspd.com; Maggie Thurber. Best method: E-mail with a press kit or summary of the issue, their position on it, etc. No response? I have a reputation for responding to all e-mails within a 24-48 hour timeframe (depending on weekends)

Invited Back? Are they entertaining radio and do they have something new to talk about or add to a current topic of discussion.

Bio of Maggie Thurber: Along with being a radio talk show host, Maggie is a former public official and avid sailor. "These are the things I do, along with blogging, while I decide what I want to be when I grow up," she says.

The FOG with Gary Gross on 1620 AM, Sandy Springs, GA, http://www.radiosandysprings.com/fog.php

Theme: Create awareness of the non-profits in our area (Atlanta, GA region).

Guest Profile: Executives from non-profits, foundations, and charity organizations. Someone who will be in the know about the organization's programs and impact on the community.

Guest from Hell: We're radio, so I need someone who talks! We had a guest who no matter how I phrased open ended questions still managed to find a way to answer with one or two words.

Contact: gary@garygross.com; 404-329-1000; http://www.garygross.com/fog; Gary Gross. Best method: E-mail or phone. I always ask for a brief Bio in advance so I can get a feel for what they are about and what the organization is about. I personally review every potential guest's website to see if they are a credible guest. Call with a pitch, send a press kit. Any form of communication works. No response? That hasn't occurred but yes they should take the initiative.

Invited Back? The interest of the topic and how they are during the interview. Fun and gregarious people work well on my show.

Guest Comments: "I am so grateful to you for having me on your show ... I wanted to tell you that a friend of mine in D.C. tuned in and a few others here in town. They all enjoyed your interview style as did I. I had a lot of fun! Thanks again my friend, I hope to see you soon."—Alison O'Neil Andrew, president and CEO, Beauty Becomes You Foundation, http://www.beautybecomesyou.org

"I appreciate the opportunity and love talking about the Center. Thanks again for thinking of us for such a special broadcast."—Dean Melcher, director of Annual Giving, Shepherd Center Foundation, http://www.shepherd.org

Bio of Gary Gross: An Atlanta resident and entrepreneur, Gary has been part of the city's fundraising and charity communities for over 20 years. As Event Chair for the 2001 Cystic Fibrosis "Single Greatest Night," Gary coordinated with dozens of vendors and contributors to entertain nearly 2,200 attendees and raise funds in excess of $100,000. He also was the narrator for the event's webcast.

Among the dozens of local and national organizations he has served as both chairperson and steering committee member are Atlanta for America's Children black tie event (raising over $150,000 for children of the 9/11 victims), and the American Cancer Society, in which he co-chaired the group's largest event—3,200 people—"Party with a Purpose" in 1999, featuring singer Melissa Etheridge. His fundraising and promotion of charity events have garnered more than $3 million in raised contributions since 1974.

As an entrepreneur, Gary has been published in Who's Who of American Inventors for his patent on a wheelchair accessory.

The Graduates with Stephanie Gerson on KALX, aired in Berkeley, CA, and larger Bay Area, on iTunes University, and GarageBand, http://www.garageband.com/user/sgerson/podcast/main

Theme: Berkeley graduate student research.

Guest Profile: Fascinating graduate students across campus, from a Master of Fine arts building a web-enabled paintball gun to a Ph.D. in energy and resources researching the effect of environmental, health, and social information on consumer behavior. Anything can be fascinating (at least, to me) so I look for passion, engagement, the ability to communicate. Obviously I want to know about their work, but more broadly about their interest in their work; e.g., you can tell a grad student is interested beyond what's required if they have a personal blog on which they discuss academic work.

Guest from Hell: A guest who has nothing to say (a grad student having nothing to say would be quite an anomaly) or rambles way too much (much more work for me in post-production).

Contact: misstephanie.qerson@gmail.com; 415-871-5683; Academic: ecnr.berkeley.edu/persPage/dispPP.php?I=1200; Facebook: http://www.facebook.com/pages/The-Graduates-KALX/11206523071?ref=ts; showerinthedark.blogspot.com; Stephanie Gerson. Best method: E-mail or phone. I'd love guest recommendations. No response? E-mail or call.

Invited Back? Unfortunately, it's a one time shot at this point. I'm trying to get as many grad students from as many different departments as usual, but I'd like to move from Terry Gross–style interview to Michael Krasny–style panels (e.g., a panel on artificial intelligence with a neurobiologist, computer scientist, and philosopher), in which case, it would be possible to re-invite guests—if they were passionate, clear, and concise.

Guest Comment: "Stephanie ROCKSSSS!!! and so does her show. It's amazing—I've learned so much by doing this. It's so hard to talk about your research to a general audience, and I feel like I rarely get a chance to practice that. Everyone should do this!"—Hania Kover

Listener Comment: "This station is sooo fab. I can't get enuff ... the shame I have to live stream and can only listen at my flat ... oh just imagine if I could listen to this in the street or in my motor ... I was listening to that programme about neuron activity.... I'm gonna experiment with that stuff in a most funky way ... I am gonna ... listen to KALX thro the night (7 hour time difference from where I am). Then I will be able to tune into KALX with my ears and play it in my head whilst out and about ... clever clever!"—Charles Lovegrove

Bio of Stephanie Gerson: Her name is Stephanie Gerson in real life, and Sequoia Hax in Second Life. She received a B.A. in science, technology, and society from Stanford University with a self-designed concentration in experience design. Afterwards, she worked professionally in new media and interactive art.

Stephanie is an M.S. candidate in environmental science, policy, and management at UC Berkeley, writing her thesis on the use of new and participatory media for environmental governance. Having graduated in May 2008, her goal is to continue producing new media events and experiences for purposes of social change.

Inside New Orleans with Midday Host Eric Asher, aired on AM 690 WIST, New Orleans, LA.

Theme: All things New Orleans: Recovery, politics, culture, sports.

Guest Profile: Anyone who fits the show's theme. Past interview experiences, credentials and sound of their voice are important as well as qualities such as smart/honest/strong opinion/entertaining.

Guest from Hell: Boring/won't take a position on topic/horrible voice.

Contact: easher@wistradio.com; 504-885-4690; http://www.wistradio.com. Best method: E-mail. Press kit is best. No response? If I don't respond I have no interest.

Invited Back? Smart/honest/strong opinion/entertaining.

Bio of Eric Asher: Neither a Republican nor Democrat, Eric is a New Orleanian first and foremost. Never afraid to ask the tough questions and an advocate for reform in Louisiana, Eric keeps track of its politicians, holding them accountable for their actions.

The Jim Brown Show on WRNO, 99.5 FM, New Orleans, La., airing Sunday, 11 AM–1 PM (CT). Rated among Talkers' 250 Top Radio Shows in 2008.

Theme: Current events, related to the South and Louisiana.

Guest Profile: Opinion makers who are lively, energetic, and use current and relevant topics. Their ideas are important — preferably something they have written to give their views.

Guest from Hell: Completely out of the mainstream. I love guests like this, off the wall.

Contact: jim@jimbrownla.com; 225-925-0997; http://www.jimbrownla.com; Jim Brown. Best method: E-mail. No response? Follow up e-mail.

Invited Back? Listeners' reactions.

Bio of Jim Brown: Jim is one of the longest serving public officials in Louisiana history and has authored many of the laws on the books today: created the strongest public records and open meetings laws in the country, wrote landmark legislation that offered more public protection for financial privacy, and many of the state's consumer protection laws; his weekly column on current affairs runs in a number of Louisiana newspapers and he hosted a cable television show for more than 14 years.

Jim is author of *Justice Denied* (AuthorHouse 2004).

He received his undergraduate degree from the University of North Carolina, attended Cambridge University in England, and received a Juris Doctorate from Tulane University in New Orleans, where he served as president of the Law School student body. He was a member of the United States Track Team in 1962–63 and maintains an avid interest in physical fitness.

Jim and his wife Gladys have three daughters and one son.

The Kaare Johnson Show on AM690 WIST, New Orleans.

Theme: Local issues.

Guest Profile: From Mayor Nagin to HUD Secretary Alphonso Jackson. Someone that is interesting ... can't be boring no matter how big the guest is. Credentials and ideally past interviews ... gotta be riveting...

Guest from Hell: Someone who is boring and won't shut up.

Contact: kaare@wistradio.com; 504-885-4690; http://www.wistradio.com; Kaare Johnson. Best method: E-mail a bio, call with a pitch, send a press kit. No response? Maybe the person should read the e-mail ... some don't require or deserve a response...

Invited Back? If they were interesting or not...

Bio of Kaare Johnson: Kaare was born in New Orleans and graduated from LSU in Baton Rouge, LA. He has been in radio since 1992, and was a sports radio host for 10+ years.

Says Kaare — "No human being can say they covered hurricane Katrina more extensively than me ... someone may, may have covered as much but no one can say they covered more ... if I never do another minute of radio again, my Katrina coverage was a lifetime worth of work."

Lunch Pail Logic with John Sylvester and Joe Wineke, aired on seven affiliates in Wisconsin, including WTDY. Producer Dan Gunderson co-hosts *The Big Wild*, which joined with *Pheasants Forever* (PF) in 2008 and features a weekly seven-minute segment, "In the Wild with Pheasants Forever" offering hunting tips, seasonal activities and conservation issues.

Theme: Working families and labor. Focuses on the issues of Wisconsin's working families.

Guest Profile: Labor, politicians, workers with an out-going personality and command of the subject. Almost every guest has been contacted via phone prior to the interview.

Credentials and personality are paramount. If we don't want to listen, the public won't want to either.

Guest from Hell: Monotone with one word answers.

Contact: dangunderson@tds.net; 608-833-2040; http://www.lunchpaillogic.com; Dan Gunderson, executive producer. Best method: E-mail, phone, snail mail. No response? See above.

Invited Back? Entertainment value. Ongoing issues that require follow-up; http://www.thebigwild.com

Bio of Dan ("Gundy") Gunderson: Dan is the founder and managing member of Big Wild Communications (BWC). He has 30 years of professional communications experience working for Fortune 100 companies, including BP Amoco, Coastal Corporation, ExxonMobil and The Pillsbury Company. Dan specializes in assisting clients with developing and implementing successful issue media relations and communications strategies.

He has been instrumental in developing a unique clientele allowing BWC to reach many seemingly disparate groups with public affairs and media support. For example, in 2001, he created the Wisconsin Hunting and Fishing Alliance, the organization responsible for coordinating the passage of the Constitutional Amendment protecting hunting, fishing and trapping rights. In 2005, the WOA Foundation, a sister organization, was created to develop and manage the Wisconsin Outdoor Education Expo. The WOA Foundation received the 2007 State Conservation Organization of the Year Award from the Wisconsin Conservation Congress.

Dan is a graduate of the University of Minnesota

and the Harvard-MIT Crisis Communications Program.

Mac's World with J. Michael "Mac" McKoy on KWQW, Des Moines, Iowa, 1–4 PM, Monday–Friday (CT); now off the air.
Theme: Local talk show ... sex, religion, lifestyle and politics.
Guest Profile: Interesting local people relatable to Iowa. The sound of their voice, experience on air, and knowledge about topics are all important.
Guest from Hell: A bleeding heart liberal.
Contact: mac@mcKoy.net; 515-229-6292; http://www.983wowfm.com; J. Michael McKoy. Best method: E-mail or phone. No response? E-mail or phone. I apologize if we keep missing each other, please try again. Thanks...
Invited Back? If they entertained, informed my listeners.
Bio of J. Michael McKoy: Mac has been a Des Moines talk show host for 32 years.
He is a local business man involved in real estate and hospitality.
Mac has been married 29 years, is father of four and a grandfather.

Madison in the Morning with Dick Alpert on 1310 WIBA, Madison, Wisconsin.
Theme: News/talk.
Guest Profile: Varies on the day. We include a variety of guests, including local government/school board officials, fun feature stories from the state, organizers of local events, local doctors and physicians, local financial advisors, the coaches for the Badgers and the Packers, a sausage runner at Miller Park ... and the list goes on. But we do sprinkle in a variety of national guests as well ... including authors. Need to know their purpose, why they want to be on. Past interviews really don't attract me. I mean ... they could be on *Oprah* ... with a topic that just wouldn't work here. As for the topic ... it really varies. But while on the air ... someone who can explain their "purpose" or "statement" in 5 minutes or less.
Guest from Hell: There you go ... you answered it ... someone who only gives one or two sentence answers. Someone who can't get out their point in 5 minutes or less. Or the guest that promises to be on ... and then backs out! That's the worst guest of them all.
Contact: dickalpert@clearchannel.com or chandralynn@clearchannel.com; 608-271-6397 (newsroom) 608-321-1310 (studio); http://www.wiba.com; Chandra Lynn (producer). Best method: E-mail. There's just no time to hear everyone's pitch over the phone. No response? Usually means we're not interested.
Invited Back? If the interview grabbed our attention ... if we were even fascinated. But usually we don't repeat guests.
Bio of Dick Alpert: Born and raised in Sheboygan, Wisconsin, Dick got his start in radio at the first high school station in the state, Sheboygan North's WSHS-FM.
"Thank goodness I took French," Dick says, "because the French teacher doubled as the radio sponsor and that's how I got in to the station."
Dick graduated from UW-Madison with a Bachelor of Arts in communications. While in Madison, he was on the air at the old country version of WMAD and later when it morphed into WWQM. He started his full time professional radio career at KFIZ in Fond du Lac. After a stint in La Crosse at WIZM Radio, Dick moved to Milwaukee and landed some part-time positions before accepting a full-time gig at WEMP in 1982. Stints at WISN, WLTQ, WZTR and WEZW followed. He also had a sales career before heading to WTMJ/WKTI in Milwaukee in May 2004.
He and his wife, Debbie, have one boy and two girls and two grandchildren, a dog, and two granddogs.

Remember When with Susan Woods on CFAX 1070 AM Radio, Victoria, British Columbia, airing Sunday, 2–3 PM (PT).
Theme: Oral history, British Columbia and Canadian history.
Guest Profile: Historians, authors, archaeologists, adventurers, senior armed forces personnel, politicians, teachers, genealogists, "regular folks" with good stories, etc.
Susan interviews guests about the people, stories and events that have brought us to where we are today. I look for good storyteller, credible, sense of humor. I like to know a potential guest's area of interest/expertise, and location.
Guest from Hell: Humorless, reads from paperwork.
Contact: suewoods@shaw.ca; 250-386-1070; http://www.cfax1070.com; Susan Woods. Best method: E-mailing a bio/ pitch and/or press release. No response? I always respond to e-mails within 48hrs. But phone calls are welcome anytime as well.
Invited Back? If there is an upcoming event related to the guest/subject (i.e., book launch/second book, etc.) or more stories/info then we had time to cover in one-hour segment.
Guest Comments: "It was a good experience. For someone like I who has never been before the public, Sue made me feel very comfortable. She doesn't use a script, nor does she have notes, you might say she just wings it. But she has a terrific grasp of how to steer an interview and by some bewitching process she manages to get through the show without being flustered. In all I have been on her show three times now and each experience has proven itself superior to the prior."— Daryl Ashby, independent historian and author of *John Muir: West Coast Pioneer* (Ronsdale Press 2005)

"I am currently writing a novel for teen-agers set in Victoria in World War II. Someone told me about Susan Woods and suggested that she might be able to help me. Although I called Susan out of the blue, as soon as I told her my dilemma, she invited me to be a guest on her program *Remember When*. I felt very shy about being on the radio, but she was very relaxed and welcoming as a host. The time flew by. Nine people phoned in who were willing to visit with me afterwards, and this was a great help to my work. The warmth and support I felt from the people who called in was entirely consistent with Susan's own warmth and generosity. Her program is immensely popular in the Victoria area. I can only suppose this is due not only to Susan's having seen and filled a need for facilitating community, but also to her own particular skills at bringing people together and giving them a safe place to share."—Nan Gregory, a professional story teller and award-winning author of three picture books for children. Her novel, *I'll Sing You One-O* (Clarion Books 2006), is for ages 9–12.

Bio of Susan Woods: Susan is a professional writer with 25 years' experience as a broadcast journalist and magazine publisher. She recently received the Hallmark Society's 2006 Heritage Preservation Award for her radio show, and was a finalist for the 2004 Victoria Women of Distinction Award.

Santa Fe Radio Café with Mary-Charlotte Domandi on KSFR 101.1 FM, heard in Santa Fe, NM, from 8:06 to 9:00 AM Monday through Friday, streaming live on the web at http://www.ksfr.org and podcasting at http://santaferadiocafe.org

Theme: General interest, with focus on Santa Fe, NM.

Guest Profile: Authors welcome. Specialties are the arts, politics, music, environment, science — a bit of everything. Special consideration to New Mexico authors and themes, and authors who are speaking in Santa Fe. No self-help or relationship books. Fiction only if there's a southwestern connection. Intelligence, fresh ideas, importance of topic. Credentials. Pre-interview preferred, but not necessary. If they're an author, I need the book.

Guest from Hell: Monosyllabic, axe-to-grind, arrogance

Contact: radiocafe@ksfr.org; http://santaferadiocafe.org; withheld upon request; Mary-Charlotte, host and producer. Best method: E-mail a request. Put my name on it. I tend to pass over bulk e-mails. No paper. No response? E-mail again.

Invited Back? If they have something new to add to the first interview, and if it went well.

Guest Comments: "Before any more time passed I wanted to tell you that I was deeply touched by the effort you made to read my book and make its key ideas come to life on air. Few authors can resist the magic of such rare, sophisticated sympathy for their work. I count myself lucky to be the beneficiary of your professionalism."—John Brady Kiesling, author of *Diplomacy Lessons: Realism for an Unloved Superpower* (Potomac Books 2007)

"I love these questions, they're fantastic. Thank you for thinking so carefully and deeply about the book."—Eve Ensler, author of *The Vagina Monologues* (Virago Press 2001)

Bio of Mary-Charlotte Domandi: Mary-Charlotte is a graduate of Yale University and received her Masters Degree at St. John's College. She was the general manager of Mobius, an artist-run performance and exhibition space in Boston, and worked in video and audio production in Santa Fe. A salsa dancer and DJ, she entered her radio career as a Latin music program host. She has been hosting her morning interview show, which broadcasts from a popular local cafe, since 2003.

Welcome to My World with Walks with Thunder Andy Rodriguez on Tuesdays at 10 AM (PT), Bellevue, Washington on Contact Talk Radio.

Theme: Non-traditional shaman, views of this paranormal life.

Guest Profile: Local psychics, authors, readers, energy healers. I look for someone who has something to say and I don't have to drag it out of them. I have to have a good feeling about them.

Guest from Hell: They have something interesting to say but just can't get it out, without most of the show being about getting what they should have said in the first five minutes.

Contact: walkswiththunder@msn.com; 253-350-5755; http://www.walkswiththunder.com; Andy Rodriguez. Best method: E-mail and then set up a time to call on phone. No response? My weekends are busy — give me five days then call me.

Invited Back? What kind of response did we get for them?

Client Comments:—"I recently attended a Walks with Thunder's Energy Body class. That evening I had occasion of utilizing his techniques to rid my daughter of a headache. His methods are simple but profound and work even in my hands.

"This is a class all should take if not for themselves then for those who cross their paths. It is indeed time well spent. Thank you Walks with Thunder for sharing your wisdom."—Linda, Issaquah, WA

"Right before our 'Introduction to the Stone Nation' workshop started at Spirit Journey gift shop in Issaquah, my wife felt compelled to purchase a rose quartz heart for me. During the workshop, she understood why she was so directed. Andy taught us about the healing wisdom of the stone nation. That night, my wife blessed the rose quartz heart as Andy taught us, and gave it to me to wear in my pocket. I've been undergoing some releasing and healing of heart-related issues. While wearing this blessed rose quartz heart in my pocket, I have handled several situations differently, with compassion and understanding instead of anger."—Larry, Vashon Island, WA

Bio of Walks with Thunder, Andy Rodriguez: Walks with Thunder is Shaman born. His grandfather was a Shaman for the Caddo tribe, as was his father before him. Andy has been able to see Grandfather Spirits since the age of two, and could bi-locate (literally in two places at once) at 14. "I didn't know those things were special. I thought everyone could do it. The classes I teach are based on this. I have been on the Red Road a long time — before I even knew there was a Red Road."

He lives a spiritually pure life, abstaining from alcohol and tobacco (except for an occasional ceremony), doesn't drink coffee and uses no recreational pharmaceuticals. "I didn't learn the way of the Shaman from another Shaman. The Spirits teach me gently when I sleep."

Walks with Thunder teaches classes throughout the Puget Sound region. "My beginner's classes help many take control of the 'gifts' we possess, opening the suppressed power of our lives that sets some apart from the norm. When you take control of your own hidden powers, you don't have to be victims any longer. Everyone can do what I do. Just like the Spirits who teach me, I can't keep a good thing to myself. Come learn with me."

Relationships

Ask Dr. Jackie with Dr. Jackie Black on iTunes and http://www.AskDrJackie.com. She also hosts *The Dr. Jackie Black Show.*

Theme: Relationship-oriented topics.

Guest Profile: Authors and experts: dating; marriage; divorce; parenting; step-families; sex and intimacy; guests are from around the world and freely share their insights on real and complex issues of dating smarter, where to meet other singles, money, sex, living together, reducing conflict, commitment and committed relationships, rebuilding after an affair, divorcing, deepening intimacy and trust, making a great relationship better and lots more! I want to read their books or material that will tell me about their point of view or the compelling message they are delivering.

Guest from Hell: I am very curious; good at putting people at ease; and can talk to anyone about anything. The guest from hell comes with an agenda to deliver sound bites; and isn't interested in engaging in a conversation.

Contact: DrJackie@DrJackieBlack.com; 760-346-9795; http://www.DrJackieBlack.com; Dr. Jackie Black. Best method: E-mail a One Sheet with a brief bio about the author and a brief synopsis about the book; followed by sending a review copy of the book. No response? Won't happen. E-mailing again is fine; calling is fine

Invited Back? If they are interesting, engaging; have something meaningful to say to listeners.

Bio of Dr. Jackie Black: Jackie is an internationally recognized relationship expert, educator and coach who attracts clients from all over the world. She inspires and encourages people to risk again; to move through the challenges and pitfalls of dating, loving and building long-lasting, committed relationships in today's fast-paced world.

Her mission is to support and mentor you, whether you are single and never-married, divorcing or divorced, widowed or in a committed relationship that is challenging and just doesn't met your needs yet.

In addition to her private relationship coaching services for individuals, couples and families, Dr. Jackie offers on-going coaching groups and short-term coaching programs focusing on specific areas of relationship life. She is also launching the Ideal Match Coaching Club for singles who are committed to dramatically increase their ability to find that special person; and singles and couples who are committed to build long term, strong and stable loving relationships.

She is a popular newspaper, magazine and Internet syndicated columnist, radio personality and a veteran lecturer and educator. In addition to her Individual and Couples Relationship Coaching business, Dr. Jackie is on the faculty of Coach Training Alliance (http://www.CoachTrainingAlliance.com), one of the top 10 coach training organizations in the world.

Dr. Jackie's first book is *Meeting Your Match: Cracking the Code to Successful Relationships* (AuthorHouse 2007).

Bride's Night Out with Pamela Yager on http://www.bigmediausa.com

Theme: Pre-wedding /bachelorette party planning.

Guest Profile: Experts and vendors in the wedding industry, restaurants, nightclubs, and limousine service companies. A potential guest should be a professional in their field, well spoken and knowledgeable about their industry and about servicing the pre-wedding event clientele.

Guests from Hell: A "guest from hell" is someone who is late to their interview, rude to the host, or unprepared to discuss their industry.

Contact: pamela@bridesnightout.com; 323-939-2293; http://wwwbridesnightout.com; Pamela Yager. Best method: Phone. Guests should provide an updated bio with work background, credentials and past media (internet, radio and tv) experience. If someone is interested in being a guest, they should either send an e-mail with media kit files attached or send a media kit via USPS. Also, it is helpful for guests to provide a few "talking points"; topics they are well versed in discussing. A phone screening is the next step, to find out about their voice talents (confident, and clear). No response? A follow-up e-mail or phone call is fine.

Invited Back? Guests are invited back if they are not only knowledgeable about their industry and supportive of Bride's Night Out, Inc. services, but are also fun and witty interviewees.

Bio of Pamela Yager: Founder, president, and CEO of Bride's Night Out, Inc., Pamela is considered to be the nation's foremost bachelorette party planning expert, creating celebrations for celebrities and hundreds of women across the country.

Her events have been seen on VH1's "Ball Before the Chain," "The Montel Williams Show" and ABC Family's "Movie XTRA," as the recurring party planning expert and co-host. She has also been featured in numerous publications including *Los Angeles Weddings Magazine, Modern Bride* and *People Magazine.*

Bride's Night Out, Inc. provides custom party planning services for pre-wedding and bachelorette parties. Pamela believes the key to a truly special event lies in creating unique and entertaining elements that reflect the style and personality of the bride. Pamela admits, "I'm living my dream of providing women with exciting new ways in which to celebrate their last moments of being single."

Pamela has over 15 years of event planning experience. Her specialty in pre-wedding party planning stems from her educational background in sex and marital therapy (Sarah Lawrence College) and over 20 years as a veteran of the entertainment industry — a professional stand-up comedian and reality television producer.

A Fresh Start with Sallie Felton on 106.9 FM HD Channel 3, Seattle, WA and Contact Talk Radio.

Theme: It's all about taking fresh starts: life transitions, individuals dealing with professional issues, personal relationships, self-development, organization and clutter.

Guest Profile: Authors, seminar facilitators, professional experts, representing such specialties as ADHD, organization/clutter, imagery, relationships, adoption and transition specialists, small business marketers, founders of companies, psychics, psychologists, neuros, testing experts, spiritual leaders, personal and professional coaches. Their ability to have something to GIVE to my listeners ... I want a guest that will provide advice, tips, information that listeners might take action on. They must have a topic that has to do with empowerment. I have a very strong intuition, so I can sense from their bios, past interviews and credentials if they would be a fit.

Guest from Hell: I have only had one such guest. It was all about selling his product and giving nothing in the way of FREE advice to listeners. If you wanted more, you had to call him directly. UGH.

Contact: sallie@salliefeltonlifecoach.com; 978-626-0090; http://www.salliefeltonlifecoach.com; Sallie Felton. Best method: I very much like to have an e-mail with a bio, press kit and if they are authors ... a copy of their book. No response? Yes, please keep after me, I will respond, but sometimes find that the e-mail box gets overloaded.

Invited Back? If I find that they are a real match and listeners are requesting that they come back on, I don't hesitate. However, if I find that the topic is one that can be heard again or if they have another, I will invite them once again

Guest Comments: "Sallie! Sallie! Sallie! I have done countless radio interviews and that was by far the very best, most thorough, insightful interview I have had! I can't thank you enough! Let me know what I can do to help YOU!"— Peggy Collins, author of *Help Is Not a Four-Letter Word: Why Doing It All Is Doing You In* (McGraw Hill 2006)

"Thank you sweet one! I absolutely loved being on your show today Sallie. Thank you ever so much."— Shoshanna Katzman author of *Qigong for Staying Young: A Simple 20 Minute Workout to Cultivate Your Vital Energy* (Avery Penguin Group 2003) and co-author of *Feeling Light—The Holistic Solution to Permanent Weight Loss and Wellness* (Avon Books 1997)

Bio of Sallie Felton: Sallie is living proof that people can go through a major life change and can not only survive, but can thrive. After years of frustration and searching for her purpose, she decided to leave her proper Yankee upbringing, traditional education and competitive sports career behind to pursue her true passions. It's been 20 years and she hasn't looked back.

Now she helps other New Englanders do the same. Like leaves on a tree, life is a collection of changes stemming from old roots and exciting new leaves — from single woman to wife, employee to employer, wellness to illness and spouse to widower. For example, how often do you hear of a woman who has a hard time meeting the challenges of menopause or men who need to free themselves of disastrous clutter? And how about those empty nesters and baby boomers, what are their next game plans?

Sallie draws on her personal experience, strong intuition, nearly 10 years of experience in deep imagery/visualization and hypnotherapy, world-class training from MentorCoachLLC, and education to help others achieve their goals. She received her postgraduate certificate from the International Institute of Visualization Research, her B.A. from the Gibbs School and studied at both L'Université de Grenoble and L'Université de Clermont-Ferrand in France.

Sallie and her husband have three grown children and live in the Boston area.

Infinitelove Talk Radio with Doug and Jackie Christie on Blog Talk Radio.

Theme: To empower and inspire and to send a positive message about marriage and relationships.

Guest Profile: Everyday people, celebritys, sports icons, authors, entertainers, teachers and general. We look for outspoken people — someone who has a clear idea of what they feel and has an open mind to learning new things. We also look for an interesting guest with an engaging personality. We want to know their past interview experiences, credentials and sound of their voice, and also their background and credibility;

that's important as you want your audience to get truthful information from everyone involved. We also look for interesting people from prior shows that we found to be an ideal guest.

Guest from Hell: A person that is argumentative and hard to talk to or relate to; someone who is standoffish and only offers one word answers, and is close-minded.

Contact: info@infinitelovepublishing.com; 888-733-7105; http://www.blogtalkradio.com/christiedandj; http://www.jackiechristie.com; Jenifer. Best method: Either. No response? Yes, they can follow up. We won't have a problem with that — we have every intention to respond ASAP to all requests.

Invited Back? Their personality, how engaging they were, and were they able to answer the questions fully and comfortably and overall how did our audience respond to them.

Bios of the Christies: Jackie and Doug are Seattle natives and their story is one of love at first sight. They are best friends and soul mates who share what they call "infinite love" — the kind of love that can never be broken. Although their marriage has been publicly criticized by the sports media, their love remains strong, due in part to prayer, and the strength and comfort they find in one another. Each year, in celebration of their love, Doug and Jackie remarry with a full wedding ceremony where they renew their vows to each other.

Jackie is also a fashion designer and recent author. She realized her passion for fashion as a child and is an avid reader. She has always aspired to be a writer and now has realized a dream. Her book is *No Ordinary Love: A True Story of Marriage and Basketball* (Infinite Love Publishing 2007).

Love by Intuition Show with Deborah Beauvais on Dreamvisions 7 Radio Network at WARL 1320am, Wednesday, 8–9 PM (ET), aired in Rhode Island and Southeastern MA, and streaming via Internet. http://www.lovebyintuition.com and http://www.dreamvisions7radio.com are now welcoming new hosts who would like to empower the universe. "Our mission is for all our radio hosts to have the common goal to deliver positive messages ... infused with spirituality, love and a desire to bring listeners to a place of divine enlightenment," says Deborah. Call 508-226-1723.

Theme: Self love, partner love and universal love — healing self and finding love within — how to date successfully — keeping the marriage cemented in love.

Guest Profile: Authors of self help books, psychic mediums, astrologists, educators, aura readers. People who help bring awareness to mankind. I enjoy having guests who share ideas on self awareness and how to bring hope, love and peace to the planet. I like to speak to all guests prior to the show ... when we are live ... I ask them to share how they got started, their vision and then let it flow. It makes for an exciting, spontaneous show. Guests have included Joan Countryman, the first head mistress of Oprah's Leadership Academy for Girls in South Africa.

Guest from Hell: I don't believe anyone is from hell but I do like guests who are respectful and understanding of who is the host of the show.

Contact: empoweredconnections@yahoo.com; Deborah@dreamvisions7radio.com; 508-226-1723; http://www.lovebyintuition.com http://www.dreamvisions7radio.com; (Deborah is owner of Empowered Connections and Dreamvisions7Radio Network); Deborah J. Beauvais. Best method: I like connecting on the phone, hearing sincerity, honesty and a direct message. No response? I always respond unless something major happens ... call or e-mail.

Invited Back? If there is a connection, excitement, flow and joy ... one can usually feel it.

Guest Comments: "Deborah is a gracious host and she gave me the full opportunity to get my information across to the audience. She asked good questions and was totally engaged in the conversation." — Rita Berkowitz; http://www.theSpiritArtist

"*Love by Intuition*, the brainchild of Deborah Beauvais, is a remarkable hour apart from a world held spellbound by ego's definition of love. Though love plays out in so many scenarios, Deborah brings her listeners to an expanded awareness of relationships one interview at a time. Just finding a partner and sticking with them for a lifetime does not make a success of a relationship. Combining her unique counseling and insight with interviews from today's leading luminaries and relationship specialists, listeners learn relationships are successful only if they provide both parties with a way to keep learning about themselves and the world around them; that all love begins with loving self before it can be reflected from without. Kudos to Beauvais for cracking open the inner heart of the soul!" — Angelina Heart, author of *The Teaching of Little Crow: The Journey of the Soul* (Heart Flame Publishing 2005). http://www.angelinaheart.com

Bio of Deborah Beauvais: Deborah's life has always been about love. She knew intuitively as a child, but was unaware of the scope of love or how it would be manifested. "My journey in life has encompassed many lessons followed by much inner work ultimately leading me to my purpose... Teaching others to connect to their own *Divine Love Within* ... awakening to the limitless power of the light and bringing illumination to each individual's purpose and path," she says.

Empowered Connections was created out of love and desire to help singles connect to their inner love — better preparing them for a partner. As a professional personalized matchmaker and relationship consultant for five years, she loves assisting people in their quest for love at all levels.

"I so look forward to a time when the universe radiates with love," she says.

Love Mechanics with Renee Piane on WomensRadio, iTunes and on numerous pod casting sites, including Yahoo, Podnova, Newsgator, Net Vibes, Odeo, Google, PageFlakes, Google, and miniQ.

Theme: This bi-monthly radio show offers direct dating advice and Hot interviews with the top experts in all fields relating to love, dating issues, sex and relationships with your host, internationally known dating and love coach Renee Piane (author of *Love Mechanics*) and president of Rapid Dating.com. You can send in your love and dating dilemmas to Renee at Renee@LoveMechanics.com

Guest Profile: Interactive authors, experts, matchmakers in fields relating to love and relationships, sex, divorce, health and wellness, spiritual practices related to relationship, people with love and dating challenges who want a love tune-up! Love stories are always great. Fun, organized, energetic guests who are credible, believable, can speak English clearly, and are able to focus and deliver their information/conversation — preferably without the need for a lot of editing (not too many spaces, uh's, ah's, and's, well's, etc.).

Guest from Hell: Experts who do not have bios/photos/questions or do not call on time. Call-ins from flakey angry people (I get rid of them rapidly). These shows are a great way for promotion ... be grateful.

Contact: Renee@LoveMechanics.com; 310-827-1100 office; http://www.Rapid Dating.com, http://www.Love Mechanics.com; Renee Piane or one of her staff. Best method: We request that they send a short, succinct e-mail with pertinent information about the proposed guest, the book, the situation, why that person is an authority (if it's about an issue), and the topic that is important to cover with some good questions. We appreciate sending products, books and any info to our address listed on the site. No response? We receive a hundreds of inquires and "pitches" from publicists. They get the message if we don't respond and we normally add the info into a special quest section for future shows so it is good if they send an e-mail or call to follow up. Those that feel they have the "perfect" guest will usually follow-up. Most people that contact me are in the love field in some form or another and we appreciate their follow-up. If we don't think that the person or topic is suitable, we will let them know — usually by return e-mail ASAP.

Invited Back? If they are going through a process and we want to follow up with progress reports. and if the audience enjoys them and I get feedback.

Listener Comments: "I heard Renee on her *Love Mechanics* show and it inspired me to make some big changes in my life! With Renee's book and a complete makeover, I've transformed my wardrobe, my home and my way of thinking. Now my biggest problem is finding enough time for Dating!" — Peter, engineer

"I was running through life with my eyes closed and Renee Piane opened them up with her easy *Love Mechanics* step by step techniques. I've begun a new exciting life and expanded my mind. I listen to her online all the time and pass on her great advice to all my friends struggling with relationships. You will see what magic her coaching and makeovers can do for you!" — Michael P, Massage therapist

Bio of Renee Piane: Renee has 20 years' experience in front of and behind the camera. She has professionally trained in broadcasting and TV production, communications and marketing. Renee has been a featured guest on 27 national TV programs, including the "Today Show" and CNN "Headline News." A page of testimonials from TV producers, authors and seminar leaders raving about her guest appearances speak volumes about Renee's boundless energy and passion for the dynamics of the dating game.

She is president of Rapid Dating, the fastest growing dating experience for singles in America. In addition to writing more than 400 singles love advice columns for newspapers and online sites, she is author of *Love Mechanics — Power Tools to Build Successful Relationships with Women* (Love Works Publishing 2001). Renee is writing a new book called *Secrets into the Minds of Men* based on her work with single men.

Renee is a graduate of the American Seminar Leaders Association and has been professionally media trained by Joel Roberts. She is also certified in NLP (Neuro Linguistic Programming), Time Line Therapy and Hypnotherapy.

Passion with Dr. Laurie Betito on CJAD 800, Montreal and CFRB 1010, Toronto.

Theme: Sex and relationships.

Guest Profile: Anyone who writes or is involved in sex or relationship related activities with experience in the field and interesting topics. Credentials are a must, the book in hand, a list of topics/issues they are comfortable addressing

Guest from Hell: One who only answers the questions asked in a perfunctory manner ... I like to have conversations, not interviews.

Contact: laurie@drlaurie.com or passion@cjad.com; 514-984-5910; http://www.drlaurie.com; Laurie Betito. Best method: E-mail a bio, send me a book/press kit. No response? E-mail again.

Invited Back? If they have a lot to say, are dynamic, and an easy interview.

Bio of Dr. Laurie Betito: Laurie is a psychologist with a specialty in sex therapy, and has been a practicing psychotherapist for 18 years. Before then, she began a career in radio when, as a co-host, she joined the team of MIX 96 in Montreal — a station that broke barriers when it introduced a call-in show (*The Love Line*), airing once per week, all about sex and relationships. In 1999, she joined CJAD 800 with her own talk show (this time nightly), once again about sex and relationships. This show, *Passion*, has soared to take the number one position in its time slot, and it is the only show of its kind on Montreal airwaves.

Laurie has appeared on TV, both as a host of a national show called "Let's Talk Sex" and as a commentator and regular "sexpert" on many other sex related programs.

She is affiliated with the Montreal General Hospital's Human Sexuality Unit, and is a senior member of their specialized team.

Quality of Life with Brian O Lynch on Blog Talk Radio, http://www.blogtalkradio.com

Theme: Relationships and life changing issues.

Guest Profile: The program interviews authors, singers and people with a compelling life changing story to share with others. I usually get an excerpt of what they have to present to the audience.

Guest from Hell: A guest who doesn't show up for an interview.

Contact: executive@valsonwritings.com; 704-532-1090; http://valsonwritings.com; Brian. Best method: E-mailing a bio. No response? I usually reply to my e-mails within 36 hours. It would be ok to e-mail me again if they didn't get a reply within that time.

Invited Back? That is usually done by request from guest, audience or if we felt as if they had more to share.

Bio of Brian O Lynch: Brian's deep conviction of relationships was deeply rooted by his Christian background. As a young boy he was taught the basic principles of what a relationship should be. Migrating to the United States in his late teens he was soon influenced by the wrong ideas and had soon turned to practices contrary to his Christian belief.

Thanks to his single mom and the spirit of God working through both of them he was set on the right path again. His deep convictions were once renewed into his way of life. Assuredly no one is perfect so over the years he has learned valuable lessons when he turned away from God. His passion to find a relationship of love, romance and the quality of life has driven him to get deeper in the subject of relationship.

He credits the guidance of the Holy Spirit as the source of his knowledge. His writings are based partially on his own relationship experiences and of numerous researches that were carefully conducted over the years. His passion to see a better life for single mothers was also a strong inspiration for his writings. His greatest hope is as you read his writings you will allow it to point out where you are in seeking your relationship of love, romance and a better quality of life.

Brian is author of *The Rules to Love* (PublishAmerica 2007).

Relationships for Life with Drs. Joseph Dooley and Sabra Brock on http://www.VoiceAmerica.com, Health and Wellness Channel, and http://www.success-talk.com

Theme: Relationship issues, with the underlying thesis that men and women are very different, but if you know and understand those differences, you can get along better with the opposite sex. We devote the entire hour to one author's ideas and look for interesting, informative and entertaining discussion, not sound bites. We balance research-based expertise with edgy relationship advice.

Guest Profile: Almost exclusively authors — who have something to say about how men and women are different and how to use that knowledge to improve all your relationships with the opposite sex, at home, work and play. We treat our guests with courtesy and curiosity. Ideal guest is a celebrity who is talkative, intelligent and has something to say about how men and women relate.

Guest from Hell: The guest from hell is a person who gives one-word answers.

Contact: Sabrabrock@aol.com; JosephD643@aol.com; 917-915-5177; http://www.Relationshipsfor Life.net; Sabra Brock. Best method: E-mail with press kit that includes a short bio. I do a 1-minute communications check with guest before show. No response? E-mail again

Invited Back? Articulate, lively with interesting stories.

Bios of Joseph Dooley, Ph.D and Sabra Brock, Ph.D: Joseph is a leading expert in biotechnology and human management techniques. He is president and managing partner of BioTechnology Associates, Inc. He has been affiliated with medical schools and lectured on medical and management subjects around the world. Dr. Dooley is the author of more than 30 professional publications and with his company has written 20 book length reports on management and human biology for private clients.

Sabra is a leader in the area of change management and innovative business thinking. She is the president of The Training Advantage, which specializes in consulting with multinational corporations, as well as individual, on managing personal and professional change. Her clients include Colgate-Palmolive, the Federal Reserve Bank of New York, Meridian France, Verizon, and the U.S. government.

Joseph and Sabra are authors of *Men Head East, Women Turn Right: How to Meet in the Middle When Facing Change* (Adams Media Corporation 2004), and *The Relationship Advantage* (TriMark Publications 2004).

Sex with Emily with Emily Morse was on 106.9 FREE FM/CBS radio in San Francisco from 2005–2007, when it changed to classic rock. Emily is in the process of syndicating her show. About 80 podcasts can be heard at http://www.sexwithemily.com and/or downloaded through itunes.

Theme: Talk about sex, relationships, and everything in between (dating, cheating, marriage, tysts, methods, mistakes lovers, love), "changing the world one orgasm at a time."

Guest Profile: Live in-studio and call-in guests ranging from sex and relationship authors, experts, doctors, therapists, coaches, phone sex operators, exotic dancers, and "real people" including — happily married couples, couples living alternative lifestyles, single men and women, recent divorcee's. Guests are gay, straight, lesbian and transgendered etc. Someone one who is open, honest, articulate and willing to share their personal experiences beyond their expertise. Previous interviews, credentials and sound of their voice are important. However, pre-interviews are key. I've rarely had a guest on without speaking with or meeting them first.

Guest from Hell: A guest who misrepresents themselves and uses the show simply as a tool to advance their own agenda.

Contact: feedback@sexwithemily.com; 415-401-8122; http://www.sexwithemily.com. Chickflick Productions, LLC: 415-401-8122. Best method: E-mailing and mailing press kit is preferred. No response? Be persistent. E-mail me again. Sometimes people get lost in the shuffle and it never bothers me, in fact I prefer it when people follow up. The squeaky wheel gets the grease.

Invited Back? If we had a good chemistry and was able to translate to the listeners. Someone who had a new or alternative perspective that was beneficial to our audience.

Bio of Emily Morse: Emily is the creator of her show and her mission in life is to ask the questions you wanted to but weren't ready to ask. She realized a few years ago that no matter where her conversation starts it ends with relationships and sex. Is he the one? Is she the one? Did I pick the wrong one? And so Sex with Emily was born and has was in the top 20 downloaded podcasts on iTunes and had over a million listeners the first year.

Emily has a television show in development based on the weekly production of her radio show. She has also appeared as a guest or co-host on other radio stations around the country, including the *Jamie Foxx Show*, the *Tom Leykis Show*, *Playboy Radio* and *Date Night on TMC*. She has been featured in the *New York Times*, *Los Angeles Times*, and *Wired News* and was selected as one of the "Hot 20 under 40" in San Francisco's *7 × 7 Magazine*.

Emily began her career in electoral politics running campaigns. She later parlayed her experience in politics into an award winning documentary about the 1999 San Francisco mayoral election. As founder of Chick Flick Productions, LLC, she directed and produced the award winning documentary, "See How They Run," which aired on PBS and played at film festivals around the country. Emily also produced and hosted shows for networks including PBS, OXYGEN, TMC, Court TV and Current TV.

As a model, Emily has been featured in dozens of national commercials and in print advertisements for national brands. She appeared as the lead in Caveh Zahedi's award winning film *I Am a Sex Addict*.

Emily graduated with honors from the University of Michigan.

Check out her electronic press kit at http://www.sexwithemily.com/node/195

Listener Comments: "I am a carpenter living in Santa Barbara. I often listen to your podcasts on my iPod during the work day. Imagine doing trim work in luxurious 7,000 square foot celebrity mansions as I chuckle over Eva the Urban Cougar's exploits, online dating disasters and Dating Dahling's Do's and Don'ts. Thank you for your show."—Chris, Santa Barbara

"Thank you for a fantastic show. It has really opened up for the whole area of sex and loving. I'm recently divorced after 20 year marriage and getting back into the swing of dating. I've been listening to your radio show for 6 months. I found for the first time in my life that I am able to express myself is a very sexual way. Thank you for a very informative and exciting show."—Pete, Santa Fe

Sex with Sassy Radio Show with Sassy Tease on All Talk Radio, http://www.alltalkradio.net

Theme: Sex, fantasies, lifestyles, sexual experiences, adult products, books, up and coming talent and websites, etc.

Guest Profile: Authors, actors, models, singers, dancers, celebrities, pornstars, other talent, business owners and everyday people. Anyone who is open to talking about sex or sex related topics. I look for guests who are open minded and willing to talk openly. I like my guest to have fun, enjoy themselves and play along If I flirt or make comments, respond back or laugh — something is better than dead air, after all this is entertainment. My guest(s) don't have to have been on TV or even had any experience, but if they do I like to know who has interviewed them on TV, radio, print media, Internet, etc. I also like to know a little bit about my guest's background — a bio, previous interviews, experience — and what they are trying to promote. Also knowing about their personality helps me when I am interviewing and for the comfort of everyone involved.

Guest from Hell: If a guest doesn't talk or gives one word answers that's the worst. Also those who are too up-tight about the show topics — remember your fans and potential fans are listening and you want to give them something to talk about.

Contact: sexwithsassy@gmail.com; Withheld upon request; http://www.sexwithsassy.com; GIGP Management or Sassy Tease. Best method: E-mail. Just make sure to include as much information as possible about you and what you do, what you'd like to promote or talk about include a promotion picture if you have one for promotional use, press kit, bio, website link, e-mail address, phone number and send a copy of your book or product if you have the ability to do so. If you do not have some or any of the above a simple e-mail will do. Also please mention which topics you are open to talking about when it comes to. No response? You can send another e-mail; sometimes things get lost. The best way to make sure I get the e-mail is to make sure the subject line says "Be a Show Guest," or "Show Guest." Then I will read it fairly quickly.

Invited Back? If my guest(s) have a website and they list me in their press/interviews section and posting interview or a link to it or just the show on the website. Guest(s) who send out press releases, send e-mails to their fans and e-mail lists about their interview. Guests that play along and have fun with it are always welcome back. Also if they are fun and talk openly about the show topics. If they actually show up or call in that is helpful. Just to name a few things

Guest Comment: "Sassy, in my mind, is the ideal radio host, as well as a knowledgeable, exciting advocate on the topics of sexuality and adult entertainment. She shows a keen interest in her guests and puts them immediately at ease; in addition, she blends professionalism with a very accessible, down-to-earth persona.

When I appeared on Sassy's show to discuss my group, the Playgirl Posse, and my work with *Playgirl* magazine, I felt that Sassy put her show to work for me — she worked with me to get my message out there; plus we had a good laugh and a lot of fun. When I'm interviewed by Sassy, I feel like I'm talking to a classy, very hip friend with many stories to share, and with a keen interest in the stories and experiences of others." — Megan Hussey, Possemeister Playgirl Possee, http://goldenmuse.tripod.com

Bio of Sassy Tease: Sassy has been a traditional, mainstream AM/FM radio host since the 90's, on KCEP, KCEG, KSBR, KLAV. She's been doing her Internet show since 2003.

She's also a TV host, web designer, public relations and marketing specialist, author, singer songwriter, choreographer, and dancer.

Single Talk with Aliza Silverman/Michele Economou on World Talk Radio and Blog Talk Radio; now off the air.

Theme: Single life — love, life, and dating.

Guest Profile: Authors, dating industry professionals. A good guest for us is someone who has anything to say about any aspect of single life and dating. If they have a little different take or edge on a topic, even better. If they have energy and passion, we're elated. Credentials important — what they have to say, if it is within the scope of our show.

Guest from Hell: The guest from hell is the guest who gives one word answers to questions, has no passion or energy, and nothing much to say about anything. We've had them, it's not fun.

Contact: Singletalk@roadrunner.com; Withheld upon request; http://www.modavox.com/WTRStudioA/HostModaviewForWTR2.aspx?HostId=304andChannelId=14andFlag=1; Website for Blog Talk Radio (coming soon); http://www.blogtalkradio.com/Singletalk; Aliza or Michele. Best method: E-mail first. No response? E-mail one more time. If we don't respond, it is because we are not booking at that moment or the guest is not right for our show, but we try to respond to everyone.

Invited Back? We like the chatty, fun, yet informative type of guest.

Bio of Aliza Silverman: Living in Los Angeles or any huge metropolitan city makes it difficult to meet a prospective mate. Aliza wants to lend a voice to the single people out there who would appreciate a forum to discuss their lifestyle, and the frustrations as well as the joys that go along with it.

She has a degree in drama and loves the theater scene.

According to Aliza, "there are 95,000,000 people living solo in America, so, I take comfort in knowing that although single, I am not alone."

Your Dream Wedding with Cindy Marinangel on http://www.BigMediaUSA.com (http://www.bigmediausa.com/show.asp?sid=346)

Theme: Weddings.

Guest Profile: Brides, authors, bridal shops, DJ's, limo drivers, colorists, beauty salons, officiants, etc. I look for an unusual wedding story or wedding vendor. Something that a bride-to-be can find helpful when formulating their own idea of their dream wedding. I like to know about their history in the business, what makes their services unique, how their services work and what their range of fees are. For brides, I like to know about their planning process, whether they started with a budget or not, how the actual ceremony went, what the details of their weddings were/are.

Guest from Hell: Anyone who doesn't show up or fails to call. Anyone who does not talk a lot in response to a question.

Contact: cindymarinangel@sbcglobal.net; 310-927-1999; http://www.cindymarinangel.com; Cindy Marinangel, host and producer. Best method: Phone after 11 AM (PT) or e-mail is fine. A phone call or e-mail is ok. I love referrals. No response? E-mail or call.

Invited Back? If there is another topic they are knowledgeable on or if they were vendors, they are welcome to come back with a wedding story if they or someone in their family are getting married, or vice versa.

Guest Comments: "Cindy makes her show fun and fills it with great info that her listeners can immediately incorporate into their lives. She achieves this with her spot on questions and her fantastic energy. Her genuine interest in her guest is apparent and doing her show was an absolute blast!"— Jill Kirsh, http://www.jillkirshcolor.com

"As far as radio hosts are concerned Cindy Marin Angel is fantastic! She is comfortable and fun to interview with! I had a blast doing her show, because Cindy guided the interview in a professional way and also got to the heart of the matter by asking the most interesting questions. I can't wait to do another interview with her!"—Donna Spangler, actress, model and author of *How to Get a Rich Man* (Boonie Publishing 2007), http://www.donnaspangler.net

Bio of Cindy Marinangel: Cindy is a Chicago Second City graduate and was just accepted as a lifetime member into the esteemed Actor's Studio. She just starred in her sixth theatrical world premiere in Los Angeles. On film, Cindy has starred opposite Fred Durst and Tim Bagley, and can be heard narrating E! Entertainment's special "Beyonce Uncut."

Cindy has portrayed Princess Diana, been on "Good Day LA" as a "wedding expert," and was just interviewed on the TV show "The Method Actor Speaks." She has had several leading roles in TV pilots and independent films that have run the festival circuits.

Religion and Atheism

The Allen Hunt Show on News Talk 750 WSB, aired in Atlanta, Jacksonville, Dayton, Richmond, Charlotte, Winston-Salem, Virginia Beach.

Theme: Where real life and faith come together.

Guest Profile: Wide variety of folks — from porn producers to professional athletes to women who have had abortions and the list goes on extensively. Someone doing something extraordinary by faith or experiencing a real life struggle.

Guest from Hell: Dull.

Contact: allen@allenhuntshow.com; 770-851-4542; http://www.allenhuntshow.com; Allen. Best method: E-mail with overview and bio. No response? E-mail.

Invited Back? My impression of their authenticity and helpfulness.

Bio of Allen Hunt: Allen is passionate about a few things: God, family and a full life of joy.

Talk radio is a natural fit for Allen. He loves to talk, and he loves people. Plus, he is full of opinions (and maybe a little wisdom too). As a pastor of one of the largest Methodist congregations in the world, he has learned a lot about faith. As a former businessman, he has experienced a lot of life. As a father of two teenage girls, he has learned a lot about real life and faith.

Allen was born at a very young age (ok, I think Allen thinks he was funny when he told me this, just laugh along). He grew up in the mountains in Brevard, North Carolina, and then graduated from high school in Lakeland, Florida. As a kid, he loved baseball and all things athletic. But the Church has usually (but not always) been a significant influence in his life.

Before entering the ministry, Allen worked in business and wandered away from God's plans for a while. Allen quickly discovered that a life serving himself, his own pleasures, and his own plans did not result in much. One day, while entering a Wall Street highrise in New York, Allen stepped over a homeless man lying on a subway grating for warmth. At that pivotal moment, God taught Allen that it was time to leave behind his own plans and embrace God's plans for his life. A life of serving others and following Jesus. Allen then became a minister. And he has never looked back.

Allen and his wife, Anita, met in college at Mercer University in Macon, Georgia. Along the way, Anita helped Allen earn a Ph.D. in New Testament from Yale University. They have two daughters, SarahAnn and Griffin.

Answers in Atheism with Edwin Kagin on http://www.answersinatheism.net, airs Thursday at 7 PM (ET).

Theme: Interactive talk radio on issues of interest to atheists showing that there are answers in atheism.

Guest Profile: Authors, scientists, activists, writers, educators, entertainers, and other persons interested in advancing science and rational thinking over supernatural explanations. Someone who has interesting things to say and can say them in an entertaining manner. Such a person should be able to inspire others to do something other than complain. Interested to know what they have done, or are doing, things that have furthered the interests of persons who view themselves as Atheists. They may be well known, or controversial, or worthy of becoming known. They should also be able to converse in such a manner that the audience is not bored or disinterested.

Guest from Hell: A person who answers in monosyllables and has to have every thought coaxed out of them. Or who thinks they are the most brilliant and creative person who has ever lived.

Contact: theshow@answersinatheism.net; 877-814-9287; http://www.answersinatheism.net; John or Fran Welte, producer, at welte@fuse.net. Best method: e-mail. No response? Please e-mail again. If there has been no answer, it is unintentional, and e-mail does get lost.

Invited Back? Whether they did well on the show; whether they have done any thing of interest since the show; whether listeners have asked that they come back.

Bio of Edwin Frederick Kagin, J.D.: The son of a Presbyterian minister, Edwin was born in Kentucky, and is an attorney in Union, Kentucky.

He attended The College of Wooster in Wooster, Ohio; Park College in Parkville, Missouri; the University of Missouri at Kansas City in Kansas City, Missouri; and the School of Law of the University of Louisville in Louisville, Kentucky.

He is co-author of *The Fundamentals of Extremism: The Christian Right in America* (Kimberly Blaker, ed; New Boston Books, 2003), available in English and Arabic. He was a founder and former board member of Recover Resources Center, which provides alternatives to Alcoholics Anonymous for addiction recovery.

Edwin and his wife, Helen McGregor Kagin, a Canadian of Scottish descent and a retired physician, were awarded the "Atheists of the Year" award for 2005 by American Atheists. The couple has four children, Stephen, Eric, Heather, and Kathryn, a stepdaughter, Caroline, a granddaughter Maren, and two grandsons, Ethan and Quinn.

Full bio at http://en.wikipedia.org/wiki/Edwin_Kagin

Awake, Alive and Jewish with Rabbi Shmuel Kaplan and Gary Siegel on WMET AM 1160, covering Washington, D.C., suburban MD, and northern Virginia; www.wmet1160.com

Theme: Talk, music, interviews and information geared to the Jewish community; Michael Hoffman, producer, at michaelchoffman@msn.com.

Guest Profile: Authors are more than welcome. The focus is to increase observance. Most guests have done something themselves/written something/or researched something in that area. We rarely do fiction. Someone who has either written, televised, broadcast, filmed or done something to promote traditional Jewish observance. What they've done that will interest our vast listener audience.

Guest from Hell: Someone heavily accented who can't be understood. Best method: E-mail a press release. No response? E-mail or call.

Invited Back? They've done something new that interests us.

Bios of Rabbi Shmuel Kaplan, Gary Siegel and Michael Hoffman: Rabbi Kaplan is a noted Torah scholar and director of Chabad-Lubavitch of the Maryland region, and a lecturer at the University of Maryland.

Gary was born and grew up in Scranton, Pa., where he was among the original students in the Hebrew Day School, beginning in 1948. He served in both the Viet Nam War and Desert Storm. A graduate of the U.S. Naval Academy in Annapolis, MD, Gary served in the Navy Supply Corps in USS *Sterett*, CG-31, in Naval Support Activity, DaNang, RVN ('68–'69), and at Naval Air Systems Command Hq in DC. He then became a Navy reservist and graduated from the Columbus School of Law, Catholic University of America. After more than 32 years of trial practice — mainly personal injury claims and family law — he closed his office in June 2006 and is now trying to get into the voice-over field.

Gary has been on the show with Rabbi Kaplan since June 2005 and describes his role as "being the rabbi's comic relief, as well as selector of music and news from Israel."

Michael has had three years of college radio experience and 27 years of weekly Jewish radio experience.

Bob Enyart Live with Bob Enyart on Bel, AM 670 KLTT, Denver, Colorado, covering 90 percent of Colorado (4.2 million) and reaching into seven bordering states. The show airs weekdays, 3 PM (MT).

Theme: Conservative news talk radio with a biblical Christian perspective.

Guest Profile: Liberals, atheists, etc., basically anyone with an opposing Christian biblical view. Bob also interviews people who agree or at least think they will agree with him. Their point of view, their popularity, and people who are extremely knowledgeable in their topic/field.

Guest from Hell: One who would use profanity and be vulgar, such as Bill Maher. Bob was on his show ("Politically Incorrect") eight times and has a DVD called "Bob debates the stars."

Contact: Bob@kgov.com; 800-836-9278; http://www.kgov.com and http://www.kgov.com/bel/affiliates; Ray Greybar, producer, Rjrossmountain@aol.com or Michelle Ross, associate producer at MMRossmountain@aol.com. Best method: Phone. No response? E-mail either Ray or Michelle and then if it is a topic/person Bob wants to have on his show we will contact them back. If a person needs a phone contact, Ray will take calls at 970-224-2964.

Invited Back? If the show is worthwhile.

Guest Comment: John Henderson MD debated a right wing fundamental preacher on the subject of "Does God Exist." Prior to airing the show, John spoke to producer Ray Graybar, recalling: "We had a nice chat over the phone, and, for a Christian, he was surprisingly tolerant of my views. He didn't even threaten me with hell when I said that I was not a big fan of Jesus."— John Henderson MD is author of *God.com: A Deity for the New Millennium* (Dorrance Publishing 2002) and *Fear Faith Fact Fantasy* (Parkway Publishers 2003), http://www.johnhenderson-god.com

Bio of Bob Enyart: Bob is an American television and radio talk show host, pastor and author, based since the 1980s in Denver, Colorado.

He calls himself a conservative, Christian, advocate of non-orthodox Open theism, and frequently introduces himself as "America's most popular self proclaimed right-wing, religious fanatic, homophobic, anti-choice talk show host."

The Christian Women's View with Sarah Goebel and Sandra Stanford on WLGT "We Love Girl Talk" Radio on Blog Talk Radio.

Theme: Christian women guests and listeners who call in to discuss the "real life" challenges, joys and journeys of "real Christian" women from a Christian woman's perspective. Each show is spiritually enriching.

Guest Profile: Christian authors, Christian testimonies, discussions on real life issues and challenges from a biblical perspective. We look for guests who glorify the Lord through their book, ministry or testimony and through their lives. What we want: Past interviews, credentials, name of book or ministry and if an author we like to have a copy of the book mailed to us along with suggested interview questions.

Guest from Hell: Someone with nothing to say or someone who doesn't love the Lord.

Contact: wlgt@nc.rr.com; Withheld upon request; http://www.wlgt.org; http://www.DeclaringHisAnswer.com; Sarah Goebel. Best method: Someone desiring to be on our show should send us a press kit or e-mail us a bio and request. Include website information if have one. No response? E-mail us again.

Invited Back? Slot availability, public interest, does it fit into our planned topics?

Bio of Sarah Ann Goebel: Dedicated to the service of Christ and His household, Sarah is a CLASS graduate, founder of Declaring His Answer Ministries, Int'l, BreakThrough University for Women, The Christian Women's View Blog Talk Radio Show, member of the Women on Assignment Conference Ministries Team, pastor's wife, mother of two and grandmother to one. She serves on the staff at Manna Church of Lumberton as Minister to Women and published her first book, *Satisfied Woman — Discovering True Worth, Peace, Fulfillment and Abundant Living* (Xulon Press 2006), which resulted in extensive national and worldwide press via radio and television interviews.

Other published writings by Sarah include *My Knight in Shining Armor*, which won a place in Xulon Press' book release How I Met My True Love and she won the Editor's Choice Award from the International Society of Poetry in 2007 for her poem, "You Have Set Me Free."

Sarah believes that all of us are able to conquer our pasts and fulfill God's destiny when we learn how to trust God. Among her many life challenges, she was abandoned by her husband, left with two teenagers to raise alone. God provided by giving her an idea for a business of which, although launched on a shoestring, soon became a thriving company expanding into three locations. She left the life of a successful business owner when called to full time ministry.

Sarah's passion in addition to spending time with God and her family is to encourage and equip women to persevere to the abundant destiny Christ has waiting for them by leading them to a place of recognition of God's presence in their lives and assisting them through the principles that result in leaving the past and its strongholds behind and moving forward into a permanently changed, purposeful and prosperous life in Christ.

The Christian Worldview with David Wheaton presented by Summit Ministries on AM 980 KKMS Minneapolis/St. Paul and SIRIUS FamilyNet Channel 161; 13 terrestrial affiliates; streaming at www.KKMS.com; podcast at www.DavidWheaton.com

Theme: News, culture, and faith from a biblical perspective with the mission of sharpening your Christian worldview.

Guest Profile: Christian leaders and pastors, A-list guests in any field. Someone who's well known or has credibility and can articulate their point in a compelling manner.

Guest from Hell: Someone who has low energy and low enthusiasm or someone who won't stop talking and rabbit trails.

Contact: david@davidwheaton.com; 651-289-4439; http://www.DavidWheaton.com; David Wheaton. Best method: E-mail me or send press kit and books/material to radio station: Salem Twin Cities, c/o The Christian Worldview with David Wheaton, 2110 Cliff Road, Eagan, MN 55122. No response? E-mail me once more and then take the hint.

Invited Back? How good they were the first time.

Bio of David Wheaton: David is an author, speaker, radio talk show host, columnist and professional tennis player.

His first book, *University of Destruction* (Bethany House 2005) has reached as high as #25 on Amazon.com. He is a contributing columnist for the *Minneapolis Star Tribune*. Formerly, David was one of the top professional tennis players in the world attaining a world ranking of #12, winning the Grand Slam Cup, reaching the semi-finals of Wimbledon, representing the United States in Davis Cup competition, and scoring victories over such players as Andre Agassi, Jimmy Connors, Ivan Lendl, Stefan Edberg, Jim Courier, and Michael Chang.

God Unplugged with Amy Hammond Hagberg on Blog Talk Radio; http://www.blogtalkradio.com/godunplugged. Amy also co-hosts with Candace House an Internet talk show called *It's Time to Breathe* where they interview guests who are living their life's purpose.

Theme: Show explores how God impacts our daily lives and features interviews with Christian celebrities about their faith.

Guest Profile: Well-known actors, recording artists, authors and professional/Olympic athletes. I interview Christian celebrities who have had dramatic encounters with God — most of them were featured in my books. I would need to know how they came to know Christ.

Guest from Hell: I haven't had any of them, but it would be someone who is too nervous to share their personal journey candidly.

Contact: amy@amyhagberg.com; 612-616-4414; http://www.hesreal.com; http://www.amyhagberg.com; Amy Hagberg. Best method: E-mailing a pitch and press kit would be best. If the prospect is a recording artist or author, I would need a review copy of their work. The address can be obtained by e-mailing me. No response? I will respond to them either way: e-mail or phone.

Invited Back? If my listeners let me know they wish the program had been longer, I will definitely invite the guest back.

Bio of Amy Hammond Hagberg: Amy has more than 20 years experience as a writer, speaker and sales/marketing executive. She has worked in the advertising agency, non-profit and corporate arenas and in industries as varied as yellow pages, energy, information technology and software promotions. She also provides sales training and consulting services to small businesses.

She is a frequent contributor to publications around the world and writes a monthly column on three popular websites, http://www.positivelyfeminine.com, http://www.soulshine.ca and http://www.christianeducation.ca.

A sought-after speaker at churches all over the country, Amy is a member of the Evangelical Press Association and served as a judge in their 2006 and 2007 Awards of Excellence. She is co-editor of the Author's Co-op, an online community of writers and involved in numerous writer's groups.

Amy is author of a three-book series, *How Do You Know He's Real: Celebrity Reflections on True Life Experiences with God* (Destiny Image Publishers 2006), *How Do You Know He's Real: God Unplugged* (Destiny Image Publishers 2006), geared for teens and young adults, and *My Favorite Christmas* (Integrity Publishers 2006).

She's been married for over 22 years and has two teenagers.

The Infidel Guy Show with Reginald V. Finley Sr. aired Thursdays at 8 PM, ET, on http://www.infidelguy.com

Theme: Critical thinking/religious history/science.

Guest Profile: Authors are welcome. Scholarly research and discussion in various fields: religion, science, philosophy, social issues and critical investigation. When looking for great guests, I hope that they are experts in their field and/or highly entertaining as well as educating. I prefer to read something by them which usually gives me an idea of whether or not to have them on.

Guest from Hell: A guest from hell for me (and I've had a few), is a guest that's condescending, rude, arrogant, pompous, ignorant, unqualified, lack of etiquette. I don't like it when my guest is yelling and talking over me or the callers. I'm more offended when it happens to my callers. :)

Contact: infidelguy@infidelguy.com; 888-503-0802; http://www.infidelguy.com; Reginald Finley Sr. Best method: E-mail. I'm more impressed when I receive e-mails or a call from fans of a potential guest. I'm rather turned off when someone asks to be on the show. I have had a few guests that have simply e-mailed me promotional material. If done well ... and if it's convincing, I might bite. But, "Hi, I'm really smart. Have me on," will not cut it. No response? Persistence is a virtue. I'd tell any potential guest to be persistent. Never assume the host isn't interested. Sometimes, we are just damned swamped and push stuff to the side. You have to learn how to stick-out without being a pushy jerk. The best way I recommend is to send in quick, interesting, easy-to-read word bytes about your work. Time is essential to a broadcaster. If you respect that. You may get some recognition.

Invited Back? Listener response is a pretty good indicator of whether to have a guest back on. I go off that mostly. Usually, what I like and what they like mirror fortunately.

"I always have a great time on *The Infidel Guy Show*. He listens and lets you talk without all of those annoying commercials." — Dr. Robert Price, theology professor

"I am having such a great time on your show. You are really a smart guy Reggie. Handsome too." — Acharya S., author of *Christ Conspiracy* (Adventures Unlimited Press 1999), http://www.truthbeknown.com

Bio of Reginald Vaughn Finley, Sr.: Reginald is considered a pioneer in Internet broadcasting as he is the first non-corporate entity to earn a living doing an Internet broadcast from home. For over a decade, he has been very active in freethought communities and education activism.

He was raised to always question everything and look up information independent of what his parents would say. He grew up knowing that often times, people just don't have all the answers, so he should look it up for himself. After taking a few religion and philosophy courses in college, Reggie quickly discovered his new calling: educating the masses.

His family appeared on ABC's reality show "Wife Swap" on November 28, 2005. Reggie and his wife are both freethinkers and are currently raising three young critical thinkers.

Interfaith Voices with Maureen Fiedler, syndicated in Washington, DC; Chicago, IL; Alabama (statewide); Western Michigan; 43 total stations in the U.S. and Canada (Halifax, NS and Winnipeg, MB). Complete list online at http://www.Interfaithradio.org/stations

Theme: We cover religious and spiritual news, current affairs, and history.

Guest Profile: Our typical guest is a reporter, author, professor or other expert on subjects of religion and spirituality. We look for guests who have a compelling story to tell about interfaith religion and spirituality. The show strives to show the many facets, faces, and issues of faith in North America and around the world. We look for the quality of interfaith understanding and hope to educate and inform the audience every week. We have had many people on the show who have not previously done radio interviews. We want people who can speak passionately and compassionately about personal, communal (organizational or denominational) and international spirituality and religion. We are not interested in people who are one-issue oriented. Tell us how your issue is on the avenue of faith and how it helps your community. We have hosted Starhawk, Tony Campolo, Richard Cizik, John Shelby Spong, Richard Land, many leaders of major faith traditions; many first-time and multiple published authors including Christopher Hitchens.

Guest from Hell: If the guest is not succinct or is uninformed, we will probably not air the interview. We never book novelists, "chicken soup"— types and rarely book inspirational speakers or authors.

Contact: Maureen@interfaithradio.org; 301-699-3443 ext 105; http://www.interfaithradio.org; Maureen Fiedler. Best method: E-mail with a pitch or send book. No response? Suggest agent call; but not every book will get a response. We usually respond in two to five weeks. If it is a timely story, we suggest that you send a press kit or a pitch via Religion News Service, a non-profit, or another PR outfit.

Invited Back? Guests are often not invited back immediately. We wait to see what the guest accomplishes, be it a book, essay, public role, etc.

Bio of Maureen Fiedler, SL: Maureen has hosted *Interfaith Voices* since it debuted in 2002. She presents interviews, features, and commentaries with an informed and engaging style appreciated by our listeners.

Jewish Digest with Leslie Lutsky on CINQ, Montreal and Internet.

Theme: Jewish topics.

Guest Profile: Authors, musicians, political activists, people from diverse Jewish communities or people representing a host of social and unusual Jewish groups — example — Jewish motorcycle club, Jewish punk band, Jewish ecological movements, Jewish labor organizations. Anyone who has a story, song or something interesting to say. I don't need to know their past interview experiences or credentials since I would have read their book or done research or heard them speak. Guests are interviewed in the studio, a hotel or a quiet space while they are in Montreal or on the phone.

Guest from Hell: A guest from hell is one who speaks only in yesses and nos.

Contact: leslieljd@yahoo.com; 514-272-5064; http://www.rtscanada.ca/CINQ.htm; http://www.radiocentreville.com; http://www.klezmershack.com; Leslie Lutsky. Best method: E-mail or phone. Calling with pitch, e-mailing a bio and press kit all work, although a simple phone call is good. No response? Usually I reply as soon as I can. I do not have a computer so I have to go to a library to use one. They can call me or e-mail me.

Invited Back? If they write another book or put out another cd or made a new film.

Bio of Leslie Lutsky: Leslie has training in bookkeeping and experience as a vegetarian cook and a hobby of photographing former shul buildings.

The Jewish Experience with Reb Hirsh Dlinn on WEDO-AM 810, aired in Pittsburgh, PA and vicinity; now off the air.

Theme: Authentic jewish variety.

Guest Profile: Anyone that impacts the Jewish community in Pittsburgh and around the world. Even better if they relate to what's happening now in the Jewish community.

The program features nationally-known rabbis providing lessons in Torah, Jewish history, news from Israel National News, community announcements and events, interviews with personalities that affect the Jewish community, the feminine perspective and inspiring classic Jewish stories. Authentic Jewish music fills out the hour-long weekly program. I normally require a backgrounder to include credentials. I want to be sure that the guest has credibility.

Guest from Hell: Anyone that gives one-word answers to general questions, can't follow a conversation and mumbles.

Contact: jewishexperience@verizon.net; 412-979-5770; http://www.jewishexperienceradio.com; Hirsh Dlinn, host and producer. Best method: I would prefer e-mail at first. Then I will call the prospective guest to discuss the possibility. No response? The person should e-mail again. I usually respond to all e-mails even if it is a negative response.

Invited Back? Their ability to deliver information in a clear and entertaining manner.

Guest Comment: "Hirsh Dlinn's radio program was one of the first programs on which I was invited to speak since being elected. He has a knack at examining the human side of a story and the Jewish side of a story, not just the political side. Though I knew the interview would be broadcast all over the country and the world, I felt like it was just the two of us having a private conversation. I'm glad that Dlinn is on air and I wish only that he should go from strength to strength." — Yehoshua (Jason) Bedrick, Jewish State Rep from New Hampshire and the first Orthodox Jew to hold elective office in the state

Bio for Hirsh Dlinn: Prior to hosting his current show, which he calls "the fastest 60 minutes in Jewish radio," Rabbi Dlinn hosted other radio programs dealing with religion and politics.

He is the president of Senior Wealth Management, LLC, a financial services firm specializing in estate/retirement planning, long-term care and fee-based portfolio management and has more than 14 years experience managing investments for select clients nationwide. Previously he was a co-founder of Hayden Stone and Co., LLC and worked for Wachovia Securities and Prudential Securities.

The rabbi has a long track record of political/community activism and has received many honors and awards, including the Marjorie S. Eiseman Community Leadership Award.

He earned a bachelor's degree in physics from the University of South Carolina, where he achieved a master's degree in mass communications. From 1974 to 1978, he served as a commissioned officer in the United States Navy. Starting in 1979, he was a public affairs officer in the United States Naval Reserve and retired in 1995.

He and his wife have six children.

The JPEG Show with JP and Peg (Peuster) has aired on more than 30 stations in the Midwest.

Theme: Christian programming.

Guest Profile: Authors, leaders, sports, Christian-religious, entertaining, educational, open for deep questions. Some credentials — mainly experiences.

Guest from Hell: We would never interview someone from hell.

Contact: jp@thejpegshow.com; 816-739-2066; http://www.thejpegshow.com; JP. Best method: E-mail-send book. No response? E-mail or call.

Invited Back? Response.

Bios of James and Peggy Peuster: James was a radio DJ in KC through college but got out of it to pursue a career in management. One night God woke him up and provided the foundation for *The JPEG Show*. JP and Peg combined for the name and the premise is to "bring you a snapshot of heaven on Earth." James's quick wit and thirst for humor provides the listener pure enjoyment while still providing Christian insight and guidance.

Peg is the musical brains of the two. While researching for hours at a time to get the right music for the show, she also represents the serious side of life while hitting some tough issues head on.

Need a Word with Lynette M. Johns on Big Media USA.

Theme: Christian teaching.

Guest Profile: People moving in the Kingdom. I look for experience in the subject I'm presenting and that they are serious about the show. Approach me with a realness. Don't lie and scheme.

Guest from Hell: A person who refuses to stay in sync with the host.

Contact: lynettejohnsministries@gmail; 951-858-7224; lynettejohnsministries.org; Lynette Johns. Best method: E-mail. No response? Send the e-mail once more.

Invited Back:? If there is a need to bring them back on.

Bio of Lynette Johns: Prophetess is her position, preaching is her call, praying is her passion and loving souls into deliverance is her mission. Lynette is a woman of obedience, freedom, faith, and power! She is a soldier skilled in warfare against demonic forces and witchcraft. She has been committed and dedicated to God and in service for 30 years.

Wife and mother of five, ranging in age from 21–10, Lynette believes in God's order, "God first, family, then career."

The Steve Duignan Show with Steve Duignan on KSFA AM950 in Fort Smith, Arkansas.

Theme: Talk radio for Christians.

Guest Profile: All topics relating to Christianity. Passionate, well-motivated people make the best guests, regardless of their training and expertise. If they want to get their message our, we want to talk with them. As a guest, the most important thing is to enjoy yourself. When you do, there are overtones and intangibles that shine brightly ... to the host and the audience. I once interviewed Peter Marshall on his American history book *The Light and the Glory* (Revell 1980). His familiarity with the material and relaxed conversational style made my job very enjoyable. His responses were well paced, properly timed, and ended with obvious phrasing that let me know he had finished the thought. We talked for an hour, but it seemed like five minutes. For our goals of informing and encouraging Christians, it helps if they have been interviewed before, but it is not necessary. The message they present is the centerpiece of the interview.

Guest from Hell: The "feast or famine" guests are the worst. If you can't get another question or comment in edgewise, it's bad. Worse, however, is when their only answers are "yes" or "no" (followed by silence).

Contact: steve@talktosteve.com; 479-646-6700; http://www.talktosteve.com; Steve Duignan (pron. DEHG-nuhn), host and producer. Best method: I respond best to e-mails with a short pitch, limited bio/credential info, and any limitations on availability (time-frame). No response? With the quantity of e-mails, it is easy to overlook or completely miss e-mails. I recommend sending three, spaced three to five days apart.

Invited Back? It is generally based on the value of their story and if they communicated well.

Bio of Steve Duignan: From both Irish and Pilgrim immigrant stock, Steve is originally from the St. Louis, Missouri, area. The year he entered Southern Illinois University he heard the clarion call of radio. During his college years, Steve worked full time for area radio stations including a position as overnight news editor for CBS-owned KMOX in St. Louis, arguably the most successful radio station of all time.

After marrying Joyce, the couple moved to Western Wisconsin where Steve helped design, build, and run WWIB, the area's first Christian radio station. So began a life in Christian broadcasting. His show began in 1997.

Steve and Joyce have two grown children and have lived in Western Arkansas since 1980.

This Gospel of the Kingdom with Pastor Tim (Zimmerman) on AM Christian Radio Stations: KXKS, Albuquerque, NM, WYYC, York/Harrisburg/Lancaster PA, WITK, Wilkes Barre/Scranton PA, WSKY Asheville NC, WELP, Greenville SC, WLMR,

Chattanooga TN, KLNG, Omaha Neb. and *I Saw The Light Ministries* on BlogTalkRadio, http://www.blogtalkradio.com/isawthelight

Theme: Religion, Bible, God and world events.

Guest Profiles: Authors, pastors, ministers. I am interested in guests that bring an intelligent conversation with common interest and agreement. I desire guests that do not wish to sell a product. I want to know their past Interview experiences, credentials, and how they feel about the topic to be discussed.

Guest from Hell: It is displeasing if a potential guest states their beliefs one way before the show and then preaches something else on or after the show.

Contact: timcar@bellsouth.net; 423-581-5932; http://www.isawthelightministries.com; http://blogtalkradio.com/isawthelight; Pastor Tim (Zimmerman). Best method: Call or e-mail with truth and honesty about WHY they want to be on the broadcast. No response? They may e-mail me.

Invited Back? Whether they actually bring something to the table that was worth the hearing.

Guest Comment: "Being an 'End Time' writer I was happy to be interviewed on *I Saw The Light Ministries* and be able to talk about the world events and how they are unfolding before ours eyes." — Dr. Alfred Adams, author of *Nearing Midnight* (Xlibris Publishing 2004), http://www.nearingmidnight.com

Bio of Pastor Tim Zimmerman: Pastor Tim was born in Morristown, TN, where is pastor of Ecclesia Theos. He spent many years in North Carolina and Pennsylvania, always on the pursuit of truth behind the curtains.

WJEW Talk Hour with various Temple Israel Teen DJs, on WJEW, http://www.wjew.net

Theme: Jewish topics for young people.

Guest Profile: Recording artists, playwrights, media personalities, Jewish figures, involved Temple young people. Name recognition that will make young people want to tune in. Credentials are great. We also interview young leaders at our temple as a great way to get them more involved.

Guest from Hell: No such thing. Every person on the planet has a fascinating story if you really listen for it.

Contact: msmolash@temple-israel.org; 248-661-5700; http://www.wjew.net; Cantor Michael Smolash. Best method: E-mail. As to calling with a pitch, e-mailing a bio or sending a press kit, any approach is fine. No response? Polite persistence is welcome by e-mail or phone. Everyone is busy and needs an extra nudge sometimes.

Invited Back? If the interview gets good ratings in terms of low listener drop off on the internet.

Bio of Michael Smolash: Michael is thrilled to be the cantor of Temple Israel in West Bloomfield, Michigan, which, at 13,000 congregants, is the largest Reform synagogue in the world. He arrived after having served for seven years as Chazzan Sheini at Holy Blossom Temple in Toronto, while working concurrently in musical theatre. The cantor received his Bachelor's Degree with great distinction from Concordia University's voice department. He is a full member of the American Conference of Cantors, and the first Canadian to have completed the ACC's certification program. He serves as the president of the Michigan Board of Cantors. He also created WJEW: the first twenty-four hour synagogue Internet radio station, which is run by Teens at Temple Israel, and has listeners in over 20 countries.

On the concert stage, Cantor Smolash is a sought after artist both for new commissions and gala musical events. He is also a stage actor, having starred in such roles as Sparky in *Forever Plaid*, Billy Lawlor in *Forty Second Street*, and Matt in *The Fantasticks*. Cantor Smolash's most recent theatre gig was *The Producers* in Toronto, where he covered the lead role of Leo Bloom, as well as those of the entire male cast of singers, actors and dancers.

Cantor Smolash and his wife, Jen Green, a practicing naturopathic doctor, have a daughter, Ayla Miriam.

Science

Biota Live with Tom Barbalet (podcast).

Theme: Artificial life — simulated biological environments through software, hardware or biological agents — past, present and future.

Guest Profile: Academics, developers, philosophers, users. Someone who can speak with passion on the subject of artificial life or a related field. A user of artificial life who has a particularly interesting take or story to tell is always applicable too. Almost all the guests I have interviewed to date have online examples or introductory/biographical text online. If they are active academics or developers of note, they have probably spoken in front of small-large crowds and thus should be reasonable interviewees.

Guest from Hell: Someone who can't speak for more than a couple of words or someone who says um excessively. Aggressive or angry guests are difficult too.

Contact: tom@nobleape.com; withheld upon request; http://www.biota.org/podcast/; Tom Barbalet. Best method: E-mail only. A relatively brief introductory e-mail with some link to their work or additional information. No response? This will never happen. I'm prompt on e-mail.

Invited Back? If we run out of time or if they are doing something exciting or topical in the next six months.

Bio of Tom Barbalet: Tom is the creator of *Noble Ape*, editor of Biota.org and co-chair of the IGDA Intellectual Property Rights SIG.

Born in Australia, he developed a series of interpreters, compilers, anti-viral programs and the Schmuck Quest series of graphics/text adventure games in the late 1980s and early 1990s.

In June 1996, as an undergraduate, Tom put a collection of his landscape viewing and cognitive simulation demo programs together and created the artificial life development Noble Ape (originally called the Nervana Project)—which continues to this day.

He lives with his wife in Las Vegas.

Full bio at http://en.wikipedia.org/wiki/Tom_Barbalet

The Groks Science Show with Charles Lee and Frank Ling on WHPK 88.5 in Chicago and syndicated nationwide.

Theme: Science and technology.

Guest Profile: Scientists, technologists, authors, entrepreneurs. We look for someone passionate about their subject. Credentials are important.

Guest from Hell: The person who gives one word answers to all questions. Verbosity and a sense of humor are much appreciated.

Contact: groks@hotmail.com; 773-702-8289; http://www.groks.net; Charles Lee or Frank Ling. Best method: E-mail. A press kit or synopsis of a book, if applicable. No response? Please try e-mailing again. Sometimes communication gets lost in the shuffle. Call as a last resort.

Invited Back? We rarely repeat guests on the show. However, if they have something new to talk about, we may rebook an interview.

Bios of Dr. Charles Lee and Dr. Frank Ling: Charles earned his Ph.D. in neurobiology from the Department of Molecular and Cell Biology, and Frank earned his Ph.D. in chemistry from the Department of Chemistry at U.C. Berkeley. Both Charles and Frank received their undergraduate degrees from the California Institute of Technology.

Infinite Consciousness with Eva Herr on BBS Radio, http://www.BBSRadio.com

Theme: Cutting edge science related to human consciousness, alternative energy, world peace and alternative medicine.

Guest Profile: Scientists, typically physicists, biologists, psychologists, physicians and engineers. I look for an open minded individual who looks at the big picture, combined with credible, factual information. I want, in advance, a copy of their curriculum vitae and a copy of the book, paper or movie we are to discuss.

Guest from Hell: LOL, that's an easy one. 1) A highly opinionated guest who has not really done his homework. In other words, my show is designed to educate my listeners and if someone comes on the show with information that is more "opinion" than fact, it will come out in the interview because I try to stay on top of the topics on which I interview; and 2) a guest that I have to pull information from. It's hard when you have a guest answer a question and then just sits there in silence. They obviously have a lot to say on a topic or I would not have invited them on my show.... Say Something.

Contact: evaherr@gmail.com; 404-513-2895; http://www.bbsradio.com/bbc/infinite_consciousness.php; Eva Herr. Best method: Send me an e-mail with a brief synopsis of the topic you wish to discuss. Make sure it fits the general theme of my show. My show is a science/medicine based show and people who send books that are off topic are wasting their resources if they don't fit the scope of the show. No response? If your topic falls within the scope of my show, please e-mail me again. If you want to get on a show, it is important to select shows that carry your material; otherwise you may not get a response.

Invited Back? How well they presented on my show, i.e., the quality of their presentation about the work they are doing.

Guest Comment: "Thank you so much for the opportunity to be interviewed on your show. You have a wonderful interviewing style which is a pleasure!"— Dr. Shoshanna Bennett, post-partum depression authority, http://www.drshosh.com

Listener Comment: "Eva, it is a real pleasure to listen to your interviews. The changes in me and my life are immense. You and your work are a blessing to us all."—Anna

Bio of Eva Herr: Eva Herr is a paralegal and expert witness in the area of civil litigation. She is also a highly respected medical intuitive, author of *Agape: The Intent of the Soul* (New Freedom Press 2005). She has a deep understanding of the science behind consciousness, and is revered amongst today's most forward thinkers.

Her radio show gives her an opportunity to compare notes with the likes of Amit Goswami, William Tiller, Dean Radin, Henry Stapp, Stanislov Grof, Norm Shealy, Ervin Laszlo, Charles Tart, Brenda Dunne/Robert Jahn and Fred Alan Wolf among others.

Planetary Radio with Mat Kaplan, aired on about 110 public stations, along with XM Satellite Radio — reaching all of North America and Stockholm.

Theme: Space exploration.

Guest Profile: Astronomers and other space scientists, mission engineers, astronauts, non-fiction writer about space topics, science fiction writers, space agency officials, sometimes actors and filmmakers. Two popular guests have been Hugo and Nebula award-winning author Kim Stanley Robinson, and Alan Stern, associate administrator at NASA and head of the New Horizons mission to Pluto. Someone who is connected to an ongoing or recent development in space exploration who knows how important it is to communicate their passion to intelligent laypeople. Even better if they have a sense of humor and fun regarding their work. Also, visionaries in the arts who are well-grounded in real space science. (Sometimes do special event coverage.) How they are connected with a project or effort to be discussed. If foreign, relatively good English skills. An updated online bio that is relatively easy to find.

Guest from Hell: Arrogant, just the facts, no sense of magic and excitement about their work. No UFOlogists, alien abductees, astrologers, or people who know exactly how Einstein was wrong about everything.

Contact: kaplanmr@earthlink.net or mrk@planetary.org; 562-760-4152 (cell) 626-793-5100 (The Planetary Society, but I'm not there much); http://planetary.org/radio; Mat Kaplan, host and producer. Best method: Generally not thrilled with phone calls. E-mailed pitches are welcome, especially if they contain links to a site or sites that will tell me more. Press kit is okay. (I find most of my guests.) No response? E-mail.

Invited Back? New developments in project or a new project that is intriguing, along with ability to hold up their end of an interesting conversation.

Bio of Mat Kaplan: Mat was just 17 when he got his first job in broadcasting. He has reported on space exploration for more than 30 years, beginning at his college radio station. It wasn't until *Planetary Radio* that he was able to combine his love of space exploration with the fun and excitement of a regular series.

A Planetary Society staff member for seven years, he lives in Long Beach, California, with his wife and daughters, and also works as a technology and media manager for a local university. His extensive background in journalism has ranged from public radio reporter covering the political conventions to movie reviewer for an international magazine. One or two people may even remember him as a correspondent for a couple of pioneering national TV series about computers.

This Week in Science with Kirsten Sanford and Justin Jackson on KDVS 90.3 FM, Davis, CA, CJUM 101.5 FM, Winnipeg, Manitoba, Canada, Internet Partnership Radio, and podcast internationally.

Theme: Science news and discussion.

Guest Profile: Usually scientists, but we also invite science fiction authors and science writers onto the program. I look for people who are doing interesting research, or are writing about interesting scientific subjects. Also, they should also have a radio-friendly voice, and be able to talk about their subject in a non-academic manner. I usually look to see if they have ever done interviews before, but that isn't something I think is necessary for inviting them onto the show. The most important thing to know is that they know their subject backward and forward, that they are experts on the subject I'm inviting them to talk about.

Guest from Hell: To me a guest from hell is someone who never stops talking long enough for me to get a word in edgewise, or who has a thick accent that I can't understand, or who is so pedantic as to make a really interesting subject seem boring.

Contact: kirsten@thisweekinscience.com; 415-948-3589; http://www.thisweekinscience.com; http://www.kirstensanford.com; http://www.kirstensanford.com/kirsten_sanford.html; Kirsten Sanford. Best method: E-mail followed by phone. I appreciate pitches or bios sent to me by e-mail. If I am interested, I will get back to the agent. Don't call me. I will just ask you to send me an e-mail. No response? Definitely, e-mail me again. My e-mail inbox is a bottomless pit that things get lost in if I am not careful.

Invited Back? If the interview went well, I'm more likely to invite someone back, but other than that it depends on what topics seem to require revisiting, the timeliness of a topic. For example, we talk about the Large Hadron Collider a lot, and recently interviewed someone involved in its production. We will probably invite them on again when the LHC comes on line in 2008.

Guest Comments: "I had a lot of fun...! Time just flew by! ... Even knowing your show so well now, I still was very impressed with your questions and examples. Either you both are extremely well-prepared or extremely smart or both! And that's no flattery, just saying what I feel"—Dr. Bjorn Brembs

"Thanks for having me on the show, I enjoyed it!"—Dr. Martin Amos

Bio of Kirsten Sanford: Kirsten has been interested in science for as long as she can remember, but it was somewhere in the middle of graduate school that she realized she didn't want to be a scientist for the rest of her life. Realizing that she was good at teaching and that her experience in science research enabled her to help others understand it, she decided to become a science journalist and media personality, and in doing so infiltrate print, broadcast, and internet mediums with science.

In 1999, Kirsten started her radio show with a good friend, who has since moved on. In 2006, she worked at WNBC-TV in NYC as a producer for the medical/health reporter, Dr. Max Gomez. "TV is quite a different world from radio, but my whistle is whetted," she says. "I'm definitely going to pursue more science television programming employment options in the future. I started this blog this year as well so that I could practice and sharpen my writing skills, and share my thoughts with others."

Kirsten received her Ph.D. in physiology with an emphasis in neurophysiology in December of 2006 from UC Davis, with her area of specialization avian leaning and memory. Her dissertation topic was on spatial memory in non-storing songbirds. "Don't tell me any jokes about bird brains, please," she says. "I have heard them all."

X-Squared Radio with Brooks A. Agnew, Ph.D. on BBSRadio.com and Steeleyeradio network.

Theme: Scientific talk radio of the mysteries of the universe and of the earth.

Guest Profile: Patented commercial scientist with three top-selling books and multiple films whose claim to fame is his intense desire to explore the Earth and interview the best guests on leading scientific issues of the day. Strong science or evidence and some kind of publication such as a book, a DVD, or a patented technology that might open the mind of a listener. We look for a great conversation with the author of a new idea or discovery.

We look for content. Some of the most brilliant minds on Earth could not last five minutes with a professional broadcaster, but we are scientists in interviewing scientists. We like to read the book and make out about 90 questions to ask in 180 minutes that will engage the listener in an education that will prove to them that their potential is unlimited. After more than 150 guests, we have not had a dull interview from a single one.

Guest from Hell: That's easy. A guest from hell is one who has stolen an idea, or who has represented something to be true that is phony or fiction. The second type is one who converts your program into one huge infomercial.

Contact: bagnew@x2-radio.com; 270-875-3777; http://www.x2-radio.com; Brooks A. Agnew. Best method: Our listeners have sent us 70 percent of our guests. They hear them somewhere or know their book or something, and then we call them up and ask them to come on the program. We research the latest science news and breakthroughs and try to get the actual scientist to come on the program and tell about it. Mailing us a book is a great way to get on the program, but we are very tight on our genre. We don't do ghosts and we don't do conspiracy theories as a theme. We focus on a positive and completely open message of growth and trust in science. No response? We respond within 12 hours of any e-mail. We have given out perhaps 150 free subscriptions to listeners who were offended that we started charging for archives. We value them much more as a listener than we do as a source of financial support.

Invited Back? We invite guests back when they publish something new, or come out with a new film. We cover a story so well in three hours there is nothing left to tell of their ideas when we are done, unless they generate something new.

Listener Comment: "In my humble opinion, I think Dr. Brooks Agnew's program has added a lot to human knowledge since the dawning of modern day man. I hope to hear more through BBS radio.

"I can't get enough information about our past history as I have gotten from his programming.

"Thanks for moving us forward into the pass."— Kymond Gee

Bio of Brooks Agnew: Brooks is a Renaissance man: scientist, engineer, teacher, musician, author, public speaker, earth explorer and champion of discovery and peace. His books tell the story of creation in great detail and coordination between nearly every discipline. His processes and engineering have saved or generated more than ten thousand jobs. His designs are operating to bring us a continuous flow of knowledge from two planets and the space in between. He continues to explore the Earth and will yet reveal many things about our world that no scientist has yet seen.

Science Fiction

SyFy Radio with Michael Hinman on Blog Talk Radio, www.blogtalkradio.com/syfyradio

Theme: Science-fiction television/movie entertainment news and comment.

Guest Profile: Sci-fi writers, journalists, television producers, actors, famous names in science-fiction. Using the 10 years we've been covering the Web, we like to try and bring in television writers, producers and actors, but we also want to create a forum for other entertainment journalists, as a way that can cross-promote both the show and their site.

Basically, the entertainment value that I alluded to before, and also what kind of new information they could provide in an on-air environment that they couldn't provide in print. The first official guest was Daniel Malen, who runs the popular *TV Addict* (http://www.thetvaddict.com). A recent guest was Eugene W. Roddenberry, son of the late "Star Trek" creator Gene Roddenberry, who runs http://www.roddenberry.com

Guest from Hell: One who really has nothing interesting or entertaining to offer. It's one thing to be knowledgeable, but it's more important to be entertaining and engaging. Knowledge is good for books and print, but entertainment is almost required to do something audio or visual.

Contact: mhinman@syfyportal.com; 813-245-5371; http://www.syfyportal.com; Michael Hinman. Best method: Best way is to drop me an e-mail on what exactly they or their client does, and what they would like to talk about in our forum. No response? They should try to e-mail again. Usually, if I don't respond, it's because the e-mail may have been accidentally misfiled. I respond to all e-mail.

Invited Back? First of all, if they want to come back. But it is important to be on-time, to not talk over the host, to be engaging with the audience, and to be able to wrap up when it's time for their segment to end.

Bio of Michael Hinman: Michael started *SyFy Portal* in 1998 as a science-fiction fantasy news and rumors site, and it's practically followed that same format ever since. "We are considered a 'glorified fan site' as we are independent of any other network or major media outlet, but at the same time provide quality that rivals them, thanks to the fact that myself and key members of our staff are professional journalists outside the site, or have been trained directly by me," says Michael. "At the same time, however, I do not remove myself from our readership (despite the ability to do so), and I'm always accessible to each and every one of the more than 12,000 daily unique visitors the site receives, and the radio show is more of an extension of that.

Michael is a business newspaper journalist in Tampa, Fla., and has worked in radio off and on since 1993.

Self Help

"Human beings are magnificent creations. Together we will find the Magnificent You."— From Brad Richard's mission statement

Alivewiredu Talk Radio Show with Brad Richard on Blog Talk Radio, http://www.blogtalkradio.com/alivewiredu

Theme: Self help/self improvement/personal growth.

Guest Profile: Open—format/appropriate. A guest that has a positive message to share and/or a life experience that could benefit others. Want to know their background, book titles, experiences, successes and failures.

Guest from Hell: A guest who has not lived their own advice or one who has not followed their own advice.

Contact: brad@bradrichard.com; 715-808-0130; http://www.bradrichard.com/radio; Brad Richard. Best method: E-mailing a bio, press kit, photos, book copy for review. No response? Call me.

Invited Back? New information and/or new material to cover of a benefit to my listeners.

Guest Comment: "Thank you so very much for a very enjoyable discussion. I've been enjoying your show and was honored to be a part of it today. I'll be tuning in regularly."—Lillian Brummet, author, http://www.sunshinecable.com/~drumit

Bio of Brad Richard: Brad has worked in various public service industries, including: food and beverage, performing arts, entertainment and public speaking. Brad's motivation for helping and teaching people stems from him being a survivor of childhood abuse and wanting to help others deal with their fears, growth, learning and personal development.

His mission statement is: I have committed to myself to help and teach people through seminars/workshops, radio and TV shows to look within themselves and discover their purpose, light and passion. Human beings are magnificent creations. Together we will find the Magnificent You.

At Home with Cheryll Gillespie on CJOB-Winnipeg, CHED-Edmonton, QR-Calgary broadcast on the Corus Radio Network. Cheryll also hosts *Interiors by Cheryll,* airing in over 20 markets, www.cjob.com, www.630ched.com

Theme: Lifestyle.

Guest Profile: Everyone from Hugh Hefner to Jane Seymour to anti-aging doctors. Knowledge, information that makes life better, enthusiastic and passionate about their area of expertise. Want their past interview experiences, credential, sound of their voice, ... plus web address and press materials, including preview copies of books.

Guest from Hell: Someone who really doesn't care whether they are there or not, a guest that does not even take the time to find a little bit out about the show before the interview, too dry, no energy, some one who wants to blatantly plug a product, as opposed to sharing general information.

Contact: cheryllgillespie@shaw.ca; 250-864-3409; http://www.cheryllgillespie.com; Cheryll. Best method: E-mail a bio and then forward press kit upon request. No response? Resend the e-mail.

Invited Back? Quality of the interview, listener response.

Bio of Cheryll Gillespie: Canada's design diva, Cheryll is famous for her creative verve and magnetic approach to fashion.

Her star is rising in the enormously popular lifestyle genre of television, radio, print, and personal appearances. Cheryll is also host of CNBC TV's, "Let's Shop," which also airs on Wealth TV in America, CTV Travel and OUTtv in Canada, FOX Japan and xclusive TV in Latin America.

She has been a weekly home trends reporter on Calgary's CFCN's "Friday News," has anchored a weekly series for Access Television and has appeared in numerous newscasts, talk shows, and television commercials.

Her nationally syndicated columns on design and décor are published extensively throughout North America, including *The Toronto Star* as well as online at http://www.canoe.ca and yahoo.ca

The BottomLine with Larry Arnette on 88.3 WAIF-FM in Cincinnati, Ohio broadcasting to Cincinnati and Northern, KY, telecast twice weekly on the Time Warner Cable system in Cincinnati.

Theme: Crime, current events, the media, relationships with a cut to the chase perspective and a unique blend of blunt truth and wit. I'm quite political but a pragmatist who sees through the never ending BS that comes from both political parties. Much of the American electorate fall for the same con and phony sense of purpose from politicians whose primary concern is for money and reelection.

Guest profile: Authors, politicians, political activists, relationship experts. I prefer non-fiction and topics that reflect many of the above topics talked about on my show. Passionate person with personality who can communicate in brief, concise sentences and viewpoints.

Guest from Hell: A person who rambles on or responds in one word answers, speaks too low with no enthusiasm for the topic.

Contact: larrysbottomline@aol.com; 513-631-7980; Larry Arnette. Best method: Preferably by e-mail, with a brief synopsis of person and their topic and a bit of a bio. No response? Call or e-mail.

Invited Back? A continuing interest in topic, their enthusiasm on the air and when they are easy to reach and book.

Bio of Larry Arnette: Larry began in radio hosting the original version of his show on an AM station, late night in Los Angeles; returned to Cincinnati in 1993 and has been hosting his show here since that time. His primary career is in the cable TV industry, where he also produced/hosted a few TV shows as well as working in commercial sales/marketing.

The Brad Neufeld Show with Brad Neufeld on Grapevine Talk Radio Network http://www.grapevineradio.com

Theme: Winning habits radio — overcoming the challenges of life.

Guest Profile: Any person who has overcome a personal challenge and can share their experiences about their challenge in a somewhat passionate way (i.e., how they conquered the challenge, what can others do to overcome a similar challenge, etc.). A person with a true desire to share their story with the world. A person who has a passion to help others.

Mostly, I like to know the approach the person took to discover the challenge, and then the steps that were taken to come to the solution. The more detail the better. I usually like to have a casual phone conversation with the person prior to the radio interview. In this interview I am looking more for "How should we approach and present the subject matter?" than "Is this person the perfect guest?" I also enjoy working with "first time" guests as well. The show is dedicated to "Overcoming the Challenges of Life" and the fear of public speaking is one of those challenges I like to help people with.

Guest from Hell: A person who doesn't give very much detail or gives short answers to the questions asked. When I have a guest on, I like them to do most of the talking. It's been my experience that the audience likes to hear the views and opinions of the guest. When short, low content answers are given, the guest's credibility is lost and then I have to work extra hard to help restore it. I prefer it when the guest shines and the audience comes away feeling like the guest is the expert in their chosen subject.

Contact: bradjneufeld@msn.com; Office: 435-843-5698 Mobile: 435-830-6945; http://www.bradjneufeld.com and http://www.affinityeducationservices.com. Best method: E-mail or phone. No sales pitches, please. Get to the point of what you want to present and what your desired outcome is for the interview (even if it's just "I want to share my story and see what happens"). I am very much a "people person" and I want to help the guests of my show get their message out to the world anyway I can. Sending me a copy of your book, e-mailing me a bio and/or sending a press kit are all great ways to approach me. No response? I apologize for putting this responsibility on my potential guests; however, keep e-mailing me until I do respond. Even if it's every day. Never think that you are being a nuisance. I get busy from time to time (as we all do), and may be a little slow in responding. I do receive all of your e-mails and I welcome them. I assure you that I will get back to you as soon as possible.

Invited Back? I pretty much leave this up to the guest. If they want to come back onto the show and they have made new strides, discovered new methods of working with their chosen subject matter or just want to give a "progress report," I am open to it.

Bio of Brad J. Neufeld: Brad is the founder and CEO of Affinity Education Services and the developer of the Positive Self-Management Learning System. http://www.affinityeducationservices.com. He has over 20 years of experience in assisting others with overcoming personal challenges and helping them succeed with their own personal goals and desires. His basic belief is that all human beings possess talents and passions, yet few ever discover what they are truly capable of during their lifetime. Brad's passion is to provide effective means for individuals to discover their own self-worth, talents and value, and create for themselves success filled lives, which, in turn, will enable them to be responsible adults, effective parents, and major contributors in society.

Dedicating much of his time and energies to working with youth, particularly "At Risk" youth, Brad played a major role in the creation of Youth Visions, a non-profit organization dedicated to providing education, tools, skills and any other resources necessary for a youth to have success regardless of their backgrounds or current circumstances. http://www.ouryouthvisions.org

Brad also has many years of experience in sales and business, which has used in the development of effective methods for coaching and training for adults.

Bright Spot! with Dot Blum on Fridays 3–4 PM, EST on AM 1620, Sandy Springs, GA, and http://www.radiosandysprings.com

Theme: Focusing on the positive.

Guest Profile: Artists, non profits, musicians, new business models, new ideas). People who educate, entertain and enrich our lives. Someone who focuses on the positive or talks about their passions. Sound of their voice and how they express their passions.

Guest from Hell: Someone who does not enunciate clearly or who has no personality and passion.

Contact: DotBlum79@mindspring.com; h: 770-435-7191; c 404-210-4143; http://www.radiosandysprings.com; Dot Blum. Best method: E-mail. No response? If I do not respond within a week, please feel free to call me. I travel a bit so I might not respond very quickly periodically.

Invited Back? If they entertain and enrich our lives and if the listeners respond to them.

Guest Comments: "I'm so glad our paths crossed,

and delighted to have met you. You do a bang-up job interviewing (my mother's word!), and I take my hat off to you for doing it every week. I also appreciate your making me look good.

"And if I can ever help remove a thorn from your paw, please let me know." — Lynne Alpern, writer and comedian

"You made it all so easy. What a good time I had with you. I look forward to having you come and see what we are doing. Please call me when next you have time to come into town and have an hour with us and then maybe lunch." — Anita Beaty, director, Taskforce for the Homeless

Bio of Dot Blum: Dot's expertise includes marketing, advertising, fundraising and consulting. Her broadcasting career began at WQXI AM/FM (previously 94Q/now Star 94). She was a founding member of FunDraisers, a group of 40 volunteers, who perform good deeds for local charities, a founding member of Say-So, a conversation salon, and was instrumental in the formation of a neighborhood watch in her own community.

Dot is an artist, whose hobbies include American Indian drumming, reading energy, travel, listening to music, walking her dog, entertaining family and friends with stories and laughing gleefully. Married to former broadcast executive, Jerry Blum, parent to four stepsons, and 6 grandchildren, a Sandy Springs resident for 20 years, she now resides in Smyrna, Georgia.

Celebrating Your Potential with Revvell P. Revati on Fresh Talk Radio, http://www.CelebratingYourPotential.com (the show is taped weekly so it can be archived and listened to 24/7/365). Revvel also has a podcast at http://podcast.TheBookCrawler.com just for authors, publishers, publicists ... anyone having anything to do with books.

Theme: How did the guest get from where they were to where they are (mostly).

Guest Profile: Mostly authors who write books on health, healing, motivation ... and raw foods. Their topic, book popularity, our connection and their willingness to actually talk. What their database is. As this is not like AM/FM radio, I (or, my sponsors) pay for everything so a posting on their site and a blast to their database means a lot.

Guest from Hell: One who gives one-word answers and counters everything I ask — have had VERY good rapport with everyone I've had on so far.

Contact: Revvell@CelebratingYourPotential.com, put "interview" in the subject line; 818-824-4422; http://www.CelebratingYourPotential.com; http://www.bigmediausa.com/stationhome.asp?stid=10; Revvell. Best method: Phone because it may be better to schedule without going back and forth too much. Mostly I get people from books I've read; books they send me (after an e-mail/phone exchange) or word-of-mouth; openings I've been to; book-signing, etc. No response? A call is better. I may have flagged their e-mails and still not gotten back with them.

Invited Back? Their attitude — are they fun? Informative? lively? congenial?

She has a website where she features the authors she interviews at http://www.TheBookCrawler.com

Guest Comments: "My experience being interviewed by you was excellent. Your style of interacting allowed me to be fully expressive, honest and open about matters in ways I rarely am." — Herb Goldberg, Ph.D., licensed psychologist and author of *What Men Still Don't Know About Women, Relationships and Love* (Barricade Books 2007)

"Being a guest on your show today was a blast. Our discussion targeted all the messages I wanted to deliver. I appreciated your ability to ask great questions." — Arlene Rosenberg, Leading Achievers, http://www.leadingachievers.com, award-winning finalist, Best Books 2006 National Book Awards for *Say It, See It, Be It: How Visions and Affirmations Will Change Your Life* (Book Marketing Solutions 2006)

Bio of Revvell P. Revati: Revvell is author of *Revvellutionize Your Life in 30 Days — A Self-Empowering Playbook* and *Smoothies and Smoozies for Life*, both published in 2006 by Revvellations Publishing. On her radio program, she takes guests into realms they usually don't go in a very relaxed and informal manner eliciting responses beneficial to her listeners so they can realize their own potential.

Revvell is also a seminar and workshop leader sharing her smoothies with the elderly in residential care facilities; going to schools and speaking on suicide and choices; and also going to women's groups asking the question: "Who Would You be if Society Had Not Interfered?"

You can also hear Revvell on her other online radio show at: http://rawcast.rawkinradio.com/

Conscious Discussions with Lillian Brummet (occasionally joined by her husband Dave, who has co-hosted a few shows as his schedule allows) on Blog Talk Radio http://www.blogtalkradio.com/consciousdiscussions, airing Tuesday at 10 AM (PT). Lillian and Dave also host Authors Read at www.blogtalkradio.com/authorsread.

Theme: Focuses on inspiring listeners to become more proactive in their daily lives by sharing real-life, positive stories. Discussions vary between the world of writing, volunteer community involvement, waste management and reduction alternatives (composting, refuse/recycle/reuse/reduce), alternatives for consumers and sustainable business practices. With the varied topics and guests on the show listeners will realize their value as individuals and become more aware of the fact that they can make a real and visible difference. The show is recorded live, commercial free and archived.

Guest Profile: Guests range from environmentalists, authors, volunteers and water conservationists to book promotion experts; the guests are spoken to live from across the globe — including West Africa, Canada, the U.S. and the U.K. We want someone who is passionate about what they do and will inspire our listeners to become more proactive in their own lives, while discussing an important issue. We do not require past experience or samples of previous interviews, although most hosts prefer guests who have some experience. People who want to appear on our show as a featured guest simply query us and explain how their cause, book, topic or endeavor fits in with the focus of our show. If they are passionate and we feel strongly about their message then we welcome them to appear on *Conscious Discussions*. After all, our show is not about finger pointing, but more saluting those individuals making positive changes we all want to see in this world. We want to know why our audience would find them interesting as guests.

Featured guest application is as simple as clicking on the "contact us" button on http://www.sunshinecable.com/~drumit/conscious.html and sending us your query application today.

Guest from Hell: One who over-talks the host and doesn't leave room for the host to respond. Clearing of throats, typing on a keyboard and excessive background noise during an interview are all disruptive. It is also offensive to listeners when a guest breathes into the phone or has the phone so close to their mouth that "f's," "p's," "s's" and "sh's" sounds become offensive and abrasive.

Contact: drumit@shaw.com; http://www.sunshinecable.com/~drumit; http://www.brummet.ca; http://blog.myspace.com/canadianauthor; http://www.myspace.com/canadianauthor; Lillian Brummet. Best method: Bios and press releases are nice, but not necessary. Because our time is very limited, we prefer to hear from them in their words why they should be on our show and refer us to their website — and this should be where their bio, credentials, awards, press releases, present endeavors and so forth would be available for us to browse. Authors who are looking to query a program director or the host of a radio show should be aware of the fact that sending attachments along with query letters is considered bad etiquette. No response? Don't e-mail or call. We always respond even if it is to say "no thanks." However, if the person has experienced technical glitches with their Internet server or computer and is worried the e-mail did not go through — they can write and explain this, and we would understand that. When someone writes asking us to promote them or writes a query letter in an unprofessional manor, we are unlikely to respond in a positive way. Guests should be aware what their own time zone is and not pester the host with questions like how long the show is when that information is usually available on the program's website and in the information package that approved guests receive. If the applicant hasn't listened to the program or researched the site, it shows.

Invited Back? We have invited guests to appear again in future shows for three reasons. First, they were very passionate about their topic and inspired enthusiasm in our listeners and us. Secondly, if the show seems to end too quickly and we feel that they could have covered more information than they were able to during that first interview. Finally, the company or individual may have created a new product or endeavor that would be of added interest to our listeners.

Guest Comment: "Thank you — what a great show and I am going to put the word out about your radio program ... we have about 700,000 people on our opt-in list! ... And thank you for allowing me to offer my solution to the world!" — Spencer T. Brown, founder and inventor; owner of http://www.EarthFriendlyMoving.com

Bios of Dave and Lillian Brummet: Award winning authors Dave and Lillian have been writing professionally since 1999 and have published three books: *Purple Snowflake Marketing — How to Make Your Book Stand Out in a Crowd* (2007; e-book) shows authors how to create an effective, frugal marketing plan and includes more than 500 live links for authors to use immediately simply with a click of the mouse; *Trash Talk — An Inspirational Guide to Saving Time and Money through Better Waste and Resource Management* (PublishAmerica 2004) shows readers how they can save money while making their community become a more prosperous, attractive and healthier place to live; *Towards Understanding — A Collection of 120 Poems* (PublishAmerica 2005) depicts the healing process one goes through and the steps taken to get past the pain of a troubled upbringing and strive towards understanding of both purpose in life, and the value of it.

Lillian is a poet and a book reviewer, while Dave is a photographer, musician and lyricist. Together they have done numerous free-lance writing projects.

Conversations Live with Vicki St. Clair on KKNW, aired in the Pacific Northwest (from Seattle to Victoria and down to Olympia) ... also simultaneously streamed worldwide.

Theme: Conversations with people who have something worthwhile to share.

Guest Profile: Armchair conversations with guests whose work, expertise and life-experiences help to inspire, inform, and stimulate. We talk with authors, filmmakers, journalists; innovative leaders in the medical and business professions. And ordinary people, leading extraordinary lives. Guests must have personality, be good conversationalists, engage an audience, have past interview experiences and have a good speaking voice. And if they've written a non fiction book on a particular subject, they should have the credentials to back it up.

Guest from Hell: Someone who's dull and answers in monosyllables. People who don't know their own topic (it happens).

Contact: info@conversationslive.net; 253-302-3286; http://www.conversationslive.net; Vicki St. Clair. Best method: Send press kit, book, etc and follow up a week later. No response? E-mail.

Invited Back? Content and personality. But content is king.

Bio of Vicki St. Clair: After hosting *The Vicki St. Clair Interviews* for almost three years, Vick is now the executive producer and host of her current show.

Vicki is a professional writer, correspondent, and producer. She works in all media, including film and video, and has successfully created and managed an extensive range of commercial, editorial, and communications projects.

Vicki's strong business management background comes in useful every day. "Nothing you learn is ever wasted," she says to those who wonder how she got from banker to writer/producer/talk radio host. "The principles of business, communications, and customer service are basically the same no matter what kind of work you do. I'm just serving a different audience now ... and I love it."

In addition to her weekly KKNW broadcast, Vicki is currently writing a nonfiction book, and regularly consults on a wide-variety of editorial and communications projects.

The Creativity Salon with Neil Tepper, aired Thursday at 6 PM (ET) on 1620 AM, Sandy Springs, Ga. and streaming on the Internet at http://www.radiosandysprings.com

Theme: The creative arts and the art of living a creative life.

Guest Profile: Artists, business people, authors, anyone who is progressive-thinking and approaches their life with creativity and consciousness. In addition to them embodying the theme (see above), they should have energy and enthusiasm for their subject and be able to articulate it in simple, direct language. They should feel comfortable engaging in a conversation rather than just an interview.

Guest from Hell: One who mumbles, who answers questions in one or two words, who is always trying to sell something and who doesn't answer my questions fully.

Contact: neil@neiltepper.com; http://www.neiltepper.com; http://www.thelogicalcreative.com; 770-730-9990; Neil Tepper. Best method: E-mail. Best is to send current bio or press kit and then I'll speak with them on phone before booking them. No response? I'm fairly responsive, but if they don't hear, they should e-mail me again.

Invited Back? If I had a good time on the air with them and if there's more to say that we did not cover.

Bio of Neil Tepper: Neil is a former creative director with the Coca-Cola Company, Universal Television, and the 1996 Olympics. Since his corporate career, Neil has been a coach and consultant as well as a TV producer and award-winning songwriter and photographer.

Also known as "The Creativity Doctor." Neil's forthcoming book, *Open Your I's: 10 Steps to Unleashing Your Inner Creative Power*, helps people solve problems in new ways, overcome blocks that impede peak performance and tap into the source of creativity that flows within each of us. Neil believes that creativity is not just for artists and so dedicates his radio show to the creative arts and the art of living a creative life. In addition to interviewing people who embody that theme, each show offers prescriptions to help listeners unleash their own inner creative power.

The Daring Dreamers Showcase with Angela Treat Lyon, on http://www.IDareYouRadio.com

Theme: Dedicated to helping and supporting people who dare to live their dreams — through inspirational shows and the practical application of success principles, energy therapies and excellent products. The shows are intended to inspire, support and offer uncommon resources to daring women (and yes, you men too!) in business, as well as healers and EFTers and energy practitioners everywhere.

Guest Profile: Authors, psychologists, healers, EFT practitioners, coaches, artists, business experts. A good, hearty, upbeat (but not woo-woo or sappy) passion for life with a tendency to lots of belly-laughter. Strong understanding of how to make spiritual principles work in life. A strong voice and an ability to be concise, articulate and fairly fast-paced. Strong life-experiences that helped them be who they are today. An ability to go emotionally deep — happily — in an interview without collapsing. If they also have something we can do a JV or an affiliate set up with, they get an instant 20 percent increase in my interest rating — got to pay the bills.

Do they actually DO what they are teaching/coaching? Walk their talk on a daily basis? Have a good, sound, strong voice without being a loud bully? Who have they been on with before (if anyone — newbies welcome)? Finally, if they can provide inspiration for living the Dream, if they ARE living the Dream, I'm totally willing to check them out. They must have a website and e-mail connectability.

Guest from Hell: Anyone who talks incessantly without pausing for my questions or runs over or interrupts me; anyone who can't think on his feet, with lots of uhs and ahs and blah answers or tries to make me not believe in what I believe, rather than converse; anyone who is blindly in love with himself, talking non-stop, argues rather than discusses, pitches products/services/self non-stop. If they call and wake me up in the middle of the night because they haven't checked time zones, they get an instant 50 percent off the excitement rating (I live above my office so I hear the phones).

Contact: Lyon@IDareYouRadio.com; 808-261-0941 (in Kailua, Hawaii, where it's six hours earlier than Eastern time); http://IDareYouRadio.com; Angela Treat Lyon. Best method: E-mail first, then phone. They need to look at my website and see/feel if they are resonant with what's there. If they feel that they can offer value to my listeners, then they can either e-mail or call me. If they are referred by someone who knows me, that can help too. If they have an agent or rep, that person must be contactable too. Non-communication doesn't get it.

Absolutely no pitches during the show. I detest sell sell sell. I only want to hear about what they have to offer after I feel like I have a personal connection with them. I will not interview someone I don't like; I don't care how famous they are. Of course I will mention the website and products, but only one or two times during the show.

No Response? My assistant and I are human with inhuman schedules — translate: regularly swamped. So if we don't get back within four or five days, please e-mail again. You can call between 10 AM and 5 PM Hawaii time, but I do prefer e-mails first so I can look at your site before we talk so I can be somewhat intelligent about your work.

Invited Back? If we break the fun meter together, and/or provide lots of value, have fantastic products and/or services my listeners love, I'll want to invite them back.

Guest Comments: "Angela provided both a great starting point: a 4-question context for the interview as a whole. Then she easily and humorously went with the flow in ways that brought out both the best in me (it was fun!) and the stories and details that informed and entertained her listeners." — Rick Wilkes, emotional freedom coach and EFT specialist, http://www.thrivingnow.com

"I still feel so honored to have been a guest on your show ... it was sooo much fun and has made me smile, inside and out. I listened to the interview again today ... in a more relaxed manner, and kept appreciating your magical, wonderful way of not only 'interviewing' your guests with specific and pointed questions, but most especially your easy, engaging, and delightful energy and presence with your guests ... you are a great listener offering valuable feedback, asking insightful questions while effortlessly and easily doing what you enjoy...and it shows." — Jeanie Ward, whole body coach, http://www.jeanieward.com

Bio of Angela Treat Lyon: Angela is an EFT (Emotional Freedom Techniques) business and success expert, practicing and instructing internationally and in the U.S. She is an Avatar Master, a published author and speaker on personal and business success and wealth-building.

An award-winning professional artist, her paintings and sculpture are in private collections and galleries from China, Japan and the South Pacific to the U.S., Argentina and Europe.

The Donna Seebo Show on http://www.BBSRadio.com

Theme: Personal empowerment.

Guest Profile: Authors preferred. Publications dealing with empowering people on all levels of life from gardening to metaphysics. I only interview after reviewing the material sent to me. Good substance, stories and other information that will empower my listeners in a positive way. I want a press release giving a basic bio on their background along with pertinent contact information. I appreciate their putting a business card on the front inside page of the book so if the press release is misplaced contact information is available.

Guest from Hell: One who isn't prepared and only answers with yes or no answers. Worst of all not being available for the scheduled interview and doesn't call to cancel.

Contact: donna@delphiinternational.com; 253-582-5604; http://www.delphiinternational.com; Donna Seebo. Best method: E-mail and phone. Send a copy of published book with press release. Allow six weeks and then call my office to see where I am in the reviewing process. I do not accept e-books. No response? Call my office. Many times e-mails end up in cyber space or corrupted. Follow up with a phone call.

Invited Back? If they publish another book that had good substance.

Guest Comments: "It was a great pleasure to be on your program, and I appreciate your advance preparation, excellent comments and questions, and enthusiasm for my work." — Jo Stepaniak, Grassroots Veganism, http://www.vegsource.com/jo

"I want to thank you for allowing me to share my stories, talk about the book and promulgate the importance of taking care of one's health." — Lorena Drago, author of *Beyond Rice and Beans: The Caribbean Latino Guide to Eating Healthy with Diabetes* (American Diabetes Foundation 2006)

Bio of Donna Seebo: Donna is a psychic/mental practitioner, counselor, speaker, teacher, award-winning author, and minister. She has a real passion for bringing information and education to her listening audience that will help better their lives and understanding on multiple levels.

She has been involved in the study and demonstration of mind skills for more than 40 years. Broadcasting evolved in 1980 and she has been on radio and television ever since.

The Dr. Pat Show with Dr. Pat Baccili aired in Greater Seattle, Boston, Tampa, Australia, and on Voice America, BBS, HealthyLife.net

Theme: Talk radio to thrive by, inspirational talk radio, the new mainstream. Our goal is to offer a positive "new paradigm" vision of our collective future. We are all experiencing a powerful wave of personal shifts and cultural change as we break through to greater levels of awareness. *The Dr. Pat Show* seeks to be a force for meaningful change by establishing a mainstream media entertainment venue not afraid to address the important issues of our times from an open-minded perspective of higher consciousness. The show is all about being informed, savvy, and open to the possibilities of the spiritual world. It's about how to develop strategic relationships and understanding the law of attraction and how to put it to use in your life. But mostly, it's about demystifying spirituality. "You don't have to be a monk living in a monastery and meditating daily to understand that you are truly a divine spiritual being.

Guest Profile: Best-selling authors, motivational speakers, leading-edge scientists and futurists, environmentalists and educators, world-renowned spiritual leaders, inventors, filmmakers, artists, mystics, and healers that are stimulating and supporting individual and collective growth, positive cultural shifts, and making a meaningful difference in the world.

Leading edge movers and shakers who are doing more than simply focusing on a problem. We are looking for solutions to problems and those people who can inspire, lead, and motivate people to live powerful and fulfilling lives.

What makes them different from anyone else who knows about their topic, and what benefit can they offer our listeners? How prepared are they and if they have expectations, what are they? I would like to know if they are comfortable being on-air, and if they would like to take calls from our listeners during the interview. Also, if they are giving away copies of their books, products, or service to our callers. We prefer to "partner" with our guests to create win-win relationships, so we always seeking like-minded guests.

Guest from Hell: Someone who doesn't show up for the interview, who doesn't send us requested materials prior to the interview, and someone who simply rants about an issue without offering solutions for improving the situation. We want our listeners to receive a benefit from tuning in so there should always be something the guest can offer to help improve the world, even one person at a time.

Contact: pat@thedrpatshow.com; 206-523-5522; http://www.thedrpatshow.com; Bobbie Baxter at bbaxter@thedrpatshow.com. Best method: I prefer an e-mail containing enough information for me to quickly decide if they are a good fit. I would like to receive a topic idea, topic description containing benefits to our listeners, the url for the guest, and even a photo. I tell about by photos, so when they are included, it is often very helpful. A real plus is when a potential guest lists an additional topic they can offer so I can get a real sense of how well-rounded they are. Since we are on 13 hours live each week on several networks, it helps to know which of our shows might be a good fit. No response? I prefer that they follow up with an e-mail indicating this is a follow up e-mail. We receive so many interview requests each week that it isn't possible to speak with everyone by phone.

Invited Back? How our listeners perceived them, how well they engaged our host and listeners, the level or depth of the interview, so further exploration of that topic or guest would warrant another interview. Or is this guest able to talk about additional topics of interest.

Bio of Dr. Pat Baccili: Called "The Oprah of Radio" by her listeners, award-winning host, Dr. Pat, is blowing the doors off of traditional talk radio shows with her energizing delivery and powerful interviews with renowned leaders in the field of human potential. Her fresh, new perspective on living life full out has catapulted her show to the top position in alternative talk radio.

She's a "CAN-DO" kind of gal who will help you break free from everything that's keeping you stuck in. Dr. Pat brings her cut-to-the-chase attitude and delivers a common sense approach to spirituality using common language that is powerful and entertaining.

The Father John Walsh Show on CJAD 800, Montreal's News Talk Leader, airing Sundays, 6–7 PM (ET) in Quebec, border states and on http://ww.cjad.com

Theme: The humanization of the world.

Guest Profile: The guests I welcome are those who are making a difference, those who are contributing by making this world a better world in which to live, by serving peoples' needs. The guests are usually those who have found a way to solve a societal problem, be it loneliness, street kids or adults, lack of food, lack of love, or simply people who cannot find a listening ear. The primary qualities are passion and enthusiasm for the topic to be discussed. Some background material so that there are no surprises. Claude Ryan, provincial political leader of the Opposition, and Paul Martin, prime minister of Canada, have been his guests.

Guest from Hell: A person who gives one word answers, "yes" or "no," and then stops and looks at you with a blank look.

Contact: fatherjohn@johnbrebeuf.ca; 514-366-0131; http://www.cjad.com; http://www.johnbrebeuf.ca; Father John Walsh. Best method: I have been contacted personally. By phone, e-mail. Etc. ... it doesn't matter. No response? No problem if they do so.

Invited Back? The quality of the interview.

Bio of Father John Emmett Walsh: Father John was born and educated for the most part in Montreal, except for one year in PEI (Prince Edward Island) at Saint Dunstan's University; now University of PEI.

He spent three years in Rome at the Pontifical Biblical Institute and a year at Hebrew University in Jerusalem.

Father John completed Licentiate in Theology (U de M) and a Licentiate in Sacred Scripture (Rome) and has served in parishes, schools and as chaplain of Police and Fire Departments. He is Pastor of Saint John Brebeuf Parish in LaSalle.

He completed two-year terms as president of Missing Childrens Network Canada and as president of the Board of Catholic Community Services.

The Florida Show with Rhett Palmer on 1370 AM, WAXE, Vero Beach, Florida, airing weekdays, 6–10 AM (ET) with a repeat of the 8–9 AM slot at 3 PM right after RUSH.

Theme: Inspirational talk.

Guest Profile: U.S. presidents to movie stars, *New York Times* best selling authors, motivational/sales consultants. Passion and profound enthusiasm. History, briefing on subject matter, short that is, and perhaps potential question. mmmmm.... NOT perhaps ... I love potential questions though I may not use them.

Guest from Hell: One word answers describes the guest from Hell.

Contact: radiorhett@aol.com; http://www.rhettpalmer.com; Rhett Palmer. No response? You cannot e-mail too often. It is a great way to bug someone. The squeaky wheel gets the oil.

Invited Back? Call Back? Did they deliver the goods? Did they give information that either educated or inspired or entertained? Best method: I hate the phone to ring but it works. E-mails are the only way you are confirmed on my show and an e-mail to remind host near air date is recommended. A press kit in the mail with the book, not a cover or prepress copy that is half baked, and something that suggests the author has a story or stories. Tell me a truth, I will believe, tell me a fact, I will learn, Tell me a story and it will live in my heart forever — blasting out cold facts dies a quick death.

Bio of Rhett Palmer: Rhett is an award-winning talk show host, singer/songwriter and 1st Place Vocalist in Nashville's Music City Festival, winner of two prestigious Gold Addy Awards, public speaker and so devoted to his country he has been dubbed "Patriotic Palmer."

Goddess Radio with Carly Newfeld on KSFR 101.1 FM, Santa Fe, New Mexico and live webcast http://www.ksfr.org; now off the air.

Theme: Lively and respectful "conversation on the air" with women and men of awareness who lean towards liberal and open minded thinking and who are willing to take action to implement positive change.

Guest Profile: Anyone could be a potential guest — well known or unknown — whatever their topic. As long as my guests are willing to live or learn to live as they speak and have integrity, heart, and honesty. I usually glean everything I need to know from their website and/or books. I give priority to local guests or those coming into Santa Fe for an event or booksigning.

Guest from Hell: Someone who is full of themselves, doesn't listen, is arrogant and has a prepared monolog not willing to answer my questions.

Contact: goddess@ksfr.org; 505-670-4721; http://www.ksfr.org; Carly Newfeld, Producer and host. Best method: E-mail initially. E-mail PR and include a personal note. No response? Please e-mail again.

Invited Back? Feedback I receive from listeners.

Bio of Carly Newfeld: Carly grew up in England and lived for many years at the legendary Findhorn Community in Scotland. She is the author of the *Findhorn Book of Guidance and Intuition* (Findhorn Press 2003) and co-authored *In Search of the Magic of Findhorn* (Findhorn Press 2002) to celebrate the spiritual community's 40th year.

Carly set her sights on radio in 1982 and has been in radio production in Santa Fe since the early 90s. She has hosted her show since March 2001.

Good News Broadcast with Paul Sladkus on the Internet and TV Cable.

Theme: Only good news, life affirming.

Guest Profile: Authors and others doing good for the world and are happy with their Good News. Credentials and past interviews are not important. It's all about them; what they want to share.

Guest from Hell: Someone who wants to bash other people or corporations.

Contact: paul.sladkus@goodnewsbroadcast.com; 212-647-1212; http://www.goodnewsbroadcast.com; Paul Sladkus. Best method: E-mail or press kit. No response? E-mail.

Invited Back? If they have more Good News to share and we have time.

Bio of Paul Sladkus: A 30-year award-winning veteran of the communications industry, Paul founded Good News Broadcast (GNB) in 1998 and oversees its daily operations. For 14 years prior to GNB, he was an executive with CBS and PBS Television, working on more than 150 television shows and series, including "All in the Family," "Carol Burnett," "Love of Life," "Sonny and Cher," "Good Times," and "Captain Kangaroo."

The Harry Wolf Show on WNJC 1360AM and http://www.WNJC1360.com aired in Philadelphia and South Jersey, Tuesday, 7:30 PM (ET).

Theme: Humor — slice of life stories about being a 12 to 15 year old kid in the 60s. My shows are modeled somewhat from Jean's Shephard's 1964 to 1971 radio show on WOR.

Guest Profile: Anyone who has a good, funny, touching story with some relevance about coming of age or to present events. Have a concise story that fits into larger story.

Guest from Hell: I pre-record these, so guests from hell are not aired.

Contact: Harrywolfshow@aol.com; 856-261-2941; http://www.Harrywolfshow.com; Harry Wolf. Best method: Just e-mail me and we will set up a time to talk on the phone. No response? E-mail again.

Invited Back? Would like a running character/story.

Bio of Harry Wolf: Harry has been doing this weekly 30-minute show for more than six years. He had a local jewelry business but his first love has been radio (Temple University Radio in college) and writing.

In the Know with Tony Reeves, Esq. on Blog Talk Radio. http://www.blogtalkradio.com/intheknow. Anthony also hosts a call-in show, *LegalBeat in the Morning!* on Blog Talk Radio — a dose of information with a legal twist — giving you the chance to ask any question and get answers about general legal information. http://legalbeat.anthonyreeves.com

Theme: Provides information about the great things that good people do.

Guest Profile: Doctors, lawyers, presidents, activists, CEOs, non-profit leaders. Someone who has useful information that can be beneficial to my listening audience. Someone who can provide useful answers to a problem.

Guest from Hell: Someone who is more interested in promoting themselves instead of providing useful information.

Contact: reeves@anthonyreeves.com; 813-767-7147; http://www.anthonyreeves.com; Anthony Reeves, Esq. Best method: E-mail or phone. E-mail with a bio and/or press kit. No response? They should e-mail me.

Invited Back? All guests are extended the opportunity to re-appear.

Bio of Anthony Reeves, Esq.: Anthony is the owner and CEO of the A.nthony R.eeves E.xperience in Kissimmee, Florida. Surmounting great odds on his road to success, he is an avid motivational speaker, addressing the keys to self empowerment, self achievement, and personal excellence. Reeves is also a passionate supporter of youth initiatives and youth programs.

A senior partner in the Reeves Law Firm, P.A. http://www.reevesfirm.com, Anthony actively serves on the board of directors for four different organizations, works with four different 501c3 Non Profit organizations, and volunteers his legal experience as legal counsel to a martial arts federation, as well as a 501c3. Anthony has also served as co-chairperson for a large regional youth competition.

The Inez Bracy Show: Living Smart and Well on blogtalkradio.com/InezBracey

Theme: Creating and living your best life.

Guest Profile: Authors, doctors, holistic practitioners. Knowledgeable, interesting expert in the area. Want to know their past experiences, sound of voice, "spirit."

Guest from Hell: One who tries to monopolize the show, is not familiar with their material, patronizing.

Contact: inez@livingsmartandwell.com; 386-626-6652; http://www.thebracygroup.com; Inez Bracy. Best method: E-mail. Send press kit and bio. No response? Send second e-mail as reminder.

Invited Back? How they engage with the audience, knowledge, "spirit."

Bio of Inez Bracy: Inez's passion is helping others live their best life. She is a masterful coach, engaging keynote speaker, trainer and seminar presenter.

Her book, *Rejuvenate Your Life in 21 Days*, a powerful guidebook for creating, revitalizing and living your best life, can be purchased at www.justbeingyourbest.com

The Iris Fanning Show on Quiet Time World Radio, http://www.qtworldradio.com

Theme: A fast paced, entertaining, energetic program focusing on you as a whole person. Topics include: business, career, love and relationships, spirituality, communication, parenting, health and well-being, emotional balance and much, much more. Every show has a different focus. Listen in regularly and learn how to be happier, more successful, more energetic and in love with your life.

Guest Profile: Over half my shows I do as a workshop format much like Wayne Dyer or Deepak Chopra. So, I don't include guests in those shows. The other half of my shows I invite guests who have expertise that leads to better living for my listeners. This can include: authors, psychologists, ministers, financial advisors, alternative health care providers, exercise and nutrition experts, scientists, inventors, musicians, artists etc. I am interested in people who have a message about living at a higher more fulfilled conscious level. I look for someone who has some media experience and a clear, concise message: A person who can dialog but not interrupt the host or try to take over. I also want someone who is passionate about their field who has a nice sense of humor. The focus is on the *listener* and what the listener can learn and implement — not the ego of the guest. I want to know: credentials, experience, past media work, pre-interview of a consistent message, can they take instructions and follow my lead. It is not always necessary to have media experience (everyone has their first break somewhere). I do want to know that they have learned about media work by either reading, classes or working with a media expert.

Guest from Hell: A guest from hell is either someone who monologues, talks over the host, interrupts the host ... or the opposite, someone who gives a two word answer and doesn't dialog well. The other big NO is someone who promotes their book, product or service. It's my job to let listeners know about the guest. Self promotion kills the guest's chance of being credible or invited back on the show.

Contact: coachiris@hotmail.com; 505-263-1854; http://www.irisfanning.com; Iris Fanning. Best method: E-mail a media bio, press kit if they have one and a short one paragraph or less pitch. No response? E-mail again ... politely.

Invited Back? If the person is great in a dialog, sensitive to listening to the host and when the host is asking a new question, listener focused, engaging, great well spoken ideas and entertaining.

Bio of Iris Fanning: Iris is a coach, speaker and author of *Do What You Love and Get Rich* (Lulu.com 2007, 2006) and *Change Your Life Right Now* (Lulu.com 2007).

She holds a Master of Arts degree from the University of Northern Colorado, and Graduate of Coach University. She has an Honorary Doctorate of Divinity, Universal Life Church.

Iris has 25 years' experience in counseling individuals and groups, speaking, team building, developing and leading trainings, and seven years of experience as a small business owner of Fanning Success Systems individual and group coaching with clients nationwide.

Journey to Self with Tonya Ramsey on Blog Talk Radio, http://blogtalkradio.com/journeytoself

Theme: The theme of the show is to provide advice, tips, tools and resources for people that are striving to create/manifest the life and the person they want to be.

Guest Profile: I have had a variety of guests; most of them have authored at least one book and are in the field of assisting others in helping them create the life they want. I have had professional coaches, mentors, and guests in the business service industry. I am looking for guests that are passionate about what they do, that are passionate about helping others bring about what they want in their lives. Regarding potential guests, I would like to know about their business, their credentials, links to their website and if they are authors a sample of their work.

To view guests and topics of past shows you can visit http://journeytoselfshow.wordpress.com/archived-shows/

Guest from Hell: Someone that I have to drag the information or answers out of.

Contact: Tonya@lifebydesignsite.com; 608-554-1235 (home phone: 608-207-3535); site for *Journey to Self* (http://journeytoself.info); *Journey to Self* is a part of my main business Life by Design (http://lifebydesignsite.com); Tonya Ramsey. Best method: The best approach is to e-mail me an introduction of themselves, their business, with their credentials. It also helps if they list a couple of topics that they would like to talk about. Even though I allow my guest to be center stage, it is less of an interview and more of a discussion. No response? If for some reason I do not respond to e-mails, calling me would be the best. I am usually able to answer e-mails within 24 hours.

Invited Back? There are many things I consider, the main factor is how the show went, did they contribute to capturing the audience, did callers call in to talk to them, what kind of information did they give, were they excited and passionate during the discussion?

Bio of Tonya Ramsey: Tonya is student of the Law of Attraction (LOA) and the universe and able to see the positive results of applying the principles to her life.

She started Life by Design to provide one-on-one coaching, group coaching and classes on the principle of prosperity through a strong healthy foundation of self. Her passion is helping women find self-empowerment in order to make their goals a reality. "When we understand ourselves, take care of ourselves, and are aware of our own behaviors, then we can start creating the life that we want," Tonya tells her clients.

As a team leader for Digital Moms, Tonya provides training and support to team members as they work together to prosper by working from home. As a writer and speaker, she uses her talents to help women find the help they need to change their lives. "Knowledge is empowerment, to learn something that you did not know before is growth. Together they are powerful keys to changing your life."

Tonya is a full time student at the University of Wisconsin, and is married with a toddler son.

Let's Talk It Through with Duane Bowers on Healthy Life.net, http://www.healthylife.net

Theme: Discussion of ways to improve our reality or our life.

Guest Profile: Someone with expertise in ways we can use to improve our reality. Expertise in some way, method, modality of improving our individual reality or life.

Most important is their personality and how well it will come across on radio.

Guest from Hell: A guest that answers in single words or short phrases and is not willing to expound on a point.

Contact: dtbowers@att.net; 202-236-5452; http://www.duanetbowers.com. Best method: 1) e-mail, 2) phone E-mail me with a pitch, an idea that you are excited or passionate about discussing. Then we'll talk by phone. No press kits unless requested. No response? A follow-up e-mail will suffice.

Invited Back? How well the two of us worked together on air.

Bio of Duane T. Bowers, LPC: Duane is a personal development counselor and educator in private practice, and author of *Guiding Your Family Through Loss and Grief* (Fenestra Books 2005). His specialty is working with survivors of traumatic death and suicide, which includes assisting families who must identify loved ones at the DC Office of the Chief Medical Examiner, through the Wendt Center for Loss and Healing. He also provides support to families of abducted, missing, exploited and murdered children through the National Center for Missing and Exploited Children (NCMEC). In addition, Duane serves as a training consultant to NCMEC, and is deployed by them to provide crisis intervention at Amber Alert sites with Team Adam. He also serves as a consultant and trainer for Team HOPE, a telephone support line for parents of missing children, and has provided services to AMECO (Association of Missing and Exploited Children Organizations).

Duane teaches seminars on dying, death and grief, as well as trauma, post traumatic stress disorder (PTSD), and traumatic loss. He has served as an adjunct professor of counseling at Trinity College in Washington D.C.

Lisa's Walk the Talk Show with Lisa Loucks Christenson on vets.fm, and also aired on terrestrial stations through about 27+ affiliates.

Theme: Talk About Topics! is our tag. One hour format, featured guests inside story of struggles to success as they reached their dreams.

Guest Profile: Indie artists, major artists, entertainers, best-selling authors, various theme/event/attractions. When we do the major or indie artists, we play 3–5 of their songs inside the interview. When we do authors, we have them read excerpts from their book. We do free give-away books or CDs (or other products) to the listeners for guests that are on the show. The authors or agents/publishers will send us copies of the book to give away and one for our review (I write reviews for authors). We cover most genres. We want story first from guests. What struggles to triumphs they've endured, what message they have to encourage another. Talent, how their story can benefit others struggling to reach their goals. I work with all guests, from beginners to super stars; ideally the guest has an irresistible story and talent to share with our listeners, or a message of hope to deliver.

Guest from Hell: I've never had a guest from hell; we work with all people, from all walks of life and find that gem inside.

Contact: LisaWTTS@gmail.com; 866-562-5125; http://www.LisaLC.com; Lisa Loucks Christenson. Best method: E-mail, and press kit. I don't take calls until the first interview. No response? E-mail me again, and again if necessary. Calls are usually booking agents and talent coordinating their times with my PR people.

Invited Back? Guests coming back are usually ones that have a theme-oriented song or story, a new CD, new book, new "something" to share, or they are invited as a co-host.

Guest Comment: "I think Internet radio is the wave of the future. *Lisa's Walk the Talk Show* was one of the first I had done for my new CD *American Man*. I was surprised at the energy that was flying around over the phone. It was like the days when you would finally get an interview and you had so much to say you just couldn't wait to get it all out. What a blast, faster than the speed of light. Now radio and radio politics can't slow us down, just press play and it's faster than the speed of light..."—Terry Lee Bolton, singer, song writer, guitarist, drummer, bassist, percussionist, entertainer, arranger and producer, http://www.terryleebolton.com

Bio of Lisa Loucks Christenson: Lisa is a national award-winning author, photographer and national speaker and mentor. She owns Ecompass Business Center and Alarm, LLC, a 20-year-old communications company serving clients' business support needs, and is the publisher of Loucks Christenson Publishing, LLC, a small independent publisher specializing in children's books, and her nationally known wildlife documentaries.

Her wildlife gallery and studio is located in Rochester, Minnesota.

Live the Day with Rachelle and Christen Resmo on KKZN 760 AM, Denver Colorado, airing Sunday, 8–9 AM (MT), www.am760.net

Theme: Motivation, inspiration and information.

Guest Profile: Authors/speakers who focus on self development, self help and positive living. Someone that is considered an expert in their field, is articulate and excited about their topic. I always talk to the guest beforehand to make sure they are prepared, have a set of questions we could ask if we need to, and are open and friendly.

Guest from Hell: I have had a few and those are the guests that don't talk. I can't stand yes or no answers. I like a guest that will engage the audience, share what they know, not just sit there with dead air.

Contact: rachelle@livethedayradio.com; 303-617-6196; http://www.livethedayradio.com; Dr. Rachelle Disbennett Lee. Best method: E-mail is preferred as a first contact just letting me know they are interested and a little about them. I then visit their website and if it looks like they fit I will ask for additional information and see if I can set up a call with them just to get a feel if they would be a good guest for us. No response? They could e-mail or even call me, I have had a few misses where I didn't get the person's e-mail so it is best to follow up if they don't hear from me within a couple of days.

Invited Back? If they support the show and share that they have been on it and are willing to help us grow. Also if they were popular with the audience and had a powerful message that just couldn't be captured in one show.

Guest Comments: "*Live the Day* is a breath of fresh air in content and the hosts. The majority of talk radio is some form of people bashing. Live the day provides practical and positive tools and inspiration that help us get through the day and have fun! I highly recommend this show."—Ed Tate, world speaking champion, http://www.edtate.com

"Christen and Rachelle—I wanted to say thank you again for the wonderful time I had with you in the studio. I appreciate the opportunity to share the story of Grace Flight and to let our neighbors know that we are out there to help. Your show is so uplifting and positive—I always have a big smile on my face after listening and I'm energized to positively impact the day. And having the show archives on the web works well with my schedule so that I can listen anytime." — Lori Eddlemon, *Grace Flight of America*, http://www.graceflight.org

Bio of Dr. Rachelle Disbennett Lee (Coach Lee): Coach Lee is an advocate of daily action and the power it wields. Her award-winning newsletter, *365 Days of Coaching*, has been published every day since 1998. Her first book, *365 Days of Coaching — Because Life Happens Every Day (Universal Publishers 2004)* was a best seller on Amazon.com. She is a contributing author to *A Guide to Getting It, Self Esteem* (Clear Vision Publishing, 2002).

Coach Lee earned her doctorate degree from Walden University in applied management and decision sciences with a specialization in business coaching.

Live! With Lisa Radio with Lisa Wexler on WYBC Friday, 10 AM to noon (ET) and Saturday on WSTC/WNLK (1350 and 1400 am), 10:30 AM to noon (ET). Lisa also hosts a local cable television program called "Connecticut Conversations," featuring CT State Representative Thomas Drew, which discusses public policy issues with various experts and elected officials.

Theme: Respect: "I respect the opinions of my audience and my guests, as opposed to a lot of other talk shows who don't know any respect for anyone."

Guest Profile: Extremely diversified. Anyone that I think has an interesting story to tell or who can teach me something. Someone whom I can learn from. Credentials; also I read the book beforehand, so I try not to have authors whose books I don't personally like. My only criteria for guests is that they be people who are doing something with their lives that they are passionate about and who wish to share something interesting or important with others. My passion is to host authentic conversations among guests and the audience about topics not typically discussed on the radio while showing respect for a variety of opinions on the same subject. I particularly love politics, all things green, children's issues, the advancement of women's rights, and the theater. I also love to laugh.

Guest from Hell: Someone who has no sense of humor.

Contact: lisa@livewithlisaradio.com; http://www.lunchwithlisa.com. Best method: I prefer e-mail. That way I can respond in the middle of the night, when I catch up. They can send me their book, unsolicited, or an e-mail. Pitches and press kits have not impressed me to date. No response? That happens sometimes — sorry for that. Just e-mail me again, but not a nasty one. (I got a nasty one once — I'll never have that person on.)

Invited Back? If they were funny, bright, and if they are working on something else of interest.

Guest Comment: "I enjoyed talking to you. Thanks for the interview. Yes, the subject is too complex ... the interview time is short. I would love to join you again in the future." — Saul Silas Fathi, author of *Full Circle: Escape from Baghdad and the Return* (Xlibris Corporation 2005)

Bio of Lisa Wexler: The show was the realization of Lisa's dream to host a radio show that would be live, informative and entertaining. She was born in Brooklyn, grew up on Long Island and graduated with honors from Johns Hopkins University, where she co-hosted a radio show called *Showstoppers* for four years. She obtained a Juris Doctorate from New York University School of Law in 1984, and while there won the American Jurisprudence Award for Excellence in Constitutional Law. Admitted to the New York and Connecticut Bars, Lisa owned her own law firm for many years, concentrating on real estate, trusts, wills and probate.

Lisa is married to her college sweetheart, Bill Wexler, for 25 years. Son Jon is studying at Northeastern and daughter Joanna is in the eighth grade. The family lives in Westport, CT, and share their home with their beloved Bichons — Snuggles and Sugar.

Wanting to graduate from a turntable to the digital age, she attended the Connecticut School of Broadcasting, completing their curriculum in January of 2006.

Living and Loving Life with MaryAnn Swanson and cohost Debbie Friedman, on BBS Radio, http://www.bbsradio.com/bbc/living_loving_life.php; now off the air.

Theme: Inspirational. A fun program with powerful insights and messages allowing you to completely fall in love with life once again.

Guest Profile: Fun and uplifting people who love life and would like to share their unique experiences of living life with joy, happiness, and success. Fun, outgoing people who have reconnected with the true wonderment and joy of life. Have wonderful, positive messages to share with others, exceptional inner experiences, and ability to inspire and empower others. Credentials are not the most important. The desire and courage to take the step to share with others what has inspired them so in life.

Guest from Hell: Angry, negative people who complain and curse about what they do not like. Guests with short, one sentence answers.

Contact: maryannswanson07@yahoo.com; 360-901-8012; http://www.freewebs.com/livingmybliss; MaryAnn Swanson. Best method: E-mail first, then phone. No response? Call us.

Invited Back? They have an air of fun that comes across the radio, and have much to about their incredible journeys. And what they say motivates the audience to respond.

Guest Comments: "[The program] was so much fun, I could have kept on going for hours ... I wished it would never end." — Mary Pat O'Rourke, Laughter Yoga Therapist http://www.freewebs.com/laughingwithlife

"The show was loads of fun, and whenever you

want, I would love to come back on. You made me feel so at ease." — Richard D. Blackstone, author of numerous books, including *Nuts and Bolts Spirituality* (Trafford Publishing 2006)

The Louie Jones Show on WCFJ AM 1470, Chicago, IL.

Theme: Personal development/motivation/inspiration.

Guest Profile: Wide variety. Those who have a positive spirit and/or have valuable insight to bring to the audience. I look for a guest to be entertaining, lively and be able to provide valuable information to the listeners in a method that the majority of the listeners can relate to. I would like to know their credentials, but more importantly, I would like to know how their life's experiences relate to the theme of my show.

Guest from Hell: Someone who is mundane, uncertain of themselves. Another guest is someone who does not want to discuss their book directly for fear of "giving it away."

Contact: louie@louiejones.com; 847-991-8628; http://www.louiejones.com; Louie Jones. Best method: The best method is by e-mailing a bio/EPK. No response? If I haven't responded within a week, the person should follow up with another e-mail.

Invited Back? If there is a connection and if the guest is engaging.

Guest Comments: "You've made my life richer." — Janis Kearney, personal diarist to President Clinton

"It was a blast interviewing with you on your radio show. That interview even boosted my career (upward)." — Brian O'Neal, recording artist

Bio of Louie Jones: Louie's purpose, via his radio show, personal writings and business mentoring, is to help you to develop or enhance some key life skills to aid you in creating a life of distinction. "I've found out that there are many things that hold people back in life, and, hopefully, I can offer some encouragement that will help the listeners to elevate themselves to greater heights," he says.

Louie feels fortunate to have a variety of experiences. He's been an Army officer, where he had the benefit of learning about leadership and people from some of the world's most forward thinking leaders. He's also had the honor of leading some of the brightest soldiers. He's done training for major corporations. He's lived and worked abroad in three countries, Germany, Korea and Japan.

"Wherever I am, I always try to find out what motivates people to behave as they do ... what drives them to achieve what are their dreams and fears," says Louie. "I'm also interested in belief systems ... and most of all philosophies. In the process, I've developed a love and respect for humankind ... I've come to learn the significance of the words by John Donne that 'No man is an island.'"

Never Settle for Less with Howard Spiva, Esq. and Ed Spiva on WTKS 1290am, Savannah, GA, on Saturdays, 10 AM–Noon (ET), http://www.Spivalaw.com

Theme: Motivational and self-improvement talk show, where the topics are intended to make you ... healthy, wealthy and wise. Topics include: financial — self improvement, investing, real estate, law, health, the Savannah economy, legal entities, tax saving, estate planning.

Guest Profile: All guests are welcome. Interesting, willing to be flexible and answer questions yet a sense of humor. John Edwards, presidential candidate, was a guest on the show.

Guest from Hell: I don't like short answers. However, I love all guests; 912-947-1290 (radio); 912-920-2000 (office).

Contact: howard@spivalaw.com; http://www.wtksam.com; http://www.neversettleforless.net; Howard Spiva. Best method: E-mail. Don't need to send a press kit or call with a pitch. Just ask. Try to not make your message so commercial. No response? E-mail or phone calls are fine. I answer both.

Invited Back? Listener response determines returned guest.

Bio of Howard Spiva: Howard is a Savannah personal injury trial lawyer, trial attorney, real estate broker, investor and professional seminar speaker. He is certified for instructing continuing education classes by the Georgia Real Estate Board.

In addition to building a sizable net worth through buying and selling an ever-increasing number of residential and commercial properties, Howard holds numerous record-setting verdicts and settlements in Georgia.

He has taught courses to thousands of real estate investors and business owners and is frequently invited to speak at various professional organizations, schools, and trial attorney associations. He is president-elect of the Southern Trial Lawyers Association.

Howard is a graduate of the Woodrow Wilson College of Law in Atlanta, GA, and was admitted to the Georgia Bar in 1984. He enjoys the highest rating ("AV") in both legal professional ability and ethical standards given by the Martindale-Hubbell Law Directory.

Howard is married with two children. His oldest son is a lawyer and practices with Howard.

Bio of Carl "Ed" Spiva: Carl is a veteran law enforcement officer with over 33 years experience and has trained law enforcement officers in 45 states, Canada, Central America, Australia and the Bahamas. He is a P.O.S.T. certified senior instructor in the State of Georgia, with 11 years experience as a undercover narcotics officer with the Chatham County Police Department, Savannah, GA. Ed also served TDY on the D.E.A. drug task force and U.S. Marshal Fugitive Squad.

On the Verve with Rachael Cadden on World Talk Radio, airing Tuesdays at 5 PM (PT) on Studio B.

Theme: Igniting, championing and leaping into greatness and vitality.

Guest Profile: Those who have found and are living their mission and passion and experts on living an extraordinary life and holistic elevating greatness in body, mind and soul/spirit. Forward thinking individuals who have found and are living their mission and passion along with experts on areas of personal growth and development ... those who train and inspire us to live an extraordinary life. Personally, I want to speak with them first or at least have heard or seen them being interviewed to see. My show is fun and energetic and even if there is an expert out there who does not have a "presence" or energy, I will not interview them. It's important not only to relate to the audience but connect, so I look at past interviews or even their ability on the phone. Typically, I will have found my guest from my own research or experience with their services or product.

Guest from Hell: Great question, one who is unable to hold a conversation or expound on a point or subject ... one who is unable to run and carry a point and has limited expression.

Contact: Rachael@VerveEnterprises.com; 949-713-4755 Voice; 949-680-7228 Cell; http://www.YourVerveCoach.com; Rachael Cadden. Best method: E-mail or phone. Personally, an e-mail about them and why they want to be on my show. A press kit and bio are helpful, but if someone does not have one and they include information and refer me to a link or site or past interview that is helpful. I want to know about them and not in a sterile way. I want my guests to be authentic and who they are and even if they are raw and no-nonsense, I appreciate it. I might be the majority to the rule, but it's who I am and important in the guest I have.

They don't necessarily have to be rock n' roll ... but be comfortable with who you are regardless of your personality type. No response? I appreciate tenacity. A follow e-mail is fine. A call, probably not. I would be a little irritated and if I have not responded it would be for good reason ... that I am busy. I will always let someone know if they perhaps are not a fit for my show and wish them well rather than ignore.

Invited Back? Their overall attitude and willingness to "show up" at the interview. I recognize these folks are extremely busy, but putting your all into the interview and being present and fun and have the ability to be relaxed and expound on a whim with wit will always return on my show.

Guest Comments: "You were a great host, it would be my pleasure to be on your show anytime, Rachael."— Topher Morrison, author of *Settle for Excellence* (Topher Morrison 2006). http://www.settleforexcellence.com

"That was great fun, thanks for putting me at ease ... that was a blast!"— Ryan Higgins, creator and owner of Mind Movies, http://www.MindMovies.com

Bio of Rachael Cadden: Rachael is an editor/author, radio host, verve life coach, motivational speaker, fitness enthusiast, adventure seeker, world traveler, music lover and amateur shutterbug. Founder of Verve Enterprises, she offers personal coaching and other services. She began her coaching career mentoring inner city youth in the early 1990s; this passion extended into opportunities to inspire others to reach their greatest potential through awareness. Her approach is primarily holistic, taking all aspects of life into account while guiding you through life transitions and improving your well-being in addition to moving forward and creating an extraordinary life.

"Along with polishing up my golf swing, I do a mean one-legged running man and am elated to be living my passion and purpose of igniting and championing vitality and brilliance in the lives of others," she says.

Point of Life with Michael Levy on Blog Talk Radio, http://www.blogtalkradio.com

Theme: Life.

Guest Profile: Everyone with an authentic message for humanity. A person who lives what they talk about.

Guest from Hell: One who shortens the word hell-o.

Contact: mikmikl@aol.com; Withheld upon request; http://www.pointoflife.com; Michael Levy. Best method: E-mail. Nothing but a bio and their latest project are necessary. No response? I reply right away to all e-mails unless I am on vacation.

Invited Back? Time.

Bio of Michael Levy: Michael is author of eight inspirational books and his poetry and essays grace many web sites, newspapers, journals and magazines throughout the world.

He speaks on health maintenance, stress eradication, wealth development, authentic happiness and inspirational poetry. His latest book is *The Inspiring Story of Little Goody Two Shoes* (Point of Life 2007).

Positive Changes with Dr. Panney Wei, N.D. C.Ht. on KCAA 1050 AM radio, airing in 240 countries, and on the worldwide Web.

Theme: Personal growth and empowerment.

Guest profile: *NY Times* best-selling authors, award-winning filmmakers, international motivational speakers with a strong following, experts in their particular fields, experts in the field of human potential and consciousness, women in leadership, experts in women's health and wholeness. I look for a guest who is passionate about what he or she does, is probably an expert in their field and can offer a unique or different perspective about a topic matter that we haven't heard of before, and is making a difference in the world. Celebrities are also fun and entertaining to have on the show as well because, chances are, they are meant to serve the world in a bigger way and being on my radio show serves their purpose, serves the people listening, and serves my intentions as the writer/producer/host of my radio show as well. I would like to get their bio, a copy of their recent book or product they are promoting, a good list of where they've appeared on radio or TV before, credentials, and if possible, have a decent conversation with them to establish rapport before we book them on the show.

Guest from Hell: My idea of a guest from hell would be a person that isn't resonating with me, isn't answering my questions with an earnest sincerity to help the audience or is just interested in over-promoting themselves without really having a good conversation with me. I will always be there to help promote them but it's especially frustrating when the guest wants to overtalk me and try to run the show.

Contact: panneywei@yahoo.com; 310-869-3832; http://www.panneywei.com; Dr. Panney Wei, N.D. C.Ht., Host/Writer/Producer. Best method: E-mail or phone but e-mail first. A person who is interested in appearing on my show should e-mail me first and send a bio and brief intro about themselves. If they have an electronic press kit, I'm open to receiving that too, since I read everything. No response? I always respond to my e-mails from prospective guests with an answer "yay" or "nay" on whether they will appear as a guest on my show, but I always respond, as I appreciate the effort it took for them to e-mail me. It may take up to a week to respond at times.

Invited Back? Guests are invited back if I feel I resonate with them, if I get great feedback from my audience, or if their topic matter is very inspiring or particularly resonates with me.

Guest Comments: "Panney Wei has an electrifying blend of east-meets-west wisdom, experience, and heart filled fun personality that inspires me week in, week out! *Positive Changes* with Panney Wei is a show that will open your heart and inspire you to radical action!"—Debbie Ford, author of *The New York Times* bestseller *The Dark Side of the Light Chasers* (Hodder and Stoughton 2001)

"If you're gonna want to have some fun, if you want to be able to play, if you want to have some inspiration, and you want to have a greater life, just listen to Panney Wei on Contact Talk Radio. What an amazing show!"—International motivational speaker, Dr. John DeMartini, from the hit film *The Secret* and bestselling author of *The Breakthrough Experience* (Hay House 2002) and *How to Make One Helluva of a Profit and Still Get to Heaven* (Hay House 2004)

Bio of Dr. Panney Wei, N.D. C.Ht.: Panney is an award-winning artist, author, speaker, and TV-radio personality whose heritage is deeply rooted in Chinese history as a proud descendant of one of China's greatest heroes, General Tso Tsung-Tang, forever immortalized by his famous cuisine, "General Tso's Chicken."

With her background in alternative medicine gained from surviving a near-death experience with the life-threatening illness, bulimia, Panney has first-rate knowledge about the power of the mind-body connection, living life with purpose and passion, and the ability to achieve anything in life. She healed herself without the help of doctors, and after quitting her cushy job as an executive in the entertainment industry, pursued her passions to become a doctor of naturopathy and certified practitioner of several powerful healing modalities, including hypnotherapy, neuro-linguistic programming, life-coaching, and Reiki energy healing, and now maintains a thriving practice helping women, children, and entrepreneurs with successful strategies empowering them to discover their life purpose, achieve their dreams, and live a powerful, fulfilling life.

Nationally recognized as a Presidential Scholar for exceptional talent in the arts, Panney began her entertainment career as a professional figure skater, but parlayed her talents into TV-radio hosting, motivational speaking, and writing, and inspiring others by entertaining, empowering, and educating through the media, where her true passions shine.

Recognized as "The Asian American Entertainer to Look Out For" by APEX, she has hosted for *NBA TV China*, *The Money Show*, and *The Discovery Channel*, and her live weekly radio show has been ranked TOP 100 Best Podcasts on Itunes in Spirituality.

Her upcoming novel is *The Jade Princess Warrior*, an inspiring coming-of-age and mother-daughter story based on true events; of overcoming abuse, loss, and redemption and bridging the mystery and richness of the East with the West.

Positively Incorrect! with Scott Cluthe on www.lime.com/radio/positively_incorrect_with_scott_cluthe and on www.blogtalkradio.com/positively_incorrect

Theme: A daily variety of guests and topics on all aspects of living a more fulfilling, balanced, happier life in relationships, health, work, and more with national guests on a wide range of themes. With call-ins.

Guest Profile: Authors, psychologists, doctors; look for a guest who has both something original to say, or is working with something that needs to be said again. Credentials are obviously important to a point, and well published guests do get my attention, but only if I find their materials relevant to sharing with the audience. Some of notable guests have been Deepak Chopra, Andrew Weil, Greg Baer, M.D., Lama Surya Das, Michael Lutin, and Sandra Anne Taylor.

Guest from Hell: Someone who doesn't show up for the show, or begs out at the last minute.

Contact: positivelyincorrect@lime.com; 713-665-3969; http://www.evoradio.net; Scott Cluthe. Best method: Call with pitch, e-mail a bio, send a press kit. All of these approaches will/or will not work. No response? E-mail or call. I am human and lose e-mails and of course get lost in the time/space continuum.

Invited Back? The quality of the interview and their interaction with both me and the audience. And of course lots of free books for listeners

Guest Comment: "One of the best interviewers in the U.S."— John Gray, Ph.D., author, *Men Are from Mars, Women Are from Venus*

Listener Comment: "Just wanted to say thank you for your interview with Mariel Hemingway today— I just talked to her and she enjoyed it very much. Thanks again!"— Krista Holmstrom/HarperSanFrancisco

Power Talk with Frank Gasiorowski on Blog Talk Radio, http://www.BlogTalkRadio.com/PowerTalk and on AACTV for TV show. Frank has another interview program on Blog Talk Radio called *Today's Guest*, Monday through Friday, with a different host each day. These hosts are known as the FAB-5.

Theme: Interview guests on goals and dreams.

Guest Profile: All people achieving goals. Inspiring, motivating, enthusiastic and a person who accomplished their dreams/goals. I do a pre-interview to learn about past interview experiences, sound of voice, and credentials.

Guest from Hell: A person who cannot answer questions or has short answers.

Contact: Frank@90DayGoals.com; 410-590-0966; http://www.TodaysGuest.com, http://www.90DayGoals.com 1251; Frank Gasiorowski, "Mr90DayGoals." Best method: E-mail a bio, call with pitch, and/or send a press kit. Calling is the least best method for me. No response? E-mail or call.

Invited Back? How much fun we had, how much the audience responded and lead sign-up e-mail received.

Guest Comment: "Frank is very professional and organized both before and during his show. He freely promotes his guests, is very knowledgeable when asking or setting up questions and provides his guests with ample time to respond.

From my point of view, definitely a worthwhile activity. I highly recommend his show."— Roger Ellerton Ph.D., CMC, author of *Live Your Dreams Let Reality Catch Up* (Trafford 2005) http://www.live-your-dreams.biz http://www.renewal.ca

Bio of Frank Gasiorowski: Frank's earliest recollection of being an entrepreneur was 6 or 7 years old. He found attending large weddings with his parents boring, but looking for something to do he landed a job in the cloak room. "I incorporated a basket at the drop-off/pickup window," recalls Frank. "Magic happened. Whenever anyone dropped off a coat or picked up a coat, they gave me a tip in the basket. Boring weddings got me excited — changed my perception and doing what other people were not willing to do, make money."

At 15 years old, he had 90 days to come up with enough money to go to Spain and Italy with the Explorer Scouts. Within 90 days, he had more than enough money to make the trip through a business brainstorm of a snowball stand in his basement. "That was my first experience with 90 Day Goals," he says.

As he got older, Frank read more than 3000 motivational books and attended seminars by the most popular mentors of the day. When he had a difficult time in his industry of large-scale photo-processing equipment, he attended a one-day seminar hosted by Anthony Robbins. Following his advice to set a few goals that must be attainable in 90 days, he eventually grossed $280,000 in sales at the end of that period. Co-workers started calling him the "Golden Boy" and others labeled him "Mr. 90 Day Goals."

What really changed his life around was his heart attack in 1998. Nine months later while working a convention in NYC, he had chest pains again. The doctor told Frank's wife that she had one hour to get all of their affairs in order because they were going to do life saving quadruple by-pass open-heart surgery. The successful surgery caused Frank to re-evaluate his life and to give back to others. He found his life's purpose, his voice, and started interviewing people who have achieved their dreams and goals. If you have achieved your big dream, Frank wants to talk to you.

Full bio at http://www.90DayGoals.com

The Power Within You with Kathleen Graham on Contact Talk Radio, http://www.contacttalkradio.com, Wednesday at 1 PM (ET).

Theme: Self help, self empowerment.

Guest Profile: Motivational, spiritual coaches. Someone who has helped people improve themselves to obtain the success they deserve in life. I like to conduct an interview to discuss various topics before making my decision. You can get a sense of a person in the tone of their voice and how they handle themselves during a conversation.

Guest from Hell: A person who is not open to the opinions of others; who thinks they are always right on all subjects. A person who doesn't listen but who only wants to be heard.

Contact: kgraham@successinu.com; 770-625-5038; http://www.findsuccessinu.com; Kathleen Graham. Best method: E-mail. An invitation to read a book they wrote or listen to a show they have been a guest on, etc. No response? Patience is a virtue. Many hosts have other business related responsibilities outside of their shows. If a host is interested in you because you would be a good fit in regard to the message been given to their audience, they will be happy to get back to you as soon as they can.

Invited Back? Is there good chemistry? Does the guest have something to offer my audience?

Bio of Kathleen F. Graham: Kathleen is founder and president of Success In U, LLC, a personal professional coaching firm located in the suburbs of Atlanta, GA. The firm provides personal and professional growth services to individual clients and various organizations world-wide.

For the past 25 years, Kathleen has mentored individuals and organizations all over the country. With her background in personal growth, career development and planning, time management, and IT/financial consulting, Kathleen has gained expert knowledge regarding the power of the mind-body connection, living a joyous and fulfilled life, and the ability to teach how to create and receive anything you desire in life. By using the power contained within all of us, she was able to rise to personal heights she never thought possible.

She went from growing up in a family on welfare and food stamps to president of a multi-million dollar company. Despite starting out in a male dominated corporate world, she was able to overcome obstacles and climb the corporate ladder to success. In the process she had the opportunity to coach both individuals and corporations on how to achieve their own successes.

Among the organizations she has assisted during her coaching/consulting career are BellSouth, The Weather Channel, Coca-Cola, and Lucent Technologies. This amazing experience has led her to be a successful author and an effective personal professional coach. Throughout her career, Kathleen has received numerous awards for customer service, quality assurance, and coaching and leadership excellence.

Radio Good Spirited with Caryn Colgan on Blog Talk Radio, http://www.blogtalkradio.com/caryncolgan, aired the 1st and 3rd Mondays at 2 PM (PT).

Theme: Expand your spiritual, environmental, and mental awareness and use your free will to make positive changes.

Guest Profile: Guests are typically authors, editors or activists who are leaders in interpersonal or environmental changes for a more balanced world. Each guest provides easy tips that any listener can implement. Credentials are key. What makes this person an expert on their topic? Another key element is: can this guest convey their message in a concise and meaningful way.

Guest from Hell: A poor guest would be someone who is not positive and peaceful in demeanor. The worst type of guest is someone who drones on and on and does not allow for a more conversational exchange of ideas. I'm not interested in obvious self-promotion. Rather, a great guest is one who intends to help others help themselves and/or the environment.

Contact: ancientpact@gmail.com (Please do NOT post this on an unprotected website without proper anti-spam measures. My e-mail addresses have been ruthlessly used by spammers); 866-365-4441; http://www.caryncolgan.com; Colleen Schone. Best method: I prefer e-mail with their pitch. They should include the tips they intend to share and a short, concise bio. Once I've invited them to be a guest I send them to my webpage that includes everything I need from a guest prior to the show. No response? E-mail. This hasn't happened but I would assume they are either not interested or involved in life. I would schedule another guest.

Invited Back? The most important elements of a good show is whether or not the interview was entertaining and helpful to listeners.

Bio of Caryn Colgan: Caryn earned a Master of Science in accounting in 1984, joined the firm of Ernst and Young as a tax consultant before moving on to a private firm.

In 1991, after almost ten years as a corporate tax consultant and CPA, Caryn began her present career as an international speaker and workshop facilitator. She has conducted team-building and diversity awareness workshops for the Anti-Defamation League and National Conference for Community and Justice. Additionally, Caryn has delivered workshops and career coaching throughout the U.S. and Europe for major companies like McKinsey and Company, McDonnell Douglas (Boeing), Ralston Purina, MCI and Monsanto.

She earned a CTM (Certified Toastmaster) in 2006 and is working toward advanced certification (ATM). In 1998 she completed the mentoring program with the National Speakers Association.

Reaching Peak Show with Joseph Price on WTAN, aired in Tampa / Clearwater, Florida.

Theme: Personal development.

Guest Profile: Authors, personal development, psychiatrists, counselors, life coaches, motivational speakers. Story of overcoming seemingly insurmountable challenge, experience extreme personal growth, provide a service to humanity for growth, personal profile of reaching peak life, successful entrepreneur overcoming big challenges. We interview guests to find out what they have in common with our program, personal development knowledge, success story, personal growth epiphany.

Guest from Hell: Misrepresented themselves or lied about who they are or what they stand for.

Contact: contact@reachingpeakshow.com; 813-984-7325 or 813-938-4367; http://www.reachingpeakshow.com; Karen Price at Karen@reachingpeak.com. Best method: E-mail an introductory pitch with the way to contact them. Include how you are related to our show purpose. No response? E-mail again and call.

Invited Back? Knowledge and contribution to the good of the show, which is contributing to the good of the community and society.

Guest Comments: "Joseph was the consummate professional, an engaging host and made me feel welcome and valued as a guest on his show. I thought the format and flow of the show was very professional and well done. It was my first radio appearance ever and while I was a bit nervous before the call, once Joseph started the show, I felt calm and ended up really enjoying myself. Thank you Joseph for such a fun and enjoyable experience!"—Carey Powell, certified transformational life coach, owner, Fearless Soul Life Coaching, http://www.fearlesscoaching.net

"Joseph Price made me feel welcome at every stage of the process. He is professional and stands by his word. His *Reaching Peak* program is filled with energy, enthusiasm, and valuable content. And he works really hard to help me shine and make me feel at ease. He definitely understands and voices the value that having me as a guest brings to the relationship. Simply put, he had me at "hello." I look forward to a continued relationship with Joseph and Reaching Peak Radio."—Kelly Swanson, http://www.kellyswanson.net

Bios of Joseph and Karen Price, managing partners, Reaching Peak, LLC: Joseph started his journey in the self-improvement movement about 29 years ago when not too many people were discovering its power. His first sales job was selling *Encyclopædia Britannica*. "In the business of sales we believe in personal growth," he says. "Generally sales people do personal development daily to improve performance. There, Mr. Hale was one of my greatest mentors. In the first week he told me to go in an office and listen to a six-tape album by Denis Waitley called *The Psychology of Winning* and not to come out until I was finished. I was young, ambitious and eager to excel, so I did as I was asked. I was completely overwhelmed by this information that could help me grow and become a better person. I developed a passion for life and a commitment to excellence."

Joseph's passion for personal growth led him to create his radio show to provide motivation for individuals, companies, and organizations. Utilizing powerful delivery and an abundance of knowledge in peak performance, Joseph teaches, inspires, empowers, encourages, and guides listeners to overcoming challenges and reaching their peak life desires.

Karen's role is to manage the marketing of the show as well as oversee web services. She brings a wealth of experience in product management, marketing, and public relations for small and large corporations. Predominantly, her experience is in marketing and product management roles at companies such as Magnetic, Exostar, eMerge Interactive, and CommerceQuest.

In the past, she has provided volunteer public relations and fundraising to charitable organizations such as Cystic Fibrosis Foundation, Neurofibromatosis (NF), and Loudoun Area Agency on Aging.

Karen graduated from the University of South Florida, Tampa, in 1998 with a Master's degree in business administration, with focuses in Entrepreneurship and management information systems.

For complete bios, visit http://www.reachingpeakshow.com/about.html

Results Radio Show with Tony D. Baker, Annica Westphal, airing Sundays at 12 PM on KFAQ 1170am, Tulsa, Oklahoma, and broadcast across the entire Green Country area, which includes Oklahoma City, Ft. Smith, Arkansas; and Joplin, Missouri.

Theme: Achieving success in business and beyond.

Guest Profile: Internet marketing experts, motivational speakers, life coaches, health experts and others. People that will keep the audience interested that have excitement and passion about their topic. Also, what information they have to offer my audience.

Guest from Hell: Extremely opinionated with no information.

Contact: tony@xeal.com, annica@xeal.com; 918-491-4731; http://www.resultsradioshow.com; Annica Westphal. Best method: E-mail. No response? E-mail or call.

Invited Back? A good show.

Listener Comment: "I felt Annica Westphal represented her audience well. I appreciated that she asked the type of questions the general public listening would be interested in having an answer for. I also liked her enthusiasm and reinforcing comments to the interviewee."—Jeanette Jacono

Guest Comment: "What a great concept! People are always seeking results—in life, in ventures, in business, in love. *Results Radio Show* isn't afraid to step just outside that box and ask some tough questions. I loved being interviewed. It was a real opportunity to encourage others tasting failure to wash it down with perseverance."—Tara Lynn Thompson, http://www.taralynnthompson.blogspot.com/

Bio of Tony Baker: Tony is Oklahoma's leading Internet marketing expert with more than 1,000 clients and over 10 years of Internet marketing experience.

As an author and public speaker, he has written several ebooks and has spoken at conferences throughout the United States.

Seeing Beyond with Bonnie Coleen, on KEST 1450 AM, aired in the greater SF Bay area for more than 18 years.

Theme: Personal growth.

Guest profile: Anyone talking about personal growth. Click "Guest Contact Information" at the top of the website for former guest information. I look for someone who is interested in marketing what they do and believe in. I want people who are pioneers—people doing something different to make a difference. It helps if they are passionate about their topic and work. Among the prominent guests on the show were Wayne Dyer and Charles Thomas Cayce, Edgar Cayce's grandson. I want for them to send me a detailed introduction about them. I usually have a short conversation with potential guests before I book them.

Guest from Hell: The guest from hell is the one with low affect—one who lacks the ability to speak with verve and passion. Believe it or not, I had a very well known personage on the program—one who's written many best sellers and is dynamite on the stage — who totally flopped on the show because he talked in a monotone and lacked energy for his subject — It was, quite frankly a shock and a disappointment.

Contact: bonniecoleen@yahoo.com; http://www.seeingbeyond.com; 510-501 1803. Best method: Just giving me a call or e-mailing through http://www.seeingbeyond.com is sufficient. They may send press kits to: KEST, c/o Bonnie Coleen, 145 Natoma Street, 4th Floor, San Francisco, CA 94105. No response? If for some reason I don't respond to an e-mail, the best way to get my attention is by calling and leaving a short message at 510-501-1803. BE SURE to leave your number twice.

Invited Back? The response from the audience is the number one indicator of who comes back. I feel that any program needs to be a triple win, one for the guest, one for me and one for the audience. I believe that if it's a win for the audience, the guest and I need not worry; it will be a win for both of us.

Bio of Bonnie Coleen: Bonnie started her broadcast career in Santa Cruz, California, but moved her radio program to San Francisco in 1994.

Always a pioneer, Bonnie graduated from college and then gave birth to her first daughter, Michelle, three months later and her second daughter, Catherine, that same year.

During that time, Bonnie was also co-owner of a very successful business that sold office equipment out of three locations. She left the business in 1982 to return to school, attending UCSC to get her teaching credential. Finding that she was a natural born teacher, Bonnie taught high school full time while producing and hosting her daily show.

Psychic herself, Bonnie feels that her greatest gift is the ability to truly HEAR what her guests are saying and help them to communicate their information and inspiration to her listening audience. "In short, I call myself a catalytic converter — one who is constantly encouraging my listeners to discover more about who they are and why they are here."

Shelia Smoot on Your Side with Shelia Smoot on WAGG 610 AM (Cox Owned), Birmingham, AL, weekdays from 2–3 PM. Shelia also hosts a weekly statewide program, *Know Your Rights with Shelia Smoot.*

Theme: Consumer and problem solving, self help.

Guest Profile: All guests are welcomed who are snappy, funny, informative. Boring is out. Want to know their credentials.

Guest from Hell: Someone who can't hold a conversation.

Contact: smoots@jccal.org; 205-966-9683; http://wagg610.com/info/sheliasmoot.html; Toya G. or Shelia Smoot. Best method: Press Kit, Bio, or call. No response? E-mail back or call.

Invited Back? If they are engaging.

Bio of Shelia Smoot: Commissioner Shelia is the first African American female to serve on the five-member Jefferson County Commission and the youngest person elected to the position. During her first term, she oversaw the largest of the county's departments and with her staff championed several large projects in economic and community development. She oversees the departments of Information Technology and Environmental Protection.

Shelia is a 2000 graduate of Leadership Birmingham and a 2004 graduate of Leadership Alabama.

A native of Flint, Michigan, Shelia holds a bachelor's degree in telecommunications and a minor in political science from Michigan State University.

Shrink Rap Radio with "Dr. Dave" (David Van Nuys, Ph.D.) on http://www.shrinkrapradio.com and iTunes.

Theme: Interviews with interesting people in and around the broad field of psychology, personal growth, self-help, etc.

Guest Profile: If authors: psychologist/mental health type authors, self-help. Guests who are interesting and articulate, don't require too much prompting, and have credentials and an area of expertise.

Guest from Hell: Like pulling teeth, speaks in monotone, not self-disclosing, says "uhhhh" too much.

Contact: shrink@shrinkrapradio.com; 707-585-7363; http://www.shrinkrapradio.com and http://wisecounsel.mentalhelp.net; David Van Nuys. Best method: E-mail a query with some info about guest. No response? E-mail or call.

Invited Back? Don't usually do.

Bio of David Van Nuys: When outside of the pod, "Dr. Dave" is also known as David Van Nuys, Ph.D. He is emeritus professor of psychology at Sonoma State University and for seven years served as chair of that department, which has a longstanding reputation for commitment to humanistic, transpersonal, and existential approaches to psychology. David received his doctorate in clinical psychology from the University of Michigan and has worked as a licensed psychotherapist in both California and New Hampshire.

He has also taught psychology at the University of Montana, the University of Michigan, and the University of New Hampshire. He has served as a dissertation advisor for doctoral students at Saybrook Institute and the Institute for Integral Studies.

David also runs a market research consulting business — http://www.e-focusgroups.com — which has served such distinguished clients as *The New York Times*, Apple Computer, IBM, Hewlet Packard, and QuickenLoans.

He co-authored the book *This Is the Zodiac Speaking: Into the Mind of a Serial Killer* (Praeger Trade 2001). HBO picked up an option on the book with the idea of possibly using it as the basis for a mini-series.

In addition to his own show, David is a regular

call-in guest for a drive-time radio show in L.A. on KLAC-AM.

Something You Should Know with Mike Carruthers aired on 200+ radio stations throughout the U.S.

Theme: Very self-help, practical and for "everyday folk."

Guest Profile: Authors and experts. We need credentialed experts, particularly when it comes to any health related stuff. Enthusiasm, knowledgeable and media savvy. That they know how to do an interview and are prepared.

Guest from Hell: Someone who just talks about their book.

Contact: mike@somethingyoushouldknow.net; 203-254-9914; http://www.somethingyoushouldknow.net; Mike Carruthers. Best method: First contact—E-mail a pitch with some background material. Then follow up with a phone call. No response? Call me

Invited Back? See Guest Profile.

Guest Comment: "I have appeared twice on *Something You Should Know* hosted by Mike Carruthers. Each time I found him to have the wonderful quality of asking the right questions to cause you as a guest to sound smarter and wiser than you probably are. Whatever the case, the real beneficiaries are his listeners who take home information that is not just "something they should know," but something they can use immediately to make their lives better."—Mark Goulston, M.D. author *Get Out of Your Own Way at Work* (Perigee Trade 2006) and *Post Traumatic Stress Disorder for Dummies* (For Dummies 2007), http://www.markgoulston.com

Bio of Mike Carruthers: Mike began his radio career over 25 years ago and has worked on the air at KBIG, KIQQ, and KLSX in Los Angeles, as well as several other stations in the U.S. He has also hosted radio specials for Westwood One and ABC Radio and has voiced television projects for 20th Century–Fox, Superstation WTBS and Baywatch.

Starstyle: Be the Star You Are! with Cynthia Brian and Heather Brittany on World Talk Radio/Modavox/Voice America, and terrestrial internationally.

Theme: Positive uplifting authors and books, tools for living a gracious life.

Guest Profile: Upbeat non-fiction authors and books, tools for living a gracious life. Positive, upbeat, energetic, enthusiastic. Someone who gives great show and lets us promote the book. We don't want to hear the words, "Well, in my book, I say...." I personally read every book cover to cover so if a guest is invited on the show, although I can't guarantee sales, I promise them great publicity and a first rate interview—every time.

We have been broadcasting since 1998 so we know good guests. Send us your book, bio, press kit and a follow-up e-mail. Be easy to work with, we'll do the rest. Please, no phone calls, unless asked to call.

Guest from Hell: We've never had a guest from hell as we pre-screen; however, a guest from hell would be a no-show or someone who was not enthusiastic, outgoing, or fun. As a host, I make all my guests feel at home and comfortable. We pride ourselves on reading every book cover to cover so we are always ready to rescue a frightened author. The compliment we most often receive from our guests is that they felt at ease, like they were talking to a best friend over a cup of tea.

Contact: Cynthia@star-style.com; 925-377-STAR (7827); http://www.star-style.com; Cynthia Brian. Best method: Pitches can be e-mailed; however, we have to read the book before we decide to invite a guest on the show. Send books, bio, and press kit to Cynthia Brian, Starstyle—Be the Star You Are!, 1660 School St. #101B, Moraga, Ca. 944556. No items will be returned. All books are donated to Be the Star You Are! charity which empowers women, families, and youth through improved literacy. No response? Unless we are out of the country, we are incredibly fast responders-usually within 24 hours. Feel free to send another e-mail if you do not receive a response. We truly don't have time for phone calls, so please don't ask to speak on the phone unless you want to buy media coaching time.

Invited Back? When a guest has a new book, always contact us. We also re-consider guests who support *Be the Star You Are!* through donations.

Guest Comments:—"I have been interviewed by thousands of interviewers and Cynthia Brian is one of four of the top interviewers in the country today. I feel like we are two bodies in one soul."—Jack Canfield, co-founder *Chicken Soup for the Soul Series*, star of *The Secret*

"About your radio show—I have never been interviewed by a more energetic or well-prepared host. It was such a pleasure."—Carolyn Howard-Johnson, founder, Author's Coalition, author, *The Frugal Book Series*

Bio of Cynthia Brian: *New York Times* best selling co-author of *Chicken Soup for the Gardener's Soul*, author of *Be the Star You Are!*, *99 Gifts for Living, Loving, Laughing*, and *Learning to Make a Difference*, *The Business of Show Business*, and *Miracle Moments*, Cynthia ASID is an internationally acclaimed key note speaker, personal growth consultant, host of radio and TV shows, syndicated columnist and acting coach.

Often referred to by the media as "the Renaissance woman with soul" and to her radio guests as "the Oprah of the Airwaves," Cynthia is a world traveler who speaks French, Spanish, Italian, and Dutch. With nearly three decades of experience working in the entertainment field as an actor, producer, writer, coach, designer, and casting director, she has had the honor of performing with some of the biggest names in the industry.

Cynthia is a certified interior designer and has had her interior and garden design projects featured in TV, commercials, books, and numerous publications. Cynthia is a much in demand speaker on luxury cruise lines and spas around the world inspiring others to be the stars they were born to be by creating a life they design.

Because of her devotion to increasing literacy and positive messages in the world, Cynthia founded and is CEO of the 501(c)(3) charity, Be the Star You Are! (http://www.bethestaryouare.org) empowering women, families and youth at risk. Her motto is "To be a leader, you must be a reader."

Born on a farm in the Napa Valley in Northern California, the eldest of five children, she raised chickens and sheep, drove a tractor and picked fruit to earn enough money to pay her way through college. After being honored as the Outstanding Teenager of California, she was named teenage ambassador to Holland and served as a foreign correspondent for several newspapers. Her travel expeditions gave birth to her writing, speaking, and coaching career.

Take Charge of Your Life with Ellie Bobrow on WDIY 88.1 FM and WXLV, Bethlehem, Pa., aired Monday, 6:30–7:00 PM (ET).

Theme: People doing things to improve their lives or others.

Guest Profile: Wide array, including authors, psychologists and medical doctors. Someone who can speak clearly and succinctly about the topic. Our guests should be able to provide concrete examples of their experience—no platitudes.

Guest from Hell: Guests who speak too generally and in a self serving manner.

Contact: info@wdiy.org; Phone withheld upon request; http://www.wdiy.org; Ellie Bobrow. Best method: Basic resume is fine. Press kit is OK. E-mailing an inquiry is OK. No response? Do not e-mail or call.

Invited Back? The relevance of their topic or topics.

Bio of Eleanor Richman Bobrow: Eleanor has been host of her show since the inception of the station in 1995 as Lehigh Valley Community Public Radio, an NPR affiliate. Her program was inspired by her late husband, Rabbi Jerald Bobrow. During her insomniac years while living in Easton, Pennsylvania (where she still resides), Elly remarked to her husband, "I wish they had an all night radio talk show for insomniacs like me like they do in New York City." Her husband Jerry replied, "That's a great idea! Why don't you do it!?" She replied, "Why me?" To which he replied, "Why not you? It's always been your dream to have a radio talk show. Why not you?" Elly heard the enthusiasm and confidence that her husband had in her, but she put the idea on hold without taking any action. A year later, Jerry died. Elly realized that life was precious and it was important to make every moment count.

After attending a workshop on making dreams and possibilities come true, Elly came home and decided to contact local radio stations. She was given an hour slot on a local news/talk radio show that lasted as long as the station had this format. One day Elly arrived to do her show and was told no more talk/news or info, we're going country — good bye.

She approached WDIY Lehigh Valley Community Public radio and began broadcasting. She also does a monthly hour-long feature show featuring a panel and a call-in on topics of community interest.

Her show has a clear philosophy, "Many events happen to us in life over which we have no control — our only control is our response to life's situations."

Although Elly is a Pennsylvania licensed clinical social worker and marriage and family therapist in practice for 25, she is not the focus of each program. The focus is a topic of interest to all with resources of the community available to help with problems focused upon during the program.

In 2007 she was awarded Professional Woman of the Year by the Business and Professional Women's Society of the Lehigh Valley for her contribution to the awareness of women's issues. In 2004 she was named Social Worker of the Year by the Pennsylvania Division of Social Workers. In 1999 she was awarded third place, with her producer Neil Hever, for her work on a program with survivors of *Kristalnacht*.

U Smile Radio with Lesly Federici on Blog Talk Radio, http://www.blogtalkradio.com/usmile. Lesly also hosts the *New Mom Radio Show*.

Theme: Inspirational life stories, personal achievements, life lessons, etc.

Guest Profile: Athletes, authors, artists, NLP practitioners, life coaches, healers, holistic accountants, perfume designers, all answering the question — how did they get to where they are today? Accessibility in sharing their life story, something to offer others through life experiences. Interested in their life; name dropping is not that important to me, their personal life story is and how it may help someone else.

Guest from Hell: Haven't had one yet. There's something good in everyone-just need to find it

Contact: artles@msn.com; 908-755-3199; http://www.usmileservices.com; Lesly Federici. Best method: E-mail a bio, call with a pitch, and/or send a press kit. No response? I usually get back within a few days. They can always check in.

Invited Back? Scope of topic, attitude and interest to come back.

Guest Comment: "*New Mom Radio Show* shares my passion to empower moms by offering down-to-earth information in an upbeat manner! It was an absolute pleasure to be interviewed about preventing and recovering from postpartum depression."—Dr. Shoshana Bennett, author of *Postpartum Depression for Dummies* (For Dummies 2007), http://www.DrShosh.com

Bio of Lesly Federici: It's been said that Lesly is an inspiration to others. In spite of her being "legally blind" she reinvented herself by creating a radio show that explores and highlights the magnificence of others. Lesly believes everyone has a story to tell, and anyone who listens learns from them. Her show was created to share one's voice, their "wealth" of inspiration to others.

A Rutgers (NJ) graduate, RN, wellness coach and a Reiki master, Lesly has prepared expectant parents for parenthood for more than 10 years. She is an advocate in raising awareness of the prevalence and management of "Baby Blues" in new mothers. She coaches new moms and others interested in wellness of mind and body. She also teaches Reiki and is an artist.

Ms. Federici lives in New Jersey with her family.

Seniors

Sharing the Wisdom of Age for a Better World — Third Age Foundation's tagline

Aging Outside the Box with Shirley Mitchell and O. E. Cruiser Small, on http://www.agingoutsidethebox.net Also Aired; WMA, RP, MP3, POD, CD.

Theme: Aging outside the box with power, style and vitality.

Guest Profile: We interview authors, writers, speakers and medical experts with specialties in aging, baby boomers, nutrition, diet, exercise, faith, women's issues, women, health and medical information, travel, entertainment and culinary. We look for professionalism, excitement, a positive attitude, passion, organization, and a willingness to share information and expand horizons. We ask for their resume, background, accomplishments, websites to check, works that have been published. We also call them prior to the show airing to do a voice check and go over the show with them.

Guest from Hell: Someone who is negative and unorganized. Who takes off with the show and disregards the host or tech people.

Contact: Agent@lighthousecoastalliterary.com; http://agingoutsidethebox.blogspot.com; http://www.artistfirst.com/Aging.htm; http://fabulousafter50.blogspot.com; http://www.sensationalafter60.com; O. E. Cruiser Small, Agent/Director/Producer; 678-471-6092. Best method: I would prefer an e-mail requesting information on our show and telling us why they want to be a guest, and what they have to offer our listeners. No response? We always answer our e-mail on a daily basis unless we are on the road traveling to events. Send a second e-mail if you do not hear back from us within three days.

Invited Back? How well the show goes, how well the guest interacts with the host, and how much information they share.

Bio of Shirley Mitchell: Raised in the South on a tenant cotton farm, Shirley had a passion to make her life and others' lives more productive. Seeing what aging did to those, her quest has been to "Promote Positive Aging" for all, especially for those who are approaching or are Golden 50 or beyond.

A national author/columnist/speaker and radio host, Shirley is known as "The Golden Egg of Aging" and the "Original Baby Boomer Promoter" because of her tremendous insight years previous to the coming of the baby boomer wave of aging younger. She's a mother of three and a grandmother of eight. An unexpected divorce later in life promoted a more positive approach to her future and what was to play in it.

Her books are *The Beauty of Being God's Woman* (Strode Publishers 1981), *Spiritual Sparks for Busy Women* (Strode Publishers 1982), *The Christian Writer's Diary* (self-published), *Fabulous After 50* (New Leaf Press 2000) — the first book in the series of inspirational and motivational books, with two more slated for publication, and *Sensational After 60* (New Leaf Press 2005). Shirley is also the co-author of three books — *Love Notes for Mom, Love Notes for Dad* and *101 Great Ways to Improve Your Life.*

Her weekly newspaper column, "Fabulous after Fifty," in the *Sand Mountain Reporter* has been going on strong now for over 15 years, and is the model for her on-line syndicated column, "RE-FIRE not RE-TIRE." She also has an on-line newsletter called "Passionate Sparks." Shirley is a regular contributing columnist for the on-line "Senior LifeStyles Magazine" out of Westminster, Colorado, and a featured columnist-writer for the on-Line "Passionate for Life Magazine" out of California.

Senior Legal Strategies with Henry Carpenter on WBCB 1490 AM, aired In Studio and at Attleboro Retirement Village, aired Tuesday at 9 AM (ET).

Theme: Legal and life advice for seniors.

Guest Profile: Individuals who provide useful, practical advice for seniors and persons caring for them — care workers, doctors/nurses, home care services. We investigate their business/organization to confirm they truly care for the clients/listeners.

Guest from Hell: Someone aggressively promoting themselves or their service, rather than providing useful knowledge for the listeners.

Contact: henryc@haciilaw.com; 215-493-0727; http://www.buckscountyelderlaw.com; Henry Carpenter. Best method: E-mail or phone. I prefer the personal touch — a call or office visit to introduce self and service is usually best. No response? Absolutely call or e-mail; even with the best intentions sometimes my paying job takes precedent and radio matters slip through the cracks.

Invited Back? If they provide useful information and handle themselves reasonably well on air.

Bio of Henry Carpenter: Henry and Bucks County Elder Law LLC, the law firm he created, specialize in the areas of elder law and estate planning. With over 20 years experience, his practice focuses on the client and emphasizes providing individualized, caring counsel to Seniors and their families in all areas, including long term health care, asset protection, medicaid eligibility, estate planning, tax planning and estate administration.

Henry practices in Pennsylvania and New Jersey, with offices in Yardley. He is a member of the Pennsylvania, Bucks County and New Jersey Bar Associations, the Elder Law Committee of the Pennsylvania Bar Association and the National Academy of Elder Law Attorneys.

The Third Age with David Debin and Peter Brill, MD on KZSB 1290 AM, Santa Barbara, CA, and Ventura County; now off the air.
Theme: Aging gracefully.
Guest Profile: Authors, doctors, experts on aging, representatives from aging organizations, financial advisers, vocational. Knowledge, experience, sense of humor. We want credentials and a short bio. Some prominent guests have included Eric Olsen, president of AARP and David Simon, Deepak Chopra's partner.
Guest from Hell: Won't stop talking to hear the next question.
Contact: contact@thirdagefoundation.com; 805-969-9794; http://www.thirdagefoundation.com; David Debin. Best method: Through website. No response? Try it again.
Invited Back? How much we learn, how enjoyable it is
Bio of David Debin: David enjoyed a long and successful career in Hollywood as a writer and producer in television, collaborating with such talents as Rock Hudson, Suzanne Pleshette, Ron Silver, Jason Alexander, Melanie Griffith, Sally Struthers, and Billy Campbell. He produced an Emmy-nominated inspirational movie about a deaf stunt woman, *Silent Victory: The Kitty O'Neil Story*, starring Stockard Channing, James Farrentino, and Brian Dennehy.

"At the age of 48 I was producing TV shows at MGM," he says. "I had been in the business for 25 years and though highly successful, no longer felt fulfilled."

Thus, he began a second career in writing. *Nice Guys Finish Dead* (Random House 1992) was followed by other books, earning David a place on radio and television shows. He was then asked to teach creative writing at a local university and with the combination of writing and teaching found the meaning and fulfillment he'd been missing in life.

For the last several years David has taught his "Reinforcing Creative Confidence" course to students of all ages. His work caught the attention of Deepak Chopra, author of *Ageless Body, Timeless Mind: The Quantum Alternative to Growing Old*, who wrote, "In his creative writing course, David Debin links students' spiritual awareness to their center of creativity and empowers them to express themselves in new and profound ways."

Bio of Dr. Peter Brill: A physician and psychiatrist, Dr. Brill studied organizations at the Wharton School of Business, and marriages at the Marriage Council of Philadelphia, and continued as a professor in two departments at the University of Pennsylvania. He was also a consultant to 150 organizations, and ran two national companies, while carrying on a private practice.

A best-selling author, Dr. Brill wrote *Taming Your Turmoil: Managing the Transitions of Adult Life* (Prentice Hall Trade 1981). He also writes a newspaper column on the same subject. He is married, has two children, 20 and 15 and lives in Santa Barbara, CA.

"One Sunday afternoon I was sitting in my living room anxiously waiting for the workweek to begin. At this time, I was running two different national companies I had started, working 12 to 14 hours a day. I was exhausted. I was too overwhelmed to even notice simple pleasures: the beautiful fall leaves changing color outside my window. A voice in my head said, 'If I had a heart attack—I would change my life.'

"But a sudden revelation hit me—I realized that I didn't need to get sick ... I could just change! Without realizing it, I had just entered the Third Age—where money, power and status were no longer fulfilling to me. There was a new passion and joy to living life differently. Life had a new purpose.

"Now I was eager to find out what other people had done to deal successfully with this time of life. To that end, I started a radio show called *The Third Age*. In more than 400 interviews conducted for the show, I learned how other people had gone about finding passion, purpose and joy in the Third Age. (In further research I also discovered that people who found these values in the Third Age live at least 7 to 8 years longer!)"

Sports

"There is no luck except where there is discipline."—Translation of a German quotation from website of Lou Krieger, an expert poker player

The Adventure Show with Mike Falcon and Sean Millington, nationally syndicated in Canada.
Theme: Adventure lifestyle.
Guest Profile: World's leading adventure athletes, coaches, trainers, nutritionists.
Guest from Hell: The ones where every answer is 10 minutes long.
Contact: mike@theadventureshow.com; http://www.theadventureshow.com; Mike Falcon. Best method: E-mail. No response? We respond to all e-mail related to the show.
Invited Back? Must be very engaging/doesn't happen often.
Bio of Mike Falcon: Mike wanted to be a fighter pilot, but circumstance and timing dictated other-

wise. The first call-up came while nursing a broken femur after bouncing off a tree in an otherwise uneventful ski race. The second call to duty occurred while incommunicado in war torn Beirut. The third call never came, so he pursued a life of adventure.

As a world traveler, he's experienced many adventures, some foolish, others challenging, but all rewarding. Along the way, often accompanied by incredibly talented athletes, he skied, surfed, swam, kited, kayaked, rafted, hiked, biked, bungeed, climbed, dropped into crevasses, raced cars and flew in fighter jets. So, hosting an adventure show is a pretty good fit for one whose skill set evolved from a life at play. "Truthfully," he says, "it's likely the only real job I'm qualified for."

BDD Talk Radio with Eric SanInocencio on Blog Talk Radio

Theme: Professional and amateur baseball.

Guest Profile: Major League Baseball personalities. We look for guests who have some sort of expertise in relation to baseball. The only thing we really want to confirm about potential guests is that they are tied to professional baseball in some way. Our audience is not all that concerned with the sound of their voice or past interview experience. Our definition of expertise is broad, though, so we're happy to have guests such as baseball players, executives, authors, and reporters. My personal favorite was Kansas City GM Dayton Moore.

Guest from Hell: Unfortunately, for our show, it requires the guests to call into our switchboard. It can leave you on pins and needles hoping to see their number pop up in queue. That transition is always difficult. So tardiness is inevitable.

Contact: gscassistantsid@mindspring.com; 205-914-5146; http://www.blogtalkradio.com/baseballdigestdaily; Eric SanInocenio. Best method: A potential guest could contact us by any of the above mentioned methods (pitching over the phone, e-mailing a bio, or shipping us a press kit). We're pretty liberal about getting guests on the show.

No Response? I recommend the guest e-mail again AND call. I've found that spam filters these days will reject unknown messages from time to time.

Invited Back? We generally have a good sense of how well an interview goes. Since most of our guests are high profile in nature, we're generally happy to have them back at any time.

Bio of Eric SanInocencio: Eric is the assistant sports information director of the Gulf South Conference and the man behind MVN's Rays Anatomy. http://mvn.com/mlb-rays. Eric came to the GSC from the University of Alabama in Birmingham, where he served as the assistant director of media relations beginning January 2006.

While at UAB, Eric was the primary contact for baseball and volleyball and also assisted in game operations for men's basketball. Prior to then, he was the media relations intern for the Southeastern Conference in Birmingham, serving as the primary contact for volleyball, swimming and diving, track and field and softball. He was also on staff to work the Nokia Sugar Bowl and the first and second rounds of the NCAA Men's Basketball Tournament.

The Bronx, NY, native is no stranger to the GSC, graduating from the University of Montevallo in 2003, where he was a four-year letterman in baseball and earned a Bachelor of Arts degree in mass communications.

Bios of former hosts Joe Hamrahi and Craig Brown: Joe is a licensed CPA with an MBA in accounting. He currently works as the controller for a Manhattan public relations firm; married with three children, he lives in New York.

In 2004, Joe came up with the idea of starting a web site that focused on all facets of baseball, from news to statistics to analysis and player development. He partnered up with a long time friend and colleague, Matt Gabriel, and together they developed what we now know as *Baseball Digest Daily*. Over the past few years, Joe has become well known within the media circles of major and minor league baseball. He represented *Baseball Digest Daily* at the 2005 All-Star Game in Detroit and has interviewed countless professional players and executives including Mike Piazza, Jeff Francoeur, Mariano Rivera, Rickie Weeks, Josh Beckett, John Schuerholz, Doug Melvin, Bill James, and the legendary Johnny Podres.

Craig is a senior writer for *Baseball Digest Daily* and co-host of *BDD Talk Radio*. He began blogging about the Royals prior to the 2005 season, which was just in time to chronicle their franchise record 106 loss season. Since he began jotting down words on the cyber pages, he's contributed to *Creative Sports*, *HEATER Magazine* and *The Hardball Times*. Currently, Craig's Royal musings appear on the Most Valuable Network at Royals Authority. A lefthander, Craig is disappointed he didn't understand the value of being a LOOGY until it was too late. When not thinking about the Royals, Craig works as a post production video editor in Kansas City where he lives with his wife and two daughters.

Big Nation Radio with Jason Stern, a/k/a "Special Ed" on BlogTalkRadio, http://www.blogtalkradio.com

Theme: Fitness, bodybuilding, MMA, powerlifting.

Guest Profile: Pro athlete, trainer, expert. I look for someone who is well-spoken with something interesting to talk about. I find that natural Storytellers make the best guests.

I don't care about past interview experiences at all. Everyone has the potential to be a great guest. I do attempt to pre-interview all guests to gauge such things as listener comprehension, sound quality, and their background/credentials. Recent guests were NFL Pro Bowl linebacker Demeco Ryans of the Houston Texans and former 3-time All-American running back and current pro bodybuilder Charles Dixon.

Guest from Hell: A guest who gives one or two word answers is almost as bad as the guest who gives run-on, 5-minute rambling answers to simple questions. Also, a guest who is promoting a product or service and makes reference to that product or service in every answer needs to be put to sleep.

Contact: jay@bignationradio.com; 917-922-0835; http://www.bignationradio.com. Best method: E-mailing a bio and a suggested topic is the best idea. A press kit isn't necessary and neither is a phone call. On *Big Nation Radio*, we're very open to hearing from potential guests. No response? We try to respond to all inquiries. If we don't feel a particular guest is "radio-worthy," we'll usually just thank them for contacting us. If they are "radio-worthy," we will usually let them know that they're in our future guest pool and we will contact them when we need them.

Invited Back? Two things determine if invited back: Audience feedback and demand, or my own determination that someone has a unique insight that will always make for good radio.

Bio of Jason Stern: Jason is an entrepreneur and motivational speaker who has appeared on numerous television shows, including "Good Morning America," "CNN Headline News," "Montel Williams," and the front page of *The New York Times*.

In addition to being a former NFL agent, he is a former competitive bodybuilder, Brazilian Jui-Jitsu practitioner, and Golden Gloves boxer who has interviewed some of the world's top professional athletes including World Boxing champions Evander Holyfield, Miguel Cotto, Shane Mosley, and Zab Judah, NFL stars Vernon Davis and Joseph Addai, and WWE/UFC star Brock Lesnar. He has written for *Fightnews*, *MMA News*, *Sherdog*, Bodybuilding.com, *Muscular Development*, *Kaged Muscle*, and the *Press of Atlantic City*.

The Big Wild with Gundy and Big Red aired on 16 affiliates in WI and MN. Dan "Gundy" Gunderson also produces *Lunch Pail Logic* (page 217), where you'll find his bio.

Theme: Hunting, fishing and eating.

Guest Profile: Anyone who has ever picked up a fishing rod or firearm with an out-going personality and sense of humor. Almost every guest has been contacted via phone prior to the interview. Credentials and personality are paramount. If we don't want to listen, the public won't want to either.

Guest from Hell: Monotone with one word answers.

Contact: dangunderson@tds.net; 608-833-2040; http://www.thebigwild.com; Dan Gunderson. Best method: Call with a pitch, e-mail a bio, send a press kit. No response? See above.

Invited Back? Entertainment value.

Broad Minded Poker with Susie Isaacs and Gavin Jerome on Hold 'Em Radio, http://www.holdemradio.com; now off the air.

Theme: Poker, mostly human interest.

Guest Profile: Anyone with anything to say on the subject of poker. Someone who will talk and has something to say: good stories, personal achievements, the good, the bad, the ugly of yesterday, today or tomorrow in the wacky wonderful world of poker. Poker players, famous and not-so-famous, have many great stories. It's great if I can google and learn something about them so I can keep the interview flowing.

Guest from Hell: One who answers questions with one or two words. One who you feel you have to open their mouths and pull out words.

Contact: susieismspoker@aol.com; 702-361-4505; http://www.susieisaacs.com; Susie Isaacs. Best method: E-mail or phone — but not their agent; I want to talk directly to them so I will know if they will be good on the radio. No response? Either I or my assistant will get back to them. If this does not happen, they should follow up with an e-mail or phone call.

Invited Back? My response to them and how the audience responds.

Guest Comments: "I enjoyed being a guest on Susie Isaacs' talk show. She is very passionate about poker and knows her subject well. Susie is a great interviewer and the hour passed too quickly." — Linda Johnson, Just Pack — We'll do the rest!, http://www.cardplayercruises.com

Bio of Susie Isaacs: Susie is best known for being the first woman to win the World Series of Poker ladies championship back-to-back in 1996 and 1997. In 1998, she placed 10th in the World Series of Poker $10,000 main event vying for the one million dollar first prize. She became the second woman in history to accomplish such an outstanding finish.

In the 2006 World Series main event she managed to place in the top five percent out of a record breaking field of 8,773. In 2007 she placed 35th in the ladies event out of a field of almost 1,300. That score combined with the many other money finishes in that particular event at the WSOP gave her the distinction of being the highest scoring woman ever in the ladies world championship event.

Susie is a professional tournament poker player. She has won various titles and placed in the money numerous times over the years. She was invited to play on the Pro Poker Tour of the World Poker Tour in 2005. You may have spotted her on TV in a variety of poker shows. She is a regular freelance columnist for a variety of publications where her popular column "Chip Chatter" is featured.

Books by Susie Isaacs: *MsPoker: Up Close and Personal* (DB Graphics 1999). The follow-up, *MsPoker:*

I'm Not Bluffing (Mimi Mc Corporation 2006) is a two book series. Part I includes her personal story and great true stories from the green. Part II is solely poker tournament strategy. She is also the author of *1000 Best Poker Strategies and Secrets* (Sourcebooks 2006), and *Queens Can Beat Kings Broad-Minded Poker for Winning Women* (Kensington 2007).

Dick Santino's Fantasy Sports Show on Tribeca Radio.Net now NYTALKRADIO with Dick Santino, www.nytalkradio.net

Theme: Fantasy sports talk show.

Guest Profile: Specific information on key areas of fantasy sports. We look for guests who have specific information that can help out our listeners gain valuable information. Their experience level and success are the best indication of what they have to offer our show. We like guests who are not mainstream or high profile.

Guest from Hell: A guest who does not back up their opinions with facts.

Contact: DickSantino@comcast.net; 516-316-5324 (Personal Company Number); www.DickSantino.com. Best method: E-mail or phone is ok. A bio or a referral will do fine. No response? I got to this point by hustling and never quitting. If I overlook a reply or if I do not respond in a timely manner. Staying on top of me is ok, unless I flat reject an e-mail or solicitation.

Invited Back? The flow we have with them on the air.

Bio of Dick Santano: Dick is all about the sports. He has been playing fantasy sports for over 15 years and has won numerous titles. He plays Fantasy Baseball, football, basketball, racing, golf, horses, international soccer, fishing, and WNBA. There is not a sport he will not research and compete in. He has won national competitions in Fantasy Baseball, Fantasy Football and Fantasy Basketball. Dick is constantly invited to play in leagues, but he only chooses the most competitive leagues because he likes the thrill of victory against the best. He has a fountain of sports knowledge and loves to share it with others, including those he competes against. Dick says, "giving my competition a better opportunity to attempt to beat me makes me work harder to win." Listening to the show will give you an edge against your competition and put you in the money.

The Drive on Fox with Chris Myers and Sean Farnham on Fox Sports Radio Network, aired on 105 stations across America and on XM 142 24/7.

Theme: Sports and entertainment.

Guest Profile: Players, coaches, GM's, actors, sometime authors. Personality, name recognition and someone who has an impact on the sport they play.

Guest from Hell: A guy who says you know too much and doesn't seem interested. They don't last very long on our program if they are shy or not willing to display a sense of interest being on the program.

Contact: Cmyers@foxsports.net and erikp@fsr247.com; Chris Myers — 310-614-4408 (Cell); http://www.FoxSports.com; Erik Peterson, producer, 818-605-2950 (Cell). Best method: Calling, via the e-mail, sending a press release is good as well. No response? Call me.

Invited Back? If they were engaging, showed a sense of humor, and got our audience interested in the program.

Bio of Chris Myers: Chris is a sideline reporter for the NFL on Fox every Sunday, host of NASCAR on Fox, and once had an interview show on Fox Sport Net called *CMI The Chris Myers Interviews*. He also won a Grammy for his work at ESPN.

With more than 20 years of broadcasting experience, Chris has covered virtually every major sports event including the Super Bowl, the World Series, the Daytona 500, and the Olympic Games and has interviewed personalities such as Mohammad Ali, Mike Tyson, Tom Brady, Kobe Bryant, and Derek Jeter. He has also hosted shows and events on the Discovery Channel, Tennis Channel, and the Military Channel and serves as the play-by-play commentator for Tampa Bay Buccaneers pre-season games that air locally on WFLA-TV.

Chris is known for such catch phrases as: "I kid because I care." "You ... you're not good." "Crazy go nuts." ... [And That Deserves a Wow!] He is also credited with establishing the concept of "Did You Know?" As host of *Up Close*, he was the first to conduct a live interview with OJ Simpson after both his criminal trial and civil lawsuit.

Chris and his wife have two children and live in Malibu, CA.

The EquiSport Report with Les Salzman on Sirius Radio Network, Channel 125 on Tuesdays, 5:30–6:30 PM (ET), and on http://www.attheracesandbeyond.com

Theme: Horses from A to Z.

Guest Profile: Trainers, riders, breeders and practitioners as well as notable horse enthusiasts. Knowledge and personality are our two key flags. Voice is important but passion is more important. We want the guest to have energy and if we can hot their target we're in good shape.

Guest from Hell: My ex-wife ... only kidding. Self absorbed guests make for boring radio.

Contact: Ls9495@gmail.com; 561-317-4500; http://www.lwsracing.com; Les Salzman. Best method: Call with a pitch, e-mail a bio or send a press kit. No response? E-mail or call.

Invited Back? If I haven't offended them. Actually, we get a pulse of what will work and will go back if we think the audience will enjoy it.

Bio of Les Salzman: For more than two decades, Les has been a certified equestrian appraiser, thoroughbred and standardbred trainer, bloodstock agent (responsible for purchasing and/or breeding of numerous stakes winners), manager of major breeding farms, and newspaper columnist. He has co-hosted both radio and television series over several networks including Fox and Sirius. He operates a public racing stable in Florida.

Les has a Masters of Education degree from the New Jersey Educational Consortium, Princeton, NJ.

The Extreme Scene with Cyrus Saatsaz, Steve Blankenship and Omar Etcheverry on KNBR 1050 AM, aired in San Francisco, Northern California, and on the Internet.

Theme: Action sports talk radio.

Guest Profile: Athletes, writers, filmmakers, pretty much anyone associated with action sports. Name recognition first (to attract an audience), talent a close second, personality a close third. Sound of their voice isn't important. Biography is most important, followed by what they're promoting (if they're promoting anything).

Kelly Slater, surfing superstar, Molly and Mason Aguirre, Olympic snowboarding champions, and actor Johnny Knoxville have been guests.

Guest from Hell: Some chick who's all high and mighty about herself, won't play around with our jokes. Conservatives.

Contact: extremescene@knbr.com; 415-995-6871; http://www.knbr.com/extremescene; Cyrus Saatsaz, producer. Best method: E-mail bios and press kits. No response? A follow-up is always good. If a guest doesn't hear back after the second or third time, they should get the hint.

Invited Back? Repertoire with the hosts, listener feedback.

Bios of Cyrus Saatsaz, Steve Blankenship and Omar Etcheverry: The concept for the action-sports talk show originated more than five years ago. After entertaining their friends one night with their typical couch banter, old college friends Cyrus and Steve decided to take their passion for action sports and ability to communicate themselves in an entertaining, intelligent and witty fashion, to the next level.

Six months later, the show debuted, with Kelly Slater joining them in-studio for the inaugural program. Pro surfer Omar Etcheverry officially joined the program as a host in 2007, developing a relationship with Cyrus and Steve that started at the 2003 Cold Water Classic, a traditional surf contest in Omar's hometown of Santa Cruz.

From the moment Cyrus hit the San Diego waters in his teenage years, catching waves has become an obsession for the young host. Born and raised in the Bay Area, Cyrus frequently visited San Diego and began surfing at the age of 15, falling in love the moment he attempted to ride his first wave.

Born in Weed, CA, and raised in Redding, Steve starting snowboarding at nearby Mt. Shasta Ski Park at 13, when boarding was still banned at virtually all Lake Tahoe ski resorts. At 18, Steve was a sponsored rider for the next couple of years. He's been charging it on the mountain ever since.

Once he moved to San Luis Obispo, CA, he began surfing up and down the Central Coast, and traveling to the likes of Hawaii, Mexico, and Costa Rica.

Born and raised in Santa Cruz, Omar "O-Dog" Etcheverry began surfing at age 11. A formidable competitor from the get-go, he was named to the 1996 U.S. Surf team and helped them clinch a long-awaited World Championship title.

Out of the water, O-Dog and his brother aka The Etch Bros are blowing up the Santa Cruz night scene, producing and spinning dance music and promoting shows. When The Hook's inside sections are firing, you'll find him threading his remote-controlled surfer through heaving one-foot barrels.

Fightin' Words with Aaron Jaco and Bob Carroll on WWPR 1490AM, Tampa, FL.

Theme: Boxing, sports.

Guest Profile: Athletes, boxing writers. Someone involved in the sport of boxing, like a boxer, promoter, manager, trainer or writer. We don't need to know a whole lot beforehand — we research the guests before we have them on air. Some of our best guests have been WBO Heavyweight champion Shannon Briggs, not only a good fighter, but possibly the funniest guy we have ever had on the show, Light Heavyweight champion Stevie Cunningham, and Alex Ramos, president of the Retired Boxers Foundation who is spearheading a pension plan for retired boxers.

Guest from Hell: Someone who gives yes and no answers to a question and seems like it is bothering them to be on the air. (We have had that happen more than once)

Contact: fightinwords1490@yahoo.com; 941-518-4935; http://www.fightinwordsonline.com; Bob Carroll. Best method: The best way to approach us is by sending an e-mail with a small bio and contact number. We rarely turn down an interesting person for an interview. No response? We answer all e-mails, but should one slip by, e-mail us again.

Invited Back? The way they interact with us.

Guest Comment: "Being on the *Fightin' Words* radio program was one of the most satisfying experiences I have had as founder and president of the Retired Boxers Foundation. Both Aaron and Bob were interested in what I had to say and they were so respectful of me and of the Retired Boxers Foundation. I have been on hundreds of radio shows and this one was the most meaningful because of the hospitality of the hosts and their genuine interest in what I had to say. As a matter of fact, Bob Carroll is now one of the RBF's area representatives! I consider him a friend as a result of that radio show and the concern he expressed off the air as well." — Alex "The Bronx Bomber" Ramos, founder and president, Retired Boxers Foundation, http://www.retiredboxers.org

Bios of Aaron Jaco and Bob Carroll: Aaron is a

light heavyweight fighter with a current record of 14–2, and holder of the NBA Junior Intercontinental Light Heavyweight Title. He is a cruiserweight with a deceiving 2–2 record.

Aaron and Adam bring the show a perspective from inside the ring and what happens before and after a fight. They are the sons of 1980–90's heavyweight contender David Jaco. Aaron and Adam also provide boxing training. Bob, his wife Kathy and his father Butch are all training at the Jaco gym. To learn more about the training and how you can train in boxing, see the Jaco Boxing website at http://www.teamjacoboxingfitness.com.

Bob is a longtime boxing fan who brings the perspective from a fan's point of view. As a native of Philadelphia, his views can be vicious and to the point. Bob has been a fan of boxing since he saw *Rocky* in 1976.

The Golf Connection with Loyce Smallwood is aired Thursdays, 9–10 AM on KAHI AM 950, Auburn, Ca. Loyce also hosts *The Music Connection*. See the show entry under Entertainment for bio.

Theme: Golf.

Guest Profile: Instructors and country club staff and low-handicap players. Authenticity; personality; color; background. Will they show up?

Guest from Hell: I don't have boring, one-dimensional, self-serving people.

Contact: loy@foothill.net; 530-906-4502; http://www.kahi.com/Loyce-tips.htm; Loyce. Best method: E-mail with bio. No response? I always respond.

Invited Back? If they show up and show appreciation.

Hockey Hour/Canadian Sport with Jon Waldman, Russ Cohen, Shane Malloy, Steve Feldman and others on *Canadian Sport—The Magazine* (the radio show with Jon Waldman, Russ Cohen and Jeffrey Morris on http://www.sportsology.net)

Theme: Discusses all sports across Canada.

Guest Profile: Sports or sports-related, including wrestling, MMA, etc. For me, a guest needs to be able to talk more than I do. They need to take my 10 to 20-word question and turn it into a 100-word answer. There's enough time that people hear my voice on a show.

I like to know as little as possible about my first-time guests. If I know about them beforehand, chances are a lot of their hardcore fans do as well.

Guest from Hell: Someone who takes sports too seriously. You have to realize that sports are ultimately about leisure and entertainment; http://www.sportsology.net

Contact: Bookings are done through Russ—rcohen@sportsology.net or Jon at jwaldman@mts.net; Phone — Withheld upon request; Jon Waldman, Russ Cohen, Shane Malloy (XM) or Jeffrey Morris (Canadian Sport). Best method: Best way is to either shoot me an e-mail with a press release. Out-of-the-blue is best done today electronically, hands down. No response? If that happens, send a second e-mail with a high priority marker. That will catch my eye, even if it's in a junk mail bin.

Invited Back? While there are guests I can talk to over and over because I've built a kinship with them, I always like to have someone on who has news or a deep perspective that can be applied to an ever-changing topic, such as new rules in hockey or innovations in the hobby.

Bio of Jon Waldman: Jon has been a co-host on the Sportsology Radio Network for three years, and XM Radio for one year. He has been a regular contributor to *The Hockey News, Hockey Business News, The Hot Dog Hockey Post, The Winnipeg Free Press, The Winnipeg Sun, Winnipeg Men's Magazine, SLAM! Sports* and others since graduating from Ryerson University in 2002. Jon is also an editor with Matrix Group Inc., a trade publication company, and has done contract work for Sport Media Group and Topps among others.

Jon lives in Winnipeg with his wife, Elana.

Kidz 'n' Sports with Mike Davis aka Coach Mike, on 1680 AM KDSV, Whittier, CA, on 1680 AM, and on http://www.AdrenalineRadio.com

Theme: Youth sports.

Guest Profile: Coaches, players, officials, administrators, recruiters, sports organizations etc. I look for guests who have some involvement in youth sports and who have something to offer parents to help their children have a better youth sports experience.

What do they have to offer youth sports? A long time coach perhaps with many lessons to learn from (such as Coach George Rykovich, head football coach at Manitou Springs HS in Colorado Springs, CO, for 36 years); umpires, players experiences, etc.

Guest from Hell: That's hard to say. I've had one or two guests who were tough interviews, i.e., stumbled for answers, unprepared, poor communicators.

Contact: coachmike@kidznsports.com; 562-416-5102; http://www.kidznsports.com; Mike Davis. Best method: Initially by e-mail or website form about what you have to offer that benefits youth sports, either for the kids or the parents. No response? Usually it's because I didn't see the first e-mail. Perhaps it went into a spam filter or something. If you don't receive a reply within a day or two send the e-mail again. Even if the guest is not someone I would want to bring on I will still reply to their e-mail.

Invited Back? Usually if the guest is a good, interesting interview which is often signified by the fact that we could have done another hour because we had so much information and lots of fun.

Bio of Mike Davis: Mike has been coaching youth sports since about 1975 — basketball, baseball, and softball. He ran cross country in high school, and coached high school varsity fastpitch softball for eight years.

Full bio at http://www.kidznsports.com/coachmike.

Minor League Baseball Radio with Tim Kuda on Blog Talk Radio, http://www.blogtalkradio.com/milbradio

Theme: Sports, baseball.

Guest Profile: Sports figures, personalities, former athletes. People who are interesting and have things to say about their lives or their profession. How they interview and handle the tough questions Do they answer or do they back away?

Guest from Hell: Guest that only answers questions with yes and no.

Contact: timkuda@MiLBRadio.com; 630-464-4134; http://www.MiLBRadio.com; Tim Kuda. Best method: E-mail a bio. Or call with pitch. Or send a press kit. Anyway, I am always looking for interesting people who have something to say and others will enjoy listening to. No response? Try me again or give me a call.

Invited Back? If they hold my attention. If I am looking for a way to end the interview, they are probably not coming back.

Bio of Tim Kuda: Tim has been participating in sports most of his life. From the Chicago area and a Chicago sports fan, his baseball alliance is to the north side of town. Tim has lived and mostly died with the Cubs since the Bill Buckner days in the early 80s but don't hold that against him. Anyone can have a bad century. Tim's "real" job is an air traffic controller so he apologizes if he talks too fast.

NY Baseball Digest with Mike Silva (podcast), aired Sundays at 6 PM (ET) syndicated on 1240 AM WGBB, Long Island, www.am1240wgbb.com; also on www.blogtalkradio.com/nybaseballtalk and New York Sports Radio, www.sportsradio.ny.com. Mike also hosts *Gotham Hoops Live.*

Theme: New York baseball.

Guest Profile: Former athletes, journalist, fans, bloggers. I look for a guest that is engaging and able to carry a two-way dialogue. Usually they have a unique story that is outside what you would normally get on mainstream radio. I would like to know their past, present, and future. With my show it's about baseball. I like to set up how they got to the present time and what they hope to achieve going forward.

Guest from Hell: Someone who gives one or two word answers. The worst guests are those that will not detail their answers.

Contact: msilva126@aol.com; 646-716-8187; www.nybaseballdigest.com; Mike Silva. Best method: Phone or e-mail. Normally I get an e-mail from someone that is interested in the show. I do most of the reaching out to potential guests. Since I am less than a year on the air the awareness of a show like mine is nowhere near the mainstream. Big stations like WFAN and ESPN have people reaching out to them. I need to work a bit harder and prospect for well known names as well individuals that have talent. No response? I try to get back to all guests in a timely manner. At the very least tell them I got their e-mail and will be setting something up in the near future. I think I have done that with just about every guest with the exception of a few.

Invited Back? If a guest is invited back that means they have the ability for fresh content in the future. I never like to repeat the same story. Usually journalists are the most likely to be invited back. They have the advantage of discussing the new topics of the day by "painting a fresh word picture" on the story.

Guest Comment: "In an arena filled with ignorance coupled with intolerance, Mike Silva provides both an intelligent take on New York sports and the humility to accept other points of view. As a frequent guest on Mike's program, I am always struck by his facile ability on a range of topics, his quick wit, and his ability to treat the listener with respect. I believe that before he's finished, millions of New Yorkers will second my assessment."—Howard Megdal, *New York Observer*

Bio of Mike Silva: Mike grew up a passionate sports fan in Brooklyn, New York. His fondest memories are living with the daily drama and heartbreak of his two favorite teams: The Mets and Knicks. He lived through the "Worst Team Money Can Buy," rooted for Pat Riley's Knicks, and felt disappointment with the near miss Mets title in 2000. In 2007 he decided to jump into the world of freelance reporting by creating *NY Baseball Talk* on 1240 AM WGBB Long Island. Mike was able to produce, host, and sell ad time to keep the show afloat for the 2007 baseball season. By joining Gotham Sports Media in November 2007, he came full circle and now is part of the independent coverage of baseball and basketball in New York. He prides himself on bringing listeners a show that is fair and balanced without forgetting his roots as a sports fan. Regardless of who is your favorite team one thing is for sure: No other host connects better with his fans then Mike. If you haven't listened to him yet what are you waiting for?

The Performance Nutrition Show with Jose Antonio, Ph.D., and Carla Sanchez on 1470AM WNN, aired in south Florida and over the web as a podcast. The show alternates with *The Strength-Power Hour* (page 269) in the same time slot, Sunday 4–5 PM (ET).

Theme: Sports nutrition and fitness/figure competitions.

Guest Profile: Personal trainers, scientists, fitness and figure competitors, athletes, doctors, nutrition experts. Someone who is passionate and smart with a story to tell (related to nutrition, fitness, health, and exercise). If they have a story to tell; and if they are smart. They need to know the sports nutrition category. A simple e-mail will do.

Guest from Hell: Someone who answers in one or two words and has no "story" to tell ... and those who pause! That's the death knell of a radio show.

Contact: exphys@aol.com; 561-239-1754; http://

www.pnshow.com; http://www.joseantoniophd.com; Jose Antonio. Best method: E-mail. No response? I always respond; e-mail again if needed.

Invited Back? If they are both entertaining and educational (in that order).

Guest Comment: "*The Performance Nutrition Show* isn't your typical show. Dr. Antonio and Carla provide a refreshing, entertaining, and educational view on sports nutrition and exercise!"—Juan Carlos Santana, CSCS (http://www.ihpfit.com)

Bio of Jose ("Joey") Antonio: Jose earned his Ph.D. and completed a post-doctoral research fellowship at the University of Texas Southwestern Medical Center in Dallas. Some of his current projects include: International Society of Sports Nutrition, Javalution, Body Well Nutrition, Performance Nutrition Show, Performance Ready Team, RunFast Promotions, Sport SupplementVideos.com, SupplementCoach.com, Suzy Favor Hamilton Running Camps.

Jose's most recent books are *Fast Track: Training and Nutrition Secrets from America's Top Female Runner* (Rodale Books 2004), and *Fit Kids for Life: A Parent's Guide to Optimal Nutrition and Training for Young Athletes* (Basic Health Publications 2004).

Pit Pass Radio with Scott Casher and Tony Wenck on KXNO-AM 1460, Iowa and southern Minnesota and on http://www.pitpassradio.com. Please see Takedown Radio, page 269, for a complete entry.

Theme: Motor Cycle enthusiasts of all kinds.

Guest Profile: Riders, racers, performers, industry insiders, authors, mechanics, manufacturers.

Contact: Tony@pitpassradio.com; Scott@pitpassradio.com; 515-360-9738; 515-707-8657; http://www.pitpassradiocom; 1) Tony Wenck, 2) Scott Casher. Best method: E-mail first and then phone.

Bios of Scott Casher and Tony Wenck: Scott has been a broadcast professional since 1975, and Tony for three years.

Pratt and Taylor with Dave Pratt and Don Taylor on CKST (the team), aired in greater Vancouver on Radio/Cross Canada on TV.

Theme: Sports and entertainment.

Guest Profile: Sports and entertainment figures. We like to say "interesting people talking about interesting things." Obviously, bigger names make for more compelling radio. As long as they speak English, I don't really mind what their voice sounds like. A short bio is nice. Most of the time with the bigger name guests, we already know a fair bit about them.

Guest from Hell: Guests that don't talk, sidestep questions, don't call when they say they will.

Contact: paul.debron@team1040.ca; 604-505-3443; http://www.team1040.ca; Paul De Bron. Best method: E-mail a bio, call with a pitch, and send a press kit.

No response? Probably not a good idea to e-mail or phone. That's a fairly good sign we're not interested.

Invited Back? How entertaining they were.

Bio of Dave Pratt and Don Taylor: Pratt and Taylor has been the #1 rated sports talk show in Vancouver since Dave and Don teamed up in 2003. Both hosts have extensive backgrounds in the local and national sports media.

The Professor and Mary Ann Talk NASCAR with Sean and Mary Ann Cole on the Monks Media Radio Network, http://www.monksmedia.com, on Mondays at 7 PM (ET).

Theme: NASCAR fans talk show.

Guest Profile: Anyone related to racing, driver, family members, crew chiefs, experts on racing etc. Informed individuals who can speak effectively and are qualified to speak about the topic of interest.

Guest from Hell: One who does not talk effectively or one who says very little... One who you have to force information from.

Contact: mary@monksmedia.com; 317-565-1392; http://www.monksmedia.com; Sean Cole, Mary Ann Cole. Best method: E-mail is a quicker response, but a phone call is fine. No response? Yes, by all means e-mail or call; sometimes we get too busy and let someone slip through the cracks. Please don't hesitate to call again and again.

Invited Back? If they could effectively talk about their expertise and if the listeners enjoyed the guest.

Bios of Sean and Mary Ann Cole: Sean has been a NASCAR fan all of his life. Originally from Maryland, he transplanted to North Carolina for most of his young adult life, then moved to Indiana 9 years ago.

Mary Ann is a native of Indiana and has been a NASCAR fan for six years and counting... Previous owners of a NASCAR and Sports Shop the couple found it fun and entertaining to talk to race fans about the racing world ... and took that format to radio. Just fans talking to other fans about their favorite past time. They have hosted live remote shows and have had many guests from the NASCAR circuit in each of the divisions. "Our show is informative but casual and fun, something like gathering at the water cooler at work to catch up on all the latest news and gossip in the racing world," the Coles say.

Ringside Live with Ian Hamilton and Adam Firestorm on Blog Talk Radio, http://www.blogtalkradio.com/ringsidelive

Theme: Professional wrestling and mixed martial arts news/reviews/comment.

Guest Profile: So far, it's been pro-wrestling/MMA writers, but we've been reaching out to get active wrestlers on the show. Ideally someone who is relevant to the subject we are covering, or someone who will be of interest to our listeners (i.e., an expert on the subject, or someone connected with it — as we've had already in Keith Lipinski and Oliver Copp). Ideally we'd want the guest on the show for a reason —

not necessarily to promote something — but someone who's got a lot to talk about and is good at keeping to a time limit. Most of the guests we've had or want, we already know about their credentials, voice, etc.

Guest from Hell: Since wrestling can be a protective business, a guest from hell for us would be someone who sticks strictly to something called "kayfabe" — that is, insisting that it's real and everything we see on TV is real.

Contact: live@wrestling-online.com; ian@ihamilton.plus.com (personal account for guest bookings and general show queries); Ian Hamilton, preferably to his personal e-mail; 646-716-9721 (during the show only); http://www.wrestling-online.com/ringside. Best method: Usually it'd be done best by e-mailing ourselves — but most of the interviews we've had so far have been arranged by ourselves. No response? I'm online most days, so e-mails are by far the better option.

Invited Back? Whether they want to come back on the show for one thing. That, and whether there's a need (obviously if it's a one-time thing solely for promotion reasons, there'd be no reason for a return).

Bios of Ian Hamilton and Adam Firestorm: Ian has been watching wrestling since 1992, growing up watching WWF/WWE through the dark days of the mid 90s. He's been writing about wrestling since 1998, and has also covered MMA.

Focusing on writing rather than wrestling, Ian released a book — *Wrestling's Sinking Ship* (Lulu.com 2006), charting the events of WWE in the first five years since the sale of WCW. Ian has attended several major WWE and UFC pay-per-views and has been involved with Wrestling-Online.com since 2002.

Adam began his involvement with professional wrestling at the age of 14, working in media and PR, as well as ring crew for independent promotions in British Columbia, Canada. At 18, he added professional wrestler to the list, and over the course of the next ten years would capture several regional championships as well as the NWA Canadian Junior Heavyweight title on two occasions. He has tangled with the likes of "Fallen Angel" Christopher Daniels, Asian Cougar, Bryan Danielson, Dr. Luther, and Jason the Terrible. He was briefly managed in Portland Wrestling by "Rowdy" Roddy Piper, and holds a victory over Bryan Alvarez in their only match.

Rod and Reel Radio with co-host Wendy Tochihara on Sunday, 5–7 PM (PT) on http://www.rodandreelradio.com or live on KGIL AM 540 and 1206.

Theme: Saltwater and freshwater fishing. My goal is to encourage more women and children to participate in outdoor sports by broadcasting a fun and informative program. I want *Rod and Reel Radio* to be a truly family oriented program.

Guest Profile: Great speaker, informative, energetic, leader in their field. Can they carry on a conversation?

Guest from Hell: No manners, someone that gives one word answers/does not elaborate.

Contact: rodandreelradio@aol.com; 714-609-5544; http://www.rodandreelradio.com. Best method: Call with a pitch, e-mail a bio, send a press kit. No Response? Call or e-mail.

Invited Back? Performance

Bio of Wendy Tochihara: Wendy and her twin sister were child actresses who appeared in TV commercials and made guest appearances on "Kung Fu," "Medical Center" and "The Roseanne Show." Wendy was a regular cast member of the CBS series "The King and I" with Yul Brynner and Samantha Eggar and also performed on stage in *Anna and the King* with Ricardo Montalban and Sally Ann Howes.

As a child, she acted, played basketball and softball and went on family camping and fishing trips. Today Wendy is the national sales manager for Izorline International and competes in fishing tournaments in the Southern California area. As a tournament angler, Wendy has many impressive sponsors including Daiwa and Triton boats. She has appeared in a number of TV fishing programs, including ESPN2's "Destination Outdoors" and "Randy Jones' Strike Zone" seen on the Outdoor Channel.

Signs of Speed/Thursday Night Thunder with Jake Speed and Guest Hosts on BlogTalkRadio; now off the air. Jake started another show on Blog Talk Radio called *Hermetic Politics* covering conservative politics, education, self improvement and spiritual enlightenment.

Theme: The world of automotive racing.

Guest Profile: Fans of racing, racers, racing celebrities, anyone who loves the sport of racing or those who race themselves. Racing experience is a major plus, interview experience is great too but not required. As long as they can carry on a conversation on the phone they will be fine.

Guest from Hell: Anyone who doesn't respond to questions or those who are vulgar.

Contact: jake@signsofspeed.com; 704-455-7446; http://www.BlogTalkRadio.com/Jake-Speed; Jake Speed. Best method: Leave a message on the show, e-mail or a phone call all works. No response? Please try again. I don't always get the message or I just ran out of time. I would like to talk to all interested in being a guest.

Invited Back? If they liked being on the show is most important and those who bring something that listeners don't get to hear on other shows.

Bio of Jake Speed: Jake has been involved in racing for over 30 years and has crew chiefed in the Craftsman Truck Series, Hooters Pro Cup, Winston West, SCCA Pro Racing and many short tracks around the U.S. His perspective on racing is a little out of the mainstream and his humor makes him popular at the race rack and on the show. Jake is also in the process of compiling a fictional action packed book about racing with a co-writer.

Sports Heaven with Mark and Evan on Blog Talk Radio, http://www.blogtalkradio.com/sportsheavenwithmarkandevan

Theme: NY sports.

Guest Profile: Broadcasters and well known sports writers from local newspapers or league sites (i.e., MLB.com). Someone with experience directly with sports and NY teams such as professional sports writers or broadcasters. I like to know what they do. If they are not professionals I would not prefer them. I do not like getting guests such as bloggers. I also want to make sure they have knowledge of what I want them to talk about. My ideal guest was without question *Newsday* sports writer Jim Baumbach — one of the nicest guys you will ever meet. He responds to my e-mails within 24 hours and sometimes within minutes. He is very knowledgeable about all New York teams. He has made an appearance on my show on five different occasions just because he enjoys helping me out. He is the ideal guest — kind, knowledgeable, and quick responding.

Other guests have included NHL.com writer Evan Grossman, NY Rangers radio broadcaster and FOX announcer Kenny Albert, NBC, sports anchor Bruce Beck, New York Yankees beat writer for MLB.com Bryan Hoch and New York Mets beat writer from the *NY Post* Mark Hale.

Guest from Hell: Someone who does not know a lot about the subject I am asking about and is not a professional.

Contact: Songwriter3333@aol.com; 516-205-4234; http://www.freewebs.com/sportsheavenwithmarkandevan; Mark Elliot Wishnia. Best method: I guess I would prefer an e-mail bio or press kit. Any way is good. No response? If I do not respond it is probably because I am on vacation. I check my e-mails once every 10–30 seconds. If I do not respond within a week they can e-mail me again but it should not be an issue.

Invited Back? If they are not only knowledgeable but are very willing to come on and are very nice people. Some people are very bitter while others are very nice and have come on 4 or 5 times.

Bio of Mark Elliot Wishnia: Mark graduated Jericho High School in Jericho, New York, and in 2008 entered Penn State University to pursue a career in broadcasting where he will host his radio show. "I am a die-hard fan of the New York Yankees, New York Giants, New York Rangers, New York Knicks, and New York Dragons," he says.

The Sports Opinions Show with Matt Alvarez on Blog Talk Radio, http://www.blogtalkradio.com/thesportsopinionsshow

Theme: Wrestling news and other sports.

Guest Profile: Wrestlers, or other sports people. I look for how much a real pro is and see if they've been on other shows. His guests have included Chris Yandek, who currently represents wrestling and TV superstar Jake The Snake Roberts, and J.J. Dillon, a former referee, wrestler and manager.

Guest from Hell: Someone who disrespects the show or the fans that listen to it.

Contact: matthew-alvarez@sbcglobal.net; 510-614-8184; myspace.com/mattneedsagirlfriend, www.thesportsopinionshow.com; Matt Alvarez. Best method: E-mail or phone. If someone wants me to interview them and lives in my area, I would like it if they approach me by saying "Hi" and shaking my hand. However, if they live far away or live in another state, I'd prefer that they e-mail me a press kit and/or bio. No response? Call.

Invited Back? How well and polite I thought they were; then if I liked doing the interview, they'll be invited back.

Bio of Matt Alvarez: A lifelong sports lover, Matt began dreaming about people talking with him about sports when he was 16. But his mom (who passed away in 2000) was so poor they couldn't afford anything. Now he lives alone and is happy doing his shows. His dream has come true and he loves getting three, four or even five people calling the show.

"I really enjoy being a part of Blog Talk Radio; it makes everything else I'm feeling go away for awhile," he says.

Sports Talk Live (now ***Sports from Frankie's Point of View***) with Frankie the Sports Guy on Blog Talk Radio, http://www.blogtalkradio.com/sportsfromfrankiesview and WGBB 1240 AM, Long Island, NY.

Theme: Sports talk.

Guest Profile: Current and former sports figures, broadcasters, authors, fans. When I am booking or searching for guests, I look for a guest who will have something to say that I believe my listeners (not myself) would like to hear. I like to know how well the guest will project and also come across on an interview. If they sound intelligent and can get the point across I am happy. If the guest has a lot of knowledge but their answers are not solid or they cannot describe what they are trying to sell correctly this could be a problem and make the interview boring.

Guest from Hell: One that does not give any details, the yes or no answer guest.

Contact: Mailforfrankie@aol.com; 516-721-5486; http://www.frankiethesportsguy.com; Frankie Maniscalco, host and producer. Best method: E-mail or phone. I usually receive my requests by e-mail. A press kit is always a good idea. No response? I believe that it is important for that guest to give it at least one more try for a response. In the next e-mail, selling themselves even more than the first time may help.

Invited Back? The first thing is ratings. If a show did well b/c of the guest(s) on that show. Also, if the guest makes me comfortable and has the knowledge that I think is important to the show.

Guest Comments: "Frankie the Sports Guy is legit. I was interviewed by him for 20 minutes and enjoyed the experience. He was prepared, creative and professional. He was dogged in chasing me to appear on the show and a pleasure to work with throughout." — Bruce Beck, News Channel 4 weekend sports anchor

"Frankie does a great interview and clearly researches the topic beforehand. All that needed to be said about my role with the New York Sharks Women's Tackle Football Team was clearly covered." — Merle Exit, host of *Whirl with Merle* talk show on Blog Talk Radio (see page 281) and public relations director of the NY Sharks of IWFL (Independent Women's Football League).

Bio of Frankie Maniscalco: Frankie "The Sports Guy" is a full time music teacher in Oceanside, NY, who doubles as a sports talk host. Ever since childhood, Frankie has dreamed of calling the walk off home runs at the World Series or game winning touchdowns at the Super Bowl. As a radio host, he does not look for just the popular story, but also the one that tugs at your heart strings. Whether it is a professional athlete or fan that loves their team Frankie makes sure to treat all guests with the same intensity and emotion.

He and wife, Bridget, live on Long Island, NY, with their children, Tommy and Arianna.

The Strength-Power Hour with Jose Antonio, Ph.D. and William Kraemer, Ph.D. and featuring the "Strength-Power Princesses" on 1470AM WNN, aired in South Florida AND over the web as a podcast; www.wwnnradio.com

Theme: Strength and conditioning, sports nutrition and athletics.

Guest Profile: Strength coaches, personal trainers, scientists, athletes, doctors, nutrition experts. Someone who is passionate and smart with a story to tell (related to strength and conditioning, nutrition, fitness, health, and exercise).

Contact: exphys@aol.com; 561-239-1754; http://www.sphour.com; Jose Antonio. Best method: E-mail

For more information and Jose's bio, please see his other show, *The Performance Nutrition Show*, on page 265.

Guest Comment: "*The Strength-Power Hour* has some of the best information, hands-down in the field of strength and conditioning." —Bob Alejo, http://www.bobalejo.com

Takedown Radio with Scott Casber and Steve Foster on KXNO-AM 1460, Iowa and Southern Minn. and http://www.takedownradio.com

Theme: Wrestling, MMA enthusiasts of all kinds.

Guest Profile: Fighters, wrestlers, promoters, industry insiders, authors, managers. Guests need to have a passion for what they do and an energy in presentation. Humor helps too.

Guest from Hell: Yes or no answers to questions. Making the host feel like the guest is doing them a favor by coming on the program. No shows are very bad. You book yourself on a program, be there! We always try and talk with each of our guests prior to air to confirm and remind but also to gauge the guest's attitude, demeanor and points they would like to get across.

Contact: Scott@pitpassradio.com; 515-707-8657; http://www.Takedownradio.com; Scott Casber. Best method: E-mail first, then phone. Send an interview idea to us. Sell yourself and your idea, company, product, event to us. No response? Send an interview idea to us. Sell yourself and your idea, company, product, event to us.

Invited Back? A positive attitude, friendly, informative, prepared.

Bio of Scott Casber: Scott has been a broadcast professional since 1975. He has been a multi-sports public address voice, sports radio talk show host, actor, voice-over talent and founder of *Takedown Radio*.

"Takedown Wrestling Radio was founded seven years ago with the idea that we can promote the sport and make it available to everyone free of charge," he says. "The more fans the sport has the better it is for all of us."

Tee It Up show with Al and Adam Gottfried and Kevin Smith, syndicated on more than 50 stations from Hawaii to Syracuse, NY, airing on Sunday.

Theme: Lifestyle show with emphasis on golf.

Guest Profile: We love guests with a sense of humor and passion to talk about golf ... how they got hooked ... talk about their family ... and their great moments in golf. Celebrities, professional golfers, actors, musicians, pro athletes, singers, politicians, who are passionate about golf, i.e., Donald Trump, George Bush (former president 41), Ice Tee, Kevin Costner, Tom Selleck, Justin Timberlake, Samuel L Jackson.

Guest from Hell: Provides little ... and might even be dead air...

Contact: alang@fourteenthcolony.com; 818/8493 630 x229; http://www.teeitupshow.com; Alan Gottfried. Best method: E-mail is fine to reach out to me. No response? Calling us direct and e-mailing is the best way to get our attention for guest appearances

Invited Back? If they are type "A" celebs ... and it's at least one year ... since on air ... or if they happen to be on my favorites list ... personally.

Bios of Al and Adam Gottfried and Kevin Smith: Kevin (5 handicap), is a golf historian; Al (18 handicap) is CEO of Fourteenth Colony Productions and amateur to the game; executive producer and president of Fourteenth Colony Productions, Adam (+1 handicap) contributes by expressing his youthful insight to the game. The show is in its 13th year.

Teebox Golf Show with Rick Arnett and Craig Rosengarden on KTCK, Dallas, TX.

Theme: Golf— tour news, guest interviews, course and equipment reviews.

Guest Profile: Golf related guests. Relevant, funny, good topics, good conversationalist. We want to know the reason for the interview and the sound of voice.

Guest from Hell: Non-responsive and boring.

Contact: rick@myavidgolfer.com; 972-550-9000 x 106; http://www.myavidgolfer.com; Rick Arnett. Best method: E-mail. No response? E-mail.

Invited Back? Satisfy the requirements above.

Bio of Rick Arnett: Rick has hosted the radio show for more than 15 years. He is vice president of *Avidgolfer Magazine* and has written over 75 golf articles for SportsIllustrated.com

The Tournament Trail with Earl Burton and Jennifer Shoots on Hold 'Em Radio http://www.holdemradio.com

Theme: Tournament poker, poker in general.

Guest Profile: Players, people involved in industry, authors, others. Gregarious, knowledgeable, interesting and educational. As long as they have credibility, we'll talk to most anyone.

Guest from Hell: Someone who answers questions with one or two words.

Contact: usraider75@aol.com; 512-636-2134; http://www.holdemradio.com; Earl Burton. Best method: E-mail or phone. Call with a pitch, e-mail a bio and send a press kit. No response? Depends on what is a reasonable time! No, seriously, yes an e-mail or call would be fine.

Invited Back? Listener reaction, additional works or ideas to bring to the program.

Bio of Earl Burton: Earl is a longtime poker writer who has covered tournaments across the United States and provides insight to the latest tournament action around the world and commentary on issues in the poker community.

Twisted Metal with John "Captain Thunder" Nevins and Scott "The Big Man" Cook on http://www.captainthunderracing.com, Race Talk Radio, airing Thursdays at 9 PM (ET). Captain Thunder also hosts *Burning Rubber with Captain Thunder* on Wednesday at 8 PM (ET).

Theme: Weekly uncensored NASCAR radio show.

Guest Profile: Race car drivers, pit crew chiefs, PR reps, team owners. Someone who is willing to open up and not give the "standard issue" answers ... big name in the sport of stock car racing. I do all of my own due diligence and make sure I am prepared for the interview; I also prep them beforehand.

Guest from Hell: Someone who answers with one word responses or acts like he/she does not want to be there.

Contact: captainthunder@captainthunderracing.com; 561-702-7869; http://www.captainthunderracing.com; John Nevins. Best method: E-mail or phone or send press kit. No response? I always respond.

Invited Back? Were they entertaining ... that's the bottom line.

Bio of "Captain Thunder": "Captain Thunder" is a noted NASCAR reporter and radio personality who has been featured on many Internet and terrestrial radio shows. His racing roots go back to the 1970s and 1980s when his father was a racecar driver and he raced motocross. Captain Thunder raced all over the country and quickly became a force to be reckoned with on the motocross circuit.

The Captain has also been a weekly guest on *The Scott Ferrall Show* on Sirius Channel 101—The Howard Stern Network—since March of 2006. In addition to writing for Captain Thunder Racing.com, he writes for http://www.insidethepitbox.com and http://www.insiderracingnews.com

Full bio at http://www.captainthunderracing.com/modules.php?name=Bio

The UltraFlight Radio Show with Roy Beisswenger on http://www.ultraflightradio.com

Theme: Sport aviation.

Guest Profile: Pilots, manufacturers, FAA personnel, event organizers, association directors. Participant in the sport. Can carry an expert conversation in flying. Something to offer the audience in the way of flying information, whether it be about the rules, training, maintenance, products, or events.

Guest from Hell: One where I feel like I'm doing an interrogation instead of an interview. One with a bad phone line.

Contact: roy@easyflight.com; 618-664-9706; http://www.ultraflightradio.com; Roy Beisswenger. Best method: E-mailing the idea for a segment and their expertise in the area. No response? E-mail or call.

Invited Back? How well the interview went and whether there is more to discuss.

Guest Comment: "Ultraflight radio is becoming a great information dispersant of knowledge in an otherwise vacant realm of sport aviation. I have received numerous inquiries from your listeners in search of additional technical assistance. In most cases, available information on their respective ultralight aircraft is sparse at best. I am not aware of any other media format such as yours. Your weekly line up of well informed guests covers the entire sport aviation community. You're doing a great service for the aviation community."—Gene "Bever" Borne, Air-Tech, Inc., http://www.air-techinc.com

Bio of Roy Beisswenger: Roy is based in Greenville, Illinois, where he has operated a powered parachute training school and support services since 1993. He holds the designations of Ultralight Flight Instructor-Examiner (UFI-E) with the Experimental Aircraft Association (EAA), as well as Advanced Flight Instructor (AFI) with the United States Ultralight Association (USUA). He has trained local pilots, equipment dealers, students from other countries as well as U.S. military members.

In 2004, Roy was chosen to participate in the Federal Aviation Administration's first Designated Pilot Examiner (DPE) training class for the sport pilot program. A year later, he became the first to receive the designations of Sport Pilot and Certified Flight Instructor-Sport Pilot (CFI-SP) for powered parachutes. He also became one of the country's first DPEs for powered parachutes and first Designated Sport Flight Instructor Examiners.

Roy was a columnist for *UltraFlight Magazine* and the *EAA Experimenter* and for several years wrote an engine maintenance column for *UltraFlight*, which was picked up by the Australian magazine, *Pacific Flyer*.

Prior to his work in powered parachutes, Roy was schooled in Mechanical Engineering, graduating from Washington University in 1984. Following that, he went to work as an officer in the U.S. Army, where his specialty was maintenance and he headed a team of military personnel and civilian contractors that inspected combat vehicles to determine which were to be sent to depot for overhaul.

WSB 120 with Capt. Herb Emory on Newstalk 750 WSB Radio aired Saturday afternoons.

Theme: NASCAR racing.

Guest Profile: NASCAR drivers, owners. A good, clear, entertaining conversationist is ideal. Want to know their background and knowledge on topic interview.

Guest from Hell: One or two word answers.

Contact: herb.emory@coxradio.com; 404-897-6296; http://www.captainherb.net http://www.wsbradio.com/sports/herbnascarshow.html; Doug Turnbull at doug.turnbull@coxradio.com. Best method: E-mail fact sheet. No response? E-mail.

Invited Back? Response from audience.

Bio of Capt. Herb Emory: Herb has been a traffic, news and NASCAR reporter in Atlanta since 1979.

Yankee Fan Club Radio with Ty Hildenbrandt, Uncle Joe Colarusso, Tony Colarusso on http://www.TPSRadio.net, YankeeFanClubRadio.com, and uStream.tv (for live video simulcast); available as a podcast on iTunes as well as an array of other sites. The show is syndicated through The People's Sports Radio Network and sponsored by the Lehigh Valley Yankee Fan Club; now off the air. Ty now has a podcast co-hosted by Dan Rubenstein on www.solidverbal.com focusing on college football.

Theme: The show is dedicated entirely to the New York Yankees, created by the fans, for the fans.

Guest Profile: Prominent sports reporters and bloggers, announcers/radio hosts, everyday fans looking to give their opinions. We're looking for people that can offer unique, thought-provoking perspectives on issues that are often overplayed, as is usually the case with many Yankees-related topics. Also, since our show is very informal, we look for people that can inject our show with some humor to keep the mood light. For a smaller show such as ours, prominent names are always a plus. But I think we're most interested in guests that are credible and can improve the reputation of our show.

Guest from Hell: Either a guest who talks too much or too little. As long as a guest stays between those two extremes, we can usually mold an interview around their strengths.

Contact: radio@lvyankeefanclub.com; 610-509-4943; http://www.yankeefanclubradio.com; Ty Hildenbrandt. Best method: Either. We pride ourselves on being extremely approachable. Usually a brief introduction and some links to work on the web or other references is enough to pique our interest. No response? Usually, we are pretty good about getting back to inquiries; however, if we forget, a simple e-mail from someone works just fine.

Invited Back? Guests are invited back if we feel they are compatible with our style of broadcasting, have an extensive knowledge of our main topics, and can cogently convey their thoughts to our audience.

Guest Comment: "Yankees Fan Club Radio offers intelligent talk by true Yankees fans, and the best Uncle Joe since 'Petticoat Junction.'"—David Pinto, http://baseballmusings.com

Bio of Ty Hildenbrandt: Ty was the winner of the first ever McDonald's Next Great Sportswriter competition on FOXSports.com in 2006. He writes for SI.com and SIOnCampus.com about college sports and pop culture in a regular, off-the-cuff column titled "Campus Quick Slants."

He launched the radio show prior to the 2005 season along with his uncle, *Uncle Joe Colarusso*, in an effort to give Yankees fans around the country a voice that could be heard.

Ty is a 2004 graduate of Penn State University and lives in eastern Pennsylvania.

Technology

"What's New—What's Best and What's Next"— theme of the *Computer Outlook* radio talk show

Ask the Technology Therapist with Jennifer Shaheen on http://www.womensradio.com; now off the air.

Theme: Small business use of technology for marketing and increased productivity.

Guest Profile: Business professionals that are experts in their area and have a good personality. The voice is important and so is business experience customer satisfaction.

Guest from Hell: Someone who is too wordy or someone who can not interact with you and only gives one word responses.

Contact: ask@technologytherapy.com; 914-949-6092; http://www.technologytherapy.com; Jennifer Shaheen / Theresa Yattaw. Best method: Phone a pitch, e-mail a bio or send a press kit. No response? People should try reaching out again. Most of us try to stay on top of e-mails and calls but occasionally something is missed.

Invited Back? Audience interest in a topic.

Bio of Jennifer Shaheen: An eMarketing and Technology Therapist, Jennifer is an expert at helping small and mid-sized companies use technology to leverage effective marketing strategies and increase business productivity.

With years of in-depth technological experience, she has an understanding of how it can be used in practical businesses applications. Her techniques have boosted sales, enhanced staff productivity, and increased market share. Jennifer is a strong advocate of small women-owned businesses and has partnered with organizations such as National Organization for Women New York City Chapter, NAWBO, and Women's Venture Fund. She was appointed to the board of American Marketing Associations Southern New England Chapter for her dedicated involvement in developing and promoting eMarketing strategies. Her company, The Technology Therapy Group, also provides website development and technology support for this growing chapter.

Jennifer is a certified software trainer and educator and was one of the premier certified instructors in the area of Web development.

Jennifer is an active contributing author for Womenandbiz.com, New York Enterprise Report, and Women's Radio. She also writes a business blog which has been nominated for a bloggers' choice award.

Breakfast Bytes with Felicia King and Eric Doherty on WGTD 91.1 FM, Kenosha-Racine-Lake Geneva, WI, airing Saturday at 9:45 AM (CT).

Theme: Computers and technology.

Guest Profile: Demonstrable expertise in a computer, technology, or related field, whose expertise would be valuable shared with the listeners of the show. Past guests have been experts in some field. Experience with radio is very helpful. Generally we pre-interview people unless their reputation speaks for itself. They should at least feel comfortable having a friendly conversation rather than reading from some papers as that is the show format that is most enjoyable to listen to.

Guest from Hell: Someone with such low self-confidence that they cannot speak authoritatively on their subjects, comfortably on the radio. These people tend to hyperventilate, speak poorly, and are so tense that they are boring to listen to.

Contact: breakfastbytes@gtc.edu; 262-564-8540; http://www.wgtd.org/breakfast_bytes.asp; Felicia King. Best method: Phone. Our listeners are looking for free advice and information from experts. So it is best to approach us by presenting one's expertise in an area. No response? I don't think this has ever happened. Our show is not so huge that we can't get to e-mails.

Invited Back? Quality of presentation, quality and value of information they shared with listeners.

Bio of Felicia King: Felicia has years of experience in the computer field. She owns Quality Plus Consulting, specializing in security, disaster avoidance and recovery servers, workstations, and domain infrastructure.

Computer America with Craig Crossman, host and Carey Holzman, co-host airing on Business TalkRadio Network and the Lifestyle TalkRadio Network, Monday through Friday.

Theme: Talk show on computers and technology that shows how people can use their personal computers to become more productive and entertained. Show includes special segments ("Newsprint Live," "Wednesday Madness"), correspondents that appear on a regular basis, industry news, coverage of industry events, ongoing contests and open phone lines.

Guest Profile: Industry experts, company spokespeople, authors with credentials, and are well informed and well spoken.

Guest from Hell: Non-informed and can't speak well.

Contact: ccrossman@computeramerica.com; carey@computeramerica.com; 828-299-8967; http://www.computeramerica.com; Craig Crossman and Carey Holzman. Best method: Phone. If we want further information, we will request an e-mail follow up. No response? E-mail or call. Sometimes things get overlooked or e-mail isn't delivered.

Invited Back? If the product is something of continued interest.

Guest Comment: "On October 12, 1997, I had the privilege of visiting with Craig as he brought his special magic to the airways. Craig has a unique infectious sparkle both on and off the air. With the microphone off during one of the news and commercial breaks, Craig beamed as he told us about his new 'spinning top' which actually levitates above a specially built base. It's 'real levitation' Craig insisted, as he vividly described his newest acquisition. There are no hidden strings ... no magic tricks. 'It's true levitation.' He beamed with delight as he shared the information with us one on one.

"Yes indeed, Craig Crossman is a 'real person' and one to whom you are instantly drawn. Thanks for inviting me to your show and I look forward to visiting in the future."— Steve Singer, president of Micro Format, Inc.

Bio of Craig Crossman: Craig has been a national newspaper computer columnist since 1985. In his weekly syndicated newspaper column in the McClatchy Tribune Newspapers he does Q&A, commentary and product review. The column can also be read on the *Computer America* website (http://www.computeramerica.com).

Craig has a Bachelor's Degree in computer science from Florida Atlantic University and is a contributing editor to several computer publications.

His show has aired since 1992.

Computer and Technology Radio with Marc Cohen and Marsha Collier on WS Radio.

Theme: Technology.

Guest Profile: Anything related to technology, celebrities, anything with a battery or a plug. Clear, funny, informative, not too confusing. We want to know their background and current position.

Guest from Hell: Promoting their product without informing the audience. Long answers instead of short.

Contact: marcandmarsha@gmail.com; 818-709-6229; http://www.wsradio.com; Marc Cohen or Marsha Collier. Best method: E-mail. No response? E-mail me again.

Invited Back? Quality of the interview.

Bio of Marc Cohen: Marc has spent more than 30 years as a Southern California announcer, both on television and radio. Along with doing keynote speeches, he is called upon by such top technology companies as Microsoft, Sony and Gateway to do early technology testing. As a judge for the Codie Award, he judges the top software in the country.

Marc lives in the San Fernando Valley and graduated from Cal State Northridge University. He is managing director at Wachovia Securities.

He and his wife, Leslie, have two grown children. Full bio at http://en.wikipedia.org/wiki/Marc_Cohen

Bio of Marsha Collier: Born in New York City, Marsha is an author and educator specializing in training individuals how to use and make money on eBay and online.

Marsha has more than one million copies of her books in print (special editions for the UK, Germany, France, Canada, Australia, Chinese — and an edition in Spanish). *eBay for Dummies* (For Dummies 2006) is the best selling book for eBay worldwide and *eBay Business All-in-One Desk Reference for Dummies* (For Dummies 2006) is the best selling title on operating an eBay business. Marsha shares her eBay business expertise in streaming video at Entrepreneur.com's "Entrepreneur's Coaches Corner" and is Entrepreneur.com's online eBay columnist. She's also a featured lecturer at eBay's "eBay University" training events and their yearly eBay Live conference.

Before her eBay career began, Marsha owned and operated her own marketing and advertising firm, The Collier Company, and won numerous awards including "Small Businessperson of the Year." She got started on eBay during the site's early years and as one of the site's first successful sellers she was able to use the money to put her daughter through private school and college.

Marsha lives in Los Angeles, California.

Full bio at http://en.wikipedia.org/wiki/Marsha_Collier

Computer Corner with Gene Mitchell on WCOJ, Coatesville-West Chester, Pennsylvania.

Theme: Computers.

Guest Profile: Anyone related to computer technology with an interesting topic for general audience relating to computers. Bio, topic, and where else have they spoken.

Guest from Hell: Someone who comes on just to sell something.

Contact: gene@wcoj.com; 610-590-0451; http://www.wcoj.com and http://www.5dnet.com; Gene Mitchell. Best method: Send an e-mail that gets my attention. No response? Try again.

Invited Back? How interesting they are.

Bio of Gene Mitchell: Gene has been host of his show for four years, and is producer of *Computer Tips* on WCOJ. He's also board operator, engineer, producer, and account exec for Sunday religious programming. A graduate of Valparaiso Technical Institute, he has owned Gene's Computer Outlet for 20 years.

Computer Outlook, airs live daily 5–6 PM (PT), and is re-broadcast a week later on the World Internet Talk Radio Network (WIRN) and Sunday at the Coffee Lounge in Las Vegas, 10:05 AM to 11:00 AM (PT), broadcast on Fox News Radio Station KDOX—1280 AM and re-broadcast a week later at 5 PM (ET) on WIRN. Both shows are also on the Internet at www.computeroutlook.com and www.techoutlookcentral.com. The Sunday show is tagged "Java with John." http://www.rejavanatecoffee.com

Theme: "What's New — What's Best and What's Next" in the computer and I.T. industry.

Guest Profile: Computer/tech industry company representatives, industry analysts and other leaders in technology. The best guest for this show is anyone who can speak in plain English about their product, technology or trends in the computer and high tech industry, and maintain a contagious level of enthusiasm for what they are talking about. I want to know how they can contribute to the show's theme: "What's New — What's Best and What's Next."

Guest from Hell: I don't know if it makes them a "guest from hell," but it does make the interview more difficult (more work for me!) when the guest only responds with very short or just yes or no answers. It also makes the audience feel that the guest may not know the subject matter as well as they should.

Contact: john@computeroutlook.com; 702-471-7200; http://www.computeroutlook.com; John Iasiuolo. No response? E-mail or call.

Invited Back? If the guest has a new product or technology to talk about, or they have significant knowledge of a new or growing industry trend, we invite them back. Best method: E-mail first.

Guest Comments: "What a great concept! A nightly, one-hour, fast-paced look at the world of consumer electronics using language humans can understand. I love being a guest on John's show."—Ralph Bond, consumer education manager, Intel Corporation

"Your show has a great format ... you have a real gift for explaining technology at a level everyone can understand, for announcing new product and other Diskeeper news. *Computer Outlook* has consistently been at the top of our list for media outlets to work with." — Colleen Toumayan, director of public relations, Diskeeper Corporation

Bio of John Iasiuolo: John has a varied background in the business world, as well as a successful career in the entertainment industry. He has always been committed to hard work and striving for nothing less than his best.

Born and raised in Staten Island, New York, John moved to New Jersey for the better part of his adult life. He later moved to Las Vegas, where he has lived for 17 years.

"My career was built around education, business knowledge and the School of Hard Knocks," he says. "My data collection system consisted of index cards and notebooks — not the wonderful world of computers. Unfortunately the techie-thing came to me later in life, not through business but from family. I realized then that computers were here to stay and I better do something about that for myself."

John started his radio show in order to learn more than computer how to's and the techie talk. "I needed to understand it all in plain English," he recalls.

Digital Nation Radio with Tim Taylor on WFLA 540 AM, aired in central Florida.

Theme: Technology.

Guest Profile: Computer industry professionals and related industries. Someone who is interesting and has good information for my audience. I like to interview guests that I have heard on other programs. Since I have already heard them then I know if they would make good guests.

Guest from Hell: Someone who does not communicate.

Contact: tim@digitalnationradio.com; 407-478-6600; http://www.digitalnationradio.com; Tim Taylor. Best method: E-mail. No response? Do not e-mail or call.

Invited Back? I want to talk to them again. We did not cover everything the first time.

Bio of Tim Taylor: Born and raised in Memphis, Tennessee, Tim graduated from the University of Memphis with a Bachelor's degree in business administration and has always worked in the IT field. He spent 13 years as the head of the IT department of a large non-profit organization where his oversaw the installation of over 1,500 PCs and servers.

Tim started TaylorWorks, an IT solutions company in central Florida, in 1999 with one client and by 2006 had a staff of 12, serving more than 150 network clients.

Tim and his wife, Karissa, have three children; Jared, Brandon and Grace.

Full bio at http://www.digitalnationradio.com

Into Tomorrow with Dave Graveline airs on radio stations across the U.S., XM Satellite Radio, Armed Forces radio networks, online, podcasts, mobile networks, and various other outlets. Rated among Talkers 250 Top Radio Shows in 2008.

Theme: Talk show covering ALL consumer electronics and technology, with listener call/e-mail ins, how-to-advice, technews and more.

Guest Profile: Mainly CEO's of top consumer electronic companies. A top executive that can talk about their latest and greatest consumer electronics and technology. Past interview experiences, credentials and sound of their voice are important.

Guest from Hell: One that just wants to market their product as we try to be informative, not selling, and one who has nothing to say.

Contact: beth@graveline.com or rob@graveline.com; 239-354-9810; http://www.graveline.com; Beth Gatrell or Rob Almanza. Best method: E-mail a pitch. No response? E-mail again as we get many and try to answer best we can; we book the coolest products/services first so make sure it is exciting.

Invited Back? If they give a good interview and are upbeat and fun.

Bio of Dave Graveline: Dave is an award-winning broadcaster who initiated the concept of a high tech talk show at 610 WIOD-AM in Miami, where he created and hosted the popular show then titled *Toys for Boys*. On January 6, 1996, the program entered syndication under a new name, and the *Into Tomorrow* Radio Network launched via satellite.

Since 1970, Dave has worked for most of the English language radio and television stations in South Florida. His many pursuits include several years as news anchor and talk show host at WIOD-AM, WKAT-AM, image voice and talk show host for WINZ-AM, DJ at Majic 102.7FM, staff announcer for WTVJ Channel 4 (now NBC 6), news 1360 signature voice for WCIX-CBS (now WFOR), producer and host of several nationally broadcast television specials such as: "Florida Outdoors" for PBS, "The Grand Prix of Miami" for ESPN, "Thoroughbred Racing Reviews" for SportsChannel, the Miss Florida USA pageants, "Spring Break Reunion" in nationwide syndication, as well as many national and local television commercials, training videos, documentaries, voice-overs, and on-camera productions.

Let's Talk Computers with Alan and Sandra Ashendorf, produced in Nashville, TN, and syndicated in Tennessee, Kentucky, Alabama, Illinois, Indiana, Texas, New Mexico and on the Internet.

Theme: Computer and technology issues.

Guest Profile: Authors, CEOs presidents of tech companies. Look for people that have an interesting story about their company — product — book, etc. We try to make sure that all of our guests are legit and we have worked with most of these companies or publishers for years.

For recent guests, visit http://www.lets-talk-computers.com/pastguest/bydate/index.htm

Guest from Hell: One that just has to put down their competition.

Contact: pr@lets-talk-computers.com; 615-662-0322; http://www.lets-talk-computers.com; Alan Ashendorf. Best method: Call with a pitch, e-mail a bio, send a press kit, especially sending in a full copy — book to review. No response? Sure — we get thousands of e-mails — request — some things just get lost in the shuffle.

Invited Back? How well they come across on the air. How knowledgeable they are on their topic.

Bios of Alan and Sandra Ashendorf: Alan is CEO and president of Total Solutions, Inc. and Sandra is host of their show. Alan has a reputation as a "pioneer" of the computer radio talk show, which dates back to his early days on the air in 1989.

Alan's background in electronics began when he put together his first Altair from a kit. He is fond of remembering that when he began, "believe it or not there were no computer books out there."

He became editor of the Music City User's Group in 1985, then its president. Later he and Sandra founded the Nashville Area PC User's Group, with a mission to bring together computer users from all walks of life and assist them in learning as much as possible.

There was a huge demand for a user group, dedicated to programming languages so Alan founded the Nashville Clipper Developer's Association in 1988, dedicated to DOS/xBase programming and the CA-Clipper language.

As Microsoft Windows gained in popularity, the same type of interest occurred for a Windows programming language. So, Alan founded the Nashville Area Access/Visual Basic User's Group in 1996.

Alan also has a monthly column, "Off the Air" in the *Nashville ComputerUser*, spotlighting one of the segments from his show.

Not impressed by technology for the sake of technology, Sandra's interests are in the positive results of how that technology changes the lives of those it is supposed to serve. Both on a person and business level, she marvels at the practical applications that these great technological advances that were promised to us are now starting to have. She has seen the hope, the beginnings of fruition, of a technology that advances the well-being of everyone. These advances are seen everyday in the fields of medicine and security; in the home, in the schools, as well as in the work place.

Her "other job" as a mother of a teenage girl keeps her on the lookout for software programs that educate and help to form the next generation of "computer gurus."

My Computer Show with Ira Wilsker on KLVI, aired in SE Texas, Beaumont, Houston, SW Louisiana and Lafayette, LA.

Theme: Computers and related technology.

Guest Profile: Reps from computer hardware, software, peripheral manufacturers and distributors; authors of computer books. Guests with knowledge of subject

Guest from Hell: One who is too technical, and the listeners cannot understand.

Contact: iwilsker@sbcglobal.net; 409-898-4598; http://www.klvi.com; Ira Wilsker. Best method: E-mail a brief bio and send a press kit. No response? E-mail again.

Invited Back? How well they do on the air.

Bio of Ira Wilsker: Ira has been host of his show since 1996 and technology columnist for the *Examiner* newspaper, since 2001. He has been on radio and TV since 1968.

Podcaster Training from Two Beams with Rob White on Talkshoe and uStream.tv

Theme: Podcast and videocast training and chat.

Guest Profile: Authors of podcasting books, new media consultants, bloggers. Sincerity, reputation, knowledgeable in their field or subject are vital. I also try to bring guests on that specialize in the topic for that night to keep continuity in the show.

Guest from Hell: A guest from hell would be someone who lets you begin the interview and then immediately takes over the show and starts letting their ego come out without giving you the opportunity to regain control of our own show. I try to research my potential guests as much as possible by reading their sites, blogs, listening to past interviews they have had and definitely by their credentials.

Contact: robwhiteus@gmail.com; 765-997-1140; www.nmpnetwork.com; Rob White. Best method: E-mail. Simply contacting me and requesting an interview works the best. At that point, I will ask for more information and make a determination if I have an upcoming show that they would fit into. No response? I try to respond to all e-mails within 48 hours of receiving them. In a case where I miss an e-mail and don't respond back in a timely fashion, they should contact me again as I will most likely see the second e-mail. If they fall into a spam filter for some reason and I don't see the e-mails, a phone call or Skype message will suffice.

Invited Back? Depends on how well the interview or segment goes and by the response of the listeners.

Bio of Rob White: Rob is a certified identity theft risk management specialist and a new media consultant. In addition to his podcaster show, he hosts *Identity Theft Radio* and *Business 101: Business Chat and Views* and produces a number of instructional videos and podcasts dealing with identity theft and new media.

Rob is author of some eBooks, including *Identity Theft: EXPOSED!*, *The Identity Theft Answer Man* and *Your First eBook — A Guide to Writing and Publishing eBooks!* He is currently writing an eBook dealing with Credit Repair and Debt Management that will be ideal for identity theft victims and a joint effort eBook being written by the listeners of his podcaster training show.

Married with six children and 12 grandchildren, Rob lives in west central Indiana and works full time for INDOT, the Indiana Department of Transportation. He's been dealing with identity theft for more than six years and started after becoming a victim himself and seeing, first hand, what victims must endure to rebuild their lives.

TechForum LIVE! with Priscilla Tate, on http://www.techforum.com/techforumlive.html

Theme: Emerging trends in enterprise computing.

Guest Profile: Two kinds of guests — (1) information technology managers for Fortune 500 companies and (2) technology product and service suppliers who sell to them. Credibility and credentials are essential. We select guests who have established expertise in the subject matter of the show. If we have a problem with a very thick accent, we would not accept that guest. But we have had that problem only once in two years and the solution was to have several people involved in the discussion.

Guest from Hell: A person who speaks like a public relations briefing.

Contact: ptate@techforum.com; 212-787-1122; http://www.techforum.com/techforumlive.html; www.techforumtrends.com. Best method: E-mail us the pitch and the bio. Never a press kit. No response? If the guest is appropriately placed for our audience, they should call.

Invited Back? It is a combination of their credentials and their energy level. High energy individuals are well received by listeners.

Guest Comments (about the Tech Forum events): "We walked away with several solid leads and I do believe face time with customers is the best way to increase brand awareness." — Marketing Director, Future Forum 2004 Silver Sponsor

"I always enjoy your events and so does the NY Team. They feel this is one of the most valuable marketing activities I do for them!" — Marketing Director, Future Forum Gold Sponsor

Bio of Priscilla Tate: Priscilla is the founder and president of Technology Managers Forum (TechForum), a professional association for IT managers at large companies. She produces two conferences a year in New York for corporate technology managers and two annual TechForum Roundtables on current trends in technology management.

Since the fall of 2005, she has been the host of her weekly radio show produced by Mytechnologylawyer.com. She also manages and conducts the Technology Managers Forum Best Practice Awards program, founded in 1994, which recognizes superior achievements in IT management.

Earlier in her career, Priscilla was a technology manager at Citibank, EF Hutton and Manufacturers Hanover Trust. During her tenure at EF Hutton she became active in the Microcomputer Managers Association (MMA) and in 1994 she left the MMA to form Technology Managers Forum.

In the late 90s she hosted a weekly radio show, *PC Planet*, on WEVD 1050 AM in New York on PC's and popular culture. She continues to be a frequent guest speaker on enterprise technologies for Internet radio stations.

Priscilla graduated from Duke University with a BA in history and an MA in art history. She also studied at the Freie Universitat in Berlin with a scholarship administered by the Fulbright commission. She was a Columbia Fellow and did graduate work at Columbia University.

Travel and Living Abroad

Paradise is Waiting.... — From *http://www.travelingwithfrancoise.com*

The Chris Robinson Travel Show with Chris Robinson on Newstalk 1010 CFRB in Ontario and CJAD 800 Montreal in Quebec.

Theme: Travel.

Guest Profile: Travel executives from tour operators, airlines, travel agents, destination marketing organizations. The shows are live listener phone-in format, so it is important for guests to be both knowledgeable and spontaneous. They need to understand the balance between providing useful information and entertaining delivery, and between promotion of their organization and enthusing listeners about travel generally. Their professional background and current roles are invaluable. I would always seek to talk with them over the phone or meet them personally in advance of the show, and to thoroughly brief them on the format of the show. It is also important for me to understand the major messages that they wish to communicate during the show as this enables me to facilitate this output.

Guest from Hell: A self-publicist who doesn't understand or care about the need to entertain and provide a service to the listeners at one end of the spectrum, and an introverted mumbler who can't express the knowledge and experience that they undoubtedly possess — as they wouldn't have been invited on to the show otherwise.

Contact: Chris@ChrisRobinsonTravelShow.ca; 416-925-1437; http://www.ChrisRobinsonTravelShow.com; Chris Robinson, host and producer. Best method: Approaches are welcomed by all appropriate routes: e-mail, post and phone. No response? Occasionally I am travelling as part of my work on the shows and unable to respond promptly; when this happens a follow-up is appreciated.

Invited Back? Listener feedback is important, both by e-mail following the show and by visits to our website in the week following the show. A win/win judgment from myself as host (did the guest achieve what I listed in the first question), and from the guest (in their own PR terms, i.e. did the show allow them to get their chosen message across effectively).

Guest Comments: "I simply cannot express how grateful I am to have been given the opportunity to sprout some radio wings through the opportunity provided by CFRB. I was very nervous over the prospect ... but yourself, Helen Lovekin and the CFRB team did a wonderful job.

"Providing this opportunity to 5 Festivals and Events may have been idealistic, yet, I believe each of those 5 events received great coverage." — Ana Kirkham, executive director, Festivals and Events Ontario

"I personally, was very pleased with the entire broadcast ... excellent thanks to everyone involved. I thought you and Christina were bang on of course, and Helen, Paul and Tara made for great guests. They all knew their product extremely well. I was really impressed by Helen Lovekin's knowledge of not only the Thunder Bay area, but the Aboriginal product up North." — RoseMarie Mancusa, partnership marketing officer, Tourism Thunder Bay

Bio of Chris Robinson: Chris' professional background is rooted in travel, commencing in the UK with a geography degree from Cambridge University in the mid 70s. He joined Thomson Holidays, the world's largest tour operator, as one of their first marketing graduate trainees and spent seven years in a number of marketing roles culminating in the post of general manager.

After positions with Diner's Club UK, Avis Europe and Saatchi and Saatchi Advertising, Chris moved back to tour operating in 1991 as general manager of Sovereign Holidays at the old Owners Abroad Group, a leading UK holiday company.

For six years Chris was the national marketing director at Signature, one of Canada's largest tour operators with sales of over $½ billion per year. In 2001 he moved to lead the marketing team at Sunquest Vacations, and subsequently moved up to become marketing vice president for MyTravel Canada, part of MyTravel plc, one of the largest leisure travel companies in the world, with 15 million customers globally.

In 2004 Chris set up his own company, Chris Robinson Associates, which provides consulting services to the Canadian travel industry. Consultancy clients include Conference Board of Canada, New Brunswick Tourism and Parks, CAA Travel, Flyglobespan, Collette Vacations, Best Western and Atlantic Canada Tourism Partnership.

He advises the Canadian Tourism Commission on their Canada marketing committee. He is a professional travel writer and co-author of a textbook, *Marketing for Tourism* (Longman 1995).

The Expat Show with Tai Aguirre on WTBQ, 1110 AM, an ABC affiliate, Warwick, New York, airing in Orange County, NY and northern New Jersey, on Saturday at 12:30 PM (ET). Tai is the creator and executive producer of *The Teen Show*, a positive spin on America's youth. For and about teens, the show airs Saturday, 11 AM to 12 PM, hosted by high school students. http://www.taicoproductions.com/theteenshow.htm.

Theme: For and about the worldwide expatriate community.

Guest Profile: Experts on culture, business, law, real estate, etc. I want people who can offer relevant information for those living abroad and those contemplating same — with knowledge and enthusiasm about their work and the skill to convey that in an interview. I want to know their past interview experiences, credentials and sound of their voice. They can direct us to their website and call me to speak.

Guest from Hell: Can't follow suggestions.

Contact: tai@taicoproductions.com; producer@theexpatshow.com; 914-422-1990; http://www.theexpatshow.com; http://www.taicoproductions.com; Tai Aguirre, Executive Producer. Best method: E-mail or phone to introduce. No response? Sometimes things get busy here ... be patient and be understanding.

Invited Back? They have a long range interest and info for our audience.

Listener Comments: "Your show has great potential for introducing those of us who would like to retire overseas. I enjoy your program. Thanks so much!" — Marilyn P. on the West Coast

"Finally a radio show just for us! Thanks!" — Bill S. in the Yucatan

Bio of Tai Aguirre: Tai is an entertainer, and an early entrepreneur, winning the web site-of-the-year award from *Incentive Magazine*. He also won best new product of the year from New York's Incentive Show for his "Your Personal Song," an all-occasion music production Ebusiness. He has won critical acclaim for his original Off-Broadway musical entitled *Broadway Moon* which played at Judy's and Theatre East in New York City.

His first radio program, hosted, written and produced by him, was a news/talk exposé radio show called Could YOU Be Next? ... stories the mainstream media won't dare talk about. The show exposed high profile cases and welcomed guests who told-all, such as race car driver Bobby Unser on the frivolous $600,000 lawsuit against him by the Forest Service.

Get a Life with Françoise (now called *Traveling with Françoise*), airing Sundays, 11 AM–1 PM, on 920 KPSI in Southern California, Palm Springs to Desert Center.

Theme: The second hour covers all aspects of travel: helpful hints, hottest destinations, local resort specials, prize packages and more. Both segments feature guests. The first hour covers local events, movie reviews, book reviews, new business profiles, prize give-a-ways and a variety of specialized segments.

Guest Profile: Everyone. I like to keep it fresh and different with an eclectic assortment of guests. Enthusiasm and loves what they are doing. Basically if they are knowledgeable about the subject matter.

Guest from Hell: Someone who doesn't know the subject they are talking about, or is a know-it-all and tries to control the segment

Contact: charityhotline@aol.com and travelershotline@aol.com; 760-409-9779; http://www.travelingwithfrancoise.com; http://www.getalifetravels.com; Françoise Rhodes, host and producer; Best method: E-mail or phone explaining the subject matter. No response? E-mail or call.

Invited Back? If I find them interesting.

Bio of Françoise Rhodes: Françoise understands the schematics of radio programming, and is a professional journalist who currently writes the scripts for both of her shows. She is also a regular co-host with Rich Gilgallon on *Da Coaches Soapbox* on 920 KPSI.

She's a staff writer for *Desert Golf Magazine, Colorado Golf Magazine, Golf Divas News Magazine,* and contributing writer for *Women Poker Player* magazine, *Desert Magazine, 92260* magazine and society coverage for the *Desert Sun* newspaper.

Talking Travel on the Travel Talk Radio Network with Roy Lowey, aired in Sarasota, Florida, and online 24/7.

Theme: In depth travel multi media.

Guest Profile: Industry guests, travel journalists, authors who are product knowledgeable and offer interesting subject matter that is travel related.

Guest from Hell: Only our journalists have recollections of experiences from there.

Contact: roy@ttrn.com; 941-739-3782; http://www.ttrn.com; Roy Lowey, Host/Producer. Best method: Short detailed e-mail. No response? Send another e-mail reminder

Invited Back? Good interaction with host.

Bio of Roy Lowery: Roy is the quintessential man with many irons in the fire. He also has many years experience in the airline industry, both as marketing executive and owner.

As a pilot and retired airline executive, he has many stories to tell. Few know of his involvement as a pioneer in the travel industry, especially in terms of airlines. For example, at one point in his career he was offering the only passenger air service from California to the Baja Peninsula. His airline companies, Air Cortez and Pacific National Airways, started out by flying nine-passenger twin Beech aircraft and then DC3s to what were then little known places in the region, many of which were important getaways for celebrity sports fishermen like Bing Crosby, as well as other Hollywood figures. Roy also operated a similar service out of Las Vegas to remote communities in Nevada.

He has worked with some of the world's most illustrious travel and tourism leaders (Freddy Laker, Nicky Oberoi) and has operated every kind of tour operation you can think of, from charter jets to managing group tours to the Dominican Republic. Roy has indeed been there, and done that, but never tires of discovering new opportunities in the industry. His show is just one of his latest forays into the 21st century of travel.

Tilley Talks Travel with Marcus Tilley, host and producer, on WECX 99.9FM, airing in St. Petersburg, Tampa Bay, Bradenton, Sarasota, FL.

Theme: Travel talk.

Guest Profile: Travel industry leaders from cruise lines, airlines, accommodation properties, spas, dining experiences, tour operators, voluntourism organizations, journalists, authors, destination CVBs and other travel industry media personalities. Leaders in the field of expertise with access to a landline phone and a reasonable interview personality. Important for us to know: Are they the most appropriate spokesperson? Do they have full authority to represent their particular part of the industry? Do they have the authority to offer prizes to be given away to listeners?

Guest from Hell: Someone who calls in on a mobile phone, talks so softly that even the automatic modulation equipment can't correct for the whisper quiet voice that only answers interview questions in 2 or 3 words and getting information is even more difficult han extracting hens' teeth.

Contact: mtilley@tampabay.rr.com; 727-867-4042 (Home); 727-434-7987 (Cell); http://www.tilleytalkstravel.com; Marcus Tilley. Best method: Calling with a pitch, e-mailing a bio and sending a press kit. Many of our guests come from PR agencies and as a result of press releases or articles in Travel Industry online publications. No response? E-mail again and follow up with a phone call after that. We plan our schedule about 3 months out, but there are occasions when a last minute cancellation of a guest creates an opening at 24 hours' notice.

Invited Back? Their attitude and radio presence as well as the amount of information we didn't get to cover during the interview. The offer to become a sponsor or advertiser also has an influence.

Guest Comments: "Marcus is such a wonderful host. He has had me on the show many times now and I have even co-hosted the show with him twice where I set up the entire show (all the people he would interview) full of Alaskan businesses. He has also been extremely gracious to us by taping a commercial that is run during his show for Xtremely Alaska and our product. Whenever Marcus calls I NEVER turn him down! I have been in Alaska for many of the shows, but I've been in Hawaii for a couple as well—over there racing in Triathlon. He is so personable and ALWAYS asks how my racing is going. I truly enjoy talking with him and feel like I've known him forever.

"Something else I would like to highlight — the first time I was on the air with Marcus I was so nervous to be on live radio, I had a speech and had rehearsed so I wouldn't talk too fast (or too much, something I'm good at) and within 15 seconds of starting the show I didn't need that paper, or feel stressed at all. In fact the only thing that I remember is how much my cheeks hurt from smiling! I truly enjoyed talking with him, it was very relaxed." — Rebecca McKee, general manager/guide, Xtremely Alaska, LLC, http://www.xtremelyalaska.com

"Marcus Tilley is one of my favorite hosts. I love his attitude and excitement for travel and my travels. While we are on the radio he plugs my website more than I do. When I call in for the show I feel as if I am speaking to a close friend (who I haven't met BTW) and sometimes forget that thousands of others are tuning in." — Johnny Jet, whose site, http://www.johnnyjet.com, is where travel experts share their tips and expertise

Bio of Marcus Tilley: Marcus is a travel industry veteran of some 25 years. Having worked in the travel industry in Australia, New Zealand, Norfolk Island and the USA for some of the largest travel wholesalers in those countries, he has also owned and operated his own travel agencies.

He's been a travel broadcaster for almost as long and been a show host in each of the same countries. In the USA, Marcus has been active on various stations in Indiana and Florida.

He has written travel columns for a number of newspapers and journals as a stringer and has many testimonials published on jacket notes for a number of travel authors. In a former life, Marcus was a bookseller and publisher and by default became a proofreader for author's manuscripts; something he still chooses to do.

Travel Queen Show with Jane DeGrow on the Michigan Talk Network of Citadel Broadcasting, aired on more than a dozen radio stations in Michigan. On the Internet, and podcast.

Theme: Travel.

Guest Profile: Travel industry experts, tourist boards, travel writers, etc., who are informative, interesting and enthusiastic/dynamic. I want to know their past interview experiences, credentials, and sound of their voice.

Guest from Hell: One who never stops talking or takes a breath or one who answers only "yes" or "no" to questions. It should be a conversation.

Contact: jane@travelqueen.com or dawn@travelqueen.com; Withheld upon request; http://www.travelqueen.com; Dawn Allan. Best method: E-mail a bio. No response? Send another e-mail.

Invited Back? How dynamic they are and their on-air rapport with the host.

Guest Comment: "Jane DeGrow, the Travel Queen, is anything but the spoiled monarch when it comes to her weekly travel radio show. She is a hard working, personable and charming host who always remembers to insert just the right promotional information to make her show valuable to her author/guests. Jane faithfully asks, "Susan please remind our listeners where they can buy a copy of SMART PACKING" — every author's dream question! Most important — she features valuable travel content for listeners.

"Having chatted with Jane on air many times over several years, I see her broadcast expanding to statewide coverage in Michigan. And with good reason — she is a great promoter of the state and features Michigan destinations as well as national and international locations. I have also watched website hits increase from travelqueen.com to my site as her audience and coverage expand. The *Travel Queen Show* is a winner for listeners and for articulate authors with a travel title to promote." — Susan Foster, author of *Smart Packing for Today's Traveler* (Smart Travel Press 2003), http://www.smartpacking.com

Bio of Jane DeGrow: Jane has been host of the *Travel Queen Show* for 13 years.

The Travel Show with Erik Hastings on WABC Radio, New York City and on http://www.wabcradio.com

Theme: Travel, places, products and services.

Guest Profile: Those with an intimate knowledge of a place, service or product in the travel space. Anyone who can tell us something we didn't already know. Upbeat and passionate. Want to know their past interview experiences, credentials and sound of voice.

Guest from Hell: Boring or someone who is pushing a product gratuitously.

Contact: adamhamway@hotmail.com; Withheld upon request; http://www.wabcradio.com or http://www.erikhastings.com; Adam Hamway (Producer) at Adamhamway@hotmail. Best method: Send a press kit or e-mail story ideas. No response? Do not call or e-mail.

Invited Back? The interview itself.

Bio of Erik Hastings: Erik is doing what he was born to do: Travel, meet and interact with people in places all over the world, and get behind the biggest microphone he can find (WABC Radio-NY). Erik's company, Scripted Improv Media Inc., produces a weekly travel show for WABC Radio's tri-state listening audience. Official tourism bureaus, travel professionals and "destination experts" collaborate with Scripted Improv to ensure accuracy and relevancy of destination and travel content.

In addition to the weekly show, the company pioneered a new style of online destination videos gaining national attention with the launch of new videos for Detroit, the host city of Super Bowl XL. In writing about the success of the videos and Erik's entertaining style, *Detroit News* columnist Neal Rubin dubbed Erik the "Flip tour guide."

To date, Erik has visited over 100 destinations,

ranging from little-known places like Aberdeen, South Dakota, to places of international prominence, such as London, and has produced videos, photo montages and written travelogues for many of them.

Erik is a frequent visitor to some destinations, like Atlantic City and Las Vegas, noting, "These types of destinations are growing and changing rapidly, necessitating frequent visits to see the progress." (On hearing this explanation, friends and family give an understanding nod and recommend therapy.)

Born and raised in America's heartland (that's code for Des Moines, Iowa), Erik got his first taste of travel when, at age 13, he was invited to join the cast of the musical *Peace Child*, making its debut tour to Moscow and other cities of the former Soviet Union. That memorable trip planted the seed of what has grown to be a passion to make the most of every trip opportunity ... for education ... entertainment ... business ... or pure recreational and leisure enjoyment.

Travel Talk: Escapes! with Ann Lombardi, on 620 AM, Sandy Spring, GA, aired in the Atlanta, GA, area and with audio archiving and streaming on net.

Theme: World-wide destinations, travel tips, travelers, travel experts, and authors with an unusual angle.

Guest Profile: Travel authors, airline/travel industry experts, tourism office professionals, travelers with great stories or insight to share. I want guests with passion, energy, good sense of humor, expertise, and ability to speak in an easy-to-understand, fluid, enthusiastic fashion that entertains and informs our listeners. What do they have to offer our audience and what is their background in their area of expertise?

Guest from Hell: A person who has a lackluster voice, has nothing really to say (not fun to interview a non-conversant personality), and hems/haws to no end.

Contact: thetripchicks@mindspring.com; 404-320-3033 or 770-454-7205; http:www.TheTrip Chicks.com; http://www.radiosandysprings.com/escapes.php; Celeste Selwyn at 404-943-1620. Best method: Calling or e-mailing with pitch and brief bio would be great. No response? Call and leave a message. I could be overseas escorting a cycling group, etc. so never fear, I will get back in touch sooner or later.

Invited Back? See answer to question # 1 above.

Guest Comments: "It was an honor to be on your show."—Christopher Elliott, National Geographic Traveler's ombudsman, nationally syndicated columnist, and host of "What You Get for the Money: Vacations" on the Fine Living network

"Wow. You're very plugged in, Ann. Thanks for the chance to be on your show. Hope you'll have me back again."—Pauline Frommer, nationally-recognized travel writer, author, and travel expert

Bio of Ann Lombardi: For over 23 years, certified travel consultants Ann Lombardi and her business partner Wendy Swartzell, a.k.a. The Trip Chicks, have been sharing their savvy travel advice, traveling to 60 countries, and helping people plan stress-free trips. With both international and U.S. airlines work experience, Ann has been interviewed on NPR, CNN Travel News, and FOX TV's "Good Day Atlanta." She and Wendy often filled in for now nationally-syndicated Clark Howard on his *Friday Flyer* radio show on AM 750 WSB Atlanta.

The Trip Chicks hosted their own FOX travel talk radio show in Washington, D.C., and now moderate travel teleseminars with top national experts. Ann's articles have appeared in the *Atlanta-Journal Constitution*, travel trade magazines, two national travel humor anthologies, and regional magazines.

Recommended in the "Dummies" travel guidebooks, The Trip Chicks focus on teaching travelers smart ways to save time and money. Their trademarks are discovering off-the-beaten-path destinations and revealing the best insider travel tips. Ann and Wendy are currently co-authoring their first travel book.

Travel'n On Radio Show with Ian and Tonya Fitzpatrick, Esqs. syndicated and broadcast from the Clear Channel studios in Washington, DC. The show is also heard on Voice America and Talk Zone.

Theme: Substantive travel information presented in an entertaining and educational format. Our mission is to educate, entertain and encourage our listeners to travel and experience the world.

Guest Profile: Celebrities, government officials, tourism officials, travel writers, photographers, etc. Someone with credible experience/knowledge on a destination and/or travel topic. Guests are profiled on http://www.talkzone.com/guests.asp?sid=608

Guest from Hell: We haven't experienced this.

Contact: radio@traveln-on.com; 301-587-2676; http://www.traveln-on.com; production team at Travel'n On Media Productions. Best method: Call with a pitch, e-mail a bio or send a press kit, but we are not an hour-long infomercial for for-profit entities. No response? "Reasonable Time" is subjective. However, I'd suggest that if a guest doesn't hear back from us within 30 days I would encourage them to e-mail us again ONLY if their pitch is travel related. However, even if we don't think a pitch is a right fit we will generally communicate that. We receive an enormous number of e-mails on a daily basis and we try to sift through them as best as we can.

Invited Back? Substantive content; relevant/current topic

Bios of Ian and Tonya Fitzpatrick, Esqs.: Ian and Tonya are sought after travel experts and enthusiasts who, combined, have traveled to and lived in numerous countries around the world. Ian and Tonya are regular contributors and guests on CBS and NBC and have been featured on *The Prudent Advisor* for Retirement Living Television and also in the elegant *Private Clubs Magazine*. The Fitzpatricks are published travel writers who hold a membership in the National Press Club.

Prior to their syndicated radio show, Ian and Tonya founded Bronze World Travel (http://www.bronzeworldtravel.com), a value-based Internet travel booking company offering discounted travel packages. Both lawyers, they recognized that a better quality of life could only be achieved if they put their efforts into something that they love — travel. Now their energy is spent discovering and sharing our world through their travel brands and investing in the global community.

Ian has a long history of travel and travel industry experience, having previously served as a financial analyst in corporate planning and labor relations at Northwest Airlines. His decades of leisure and business travel experience have provided him with a wealth of knowledge on various destinations, planes and airports. As a lifelong architecture and urban planning enthusiast, Ian likes visiting cities that have notable architectural structures and, as a pseudo historian, enjoys heritage and cultural travel. He is also an adventure and sports travel enthusiast who frequently travels to see his favorite teams play and enjoys visiting newly developed or historically relevant sports arenas wherever he goes.

Tonya has sought a life full of exciting travel experiences. She has lived, studied and worked abroad in England, China, Russia and Romania and her many travels have taken her through many regions of the world including a 5-week backpacking trip through Asia where she returned to China and visited eight other countries in the region. As an avid scuba diver she gravitates to coastal areas; however, she loves adventure and desires to trek through Nepal and climb Kilimanjaro in the near future. Ian and Tonya truly believe in "Celebrating Life Through Travel."

Whirl with Merle with Merle Exit on Blog Talk Radio, http://www.blogtalkradio.com/merleswhirls Thursdays, 7–8:30 PM (ET).

Theme: Travel, food, entertainment, products, and my obsession with the NY Sharks women's tackle football team.

Guest Profile: Travel — tourism or attraction reps; chefs, product company reps, entertainers, NY Sharks staff, reps from special events that are being featured; authors.

However, the flow of the interview needs to sound "conversational." I'm not terribly concerned with interview experience as I feel that it is my responsibility to lead the conversation and make that person feel comfortable. What is important is that the person is knowledgeable about whatever the topic is.

Guest from Hell: A guest from hell would be someone who is not sticking to the topic and refuses to get back to it combined with not being able to cut the interview short enough to get the next person on.

Contact: mexit@earthlink.net; 718-849-8158; http://www.merleswhirls.com; Merle Exit. Best method: E-mail or phone. No response? What determines a "reasonable time" to me may be different than the person pitching. If the person's idea of "reasonable time" is not happening than he/she is free to e-mail me again.

Invited Back? If a similar topic comes up at later time and the guest was able to go with the flow, I would have that person back.

Bio of Merle Exit: As a native New Yorker, Merle's childhood days were spent living in a housing project in Queens. Life's educational traumas began during the first month of second grade when she was kicked out and forced to enter third grade. Teacher: (surrounded by principal, mother and teacher next door) "You can go to third grade or if you stay in second grade, you can't raise your hand anymore." "I believed it had something to do with my IQ and reading skills. I chose third grade and stopped reading," Merle recalls.

After moving to housing projects in the Bronx, Merle had the opportunity to play an instrument, but her dreams were again thwarted by the teacher.

In college, she majored in communication arts and directed school musicals, acted and sang. She wrote and performed her own solo nightclub act and changed her name to "Exit" so she could see her name up in lights.

Merle is the arts and entertainment editor of the *Queens Times* and contributing writer for *Empty Closet, Destinations for Men, La Voz Latina, Edge Publications*, as well as several local and out of town publications.

She also does publicity for the New York Sharks women's tackle football team, which has been voted the top women's football team in the country, and has assisted in the opening of the IWFL Women's Football Hall of Fame.

Women

A Wise Woman...

Recognizes
her wisdom and
that of others
Is willing to
acknowledge,
engage,
honor and
participate
in community
As a way to
educate,
empower and
inspire
each other
towards
thriving livelihoods!
— From the main page of *Wise Women Talk*, http://www.wisewomenweb.net

Amazing Women with Deb Ruggiero, airs Sunday at 8:30 AM on 630 WPRO AM/99.7 FM, 6:00 AM on

WWLI (Lite Rock 105), and 6:30 AM on 92 PROFM and Wednesday at 7:30 PM (ET) on Rhode Island PBS Television. You can also listen online ANYTIME at http://www.amazingwomenri.com

Theme: Both radio and TV shows highlight the accomplishments of women who make a difference in our community—whether in healthcare, education, politics, civic engagement, or the arts.

Guest Profile: Guests range from poets and authors like Maya Angelou, to women CEOs, political leaders, and breast cancer survivors. The show focuses on woman/women who have a compelling story to share that will create "emotional involvement." When you hear their story you, as a viewer or listener, will become inspired, enlightened, or encouraged! Someone who has a compelling story that will inspire, motivate, or encourage. It should be an issue or accomplishment that will resonate with a large portion of the audience. I want to know their background and just a little bit about their work. I want to be able to ask the kind of questions that someone listening or watching would ask if they didn't have all of the background information. I do listen to their voice on the phone to make sure they will be audible. For the TV show I try to make sure the three women on the set are all very diverse in background and in heritage.

Most guests are Rhode Islanders, but there are exceptions. "When an 'amazing woman' is in town like Maya Angelou, I will also highlight that work since it impacts ALL women," says Deb.

Guest from Hell: Someone who is glib on the phone and through e-mail and then "clams up" when the camera rolls, or the microphone is turned on.

Contact: DebRuggiero@amazingwomenri.com; http://www.amazingwomenri.com. Best method: E-mail is best because people can put their ideas on paper and I can process it and determine how to frame it for a show. No response? I will respond, but follow up with a phone call is always fine (at my office). I work a month ahead with the schedules so we may not tape immediately and research has to occur prior to any show.

Invited Back? When there is new legislation or a community issue that a past guest was working on.

Bio of Deb Ruggiero: Deb is director of community development for Citadel Radio and founding and board member of the Women's Fund of Rhode Island. She is the past president of the Lung Association of Rhode Island and serves on the Philanthropic Committee for the Rhode Island Foundation.

She also teaches broadcast advertising and marketing communications at Providence College.

Her show won the 2008 Associated Press Award for the best public affairs program in New England.

And the Women Gather Radio Show with Lorna Owens on Blog Talk Radio, www.blogtalkradio.com/and_the_women_gather

Theme: Gathering place for women around the world.

Guest Profile: Doctors, experts with energy. The sound of their voice is important.

Guest from Hell: Use the show as infomercial.

Contact: contact@lornaowens.com; 305-573-8423; http://www.lornaowens.com; Veronoca Vernon. Best method: E-mail bio and send book. No response? E-mail.

Invited Back? Fun and energy.

Bio of Lorna Owens: Jamaica-born Lorna Owens is a graduate of the University of Florida School of Law. She had her own practice since 1993 but has since reinvented herself and is now living her dreams. Lorna travels the country speaking with healthcare providers, corporations and professional women's groups about rising above mediocrity to achieving their greatness.

Bob and Sheri on WLNK, Charlotte, N.C., and syndicated by Greater Media. Rated #84 in the 2008 Talkers Heavy Hundred.

Theme: Talk targeted to females 25–54.

Guest Profile: Authors, actors, musicians and relationship experts. Someone who is compelling and can tell a good story or talk casually, with credentials and past interview experiences.

Guest from Hell: A guest that answers questions with one word answers.

Contact: todd@bobandsheri.com; 704-374-3747; http://www.bobandsheri.com; Todd Haller. Best method: E-mail with a pitch. No response? The person should feel free to send another e-mail to follow up.

Invited Back? If they're liked by the guests and the listeners.

Bio of Bob Lacey: Growing up in Old Lyme, Conn., Bob bused tables and washed dishes at his father's restaurant and fully understood that food service was not to be his life's calling.

He took his first job as a radio newsreader at the tender age of 18, after realizing that his career fronting a New England rock band would never get him on the airwaves. He says his attraction to the industry stemmed from hanging out with deviant show biz types back stage at The Doors and The Byrds shows.

Bob attended Roger Williams University in Bristol, RI. At age 22, he launched the first-ever evening phone-in show on powerhouse AM station WBT in Charlotte, NC. At 25, he was hosting a morning drive talk show and well on his way to perfecting the intellect and humor that he still manages to muster up some mornings even today.

In the 1980s, Bob hosted Charlotte's award-winning television program *PM Magazine* and served as the show's national humor reporter/producer. He is the recipient of many awards for his broadcasting and community service, including the 1986 Iris Award for Best Produced Local Television Feature in the Nation for a piece on the horrors of prom night.

Bob returned to radio in 1990, handling morning drive for WBT's struggling FM counterpart, WBCY (now WLNK). In 1991, managers launched a lengthy nationwide search to find a female co-host for the show. They listened to some 65 tapes, but Bob was adamant that they not hire a giggle box to laugh at his jokes. He wanted a partner who could really add to the mix. Bob and Sheri was born and, a decade later, their raucous, real-life humor is delighting listeners in more than 60 markets around the U.S.

Bob is the father of five children.

Bio of Sheri Lynch: Sheri began her career in television, writing and producing paranoia-inducing news teases. Having tired of warning the world about the dangers lurking in dirty restaurant kitchens and sketchy daycare centers, she agreed to create a commercial for a new radio program. Enter Bob Lacey, wearing one of his favorite preppy outfits. "Lose the red sweater," she suggested. "You don't want to look like an elf, right?" To pay her back for that disrespect, Bob invited her to be his guest on-air. That was a meeting of soul mates, and the beginning of the long, happy *Bob and Sheri* partnership.

Among her numerous honors, in 2002 and 2005 Sheri received the American Women in Radio and Television's (AWRT) highest honor, the Gracie Allen Award, for outstanding achievement in the realistic portrayal of women in media. In 2004, she won the *Charlotte Business Journal*'s "Women in Business Achievement Award." She has been named Best Local Radio Personality by *Creative Loafing* magazine for over ten consecutive years. *Bob and Sheri* has also received six nominations for the radio industry's highest honor, the Marconi Award, presented by the National Association of Broadcasters.

Sheri is author of *Hello, My Name Is Mommy* (2004), in its fourth printing and *Be Happy, Or I'll Scream!* (2006), both published by St. Martins Press.

She is married, with two young daughters and a step — or, as she prefers, *bonus* son.

Chat with Women with Pam Gray and Rochelle Alhadeff on KKNW, aired in the Greater King County Area (Seattle/Bellevue and surrounding areas)

Theme: A Forum for women and the men who love them. Inspiring, motivational.

Guest Profile: Authors, psychologists, people who have accomplished their dreams. Motivational, Inspiring. We do pre-interviews on our guests and we want to know their story.

Guest from Hell: Someone with NO personality. No energy.

Contact: rochelle@chatwithwomen.com and pam@chatwithwomen.com; 425-455-1917; http://www.chatwithwomen.com; Rochelle or Pam. Best method: E-mail. No response? E-mail or call.

Invited Back? Inspiring, motivational.

Listener Comment: "I'd like to say to both of you that you are an inspiration and have made it possible for me to follow my new life intent to do things I've never done before and what a year it's been! Thanks again. I'm dreaming big and making it happen one day at a time!— Karen Morgan

Bio of Rochelle Alhadeff: Rochelle was an at-home mom for 12 years before putting those multitasking and organizational skills to use in the convention industry as a marketing director. She switched over to telecom and became the company's number one salesperson in the country. Then her path came full circle and Rochelle put her sales and management skills to work for the family business, Apex Winery, running it with her husband.

Mother of two grown sons, Rochelle is a breast cancer survivor and advocate for Alzheimer's treatment. Her motto is "Live, Love, Laugh — and do it NOW!"

Bio of Pam Gray: After ten years as a stay-at-home mom, Pam jumped into Corporate America and climbed the ladder to become a vice president of sales, marketing and customer service in the telecom industry. After 15 years, she got off the corporate hamster wheel and joined her husband and son in managing a college town nightspot.

Five years later, Pam looked at the experience she had amassed as a mother, a sales person, and a bartender and realized that listening, finding solutions and helping people work through their problems was the common thread that pulled it all together. She reinvented herself and realized that her real skills lay in helping others discover their inner potential and live their dreams. Pam became a certified dream-coach.

Chat with Women was founded by Rochelle and Pam to change lives and explore possibilities through the power of girl talk.

Coach K! Talk Radio Show for Women with Keesha Mayes (Coach K!) on Blog Talk Radio, http://blogtalkradio.com/coachkradio

Theme: An empowerment talk radio show designed to support women in their personal and professional lives.

Guest Profile: Any guest that provides positive and practical information in personal, spiritual and professional development for women. Someone that brings a positive and practical message that uplifts and informs women in improving the quality of their lives. Their experience and credentials.

Guest from Hell: Combative and chauvinistic viewpoints.

Contact: keesha@coachkradio.com; 203-278-1988; http://coachkradio.com and http://blogtalkradio.com/coachkradio; Keesha Mayes. Best method: E-mail. They can go to my website and submit their information, either a bio or press release. No response? It would be best to call me.

Invited Back? If the show was fun for them and me. If they have new information that will support women.

Bio of Keesha Mayes: Keesha describes her life as "A Miracle Unfolding," having faced many challenges. Her first true step out on faith began when she left her abusive home at 15 years old. She spent two years in foster homes and shelters, finally settling at the Children's Center groups home in Connecticut. Just as she was about to graduate from high school and enter her first year of college, Keesha was diagnosed with systemic lupus, Sjogren's Syndrome, ITP, and rheumatoid arthritis.

Not fully realizing her personal power and inherent gifts and talents, Keesha struggled with homelessness and serious bouts with her lupus. She dropped out of college in her final year, got married, gave birth to three children and took minimal jobs that did not challenge or inspire her.

Seven years later, Keesha's life changed. She was face to face with a serious flare-up with her lupus, and had to undergo a year of pulse therapy (I.V. treatments of steroids and chemotherapy). Keesha felt her life was over at 27. Her health was rapidly deteriorating, and her dreams of health and success was slipping away from her.

One evening before her final round of pulse therapy treatments, Keesha had a powerful dream. She dreamt of a beautiful woman coming to speak with her. This woman spoke of love and strength and health for Keesha. This woman told Keesha that she had many gifts to give and receive, but she had to want to live. Today, Keesha believes that the woman that appeared in her dream was her highest self in spirit, asking her to fight for her life. Keesha took that dream and went on to transform her life.

In seven short years, Keesha went on to create the Healthy Divas, a women's empowerment group in the Connecticut Lower Naugatuck Valley, and the Divas Sanas, a women's empowerment group for Latinas. She won thousands of dollars in grant funding, and was privileged to work alongside scientists at Yale University School of Public Health and Epidemiology, co-authoring with them a breast cancer intervention research study for African American women.

Keesha completed her Bachelors degree in communications at Charter Oak State College and her Personal and Business Professional Coaching Core Competencies at Coach U in 2005. She won the 2007 Health and Leadership Fellowship from the Connecticut Health Foundation, which is a year long study program on reducing health disparities in minority communities.

In September 2007, Keesha became a non-denomination ordained minister.

Cocoa Mode with Shawna Renee on XM Satellite Radio, Channel 169, part of the Joe Madison and Friends program, airing Thursday at 8 AM (ET).

Theme: Lifestyle, womens issues.

Guest Profile: Therapists, authors, entertainers, bloggers, news-makers. Guests must be informed, energetic, compassionate, honest. Motivation, level of expertise, ability to interact with callers.

Guest from Hell: Guests who use the show as a free commercial, boring guests, condescending guests.

Contact: shawna@cocoamode.com; 240-205-1023; http://www.cocoamode.com; Shawna Renee. Best method: E-mail. I'm always interested in a good pitch. The more background information the better. I always ask authors to send a preview copy of a book before considering an interview. No response? If I don't respond within a week, I'm probably not interested.

Invited Back? Chemistry with the host, quality of information.

Bio of Shawna Renee: Shawna has dedicated her life to a career in radio. She started as a producer for the top rated African American talk show, *The Joe Madison Show*. Before long she was hired as the programming assistant for WOLB-AM in Baltimore. She went on to produce and co-host the #1 rated morning drive program at urban powerhouse WERQ-FM.

In 2000 Shawna moved to Washington, DC, where she hosted *Love Talk* and *Slow Jams* on WPGC-FM for a number of months before moving on to Satellite Radio. Shawna was hired as program director of Worldzone, the World Music Channel heard on XM Satellite Radio. After a successful three years with WorldZone, she was chosen to create and program the world's first global Hip Hop channel, FLAVA, heard on Worldspace Satellite Radio, where she was also an on-air personality.

Throughout her career in music radio she never lost sight of her goal to host her own radio talk show. In early 2006, Shawna took a break from radio to give birth to her first son. It was during this time she began researching information on natural beauty and wellness for both her benefit and that of her newborn son. It wasn't long before she discovered a way to combine her love of radio and her passion for products.... Introducing *Cocoa Mode*.

Conversations with Coach Yvonne with Yvonne Chase on BlogTalkRadio.com/coachyvonneradio

Theme: Empowerment radio for today's single woman.

Guest Profile: Authors, psychologists, experts and every day people with energy and a great story. Content; what are they bringing to the show?

Guest from Hell: Someone who clams up and cannot express points clearly.

Contact: coachyvonne@availableandhappy.com; 310-654-0609; www.availableandhappy.com; Yvonne Chase. Best method: E-mail. It's all about the story. No response? E-mail or call.

Invited Back? Content, controversy, ability to engage listening audience.

Bio of Yvonne Chase: Persuasive, passionate and powerful — those are a few words that come to mind when you see Yvonne on stage, in action. She's a dynamic, high-energy dating coach, affectionately known as "The Single Woman's Cheerleader." Her #1 mission is to create a movement of "Available and Happy" single women that enter relationships out of want and not need. "The first step in making a love connection is being the best, happiest most fulfilled YOU that you can be."

Yvonne is here to spread the word that being single is an opportunity to be pursued and to put a stop to every negative stereotype that singles have endured. Yes, she knows that living single can be challenging at times but Yvonne is here to support you, be your cheerleader, advocate and sounding board in those times. Her #2 mission is to bring the climbing divorce rate to a screeching halt by teaching singles how to date and make the best partner choice. Statistics show that one out of every two marriages ends in divorce.

She is a frequent keynoter and speaker at colleges and leads workshops that attendees say leave them "energized, empowered, and excited about life." She is the author of the *Ask Coach Yvonne E-zine* and her articles have been published in the *Brooklyn Woman* weekly newspaper, *Heart and Soul* magazine, *ESSENCE* magazine.

No stranger to the media, Yvonne has been a featured expert on "Good Day New York" (FOX), "Live with Mary Amorosa" (COMCAST NETWORK) and on New York City radio programs including *Wake-Up Club* (98.7 KISS FM), *Street-Soldiers* (Hot 97.1 FM), *Morning Show* (Power 105.1 FM), and *Conversations with Dr. Jeff Gardere* (WWRL 1600AM) to name a few.

Prior to her work as a dating coach, Yvonne launched her career in television as a reporter for Brooklyn Cable News. She later expanded her horizons by working for one of New York's leading radio stations, 98.7 KISS FM. Yvonne continued to build her career in television by working as a producer for CBS, Tribune Broadcasting, HBO Downtown Productions, and other media. She holds a Bachelor of Arts degree in TV/radio production from Brooklyn College.

Yvonne resides in Los Angeles, California.

Eve's Third Wave (hosts change periodically) on 101.5 umfm, University of Manitoba, Winnipeg, airing Tuesdays, 5 to 6 PM (CT).

Theme: Feminist spoken word radio.

Guest Profile: Community activists. We usually interview women who are creating culture or doing community activist work. We will talk to pretty much anyone though — as long as they are comfortable with it. Generally we just go with what we have — but we will research the project they are working on.

Guest from Hell: Someone who is not interested in engaging our questions.

Contact: evesthirdwave@hotmail.com; Withheld upon request; http://www.umfm.com/talk/show_descriptions.shtml?type=talk; Kim Parry. Best method: Call with a pitch, e-mail a bio or send a press kit. No response? Hopefully we will e-mail you back, but generally if you don't get a response it is because we didn't have time, but we are working on this.

Invited Back? If they are interested in coming back.

eWomenNetwork Radio Show with Sandra Yancey on WBAP 820 AM (ABC), Dallas, TX.

Theme: Each show is a showcase for introducing dynamic women from all over North America and *New York Times* best-selling authors, who share insights, strategies and ideas for personal and professional growth.

Guest Profile: Members or sponsors who can share insights, strategies and ideas for personal and professional growth. I want to know their experiences and credentials. At http://www.ewomennetwork.com/index.html click #3 "How to Join Us" to learn about membership.

Guest from Hell: A person selling boy toys.

Contact: radio@ewomennetwork.com; 972-620-9995, Ext. 1035; http://www.ewomennetwork.com; Kami Grayson, radio show coordinator. Best method: By E-mailing a bio and/or sending a press kit. No response? They should e-mail or call the show's coordinator

Invited Back? Depends how dynamic their interview was.

Bio of Sandra Yancey: Sandra is a networking expert who teaches others how to create relationships that harness great dividends. She is the founder and CEO of eWomenNetwork. Starting with just 20 women in her personal database in 2000, she has grown her organization to 113 chapters throughout the U.S. and Canada and a database of over 500,000 women business owners and professionals.

Ranked #1 by Business Women's Network as the best online community for women business owners and professionals in North America, eWomenNetwork.com receives more than 200,000 hits daily.

Sandra is the recipient of numerous national business awards, including the 2005 Entrepreneur Star award from Business Women's Network and Microsoft, 2005 Woman Advocate of the Year from the Women's Regional Publishing Association, and the 2006 Enterprising Women Advocacy Award from *Enterprising Women* magazine.

Sandra is the author of *Relationship Networking: The Art of Turning Contacts into Connections* (eWomenPublishingNetwork 2006)

Her story has been selected for the hot new *Chicken Soup for the Entrepreneur's Soul* (HCI 2006) series, which features the top entrepreneurs from North America. In fact, the eWomenNetwork logo is featured on the book's front cover.

Sandra holds a Master's degree in organization development from American University in Washington, D.C., and a post-graduate degree from the prestigious Gestalt Institute in Cleveland, Ohio.

The eWomenNetwork Foundation, which Sandra founded in 2001, has awarded hundreds of thousands of dollars in cash grants, in-kind donations and support to women's nonprofit organizations, as well as scholarships for emerging female leaders of tomorrow.

How She Really Does It with Koren Motekaitis on KDRT 101.5 FM, Davis, CA.

Theme: For women about women.

Guest Profile: Authors, columnists, women, moms, entrepreneurs, professors, financial specialists, vets, counselors. I look for guests who can inspire or teach others of the possibilities that are out there, whether financial, family balance, communication, or other issues we face in our day to day life. Want to know what their message is and how will my audience benefit.

Guest from Hell: One that does not talk.

Contact: howshe@gmail.com; 530-554-9454; http://www.howshereallydoesit.com; Koren Motekaitis. Best method: E-mail or call. No response? E-mail or call.

Invited Back? The chemistry and if they have more info to tell.

Guest Comments: "I had a blast. Was fun chatting with you."— Jeff Opdyke, *WSJ* columnist "Love and Money"

"I really enjoyed the show and the questions you asked."— Martha Beck, *NY Times* best selling author, *O Magazine* columnist, and life coach

Bio of Koren Motekaitis: Koren has always been interested in human interest stories or other peoples' journeys — especially other women. Her interest lead her to develop a talk show meant to inspire, empower, entertain — and answer the question she has often asked herself when listening and getting to know other amazing women — "How Does She Really Do It?" Each week, her show features a different topic focusing on what women face in their day to day life and provides an opportunity for women to learn from each other.

Koren is on the faculty at Sacramento City College (SCC) and runs the AquaMonsters youth swim program in Davis, California. A coach at both the collegiate and youth levels, she coached the swim and water polo teams at SCC for 11 years and developed 16 All-Americans and two state champions. As a former Davis Aquadarts youth coach, Koren also developed numerous nationally ranked kids.

As a competitive swimmer herself, Koren tallied four individual conference titles at UC Davis as well as a school record en route to becoming a Division II national champion.

Koren received her B.A. degree from UC Davis and her Master's degree in sports management from the University of San Francisco. As the proud mother and stepmother of four children, ranging in age from 5 to 20 years, and a full-time working parent, she is the first to ask "How Does She Really Do It?"

Just Between Us with Debbie Bodnarchuk: Christine Williams: Deb Smith aired in Halifax, Nova Scotia: Victoria, British Columbia and podcast on Apple I-tunes; now off the air.

Theme: A one hour program for women; about women; by women.

Guest Profile: Authors, women with interesting jobs, health professionals, beauty experts, financial experts, recording artists, television personalities, women who work from home, environmental activists, women in politics, fashion experts and everyday women doing something special, e.g., volunteering, caregiving. We look for someone who is knowledgeable and excited about their topic. Someone whose enthusiasm shows through. We always like to have a phone conversation first to see how the person comes across or at least have a good recommendation from someone. We like to have a copy of a book first before we interview an author.

Guest from Hell: We had a guest who was tipsy and didn't make a lot of sense. Didn't answer the questions we asked at all. A boring speaker is just as bad.

Contact: feedback@betweenus.ca; 902-446-0183; http://www.betweenus.ca; Deb Bodnarchuk. Best method: We prefer e-mail or a press kit. No response? An e-mail reminder is fine.

Invited Back? The topic can be seasonal ... organization tips; fashion updates and if the topic warrants further discussion, we arrange for our listeners to send in questions and we will consider having a person back.

Bio of Debbie Bodnarchuk: Debbie has been an advertising copywriter for print, radio and television. She worked for the Winnipeg Jets hockey team writing for their magazine; worked in public relations and promotions for the Special Olympics and was promotions manager for three shopping centers. She became part owner of an advertising agency and moved into media sales with Atlantic Television (ATV). Sales were in her blood and she turned to real estate, selling homes for nine years with Royal Lepage. Now she's gone full circle and is back in media, only this time behind the microphone.

Born in Toronto, Debbie spent most of her life in Halifax and now splits her time between Toronto and Halifax. She is married to Bill and has two children and two stepchildren.

Bio of Deb Smith: Deb is a Cape Breton gal, raised in Inverness County in a community called Long Point, very small (maybe 300). There is one provincial park in the area ... and a spectacular view of the Northumberland Strait.

She started in radio at age 16 at CIGO in Port Hawkesbury, working weekends in the newsroom.

Deb completed a radio-journalism program at Woodstock, NB, and got a work-term at CJCH/C100 in 1996, first as Hot line producer and currently co-hosting the morning show with Brian Phillips.

Surrounded by Scottish and Irish culture, music

and dance, Deb sang in the church choir, some local community events and, as a highland dancer, was a member of the Scotia Highland Dancers.

Bio of Christine Williams: Christine lives in Doon, Ontario, with her spouse and two sons, Zakkary and Aaron.

The Ladies Room with Lolis with Lolis Garcia Baab on KJCE 1370AM, Austin and 1650AM KHRO, El Paso, TX, aired in central and west Texas.

Theme: A show for women, about women and for women in the know.

Guest Profile: Leaders, doctors, authors, remarkable women with a remarkable story that gives our audience an inspirational or educational take away. We know the guest's past interview experiences, credentials, and sound of their voice before a show.

Guest from Hell: We have not had one ... shy guests or nervous guests are tough.

Contact: Valerie@shawtx.com; 512-423-9319; http://www.theladiesroomwithlolis.com; Valerie Shaw. Best method: E-mail. No response? Just be patient ... we receive 50 inquiries daily.

Invited Back? How relevant their remarkable story is to global and current events.

Guest Comment: "...I had the privilege of having a great conversation with Lolis Garcia regarding Hispanic Heritage Month, Latino culture, immigration, entrepreneurship in our community, Hispanic education and much more. I've mentioned the Lolis show before, and invite you to check it out and see how this amazing Mexican-American lady is setting a great example for many Hispanics to follow." — Arturo Acevedo, chief of police, Austin

Bio of Lolis Garcia-Baab: Lolis is a bilingual communications professional with a wide range of television and radio experience as a producer, writer, journalist, correspondent, and voice-over talent.

Having lived in both Mexico and the United States, she has a strong understanding of the Latino culture and its impact on mainstream society.

A mother of two children and wife of 12-year NFL veteran Mike Baab, she is a business and community leader and a graduate of the University of Texas at Austin.

Full bio at http://www.theladiesroomwithlolis.com/aboutlolis.html

The Life Lounge with Carol Lee Espy on KDKA, Pittsburgh PA.

Theme: Lounge/salon atmosphere.

Guest Profile: Female baby boomer. Quick intellect able to talk off script, on their feet, sense of humor. I need subject matter that means something to my audience, and the guest needs to sell that point. Are they interesting, do they know their subject matter, are they passionate about what they do?

Guest from Hell: A guest who takes herself too seriously and reads from a script. Someone who insists on pre-interviewing questions sent to them (they don't get on the show).

Contact: cespy@kdka.com; 412-576-3388; kdkaradio.com; Carol Lee Espy. Best method: E-mail me with info, bio, press kit, etc., also product, send the book. I don't want phone calls. No response? E-mail me again.

Invited Back? If they were interesting, excited about their subject.

Bio of Carol Lee Espy: Carol is a multi-hyphenate. She's a singer-songwriter-voiceover-talent-TV-host-producer-wife-mother and radio host. Her compositions for television have garnered multiple Emmy nominations.

Carol started her career as a voice-over talent while working as a production manager in a Pittsburgh studio. Her national voice-overs and jingle work soon became a staple for her.

She is the only female host on KDKA, the first commercial radio station in the nation, heard in over 38 states in the U.S. and Canada. Fifty thousand watts and counting.

Carol produces and writes her shows for KDKA radio and her packages for TV.

In the midst of all of it, she raises (along with her husband percussionist/composer Jim DiSpirito), her son Daniel in a flurry of soccer, football, chess club, historical re-enactments in the yard. Carol and Jim have their own production company called Wichita Blue Productions, http://www.jimdispirito.com/carol.html, http://www.jimdispirito.com/wbp.html

Loving Life Radio Show with Jane Carroll on http://www.lovingliferadioshow.com in conjunction with http://www.byforandaboutwomen.com; now off the air.

Theme: Inspiring women to love their lives wherever they are on the journey.

Guest Profile: Uplifting message for women, especially ages 35–65. Authors who have written books of encouragement, personal growth and some business topics. I look for guests who are willing to share some valuable information with the listeners. I also look for guests who have something to promote. If a listener loves the guest, they want more. I love guests who promote the show with their list. I look for past interview experiences, credentials, sound of their voice. I usually spend a great deal of time visiting their websites, blogs, podcast and anything else that will help me know them better. Having a list of questions for the media is great because it gives me a good idea of their comfort zone of topics.

Guest from Hell: A guest from hell is only promoting their product or service and doesn't give any real information to the listeners. This isn't a commercial for the guest — the more information they give, the more the listener will want from them.

Contact: jane@lovingliferadioshow.com; 256-974-7794; http://www.lovingliferadioshow.com; Jane

Carroll. Best method: E-mailing is probably the simplest way; attaching a bio and press kit or appropriate links is great. No response? By all means re-connect. E-mails get lost and misdirected all the time.

Invited Back? Audience response, how long since they were on the show.

Guest Comment: "I am fortunate enough to have been interviewed by Jane. I know firsthand that she does her homework prior to the interview. She creates the best possible show by inquiring and digging deep for excellent information pertaining to her interviewee's area of expertise."—Dotsie Bregel, founder of the number one site on major search engines for "baby boomer women," http://www.boomerwomenspeak.com, and the National Association of Baby Boomer Women, http://www.nabbw.com

"Doing a radio show with Jane is an opportunity to share your deepest thoughts and most passionate observations. And she asks great questions that make it easy to sound smart! Her choice of guests (present company included!) is stellar. A show that will be heard by millions! Thanks!! Jane."—Jennifer Louden, author *The Life Organizer: A Woman's Guide to a Mindful Year* (New World Library 2007), http://www.comfortqueen.com

Bio of Jane Carroll: Jane Carroll RN, BSN transitioned into a fulltime life coach, speaker, author, and Internet talk radio host two years ago.

Because she has experienced first-hand the effects of low self-esteem and feeling miserable in her own life, Jane has created a personal growth company geared towards providing women with the tools, information and support necessary for loving life ... wherever they are along the journey. Accompanied by her whimsical character Bertha, she offers a humorous approach to personal growth for a generation of women who prefer laughter to lectures.

Jane is author of *Bertha-Size Your Life!* (To The Letter 2005).

The mother of two grown daughters and grandmother, Jane lives in north Alabama with her cat.

Metrochick Radio with Lisa Marie is streamed over the Internet through Live365.com and on http://www.metrochickradio.com. The show is on from 8–9 AM, Monday (mompreneur show), Wednesday (business), and Friday (Successful Living).

Guest Profile: Women authors or books that would appeal to women. There is a fee. An individual segment, which runs 20 to 30 minutes, costs $225. What informative and exciting topic do they bring to the show?

Guest from Hell: Unprepared, hard to follow up with.

Contact: lisamarie@metrochickradio.com

Theme: Informative Talk Radio for Women; 248-730-4407; www.metrochickradio.com. Lisa Marie O'Sullivan. Best method: E-mail bio and business entity you will talk about. No response? Call or e-mail. I'm usually pretty good, but things can fall through the cracks. Keep trying.

Invited Back? If they are informative and excited about participation.

Bio of Lisa Marie O'Sullivan: Lisa Marie was bitten by the radio bug after a small stint on her father's radio talk show. Although growing up with a speech impediment that left her insecure about her own voice, it was after hearing herself on tape that she realized the impediment was gone. Wanting to bring empowerment to others by creating a portal for women to have a voice and talk about their businesses, their industry, or themselves, Lisa Marie got the inspiration for *MetroChick Radio*.

Along with her formal education at Mesa College in San Diego and Baker College in Auburn Hills, Lisa Marie likes to say that much of her knowledge comes from her life experiences, including entrepreneurship, single parenting of three daughters, finance, travel and dating issues. A strong advocate for volunteering and working with non-profits, her favorite motto is "It is through helping others that we ultimately help ourselves."

She enjoys working weekends as a much sought-after face painting artist.

The Mother Daughter Club, a segment of By For and About Women Radio Network with Kathe Gogolewski, www.themotherdaughterclub.com

Theme: All things that matter to women.

Guest Profile: Versatile—generally inspirational. I look for a guest with a powerful message that will appeal to women and inspire them to some kind of action. Guests who are experts in their topic is always nice, but sometimes it's just a moving story that someone has to share. I would like to have some evidence that they have successfully shared their story or news and created interest, but this isn't necessary. First time interviewees are welcome, but I need to speak to them first on the phone.

Guest from Hell: A guest from hell would be someone who did not speak with sincerity. Disingenuine sharing is generally transparent; listeners can tell when someone doesn't care about a topic.

Contact: kgogolewski@sbcglobal.net; 760-643-9019; http://www.tri-studio.com; Kathe Gogolewski. Best method: Start with an e-mail and query. List any experience or credentials, if you have them. Most of all, convince me that you have passion about your topic. No response? It's okay to e-mail me again if you don't hear from me in a couple weeks. Some e-mail goes to my bulk folder, and I never get to read it.

Invited Back? If it feels like the message bears repeating, or if they created enough interest in the topic that more information is desired.

Guest Comment: "It's incredible to have a Mother Daughter Club! You are wonderful and this is a fabulous gift to the universe. I am delighted that you have invited me to be on *The Mother Daughter Club.*

I am so grateful to be a part of it. Thank you so much!"—Cynthia Brian, author of four books, actor, model, interior designer and host of *StarStyle—Be the Star You Are!* (see page 256)

Bio of Kathe Gogolewski: Kathe is an award-winning author of fiction for both children and adults. She has written three novels and numerous short stories, some of which are published on Amazon Shorts. She also writes for *Ranch & Coast, San Diego's Lifestyle Magazine*, and publishes an ezine for writers, *The Fiction Flyer*.

A retired schoolteacher, Kathe volunteers in the schools as a science and writing teacher. She's also an artist, and creates illustrations and book covers for Red Engine Press. She paints murals around San Diego, including several at San Diego Children's Hospital.

Roaring Women Radio with Mandie Crawford on Blog Talk Radio http://www.blogtalkradio.com/roaringwomenradio

Theme: Business women — success strategies — success stories.

Guest Profile: Varied. Ability to convey a solid message, topic relevant to our audience, innovative ideas, outside the box thinking and energy. Want website info, accomplishments, future plans, that they understand what we do as well.

Guest from Hell: Monotone voice, one word answers, inability to stay on topic, blurting inappropriate comments, background noise in phone interviews.

Contact: president@roaringwomen.com; 888-726-3361; http://www.roaringwomen.com; Mandie Crawford, or Monica Velt at monica@roaringwomen.com. Best method: Call with a pitch, e-mail a bio and send a press kit. No response? Send another e-mail.

Invited Back? Content and ability to convey their message. Feedback from listeners.

Bio of Mandie Crawford: Mandie is an energetic entrepreneur with a passion for women in business. A former police officer, she is a mother of four with an adventurous spirit and a willingness to risk all for projects she believes in.

Mandie's gutsy approach to business includes issuing of press releases speaking to many areas of business, including integrity in business, business women and risk, and marketing strategies. She speaks at her own events, at trade shows and for organizations such as chambers of commerce and business enterprise centers.

She has self published two business books and is currently working on a third, *Business Bling*, which will help business owners understand the principles behind building businesses that stand out from the crowd. She also penned a weekly column for the *Hamilton Spectator* for three years.

Mandie is president of *Roaring Women* and also the visionary for the organization. Constantly looking for new ways to promote the company, she has recently embarked on taking *Roaring Women Radio* from traditional radio to a weekly internet radio program — with call-in features and the ability to have shows archived on the web as well as downloadable to ipod. Her love for technology keeps her on the leading edge — passing opportunities on to members and subscribers alike.

"You need to have your full mental gear in overdrive to keep up with the tornado that is Mandie Crawford" was a recent radio show's observation of Mandie.

Mandie has been twice nominated for the women's leadership award, Athena, and has recently been nominated by Women's Entrepreneurial Network as "Top 100 most powerful women in Canada" and the Royal Bank's Entrepreneur of the year.

Speak Up! with Pat Lynch, editor in chief, WomensRadio on http://www.WomensRadio.com

Theme: Talking about issues in life that affect women's lives and topics which take some courage to address.

Guest Profile: Authors, experts, accounts of incidents that affect women and/or children, heads of organizations that serve women — who are talking about issues in life that affect women's lives and topics which take some courage to address. Want to know that they are credible, believable, can speak English clearly, and are able to focus and deliver their information/conversation — preferably without the need for a lot of editing (not too many spaces, uh's, ah's, and's, well's, etc.).

Guest from Hell: People who are not cooperative in preparing for this unique opportunity.

Contact: editor@WomensRadio.com; 888-658-4635 x225; http://www.WomensRadio.com; Liana Ramos, Producer, at Liana@WomensRadio.com; Pat Lynch: 2533 N. Carson Street, Suite 3003, Carson City, NV 89607-0147; Fax: 888 658 4635; Pat@WomensRadio.com. Best method: We request that they send a short, succinct e-mail with pertinent information about the proposed guest, the book, the situation, why that person is an authority (if it's about an issue), and the topic that is important to cover. No response? We receive a number of "pitches" from publicists. They understand that if we don't think that the guest is our cup-of-tea, we don't respond. Those that feel they have the "perfect" guest will usually follow-up. If anyone has visited the site and has a sense of our audience and approaches us by letting us know that they know our audience and think our audience will be interested, that helps — and because we have more to do than we have arms and legs, we are never offended when people follow-up, and appreciate their follow-up. If we don't think that the person or topic is suitable, we will let them know — usually by return e-mail ASAP.

Invited Back? We seldom invite any guest back unless we invite them to become contributing editors or hosts.

Guest Comment: "Pat Lynch was well-prepared and asked great, probing questions. A total pleasure." — Patricia Aburdene, author *Megatrends 2010*

Bio of Pat Lynch: Pat is first and foremost an innovator and women's advocate who founded the Women's Online Media and Education Network in 1996 to "give women a greater voice." Her company produces WomensRadio.

She followed this feat in 2001 by establishing the *WomensCalendar* that today has become the largest databank of women's events in the world, #1 in all the major search engines and reaching hundreds of thousands of women leaders each week. In 2004, Pat's company launched the SpeakerSpot, a dynamic speaker referral program. Most recently her company introduced a new audio production tool for the Web: AudioAcrobat, which enables everyone to have audio streaming in their e-mails and on their Websites. Coming soon is the new WomensRadio Channel, a syndicated 24/7 all-talk Web radio for women.

Pat believes her forte is in public relations and began her career directly out of college as press secretary for a U.S. senator and a congressman. At the age of 25, she founded the first woman-owned advertising/marketing agency in the south (Atlanta, GA). Eight years later she had been listed twice in the World's Who's Who of Women and most recently in the International Who's Who and Strathmore's Who's Who.

Strong Woman Hiding (now ***Live Courageously***) with Terri Cadiente on http://www.BigMediaUSA.com

Theme: The masks women wear to cover fear, shame and how to choose a healthy whole identity.

Guest Profile: My guests are experts in their fields leading to whole identity — dealing with choice, individual strengths, actions, quality self talk/quality life. Integrity, excellence in professionalism. I want to know that they WANT this interview. I consider my time in airwaves a privilege and to bring anything less than commitment doesn't work for me.

Guest from Hell: I have not encountered one. The closest I could say would be the one who might be less experienced in interviews or interaction between sound booths, it still turns out authentic and the vulnerability that is conveyed; brings safety to listeners and an element of being touched and more so-moved to action in their personal endeavors.

Contact: info@strengthandgracecoaching.com; 661-294-7841; http://www.strengthandgracecoaching.com; Terri Cadiente. Best method: I prefer e-mail and if I am interested, I will connect and invite one to send more. No response? I will respond within 24 hours or you know I did not receive e-mail.

Invited Back? Depends on my advance scheduling.

Bio of Terri Cadiente: A former Factory Kawasaki race team rider in jet skiing, Terri overcame a life of pain, and drug addiction to compete throughout the U.S. and internationally including; Budweiser World Tour, Anheiser Busch World Cup Champion Test Rider for Kawasaki in Japan, and Silver Medalist in Australia. She currently holds a 14-year world record.

Taking with her the demand for physical fitness, intense focus and courage, she commands life as a Hollywood stuntwoman. She is a mother of two and married to a 2nd generation Stuntman, a two-time Emmy nominated stunt coordinator, and 2nd unit Director.

"My years of working with the professional entertainment industry, elite athletes, along with my background and training, afford me the privilege to offer my clients a unique and powerful blend of life coaching – with a compassionate edge," she says.

Along with her soon-to-be-published book, *Live Courageously*, Terri is committed to her private coaching, public speaking, hosting her Internet talk show, and her philanthropic efforts of Ragdoll Restoration Foundation.

Timeless Women Speak with Dr Nancy O'Reilly, PsyD and Maggie Castrey on VoiceAmerica, Women's Network.

Theme: Timeless Women speak about health, finance, relationships and aging issues ... staying youthful at any age.

Guest Profile: Female authors who have written books about women and for women issues especially females authors who empower women of all ages. Women guests who are interested in helping women be all they can be ... empowerment, educating women about health, finance, relationships and aging concerns. I typically do a pre-call to see how they sound, explain themselves, if they come across as friendly, engaging and someone I like and want to talk with over and over again.... Pretty easy to find out if a guest is going to be good on the radio ... every now and then I have been surprised when a guest I have chosen goes south on me ... usually we have a good time....

Guest from Hell: A guest who cannot enjoy her interview and has few if any good things to share ... no personality, and no way of entertaining the listeners ... a bomb....

Contact: drnancy@womenspeak.com; 417-886-7061 office; http://www.Womenspeak.com; Maggie Castrey, Womenspeak editor at mcastrey@sbcglobal.com. Best method: All of the above ... we have many people e-mail us from the web site and we ask for their books, press kits, web site url and then have a recorded pre-call we can listen to and evaluate if we match up and we feel she will interest our listeners ... if not we move on ... one women I spoke with had the right credentials ... but her voice sounded like Minne Mouse ... too bad for her ... hard to do much about her voice.... No response? We contact guests in a responsible and consistent fashion and feel we respect them and treat them as we would want to be treated.

Invited Back? All of the above ... answers ... must be fun, good personality, good information, and eager to share and move our listeners.

Bio of Nancy D. O'Reilly, PsyD: Nancy is a clinical psychologist, researcher and founder of the online resource WomenSpeak.com, based on a decade of research. A member of the American Psychological Association with more than 25 years of experience, Nancy counsels clients on topics ranging from mental health and stress to relationships and careers. She is author of *Timeless Women Speak: Feeling Youthful at Any Age* (Women Speak Press 2008).

Whatever Live! with Beverly Mahone on Blog Talk Radio, www.blogtalkradio.com/whateverlive

Theme: Baby boomers. Theme centers around the topics in Beverly's book, *Whatever! A Baby Boomer's Journey into Middle Age* (Benoham Publishing 2006), in which she discusses such issues as growing older, menopause, middle age dating, raising children, and spirituality.

Guest Profile: Authors and other experts whose messages relate/pertain to baby boomers. I want to know how they come across verbally when I speak to them. I can usually tell within the first few minutes if they will make a good interview.

Guest from Hell: I'm of the opinion that no guest is boring—because I'm not boring. I believe a good radio host can bring out the BEST in a guest. When I get the guest from HELL, I'll be sure to let you know.

Contact: bmahone@nc.rr.com; http://www.talk2bevpodcast.com. Best method: I prefer e-mailing a bio with a follow up phone call. Once I talk with a potential guest on the phone, I'll know whether or not I want to interview them. No response? That's one of the things I teach in my teleclasses. FOLLOW-UP. Be persistent.

Invited Back? I will invite a guest back if the interview was going really well and we ran out of time; If the guest was a great interview and has another book or message to share. The bottom line is the guest must come across exceptionally well during the interview because I am a stickler about upbeat, lively interviews. If you're dull and boring you definitely won't be invited back.

Guest Comment: "We taped Beverly's radio show [for a series on various issues affecting women's health]... She seemed very pleased. Time flew by."—Bobbi de Cordova-Hanks, co-author with husband, Jerry, of *Tears of Joy* (Infinity Publishing 2003)

Bio of Beverly Mahone: Beverly is a graduate of Ohio University with a degree in journalism and more than 25 years in radio and television. She is the author of *Whatever! A Baby Boomer's Journey into Middle Age* (Benoham Publishing 2006). Her favorite quote is: "I'm not a writer because I wrote a book. I wrote a book because I was inspired by God to write."

Wise Women Talk with S. Kya Supers on http://www.byforandaboutwomen.com/wisewomen.html

Theme: Mind, body, spirit lifestyle.

Guest Profile: Guests must be members of the Wise Women Web and able to speak clearly and effectively on their area of expertise. Authors of mind, body, spirit type publications, holistic health care practitioners, teachers, and spiritual leaders are welcome. Someone who is confident, well-spoken, inspiring and able to generate interest around their field of expertise. We welcome first-time interviewers; however, we do like to know the guest's reputation for their area of expertise—usually we look at their web site and promotional materials to determine a match.

Guest from Hell: Someone who is nervous and needs a lot of "hand-holding." Someone who is unsure of what to say or how to say it.

Contact: WomenHealers@aol.com; 202-372-7351; S. Kya Supers. Best method: First the person should be a member of the Wise Women Web (info on our web site) and then they can contact by e-mail with their interest and suggest areas of discussion. No response? Should the person e-mail or call you? E-mail please.

Invited Back? Length of time since last interview, variety of topics the guest is able to speak on and level of interest from our listeners on initial interview.

Bio of S. Kya Supers: Kya is the founding director of the Wise Women Foundation featuring the Wise Women Web network of women in the healing-arts. She is a community activist with a vision to create a sustainable way of life from which all people can live from their wisdom and as the host of her show she hopes to provide women an opportunity to share their wisdom with others around the world.

She is also the producer of the Soul Searching Conferences, Wise Women FestivALLs and Women's Retreats.

A Woman's Spirit with Vanecia Wills-Leufroy on 1620 AM, Sandy Spring, GA, and http://www.radiosandysprings.com

Theme: *A Woman's Spirit* offers greater insight regarding the spirit and spirituality of women. Because a woman's spirit and spirituality is impacted by her daily interactions, topics are discussed that assist her in her daily life. *A Woman's Spirit* is an opportunity for a woman to learn more about herself in order to make better choices.

Guest Profile: Individuals who range from the professional to the unique to someone who may appear to be ordinary and have one commonality: they are aware of their spirituality and how their spirit is impacted by what they are doing in this world. A spiritual perspective, a positive approach to their subject, a personal experience regarding their topic, and a topic that assists women in making better choices in their lives. Bio, resume, their journey related to the topic, energy level, and past interview experiences.

Guest from Hell: I only attract great guests.

Contact: clrvsion2@aol.com; 678-427-0009; http://www.radiosandysprings.com; Vanecia Wills-Leufroy. Best method: An e-mail describing the subject matter, phone number, web site or article about them and their subject matter. I will contact the person to let her/him know the subject is a good fit for the show. No response? An additional e-mail will suffice.

Invited Back? Energy level and subject matter.

Guest Comment: "Vanecia Wills-Leufroy embodies the name of her show—*A Woman's Spirit*. She states in her mission that we believe: Everyday is an opportunity to have a clear vision about who you are and what you want.

"In my experience as a guest on her show, I found that all that we strive to be and become as women is evidenced in her passion for bringing just that out in her listening audience and her guests.

"Vanecia's style of interview is organized yet free-flowing. Her gift is in guiding the interviewee to the answers, which move her audience the most. As a guest, I witnessed her ability of putting one at ease while at the same time energizing them to genuinely express the level of passion they feel regarding the topic of interest.

"Beauty becomes you."—Alison O'Neil Andrew, president and CEO, http://www.beautybecomesyou.org

"Ms. Leufroy created an effortless ambience with insightful questions and unexpected dialogue. It was the most well prepared and presented radio interview I have ever experienced. I am certain *A Woman's Spirit* will become a force in years to come. It fills a much needed gap in identifying inspiring subjects and subject matter."—Nea Anna Simone, whose latest book is *Reborn* (Kimani Press 2007), http://www.neasimone.com

Bio of Vanecia Wills-Leufroy: Vanecia has a passion for spiritual development. It is the nucleus for her life. She has taken the opportunity to live this passion as a life facilitator and spiritual practitioner. During individual and group sessions, Vanecia uses a proven three-step process that provides her clients with tools to decrease self-doubt, increase self-trust, and utilize their creative mind to increase success. From her spiritual practitioner perspective, Vanecia assists individuals in creating a new way of thinking. She adheres to the philosophy, "Change your thinking, change your life."

Vanecia believes "Everyday we have an opportunity to learn more about ourselves and to make better choices. As we do this, we can live our lives at a greater level." *A Woman's Spirit* is one of these opportunities. Through *A Woman's Spirit*, Vanecia interviews people who speak to and support the emotional and spiritual nature of women. She also provides information and tools that help her listeners relate to topics and events that are shaping their lives every day. Vanecia often says, "Beliefs determine our perception of the world, ourselves, and what we create in our lives. As soon as we learn we can change our beliefs, the process of transformation begins. We can change our life by changing how we think about our life and about ourselves."

Women Power Talk Radio with Raven Blair Davis on 1320 WARL AM. Note: Raven produces and hosts three dynamic radio shows, all podcast under the WPR Talk (Women Power Radio). Her second show, *Mentoring from MLM Divas*, is designed to inspire the women in direct sales, MLM and network marketing to get to the next level of their business faster rather than slower. Each week Raven interviews the top women in that industry and they share their formulas for success and strategies with her listeners. Her third show is for business women of all ages called *Amazing Women in Business*. Her newest show is *Careers from the Kitchen Table*, www.careersfromthekitchentable.com

Theme: Empowering women in their 40s, 50s and 60s to go for their dreams and visions "Life is just beginning and the best is yet to come."

Guest Profile: Boomer women or older, with a story and a solution to inspire and empower others that they too can turn their challenges into triumphs. Someone who has an inspirational story or message. Offers a step by step solution for the problem that will empower my listeners; they need to be entertaining, and enthusiastic. Have lots of good content that they're eager to share. Mainly I want to know if they took the time out to listen to my show and understand my format, then what exactly their message is, are they just trying to sell their product or service; if so, it might be better for them to advertise on my show instead of being my guest. I want to know or prefer to listen to other interviews they've done. I want to hear the excitement and enthusiasm of their voice. If they talk soft or have a strong entertaining powerful uplifting voice and if they can relate to my audience or are they speaking tech-no-babble where only people in their industry can relate. I like to hear past interviews so I can see how they interact with the host. I want to know a little about their story, what makes them an authority on the topic. How they got from where they were to where they are now and if they can pass my 3 P's test: Passionate about their message, have power and passion in their voice when speaking and do they have a personality that will grab my audience/listeners? Raven has interviewed such notables as Diana Nightingale, widow of the legendary Earl Nightingale; Dr. Joe Vitale, marketing guru; and Bern Nadette Stanis, Thelma from "Good Times."

Guest from Hell: No personality, more interested in them selling their product and service than reaching and empowering the listeners, someone that talks over you and does not pause, someone who you have to drag the content out of them, someone that doesn't speak up and holds back because they're afraid of giving too much content away for free. Sounds too much like a salesman throughout the interview.

Contact: raven@womenpower-radio.com; 281-345-9594; http://www.womenpower-radio.com; Raven Blair Davis. Best method: I prefer they e-mail me first, then if I like the e-mail they sent I'll e-mail them asking that they connect with me by phone. And if they have a book or audio book include in their media kit. No response? I would recommend a second e-mail saying that they weren't sure I received the first e-mail and....

Invited Back? The feedback I get from my listeners through e-mails or the amount of downloads. Also how well we connected and how inspiring their story and delivery of their content. Did they give my listeners a lot or did they hold back in order to sell their product or service?

Guest Comments: "I've known Raven for a few years now and I must say, I'm honored to be associated with such a phenomenal woman! Being interviewed by Raven was so inspiring. I knew when Raven interviewed me, she was not only interested in what I had to say, but she has a gift of being able to tap into your desires and bring them to life. I've listened to many of Raven's shows simply because I know she's bringing substance to internet talk radio while interviewing some of the pioneers in the industry.

"Blessings for continued success Raven!"— Regina Baker, executive producer, http://www.ChristianBusinessTalkRadio.com, "where Christians TALK business!"

"I can't say enough about the power of women talking to other women about our experiences, our vision and our blessings. Raven Blair's *Women Power Radio* is a wonderful forum for just that!

"It was both a delight and an honor to be interviewed by the wonderful Raven Blair. She's an ace interviewer, skillfully asking the questions she knows women want answers to. As a literary advocate and entrepreneur, it is always wonderful to be given the opportunity to speak to other women at the crossroads of their lives and their careers; to share experiences, as well as vocalize the challenges of being a woman whose mission in life is to make a difference in our world.

"Thank you, Raven Blair. It is my hope and prayer that she 'keeps on keeping on' for American women certainly need her voice."— Janis F. Kearney, former diarist to President Clinton, founding president, Writing Our World Press, http://www.writingourworldpress.com

"It was such a pleasure being interviewed by you on *Women Power Radio*. I enjoyed so much being able to share the business of etiquette and manners with your listeners. Your interviewing style allowed me to feel relaxed and 'at home.' Thank you once again for allowing me to share my passion. As women in business we must always be prepared to outshine the competition ... When Manners Matter."— Christine Chapweske, president, The Etiquette Professionals, http://www.EtiquetteProfessionals.com, Christine@EtiquetteProfessionals.com

"Thanks for making my interview such a pleasant and valuable experience. You asked the questions your listeners wanted answered. You listened to my answers and probed deeper. You really delved into the heart of the interview.

"From the first contact through the interview to the replay, you displayed your professionalism and caring attitude at every step — and I appreciate it!"— Jeanette S Cates, Ph.D., author, *Online Success Tactics*, http://OnlineSuccessSecrets.com

Bio of Raven Blair Davis: Raven is a recognized speaker, coach and trainer whose mission is to assist home based businesses in discovering and pursuing their true passion and dreams in a home based business.

She has more than 25 years experience in telecommunications, tele-sales/telemarketing, customer service and management and has been responsible for training and coaching hundreds of people in that industry. She has won many awards with such Fortune 500 companies as MCI and Cendant.

Known by friends, family, clients and associates as "The Telephone Diva," Raven feels you can do any job or create business over the phone, once you learn and master the art of tele-connecting. After spending 3 years with a local business television show, "inside Houston," she realized her dream was to have a talk show on radio or TV. That dream, 20 years in the making, was realized April 23, 2006.

Raven was born in Cleveland, Ohio, and lives in Houston, Texas, with her husband, Larry.

The Women's Community Talk Radio with Denise Trifiletti on http://www.womenscommunity.com, Mondays at noon (ET); now off the air.

Theme: How to grow through the power of partnerships.

Guest Profile: Expert on partnerships, strategic alliances, joint ventures. Successful women business owner with a focused niche market. Interested in their past interview experiences, credentials, sound of their voice.

Guest from Hell: Someone who is unfocused or not clear on their unique strength and ideal target client.

Contact: denise@WomensCommunity.com; 828-295-3369; http://www.WomensCommunity.com; Denise Trifiletti. Best method: E-mail a media release, bio, press kit including interview questions. No response? Call.

Invited Back? If they provide practical (vs. hype) strategies and tips relevant to my listeners' needs.

Bio of Denise Trifiletti: Denise founded WomensCommunity.com to help business women to grow, personally and professionally, through the power of partnerships.

After years of corporate sales and training success, she learned from sales and performance experts like Dr. Stephen Covey the secrets of her success. She left the corporate world and established Dynamic Destiny Partnerships (http://www.D2Partners.com) to help others to grow their sales.

Her clients became mostly women who were not only struggling to grow their sales and business, but also struggling, juggling, and attempting to do it all. Denise coached women 1-1 and in groups sharing her formula for success: The 3-Step Power Partnership System including a partnership with yourself, your time, and others. She knew that these 3 key power partnerships were the keys to both a joyful life and exponential business growth.

Coming from high tech, she knew that the Internet was how she would reach women globally so that she can make a difference, and leave a legacy — achieve her destiny. Thus the birth of WomensCommunity.com

Denise is a speaker and author, along with Brian Tracy, Mark Victor Hansen, et al., of *Create the Business Breakthrough You Want* (Mission Publishing 2004). Included in her book are the proven ASK, GROW and RESULTS models that she invented along with her partner, Don. She is a collaborator, leader, and visionary and is on a mission to help women across the globe to achieve their destiny.

APPENDICES

1. The 100 Top Talk Shows

The editors of the monthly *Talkers Magazine*, with comment from industry leaders, annually select the 250 Most Important Radio Talk Show Hosts in America. The top of that list is what has come to be known as the "Heavy Hundred." Some of those 250 shows welcome guests, and I have collected information on the shows that do. Questionnaires were emailed to all those that welcome guests; when I did not hear back, I provided only basic information.

Networks and Syndicates

ABC Radio Networks, New York, NY, 212-735-1700
Air America Radio, New York, NY, 212-871-8100
Astral Media, Montreal, Quebec, 514-939-5000
Buckley Broadcasting, Greenwich, CT, 203-661-4307
CBS Radio, New York, NY, 212-846-3939
Citadel Broadcasting, Las Vegas, NV, 702-804-5200 and New York, NY, 212-887-1670
Clear Channel, San Antonio, TX, 210-822-2828
Corus Radio, Toronto, Ontario, 416-642-3770
Cox Radio Network, Atlanta, GA, Paul Douglas, managing director, 404-962-2078, dougatl@earthlink.net or paul.douglas@cox.com
Crawford Broadcasting, Denver, CO, 303-433-5500
Fox News Radio, New York, NY, 212-301-5439
Gap Broadcasting, Dallas, TX, 214-295-3530
Greater Media, Braintree, MA, 781-348-8600
Houston Broadcasting, Jefferson, TX 903-665-3701
Jones Radio Network, Seattle, WA, 800-426-9082; Denver, CO, 800-609-5663; Washington, DC, 800-611-5663.
National Public Radio, Washington, DC, 202-513-2000
Pacifica, Berkeley, CA, 510-849-2590
Premiere Radio Networks, Sherman Oaks, CA, 818-377-5300
Radio America, Arlington, VA, 703-302-1000
Republic Broadcasting Network, Round Rock, TX, 512-246-9549
Salem Radio Network, Irving, TX, 972-831-1920
Talk Radio Network, Central Point, OR, 541-664-8827
USA Radio Network, Dallas, TX, 800-829-8111
Westwood One, New York, NY, 212-765-1807
Wilbur Entertainment, Fresno, CA, 866-534-2998
Wilkins Communications, Spartanburg, SC, 888-989-2299
WOR Radio Network, New York, NY, 212-642-4500

Shows That Feature Guests

Sean Hannity, ABC Radio Networks
  Theme: Conservative host talks topical issues
  Phone: 541-664-8827
  Website: http://www.hannity.com
  Email: seanshow@abc.com
  Contact: Producer James Grisham at james.grisham@citcomm.com
  Guests: Yes

Michael Savage on the **Savage Nation**, Talk Radio Network
  Theme: Controversial conservative host covers topical issues in politics, history, culture (food, books, television), and health
  Website: http://www.michaelsavage.com
  Guests: Yes
  To be a guest on his show, write to Michael at P.O. Box 3755, Central Point, Oregon 97502

Glenn Beck, Premiere Radio Networks
  Theme: Politics, family, faith, pop culture
  Website: http://www.glennbeck.com
  Email: me@glennbeck.com
  Contact: Exec.producer Stu@glennbeck.com
  Guests: Yes

Laura Ingraham, Talk Radio Network
  Theme: Politics and culture
  Website: http://www.lauraingraham.com
  Contact: Producer Mike Kincaid at producer@talkradionetwork.com
  Guests: Yes

Appendix 1

Imus in the Morning with Don Imus, ABC Radio Networks
Theme: Mixed bag from politics to sports and music
Phone: 212-613-3800
Website: http://www.wabcradio.com
Contact: Producer, Bernard McGurk
Guests: Yes

The Ed Schultz Show, Jones Radio Network
Theme: Progressive host covers newsworthy topics
Phone: 701-237-5346
Website: www.bigeddieradio.com
Email: Program manager Vern Thompson at vern@edschultzshow.com
Guests: Yes

The Mike Gallagher Show, Salem Radio Network
Website: http://www.mikeonline.com
Email on line
Contact: Exec. Producer Lance Anderson at landerson@mikeonline.com
Guests: Yes

Neal Boortz Show, Cox Radio
Theme: This Libertarian "Mouth of the South" and inactive attorney discusses current issues
Phone: 212-302-1100
Website: http://boortz.com
Contact: Producer Belinda Skelton at Belinda.Skelton@coxradio.com
Guests: Occasionally

The Dave Ramsey Show
Theme: Financial topics
Phone: 877-410-3283
Website: http://www.daveramsey.com
Email: info.radio@daveramsey.com, daveonair@daveramsey.com
Guests: Occasionally

The Howard Stern Show, Sirius Satellite Radio
Theme: Shock jock focuses on a gamut of issues, ranging from world affairs to problems among his own staff.
Website: http://www.howardstern.com
Contact: Agent — Don Buchwald at Don@Buchwald.com
Guests: Yes

Mancow
(see page 194)

The Alan Colmes Show, WWRL 1600, Fox News Radio
Theme: The liberal host has a news-oriented show
Phone: 212-301-3000
Website: http://www.alan.com
Email: alan@alan.com
Contact: Joel Morton, producer, at alancolmesradio@foxnews.com
Guests: Yes

The Black Eagle with Joe Madison, WOL, Washington, D.C.
Theme: This radio activist challenges the status quo while covering current affairs, political events, civil and human rights.
Phone: 301-429-2631
Website: http://www.joemadison.com
Email: jmadison@radio-one.com
Contact: Producer Darrell Greene at dgreene@radio-one.com
Guests: Yes

Bill Handel, KFI
(see page 178)

Michael Medved Show, Salem Radio Network
Theme: Social, political and cultural issues
Phone: 206-621-1793
Website: http://www.michaelmedved.com
Email: On-line
Contact: Jeremy Steiner, producer at Jeremy@medvedshow.com
Guests: Yes

Doug Stephan's "Good Day," Stephan Productions
Theme: Libertarian host features current events, politics, business reports, entertainment news
Phone: 650-564-3969
Website: http://www.dougstephan.com (NG)
Email: doug@dougstephan.com
To offer a guest idea: ken@dougstephan.com
Guests: Yes

The Jim Bohannon Show
(see page 190)

The Thom Hartmann Radio Program, KPOJ, Portland, OR, Air America Radio
Theme: Liberal host discusses current affairs
Phone: 503-323-6400
Website: http://www.thomhartmann.com
Email: thom@thomhartmann.com
Contact: Shawn Taylor, THproducer@gmail.com
Guests: Yes

Jerry Doyle, Talk Radio Network
Theme: This conservative-minded TV actor covers current issues
Phone: 541-664-8827
Website: http://www.jerrydoyle.com
Email: askjerry@jerrydoyle.com
Contact: Producer Joe Vollono at rjvollono@gmail.com
Guests: Yes

Bill Bennett's Morning in America, Salem Radio Network
Theme: One of the nation's most prominent political figures, this host naturally discusses politics.
Phone: 703-248-9413
Website: http://www.bennettmornings.com

Email: on-line
Contact: Seth Leibsohn, Executive Producer at seth@bennettmornings.com
Guests: Yes

Coast to Coast AM with George Noory, Premiere Radio Networks
Theme: Exploring the unexplained, the unusual, paranormal
Phone: 818-377-5323; cell 818-281-3902
Website: http://www.coasttocoastam.com
Email: george@coasttocoastam.com
Contact: Tom Danheiser, associate producer at tdanheiser@premiereradio.com
Guests: Yes

Lars Larson, Westwood One/KXL
Theme: Topical issues
Phone: 503-243-7595
Website: http://www.larslarson.com
Email: Lars@larslarson.com
Contact: Producer Matthew Trom at matthew.trom@KXL.com
Guests: Yes

The Stephanie Miller Show, Jones Radio Networks/WYD Media
Theme: Progressive talk host whose background in stand-up comedy heavily influences her show.
Website: http://www.stephaniemiller.com
Contact: Producer Chris Lavoie at Chris@stephaniemiller.com
Guests: Occasionally

The Jim Rome Show, Premiere Radio Networks
Theme: Sports
Phone: 818-461-8057 (Rachel Nelson)
Website: http://www.jimrome.com
Email: rome@haveatake.com
Contact: Travis Rodgers at 818-377-5300
Guest: Yes

The Clark Howard Show, Cox Radio
Theme: Consumer issues
Phone: 404-897-7500/404) 872-0750
Website: http://www.clarkhoward.com
Contact: Producer Christa at Christa@clarkhoward.com
Guests: Occasionally

The Lionel Show
(see page 193)

The John and Ken Show, KFI, Los Angeles, CA
Theme: Local issues
Phone: 818-559-2252
Website: http://johnandkenshow.com
Email: johnandken@johnandkenshow.com
Contact: Producer: Ray Lopez at raylopez@clearchannel.com
Guests: Yes

The Jack Rice Show, WCCO, Minneapolis/St. Paul, MN
Theme: Former CIA officer and prosecuting attorney discusses current issues
Phone: 612-370-0611
Website: http://www.thejackriceshow.blogspot.com
Email: jrice@wccoradio.cbs.com
Contact: Producer Susan Blanch at sblanch@cbs.com
Guests: Yes

The Dennis Prager Show, Salem Radio Network
Theme: Everything from politics to religion to relationships
Phone: 818-956-5552
Website: http://www.dennisprager.com, http://www.PragerRadio.com
Email: dennis@PragerRadio.com
Contact: Eva Vayntraub, ass't producer at eva@salemla.com
Guests: Yes

The Spike O'Dell Radio Program, WGN, Chicago, IL
Theme: Politics, entertainment, sports and pop culture.
Website: http://www.wgnradio.com
Contact: Producer Jim Wiser at jimwiser@wgnradio.com
Guests: Yes

Bev Smith
(see page 5)

Rusty Humphries, Talk Radio Network
Theme: Current affairs
Phone: 541-664-8827
Website: http://www.talktorusty.com
Email: on line
Contact: Producer Mike Kinney at mike.kinney@talkradionetwork.com
Guests: Yes

The Michael Smerconish Morning Show, WPHT, Philadelphia, PA, and WOR 710, New York CBS Radio
Theme: Philadelphia lawyer turned political commentator discusses current events and entertainment
Phone: 610-668-5800
Website: http://www.mastalk.com
Email: on-line
Guests: Yes

The Bob and Tom Show, with Bob Kevoian and Tom Griswold, Premiere Radio Networks
Theme: Comedy/variety show
Phone: 317-257-7565
Website: http://www.bobandtom.com
Email: bobandtom@bobandtom.com
Contact: Joani Downing at 317-475-7431
Guests: Yes

The Dennis Miller Show, Westwood One
Theme: http://www.dennismillerradio.com

Phone: 212-641-2000
Contact: Email producers on line
Guests: Yes

The G. Gordon Liddy Show, Radio America
Theme: Watergate mastermind and former high government official turned talk show host covers world affairs, including the military and FBI
Phone: 703-302-1000
Website: http://www.liddyshow.com
Contact: Producer Franklin Raff at fraff@radioamerica.org
Guests: Yes

Ronn Owens, KGO, San Francisco, CA
Theme: Everything from local politics and popular culture to current events, personal issues, or just plain gossip
Phone: 415-954-8142
Website: http://ronn.com
Email: sfowens@gmail.com
Contact: Producer Mark Silverman at mark.silverman@citcomm.com
Guests: Yes

Howie Carr, WRKO, Boston, MA
Theme: Conservative host discusses current affairs
Phone: 617-779-3400
Email: howiecarr@wrko.com
Website: http://www.howiecarr.com
Contact: Producer Nancy "Sandy" Shack — nshack@wrko.com
Guests: Yes

The Greg Knapp Experience, KLIF, Dallas, TX, Radio America
KLIF programming — 214-520-4365
Theme: Conservative host discusses hot topics
Website: http://www.gregknapp.us, http://www.radioamerica.org/PRG_gregknapp.htm, http://www.klif.com/host-knapp-new.htm
Email: greg@klif.com
Contact: Producer Lance Anderson at landerso@dfwradio.com
Guests: Yes

Jay Severin, WTKK-FM, Boston, MA
Theme: Political analyst host discusses hot topics
Website: http://www.wtkk.com
Contact: John Parker at jparker@969wtkk.com or 617-822-6830
Guests: Rarely

Quinn and Rose
(see page 200)

The Kathy and Judy Show, with Kathy O'Malley and Judy Markey, WGN, Chicago, IL
Theme: Variety of topics
Phone: 312-222-4700
Website: http://www.wgnradio.com
Email: on line

Contact: Producer BethSwierk@wgn.com
Guests: Occasionally

The Tom Sullivan Show, Fox News Radio
Theme: Topic-driven look at news and issues
Phone: 212-301-5900
Website: http://www.foxnews.com/radio/tomsullivan/index.html
Email: tomsullivanradio@foxnews.com
Contact: Producer Matt Pascarella at 212-301-5979
Guests: Yes

Jim Gearhart, 101.5 WKXW-Fm, NJ
Theme: "Watchdog for the people of New Jersey" discusses everything from politics, and taxes to SUV's.
Phone: 609-956-5552
Website: http://www.nj1015.com
Email: gearhart@nj1015.com
Contact: Producer Irene Lenhart at Irene.lenhart@nj1015.com
Guests: Rarely

Bill Cunningham Show, WLW, Cincinnati, OH, Premiere Radio Networks
Theme: Conservative host discusses national and local news and politics.
Phone: 513-686-8300
Website: http://700wlw.com/pages/onair_willie.html
Email: willie@700wlw.com
Contact: Rich Walburg at rwalburg@700wlw.com
Guests: Yes

The Lee Rodgers Program
(see page 190)

Fred Honsberger, KDKA, Pittsburgh, PA
Theme: Local and topic issues
Website: http://www.kdkaradio.com
Email: on-line
Contact: Promotions director Amy Mauk at 412-575-2200
Guests: Yes

The Roe Conn Show, WLS, Chicago, IL
Theme: General issues and local stories
Phone: 312-984-0890
Website: http://www.roeconn.com
Email: on-line
Contact: Producer Todd Ronczkowski
Guests: Yes

The Mike Rosen Show, KOA, Denver, CO
Theme: Conservative host discusses politics, news and reviews movies
Phone: 303-713-8000
Website: http://www.850koa.com
Contact: Producer David Lauer at davelauer@clearchannel.com
Guests: Yes

The Marc Bernier Show, WNDB/WNDA/WFHG-AM-FM, Daytona Beach, FL, Bernie Broadcast Services
Phone: 386-257-1150, ext 319
Website: http://www.marcberniershow.com
Contact: Producer Phil Kincaid — pkincaid@wndb.am — and Jennifer Worley, Jennifer@supertalkwfhg.com
Guests: Yes

Bob and Sheri
(see page 282)

Midday with Mike, 700 WLW, Cincinnati, OH, Premiere Radio Networks
Theme: A broad range of topics from "in the news" social issues to avant-garde extreme subjects.
Website: http://www.700wlw.com
Contact: Rich Walburg, ass't program director/exec producer at WLW
Email: richwalburg@clearchannel.com
Guest: Yes

Ankarlo Mornings with Darrell Ankarlo, KTAR-FM, Phoenix, AZ — current issues
Website: http://www.ktar.com
Phone: 602-274-6200
Email: dankarlo@ktar.com
Producer: Rob Hunter at rhunter@ktar.com
Guests: Yes

The Allen Handelman Show, WZTK-FM/Rock Talk
Burlington, NC
Theme: Everything from the paranormal and politics to the rock culture
Phone: 704-596-4718
Website: http://www.ifitrocks.com
Email: ahandelman@curtismedia.com
Guests: Yes

Malzberg Talk with Steve Malzberg, WOR Radio Network
Theme: Political talk and issues with this conservative host
Website: http://www.malzbergtalk.com, http://www.wor710.com/
email on-line
Guests: Yes

The Big Show with Glenn Ordway, WEEI, Boston
Theme: Sports
Website: http://www.weei.com
Email: thebigshow@entercom.com
Contact: Producer Brett Erickson at berickson@entercom.com
Guests: yes

Dan Yorke, WPRO, Providence, RI
Theme: Local issues
Phone: 401-433-4200
Website: http://www.630wpro.com
Email: dan@630wpro.com
Contact: Producer Tony Cornetta at tony.cornetta@citcomm.com
Guests: Yes

Jeff Katz
(see page 189)

The Diane Rehm Show, National Public Radio
Theme: Conversations on an array of topics with many of the most distinguished people of our times.
Phone: 202-885-1200
Website: http://www.wamu.org
Contact: Producer Tonya Weinberg at tweinberg@wamu.org
Guests: Yes

The Larry Young Morning Show, 1010 AM WOLB, Baltimore, MD
Theme: Station geared to African Americans with round-table discussions about current news, political, health, business, and family issues
Phone: 410-332-8200
Website: http://www.wolb1010.com/home.asp
Contact: Producer James Johnson at lyoung@radio-one.com
Guests: Yes

The Bill Press Show, Jones Radio Networks
Theme: Liberal host covers the pulse of politics and pop culture
Phone: 254-773-5252
Website: http://www.billpress.com
Email: Click "Contact Bill" to leave on-line message
Contact: Producer at inforadio@billpress.com
Guests: Yes

The John and Jeff Show, with John Boyle and Jeff Carroll on KLSX-FM, Los Angeles, CA, Wilbur Entertainment
Theme: Covers today's news, issues, pop culture, and personal relationships
Phone: 323-971-9710
John and Jeff direct line — 877-975-6465
Website: http://www.johnjeff.com
Email: johnandjeffshow@aol.com
Guests: Rarely

Morning Source with Alan Stock, 840 AM KXNT, Las Vegas, NV
Theme: Local and national issues
Phone: 702-889-7300
Website: http://www.kxnt.com
Email: alan.stock@cbsradio.com
Contact: Producer Patrick DiFazio at Patrick.difazio@cbsradio.com PDiFazio@cbsradio.com
Guests: Yes

The Junkies, WJFK-FM, Washington, DC
Theme: Sports with John Auville, Eric Bickel, Jason Bishop and John-Paul Flaim

Website: http://www.junkiesradio.com
Email: junksmail@aol.com
Contact: Producer Bret Oliverio at bret.oliverio@cbsradio.com
Guests: Yes

The Talkers' 25 (101–250)

Allman and Crane in the Morning with Jamie Allman and Crane Durham, KFTK 97.1FM, St. Louis, MO, Fox News Radio
Theme: Topical issues
Phone: 314-231-9710
Website: http://www.971talk.com
Contact: Executive Producer Max Foizey on-line. Click Max on Movies under "Weekends"
Guests: Yes

The Tom Becka Show
(see page 207)

Jim Brown in the Morning
(see page 217)

This Is America with Jon Elliott, Air America Radio
Theme: Liberal host focuses on politics
Website: http://www.jonelliottshow.com, http://airamerica.com/thisisamerica
Email: jon@jontalk.com
Contact: Producer: Norman Flint at Norman@jontalk.com
Guests: Yes

The Dave Elswick Show
(see page 184)

The Todd Feinburg Show
(see page 207)

The Mike Fleming Show, WREC, Memphis, TN
Phone: 901-259-1300
Theme: Local and national affairs
Website: http://www.wrecradio.com
Email: mike@600wrec.com
Contact: Producer Brian Jay at brianjay@600wrec.com
Guests: Yes

Greg Garrison—WIBC, Indianapolis
Theme: Attorney and conservative host discusses politics
Website: http://wibc.com/garrison
Email: ggarrison@indy.emmis.com
Contact: Producer Matt Hibbeln at mhibbeln@wibc.emmis.com
Guests: Yes

John Gibson—Host of John Gibson Radio and The Big Story w/ Gibson and (Heather) Nauert, Fox News Radio
Theme: News and politics from a conservative viewpoint
Website: http://www.foxnews.com/radio/johngibsonradio, http://www.johngibson.com
Email: myword@foxnews.com, john.gibson@foxnews.com
Contact: Senior producer Rich Carbery at Richard.carbery@foxnews.com
Guests: Yes

Steve Gill Show
(see page 205)

Dom Giordano
(see page 184)

The Dave Glover Show, KFTK-FM 97.1 FM, St. Louis
Theme: Topical issues
Website: http://www.971talk.com/Glover/index.aspx
Contact: Email co-host and executive producer Tom Terbrock on-line (beneath the photos of staff members).

Darla Jaye—KMBZ, Shawnee, Kansas
Theme: Topical issues, local and national
Website: http://www.kmbz.com
Email: darla@kmbz.com
Contact: Producer Brian at bmalicoat@entercom.com
Guests: Yes

The Les Kinsolving Show—680 WCBM, Baltimore, MD
Theme: Political talk with this White House correspondent and movie actor
Phone: WCBM Office: 410-580-6800/Home: 703-759-5704
Website: http://www.wcbm.com
Email: les@leskinsolving.com
Contact: Producer Rock Applebaum at RockApplebaum@wcbm.com
Guests: Rarely

Mike Malloy—Nova M Radio Network
Theme: Left-of-center host focuses on politics
Website: http://www.mikemalloy.net, http://www.mikemalloy.com
Email: mike@mikemalloy.com
Contact: Producer—Kathy Bay (his wife)—MalloyProducer@aol.com

John Resnick
(see page 47)

Dave Graveline
(see page 274)

Bobby Likis
(see page 61)

2. 33 Interview Tips (by Scott Lorenz*)

The key to success in any interview is following the lead of the host. Do not try to control the conversation. If the guest is well informed, he can follow the host into any relative subject and discuss it. If the guest is not knowledgeable, say so. Do not try to wing it. — Lee Boyland, author of *The Rings of Allah* (AuthorHouse, 2004) and *Behold, an Ashen Horse* (Booklocker, 2007).

You've landed the radio interview and it's time to get ready to actually do it. Now what? I have booked my clients on thousands of radio interviews; here's a list of tips I give them prior to their interviews.

1. Go to a quiet room in your home or office; be sure staff and/or family know you are on a radio interview and cannot be interrupted.
2. Turn off other phones, cell phones and anything else that could create background noise including air conditioners and the radio, etc.
3. Have a glass of water nearby; there's nothing worse than dry mouth on a radio interview.
4. Disable call waiting: dial *70 and then call the studio number. This disables call waiting for the duration of the phone call. As soon as you hang up, it will be reactivated.
5. Be on time. Call the station exactly at the time they tell you, or be at your phone waiting if the station is going to call you.
6. Use a land line phone for best quality. Some stations won't allow a cell phone interview. If it is not possible to reach a land line then use a cell phone in a stationary location and not while you are rolling down the road as the reception could be interrupted mid interview.
7. Do not use a speaker phone or a headset; again, it's about good sound quality.
8. Be self-assured. Remember, you know your topic inside and out. Be confident in your ability.
9. Smile, smile, smile, whether on radio or TV — smile. You'll feel better, and for TV you'll look better too.
10. Put some pizzazz and energy into your voice. Try standing while you speak to liven things up a little.
11. Research the show and tailor your message accordingly. Just Google the host's name and station and check out their web site. Is it a national audience or a small town in Ohio? What is their format? Is it News/Talk, NPR or Classic Rock or something else? You need to know.
12. KNOW exactly how much time you will have on the air as a guest, three minutes or 30 minutes... so you can tailor your answers to the time allotted.
13. Practice your sound bites — **out loud** before the interview. Communicate your main points succinctly. Practice this **out loud.**
14. Be informative and entertaining without directly pushing your book, product or service. Make the audience "want more."
15. A kind word about the host can go a long way. It's good manners and good business.
16. A person's name is sweet music to them so commit to memory or jot down the name of the host and use it throughout the interview. When taking calls, use the names of callers too.
17. Be prepared for negative comments, from the host or listeners.
18. Be careful not to slide into techno-babble, jargon or acronyms that few know about.
19. Never talk down to your audience.
20. Be respectful of the host because everybody starts someplace. Today they're interviewing you from a college radio station; in a few years they could be a nationally syndicated host.
21. Don't oversell. Remember you are on the air to provide useful information to the listening audience. If you are an author or selling something, limit yourself to two mentions of the book, product or service. You must make it interesting without the commercialism. It takes finesse but you can do it. Often times the host will do this for you and you won't need to mention it.
22. Think of a radio interview as an intimate conversation with a friend and not a conversation with thousands.
23. Radio interviews require verbal answers, not head nodding or uh-huhs. Hand gestures don't count in radio either.
24. Radio will often use interviews live and later cut them up for use throughout the day giving you more airplay. So keep your answer to a 10 to 20 second sound bite. You can say a lot in that amount of time and then you don't sound like you are babbling on. Don't go on more than a minute without taking a break.
25. Don't just answer questions. Tell listeners something you want them to know, something they wouldn't know unless they were tuned in, with the promise of more of the same when they buy the product or come see you!
26. Have three key messages. Short, not sermons. Sometimes the host opens the door, other times you have to answer a question and segue to a key message. A compelling message will have the host asking for more. Usually people can get in two key messages; the pros can get three. But even if you get in only one, you get a big return for the time invested.

---

*Scott Lorenz is president of Westwind Communications, a public relations and marketing firm for numerous authors, doctors, lawyers, inventors and entrepreneurs. (Contact www.westwindcos.com/book or scottlorenz@westwindcos.com or telephone 734-667-2090.)

27. Lazy hosts open with a lame: "Thanks for being here." Boom! Give a 15 to 20 second summary message. If the host introduces you with a question, be polite, deliver your summary message, then answer the question. "Thanks, (use name), for the opportunity to talk about.... Now, to your question (name)..."

28. Maintain a positive attitude. Be genuine or transparent. Don't fake enthusiasm or sincerity. If you're in a bad mood cancel the interview. Don't pretend to know stuff you don't.

29. Re-read the press release or pitch that got the booking since the host is going to be using that as a starting point. Often a book publicist such as myself will tie into a breaking news event that relates to your expertise. Be aware of that tie-in.

30. After the interview write a thank-you note. Since so few people do this, you'll really stand out from the crowd. And most importantly, you may get invited back.

31. Whether the interview is live or taped-live, if you stumble, or flub up, just keep going. Often what you perceived as a mistake, the listeners won't even notice.

32. Ask for an MP3 of the recording before the interview. Often if you ask ahead of time the producer will record the interview and then you can use it on your web site. Be sure to listen to it later and critique your performance.

33. Ask for a testimonial. Often that MP3 will arrive with a note from the host saying how much they enjoyed the interview, or that "Scott Lorenz was a great interview, he really kept our audience engaged," or "the phones rang off the hook when Scott Lorenz was being interviewed." You can use those testimonials in future pitches and on your web site, blog etc.

At my book marketing firm, we'll prepare questions for our author clients ahead of time and include those in our press kits emailed to the stations. Often the radio host will read those questions right in order. Other times they refer to our questions and include some of them. We do this to help the host in case they've not had a chance to read the book, which is often the case.

Make sure you know your own material inside and out and are comfortable with everything in it. You are the author of the book, and they'll ask you, "What did you mean about this or that?" You need to have the answer. You don't want any surprises.

The bottom line: relax, you'll do fine. The butterflies you're feeling are what will drive you to do your best! Just follow these helpful tips and you'll be a radio interview star!

3. Top 10 Telephone Tips (by Joe Sabah*)

1. Have a glass of water handy (room temperature). When your throat is lubricated it's easier to talk. Plus the water serves as a "cough button" if needed.

2. Stand while speaking. Pretend you're presenting a seminar. Your voice will carry further. And you'll sound more animated.

3. Have a copy of their state map on your wall. Refer to cities in the radio station's surrounding area. This helps make you feel like you are "one of them." I once made the mistake of referring to South Bend as "South Bend, Indiana." The host reminded me that I was talking on a radio station in South Bend, Wisconsin. Oops!

4. Listen to their weather and traffic report. This allows you to personalize your presentation. For example: When I was being interviewed on WHIO in Dayton, Ohio, I noticed during the breaks they were referring to their metro area as "the Miami Valley." So it became a natural for me to say "I believe we can help some folks in 'the Miami Valley' get their perfect job this afternoon." What a difference the right words make.

5. Get your listeners involved. For example, before the last commercial break I ask them to get pencil and paper to write down the three tips I guarantee will turn every job interview into a job offer. Then they have pencil and paper ready when I later give out my 800 number.

6. For those who are driving around without writing tools handy, ask your host if the listeners can call the station for the 800 number. As soon as you're off the air, you call the station's receptionist and give her or him your 800 number plus the title of your book.

7. Give the host some quotes from your book to use as segues. I offer quotes like: "Are You Singing The Song You Came To Sing?" And "If You Do What You've Always Done, You'll Get What You've Always Gotten. Is That Enough?"

8. After the host uses these Inspirational Postcard Quotes on the air, I also offer them to listeners who order my book. Another bonus to increase orders.

9. Always thank both the host and the producer for the good job they are doing. After the show, also send each of them a handwritten note of thanks and an offer "Let's do it again."

10. You may also want to record your show by using a device available at most phone center stores, that will record both sides of the interview. Then listen to your show to see how you can improve the next one. Keep on learning.

From Joe Sabah's How to Get on Radio Talk Shows All Across America Without Leaving Your Home or Office. *More tips and information at http://www.sabahradioshows.com, 800-945-2488.*

4. Getting Invited Back (by Judith Sherven and Jim Sniechowski*)

Judith and Jim strongly recommend collecting the contact information — especially email addresses — for the hosts/producers of the shows you've been on. Then when a news event, holiday, or other reason arises, it's easy to propose being on again.

Great hosts know the value of great guests. Not only do they get entertaining and informative interviews when their guests are sharp and media savvy, but it also makes their work easier. That's why we almost always get invited back by great radio hosts like Dr. Laurie who does her relationship show *Passion* out of Montreal and Larry of *Larry's Bottom Line*.

They are both bright, experienced professionals who are a dream to work with! Why? Because they respect and value their guests And they're both personally available to connect with and get down to sincere, exciting, dynamic conversation!

Authors of The Smart Couple's Guide to the Wedding of Your Dreams *(New World Library, 2005),* Be Loved for Who You Really Are *(St. Martin's Press, 2001),* The New Intimacy *(Health Communications, 1997), and* Opening to Love 365 Days a Year *(Health Communications 2000)* http://www.judithandjim.com

FURTHER READING

Magazines

Talkers Magazine, Ten issues a year at $75 ($100 outside USA): Talkers Magazine, 650 Belmont Avenue, Springfield, MA 01108; Tel: 413-739-8255.

Radio station periodicals

Accuracy in Media publishes a Talk Radio Directory that includes the address, telephone and fax numbers and website of each station, divided by states. It can be downloaded to Acrobat Reader. Type "Radio Talk Show Directory" in search box on site. http://www.aim.org, info@aim.org; 202-364-4401.

Joe Sabah offers his 19 chapter book *How to Get on Radio Talk Shows All Across America Without Leaving Your Home or Office* and current database on CD (for PC or Mac) of 1,000 talk shows with call letters of the stations, addresses and phone and fax numbers, the number of watts, name of the talk show, and the name of host and producer in charge of each show. Web address and e-mails on many of these shows. He updates the database yearly. The cost is $147. Joe@JoeSabah.com, http://www.JoeSabah.com, http://www.sabahradioshows.com; 303-722-7200.

The Radio Book, 2008–2009 Edition, covers more than 14,000 U.S. and Canadian radio stations in more than 900 pages. Radio stations in U.S. and Canada include personnel, Arbitron rating and frequency. Cost: $89.95 *(plus $9.00 S&H)*, international shipping rates may vary. http://www.insideradio.com/radiodirectory.asp

Internet directories

http://www.RadioRow.com — has links to radio stations by format, including Internet shows

http://www.ontheradio.net — you can search for a radio station by ZIP code or city/state or view all stations by state or metro area

http://radio-locator.com — you can search by format, city, state, province or country. Offers two databases for $299 (U.S. non-commercial stations) and $599 (U.S. commercial stations)

http://www.kidon.com\media-link\usa.php — has links to radio stations around the world

INDEX

Aboriginal Connections 214
Abrams, Hal 7
Action Point 174
Acupuncture 3, 4
Addictions 3–5, 132; alcohol 4; food 4; gambling 4; nicotine 4; prescription 4; prevention 3; sexual 3
Adirondack Book House 2
Adlam, Jenn 196
Adler, Andrea 145
Adoption 170
The Adventure Show 259
Aga, Susie 7
Ageless Lifestyles 125
Aging Outside the Box 258
Agnew, Brooks A. 235
Aguilar, Rose 211
Aguirre, Tai 277
The Alan Colmes Show 296
Alhadeff, Rochelle 283
Alivewiredu Talk Radio Show 237
The All Pets Radio Show 6
All Things That Matter 126
The Allen Hunt Show 227
Allman, Jamie 300
Allman and Crane in the Morning 300
Alpert, Dick 218
Alvarez, Matt 268
Alvarez, Melissa 11, 30, 162
AM South Florida 175
Amazing Women 281
Amber, Keith 145
Amber, Sharmai 145
Ambler, Aldonna R. 43
America on the Road 60
The American Dream 2
America's Dining and Travel Guide 82
Ancel, Judy 120
And the Women Gather Radio Show 282
Andelman, Bob 74
The Andrew Carter Show 175
Angels 127, 130, 137, 144, 150, 152, 159
Animals 6–14; behavior 7, 14; bond 8–9; breeds 10; communication 13, 154; events 14; health 8–11, 14, 128; industry 14; rights 116; training 7, 10
Animal Hour 7
Animal Radio 7
Animal Rescue 7

Animal Talk Naturally 8
Animals Aloud 9
Ankarlo, Darrell 299
Ankarlo Mornings 299
Another Reality Show 126
Anshara, Sherry 132
Anson, Mike 60
Answers in Atheism 227
Antiques 14–17; collectibles 16; comics 16–17; estate auctions 15; memorabilia 15; stamps 14
Antonio, Jose 265, 269
APS Stamp Talk 14
Arbor Talk 92
Architecture and city planning 21
Army Wife Talk Radio 123
Arnett, Rick 269, 270
Arnette, Larry 237
Arrington, Lael 207
Art and design 17–22; architecture 21; cities 21; feng shui 19, 133, 146; home 17, 19, 21; landscape 19; office 19; scrapbooks 20
Art and Technology 17
The Art Full Life 18
Arts 17–21, 187, 241, 282
As You Wish Radio 161
Ash, John 86
Ashendorf, Alan 274
Ashendorf, Sandra 274
Asher, Eric 216
Ashley, Steve 123
Ask Dr. Jackie 220
Ask the Psychic 127
Ask the Technology Therapist 271
Astrology 127, 137, 142, 146, 153, 154, 156
At Home with Cheryll Gillespie 237
Atheism 227, 228
Atwater, Brent 128
AuthorB-Known 22
Authors 22–35; bestselling 23, 25; children's 24, 172; literary fiction 28–29, 34; poets 30, 33; storytellers 29
Author's Voice 23
Autism 97, 114
Autism: Help, Hope and Healing 97
Automotive and aftermarket products and services 60, 61
Auville, John 299
Aveni, Louise 149
Awadu, Keidi Obi 5

Awake Alive and Jewish 228
Axisa, Suzanna 142

Baab, Lolis Garcia 287
Babbitt, Beth 93
Baby boomers 70
Baccili, Dr. Pat 242
Backman, Sherry 36
Badnarik, Michael 192
Bailey, Maria 173
Baker, James 167
The Balancing Point 97
Ball, Magdalena 28
Barbalet, Tom 233
Barry Reisman Show 65
Baskin, Darryl 211
Bates, Todd 164
Battle Line with Alan Nathan 175
Bauer, Michelle 39
Baughman, Alison 156
Bay, Dr. Scot 113
Bazi 138
BBD Talk Radio 260
Beauty, style and fashion 35–36; cosmetics 36; fashion 36, 76
Beauvais, Deborah 222
Beck, Glenn 295
Becka, Tom 207
Behind the News 176
Beisswenger, Roy 270
Bell, Dr. Fred 100
Bell, Robert Scott 151
Beneath the Surface 176
Bengston, Steve 52
Bennett, Bill 296
Berg, Gregory 196
Berinstein, Paula 35
Bernier, Marc 299
Berry, Licia 139
Bertok, Larry 215
Betito, Dr. Laurie 223
Between Two World Radio 127
The Bev Smith Show 5
Beyond Health 98
Beyond Reality 128
Beyond the Measuring Cup 82
Beyond the Paranormal 32
Beyond Words 23
Bickel, Eric 299
Big Nation Radio 260
Big Outdoors 160
Big Sauce Radio Show 177

307

The Big Show (with Glenn Ordway) 299
The Big Wild 261
Bill Bennett's Morning in America 296
Bill Cunningham Show 298
Bill Dwight Show 177
The Bill Handel Show 178
The Bill Press Show 299
Biota Live 233
Bishop, Jason 299
Black, Cynthia 175
Black, Dr. Jackie 220
The Black Eagle 296
Blackney, Elizabeth "Media Lizzy" 194
Blanchet, Art 213
Blankenship, Steve 263
The Blazing Grace Show 3
Blevis, Mark 172
Blog Talk Radio's Holistic Integrative Energy Medicine 128
Blogstein, Dr. 65
Bloomer, Kim 8
Blythe, Cathy 113
Bob and Sheri 282
The Bob and Tom Show 297
Bob Enyart Live 228
The Bob Frantz Show 178
Bob Tanem in the Garden 92
Bobby Likis Car Clinic 61
Bobrow, Ellie 257
Bodnarchuk, Debbie 286
Bogan, Rev. Zernial 204
Bohannon, Jim 190
Bono, Howard 50
The Book Babes Program 24
Book Bites for Kids 24
The Book Guys 25
The Book Squad 25
Book Talk 26
Boortz, Neal 296
Border Patrol Auxiliary Radio see *ProAmerica Radio*
Borsa, James 80
Botti, Phyllis 7
The BottomLine 237
Bower, Guy 86
Bowers, Duane 246
Boyle, John 299
Bracy, Inez 245
The Brad Neufeld Show 238
The Brad Show 179
Bradford, Catherine 116
Braun, Carl 200
Breakfast Bytes 272
The Breakfast Show 179
Breaking the Conspiracy of Silence 61
Breaking Through 129
Brian, Cynthia 256
Brice, Anthony 78
Brickey, Dr. Michael 125
Bride's Night Out 220
Bridging Heaven and Earth 129
Bright Spot! 238
Brightlights Pathfinders 130
Brill, Dr. Peter 259
Britton, Brent 39
Broadminded Poker 261
Brock, Sabra 224

Brodlie, Dr. Jerry 171
Brooks, Dr. Kathleen 61
Brown, Jim 217
Brown, Lindsay 80
Brown, Roxanne 99
Brown, Steve 196
Bruce, Matt 124
Bruhn, Debara 130
BullDog and The Rude Awakening Show 180
Burchard, Jeffrey 15
Burchard Galleries Antiques and Collectibles Radio Show 15
Burke, Dave 213
Burton, Earl 270
Business, finance and marketing 36–60, 296; careers 38, 46, 49, 60, 115; growth 37, 43, 44, 52; home-based 44, 59, 174; investments 37, 40, 42, 50, 55, 57, 58, 249; management 40, 45; market analysis 37; marketing 51, 52, 53; non-profits 41, 182, 215; sales 41, 52, 53; small 49, 53, 54, 58, 221; start-ups 46; success stories 36, 38, 39, 44, 47; trading 57; women 59, 289
Business at Night 37
Business in Motion 37
Business Matters 38
Business Success Coaching 38

Cabeza De Vaca, Jewel 108
Cadden, Rachael 249
Cadwell, Jeff 110
Caldes, Marlene 133
Calling All Angels 130
Calling All Authors 27
Calo-oy, Starr & Bob 98
Cameron, Rhonda 214
Canadia 17
Canadian Voices 180
Candeloro, Salvatore 154
The Candia Sanders Hour 130
Capitol Talk 181
The Captain's America 124
Card Corner 15
Career Call 124
Career Engineers Radio Broadcast 38
Caregiving 101 98
Carey, Trevor 208
Caribbean Crossroads 214
Carlson, Dean 77
Carmichael, Judy 71
Carpenter, Henry 258
Carr, Howie 298
Carrera, Margo 143
Carroccio, Joe 23
Carroll, Bob 263
Carroll, Bonnie 88
Carroll, Jane 287
Carroll, Jeff 299
Carruthers, Mike 256
Carson, Dr. Gayle 59
Carson, Katrina 170
Casher, Scott 266, 269
Cashman, Peter 12
Castrey, Maggie 290
Cates, Jim 70
Cauldwell, Lillian 22
The CBS Weekend Roundup 181

Celebrating Your Potential 239
Celebrity Stars 65
Celtic Seers 162
CEO Lounge 39
Chamberlain, Lynn Krielow 91
Change Your Home—Change Your Life 18
Chapman, Monique 157
Charlotte's Morning News Weekend 182
Chase, Jayne 35
Chase, Yvonne 284
Chat with Women 283
Cherry, Rowena 27
Cherry Picking 27
Cheslick, Allie 159
The China Business Show 39
Chit Chat with Kat 170
The Chris Robinson Travel Show 276
Christenson, Lisa Loucks 247
The Christian Woman's View 228
The Christian Worldview 229
The Chuck Morse Show 182
CHUM Radio Ottawa 182
Civil War Talk Radio 119
Clanton, Bill 6
Clanton, Steven 6
Clark, Brian 87
Clark, Nancy 15
The Clark Howard Show 297
Clifford, Doug 199
Cluthe, Scott 251
Coach K! Talk Radio Show for Women 283
Coast to Coast AM 297
Cock, Tom 55
Cocoa Mode 284
Cohen, David 53
Cohen, Lorraine 52
Cohen, Russ 15, 264
Cohn, Gail 21
Colarusso, Joe 271
Colarusso, Tony 271
Cole, Mary Ann 266
Cole, Sean 266
Coleen, Bonnie 254
Coletta, Carol 21
Colgan, Caryn 253
Collectibles 15, 16
Collectors Coach Show 16
Collins, Chris 209
Colmes, Alan 296
Colvard, Kimberly A. 46
Combs, Rick 160
Comedy 65, 67, 72, 77
Comic Zone 16
Comics 16–17
A Community Affair 182
The Compulsive Reader 28
Computer America 272
Computer and Technology Radio 273
Computer Corner 273
Computer Outlook 273
Conn, Roe 298
Connect 131
Connecting the Dots 183
Connecting the Light 132
Connelly, Valerie 27
Conscious Discussions 239
Conscious Healing 132

Index 309

Conscious Rasta Report see *Culturally Conscious Communications*
Constantine, William 135
Conversations from Beyond 133
Conversations Live with Vicki St. Clair 240
Conversations of the Quantum Age 133
Conversations w/Coach Yvonne 284
Coping with Caregiving 99
Cosmolicious with Diana 122
Costa, Lydia 18
Cover Your Assets 40
Cowgill, Rich 21
The Cranky Middle Manager Show 40
Crawford, Dana 52
Crawford, Don 186
Crawford, Mandie 289
Create Abundance Now! 99
Creating a Family: Talk about Infertility and Adoption 170
Creative Health and Spirit 134
The Creativity Salon 241
Creighton, Zoe 180
Crime and Child Abuse 61–63
Crime and Punishment 62, 237
Crooks, Tara 123
Crossman, Craig 272
Cuddy, Alison 214
Culinary Confessions 83
Culturally Conscious Communications 5
Cunningham, Bill 298
The Curious Cook 84
Cuthbert, Mike 25

Dailey, Brian 121
The Dailey and Stearn Law Show 121
Daoust, Danielle 127
The Daring Dreamers Showcase 241
Dark Matters Radio 162
The Dark Side 183
Darkness on the Edge of Town 163
Darko, Rev. Damien 183
Darla Jaye 300
The Dave Elswick Show 184
The Dave Glover Show 300
The Dave Ramsey Show 296
Davenport, Dawn 170
David, Mike 77
Davis, Mike 264
Davis, Raven Blair 293
Davis, Rick 207
Daywalt, Ted 124
Deace, Steve 184
Deace in the Afternoon 184
DeAngelis, Jack 16
Debin, David 259
Deborah "Doc" Watson 99
DeGrow, Jane 279
DeMarco-Barrett, Barbara 34
Demystifying Non-Profits 41
Dennis, Tim 163
The Dennis Miller Show 297
The Dennis Prager Show 297
DePew, Dave 101
Design Talk 19
DeWitt, Roger 210
The Diana Falzone Show 122
The Diane Rehm Show 299

Dick Santino's Fantasy Sports Show 262
Digital Nation Radio 274
Digital technology 17
Dillon, Ilene 102
DiMele, Armand 112
Dimensions of Light 134
Disabilities 63–65
Disability Beat 63
DiSanza, John 66
Divine Awakening 135
Divine Manifesting 136
Divinski, John 204
The Divorced Fathers Network Radio Program 123
Dlinn, Reb. Hirsh 231
Dobbins, Cheryl 148
Dr. Anne Marie Evers Show 136
Dr. Blogstein's Radio Happy Hour 65
Dr. Carol on Pets 11
Dr. Fred Bell's Health, Science and Energy Show 100
Dr. Maxine 29
The Dr. Meg Jordan Show 101
The Dr. Pat Show 242
Dr. Shawn—The Natural Vet 11
Dr. Tea! Show 85
DogCast Radio 10
Doherty, Eric 272
The Dom Giordano Show 184
Domandi, Mary-Charlotte 219
The Donna Seebo Show 242
Dooley, Dr. Joseph 234
Doty, Juli 212
Doug Stephan's "Good Day" 296
Douglas, Tom 89
Doyle, Jerry 296
DRC-FM Morning Show 66
Dreams 146, 153
The Drive on Fox 262
Duglin, Gary B. 67
Duignan, Steve 232
Dunne, Marguerite 90
Durham, Crane 300
Durning, Daniel 17
Dwight, Bill 177
Dynamic Transformations Where Intuition and Inspiration Collide 137

Eagle and Child see *The Flipside Show*
Earp, Charles 212
Earth Angel 137
Earth Harmony Divinations 138
eBay Radio 41
Ecker, Don 162
Economou, Michele 226
Ed Hitzel's Radio Show 85
The Ed Schultz Show 296
Eight Forty-Eight 214
El, Stanley 36
Elliott, Jon 300
Elswick, Dave 184
Embracing Mother Earth 138
Emory, Capt. Herb 271
Empowered Black Perspectives 6
England, B.K. 12
Entertainment 65–80, 184, 190, 297, 300
Entertainment and the Arts 66

Environment 80–81, 129, 156, 184, 195, 197, 219, 239
The EquiSport Report 262
Equity Strategies 55–56
Espy, Carol Lee 287
Etcheverry, Omar 263
Evening Edition 184
Evers, Dr. Anne Marie 136
Evers, June 12
Everyday People's Entertainment Guide 67
Eve's Third Wave 285
Ewen, David 32
Ewing, Cher 110
eWomenNetwork Radio Show 285
Exit, Merle 281
The Expat Show 277
The Expert Witness 121
The Extreme Scene 263
Eye on Toledo 215

Face the Tribune 184
Falcon, Mike 259
Falzone, Diana 122
Fanning, Iris 245
Farias, Jeff 188
Farnham, Sean 262
Farrelly, Margot
A Fashionable Life 35
The Father John Walsh Show 243
Feder, Andrew 158
Federici, Lesly 257
Feinburg, Todd 207
Feldman, Steve 264
Feldsott, Lenny 133
Ficarra, Barbara 105
Fiedler, Maureen 230
Fields, Bea 210
Fightin' Words 263
Financial Wisdom with Gabriel Wisdom see *The Gabe Winston Show*
The Finer Things in Life see *Business Matters with James Max*
Finley, Reginald Vaughn, Sr. 230
Firestorm, Adam 266
First News with Bob Steel 185
A Fistful of Quarters 67
Fitness 39
Fitness and Nutrition Radio 101
Fitness Business Radio 102
Fitzpatrick, Ian 280
Fitzpatrick, Tonya 280
Fix Your Conflicts! 185
Flaim, John-Paul 299
Fleming, Todd 300
The Flipside Show 186
Flisher, Chris 156
Florida Gardening 93
The Florida Show 244
Floyd, Tom 45
Focus580 and *The Afternoon Magazine* 186
The FOG 215
Food 82–91, 239
Food Chain Radio 85
Forchuk, Rick 77
Forker, Sean 167
Foster, Steve 269
Fowler, Don 76
Fox, J.T. 212
Fox, Laura 89

310 Index

Francis, Judy 7
Francis, Dr. Raymond 98
Frantz, Bob 178
Franz, Catherine 48
Free Forum 186
Free Range Thought 187
Freedom Works! The Paul Molloy Show 187
A Fresh Start with Sallie Felton 221
Friedman, Brad 179
Friedman, Debbie 248
Friend of the Family 171
Friesian Ink Radio 11
Frishman, Rick 56
Full Power Living 102
Furr, Pamela 199
The Future of Real Estate 211

G. Gordon Liddy Show 298
The Gabe Wisdom Show 42
Gabreael 164
Gainor, Captain Lou 125
Gallagher, Mike 296
Galt, Melissa 18
Garden Girls 93
Garden Mama 94
The Gardener 94
Gardening 92–96
Garner, Steve 86
Garrison, Greg 300
Gary B. Duglin Talks with the Stars 67
Gasiorowski, Frank 252
Gatto, Tim 192
Gazdovic, Olga 190
Gearhart, Jim 298
Gerson, Stephanie 216
Gerstner, Richard 74
The Gestalt Gardener 94
Get a Life with Françoise 277
Ghostly Talk 163
Giacoboni, Julia 182
Gibbs, Joel 73
Gibson, John 300
Gibson, Ray 179
Gilbere, Gloria 106
Gill, Steve 205
Gillespie, Cheryll 237
Gilliard, Judy 88
Gilliland, James 161
Giordano, Dom 184
Giorgio, Greg 120
A Glimpse Through the Veil 164
Glover, Dave 300
God Unplugged 229
Goddess Radio 244
Goebel, Sarah 228
Gogger, Michael 147
Gogolewski, Kathe 288
Going Global for Spirit 139
Golbom, Larry 4
Goldberg, Gary 50
Goldman, Jonathan 104
Goldseek Radio 42
The Golf Connection 264
The Good Food Hour 86
The Good Life 86
Good News Broadcast 244
Goodkind, Jennifer 35
Goodwin, Derek 91

GoofyGoddess Radio 139
Gordon, Greg 96
Gottfried, Adam 269
Gottfried, Al 269
Grace, Jay 69
The Graduates 216
Grady, Bill 210
Graham, Kathleen 252
GrapeRadio 87
Grapevine Radio 87
Graveel, Dean 68
Graveline, Dave 274
Graves, Jayson 3
Gray, Pam 283
Greene, Ryan C. 53
The Greg Knapp Experience 298
Griffin, Dennis 62
Griffin, Jim 41
Grip Strength Radio 101
Griswold, Tom 297
The Groks Science Show 234
Gross, Gary 215
Growing Up with Dr. Jerry Brodlie 171
The Growth Strategist 43
Gunderson, Dan 261
Gustavson, Dr. Kent 32
Guy, Carol 137

Hagberg, Amy Hammond 229
Haim, Mark 184
Hallows, Kristen 46
Hamilton, Ian 266
Hamilton, Dr. Sue 93
Hammond, Margo 24
Hampson, Danielle 49
Handel, Bill 178
Handelman, Allen 299
Hannity, Sean 295
Happy Hour Radio 140
Harris, Philip 126
Harrison, Francina R. 38
The Harry Wolf Show 244
Hart, Chip 160
Hartmann, Thom 296
Hastings, Erik 279
Haunted Voices Radio 164
Hawk, Golden 126
Hayes, Dr. Gianni 197
Heal Yourself Talk Radio 103
The Healing Sounds Show 104
Healing the Earth Radio 80
The Health and Beauty Revolution Show 104
Health and fitness 72, 81, 32, 97–119, 132–133, 144, 197, 242, 282; alternative 106; doctor-patient relationship 118; education 105, 111, 113; healing 103, 104; mental health 112–113, 115, 255; nutrition 101, 102, 105–107, 111, 114, 125, 151; pain reduction 110; patient advocacy 111; toxins 117; weight loss 110
Health in 30 105
Health Matters 106
Health Matters with Dr. G. 106
Healthy Lifestyles 106
Healthy Planet, Healthy Me! 81
Healthy Talk Radio 107
Healthy Woman 107

The Heart and Home Healing Show 140
The Heartland Labor Forum 120
Hebert, Greg 37
Heller, Charles 192
Heller, Meria 195
Heltzel, Ellen 24
Henwood, Doug 176
Herb Talk Live 108
Herr, Eva 234
Hildenbrandt, Ty 271
Hill, Marlon 214
Hill, Tassy 130
Hinman, Michael 236
History 119–120, 295; British Columbia 218; Canadian 218; Civil War 119; collectibles 16; pre-Columbian 119; religious 230
Hitzel, Ed 85
Hochberg, David 213
Hockey Hour/Canadian Sport 264
Holden, Kevin 172
Holder, Peter Anthony 68
Holder Tonight 68
Home Base Business 101 44
Home/office design 18–21
The Home Show 19
Honsberger, Fred 298
Horse Talk 12
Horses 11, 12
Hovey, Melissa 167
How She Really Does It 286
Howard, Clark 297
Howard Monroe and the Morning Show 188
The Howard Stern Show 296
Howie Carr 298
Humphries, Rusty 297
Hunt, Allen 227

Imus, Don 296
Imus in the Morning 296
In Short Order 108
In the Kitchen with Tom and Thierry see *Seattle Kitchen*
In the Know 245
Indie Business Radio Show 44
The Indie Music Showcase 68
The Inez Bracy Show: Living Smart and Well 245
The Infidel Guy Show 230
Infinite Consciousness 234
Infinitelove Talk Radio 221
Ingraham, Laura 295
Inkstuds 17
The Innovation Zone 45
Inside New Orleans 216
Insight on Coaching 45
Insights 109
Integrity in Business 46
Interfaith Voices 230
Interiors by Cheryll 237
Into Tomorrow 274
Intuitive Living 140
Investing 37, 42, 50
Inzerillo, Therese 140
Ireland, Elaine 139
The Iris Fanning Show 245
Isaacs, Susie 261
It Takes a Village 188
Izzard, Calvin 181

Index   311

Izzard, Jon 181
Izzard, Parthenia S. 157

The Jack Rice Show 297
Jaco, Aaron 263
Jahi, Baba Sitawi Kiongozi 44
Jay Grayce Variety Show 69
Jaye, Darla 300
The Jeff Farias Show 188
The Jeff Katz Show 189
Jefferson City's Morning News with Jay Kersting 189
Jerome, Gavin 261
Jerrigan, Rebecca 165
Jerry's Shopping Show 197
Jewish Digest 231
The Jewish Experience 231
The Jiggy Jaguar Show 69
Jim Bohannon Show 190
The Jim Brown Show 217
Jim Cates Show 70
The Jim Rome Show 297
Job You Deserve Radio 46
Jones, Louie 249
The John and Jeff Show 299
The John and Ken Show 297
Johns, Lynette M. 232
Johnson, Donna Maria Coles 44
Johnson, Kaare 217
Johnstreet, Robert 187
Jones, Norm 199
Jordan, Dr. Meg 101
The Jordan Rich Show 70
Journey to Self 246
Journeys with Rebecca 165
The JPEG Show 232
J.T. Foxx Show 212
Judy a la Carte 88
Judy Carmichael's Jazz Inspired 71
The Junkies 299
Just Between Us 286
Just Energy Radio 141
Just One More Book! 172

The Kaare Johnson Show 217
Kaehr, Shelley 128
Kagin, Edwin 227
The KAHI Corral 12
Kall, Robin 31
Kaplan, Mat 234
Kaplan, Rabbi Shmuel 228
The Kathleen Show 72
Kathy and Judy Show 298
Katz, Jeff 189
Katz, Michael 29
Katz Pajamas 29
Kay, Steven 48
Kazarosian, Marsha 122
Kennedy, Deirdre 9
Kersting, Jay 189
The Kevin and Trudie Show 172
Kevin Smith Show 165
Kevoian, Bob 297
Kids 'n' Sports 264
King, Felicia 272
Kinsolving, Les 300
Kiongozi, Baba Sitawi,
Kirby, Dave (Doc) 29
Kiricoples, Georgiann 129
Kirry, Alex 198
Kitching, Heather 96

Kjellberg, Carla C. 188
Klein, Pete 22
Knapp, Greg 298
KnightTime Radio Show 190
Knowing Spirit Radio 141
Koulopoulos, Thomas 45
Kovacs, Patty 104
Kowalski, John Adam 47
Kristafer, Jerry 66
Kuda, Tim 265
Kurban, Mike 65

Labor 217
The Labor Show 120
Lacey, Bob 282
The Ladies Room with Lolis 287
Lahteine, Scott 91
Lambert, Scott 163
Langhorne, Karyn 25
Lanto's Lantern 142
The Larry Young Morning Show 299
Lars Larson 297
Las Vegas and the Mob 62
Last Call 3
Laurie, Kim 83
Laurie and Olga Show 190
Law and law enforcement 121–123, 178, 198, 249, 258
Law of Attraction 134, 148, 155, 243
Learning Disabled 63
Lee, Charles 234
Lee, Nancy 143
The Lee Rodgers Show 190
Legal Beat in the Morning 245
Legends of Success 47
The Les Kinsolving Show 300
Leslie, Sean 203
Leslie Marshall Show 191
Let's Talk Computers 274
Let's Talk It Through 246
Let's Talk Makeup 36
Let's Talk Marketing Show 48
Levine, Mike 121
Levy, Michael 250
LiberalPro 192
Liberty Watch 192
Liddy, G. Gordon 298
Lieurance, Suzanne 24
Life Beyond Reason 143
Life Bites News 88
Life Business and Money with Steven Kay 48
The Life Lounge 287
Lighting the Fires of Liberty 192
Lights On! 143
Likis, Bobby 61
Lindsay, Deborah and Spencer 81
Ling, Frank 234
The Lionel Show 193
Lisa's Walk the Talk Show 247
Litzinger, Sam 181
Live Courageously see *Strong Woman Hiding*
Live the Day 247
Live! with Lisa 248
Live Your Purpose Radio 144
Living and Loving Life 248
Living Large 20
Living on Purpose 109
Lombardi, Ann 280

Longmore, Jennifer 153
Looney, Ebony 36
The Louie Jones Show 249
Louise, Dr. Rita 141
Love by Intuition Show 222
Love Mechanics 223
Loving Life Radio Show 287
Lowe, James "Jiggy Jaguar" 69
Lu, Christine 39
Lunch Pail Logic 217
Lutsky, Leslie 231
Lynch, Brian O. 234
Lynch, Sheri 283
Lyon, Angela Treat 241

Mackenzie, Linda 134
Macdonald, Laurie 190
Mac's World 218
Madely, Steve 193
Madely in the Morning 193
Madison, Joe 296
Madison in the Morning 218
Mahone, Beverly 291
Make Me Over Eb Show 36
Making a Living with Maggie 49
Making Life Easier 63
Malloy, Mike 300
Malloy, Shane 264
Malzberg, Steve 299
Malzberg Talk 299
Mancow 194
Mandel, Debbie 115
Manifest Change Now 144
Manifesting Miracles in Your Life 144
Maniscalco, Frankie 269
Mantz, Gary 50
The Marc Bernier Show 299
Marcell, Jacqueline 99
Marinangel, Cindy 226
Marino, Christina 144
The Mark and Brian Program 72
The Mark Reardon Show 194
Marketing as a Spiritual Practice 145
Markey, Judy 298
Marooney, Kimberly 152
Maroulakos, Elaine 144
Marshall, Leslie 191
Marshall, Mark 121
Martin, Brenda 66
Martin, Steven Hawley 155
Mason, Trudie 172
Mastering Ourselves 145
Matthew and Friends 166
Matthews, Carole 146
Max, James 38
Mayes, Keesha 283
McCausey, Kelly 174
McChesney, Robert 195
McConnell, Mike 299
McConnell, Rob 169
McConnell, Robin 17
McCoy, J. Michael "Mac" 218
McDaniel, Reggie 67
McDonald, Don 55
McGarry, Jo 9
McIntyre, Mike 62
McKee, John 38
McMahon, Marcia 150
McNally, Terry 186
McNeely, Rev. Claudia 155

312 Index

The Media Lizzy Show 194
Media Matters 195
Mediumship 127, 137
Medved, Michael 296
Mendez, Barbara 106
Mental Health 112, 113
The Meria Show 195
Merriman, Paul 55
The Messengerfiles 146
Messonnier, Dr. Shawn 11
Metaphysical World and Beyond 146
Metrochick Radio 288
Meyer, Hans 203
The Michael Gogger Show 147
Michael Medved Show 296
The Michael Smerconish Morning Show 297
Midday with Mike 299
The Midnight Bookworm see *Vin Smith's Midday Book Break*
The Midwatch 196
The Mike Fleming Show 300
The Mike Gallagher Show 296
The Mike Nowak Show 95
The Mike Rosen Show 298
Miles, Tuesday 167
Military 124, 298
Millard, Ethan 198
Miller, Dennis 297
Miller, Stephanie 297
Millington, Sean 259
Mills, Karen 20
Mind Your BIZness 49
Minor League Baseball Radio 265
Mirabel, Lee 41
Mistal, Maggie 49
Mr. Media 74
Mitchell, Shirley 258
Mitchell, Dr. Susan 111
Molloy, Paul 187
Mom Talk Radio 173
Money Matters Financial Network Radio 50
The Money Thing 50
Monks, Jeffrey 68
Monroe, Howard 188
Montgomery, Pat 173
Moore, Karl 33
Moore, Rose 63
Morekaitis, Koren 286
Morley, Russ 175
Morning Source 299
The Morning Show (with Gregory Berg) 196
The Morning Show (with Lee Rodgers) 191
Morris, Jeffrey 264
Morse, Chuck 182
Morse, Emily 224
The Mother Daughter Club 288
Mouthful 88
Movie Addict Headquarters 73
The Movie Show 73
Movies 73, 76, 80
Muller, Erich "Mancow" 194
Murassso, Tom 148
Murphy, Dan 3
Murray, Cathryn Michael 78
Music 65, 66, 68, 69, 70, 71, 74, 76, 184, 187, 193, 205, 219, 296; jazz 71; Jewish 65, 66

The Music Connection 74
My Computer Show 275
My Point Radio 196
My Spiritual Healer 148
Mytalkshow 197
Myers, Chris 262
Myth or Logic Radio 148

Nathan, Alan 175
Natural Body Building Radio 101
Nature's Translator 13
Nautical 125
Nautical Talk Radio 125
Neal Boortz Show 296
Need a Word 232
Nemko, Marty 60
Nerad, Jack 60
Networking with the Blindguy from Gorilla Central 51
Networks and syndicates 295
Neufeld, Brad 238
Never Settle for Less 249
New Age 125–159
New Dimensions 197
New World Order Disorder 197
"The New You" Radio Show 110
News for the Soul 149
Nieters, John 97
Nightside Project 198
NightSide with Dan Rea 198
Niswander, Vicky 63
Niven, Barbara 7, 78
No Bones About It 110
Noll, Doug 185
Noory, George 297
The Norm Jones Show 199
Now Showing with Bill Wilson 74
Now That's What I'm Talking About! 149
Nowak, Mike 95
Numerology 142, 156
Nunes, Paula 138
Nutrition and Health 111
NY Baseball Digest 265

Obrien, Tom 57
Odeen, David 196
O'Dell, Spike 297
O'Hare, Marianne 66
Olson, Michael 85
O'Malley, Kathy 298
On the Bookshelf 29
On the Verve 249
One Hour of Hope 199
Online Marketing 51
The Oopa Loopa Café 119
Ordway, Glenn 299
O'Reilly, Dr. Nancy 290
Organization Nation 20
Osborne, Dr. Carol 11
Osmon, Rick 119
O'Sullivan, Lisa Marie 288
Out and About with Richard G. 74
Outdoor Talk Network 161
The Outdoors Experience 161
Owens, Lorna 282
Owens, Ronn 298

Painter, Sally 162
Palmer, Dave 200
The Pamela Furr Show 199

Paranormal 127, 128, 150, 158–159, 161–170, 219, 297, 299; ghosts 135, 162–164, 167; UFOs and other sightings 150, 158, 161, 163–169
Parenting 170–174, 220; adoption 170; childhood disorders 171; early childhood 171; grandparents 173; infertility 170; moms 173–174; workplace issues 172, 174
Parents Rule! 173
The Party Line 200
Passion 223
Patch, Jon 14
The Patient's Voice 111
Patterson, Mark 137
Peaceful Planet Show 150
Pearlman, Debra 58
The Performance Nutrition Show 265
Perkins, Tom 102
Perry, Yvonne 34
Peter, Elizabeth 138
The Peter K Show 112
Pets Are Speaking 154
Peuster, Peg 232
Phelps, Brian 72
Piane, Renee 223
Pierre, Yvonne 64
Pit Pass Radio 266
Planetary Radio 234
Podcaster Training from Two Beams 275
Poetry & Prose & Anything Goes with Dr. Ni 30
Point of Life 250
Politics 124, 151, 158, 174–211, 212, 216, 219, 237, 282, 295–300
Pop culture 68, 76, 188, 193, 194, 198, 203, 295, 297, 299
Popp, Mary Jane 75
Poppoff 75
P.O.R.T.A.L Paranormal Talk Radio 167
Positive Changes 250
The Positive Mind 112
Positively Incorrect! 251
The Power of Attorney 122
Power Talk 252
The Power within You 252
Powerfull Living 52
Powers, Tazz 138
PowerSellingMom's Radio Show: Let's Talk eBay 52
Prager, Dennis 297
Pratt, Dave 266
Pratt and Taylor 266
The Prescription Addiction Radio 4
Press, Bill 299
Price, Joseph 253
PricewaterHouse Coopers Start Up Show 52
PRIDE Radio 76
ProAmerica Radio 200
Problems and Solutions 112
Proctor, Eileen 54
The Professor and Mary Ann Talk NASCAR 266
Prokopowicz, Gerald J. 119
Psychiatry Today with Dr. Scot 113

Quality of Life 234
Quantum Health 151

Queer FM 96
Quigley, Bill 213
Quinn and Rose 200
Quinsey, Mike 132

Radio Free Volusia 201
Radio Good Spirited 253
The Radio Host Show 76
Radio Rickshaw 76
Ramone, Rachel 31
Ramsey, Dave 296
Ramsey, Tonya 246
Ranoli, Faith 140
Raposo, Vera 20
Ratliff, Susan 54
Rautureau, Thierry 89
Raw Inspiration Radio 89
Raw Spirit Show see *Raw Inspirations Radio*
Ray, RSS 51
Rea, Dan 198
Reaching Peak Show 253
The Reader's Round Table 30
Reading with Robin 31
Real estate 211–214, 249
The Real Estate Guys 212
Real Estate, Real Advice 212
Real Talk "With the Experts" 213
The Real World of Autism with Chantal 114
Reardon, Mark 194
Red Bar Radio 77
Reeves, Tony 245
Regional 214–220
Rehm, Diane 299
Reisman, Barry 65
Relationships 122, 198, 237, 251, 264, 282, 297, 299; brides 220; dating 220, 222, 234; marriage 220, 221, 222; sex 220, 223–226, 234; weddings 220, 226
Relationships for Life 198
Religion 138, 158, 184, 197, 297; Atheism 227; Christianity 228, 229, 232; Jewish 228, 231, 233
Remember When 218
Renee, Shawna 284
Resmo, Christen 247
Resmo, Rachelle 247
Resnick, John 47
Results Radio Show 254
Rhodes, Francoise 278
Ricci, Monica 20
Rice, Jack 297
Rich, Jordan 70
Richard, Brad 237
Rick's Picks 77
The Right Perspective 201
Ringside Live 266
Rinker, Harry 17
Roaring Women Radio 289
The Robert Scott Bell Show 151
Roberts, Rosemary 111
Robinson, Chris 276
Robles, Anna 134
Rockafellow, Rachel 106
Rod and Reel Radio 267
Rodgers, Lee 191
Rodriguez, Andy 219
Rome, Jim 297
Romero, Kate 154

Ronn Owens 298
The Rose Moore Show 53
Rosen, Mike 298
Rosengarden, Craig 269
Ross, Andrea 173
The Roth Show 202
Rougberg, Adam 187
Roy, Sandip, p. 211
Ruggiero, Deb 281
Rushing, Felder 94
Rushlo, Dr. Robin 51
Russell, Don 182
Russell, Nan 59
Rusty Humphries 297
The Ryan C. Greene Show 53

Saatsaz, Cyrus 263
SAGE: Spirit, Angels and Guides Entertainment 151
St. Clair, Vicki 240
Salzman, Les 262
Sanchez, Carla 265
Sanders, Candia 130
Sandler, Don 83
Sanford, Kristen 235
SanInocencio, Eric 260
Sanson, Steve William 184
Santa Fe Radio 219
Santino, Dick 262
Santoro, Dean "Big Sauce" 177
The Sasquatch Experience 167
Sassy Sistah Radio Show 78
Savage, Michael 295
Savage Nation 295
Schemers, Kurt 57
Schiano, Rita 79
Schrader, Dave 163
Schultz, Ed 296
Schwarz, Shelley Peterman 63
Science in Action 81
The Scooter McGee Show 202
Scrapbooks 20
Scrappers Talk Radio 20
The Sean Leslie Show 203
Seattle Kitchen 89
Seebo, Donna 242
Seeing Beyond 254
Self-help 237–258
Semig, Doug 163
Senior Legal Strategies 258
Severin, Jay 298
Sex with Emily 234
Sex with Sassy Radio Show 225
Sexual abuse 61
Shackelford, Megan 91
Shaheen, Jennifer 271
Shakedown Street 203
Shanahan, Edward 169
Sheck, Mike 6
Shelia Smoot on Your Side 255
Shoots, Jennifer 270
Shore, Sandi C. 140
Show Business 101 78
Shrink Rap Radio 255
Sicile-Kira, Chantal 114
Siegel, Gary 228
Signs of Speed 267
Silberhartz, Allan 130
Silva, Mike 265
Silverman, Aliza 226
Silverman, Francine 76

Sinclaire, Moneca 214
Single Talk 226
Situation Awareness 203
Six, Ken 92
Six Degrees 78
Slattery-Moschkau, Kathleen 72
Slinsky, Jim 161
Slow food movement 82
Small, O.E. Cruiser 258
The Small Business Big Ideas Show 53
Small Business Power Hour 54
SmallBiz America 54
Smallwood, Loyce 74
Smart City 21
Smerconish, Michael 297
Smith, Ann 74
Smith, Bev 5
Smith, Corey 212
Smith, John 180
Smith, Kevin 165, 269
Smoot, Shelia 255
Snyder, Rocky 123
Soloman, Richard 56
Something You Should Know 256
Soul Connections 152
Soul Journeys Live 153
Sound Authors 32
Sound Investing 55
Sound Off Connecticut 204
Soundingboard 204
Speak Up! (with Pat Lynch) 289
Speak Up! (with the Rev. Zernial Brogan) 204
Speed, Jake 267
Spence, Terry 206
Spencer, Jerry 197
Spencer, Dr. John 114
Spencer Power Hour 114
The Spike O'Dell Radio Program 297
Spirit Connections 153
Spirit Is Speaking 154
Spiritual Hollywood 154
Spirituality 195, 197, 221, 230, 243, 291
Sports 184, 190, 216, 259–271, 296, 297, 299; aviation 270; baseball 260, 265; bodybuilding 260; boxing 263; entertainment 266; fantasy 262; fishing 160–161, 267; golf 264, 269; hockey 264; horse racing 262; hunting 160, 261; motorcycling 266; NASCAR 266, 270, 271; nutrition 265, 269; poker 270; surfing 263; wrestling 266, 268; youth 264
Sports from Frankie's Point of View see *Sports Talk Live*
Sports Heaven with Mark and Evan 268
The Sports Opinions Show 268
Sports Talk Live 268
Stanford, Sandra 228
Starstyle — Be the Star You Are! 256
Stearn, Todd 121
Steel, Bob 185
Steele, Richard 214
Stein, Dr. Alvin 110
Stephan, Doug 296
The Stephanie Miller Show 297
Stepp, Cliff 87

314 Index

Steppin' Out 4
Stern, Howard 296
Stern, Jason 260
The Steve Duignan Show 232
The Steve Gill Show 205
The Steve Yuhas Show 205
Stock, Alan 299
Strait, James 206
Strait Talks 206
The Strength-Power Hour 269
Strong Woman Hiding 290
Stu Taylor on Business 56
Stypeck, Allan 25
Sullivan, Tom 298
Sustainable living 81
Swanson, MaryAnn 248
Swedlow, Tracy 79
SyFy Radio 236
Sylvester, John 217

Table Talk 90
Take Charge of Your Life 257
Takedown Radio 269
Taking Care of Business 56
Talk It Over 206
Talk to Me … Conversations with Creative, Unconventional People 79
Talk with Your Animals 13
Talkin' Pets 14
Talking Travel 278
Tanem, Bob 92
Tarot 138
Tate, Priscilla 276
Taylor, Don 266
Taylor, Stu 55
Taylor, Tim 274
TechForum LIVE! 276
Tee It Up 269
Teebox Golf Show 269
Tepper, Neil 241
Terry, Celeste 41
Terry Nazon Talks Astrology 154
The Things That Matter Most 207
The Third Age 259
This Gospel of the Kingdom 232
This Is America 300
This Way Out 96
This Week in Science 235
The Thom Hartmann Radio Program 296
Thomas, Angela 167
Thomason, Dr. Jeannie 9
Thompson, Lynn 109
Thompson, Dr. Maxine 29
Thompson, Wendy Coakley 25
Thorne, Angela 141
Thorne, Rev. Cherise 141
Thurber, Maggie 215
Tilley, Marcus 278
Tilley Talks Travel 278
A Time to Heal 155
Timeless Women Speak 290
Tochihara, Wendy 267
Today's Author 32
The Todd Feinburg Show 207
The Tom Becka Show 207
The Tom O'Brien Show 57
The Tom Sullivan Show 298
Tomorrow Matters 81
Toms, Michael 197

Torok, George 37
The Tournament Trail 270
The Townstone Financial Show 213
Traders Nation 57
Travel 82, 85, 206, 276–281
Travel Queen Show 279
The Travel Show 279
Travel Talk: Escapes! 280
Traveling with Françoise see *Get a Life with Françoise*
Travel'n On Radio Show 280
Trevor Carey Show 208
Trey Ware Morning Show 208
Trifiletti, Denise 292
The Truth About Life 155
Truth from the Source 156
Tucker, Betty Jo 43
Turben, Susan H. 171
Turmel, Wayne 40
Turn On Your Inner Light 115
Turner, Joy 13
Turning of the Wheel 156
Tuskey, Dawn 21
Tuskey, Rich 21
TV 76, 79
The TV of Tomorrow Show LIVE 79
Twisted Metal 270

U Smile Radio 257
UFO Radio 168
Ukra, Mark 85
Ullstrup, Michael 196
The UltraFlight Radio Show 270
Ultrasonic Film 80
The Uncooperative Radio Show 208
The Unexplained World 169
Unions 120
Unlock Your Sales Potential 58
The Urban Herbalist 90
Urena, Steve 67

Vaishali 160
Van Hook, Kriss 148
Vannah and Collins 209
Van Nuys, David 255
Vegan Radio 91
Vegetarianism 116
Veterans in Politics see *Face the Tribune*
Vibrant Living 115
Vike, Brian 169
The Vike Report 169
Vin Smith's Midday Book Break 32
Visible by Numbers 156
Visibility 9-11 209
Vogen, Sue 108
Vogt, Charli 83
Voll, Donna 153
Voll, Dudley 153
Volpe, Tina 116

Waggoner, Stan 196
Wake Up America 116
Waldman, Jon 15, 264
Walking with Spirit 157
Wallace, Nancy 146
Waltzek, Chris 42
Ward, Suzanne 166
Ware, Trey 208
Warkenthien, Jack 58
The Watering Hole 122

Watson, Chip 12
Watson, Deborah 107
Weber, Sandra 59
Wei, Penny 250
Weight loss 110
Weinstein, Natalie 19
Weissman, Suzi 176
Welcome to My World 219
The Wellness Roadshow: Searching for Whole Being 116
Wellness, Wholeness and Wisdom 157
Wenck, Tony 266
Wendy's Animal Talk 14
Wennik, Taff 3
West, Dr. Ann 156
Wexler, Lisa 248
WGTD Radio Theater 196
Whatcha Got! 17
Whatever Live! 291
What's Ailing America? 117
Wheaton, David 229
When Pigs Fly 158
Where Wall Street Meets Main Street 58
Whirl with Merle 281
Whitaker, Julian, M.D. 107
White, Jeanne 131
White, Rebbekah 103
White, Rob 275
Whiteskycloud, Derrick 127
Whitney, Nicole 149
WHMP Morning News with Chris Collins see *Vannah and Collins*
Willey, Sam 168
Williams, Niama Leslie 30
Willis, Justine 197
Wills-Leufroy, Vanecia 291
Wilsker, Ira 275
Wilson, Wendy 108
Windows to Wellness 158
Wine and Dine Radio 91
Wineke, Joe 217
Wings of Love 159
Winogron, Steve 182
Wisdom, Gabriel 42
Wise Women Talk 291
Wishna, Mark Elliot 268
WJEW Talk Hour 233
Wolf, Brian 203
Wolf, David 54
Wolsey, Michael 209
A Woman's Spirit 291
Women 59, 281–294
Women in Business Radio 59
Women Power Talk Radio 292
The Women's Community Talk Radio 293
Woods, Linda 159
Woods, Susan 218
Wooldridge, Frosty 183
Work at Home Family Talk Radio 59
Work at Home Moms Talk Radio 174
Work Matters with Nan Russell 59
Work with Marty Nemko 60
Writers FM 33
Writers in the Sky 34
Writers on Writing 34
The Writing Show with Paula B. 35
WSB 120 271

X-Squared Radio 235
"X" Zone Radio Show 169

Y Talk Radio 210
Yager, Pamela 220
Yancey, Sandra 285
Yankee Fan Club Radio 271
Yorke, Dan 299
You Are the Guest 210

You Are What You Love 160
Young, Larry 299
Youngblood, Sheryl 190
Your Call 211
Your Doctor Said What? 118
Your Dream Wedding 226
Your Health Matters 118
Your Home — Your Money Mortgage and Real Estate 213

Your House Chicago 21
Yuhas, Steve 205
The Yvonne Pierre Show 64

Zimmerman, Pastor Tim 232
Zurzolo, Vincent 16

www.ingramcontent.com/pod-product-compliance
Lightning Source LLC
Chambersburg PA
CBHW081538300426
44116CB00015B/2679